Mothers on Trial

MOTHERS ON TRIAL

THE BATTLE FOR CHILDREN AND CUSTODY

PHYLLIS CHESLER

McGraw-Hill Book Company

New York   St. Louis   San Francisco
Hamburg   Mexico   Toronto
London   Sydney

1 2 3 4 5 6 7 8 9 D O C D O C 8 7 6 5

ISBN 0-07-010701-7

Library of Congress Cataloging in Publication Data

Chesler, Phyllis.
Mothers on trial.
Includes bibliographies and index.
1. Custody of children—United States.
2. Mothers—Legal status, laws, etc.—United States.
I. Title.
KF547.C465   1985   346.7301'7   85-11318
ISBN 0-07-010701-7   347.30617

Book design by Leonard Telesca

Contents

PART III: *The Study in Depth, II. What Crimes Are Committed Against "Good Enough" Mothers That Result in Maternal Custodial Victimization?*

PART IV: *Maternal Custody and the Male State*

PART V: *The Mothers Speak*

Preface

THIS BOOK is about what it means to be a "good enough" mother and about the trials such mothers endure when they are custodially challenged.

What custodial and economic rights does a traditional married mother have? Does she have the right (and the power) to prevent her husband from neglecting, abusing, abandoning, or impoverishing her? Can she legally prevent him from divorcing her—and keeping their children?

What custodial and economic rights does a non-traditional mother have? If a "career" mother introduces her child into a "tribe" of care givers (the child's legal or unwed father or grandparents, a paid house-keeper, a child-care center), does this endanger her custodial rights? If a welfare-dependent, lesbian, or impoverished mother is challenged, what custodial rights does she have?

This book is not about happy marriages or happy divorces. This book is about those marriages and divorces that erupt into custody battles; and about the state's appropriation of a mother's child.

Other books can be—and indeed are being—written about the role of exceptionally "maternal" fathers, about male longings for a child, and about a child's need for "good enough" fathering.

This book tries to clarify the difference between how a "good enough" mother mothers and a "good enough" father fathers; the difference between parental pride of ownership and parental pride of relationship; and the difference between (male) custodial *rights* and (female) custodial *obligations*.

On October 28, 1975, New York Judge Guy Ribaudo awarded sole custody of two children to their father, Dr. Lee Salk. Their mother, Kersten Salk, was not accused of being an "unfit" mother. It was clear that Kersten, not Lee, had reared their children from birth "without the aid of a governess"; and that Lee would probably require the aid of a "third party" housekeeper-governess were he to gain sole custody.

The judge used an "affirmative standard" to decide which parent was "better fit" to guide the "development of the children and their future." Kersten Salk's full-time housekeeping and mothering were discounted in favor of Dr. Salk's psychological expertise and "intellectually exciting" life-style. Dr. Salk was widely quoted:

> Fathers should have equal rights with mothers in custody cases and more and more fathers are getting custody. . . . The decision in Salk v. Salk will touch every child in America in some way. It will also give more fathers the "incentive" to seek custody of their children.[1]

This case swept through public consciousness: an ominous warning, a reminder that children are only on loan to "good enough" mothers. They could be recalled by their more intellectually and economically solvent fathers.

Although mothers still received no wages for their work at home and less than equal pay for equal work outside the home; although most fathers had yet to assume an equal share of home and child care, divorced fathers began to campaign for "equal rights" to sole custody, alimony, and child support, and for mandatory joint custody.

The year 1979 was the year of *Kramer vs. Kramer*. After seven years of full-time "single" mothering, Mrs. Kramer abandons her long-absent husband and young son. She returns eighteen months later, a well-dressed $30,000-a-year executive, who demands and wins courtroom custody.

Mrs. Kramer's victory was pure Hollywood fantasy. In reality, after years of absence, fathers, not mothers, were returning to demand and win visitation and custody. In reality, mothers, not fathers, were being custodially challenged for having careers or for moving away.

Mothers were also being custodially challenged when they accused their *husbands* of child neglect and child abuse, including incest, and of wife battering; and when they demanded alimony, child support, or the marital home.

In the decade between 1975 and 1985, at least 2 million American fathers obtained sole custody of their children by kidnapping them. An additional 1 million fathers obtained sole custody of their children judicially, in courtrooms. This statistical estimate is only the tip of the custodial iceberg.

The iceberg is about what happens when a father *threatens* a mother with a custody battle. The iceberg is about how men, individually and collectively, can either subsidize a woman's motherhood—or can prevent, regulate, profit from, or destroy a woman's motherhood.

The custodial iceberg is about maternal silence and capitulation. It is also about maternal heroism under siege.

In June of 1976 Marta consulted me as a therapist. She said she was "depressed" and "wanted to kill herself." Weeping, she told me:

> For fifteen years my children were my whole life. I did everything for them myself. Six months ago a judge gave my husband exclusive custody of our children. How could this nightmare ever happen? At first, I thought they'd come back to me on their own. But they haven't. Why should they? I have a small one-bedroom apartment. Their father was allowed to keep our five-bedroom house. He gives them complete freedom and the use of their own credit cards. I work as a salesgirl for $150 a week plus commissions. Is this a reason to go on living?

In September of 1976 my telephone rang at midnight. Would I testify as an expert in a lesbian custody trial? Laura, the embattled mother, spoke so softly I could barely hear her. During the trial, I never once saw her relax, smile, or look anyone in the eye. The judge ordered Laura's son into paternal custody. He allowed Laura to keep her young daughter "for now." Laura was convinced it was "only a matter of time" before she lost her daughter, too.

In January of 1977, Carol, a complete stranger, asked me for money.

> My husband kidnapped our six-year-old son two months ago. It's what they call a "legal" kidnapping. We're only separated, not divorced. I need money to hire a detective to find them. I need money to hire a lawyer once they're found. I only have $600 in the bank. And I'm four months pregnant.

In May of 1977, Rachel, also a stranger, mailed me a description of her custody battle. She entitled it "A Case of Matricide in an American Courtroom." Rachel had a "nervous breakdown" after she lost her battle for child support, custody, and maternal visitation.

In 1977, when I was six months pregnant, I decided to study women and custody of children.

Over the next eight years, I formally interviewed more than three hundred mothers, fathers, children, and custody experts in the United

States and Canada, and in sixty-five countries around the world. On the basis of these interviews I conducted three original studies and six original surveys for this book.

For more than 5,000 years, men (fathers) were legally *entitled* to sole custody of their children. Women (mothers) were *obliged* to bear, to rear, and to economically support children. No mother was ever legally entitled to custody of her own child.

During the nineteenth century pro-child crusaders gradually convinced the state that young children required maternal "tenderness"— but only if their mothers were white, married, Christian, and moral. The children of African slaves and Native American Indians; the children of immigrant, impoverished, sick, or "immoral" parents—all, all were "untenderly" appropriated by slave owners and by the state, clapped into orphanages, workhouses, and reformatories, or farmed out into apprenticeships—for "their own good."

By the turn of the century, a custodially challenged American mother enjoyed an equal right to custody in only nine states and in the District of Columbia; and only if a state judge found her morally and economically worthy of motherhood. Until the 1920s, no American mother was entitled to any child support. Since then, few have received any.

The maternal presumption was never interpreted as a maternal right.

The maternal presumption has always been viewed as secondary to the child's "best interests"—as determined by a judge. This "best interest" was always seen as synonymous with paternal rights. Between 1900 and 1985, judges (and everyone else) continued to view a white married mother as custodially worthy—until she committed adultery, initiated a divorce, pursued a career, or became impoverished.

The maternal presumption has also been viewed as "sexist." By the late 1970s, two-thirds of the states rejected it as a customary presumption. However, the spirit of affirmative action has consistently been used against mothers in custody contests.

For example, in 1979, a Kansas judge awarded one-year-old twins to a working father rather than to their stay-at-home mother; and a North Dakota court upheld a father's sole custody of three children.

> The mother argued that it was unfair for her to lose her children because she chose to stay at home with them, foregoing career opportunities. But the court, in a cruel twist of the customary logic, stated that it would not be more fair to deprive the father of custody because he did not stay home during the day.[2]

In 1980, in an attempt to be "sex-neutral," a judge in Oregon awarded a two-year-old son to his father. Since both parents were "fit" "an award to the mother because she was the mother, and as such the primary caretaker would violate the requirement of sex-neutrality."[3]

The equal treatment of "unequals" is unjust. The paternal demand for "equal" custodial rights; the law that values legal paternity or male economic superiority over biological motherhood and/or maternal practice, degrades and violates both mothers and children.

Our standards for "good enough" mothering and fathering differ sharply as a function of gender as well as race, class, and religion.

An ideal father is expected to legally acknowledge and economically support his children. Fathers who do *anything* (more) for their children are often seen as "better" than mothers—who are, after all, supposed to do everything.

The ideal of fatherhood is sacred. As such, it protects each father from the consequences of his actions. The ideal of motherhood is sacred, too. It exposes all mothers as imperfect. No human mother can embody the maternal ideal perfectly enough.

Given so many double standards for fit mothering and fathering and so many anti-mother biases, I decided to explore a "worst case" scenario. Could a "good enough" mother ever lose custody of a child to a relatively uninvolved or abusive father? How often could this happen?

I first interviewed sixty mothers who had internalized the Western ideals of motherhood; who had been their children's primary care givers; who were demographically similar to the majority of divorced white mothers in America; and who had been custodially challenged, both privately and judicially, in each geographical region of the United States and Canada between 1960 and 1981.*

On the basis of these interviews I was able to study how often "good enough" mothers can lose custody—*when their ex-husbands challenge them.* I was able to study why "good enough" mothers lose custody battles and how having to battle affects them.

On the basis of these interviews and on additional interviews with fifty-five custodially embattled fathers, I was able to study the kinds of husbands and fathers who battled for custody; their motives for battling; and how and why they won or lost. I was also able to study the extent

---

*I also interviewed fifty mothers who were black, brown, yellow, and red. Some—but not all—are part of this first study. They are very much a part of this book.

to which the custodially "triumphant" father encouraged or allowed the "losing" mother access to her children afterward.

Seventy percent of my "good enough" mothers lost custody of their children.

Why did so many mothers lose custody? Were they utterly without financial or emotional resources; or without resources equal to those of their ex-husbands? Were these mothers betrayed by incompetent or anti-mother lawyers? Did they even have lawyers? Did these mothers face unusually anti-mother or pro-father judges? Were their judges unique, or were they representative of most judges?

Did these mothers lose custody because they had been *married?* Do voluntarily single mothers have more custodial leverage than married mothers? Do single mothers have as much leverage, in a custody contest, as unwed fathers, sperm donors, or married couples?

In a sense, custody battles are the abortion controversy—after birth. Who controls a woman's right to have or not to have a child and to have custody of that child? Each woman for herself—or each woman's husband? Who determines the conditions under which all women are obliged to mother? Each woman for herself, each family for itself—or each family's priest, physician, congressman, and senator?

What are women's custodial rights when abortion and birth control remain under siege, and when test-tube technology remains in patriarchal and governmental custody?

Did these mothers lose custody because they were American citizens? Do women have more reproductive or custodial options outside the United States and Canada? To answer this question, I interviewed mothers (and experts about mothers) under economic and custodial siege in Europe, the Middle East, Central Asia, India, the Far East, Africa, and South America.

The trend my first study confirms—if it is indeed a *new* trend—consists of "good enough" mothers being unjustly separated from their children; and of presumably privileged (white, formerly married) mothers being treated as if they were poor, unwed, mothers of color—or as "criminals."

Once a mother has been custodially challenged, either as "unfit" or as a "criminal," no matter what the truth is, no matter what her station in life may have been, she is exceedingly vulnerable to custodial victimization.

To understand the nature of female crime and automatic custodial punishment, I studied the history of the witchcraft trials in Europe and

America, and the history of American women in prison. I also interviewed contemporary American mothers in jail.

Listening to custodially victimized mothers made me wonder if voluntarily non-custodial mothers feel the same way. I interviewed non-custodial mothers (and fathers) who were more philosophically "positive" about their non-custodial status.

I wanted to understand why we take custodial mothers for granted but heroize custodial fathers; why we sympathize with non-custodial fathers but condemn non-custodial mothers; and why we grant non-custodial fathers the right to feel angry or sad—but deny non-custodial mothers similar emotional "rights." I also wanted to compare what non-custodial mothers and fathers actually *do*, and contrast it with how they perceive themselves—and are perceived.

Must we view custodially challenged mothers only in terms of their psychological and reproductive victimization? Can such mothers also be viewed as philosophical and spiritual warriors and heroines? Gradually, I came to view them as such.

Under everyday siege, and under custodial siege, "good enough" mothers remained connected to their children in nurturant and non-violent ways. They resisted the temptation to use violent means to obtain custody of their children. This is one of the reasons they lost custody.

Children satisfy both male and female longings for genetic immortality, intimacy, authority, and family life. However, considering the human capacity for cruelty and tyranny, it is very dangerous for any human being to be "owned" or legally controlled by another human being.

Who can be trusted to nourish and protect a child without abusing their power over that child? If a mother and a father can betray their parental trust, can we expect the state to do better?

What basic rights should *every* child be guaranteed by a civilized society? Do children have the right to be mothered and fathered in loving and non-violent ways? Are children's needs being met by the patriarchal family during marriage or by the patriarchal state after divorce?

Should divorce and custody be determined by a judge or resolved privately by physical, psychological, economic, or legal violence? Who is a custody expert? Who is an expert in the *non-violent* resolution of a custody dispute?

As a society, we tend to view "custody" as a contest between a "winner" and a "loser," not as a series of questions about the conditions under which women mother, men father, and children grow up and about who determines these conditions.

Our focus must shift from resolving custody by force, and in anti-mother ways, to a more civilized resolution of our child-care arrangements.

Public hearings on custody are urgently needed. Such hearings could inform the public that *all* mothers are custodially vulnerable because they are women; that *all* fathers, including incestuous, violent, absent, passive, or "helper" fathers, can win custody, not because mothers are "unfit" or because fathers are truly "equal" parents but because fathers are men; and that all custodial mothers and children are impoverished against their will, both by individual fathers and by state legislators.

History is also the story of mothers and children lost to each other too soon and against their will.

What mother *freely* hands her child over to her "betters," to be enslaved, exploited, or adopted; to be punished for who she is or taught to despise or forget her—child of her body, bone of her bone, the apple of her eye.[4]

This book is dedicated to every mother who has ever lost custody of her children; to every mother who has ever been forced to "give up" her children for economic reasons; and to every mother whose children have been kidnapped or brainwashed against her.

Acknowledgments

THIS BOOK owes a great deal to the competent and generous assistance of Dale Kent Cabrera, Deborah Anna Luepnitz, Florence Matusky, and Joanne Schulman of the National Center for Women and Family Law, and to Ariel Chesler-Bronstein, Patricia De Rosa, and Marlene Wilks for all they have done—and gone without so that I could write this book.

I thank Gladys Justin Carr, McGraw-Hill Editorial Director; Leslie Meredith, Editor; jacket designer Judith Leeds; and photographer Jerry Bauer. I especially thank my former agent, Gloria Loomis, for her generous and loving concern and my current agent, Elaine Markson, for all our years and books together—and because we are together again.

On August 22, 1982, I was in a serious car accident. I thank the Deerfield Valley Rescue Squad, Vermont, surgeons Oakley M. Frost, Bennington, Vermont, Charles P. Melone and Ronald Levandusky, New York City, internist David Zimmerman, and chiropractor Harvey Rossell for their wonderfully humane care; Abraham Fuchsberg and Sybil Shainwald for their loving and competent legal care; and the PEN American Center for an author-in-crisis emergency grant. I thank all those who responded to my plea for help and gave or lent me money and emotional support.

The following people assisted me in diverse and valuable ways: Judith Antrobus, Ellen Barry (Legal Services to Women Prisoners in California, San Francisco, CA), Batya Bauman, Betsy Beaven, Teresa Bernardez (Argentina), Bob Broner, Esther (E.M.) Broner, Charlotte Bunch, Joyce Burland, Ellen J. Cahill (France, Ireland, Holland), Joan Cassell, Motlalepula Chabaku (South Africa), Rahel Chalfi (Israel), Lillian Chesler, Linda Clarke, Barbara Deming, Susan Deri, Ingrid Djalinous (Austria), Mary Dowler, Jehanne Dyllan, Nawal El Saadawi (Egypt), Susan Flakes, Don Flakes, Milton Foreman, Joanie Fritz, Leah Fritz, the Gainsville

Women's Health Center, Noel Giordano, Georgine Gorra, Nancy Greene (International Social Services, American Branch), Dorothea Gaudart (Austria), Mira Hammermesh, Judith L. Herman, Donna Hitchens (Lesbian Rights Project, San Francisco, CA), Sister Eileen Hogan (Prison Chaplain, Rikers Island, NY), Lucy Honig, Edith Isaac-Rose, Rivka Kashtan, Kiyomi Kawano (Japan), Lillian Kozak (Chair, New York State Now Committee on Domestic Relations), Bea Kreloff, Victoria Kummer, Judith Kuppersmith, Nancy Lemon (Mid-Peninsula Support Network for Battered Women, Redwood City, CA), Rose-Marie K. Lester (West Germany), Jill Lippett, Grace Liu-Volckhausen (Korea), Laurie Lowell, Evelyn Machtinger (Aid to Incarcerated Mothers, Framingham, MA), Larry Mandelker, Fran Matera (For Our Children and Us, FOCUS, East Meadow, L.I., NY), Margaret McGovern, Fatima Mernissi (Morocco), Naila Minai (Turkey and the Middle East), Selma Miriam, Janni Neilson (Denmark), Sonia Nussenbaum, Judith O'Neill, Cecilia Onfelt (Sweden), Rose-Marie Palli (Switzerland), Nancy Polikoff (Women's Legal Defense Fund), Toni Press (Mid-Peninsula Support Network for Battered Women, Redwood City, CA), Martin P. M. Richards (England), Roz Richter (Lambda Legal and Education Fund, New York, NY), Lily Rivlin, Sorosh Roshan (Iran), Margery Rushforth, Alma Sabbatini (Italy), Heleieth I. B. Saffieti (Brazil), Sylvia Sandoval (El Salvador), Susan Saxe (Aid to Incarcerated Mothers, Framingham, MA), Barbara Seaman, Rosalind Seigel (The East Side Community Center, serving the United Nations), Miriam Schneir, Debra Jane Seltzer, Elizabeth Shenton (the Schlesinger Library, Radcliffe, Cambridge, MA), Mtaze Singele (Zambia), Nancy Slater, Sigrid Stadler (Austria), Alexandra Symonds, Martin Symonds, Barbara Treen (Commissioner of Parole, NY State), Luisa Valenzuela (Argentina), Virginia Visani (Italy), Elaine Ward, Ellen Whitford, Shebear Windstone (Private Feminist Library, Brooklyn, NY), Laurie Woods (National Center for Women and Family Law, New York, NY), and Patricia Zayas (Argentina).

PART I

Mothers and Custody

CHAPTER ONE

An Historical Overview

By the laws of England, the custody of all legitimate children from the hour of their birth belongs to the father. If circumstances, however urgent, should drive the mother from his roof, not only may she be prevented from tending upon the children in the extremity of sickness, but she may be denied the sight of them; and, if she should obtain possession of them, by whatever means, [she] may be compelled by the writ of habeas corpus to resign them to her husband or to his agents without condition—without hope.

Let it not be supposed that this law is one which is rarely brought into operation. The instances in which it is brought before the public cognizance may be few, but [it] is ever in the background of domestic tyranny, and is felt by those who suffer in silence.

Master Sergeant Talfourd, 1837

We true, natural women cannot live without our children. We had rather die than have them torn from us as your laws allow them to be. Spirit wrongs are the keenest wounds that can be inflicted upon women. When woman is brought before our man courts, and our man juries, and has no marks of violence upon her person, it is hard to realize that her whole physical system may be writhing in agony from spirit wrongs, such as can only be understood by her peers. Spiritual, sensitive women, suffer on in silent anguish without appeal, until death. Kindly liberate her from her prisonhouse of unappreciated suffering.

Elizabeth Parsons Ware Packard, 1864

3

HARRIET BRENT JACOBS is born into slavery in North Carolina in 1818. Her "kind mistress" teaches her how to read and then bequeaths her to Dr. James Norcom.[1]

Norcom, who is fifty-two years old, sexually harasses the twelve-year-old Harriet. He threatens to rape, sell, or kill her for resisting his advances. Mrs. Norcom persecutes Harriet for "attracting" her husband's attention.[2]

When Harriet is fifteen, she falls in love with a "colored carpenter and free-born man." She asks for permission to marry. Norcom threatens to whip her—and to shoot her "lover" on sight. Harriet's grandmother sends a friend to advise her.

Samuel Tredwell Sawyer, "the friend," is a white man, a past member of the North Carolina legislature, and a future U.S. congressman. Within a year, Harriet gives birth to Sawyer's son Joseph.

Harriet's "grim tormentor," Norcom, "pitches her down a flight of stairs," and "cut[s] her hair very close to her head, storming and swearing all the time." Harriet has a second child, Louisa, by Sawyer. Norcom threatens to sell both her children if she sees Sawyer again, and so long as she continues to spurn Norcom.

Children are a woman's joy and only consolation. But a slave mother's joy belongs to her master. Norcom has fathered eleven slave children and sold every one—to "spare" Mrs. Norcom's feelings and to profit from his own "licentiousness." What would prevent Norcom from selling all of Harriet's children once she became pregnant by him?

Ah, if Harriet didn't exist, Norcom would not hold her children hostage. *Harriet escapes.* Norcom imprisons her children—and then sells them to a speculator whom Sawyer has secretly sent.

Harriet, hiding, rejoices. Her children—*her* children!—will be free. Sawyer sends Joseph and Louisa to live with their great-grandmother. Harriet flees her hiding place; walks to dreaded "snaky swamp"; and from there, swiftly, to her grandmother's house, and up into a dark and "airless" space, measuring seven by nine feet, beneath the roof.

For seven years, Harriet is entombed here. She can never stand up or walk around. All summer she is aflame with red insect bites; in winter, with "frostbite." Harriet bores a peep-hole through which, sight unseen, she can see—but not touch or talk to—her children.

On one of these sale days, I saw a mother lead seven children to the auction block. She knew that some of them would be taken from her: but they took all. The children were sold to a slave-trader, and their mother was bought by a man in her own town. Before night her children were all far away. She begged the trader to tell her where he intended to take them: this he refused to do. How could he, when he knew he would sell them, one by one, wherever he could command the highest price? I met that mother in the street, and her wild, haggard face lives to-day in my mind. She wrung her hands in anguish, and exclaimed, "Gone! All gone! Why don't God kill me?" I had no words wherewith to comfort her.[3]

Sawyer, newly married, offers to send Louisa to live with his relatives "up North," out of Norcom's scheming reach. After six long months, a letter arrives from "Brooklyn, Long Island," praising Louisa as a good "waiting maid" to her cousin. Has Sawyer sent his daughter North as a slave? Has Harriet's entombment been in vain?

Harriet must know. She escapes North by ship. Louisa is so shabbily dressed, so obviously "unattended" to, that at first Harriet doesn't recognize her. At nine, Louisa is still illiterate. Harriet immediately finds work as a domestic. She buys Louisa shoes and clothes and pays for a doctor.

I once saw a white lady, of refinement, sitting on the portico of her own house, with her youngest born, a babe of some seven months, dallying on her knee, and she is toying with the pretty gold threads of his silken hair, whilst her husband was in the kitchen, with a whip in his hand, severely lashing a negro woman, whom he had sold to the trader—lashing her because she refused to go cheerfully and leave her infant behind. The poor wretch, as a last recourse, fled to her mistress, and, on her knees, begged to have her child. "Oh, mistress," cried the frantic black woman, "ask master to let me take my baby with me." What think you was the answer of this white mother? "Go away, you impudent wretch, you don't deserve to have your child. It will be better off away from you!" Aye, this was the answer accompanied [by] a derisive sneer, [that] she gave to the heart-stricken black mother.[4]

Harriet lives in terror of Norcom's "bounty hunters." Warned of her imminent capture, Harriet flees New York for Boston. She takes Louisa with her. Once settled, Harriet sends for Joseph—who arrives one morning out of breath, "having run all the way."

For the first time in nine years, Harriet and her children live together in broad daylight. Harriet sews; Louisa studies; Joseph learns a trade. On June 21, 1853, under a pseudonym, Harriet publishes an article in the *New York Tribune,* about the separation of children from their slave mothers.[5]

A tall, hard-looking man came up to me, very roughly seized my arm, bade me open my mouth; examined my teeth, felt my limbs; made me run a few yards; ordered me to jump; and being well satisfied with my activity, said to Master Edward, "I will take her." After a while, my mother came up to me. Her whole frame was distorted with pain. She walked toward me a few steps, then stopped, and suddenly shaking her head, exclaimed, "No, no, I can't do it."

"Here, Kitty," she said to an old negro woman, who stood near, "you break it to her. I can't do it. No, it will drive me mad. Oh, heaven. That I was ever born to see this day." Then rocking her body back and forth in a transport of agony, she gave full vent to her feelings in a long, loud, piteous wail. . . . Why, I remember that when master sold the gray mare, the colt went also. Who could, who would, who dared separate the parent from her offspring?[6]

Harriet's pursuers are now willing to sell her. In 1855, when Harriet is thirty-seven years old, her friend and employer, Mrs. Willis, buys her for $300.

Those words struck me like a blow. So I was sold at last! A human being sold in the free city of New York! The bill of sale is on record, and future generations will learn from it that women were articles of traffic in New York, late in the nineteenth century of Christian religion. I well know the value of a bit of paper; but much as I love freedom, I do not like to look upon it.[7]

As a mother, Harriet longs for "marriage" and a "home made sacred by protecting law." She says so over and over again in her remarkable autobiography, entitled *Incidents in the Life of a Slave Girl. An Authentic Narrative Describing the Horrors of Slavery As Experienced by Black Women.*[8]

Harriet Brent Jacobs is right. She is also wrong. "Laws" do not keep mothers and children together. The whitest and most married of Christian mothers has no legal right to her husband's children. By law, children "belong" to their fathers.

Reverend Ware's only daughter Elizabeth is born in Massachusetts, in 1816. Elizabeth is "blest" with modesty, religious fervor, and "a liberal education." In 1839, Elizabeth marries the Reverend Theophilus Packard, who is fourteen years her senior. They move to Illinois, where Elizabeth gives birth to six children in sixteen years. She runs the household, cares for her "beloved" children, helps Theophilus write his sermons, raises church funds, and "ministers" to her husband's congregation.[9]

Theophilus Packard is "sluggish" and "clings serf-like to the old paths, as with a death grasp." Elizabeth has a more "active" and "progressive temperament." The "dull" and "crafty" Theophilus seizes upon Elizabeth's belief in a "free and open minded discussion of Original Sin" as proof that she is "insane."

In 1860, when their youngest child is eighteen months old, Theophilus has Elizabeth "forcibly" removed to the insane asylum in Jacksonville. Dr. Andrew McFarland, the asylum director, confiscates Elizabeth's clothes, books, and writing paper. He sexually harasses and threatens to kill her; throws her into solitary confinement; and imprisons her on the asylum's "worst ward."

For three and a half years, Elizabeth Packard ministers to her sisters in bondage. She washes, comforts, and prays with them, and tries to shield them from beatings and from suicide. Elizabeth finally convinces the asylum trustees that she is lucid and God-fearing. They release her.

Theophilus forbids Elizabeth to return home, or to see or speak with their children. Elizabeth decides that she must return to her husband's legal "protection." *She has no other.* She cannot see her children if she remains apart from Theophilus.

The People Ex Rel. Uriel M. Rhoades and Sophia
Rhoades, The State of New York, 1857

Mr. Rhoades has been wanting in respectful and kind attentions to his wife, and has often used harsh, profane, and vituperative expressions to her and to others concerning her, but he has been guilty of no such misconduct as would justify the wife in a separation. The only difficulty arises from their child being of tender age, and deriving sustenance, in part from the breasts of the mother. But upon the evidence, I think these circumstances form no obstacle to the father's right. [The child] was placed by the father with a competent person, [and has] been doing well and growing fleshy.

Therefore, on the undisputed facts of the case the father [has] the legal right to the custody of the child.[10]

Elizabeth arrives home one snowy November morning. Theophilus does not bother to conceal his hostility. Elizabeth embraces her children. She does not raise the subject of her psychiatric imprisonment. She has returned to "resume her domestic duties."

Theophilus forbids Elizabeth to heat water on the stove—or to hire anyone to help her clean the house. Elizabeth scours the house by herself, with cold water. Theophilus intercepts Elizabeth's mail. He forbids her to leave the house. Then, he locks her in her bedroom, both day and night.[11]

After six weeks, Elizabeth smuggles out a note. Friends take it to a judge who issues a writ of habeas corpus for her. Before Theophilus can act on his plan to psychiatrically imprison Elizabeth again, he must first prove to a jury that she is "insane."

In 1864, a jury of twelve men "acquit" Elizabeth of insanity. She returns to her husband's custody—only to discover that Theophilus has mortgaged her dowry-bought house and fled to Massachusetts with their children. Elizabeth is alone and destitute. She has no legal right to her dowry, or to her children.

> *Mrs. Charles [Catherine] Dickens was to have a settlement. Her own house, and her eldest son, Charley, would live with her. But all the other [nine] children were to stay with Dickens. They could visit their mother if they chose to, but Dickens did not encourage them to—in fact, quite the opposite. Dickens did not make his children choose between himself and their mother. He simply assumed that, as the law allowed, they would stay with him. And [for twenty years] so they did. They were happy to. He was dynamic, funny, famous, charismatic, and powerful.*
>
> *When their son Walter died suddenly in 1864, Dickens did not even send her a note. When Dickens himself died, no one troubled to invite her to the funeral.*[12]

From 1864 on, Elizabeth Parsons Ware Packard supports herself by selling copies of her autobiography entitled *Modern Persecution: Insane Asylums Unveiled* (vol. 1) and *Married Women's Liabilities* (vol. 2). She also drafts many bills on behalf of imprisoned mental patients—and of married women.

Packard "beseeches" her "brothers" in the state legislature to grant their wives a "junior partnership" in the "firm of marriage." She views "married women" as "legally a 'non-entity'" and "therefore an American slave." What she wants is "protection in the union"; and "protection from the cause of divorce."[13]

Elizabeth prepares to battle for custody of her youngest children in Massachusetts. Theophilus "yields" the children to her voluntarily, "rather than have [Elizabeth] come into possession of them by the Court's decision." On July 3, 1869, after a nine-year separation, Elizabeth "worships and breaks bread" with all her children "as one family unit." She rejoices:

It is for you, my jewels, I have lived—it is for you I have suffered the agonies of Gethsemane's Garden—it is for you I have hung on the cross of crucifixion; and been entombed three years in a living cemetery; and oh! it is for your sakes I hope to rise again. Children dear, when all the world forsook me and fled, you alone were true to the mother who bore you. . . . Thy Father, God, will not disinherit thee for loving thy mother.[14]

In 1860, the year Elizabeth Packard is psychiatrically imprisoned, Susan B. Anthony is visiting her friend Lydia Mott in Albany, New York. A disheveled and sobbing woman is admitted to the parlor. She is Mrs. Phelps, the wife of a Massachusetts state senator and the sister of a United States Senator.

Please, won't you help me? No one else will. I am a wife and mother. When I finally confronted my husband with proof of his adulteries, he beat me and had me put away in an Insane Asylum. My brother had me freed, but could not obtain permission for me to see my children. Yesterday, after a year, I was allowed to visit *one* child. I fled the state with her immediately. And now I am a fugitive.[15]

Anthony agrees to help Mrs. Phelps. She escorts her to New York City, and obtains refuge for her there.[16] State Senator Phelps threatens to have Anthony arrested during one of her public lectures. He also enlists Anthony's two most cherished abolitionist comrades, Garrison and Phillips, in his campaign against her.[17]

Anthony's comrades strongly believe that her action endangers the "woman's rights movement and the anti-slavery cause." Anthony disagrees with them. She says:

Don't you break the law every time you help a slave to Canada? Well the law which gives the father the sole ownership of the children is just as wicked and I'll break it just as quickly. You would die before you would deliver a slave to his master and I will die before I will give up the child to its father.[18]

Phelps hounds Anthony for more than a year. She remains firm. Finally, he hires detectives to locate his missing child. One Sunday morning, on her way to church, the young Miss Phelps is kidnapped on the street and "legally" returned to her father.

In 1869, the year Elizabeth Packard is reunited with her children, the well-known journalist Albert D. Richardson is shot and killed by Daniel McFarland. Richardson had been "attentive" to McFarland's *divorced* wife; and he marries the ex–Mrs. McFarland on his death bed.

The new Mrs. Richardson is seen as the "villain," although her divorce was granted because of the "brutality and instability of McFarland." The court acquits McFarland of murder on the grounds of "temporary insanity" and gives him custody of his twelve-year-old son. Susan B. Anthony and Elizabeth Cady Stanton call a protest meeting. Two thousand people attend it. Stanton speaks:

> As I sat alone late one night and read the story of Abby Sage Richardson, the fugitive wife, I tried to weigh the mountain of sorrow that had rolled over that poor woman's soul, through these long years of hopeless agony . . . and the unjust decision setting a madman free to keep that poor broken hearted woman in fear for her life as long as he lives. . . . Although by the revised statutes of this state the mother is the equal guardian of her child to-day, yet in the late trial we have the anomaly of a criminal, acquitted on the ground of insanity, walking out of court with his child by his hand, its natural protector, while the mother of sound mind capable of supporting it, is denied the custody of its person.[19]

Does Elizabeth Packard believe that a divorced woman is entitled to "joint guardianship" of her children? Does she include "adulteresses" or "free thinkers" in her pleas for the rights of married women?[20]

In 1837, in England, Master Sergeant Talfourd presented an eloquent brief on behalf of maternal visitation—for virtuous wives only. Talfourd does not want to "alter the laws" of Father Right, but to "mitigate" the mother's lot; to provide "intervals in which forsaken nature may be cheered and waning strength repaired." Adulterous mothers are beyond the pale of Talfourd's mercy. They—and "immoral" women in general—are to be "deprived of both custody and access."[21]

In 1795, Frances (Fanny) Wright is born to wealthy Scottish parents. In 1825, Fanny establishes a commune in Tennessee to educate emancipated slaves. In 1828, she is the first non-preacher woman to lecture in public in the United States.[22]

In 1830, Fanny quietly leaves America. Early in 1831, in Paris, she gives birth to her (and William S. Phiquepal D'Arusmont's) daughter Sylva. Fanny is a brilliant, accomplished, and independently wealthy woman. She is the friend and confidante of the Marquis de Lafayette, Jeremy Bentham, Robert Owen—and yet she marries Phiquepal, a "handsome" person of "no genuine distinction of either intellect or spirit," who is sixteen years her senior, in order to protect her child from "stigma."

1804 *George Sand, christened Amandine Aurore Lucie Dupin, is born.*

1821 *Upon her grandmother's death, George inherits a small fortune, a house in Paris and a country estate.*

1822 *George marries Baron Casimir Dudevant.*

1823 *She gives birth to her son Maurice.*

1828 *She gives birth to her daughter Solange.*

1831 *George leaves Casimir, who is cruel and openly adulterous.*

1832 *She begins an affair with Alfred de Musset.*

1835 *Casimir threatens George with a gun. He also begins his legal appropriation of her fortune and property. She sues for a legal separation.*

1836 *Casimir countersues. The jury is divided. George settles out of court, giving Casimir half her fortune and her Paris town house.*

1837 *Casimir attempts to kidnap their son Maurice, whom he despises as too "feminine." George manages to spirit Maurice away to safety. In a rage, Casimir kidnaps their daughter Solange, whom he addresses contemptuously as "a harlot's daughter." George discovers where Solange is hidden. George surrounds Casimir's hiding place with armed policemen.*

"Trying to look calm, [Casimir] came to the door and politely invited his former spouse to step inside, an honor she no less courteously declined. Solange was brought out and entrusted to her mother 'like a princess at the limit between two states,' as George Sand later described it. Casimir vowed that he would get Maurice back 'by authority and justice.' "

George is terrified. What if Casimir is successful? Exhausted, unable to write, George borrows 10,000 francs to sail to America with her children—if Casimir gains custody.[23]

By 1836, Fanny Wright and William S. Phiquepal are seriously "estranged"; by 1838, Phiquepal takes Sylva to Cincinnati, leaving Fanny alone and very ill in New York. Phiquepal now begins his legal appropriation of Fanny's fortune.[24]

In 1848, Fanny capitulates and grants Phiquepal her inheritance and property. He promptly announces that he and Sylva are "independent of her, and [can] do without her." He puts Fanny on a small "allowance."

In 1850, Fanny files for divorce in an attempt to recover some part of her estate. She claims that Phiquepal has married her for her money and has "alienated their daughter's affections." Phiquepal retaliates with an open letter to the newspapers. He writes:

Your life was essentially an external life. You loved virtue deeply, but you loved grandeur and glory [even more]. Your husband and child ranked only as mere appendages to your personal existence. [I] imposed on [myself] the sacrifice of attending your lectures but could not impose it on [my] child. Sylva's education has been the main object of [my] life, while [you] have often interrupted that education by the life [you] led traveling from one land to another.[25]

In 1851, Fanny is granted a divorce as an "abandoned" wife. Part of her fortune is restored to her. However, she loses Sylva forever.

Fanny's hopes for her daughter would never be realized. Though she was in Cincinnati at the time, Sylva did not see her mother in her last illness. [Sylva] became an ardent Christian. In 1874, she testified before a congressional committee against female suffrage. "As the daughter of Frances Wright, whom the Female Suffragists are pleased to consider as having opened the door to their pretensions," Sylva begged the Speaker and the members of the House committee "to shut it forever, from the strongest convictions that they can only bring misery and degradation upon the whole sex, and thereby wreck human happiness in America!"[26]

In 1873, in England, Annie Besant, the writer and publisher, separates from her husband, the Vicar Frank Besant. In a deed of separation, Frank "gives" Annie custody of their three-year-old daughter, Mabel. Annie continues to mother and to publish books and pamphlets, including those on atheism and birth control.[27]

In 1877, the government charges Annie Besant with "obscenity" for publishing a fifty-year-old pamphlet about birth control. The charges against her are ultimately dropped; but the pamphlet is banned. Reverend Besant now petitions the court for custody of his daughter. The judge acknowledges that Annie is a good mother.

Mrs. Besant has been kind and affectionate in her conduct and behaviour towards the child, and has taken the greatest possible care of her. I have no doubt she entertains that sincere affection for the child which a mother should always feel.[28]

The judge nevertheless orders Mabel into her father's custody. Annie's public affiliation with unpopular or minority opinions will "cut her off from social intercourse with the great majority of her sex. [It would not] be beneficial for any young girl to be brought up by such a woman."[29]

On appeal, Annie Besant reminds the court that every British subject is guaranteed the right to advocate their opinions and that *legally*, she is her daughter's "father," i.e., her husband has given her contractual custody.

The judge reminds Besant that, as a mother, she can never have the same rights as a father. "No such substitution or delegation is possible by our law," he asserts. Any child who is not under her father's control is (automatically) a ward of the court. No ward of a Christian court can "remain under the guardianship and control of a person who professes and teaches and promulgates [such] religious, or anti-religious, opinions."[30]

In *A Midsummer Night's Dream*, Shakespeare depicts a custody battle between Oberon, the fairy king, and Titania, the fairy queen. Titania's custodial interest in the orphaned child is "maternal"; Oberon's is "paternal."

Puck: Take heed the queen [Titania] come not
within his sight;
For Oberon is passing fell and wrath,
Because that she as her attendant hath
A lovely boy, stol'n from an Indian King;
She never had so sweet a changeling;
And jealous Oberon would have the child
Knight of his train, to trace the forests wild;
But she, perforce, witholds the loved boy,
Crowns him with flowers, and makes him all her
joy. . . .

Oberon: Why should Titania cross her Oberon?
I do but beg a little changeling boy
to be my henchman.

Titania: Set your heart at rest;
The fairy land buys not the child of me.
His mother was a votaress of my order;
But she, being mortal, of that boy did die;
And for her sake do I rear up her boy,
And for her sake I will not part with him.[31]

Titania is no Christian queen. If she were, she would not quarrel with her husband the king—certainly not over a child. Royal children, and, for that matter, any child claimed by a king, already belongs to him, and not to any queen.[32]

With some exceptions, the majority of Europe's Christian queens were breeders—not rulers. As *mothers*, queens were not entitled to any more authority over their children than that enjoyed by the king and his family. Queens rarely took lovers, or if they did, they rarely had or acknowledged their illegitimate children.[33]

In the twelfth century, Queen Eleanor of Acquitaine divorced King Louis VII of France. Their children remained behind as "the property of the French Crown." Eleanor remarried King Henry II of England, and gave birth to seven more children.

When Eleanor's oldest sons rebelled against Henry, Eleanor supported them. King Henry reconciled with his sons, but placed Eleanor under house arrest for fifteen years (1173–1189). Henry allowed Eleanor to see her children, then seven, eight, and twelve years old, and her grandchildren, only "on occasion."[34]

In the sixteenth century, Queen Elizabeth I of England had no children—and no consort. She was as directly involved in decisions of war and peace as any monarch could be. Interestingly enough, Elizabeth herself was the daughter of Anne Boleyn, one of the wives whom her father King Henry VIII had beheaded. According to one biographer, Queen Elizabeth never mentioned her mother directly; nor did she ever openly condemn her father for her own impoverished and motherless childhood.[35]

In the seventeenth century, Anne Pierrepont, daughter of the Marquis of Dorchester, married John Lord Roos. The bridegroom was an impotent alcoholic and gambler. Anne left—and became pregnant without him. Her mother-in-law, the Countess of Rutland, had Anne imprisoned until she gave birth. Anne's son was baptized "Ignoto" and taken away from her immediately. According to Antonia Fraser,

> At first Lord Roos hung on to custody of the boy saying that "although the child is not of my begetting, so long as the law reputes it mine, I must and shall keep it." But this, it is clear, was merely a manoevre in order to induce from Lady Anne a confession of the truth. Once Lady Anne had admitted her [adultery and a divorce was granted], then she could have the child and do what she liked with it.[36]

It is 1729, in Stettin, Pomerania. Princess Johanna Elizabeth, the wife of Christian Augustus, the Prince of Anhalt-Zerbst, has just given birth. The child, baptized Sophie, seldom sees her father and is "merely tolerated and often violently repulsed" by her mother, who subsequently gives birth to a son "whom she passionately loves."[37]

In 1744, when Sophie is fifteen, the Empress Elizabeth summons her to the court of St. Petersburg to become engaged to her nephew Peter, the heir to the Russian throne. Sophie finds the nobles "illiterate"; the intrigue "intricate"; and her fiancé "childish" and perhaps insane.

In 1745, Sophie marries the Grand Duke Peter—who spends "all his time playing soldiers in his room with his valets, performing military exercises and changing uniforms twenty times a day." The Empress Elizabeth "befriends" and "persecutes" Sophie; Peter neglects, bores, and abuses her.[38]

It is now 1752, and, despite Peter's succession of mistresses, he has yet to consummate his marriage. Sophie is urged to provide Peter with an heir. Her choice is Count Sergei Saltikov, a member of the old Russian nobility, a "vain" and "ambitious" man.[39]

In 1754, Sophie becomes pregnant. On September 20, 1754, after a "very hard labor," she gives birth to a son. The newborn is swaddled and immediately taken to the Empress Elizabeth. In her own handwriting, Sophie describes her royal child-bed:

> I had sweated abundantly, and I begged Mme. Vladislavov to change my linen and put me back into my own bed; she said she dared not do that. She sent several times for the midwife but the latter did not come. I asked for water and got the same response. . . . I had been in tears ever since the birth had taken place, particularly because I had been so cruelly abandoned, lying in discomfort after a long and painful labour, with nobody daring to carry me back to my bed. I was too weak to drag myself there. Four hours later, Mme. Shuvalov left the room and went to fetch the midwife, for the Empress had been so busy with the child that she would not let the midwife leave her for an instant.[40]

The empress does not permit Sophie to see her son at all. Sophie falls ill. She spends the "whole winter" in a "miserable little narrow room, about five to six feet long and four across." After forty days of "confinement," Sophie sees her son for the first time. The moment "the prayers were over the Empress had him carried away and herself departed."[41]

Sophie is next allowed to see her son at Easter, seven months later. In 1758, she is pregnant again. In December of that year, she gives birth to a daughter, Anna Petrovna, who is also appropriated by the empress. Again, Sophie is "abandoned like a miserable creature."

Sophie is allowed to have a lover and her own political confidantes—

as long as the empress is allowed to spy on her and to exile her friends regularly. Sophie is also allowed to see her children—but only sometimes.

The Empress Elizabeth dies on Christmas Day, 1761. By the spring of 1762, Czar Peter is publicly threatening to kill Sophie and their eight-year-old son, Paul.

Sophie, wearing an officer's uniform, her "hair flying in the wind," rides at the head of 20,000 soldiers to arrest the czar. Peter formally abdicates. On July 6, 1762, while in custody, Peter is "accidentally" killed in a fight—or dies of a "haemorrhoidal colic, with brain complications."[42]

Sophie—better known as Catherine the Great of Russia—reigns for thirty-four years, until her death in 1796. In her *Memoirs*, Catherine writes that

for eighteen years, (the period of my married life) I have led a life which would have rendered ten other women mad and twenty others in my place would have died of a broken heart.[43]

Is motherhood more of a curse than a blessing for those mothers who happen to be queens? Are queens more savagely separated from their children than common mothers are?

In 1562, [the English] Parliament passed the Statutes of Artificers which provided that the children of pauper parents were to be involuntarily separated from their parents and apprenticed to others [until they reached full age]. As of 1601, the Poor Law act established forced labor for the able bodied and cash relief for those unable to work. There was no need to justify legislation which controlled the labor of the lower classes, even at the expense of their family solidarity.[44]

In colonial America, it was a capital crime for a wife or a slave to defend herself against a violent husband or a master.[45] Female non-marital sexual activity was either severely punished, or treated as a capital crime.

A white colonial woman who gave birth to a black or mulatto child out of wedlock was sold into slavery together with her racially mixed child.[46] When an unmarried white woman was seduced, raped, or impregnated by her male employer, she either lost custody of her bastard or was forced into additional years of service.

The laws made (indentured) servants' pregnancies worth their masters' while; and so many unscrupulous masters bound their servants to additional years by rape.[47]

In the seventeenth century most of the unmarried mothers were bound servants who paid dearly for their indiscretions. The woman was heavily fined, and if no one would come forward to pay the fine for her, she was whipped. Furthermore, she served an extra twelve to twenty-four months to repay her master for the "trouble of his house," labor lost and maintenance of the child if it lived.[48]

If a mother wished to avoid such punishment, she would have to end or conceal her pregnancy, or, like Hawthorne's heroine Hester Prynne, live with the scarlet letter A emblazoned upon her breast.[49]

"Infanticide" (which ranged from the use of birth control and abortion to the accidental or purposeful murder of a newborn) was viewed as a special "female" crime. Such crimes were more severely punished than (white) male homicide; wife murder; or political insurrection. Concealing the death of a bastard became a capital offense in England and in the Virginia colony in 1624; and in Massachusetts in 1692.[50]

In the colonies, many fathers died young. Wives tended to outlive them, but they themselves often died in childbirth. Kinship networks were non-existent or very fragile. Something had to be done for the orphans and bastards.

Colonial orphans were usually apprenticed out. They were dependent on neighbors, friends, or surviving relatives to save their lives—or their inheritances—from an "evil" executor or stepfather. In 1678, in Maryland, William Watts died, leaving three motherless boys under the age of eight. Their executor, a merchant, apprenticed them to an overseer who

> "putts them to hard Labour Equal to any servant or Slave & keeps them without clothes," allowed them scanty food, and permitted them to be "saddly beaten & abused by ye overseer as tyed up by the hands & whipt."[51]

As potentially abusive as the apprenticeship system was, it was better than life on the streets or in the poorhouse. The poorhouse was filled with "rogues, vagabonds, idlers, drunkards, brawlers and the hopeless." It was

> the deathhouse of the pauper sick, the winter home of the diseased vagrant, the last refuge of the broken down prostitute, the asylum for the insane,

the lying-in hospital both for the feebleminded members and also for the poor unfortunate girl, the victim partly of ignorance and partly of lust, and perhaps saddest of all, the home of some independent, high-spirited persons whom misfortune or filial irreverence in his declining days left with only such a place in which to close his eyes in the last long sleep.[52]

Impoverished widows usually apprenticed their children. When they remarried, they petitioned for the return of their children—who were then at the legal mercy of their new stepfathers. Some colonial second husbands were unable or unwilling to support stepchildren; some were only too happy to do so.[53]

Stepfathers were notorious for appropriating stepchildren's inheritances. For such reasons, some colonial fathers tried to ensure their children's inheritance (if one existed) by bequeathing it—as well as custody—to their wives.[54]

In 1772 in New England, Mary Jones was convicted of stealing bread to feed her two children. She was hanged.[55] Since female sexuality *and* poverty were viewed as crimes, most women got married, remarried, and stayed married—even to violent or adulterous husbands who squandered their dowries, appropriated their wages, and neglected or abandoned them and their children.[56]

King and state had very little hold over what a wealthy father did (or did not do) for his children. A wealthy father could neglect and abuse his children—as long as he still supported them. Such a father could only be stopped by *his* own father; or by the child's maternal *grandfather;* and then only if the grandfather was both willing and able to economically support the child.[57]

In the United States, the child of a poor or impoverished father belonged to the state, or to whomever was best able to support her. In 1796, Mr. Nickols of Connecticut became the first American father to judicially lose custody of his child. Mr. Nickols had "very little property, no house," and also possessed a "very irregular temper." The court awarded custody of the Nickols child not to her mother, but to her wealthy "maternal grandfather."[58]

In 1839, a Pennsylvania mother committed her "morally unmanageable" daughter to a state house of refuge. The girl's father sought her release, arguing that commitment without a trial was unconstitutional. The court denied his petition—and, for the first time, claimed that under certain circumstances, and in its role of paternal guardian to the community (*parens patriae*), the state had the right to determine custody; and that such a right was based on—but superseded—the custodial rights of an individual father.[59]

In 1879, Mr. and Mrs. Ackley's Kansas crop failed, and both Ackleys fell ill. They and their seven-year-old son were sent to the county poor farm. Mr. Ackley recovered his health, found employment, and tried to reunite his family. However, the state had already apprenticed Ackley's eight-year-old son for ten years to a Mr. Tinker.

> Upon Ackley's petition for his son the court found the apprenticeship immune. If the county is expending funds for relief, the child is a county charge and the superintendent of the poorfarm may apprentice the child without the knowledge or consent of his parents.[60]

In 1899, the Hulls, a family of Connecticut farmers, "came on hard times" and "required public aid for medicine." The state removed five of the six Hull children to an almshouse and "forcibly removed" their parents to another almshouse. When petitioned to release and reunite the Hulls, the court stated that

> No constitutional right was violated by the proceedings in controversy. Town paupers belong to a dependent class. The law assigned them a certain status. This entitles them to public aid, and subjects them, in a corresponding degree, to public control. (So much for the families' home, their children, and their freedom to come and go as they pleased.)[61]

Racially despised parents were still custodially endangered (rather than protected) by the state. For example, when emancipation was imminent, many slave owners drew up apprenticeship agreements binding young slaves to them for long terms of service. In Maryland, on November 1, 1864, one day after the slaves were freed,

> wagonloads of black children were brought to orphan's courts throughout the state to be apprenticed to their former owners. So many children were bound out without their parents' consent that General Lew Wallace, ranking Union officer in the State, offered to intervene in their behalf. He and his aides were besieged with appeals from mothers, fathers and grandmothers.[62]

By the 1890s, the American state had exterminated most of its Native American Indian population. Survivors were imprisoned on reservations, and their children routinely taken from them and sent to boarding schools and private households for training in Christian obedience and in agricultural, domestic, and industrial servitude.

> 1890 *It has been two days since they came and took the children away. We are frightened by this sudden child-stealing. We signed papers, the agent said. This gave them rights to take our babies. It is good for them, the agent said.*
>
> *The agent was here to deliver a letter. This letter is from two strangers with the names Martha and Daniel. They say they are learning civilized ways. Daniel works in fields, growing food for the school. Martha cooks and is being taught to sew aprons. She will be going to live with the schoolmaster's wife. She will be a live-in girl. What is a live-in girl?*
>
> 1891 *They caught me as I tried to board the train and search for my babies. Where have they taken the children? Why do they want our babies? They want our power. They take our children to remove the inside of them. Our power. My daughter, my son. They are still crying for me, though the sound grows fainter. The winds pick up their keening and bring it to me. I begin howling. It is too terrible, the things that happen. A crazy woman. That is what they call me.*[63]

As we have seen, the state already had the legal right to appropriate the children of the poor. Now, under the influence of "child savers," the state gradually began to justify its child-stealing as in the "best interests" of the child.

Many child crusaders were genuinely horrified by child abuse among the immigrant poor. As white, Protestant, middle-class, conservative, and culturally ethnocentric Americans, they were also horrified by the influx of Catholic, Italian, and Eastern European immigrants.*[64]

Child savers idealized stay-at-home married mothers, and scorned unwed, impoverished, or working mothers. They had very fixed ideas about "proper" sex and class role behavior. Their motives were as mixed as their ultimate results.[65]

Child savers and the state removed children from their impoverished city parents and placed them with "respectable" farmers in the country. Charles Loring Brace, of the Children's Aid Society, referred to this program as *their* "emigration program." The children of impoverished immigrants were also placed in orphanages, state poorhouses, training schools, and in reformatories.

---

*Child savers also became anti-Irish in the 1840s after mass Irish immigration to America.

The New York House of Refuge, 1825

Superintendant [sic] Joseph Curtis intended to conduct a benevolent regime [but] children escaped and stole things. Curtis resolved [to be as] harsh as any other father to a youngster who used improper language in the presence of girls. Curtis [administered harsh physical punishment]. The fact that the boys had never known any other than "improper" language apparently had not occurred to Curtis.

Two boys escaped and were returned to the city marshal. Curtis promptly imprisoned them, one in a solitary cell, and the other in the hayloft. The boy in the hayloft chewed off his "toecloth" handcuffs and escaped. He was brought back by his stepfather, and Curtis wasted no time in clapping the (twelve-year-old) boy in irons and placing him in a cell.[66]

To some extent, the state appropriation of *abused* children was a genuine act of Christian mercy. Poor children *were* starving and dying. Some were forced to beg, steal, pimp, and prostitute themselves at extremely young ages. Some poor children were also beaten, raped, murdered, and abandoned by their parents, step-parents, and other adults.

Max Gilman was an eleven-year-old boy, who was beaten to death by his step-father, August Hetzke, in February 1888. The boy's mother died in June 1887; and from that time the brutal parent beat and starved the unhappy boy for months. A witness named Haartze heard sounds of a whipping and plaintive cries of "Papa" at eleven o'clock at night, and then a heavy fall as of a body hurled on the floor. At seven in the morning the beating renewed, and then, with a refinement of hypocrisy, the wretch bade the boy to "get his bible and read the commandments." In the afternoon he was dead.[67]

Abused nineteenth-century children also had non-immigrant, working-, middle-, and upper-class fathers. However, how could the state remove such children from their economically solvent fathers—without dislodging the principle of a father's or the state's own absolute right to custody, and without providing similar redress for abused wives?

Were judges prepared to deprive an economically solvent father of custody—in order to "save" a child? Judges rarely faced this decision. When they did, they attempted to "save" the child through clever, commonsense solutions, and without establishing dangerous judicial precedents.[68]

The state was willing to view child abuse as a poor man's—but not as a rich man's—crime. The state was unwilling to view its own separation of a child from his or her family as a crime at all; nor was the state anxious to condemn *itself* for apprenticing children to criminally abusive masters. As late as 1894, in Pennsylvania, a state "overseer" (but not the apprenticeship system) was prosecuted for

> indenturing a seven-year-old pauper child for fourteen years to a cruel farmer. The overseer was warned before and after the indenture, and visited the farmer, but reported that the boy was not maltreated. The boy died of starvation and overwork after a few months.[69]

By the end of the nineteenth century, an all-male judicial patriarchy had effectively usurped the absolute custodial rights of impoverished, racially despised, and excessively abusive fathers. Sometimes a judge even awarded an impoverished or abusive father's child to a maternal surrogate—if she was already supporting the child economically.[70]

Incredible as it may seem, *biological* mothers had fewer custodial rights than token mother *surrogates* did. Certainly no mother had custodial rights equal or superior to those already enjoyed by fathers and/ or by the state.[71]

Biological and adoptive mothers are *women*. The legal concept of parental rights was interpreted by men, for men—and against women. The concept of parental rights for bio-social mothers simply did not exist. According to legal historian Michael Grossberg,

> [the systematic] decline of paternal rights did not automatically increase maternal ones. On the contrary, the law reduced the rights of parenthood itself. Judges often biased custody determinations toward mothers. Yet they were so rooted in judicial sexual biases, that mothers could claim that preference only when they conformed to the bench's idea of womanhood. The newly instituted maternal preference remained a discretionary policy, not a statutory prerogative. As a result, it could be easily revoked any time a mother did not meet the standards of maternal conduct decreed by judicial patriarchs.[72]

The nineteenth-century judicial concept of moral motherhood had not changed since colonial times. Female "immorality" still consisted of displeasing or divorcing a husband (even an abusive one); committing "adultery"; engaging in any independent economic or intellectual activity; preaching or practicing birth control or abortion; bearing an illegitimate child; and engaging in non-marital "fornication" or "prostitution."[73]

The same state judge, legislator, or social worker who thought nothing of separating a child from his or her impoverished *father* was even more self-righteous about separating him or her from an impoverished or "immoral" *mother*.

The state was not interested in redeeming "immoral" mothers—not even for the sake of their maternally needy children. The state was interested in punishing "immoral" women and in turning the situation to state (and private) economic advantage.

The same state that refused to prohibit or condemn its male tax-paying citizens for excluding women from the "moral" marketplace was the state that refused to condemn *men* for consorting with prostitutes, and refused to subsidize the families of impoverished or unwed mothers.

In 1856, the nation's first reform school for girls was founded in Lancaster, Massachusetts. The majority of Lancaster's earliest inmates were poor Irish Catholic immigrants.[74] Some girls had been abandoned or turned over to the state by their families; some were the victims of incest and child abuse; some were sentenced to Lancaster for past— and to prevent future—fornication or prostitution.[75]

In 1858, Hannah K., "a pretty little girl" of eleven, was brought to Lancaster by her father because she was a "chronic masturbator." He and his invalid wife had not been able to "restrain her," not even by "tying her hands all night." The Lancaster matron quickly discovered that Hannah suffered from a chronic rash (erysipelas); and that she was to be "pitied" and treated "medically, and with kindness."

> Nevertheless [Hannah] was allowed to remain [at Lancaster] as a dependent of the state for eight more years. She was then indentured under the supervision of the state for another two years. Her continued incarceration may have been due to the sympathy of the authorities; it may have also been a result of their fear of what might befall a poor girl from a disrupted home. In the trustees' eyes, she was still considered potentially deviant.[76]

The state "saved" Hannah by training and indenturing her as a domestic servant. There was always a shortage of "desirable" female servants; and female "redemption" meant service to a family. In 1869, the Lancaster trustees explained why.

> [We think] domestic service is better and safer for [girls] than a trade, because housework in a private family is the only life that affords them sufficient protection after they leave the school. Allowing a girl to board, and work in a shop or factory, gives a freedom which they would too often abuse.[77]

Never at a loss for new ideological ways of blaming the victim, and of profiting from her victimization, the state now decided that *all* female sexual activity was proof of genetic "imbecility" or "feeble-mindedness." "Imbeciles" would not miss their children; and their children would be better off without them.[78]

The State Industrial School for Girls, Lancaster, Massachusetts, 1908

Beulah S. had been deserted by her parents as an infant and left to the mercy of the state. At age fourteen she mothered an illegitimate child and afterward was sent to Lancaster for theft and incorrigibility. . . . When she was twenty-six, Dr. Fernald described her as having "keen sexual propensities." Accordingly, Fernald labeled her a "moral imbecile" and consigned her to the custodial department of the institute.

Mary R. entered Lancaster reportedly as unchaste and "diseased." Her Lancaster records report her as "of average intellect." . . . The Lancaster officials did not express great surprise that Mary, after five placements in four years, had an illegitimate child. Although Mary was reportedly a good mother, the baby was sent away from its mother and placed in the infants' asylum. Soon after, Mary R. was returned to the Massachusetts Home for the Feebleminded.[79]

By the beginning of the twentieth century, an American mother enjoyed the right to custody only in nine states and in the District of Columbia; and only if a state judge found her morally and economically worthy of motherhood.[80]

CHAPTER TWO

A Contemporary Overview

Wait, wait (my governess) Big Elephant said, (your maternal grandmother's) told me exactly what you must write word for word. She leaned over me and said, Under Dear Naney write I miss you.

I MISS YOU, I wrote.

Very good darling, she said. Now under that put My mother is a rare beast. Why why why? and I started to cry. So did Big Elephant. Because, because she said, your Naney says to.

And I cried and cried as I wrote MY MOTHER IS A RARE BEAST.

Yes, there were times that summer I wanted to scream—at both of them—Stop! But already it was too late. I was in too deep. In on the plan . . . What did it matter that I didn't know the details of the plan or the nature of the plan? What I did know was that if I went along with it, Dodo Elephant and Naney Morgan would not be sent away. We three would stay together.

The stuttering had come to me in recent times, ever since the Custody trial, come to think of it, and it made complications for me in classes at Green Vale when my turn came to speak.

Gloria Vanderbilt
Once Upon a Time: A True Story

BETWEEN 1975 AND 1980, in the Midwest and in New England, Catherine, Nora, and Adele each were custodially challenged by their physician husbands. These mothers had been married for an average of sixteen years. Among them, they had mothered eleven children, in loving and highly traditional ways. Catherine and Adele were full-time, stay-at-home mothers. Nora was also a full-time mother—with a scientific career.

Adele was a wife and mother for fourteen years. She initiated a divorce reluctantly—only after she became convinced that her husband would never give up his mistress and would never spend enough "family time" at home.

Adele:	We lived in a very large house. I had a housekeeper three times a week during the day when the children were infants. The housekeeper did the laundry and cleaning. I did most of the cooking and all of the child care. The housekeeper left about four o'clock each day. At the trial, my ex-husband said I had a maid and did nothing but sleep. He said I couldn't even keep the closets as super neat as he wanted and that I never managed to cook the way his mother cooked.
A Fit Mother:	*Does Not Need a Housekeeper, Does Not Sleep, Keeps the Closets Neat, and Cooks the Way Her Husband's Mother Did.*
Adele:	My ex-husband's psychiatrist friend was one of his expert court witnesses. The psychiatrist said that I was an "awkward mother" who "tried too hard" and was "too tense" because I wasn't "biologically secure." I was an adoptive mother. That hurt terribly.
A Fit Mother:	*Is a Biological Mother. Adoptive Fathers Are More Fit Than Adoptive Mothers.*
Adele:	I was also accused of being a flaky artist. The judge was told that I couldn't support my children on what

26

I could earn and that I would probably bring other flaky artists into the home and give my children "wrong ideas."

A Fit Mother: *Is Not an Artist and Has No Artist Friends. If She Is an Artist, She Earns as Much as a Physician Does.*

Adele: It's like the old Solomon story. The true mother lets go. When my children were with me, their father pulled them to pieces. Now that they're with him, I won't pull them to pieces. I won't say, "Your Dad's no good," or, "I need you." If they complain to me about their father I say, "Yes, I know he's difficult. I know he's got a bad temper, but you've got to work it out."

A Fit Mother: *Is a Psychologist, Philosopher, and Saint, for Which She Gets No Credit.*

After ten years of enforced marital celibacy Catherine had a love affair. Catherine's husband immediately moved for both divorce and custody. Catherine began the first full-time job of her life a year before her trial.

Catherine: I did everything for my children by myself. I didn't want any babysitter or housekeeper to come between me and my children. When they were in school plays, I sewed their costumes myself, by hand. I made all sorts of fantastic decorations for every children's party. I loved every minute of it. The judge refused to listen to any of this.

A Fit Mother: *Does Not Rest on Her Laurels.*

Catherine: I had inherited a great deal of money. However, my husband controlled all my money. He refused to sign it over to me, especially after our separation. I was able to earn only the minimum wage. My husband told the judge that I couldn't afford to support the children. Only he could.

A Fit Mother: *Does Not Work for the Minimum Wage.*

Catherine: I took a job from nine to five. I couldn't get home till six-thirty at night. I shopped on the weekends and made spaghetti sauce, beef stew, casseroles—dishes that could be heated up at night. Six months before the trial, my husband started arriving home at five-thirty. He refused to heat anything up or wait until I got there. He'd be gone with the children by the time I got home. "How could I be a good mother," he asked the judge, "if I came home long after he did at night."

A Fit Mother: *Always Arrives Home Before Her Husband.*

Catherine: They said that an adulteress really couldn't care about her children. Two of my husband's witnesses, a priest and a psychiatrist, said that something was wrong with me because I committed adultery—especially since my husband hadn't.

A Fit Mother: *Remains Celibate if She Has to, Even for Ten Years. She Never Commits Adultery, Especially When Her Husband Doesn't.*

Catherine: My youngest children started questioning me. Why didn't I love them anymore? Why did I have to work? Why did I insist on hurting their father? Didn't I understand how hurt and angry he was? I said nothing to them. I didn't feel it was right to involve them in our adult problems.

A Fit Mother: *Never Works and Never Angers or Hurts Her Husband. She Never Burdens Her Children with Her Side of the Story. She Gets No Credit for This.*

Catherine: The judge was very impressed by my husband's medical credentials. He treated him with a lot of respect. I was "just a mother," who couldn't earn enough money on her own. I was also an adulteress.

A Fit Mother: *Is a Physician (Married to a Physician), Who Really Doesn't Need to Work—Except at a High-Paying Job with Very Flexible Hours.*

After years of marital discord Nora initiated a divorce. Her husband tried to kill her, kidnapped their two youngest children, fought for custody, and "on principle" refused to pay any child support or divide up their marital assets.

Nora: My ex-husband used to boast about how efficient I was as a mother and as a scientist. Yet his lawyer kept asking the judge how I could possibly be a single mother and also have a full-time career. They claimed that as hard as I worked, I still couldn't earn as much as my ex-husband did.

A Fit Mother: *Is Married and Does Not Have a Career. She Spends All Her Time with Her Children. If She Is Divorced, She Must Support Her Children on Inherited Wealth.*

Nora: I believe in respecting my children's judgment. I believe in letting them learn from their mistakes. This became proof of my unfitness. Someone testified that she'd seen one of my sons improperly dressed on a cool day. Yes. He refused to put on a jacket. And I wanted him to learn from his own mistake.

A Fit Mother: *Forces Her Children to Wear Jackets in Cool Weather. She Must Not Let Her Children Make Their Own Decisions, Nor Can She Afford to Respect Their Judgments.*

Nora: My ex-husband now believes that I'm a very wicked mother because I left him. He doesn't think he is a wicked father because he tried to kill me or kidnapped the children.

A Fit Mother: *Never Leaves Her Husband—No Matter What.*

Nora: The judge sent me to a psychiatrist, who described me as "paranoid" about my ex-husband—and "overly suspicious" of psychiatry! The psychiatric report described my husband's choking me and kidnapping the children as a "singular episode." The psychiatrist doesn't think my ex-husband represents a threat to anyone but me, and then only because I "provoke" him. The psychiatrist said that my "fear" of my ex-husband and my "refusal to forgive" him will "stunt" the children's normal emotional development. He therefore recommended that the children live with their father.

A Fit Mother: *Never Has to See a Psychiatrist.*

Question: Is a Father Who Murders His Wife Still Entitled to Legal Custody of His Children?
Answer: Yes.

Question: Is a Divorced Mother Who Lives with a Man out of Wedlock Still Entitled to Legal Custody of Her Children?
Answer: No.

On August 29, 1978, in Illinois, Lonnie Abdullah bludgeoned his wife, Anna, to death with a large kitchen knife. Mr. Abdullah was found guilty of first-degree murder and imprisoned for sixty years. The state moved to have his three-year-old son legally adopted. The imprisoned father contested the proposed termination of his parental rights.

In 1980, the Illinois Supreme Court decided that a murder conviction was not sufficient reason to automatically deprive Mr. Abdullah of his paternal rights. The dissenting judge noted: "Where a person murders his wife, thus depriving his child of a parent, the State should not be compelled to obtain that person's consent before it may place the child for adoption. By murdering the child's mother, the respondent has demonstrated his disregard for the child's best interests." [1]

This judge contrasted the court's *Abdullah* decision with its recent decision in the *Jarrett* case. In 1979, Jacqueline Jarrett, a divorced mother of three children, lost custody of her children because she had a live-in boyfriend. She appealed this decision. The appellate court returned custody to her, noting: "[Mrs. Jarrett] is a kind, affectionate mother. She had not neglected her children in any way as a result of the relationship. The schooling and religious training of the girls was being attended to. . . . It is evident that Jacqueline Jarrett, Wayne Hammon [her live-in boyfriend] and the three children function as a family unit."[2]

In 1981, Jacqueline Jarrett lost custody in the Illinois Supreme Court. The Abdullah court decided that Jacqueline's "non-marital relationship *in and of itself* was harmful to the children."[3]

Question: Can an Immigrant, Unwed, and Impoverished Mother Lose Custody of Her Child for These Reasons?
Answer: Yes.

In 1980, Christina Landaverde fled her native El Salvador. Like so many immigrants before her, she arrived in the United States destitute, pregnant, and with a "poor" knowledge of English. Social workers persuaded Christina to part "temporarily" from her newborn son, Mauricio.

The document [Christina] signed . . . contains the following unequivocal clause: "I understand that this declaration is not a consent to adoption and that in signing this document I retain rights to the custody, control, earnings and support of said child." All the lawyers and social workers assured her that she was not giving away her baby and was reserving her option to change her mind.[4]

Within three weeks, Christina wanted her son back. She was three weeks too late. The social workers had already found Mauricio a "real" family: a white married American couple, both of whom spoke English perfectly, and neither of whom worked as a "domestic."

From 1980 to 1983, Christina Landaverde waged a heroic and lonely war for custody of her son. The court confirmed that Christina had not "surrendered, abandoned, persistently neglected or been an unfit mother" to Mauricio. On the contrary.

This mother has ever been very devoted, dedicated to the struggle to regain her child—overcoming her lack of language and her paucity of funds, by her trek across America, by her persistent visits to the child, as well as by her legal efforts. . . . [It is] difficult to avoid measuring the relationship of parent and child by our own North American standards of culture, language and nature of family constellation.[5]

Nevertheless, in August of 1983 with sadness and regret, a New York court denied Christina custody of her son. The court viewed Mauricio's "future welfare" as more important than his natural mother's right to custody. Theoretically, Christina could be deported back to El Salvador—a country recently declared "unsafe." Christina still worked as a "domestic"; she was still unmarried. Mauricio's "best interests" were judicially perceived as better served by remaining in a "stable, devoted, two-parent home."[6]

> *Question:* Can a Native-born American Lose Custody Because She Lives on Welfare?
> Answer: Yes.

In 1983, Linda Gould, a divorced Wisconsin mother, lost custody of her seven-year-old daughter, Kimberly, because as a stay-at-home welfare mother she "earned" six times less than her ex-husband, Steven, who, as an engineer, earned $29,000 a year. Steven was also perceived as an "achiever." Linda was perceived as an "unemployed high school graduate."

Despite the fact that Linda was seen as a good mother, despite the fact that her daughter wanted to remain with her, the court felt that Kimberly's father could provide her with "enhanced opportunities for academic achievement, social stimulation, and formal religious instruction."[7]

> *Question:* Can a Native-born Mother Who Works (and Isn't on Welfare) Lose Custody Because She Earns Less Money than Her Husband?
> Answer: Yes.

In 1979, Audrey E. Porter, a North Dakota mother, lost custody of her three children because she earned too little money as a part-time waitress at night. In order to earn what she could, Audrey had to leave her children with a baby-sitter. She preferred to be there during the day when the children arrived home from school—but she was willing to work days, doing housework. The court nevertheless awarded the children to their father, Thomas, an Air Force captain.

On appeal, the mother argued that it was unfair for her to lose her children because she chose to stay home with them, foregoing career opportunities. But the court, in a cruel twist of the customary logic, stated that it would not be more fair to deprive the father of custody because he did not stay home during the day, as "both care and support are important."[8]

In 1980, Shirley Anne Dempsey, a Michigan mother, lost custody of her children because of her low earnings. Mrs. Dempsey had been her children's only domestically active parent. In fact, Shirley Anne initiated the divorce because her husband had no interest in family life.

The father, who was a hard earner and hard worker, frequently missed dinner with the family, worked long hours, and spent his leisure time bowling and on snowmobile trips without the family. The trial court judge, in reserving a ruling on the mother's obligation to pay child support, suggested that she might fulfill this obligation by serving as the children's regular babysitter![9]

Question: Can a "Career" Mother Lose Custody Because She Works and Isn't Poor?
Answer: Yes.

In 1977, divorced Michigan mother Esther Gulyas lost custody of her six-year-old daughter because she worked "forty to fifty hours per week (during the tax season), and ten to thirty hours per week at other times." Esther was forced to rely on "day care." For these reasons (her "career" and her reliance on "day care"), the judge awarded custody of the girl to her father—who had never assumed any child-care responsibility and who, unlike his ex-wife, could not leave work at midday.[10]

In 1978, a Kansas mother, Kathleen V. Simmons, lost custody to her ex-husband for similar reasons. Mr. Simmons was the "millionaire president of an oil company." When Kathleen appealed, the court found that "[Mrs. Simmons's] business and social interests, after the divorce, had priority over her concerns for her children. [The husband], on the other hand, had remarried and he and his wife were willing and able to offer the children a more stable home environment."[11]

In 1980, a Chicago mother, Mildred R. Milovich, lost custody of her children. In 1982 this decision was upheld on appeal. While neither parent "emerged as a monster or a saint," Mildred had presumably committed adultery, had to travel some of the time as part of her $18,000-a-year job, and was presumably less "affectionate" than her former husband to the children she had mothered.

Mildred's ex-husband, Peter, had presumably not committed adultery (but he was accused of hitting his daughter). He worked full-time for the Chicago Housing Authority—but never had to travel out of town.

Judge Charles J. Grupp noted that Mildred "is entitled to pursue her own career, but that her children were entitled to a stable environment." Peter got custody—and possession of the marital home.[12]

In 1983, Louisiana Judge Melvin Duran awarded custody of a four-year-old girl with cerebral palsy to her physician-father—because her mother, Margaret Gaines Bezou, was a lawyer. The judge derided Mrs. Bezou for being

> . . . interested first and foremost in herself and in furthering her own career . . . she gives no promise of putting an end to her career ambitions. [Mrs. Bezou has shown no signs of being] willing to sacrifice advancement of her career [for the youngest child's benefit]. This woman would move with her two daughters to American Samoa if a better job opportunity opens up.
>
> The handicapped girl has been "cursed" with two ambitious parents, especially a mother who wants to be a lawyer more than she wants to be a mother. . . . Gabrielle's illness indicated that "the Lord tried to give this mother a message to 'settle down' " but Mrs. Bezou refused to listen.[13]

Question: Can a Divorced, Remarried, Stay-at-Home Mother without a Career Lose Custody of Her Child—If Her Political Activities Offend Her Ex-Husband and the State?
Answer: Yes.

In the early 1970s, Tina married Ted Fishman, a nuclear physicist, subsequently employed by the Lockheed Missile and Space Company. Tina gave birth and was a devoted mother to her daughter Riva: she was also a "revolutionary communist." The couple divorced; Tina remarried and retained custody of Riva for the next seven years.[14]

In 1980, while Riva was visiting her father for the summer, Tina participated in a demonstration in front of the White House. She was arrested, indicted, immediately released on bail, and eventually acquitted. Ted seized this opportunity to convince California Commissioner James Browning that Tina's activities constituted an "emergency" in terms of Riva's life.

Browning decided that Riva was "unquestionably well cared for but that her mother's passion for politics" specifically constituted neglect. Browning transferred custody to Ted.[15]

For eighteen months Ted refused to let Riva see her mother. Tina and John Stevenson, her husband of seven years, fought Browning's emergency order in California, Indiana, and Illinois. In December 1982,

California Judge Gerald Ragan overturned Browning's initial emergency order. He still refused to return Riva to her mother. Judge Ragan contrasted Ted's "stable, safe, religious and orderly home" with Tina's *character*, which he found "totally absorbed by a fanatical obsession with a political cause which has blinded her to the true needs of a ten to twelve year old."[16]

Because Riva *had* been brainwashed against her mother, Judge Ragan felt the girl needed more time *with her father*, to get used to the idea of returning to her mother. Ragan therefore extended paternal custody for another six months and allowed Tina five days of maternal visitation. On September 22, 1983, Tina Fishman lost custody of her daughter for the third time. Tina says: "The whole message the court is giving is if a woman is political she's unfit to be a mother. My case is being used as a forum by conservative government machinery to punish me for my political activities."[17]

> *Question: Can an Apolitical "Career" Mother Lose Custody of Her Children Because Her Husband and a Judge Find the "Confessions" in Her Private Diary Offensive?*
> Answer: Yes.

In 1977, after twelve years of an increasingly "tense and troubled" marriage, a "professional" couple (*Anonymous* v. *Anonymous*) separated. The mother accepted a one-year university appointment at the University of West Virginia. Her husband forbade her to take their children along. She obtained an agreement in writing that her "leaving would not constitute either an abandonment or desertion of her husband and three children, all under ten." She visited her children for "long weekends" every three weeks and saw them on holidays.

In the summer of 1978 the anonymous mother returned home. Marital discord continued. For the next year the father, a well-paid astrophysicist in the space industry, kept a careful record of exactly how many weekends he spent alone with the children (twenty-eight), compared to his wife's measly fourteen. He recorded the number of hours she spent in the library working on her dissertation and how often she complained about or refused outright to cook and clean.

The anonymous father then "accidentally discovered a diary written by the mother." He read it, moved out, and sued for divorce and sole custody. "In the best interests" of the child, New York Judge Willens admitted this diary as evidence against the mother.

Judge Willens was shocked by what it contained, although he carefully stated that he was not against "career mothers"; nor did he think that "marital unhappiness [was] immoral."

The mother's handwriting states that she "dislikes housework"; yearns for a "housekeeper" to "free her from the obligations of parenting"; has on occasion lost her temper and her patience with her children, who "crowd around her like animals, like maggots"; has been in a "panic" over this situation; has "experimented" with marijuana; and has engaged in at least twenty episodes of adultery with both men and women while in West Virginia.

Judge Willens confronts the anonymous mother with her "selfishness" and "self-indulgence"—all based on her diary. The mother denies that what she has written expresses the whole "truth" of the matter. Willens decides:

> [She has also] chosen to perjure herself, amounting to a double jeopardy, self-imposed. Her love affairs with other women are her own business and do not enter into the court's deliberations. Neither does the fact that she was involved in heterosexual relationships suggest any moral turpitude. However the large number of these adulterous liaisons; the desperate quality of the relationships . . . together with her involvement with drugs . . . reflect poor judgment. . . . Concerning the right of a mother to live her own lifestyle, "this is her prerogative, but it must yield to the best interest and welfare of the child." Obviously, the same rule would apply to a father.[18]

Judge Willens admits that both parents have been "fit." On July 20, 1981, he awarded sole custody of all three children to their anonymous father, as the more "fit" parent—who was already engaged to marry a schoolteacher, "prepared to care for the children every day after 3:30 in the afternoon."

Question: Can a Wealthy, Apolitical, Non-"Career," Stay-at-Home Mother Lose Custody of Her Child—Because, Like Her Husband, She Commits Adultery?
Answer: Yes.

In 1983, Roxanne Pulitzer lost custody of her twin five-year-old sons to her husband, Herbert. In 1984, she lost her appeal. Roxanne's reliance on a governess and housekeeper whom she, not Herbert, supervised, wasn't at issue—as it once was in the more notorious Vanderbilt custody case.[19]

The presiding judge found Herbert Pulitzer's admitted "flagrant adulteries" irrelevant. The Florida judge castigated Roxanne for *her* "flagrant adulteries." In his opinion:

> This court finds that the wife's gross moral misconduct involved more than isolated discreet acts of adultery. She openly engaged in a continuous adulterous relationship with her male paramour. The marriage union is the very bedrock upon which our society is built. Flagrant acts of adultery and other gross marital misconduct demean the sanctity of the marriage and family unit and will not be tolerated.[20]

For her sins, Roxanne lost custody of her children and access to her home and "life-style." She was given limited rather than liberal visitation and was ordered to start "job-hunting."

Throughout the twentieth century fathers have continued to commit adultery and to engage in post-divorce sexual activities without experiencing their sexuality as a custodially or an economically punishable offense.[21]

Throughout the twentieth century mothers, like fathers, have continued to commit adultery. Despite the maternal presumption, "good enough," adulterous mothers continued to risk losing custody for this reason. For example, in 1948 in New York, Ethel Bunim was sued for divorce and custody by her physician-husband on the grounds of adultery. The dissenting judge described Ethel as a

> good and devoted mother; her indiscretions were unknown to the children; she was deeply concerned with their welfare; and for their part, the children returned her affection with attachment that was in the language of the trial court "almost Biblical" in its intensity. . . . [The father is] inordinately preoccupied with his professional duties; that as a result, he gave little of his time or of himself to the children; and that not infrequently he treated them brusquely, impatiently and even intemperately.[22]

Ethel nevertheless lost custody of all her children. Despite her daughters' "passionate and intense attachment" to her, the court was deeply offended by her "belief" that she had done "nothing wrong." The

> belief in the propriety of indulgence, by a dissatisfied wife such as herself, in extramarital sex experimentation [is unforgivable]. Our society is based on the absolute fundamental proposition that: Marriage [creates] the most important relationship in life, [and] has more to do with the morals and civilization of a people than any other institution.[23]

Some twentieth-century adulteresses *have* been able to win custody of their children, but for reasons having little to do with their natural or earned rights as mothers. For example, an adulteress can sometimes retain custody if she genuinely repents her *single* lapse from virtue; if she returns home to live with her parents; if she can support her children on her own or with help from her father; if her ex-husband has not supported his children; and if he has no more money than the convicted adulteress does.

In 1950, in Arizona, after reading his wife's diary and realizing that she had had an affair during his military absence, William Henry Grimditch, Jr., sued for sole custody of his children. Gioia Grimditch came from a well-to-do family and had been supporting her children from her own family funds. The judge viewed Mr. Grimditch as a "cold" husband who "abandoned his wife [in the hospital] with a badly broken body, immobilized by several casts after a car accident in which he was the driver. He returned only after a month to show her her diary, and to announce that he was taking the children."[24]

The judge awarded Gioia custody because she was a "fit" mother, had already suffered, and was now planning to live with her wealthy and socially prominent father. The judge might not have allowed her custody of "older" children. According to the court, "the same immoral conduct in the mother of older children might deprive her of custody since older children are more impressionable."[25]

What if a married mother not only commits adultery but gets pregnant and gives birth to a child that is not her husband's? In 1943, Ruth Taylor Blain, an Arkansas schoolteacher, was sued by her ex-husband for custody of their "legitimate" daughter on the grounds of adultery, which had resulted in the birth of a second and "illegitimate" child. (Blain had deserted and divorced Ruth and was himself remarried by the time of this "illegitimate" birth.)

Ruth was allowed to retain custody of her "legitimate" daughter for a number of reasons. The presiding judge was convinced that she had been guilty of only one "lapse from virtue" and that she had "genuinely reformed." He noted that the ex-Mrs. Blain attended church regularly and had regained the respect of her "community," many members of which testified on her behalf. Her own family took her back. She was also supporting both her "legitimate" and "illegitimate" children with no help from either of their fathers.[26]

What if Ruth had no family to take her in? What if she had to live on welfare or work for minimum wage? What if she and Mr. Blain were white—but her lover wasn't?

*Question: Can a Divorced Mother Lose Custody of One Child Be-
cause She Gives Birth to Another (Illegitimate) Child of the "Wrong"
Color?*
Answer: Yes.

On September 7, 1983, Kathleen Blackburn, a divorced white mother,
lost custody of her four-year-old white son, Nicholas, for the third time,
after giving birth to a half-black "illegitimate" daughter. In 1979, the
Blackburns divorced. Mr. Blackburn remarried and in 1981 won sole
custody of Nicholas after charging Kathleen with "lewd" and socially
tabooed behavior. Superior Court Judge W. C. Hawkins awarded custody to the boy's paternal grandmother, "commenting later that the
Southeast Georgia town of Millen was not ready for that kind of integration. [He denied] that race influenced his ruling."

Kathleen Blackburn appealed this decision and in 1982 won custody
of Nicholas in the Georgia Supreme Court, which, however, noted:
"The defendant's extramarital relationship resulting in the birth of an
illegitimate child should [not] be condoned. It would be unrealistic to
ignore the fact that society may stigmatize Nicholas [the boy] because
his sibling is illegitimate."[27]

Within a year the Georgia Court of Appeals upheld Judge Hawkins's
original decision. They noted that since her divorce, Kathleen had an
abortion as well as an illegitimate child. Kathleen noted that "attempts
to take Nicholas away from [me are] racially motivated since no one
tried to gain custody of [my] racially mixed daughter."[28]

*Question: Can a Divorced Lesbian Mother Lose Custody Because
She Is a Lesbian?*
Answer: Yes—Unless She Refrains from Lesbian Activities.

In 1972, two ex-husbands "ganged up" on their ex-wives, Sandra
Schuster and Madeleine Isaacson. Both mothers had previously been
awarded custody of their children—provided they did not live together.
The two women therefore took apartments across the hall from each
other.

When both Mr. Schuster and Mr. Isaacson remarried, they petitioned
the court to modify its custody decision, on the ground of "changed
circumstances." Sandra and Madeleine had begun to "stigmatize" their
children by being openly gay; they had even made a film entitled *Sandy
and Madeleine's Family.*

Also, since both husbands had remarried, they could now provide their children with a two-headed heterosexual household. The Supreme Court of the state of Washington upheld maternal custody in both cases—provided the women continued to live apart.[29]

In 1975, a California lesbian mother lost custody because she insisted on her right to engage in lesbian activities—"in the best interests" of her children. She described her children's relationship with her co-mother and lover as "mature and sensitive." She said: "My lover takes my son to Cub Scout meetings. We have a warm and stable family life. She takes him to those games much as an aunt, or a grandmother, or a mother might."[30]

The judge insisted that the female lover was acting out the "butch," or male, role and that *this* was confusing and dangerous for a boy in need of a *male* father figure.

> Question: Is Life with a Lesbian Mother Worse Than Life in a State Institution?
> Answer: Yes.

In California, in 1973, the mother of four children was arrested and released for possession of a small amount of marijuana. As the state bureaucracy began to return her children to her from various state institutions, her lesbianism was "discovered."

No one was challenging this mother for custody of her children. However, the state was upset that her children *knew* she was a lesbian and that she refused to repent of it.

The court didn't argue that her lesbianism had *had* a negative effect on her children. Instead, the court removed her children to a state institution to protect them against any *future* emotional problems. For some reason, the state allowed her to retain custody of her sons—but not of her daughters.[31]

> Question: In a Contest, Is a Sperm Donor Ever Entitled to His Paternal Rights Over the Single Mother's Objection?
> Answer: Yes—Especially if the Mother Is a Welfare-Dependent Lesbian and the Sperm Donor Says He Is Willing to Reimburse the State Partially.

In 1980, in California, a woman collected sperm in a jar from a "politically sympathetic" homosexual. She inseminated herself by "turkey baster" and, in 1981, gave birth to a son. In order to be a stay-at-home mother, she gave up her full-time job, worked part time, and received partial welfare payments. In 1982, when her son was eighteen months old, she and he accidentally met the sperm donor on the street. According to San Francisco attorney Donna Hitchens:

> The sperm donor was suddenly taken with the idea of having a real son. He hired a lawyer and sued to be recognized as the "father" and to obtain visitation rights. The mother didn't want to share her child with a man, who was essentially a stranger—and who by now was actively hostile to her. The sperm donor pursued the matter in court. Once the District Attorney and the judge understood that she was a lesbian mother on welfare; and that he was willing to reimburse the state by about $100.00 a month, the judge ordered visitation to commence immediately for one day each week. This sperm donor is now in a position to get custody—if he ever wants it.[32]

Question: What Happens When a Sexually Active Mother Is Accused of Killing Her Husband?
Answer: She Will Be Separated from Her Children, Imprisoned, Convicted and Executed for Her Sexual Activities.

In the 1920s, Ruth Snyder, a "respectable" wife and mother, fell in love with Judd Gray, a "sweet-talking" traveling salesman. According to Ruth, Judd "started asking her for money—ninety dollars here, a hundred there—suggesting that he might have to speak to Albert [her husband] if she didn't come up with it. She did as she was asked—even though she wanted to break off the affair—*for fear that in a showdown with Albert she would lose her daughter* [author's italics]."[33]

Ruth Snyder and Judd Gray both were accused of killing Ruth's husband, Albert. Gray initially confessed to the murder; Ruth categorically denied it. Witnesses testified to Gray's purchase of the murder weapon and his establishment of an alibi weeks before the murder.

On the last day of the trial Judd accused Ruth of having "incited" him to "strike the first blow." The only evidence against Snyder was Judd's testimony. It was enough—to convict Ruth as an adulteress and to sentence her to death.

Although Judd and Ruth were convicted for the *same* crime, Judd was heralded as a hero for having finally "told the truth." The district attorney called Judd a "decent, red-blooded, upstanding American." Ruth was "savagely pilloried" in the courtroom and in the press and died in the electric chair.[34]

Question: What Happens When a Battered Mother Kills Her Husband in Self-Defense?

Answer: If She Is Not Sexually Active and If She Is Lucky, She Will Be Separated from Her Children and Imprisoned for Life as "Insane."

When battered mothers kill their violent husbands, boyfriends, or ex-husbands in self-defense, they are usually imprisoned without bail and given maximum sentences. Acquittals, although newsworthy, are rare.[35]

On March 26, 1977, in Wisconsin, just after Francine Hughes had set fire to her husband's bed in Michigan, Jennifer Patri shot her husband to death, buried the body, and set the house on fire.

Jennifer was a Sunday School teacher, PTA president, and a hard-working farm wife. Her husband, Robert Patri, was violent, alcoholic, and adulterous. He had also sexually molested both Jennifer and their twelve-year-old daughter. Jennifer shot Robert when he came to demand his visitation rights—"armed with a butcher knife" and "threatening to shut [Jennifer's] mouth once and for all."

The press portrayed Jennifer as a woman who "battered back"; and as a wife who shot her husband in the back and still "enjoyed a total victory in the courtroom." In reality, Jennifer was sentenced to ten years in prison. After a year, she was also convicted for arson.

Defense psychiatrists testified that indeed Patri had been temporarily insane when she set the fire after the shooting, but the jury went the experts one better; they decided that she was still insane and should be transferred from prison to a state mental hospital. And there Jennifer Patri, having won "a complete and total victory," remains.[36]

Question: What Happens When a Sexually Active Mother Is Accused of Infanticide?
Answer: She Will Be Tried and Convicted for Her Sexual Activities. These Crimes Are Viewed as Interchangeable.

Any mother capable of leaving her husband and engaging in "promiscuous adultery" is probably capable of "anything"—including the murder of her own children.

On July 15, 1965, Alice Crimmins, a New York "working-class housewife," called the police to report that her children were missing. The first detective assigned to her case, the prosecuting attorneys, the jury, the judge, and the press—all viewed Alice as a "bitch," "tramp," and "swinger," who "deserved to die."[37]

Alice was guilty of having boyfriends—*and not being ashamed of it.*

Although Eddie Crimmins, the children's father, admitted that he "exposed himself to little girls in the park" and "hid in the basement under [Alice's] bedroom to listen to her have sex with other men," he was never viewed as capable of killing his children. Nor was he investigated.[38]

Once the children's bodies were found, Alice was arrested and held without bail. On the basis of flimsy, inconclusive, and strongly contested evidence, twelve male jurors found Alice guilty of first-degree murder in the case of her son and of manslaughter in the case of her daughter. The judge sentenced Alice to life imprisonment on the murder charge and five to twenty years for manslaughter.

For the next twelve years Alice was either in prison; working on an appeal; on trial; being psychiatrically examined by the state; or being "lewdly" examined by the press. She was not seen—or comforted—as a mother whose children had been kidnapped and murdered. Alice addressed the prosecuting attorney in this way:

> Anything you people have done to me in the past, anything you are doing to me now, and anything you may do to me in the future can't be worse than what was done to me six years ago when my children were taken from me and killed. And I just hope and pray the world will see all your lying and scheming against me. And I just hope and pray to have the chance to put you all down some day for what you are.[39]

Question: What Is Going On?
Answer: Patriarchal Law Is Going On.

In Chapter One we saw that women were historically punished for fornication, adultery, and having "illegitimate" babies. They were also punished for using birth control, having abortions, concealing the deaths of "bastards," committing infanticide—and "husband murders." These are the quintessential female crimes under patriarchy. They are often seen as interrelated. Why?

Abortion was, and still is, seen as an act of female violence against a helpless male fetus and against the fetus as private (male) property. Female-initiated abortion is "proof" that despite women's rigorous training in repression and non-violence, female nature may be no more tamable than male nature.[40]

Without maintaining a twenty-four-hour guard, how can a husband be sure his (disobedient) wife's children are really "his," not another man's? How can he be sure that her every pregnancy results in the birth of "his" child? How can a disobedient woman ever be trusted alone with children?

Any woman capable of breaking male law—sexually, reproductively, theologically, or economically—may also be *capable* of infanticide. Her *capacity* is unforgivable. The fear of the disobedient woman is the fear of the unwed mother; is the fear of the spurned wife turned rebel; is the fear of the witch; is the fear of Medea.[41]

Medea is the grand-daughter of the sun-god Helias. She is an Asian princess; a dusky "barbarian"; a powerful priestess.

Medea, strange to say, "falls in love" with Jason, a Greek adventurer. Medea marries him and betrays her blood ties and homeland to aid him in his quest for the Golden Fleece.[42]

Now, years later, Jason has abandoned the "aging" dark-skinned refugee Medea. He is about to marry King Creon's daughter, the young and "yellow-haired" Princess Glauce.

Jason's marriage is not an affair of the heart; it is a political decision. Strictly speaking, Jason is not *romantically* betraying Medea; but he is legally "demoting" her to the status of a prostitute or concubine. He is consigning both her and their sons to poverty, ostracism, and exile.[43]

Jason informs Medea that her banishment is her own fault. King Creon is afraid of her "cleverness," her "evil arts," her "anger," her "stubborn temper," her "loose talking." According to Jason, Medea should consider herself "lucky that exile is her [only] punishment."

Jason defends his marriage to Glauce as a "clever move" and in Medea's "best interest." Marriage to Glauce will make him a powerful Corinthian citizen. He will father more children. This will "benefit" Medea's children. They will be the half-brothers of princes. Jason asks Medea:

> . . . . Do you think this is a bad plan?
> You wouldn't if the love question hadn't upset you.
> But you women have got into such a state of mind
> That, if your life at night is good, you think you have
> Everything; but, if in that quarter things go wrong,
> You will consider your best and truest interests
> Most hateful. It would have been better far for man
> To have got their children in some other way, and woman
> Not to have existed. Then life would have been good.[44]

Despite everything she knows; despite who she is; Medea has forgotten herself for the sake of "love." She has used her powers to "help" one man—her husband. Medea has never committed adultery, nor has she ever disobeyed Jason. She has happily counted her children as "his." Medea's love-humbled behavior is what accounts for her tragic downfall.

By contrast, Jason has been an absent father and faithless husband. He is a spoiled and foolish man-child. Jason has used Medea as if she were a powerless Greek wife. Without pity, he is ready to move on. Jason under-estimates both Medea and her power. This is what accounts for his tragic downfall.

Medea's "heart is broken"; she wants to "die"; she is "finished." She has loved a man not worthy of her, a "civilized" man who neither loves nor honors her as the mother of his children. Jason is guilty of "the worst of all human diseases, shamelessness."

Medea calls the *women* of Corinth together. She orders them to "stay and watch how the barbarian woman endures betrayal." She will destroy the "upstart" Jason. He is not worthy of immortality—i.e., of children who are no more to him than property.[45]

Medea will also destroy her "enemies"—the mighty King Creon and Glauce, Jason's child bride. She tells the women of Corinth that it is not "bearable to be mocked by enemies."

> You there! You thought me soft and
>   submissive like a common woman—who takes a
>   blow
> And cries a little, and she wipes her face
> And runs about the housework, loving her master? I
>   am not such a woman. . . .
> I shall not die perhaps
> As a pigeon dies. Not like an innocent lamb, that feels
>   a hand and looks up from the knife
> To the man's face and dies.[46]

Medea turns Jason's inability to feel her pain against him. She asks Jason to "forgive" her and to "beg Creon that the children not be banished." She will give them up and go into exile without them. Jason, fool that he is, actually thinks this is a good plan.

From this point on, Medea cannot "compromise" with tragedy. She sends her sons to the palace bearing wedding presents for Glauce: a dress and a diadem. Glauce can't resist trying Medea's golden finery on. She and her kingly father are consumed in Medea's poisoned flames.

Corinth is in commotion. Jason rushes in to save his sons; Medea greets him in a "chariot drawn by dragons." She tells Jason that his sons are dead; their bodies are in the chariot with her.

Jason begins to "suffer"—i.e., to feel self-pity. He is destroyed. He is childless. Jason calls Medea a "hateful" and "loathsome" "thing." She is a "wicked mother, an evil monster, not a woman."

Jason is correct. Medea is no ordinary woman. She is not even an ordinary queen. She is half goddess and a powerful priestess (witch). She speaks the language of power. That is why she is capable of destroying, by any means necessary, those who betray her will, her love, or her "honor." She tells Jason:

> You had love and betrayed it: now of all men
> You are utterly the most miserable. As I of women.
> But I, as woman, despised, a foreigner, alone
> Against *you* and the might of Corinth
> Have met you, throat for throat, evil for evil, vengeance
> for vengeance.[47]

What choices does Medea, the mother, have? Can she protect her sons in exile, as she

> Wander[s] with fear and famine
> for guide and driver, through all the wild winter
> storms
> And the rage of the sun; and beg[s] a bread-crust and [is]
> derided; pelted with stones in the villages,
> Held a little lower than the scavenger dogs, kicked,
> scorned and slaved?[48]

Can Medea, the mother, protect her sons by killing herself or by killing Jason? Can she protect them by giving them up, never seeing them again, or leaving them behind "in a country that hates her, to be the prey of [her] enemies' insolence?"[49]

Can Medea, the mother, protect her sons from being killed once *she* has killed Glauce and Creon? And if Medea can save her sons and if she is willing to live with them as hunted fugitives, in poverty, can she bear to remain the mother of Jason's sons?

> Am I to look in my son's eyes
> And see Jason forever? How could I endure the end-
> less defilement, those lives
> that mix Jason and me?[50]

But how can Medea kill her own children? (They are not hers; they "belong" to their father.) But they are *her* children, too. She alone has given birth to and reared them; she alone loves them.

> I cannot bear to do it. I renounce my plans. . . .
> Why should I hurt their father with the pain
> They feel, and suffer twice as much of pain myself?
>
> I wish you happiness, but not here in this world.
> What is here your father took. Oh, how good to hold you!
> How delicate the skin, how sweet the breath of children!
> Go, go! I am no longer able, no longer
> To look upon you. I am overcome by sorrow. . . .
>
> Oh, come my hand, poor wretched hand, and take the sword. . . .
> And do not be a coward, do not think of them.
> How sweet they are, and how you are their mother. . . .
> Afterward weep; for even though you will kill them,
> They were very dear—Oh, I am an unhappy woman![51]

Medea is neither an "unfit" mother nor deranged—i.e., unaware of what she is doing. Medea, the mother, does not want to kill her sons. Medea the pagan priestess, Medea the matriarchal queen, Medea the goddess is resolved to do so.[52]

Medea's murder of Jason's children, and of those "enemies" that would crush both her and them, constitutes a stunning insurrection against patriarchal husband-rule.[53]

In Medea's time—at least in Euripides' time—only fathers, never mothers, had the legal right to kill their "own" children. Men, not women, had the right to "revenge" themselves against their "enemies" and to fight wars of "honor."[54]

How many wives dare to speak of their "honor" or have the power to revenge its loss? How many mothers *abandon* (no less kill) their children to protest maternal impoverishment and betrayal?

How many mothers kill their children to avoid having to serve a child who looks like, "belongs" to, and admires the very man who has abandoned or betrayed her?

What is the play *Medea* telling men to do? Perhaps it is telling men not to dishonor or divorce their wives. Perhaps it is telling men to mistrust their wives from the beginning and to treat them harshly—lest they are destroyed by them.

What is the play *Medea* telling women to do? Perhaps it is telling women not to "fall in love" with "shameless" adventurers, or not to marry them, or not to tell them who their children are—lest they one day find themselves in Medea's tragic position.

The crime of maternal infanticide has long been associated with Medea in the patriarchal imagination. Medea's crime is one of essential being. Medea is a proud and powerful woman. Her sacred power has been forbidden, debased, condemned—and eroticized, as a sexual crime.

The *idea* of Medea threatens men's trust in their wives. The *idea* of Medea therefore threatens all women's highly circumscribed access to a (man's) child. This may be why disobedient women are always first condemned by other women.

Who, then, is really an unfit mother? Can a mother be as fit as Medea and still kill her children? Would she have to be insane to do so or, like Medea, powerful when crossed?

Who, then, is really an unfit father? Can a father be as unfit as Jason and still hope to keep his children? How fit, how sane, is the father willing to send his children and their mother into exile or to separate his children from their mother—forever?

CHAPTER THREE

What Is a Fit Mother and Father? An Unfit Mother and Father? Who Decides?

Who ever saw a human being that would not abuse unlimited power? Base and ignoble must that man be who, let the provocation be what it may, would strike a woman: but he who would lacerate a trembling child is unworthy of the name of man. A mother's love can be no protection to a child.

It is folly to talk of a mother moulding the character of her son, when all mankind, backed up by law and public sentiment, conspire to destroy her influence.

Elizabeth Cady Stanton

While maternal devotion may be perfectly genuine, this, in fact, is rarely the case. Maternity is usually a strange mixture of narcissism, altruism, idle daydreaming, sincerity, bad faith, devotion and cynicism. The great danger which threatens the infant in our culture [is that its] mother is almost always a discontented woman.

Simone de Beauvoir

49

WHAT ARE OUR STANDARDS for parental fitness? Who determines such standards? Are they the same for both mothers and fathers; and for all classes and races? Judith Arcana, in *Every Mother's Son*, describes the

> idealized mother [as] a woman who is boundlessly giving and endlessly available. She is truly present to her son. The idealized father is practically invisible; he is almost never available, rarely giving; his sparse favor and scarce presence to his son become miraculous and precious when they do appear. He is like the unknowable Judaeo-Christian father-god, who is the epitome of this idea.[1]

Mothers are expected to perform a series of visible and non-visible tasks, all of which are never-ending. Mothers are not allowed to fail any of these obligations. The ideal of motherhood is sacred; it exposes all mothers as imperfect.

Fathers are expected to perform a limited number of tasks. They are also allowed to fail some or all of these obligations. In addition, fathers who do *anything* for children are often experienced and perceived as "better" than mothers—who are supposed to do everything. The ideal of fatherhood is also sacred; it protects each father from the consequences of his actions.

Father-starved and father-wounded sons (and daughters) rarely remember, confront, or publicly expose their absent or abusive fathers. Arcana also notes:

> We mothers watch our young boys go from expecting to be cherished and nurtured by their fathers to the sullen and bitter understanding that dad will not come across. And then, so powerful is society's sanction of that "ideal" paternal behavior, we see our sons come to an acceptance so complete that they will defend their fathers even against the criticism and anger they've expressed themselves. And all along, the boy will not—or cannot—confront his father. Young sons will not push their fathers the way they'll push their mothers—they learn early that dad's affection, such as it is, is tenuous and conditional. Most boys understand all this before they are 12 or 13 years old.[2]

When a father fails his paternal obligations, we don't necessarily view him as an example of *all* fathers, nor do we automatically hold other fathers "accountable" for one father's failure. We may be horrified when a father abuses or kills his child, but we first view him as the *exception* among fathers.

Or we make excuses for him. He didn't mean to (hit, molest, hurt, maim, or kill) his child. He is a man. Men are violent and don't know their own strength.

Or we blame his wife. Perhaps she "drove" him to it. How could any mother leave her child alone with such a man? Where was she when her child was being (hit, molested, hurt, maimed, or killed)?[3]

When a mother does irresponsibly abandon or savagely abuse her child, we are truly stunned and terrified. How could a *mother* of the human race "act like a man"? How could both biology and culture fail to ensure maternal pacifism under stress?

When one mother neglects or abuses her child, we tend to hold *all* mothers accountable for her failure. One mother's "crime" forces all mothers to prove—to themselves and to everyone else—how unlike Medea they are and how like the Virgin Mary they are.[4]

After reading several news accounts of maternal suicide and infanticide, I read about a mother who failed in her double suicide attempt. She succeeded in killing her child but failed to kill herself. Plunging headlong out the window, she "merely" broke every major bone in her body instead.

I wanted to visit her in her hospital bed. After many phone calls, I was made to understand that her own mother refused to see her; and that her husband had vowed never to speak to her again. Women who knew her and her husband tried to dissuade me from seeing her. Women said:

> Don't make a heroine out of her. She's a real sickie. You wouldn't have liked her. None of us did. She's broken her husband's heart. He's a wonderful man.
>
> Her husband was about to leave her. She knew that her son would follow his father, sooner rather than later. The bitch just couldn't let go. Why didn't she die instead of her son?

Voices without mercy; voices determined that no one comfort her on her cross. This mother was viewed not as human, or even as psychiatrically ill, but as an evil monster, a "loathsome thing," a "Medea."

I am always amazed that Medea's knife, unseen onstage, looms so much larger in our collective memories than Agamemnon's knife, with which he kills his daughter, Iphigenia, or than Laius' mountaintop exposure of his newborn son, Oedipus. The infanticidal fathers leave no bloody footprint, no haunting shadow.[5]

Are contemporary mothers and fathers as abusive to their children as parents presumably once were in the past? Historians have described medieval European and colonial American children as essentially their family's "servants." A girl was her mother or stepmother's domestic servant and her father's companion and nurse; a boy was his father or stepfather's agricultural servant. Both boys and girls were apprenticed out at young ages. Their wages belonged to their fathers.[6]

According to psychoanalyst Alice Miller, child rearing in the West was a form of "poisonous pedagogy." Harsh parental punishment was defended "for the child's own good":

> A sophisticated repertory of arguments was developed to prove the necessity of corporal punishment for the child's own good. In the eighteenth century, one still spoke of [children] as "faithful subjects" . . . child rearing manuals teach us that: "Adults are the masters (not the servants) of the dependent child; they determine in godlike fashion what is right and what is wrong; the child is held responsible for their anger; the parents must always be shielded; the child's life-affirming feelings pose a threat to the autocratic adult; the child's will must be 'broken' as soon as possible; all this must happen at a very early age, so the child 'won't notice' and will therefore not be able to expose the adults."[7]

In Puritan New England, child rearing was synonymous with "breaking" a child's (sinful) "will":

> Every child was thought to come into the world with inherent tendencies to "stubbornness, and stoutness of mind": these must be "beaten down" at all costs. One aspect of such tendencies was the willful expression of anger which was, by Puritan reckoning, the most dangerous and damnable of human affects. Children must therefore be trained to compliance, to submission, to "peace." To effect such training, drastic means were sometimes needed. Puritan parents were not inclined to spare the rod; but more important than physical coercion was the regular resort to shaming.[8]

Mothers worked hard and had little twentieth-century "child-centered" time to spend alone with each child. Although mothers (or women) were exclusively responsible for birthing and rearing children, they were not considered "expert" in this area. "Students of child-rearing literature in England and America tell us that in the 16th and 17th centuries the father was depicted as the important figure in the rearing of children, as well as being the ultimate authority in familial matters. In fact, most of the manuals of these centuries directed advice to fathers."[9]

In the mid to late eighteenth century, male experts began to address mothers directly. Formerly viewed as vain, and without souls, mothers were now viewed as their children's moral guardians.[10]

(Middle-class) mothers were encouraged to experience (biological) motherhood as the source of their greatest pride and joy. The influential Jean Jacques Rousseau viewed motherhood as a personal religious calling:

> The true mother, far from being a woman of the world, is as much a recluse in her home as the nun is in her cloister. . . . [A good mother] will not be willful, proud, energetic or self-centered. In no event should she become angry or show the slightest impatience . . . she must be taught, while still very young, to be vigilant and hard-working, accustomed at an early age to all sorts of constraints so that she costs [her husband] nothing and learns to submit all her caprices to the will of others. . . . She serves as liaison between [the children] and the father, she alone makes him love them.[11]

Throughout the nineteenth century, male experts continued to urge women into motherhood as a religious calling. However, these experts insisted that "instinctive" maternality (emotional, "soft") was harmful to children. They advised mothers to behave in more "manly" ways.[12]

By the twentieth century, male experts had told mothers to give up breast feeding and to feed their infants only at rigid intervals, not to pick up their crying babies, and to toilet-train them as soon as possible.[13]

Some male experts advised mothers to "bond" with their infants immediately at birth. According to these experts, if mothers didn't "bond," or didn't "let go" of children perfectly enough, they doomed them to "neurosis."[14] According to psychiatrist Ann Dally, mothers were tyrannized into believing that it was "dangerous" to leave their children "even for an hour."[15]

We do not know how many women actually succumbed to the tyranny of the male experts. Enslaved or impoverished mothers did not have the time, the literacy, or the resources to act on scientific opinion; wealthy and royal mothers continued to delegate their maternal responsibilities. (Perhaps some royal and impoverished mothers felt guilty about this.) Middle-class mothers were in a position to be most easily tempted by expert promises.[16]

The church fathers always assured mothers that they were important and irreplaceable. They also tried to convince men that it was anti-God and anti-church to divorce their wives or abandon their children.

The male experts shared these churchly beliefs. However, they also promised mothers "control" over the outcome of their maternal labors; and "control" over children at home in lieu of "control" over armies, parliaments, churches, or banks.[17]

What about fathers? Did they matter at all beyond their legal acknowledgment of sperm and economic support of families? Did it affect children badly, or at all, if fathers were absent, distant, or tyrannical? What is a "good" or a "good enough" father?

According to our state and church fathers, a "good" father is someone who legally acknowledges, economically supports, and teaches his children to obey the laws of church and state. The male experts—our scientific fathers—failed to consider the paternal role. When pressed, one twentieth-century expert said:

> The first positive virtue of the father is to permit his wife to be a good mother. In the child's eyes the father embodies the law, strength, the ideal, and the outside world, while the mother symbolizes the home and household. . . . The only thing one can usefully demand of the father is to be alive and stay alive during his children's early years.[18]

Some scientific fathers went to great lengths to deny the existence of "bad" fathers. Psychoanalysts, for example, were actually more eloquent about the rivalrous impulses of sons than about the murderous deeds of fathers.[19] Most psychoanalysts rarely paid attention to real-world "facts" or held real fathers responsible for anything they did—or failed to do.[20]

Psychoanalysts and other, more popular child-development experts failed to acknowledge their own expert fathering as "responsible" for an increase in maternal guilt and for turning mother blaming into a "science." For example, the phrase *maternal deprivation* has terrorized countless mothers in our century. A woman who "maternally deprives" her child is a "bad" mother. Dr. John Bowlby first used this phrase in 1951 to describe what happens to children whose state father has institutionalized them.

Bowlby did not condemn the state father for "depriving" his institutionalized children, nor did he (or his popularizers) hold the state responsible for the crimes such children might commit in the future. The sins of the state fathers were used to control maternal behavior. The specter of "maternally deprived" children kept mothers guilty and sleepless. (State orphanage employees and Members of Parliament slept quite soundly.)

Popular accounts of child abuse invariably focus on the "sensational" episode as opposed to the more entrenched forms of child abuse. A male homosexual child molester makes ready headline copy; his more numerous male heterosexual counterparts remain invisible.

A single school involved in the sexual abuse of children becomes a scandal; the high incidence of male heterosexual abuse of female children, including paternal incest, is denied or minimized.

What exactly is child abuse? Is *physical* child abuse increasing in America? Most incidents of physical child abuse are probably never reported. Nevertheless, the National Center on Child Abuse and Neglect reports a "dramatic increase" in child abuse.[21]

Naomi Feigelson Chase found that "serious" child abuse was either under-reported or atypical during the 1960s.[22] Chase and Leontine Young attempt to distinguish between severe physical neglect—lack of adequate or regular feeding—and moderate neglect, which includes lack of cleanliness, lack of adequate clothing, and failure to provide medical care.[23]

They also point out that physical neglect is not the same as physical abuse, which, in turn, may be either moderate or severe. According to Young, the prolonged physical and psychological abuse of children constitutes a category all its own, as does child murder: "Severe [physical] abuse is consistent beating that leaves visible results. Moderate abuse occurs when parents beat children under stress or when drunk. [Those in the] severe category are unable to be helped. The abusing parents' hall-mark is deliberate, calculated, consistent punishing without cause or purpose."[24]

Dr. David Gil analyzed the 13,000 *reported* cases of physical child abuse in the United States in 1967 and 1968. Of these, 3 percent were fatal; less than 5 percent "led to permanent damage"; 53 percent (6,890 cases) were "not serious"; 90 percent "were expected to leave no lasting physical effects."[25]

These studies of reported child abuse were almost *always* correlated with extreme poverty, severely "deprived" parental childhoods, mental illness, overburdened and isolated single motherhood, and unrelieved or profound stress.[26]

In view of the high incidence of and extraordinary stress associated with single *motherhood* and the great amount of time mothers have to spend with children, it is significant that both Gil and Chase found no evidence that mothers "abuse" their children any more than fathers (or boyfriends) do. On the contrary. According to Chase:

A mother or stepmother was the abuser in 50 percent of the incidents and the father or stepfather in about 40 percent. Others were caretakers, siblings, or unrelated perpetrators. However, since almost a third of the homes were headed by females, fathers had a higher involvement rate than mothers. Two-thirds of the incidents in the homes where fathers or stepfathers were present were committed by the father or stepfathers; while in homes with mothers or stepmothers, the mothers and stepmothers were perpetrators in less than half the incidents that took place.[27]

As recently as 1983, researchers studied pregnant mothers who were potentially "high-risk" physical child abusers. All these mothers were young, poor, unwed, and going through with unplanned *and* unwanted pregnancies. The study found that, as expected, one-quarter of the children were *psychologically* abused. The researchers explained this abuse in terms of the mothers, who had themselves received no "maternal nurturance" in childhood. The psychologically abusive mothers "don't know how to be nurturing. Instead of giving to the child, they look to the child to satisfy their own needs for nurturance and love, and the child cannot provide."[28]

This study actually shows that 75 percent of "high-risk" mothers do not psychologically abuse their children and that "high-risk" mothers need emotional as well as economic support in order to mother properly. The study focuses on maternal, not on paternal, abuse.

Researchers have no control over how their work is viewed or used. This study (and others like it) are used to "indict" mothers in the public imagination, to incite middle-class or married mothers to paroxysms of time-consuming guilt, and to justify the state's custodial or reproductive punishment of poor, unwed mothers.[29]

Mothers do not *physically* or sexually abuse, abandon, or neglect their children as often as fathers do.

Between 1979 and 1984, several statistically sophisticated studies confirmed that it is mainly men (fathers, grandfathers, stepfathers, boyfriends, older brothers, uncles, and male strangers) who physically and sexually abuse both mothers and children.

How many fathers and adult men beat or rape mothers? No one really knows. Research suggests that anywhere from 15 to 50 percent of all mothers in America are physically battered and/or raped by their husbands or live-in boyfriends.[30]

Some studies (and common sense) suggest that wife beaters also tend to abuse their children physically, sexually, and psychologically. The sons of wife beaters often become wife beaters; their daughters often become battered wives.[31]

How many fathers sexually abuse their own genetic or legal children and grandchildren? No one really knows. A number of first-person and clinical accounts about paternal incest have recently been published and publicized.[32]

According to incest researchers, 2 to 5 million American women have been paternally raped as children; one in every seven[33] or one in every five American children is the victim of paternal incest or of male sexual abuse[34]; 19 percent of all American women (one in six) and 9 percent of American men were sexually victimized as children.[35]

It is my impression that the majority of unfit mothers do not kill, torture, maim, rape, or abandon their children outright. The majority of unfit mothers seem *physically to neglect* and *psychologically to abuse* their children.

Mothers do spend more time with children than fathers do. Mothers also turn up in emergency rooms alone with battered children. The sight of a mother accompanying a child with a broken arm or a suspicious burn is sickening and impossible to forget.

We do not ask, "Why is she here alone?" or "Where is the child's father or other adult member of his family?" We do not comment, "Maybe the father (or a man) actually beat this child, and she's confessing in his place," or "Perhaps the absence of a supportive husband 'drove' her to it."[36]

Still, it is my impression that when an unfit mother does physically abuse her child, she may do so less forcefully, less often, and less fatally than her paternal counterpart.

Physically neglectful or physically violent mothers are more closely and critically scrutinized than physically abusive fathers are. For what it's worth, such mothers are also psychologically trained to monitor themselves for violence; fathers are not.

Such mothers have also internalized certain maternal ideals. Whether they achieve or fail them, they are aware of, and often guilty about, their imperfect or failed maternal performance.

Clearly, children are equally endangered by equally physically violent parents whether they are mothers or fathers. However, women in general are more rigidly socialized into non-violent maternal behavior *under stress* than men are.

Female socialization, the experience of pregnancy and childbirth, maternal practice, and the social "watchdogging" of mothers—all tend to reinforce maternal physical non-violence. Children tend to be *physically* safer with most mothers most of the time. Sara Ruddick has observed that most mothers are (objectively) "powerless" women who find themselves

> embattled with weak creatures whose wills are unpredictable and resistant, whose bodies [they] could quite literally destroy, whose psyches are at [their] mercy. . . . *I can think of no other situation in which someone with the resentments of social powerlessness, under enormous pressures of time and anger, faces a recalcitrant but helpless combatant with so much restraint* [author's italics]. It is also clear that physical and psychological violence is a temptation of maternal practice and a fairly common occurrence.
>
> *What is remarkable is that in a daily way mothers make so much peace instead of fighting, and then when peace fails, conduct so many battles without resorting to violence.* [author's italics]. I don't want to trumpet a virtue but to point to a fact: that non-violence is a constitutive principle of maternal thinking, and that mothers honor it not in the breach, but in their daily practice, despite objective temptations to violence.[37]

Children are potentially more *physically* endangered by fathers, whose socialization as men has predisposed them to flight or to physical violence under stress; whose socialization has forced them into a fierce dependence upon obedience from wives and children; who, as men, are not closely "watchdogged" within the house; and who, in a father-idealizing and father-absent culture, are romanticized by children. (This dynamic allows children to deny paternal violence against them or to blame themselves when it happens.)

Both nature and culture have prepared women to mother in *physically* non-violent ways under very oppressive conditions. Some observers romanticize the female ability to do this; others lament it as a virtue by default. Most mothers are usually able to absorb frustration, humiliation, unemployment, poverty, celibacy, and extreme loneliness without abandoning, seriously abusing, or murdering their children.

As such, mothers as a group are rearing their children *as well as can be expected of the human race—to date.*

Does a child *physically* need his or her father or father figure during pregnancy or childbirth, during infancy, or at some point later in childhood? Common sense and personal experience confirm that men and women do not have the same physical relationship to children.

It is crucial to remember that many children grow up without any fathers or father figures. Studies suggest that such children are no different from children with fathers—if severe impoverishment is not confused with paternal absence. Perhaps few children are *physically* fathered whether they live with fathers or not.[38]

It is also clear that fathers do have an effect on children whether they are absent or present, that fathers may influence a child directly or indirectly, and that paternal influence can be "advantageous, disadvantageous, or neutral."[39]

Recently, a number of feminist theorists and researchers have written about the psychological importance of "fathering" and about men's potential ability to "nurture." Such researchers have tried to show that a "good" father is potentially as good as (or similar to) a "good mother."[40]

These studies have essentially shown that white, middle-class, well-educated fathers can, under experimental conditions, "bond" with infants; and can perform many of the physical and emotional tasks of "maternal nurturance."[41]

However, studies also show that "good enough" fathers tend to spend radically less time with infants, toddlers, pre-adolescents, and teenagers than mothers do; that fathers tend to "play" with children rather than physically to "service" them; and that fathers tend to "mother" children for comparatively short periods of time.[42]

In real life, some (married) fathers are indeed physically "nurturant" to their children. However, unlike most nurturant mothers, such fathers are unwilling or unable to "nurture" children all day, every day, for all the years of each child's childhood.

Fathers do not get pregnant or give birth to, breast-feed, or take care of newborn infants.[43] Traditional fathers and mothers do not view these tasks as men's province.[44]

Researchers have found that "good enough" fathers are not able or willing to do what "good enough" mothers must do *physically* in related areas, in order to maintain family life. For example, studies confirm that American wives do 70 percent of the housework, whether they are employed outside the home or not.[45]

In their study of American couples during the 1970s, Drs. Philip Blumstein and Pepper Schwartz found that married men had such an intense aversion to housework that when wives insisted they do it, intense acrimony and a greater probability of divorce resulted.[46]

Even if a "good enough" father is unemployed, he does much less housework (and child care) than a wife who is a full-time employee outside the home. Letty Cottin Pogrebin noted that most recent surveys of male domestic participation do not say whether men cook, vacuum, and wash at the direction of their wives or whether they assume primary responsibility for these chores. It doesn't say what the men mean by "cook." Are they slicing tomatoes while their wives turn out four-course feasts, or are they producing a full meal solo or side-by-side? When . . . husbands say they vacuum, does that mean they do all the floors all the time? When they say they "help" or "wash dishes," is that every day, often, sometimes, or on Mother's Day?[47]

Of course, a father may be able to earn more money or physically lift more weight than a mother can. Such (innate and cultural) abilities may have nothing to do with satisfying the daily physical needs of children —directly; or with satisfying these needs in a physically non-violent way, especially at times of parental stress.

Is physical punishment always a form of child abuse? Is a slap the equivalent of a broken arm? Is *physical* abuse the most serious form of child abuse? Is a child who is made to feel "unloved" or "unworthy" more severely abused than a child who is physically punished?

What do we know about psychological mothering and fathering? "Good enough" fathers may be *psychologically* cold, cruel, demanding, rival-rous, ambivalent, smothering, and abusive toward their sons; and *psychologically* seductive and incestuous toward their daughters. A "good enough" father may also be infinitely more psychologically patient, un-derstanding, relaxed, and generous to his children (especially to certain kinds of daughters) than a mother may be.[48]

"Good enough" mothers may be *psychologically* cold, cruel, de-manding, rivalrous, ambivalent, smothering, and abusive toward their daughters (and to a lesser extent toward their sons). They may also be either more positively—or negatively—"maternal" toward their chil-dren than a father may be.[49]

Drs. Joseph Goldstein, Anna Freud, and Albert J. Solnit have noted that the "best" parent-child relationship is both "positive" and "nega-tive"; that it "fluctuates" over time; that "wanted" children may be "excessively valued," to their detriment; and that "good" parents cannot guarantee ideal child development even when they are their child's *psychological* parents—i.e., present and active in daily and physically caring ways.[50]

Most parents do not view the psychological abuse of children as an epidemic with "devastating" consequences. According to psychoanalyst Alice Miller, most parents unthinkingly "murder their children's souls." Parents suppress their children's "vital spontaneity" by the laying of traps, duplicity, subterfuge, manipulation, "scare" tactics, withdrawal of love, isolation, distrust, by humiliating and disgracing the child, scorn, ridicule, and coercion even to the point of torture. The former practice of physically maiming, exploiting, and abusing children seems to have been gradually replaced in modern times by a form of mental cruelty that is masked by the honorific term child-rearing.[51]

Miller may indeed be right. However, she rarely distinguishes between paternal and maternal behavior. She merges what mothers and fathers do (and don't do) into "parental" behavior. Also, Miller's psychologically high standards, while admirable, are rarely applied to fathers—or to mothers of all classes and races.

Unless or until we (and the "experts") are prepared emotionally to judge all parents by the same standard, several conclusions are in order about how most mothers and fathers behave today.

"Good enough" mothers behave (and are trained to behave) differently toward children from the way "good enough" fathers do. Most mothers give birth to children after "successful" pregnancies. Most "birth" and adoptive mothers do not physically abandon or physically abuse their children once they have gotten involved in caring for them.

Some mothers do physically neglect their children. A small (and unknown) percentage of mothers sexually abuse, torture, and kill their children.

All other things being equal, the majority of mothers *physically* nurture and support their children adequately, continuously, and in nonviolent ways.

All mothers are psychologically imperfect. Most? some? few? are also psychologically abusive.

Most fathers are trained to neglect their children physically. Many fathers physically abandon their children. As we have seen, perhaps one in seven fathers (and stepfathers) sexually abuses his daughters; perhaps 50 percent of fathers economically abandon their children.[52]

All fathers are psychologically imperfect. Most? some? few? are also psychologically abusive.

In a woman- and mother-hating culture, it is emotionally difficult or psychologically forbidden to acknowledge female or maternal superiority even—or especially—in the areas of female "specialization."

In a man- and father-idealizing culture, it is emotionally difficult or psychologically forbidden to acknowledge male or paternal inferiority even—or especially—in the areas of male non-specialization.

This is one of the reasons we "forget" that a "good enough" mother is different from a "good enough" father.

As adults, we respond "indignantly" to news of an abused child. We experience child abuse as something extraordinary, not ordinary; as something that *other* parents, mainly *mothers*, do; not as something that our *own* parents or *fathers* once did to us; not as something that we as parents do to our children; not as something that fathers allow to happen to large numbers of children—in their name and without their protest.

As adults, we confuse images of maternal psychological imperfection with maternal physical and psychological unfitness. For example, the idea of a mother's locking her child into a room arouses our rage and a deep sense of heartbreak. (Why? Were we all once left in rooms alone? If so, do we think that this constitutes "child abuse"? Does it?)

The idea of a mother's verbally tormenting or refusing to speak to her child at all, the idea of a mother's neglecting or beating her child provoke the greatest fury and terror in us. (Why? Did our mothers or fathers beat us? If not, why do we so empathetically identify with the image of an abused child? Are we by nature altruists?)

As children, none of us could escape or protest whatever minor or major abuse we suffered at maternal and paternal hands. Now, in one mighty adult voice, we vent our long-suppressed fury—at the *mother* in the "child abuse" headlines.

She is utterly evil and can never be rehabilitated. (How can she be? She is a "stand-in" for so many others.) She is very powerful. This time she must not escape us.

Given male violence (or indifference), how can our own *mothers* accept or defend the way things are? (And they do, they do. . . .) How can our own mothers bear to hear our cries and do nothing? How can they leave us alone in the tiny rooms of our lives?

Given male violence and our fear of it, we scapegoat mothers instead. (They are trained to "take it" without killing or abandoning us.)

Given male violence and our fear of it, we ask: How dare any mother refuse to become pregnant? How dare any mother have an abortion or abandon, abuse, or kill a child—because if she can, then there is no respite on earth, no one to bear the brunt of *our* imperfections, no one to save us, and we, the innocent, are damned.

Medea—not Jason, not Creon—is still the one we blame.

In summary, an ideal mother is very different from an ideal father. A real mother is also different from a real father.

Traditionally, an ideal mother is expected to choose married motherhood for her future at a very young age. She is expected to become pregnant, give birth, psychologically "bond" with, and assume bottom-line responsibility for her children's physical and emotional needs.

She is also expected to behave in physically non-violent and psychologically self-sacrificing ways. This female socialization into and practice of motherhood is devalued and taken for granted.

We experience the same parental abuse as "worse" when a mother performs it. We condemn mothers more than fathers for failing the parental ideal, for performing parental work inadequately, for being psychologically imperfect, and for being physically abusive.

What with such double standards and anti-mother biases, what kind of custodially challenged mother would automatically be viewed as a "good enough" mother? ("There must be something wrong with her. Why else would her husband or the state challenge her?")

Do judges, priests, politicians, psychiatrists, or social workers view unwed, imprisoned, or "career" mothers as maternally fit? Would they view their custodial victimization as unjust? Do white married mothers or white social workers view non-white or welfare mothers as maternally fit?

Most custodially challenged mothers blame themselves for being imperfect. What kind of custodially challenged mother would view herself, or be viewed by other challenged mothers, as a truly "good enough" mother?

I decided to study sixty custodially challenged, predominantly white mothers, who had internalized the Western ideals of motherhood and who were demographically similar to the majority of divorced white mothers in America. These sixty mothers were custodially challenged in every geographical region of the United States and Canada between 1960 and 1981.

I interviewed fifty mothers who were black, brown, yellow, and red. Some, but not all, are part of this study. They are very much a part of this book.

In general, these mothers had married as virgins—or had married the first man they slept with. They had married and given birth at relatively young ages. They had assumed the bottom-line domestic, emotional, and primary child-care responsibilities of traditional marriages. In general, these mothers had stayed at home until their youngest children were of grade-school age. Both psychologically and physically they had put "work" or a "career" second to motherhood.

During our interviews together, these mothers casually and matter-of-factly described performing at least twenty-five very specific maternal domestic and child-related chores—quite separate from domestic chores that are husband-related.[53]

As I noted in the Preface, I was exploring a "worst case" scenario. Could a "good enough" mother ever lose custody? Could she lose custody to a relatively uninvolved or abusive father? Could this happen more than once? Could this happen often?

In my book *Women and Madness* I allowed each of my sixty interviewees to confirm what would ultimately be a collective portrait of the mental health establishment. I employed this approach with custodially challenged mothers.

However, I also interviewed fifty-five fathers who battled for, won, or gave up custody. These independent interviews confirmed many of my conclusions about the range of paternal custodial motives.

The study you are about to read is a study of "good enough" mothers. Unbidden, silent, the mother Medea accompanied me to each interview.

CHAPTER FOUR

Do "Good Enough" Mothers Still Lose Custody of Their Children in North America Today?: The Results of an Original Study

One night in the early summer he came home with photocopies of custody judgments in which the custody of very young children was given to the father. He threw these papers at me saying, "See, this proves I'll be able to take the baby away from you." I tried to read the papers, but I couldn't understand the legal language. I tried to ignore his threats, but they were unremitting. I tried to understand what was troubling him, but it was beyond my twenty-year-old grasp. I felt overpowered, helpless, trapped. Where could I go where he couldn't follow me? What can a pregnant woman do? As he battered me with words, all I could do was cry. And as I did, he'd take my tear-contorted face and press it against the nearest mirror. "Look! See that face? It's the face of a crazy woman!"

Bonnie Lee Black, *Somewhere Child*

"Let me tell you one thing, little lady, so you better listen. No one—not you, not some fancy lawyer, not the courts, no one, is ever going to take my son away from me. I'll fight you till there's nothing left of you. And in case you have any doubts that I'm telling the truth remember that I'm the guy who spent two days in jail rather than pay a parking ticket."

Joy Fielding, *Kiss Mommy Goodbye*

IN MY STUDY, SIXTY TRADITIONAL NORTH AMERICAN MOTHERS WHO had been their children's primary caretakers were custodially challenged between 1960 and 1981, in each geographical region of the United States and Canada. On the average, these mothers had been married by the time they were twenty-one, had reared two children, remained married for nine years, completed three years of college, and, upon separation or divorce, had a median annual "income" of five thousand dollars.

In my study, 70 percent of these custodially challenged and "good enough" mothers lost custody, both in courtrooms and privately, to challenging fathers, 83 percent of whom had not previously been involved in primary child care, 67 percent of whom had paid no child support, 62 percent of whom had physically abused their wives during marriage or divorce, 57 percent of whom had engaged in anti-mother brainwashing campaigns, and 37 percent of whom had kidnapped their children. The median average paternal income upon separation or divorce was twenty-five thousand dollars.

Custody battles lasted for an average of three years and involved 141 children whose average youngest age was six at the time of battle.

This chapter discusses the major reasons that fathers fought for and won custody, and compares custodially challenging fathers with married and divorced fathers in general in North America in terms of their involvement in domestic and child-care activities, domestic violence and child abuse, and post-divorce economic support of their children.

STUDIES OF AMERICAN custody battles during the 1970s and 1980s tend to confirm that fathers custodially challenged mothers, and that many fathers arranged paternal custody privately, or won judicial or "kidnapping" custody of their children.[1]

In an excellent and comprehensive study of divorce and child support, Drs. Lenore J. Weitzman and Ruth B. Dixon found that in 1977, 63 percent of the Los Angeles fathers who fought for judicial custody were successful. The authors note that 90 percent of divorcing mothers retained child custody, but that as the result of an increase in divorce, the actual number of fathers winning custody had increased "dramatically."[2]

They also confirmed that divorce is impoverishing mothers and children, that most fathers do not pay child support, and that most judges do not order fathers to pay adequate or enforceable amounts of child support.[3]

This study is an important one. However, it is not based on interviews with the embattled parents. As such, it is unable to tell us much about the kind of father and husband who fights for custody, or about the kind of mother he challenges.

Studies of judicial trends in custody are also important. However, like statistical studies, they are also psychologically limited. Neither the case law analyst nor the appellate judge personally interviews the embattled parents, their witnesses, or their lawyers; nor do they observe the trial court judge's behavior.

Courtroom transcripts are not usually available to case law analysts. In any event, such transcripts do not convey the non-verbal behavior of courtroom participants, nor do they reveal what the trial court judge refused to "hear," or admit as evidence.

In an excellent study of case law, attorney Nancy Polikoff found that during the 1970s judges had a strong "paternal preference" in cases of contested custody. She notes:

In interpreting the significance of [certain judicial decisions], it is necessary to bear in mind that there has not been a revolution in child rearing, and mothers still bear most of the responsibility. Therefore, data showing a success rate for fathers in courtroom battles of one-third to one-half during the 1970s, suggest the possibility that men who have not been the primary child-care providers are prevailing over women who have been.[4]

67

How many fathers currently have custody of their children? No one really knows. Do more fathers have custody of their children in 1985 than had it in 1885 or 1785? No one knows.

Researchers have estimated that from 1965 to 1972 the number of households headed by divorced or separated fathers increased by 71 percent; that as of 1976, 500,000 fathers had sole legal custody of their children; that as of 1981, between 25,000 and 100,000 formal custody disputes were occurring annually; and that 40,000 fathers have won judicial custody *each year* since 1977.[5]

Such estimates never include the number of fathers who won "kidnapping" custody of their children. Nor do they include the number of fathers who privately coerced mothers into "agreeing" to paternal custody, nor the number of fathers who obtained custody because mothers became ill, were hospitalized for long periods, died, or were genuinely unfit.[6]

American mothers have probably lost more children during the 1970s and early 1980s to paternal kidnapping than to judicial decision. *Parental* child kidnapping is an almost all-male crime. Conservative estimates from the mid-1970s range from 100,000 to 125,000 child snatchings a year.[7] More recently, Dr. Richard Gelles estimated that 459,000 to 751,000 parental "child snatchings" have occurred each year.[8]

I would estimate that from 1975 to 1985, at least 2 million fathers won "kidnapping" custody, and that 400,000 won judicial or courtroom custody. In a single decade, nearly 2.5 million fathers probably won custody of their children in *quantifiable* ways.[9]

This statistical "guesstimate" does not include the number of children separated from their mothers each year by the state because either the children or their mothers committed crimes and were institutionalized.[10]

As I have noted in the Preface, such a statistical estimate not only is partial and conservative, but also represents only the tip of the American custodial iceberg. Each *publicized* custody battle terrorizes married, divorced, and unwed mothers in non-measurable and unknown ways.

A number of researchers have studied the psychological and medical consequences of divorce among both men and women, and the measurable effects of a conflicted marriage or a "bad" divorce on children.[11] The most influential (or most often quoted) of these studies focus more on fathers than on mothers, more on children than on mothers, and more on paternal rather than on maternal expressions of parental longing.

Most studies about custodial fathers concentrate more on what fathers *say* about themselves as parents than on observations of what they do. Pro-paternal-custody researchers have not viewed paternal custody historically or politically; nor have they explored how custodial fathers "parented" during marriage or after divorce; or whether they "parent" differently than non-custodial fathers do. Male custodial "parenting" is almost never compared to female custodial or non-custodial mothering.[12]

In 1982, Dr. Deborah Luepnitz published an excellent study of joint custody. Luepnitz interviewed sixteen custodial mothers, sixteen custodial fathers, eleven joint custody parents, and ninety-one children. She found that sole and joint custodial fathers fought long, hard, and "bitterly" to win custody, and had higher incomes, more support systems, and less of an "authority" problem with children than did sole or joint custody mothers.

Luepnitz's divorced mothers and fathers all adopted some "cross-gender" skills—i.e., fathers became more "domestically" competent; mothers, more "economically" competent. Luepnitz's children were measurably similar, psychologically, whether they lived with their fathers, their mothers, or with both parents in joint custodial arrangements.[13]

As a social scientist Luepnitz cannot and does not argue in favor of joint custody, nor does she "confirm" that male parenting and female mothering are alike. Ideologically, Luepnitz believes that genuine *co-parenting* would be ideal during marriage and, if practiced, should continue as joint custody after divorce. Luepnitz calls for "further research" to study whether joint custody is better, per se, for children than are other "conflict-free" custodial arrangements.

In 1982, Dr. Patricia Pascowicz published a study of non-custodial motherhood. Ideologically, Pascowicz is a champion of a woman's right to be a (good) "absentee mother" without being treated as a social pariah. Her arguments are eloquent and passionate. However, the majority of Pascowicz's questionnaire respondents (61 percent) lost or relinquished custody against their wills. The remaining mothers relinquished custody as the result of serious emotional problems (18 percent), a desire for self-realization (17 percent), or a belief that the children's fathers were more "nurturant" (4 percent).[14]

The majority of Pascowicz's "absentee" mothers both felt and *were* horribly victimized. All were treated as social pariahs. Only 14 percent ever again gave birth to or adopted children. Some of Pascowicz's mothers, however, did develop themselves, economically, intellectually, and emotionally, after becoming "absentee mothers."

In 1984, Dr. James R. Turner published the results of his interviews with twenty-six divorced fathers who had fought for and won sole custody of their children. Two-thirds of these fathers did not have "close" or nurturing relationships with their children during marriage, were "upset" by their wives' pregnancies, and were not "involved in the birth process." According to Turner, these fathers (who were in the majority) sought custody out of "anger" at their wives and/or because they felt their ex-wives were "poor parents." They "waited" an average of two years before moving for custody.

One-third of Turner's fathers sought custody immediately upon separating. Turner reported that these fathers were "pleased" with their wives' pregnancies, "involved" in the birthing process, and, according to them, "involved in at least half of the child care activities during marriage." These fathers sought custody in order to "maintain a close relationship with their children."[15]

What kinds of fathers custodially challenge a "good enough" mother? Are they similar to most other divorced (or married) fathers and husbands? Are they exceptionally nurturant—or exceptionally abusive—fathers and husbands? Do they pay child support? Do they see their children regularly, and behave in non-violent ways?

Why do these fathers fight for custody? How often do they win? Why do they win? Can a "good enough" mother really lose custody of her children? If so, why? How is the psychological parenting of mothers and fathers viewed in a custodial confrontation? How are "good enough" mothers psychologically affected by having to battle for custody—against their will?[16]

HOW DID I CONTACT THESE CUSTODIALLY EMBATTLED MOTHERS? (TABLE ONE)

Table One describes how I found my core group of sixty custodially challenged mothers. I interviewed each mother in my home or office—or in hers. The interviews lasted from two to ten hours and took from one to three days to complete. Three-quarters of each interview was taped. I also read and analyzed each mother's trial transcript, legal deposition, psychiatric report, and relevant private correspondence—when it was available.[17]

I transcribed and then analyzed the taped portion of these interviews, both statistically and thematically.

TABLE ONE.

Methods for Contacting Sixty North American Mothers Who Battled for Custody (1960–1981)*

Source	Percent of Total Population
Professional referral†	35
Referred by another interviewee	25
Interviewee answered newspaper ad placed by author	17
Interviewee approached the author voluntarily in search of therapist or custody expert	12
Interviewee contacted by author after her case appeared in law journal or newspaper	8
Author heard about interviewee privately and initiated contact	3

*Eight custody battles took place between 1960 and 1970. The remaining fifty-two battles took place between 1971 and 1981.

†I contacted lawyers, physicians, psychologists, social workers, psychoanalysts, college administrators, displaced homemaker agencies, women's centers, and shelters for battered women for referrals. The referred mothers called me first 50 percent of the time. This was also true for those mothers referred by another interviewee.

WHAT KINDS OF MOTHERS WERE CUSTODIALLY CHALLENGED? (TABLE TWO)

As a group, these mothers were married by the time they were twenty-one, and had two children by the time they were twenty-seven. Half the mothers were married between 1951 and 1964; half were married between 1965 and 1974. Their marriages lasted for an average of nine years.[18]

As a group, these mothers had completed an average of three years of college.[19] Of these mothers, 30 percent had professions in teaching, nursing, social work, psychology, science, and medicine; 10 percent were serious (unpaid or poorly paid) artists; and 60 percent had no

TABLE TWO.

Comparison of Sixty North American Mothers and Fathers Who Battled for Custody (1960–1981)*

Mothers			Fathers		
1. Religious origin			1. Religious origin		
Catholic	14	23%	Catholic	11	18%
Protestant	30	50%	Protestant	26	43%
Jewish	16	27%	Jewish	23	38%
2. Average number of years married	9		2. Paid alimony	6	10%
3. Average number of children	2		3. Paid child support	20	33%
4. Responsible for the primary child care of children under eight	60	100%	4. Involved in the primary child care of children under eight	8	13%
5. Mothering styles:			5. Fathering styles:		
Traditional	60	100%	Traditional Patriarch	36	60%
			Peer-Buddy	10	17%
			Smother-Father:	14	23%
6. Physically abused their husbands	0	0%	6. Physically abused their wives	37	62%
7. Estimated median annual income at time of separation		$5,000	7. Estimated median annual income at time of separation		$25,000
8. Had live-in stepfathers, maternal grandmothers, or live-in boyfriends	9	15%	8. Had live-in stepmothers, paternal grandmothers, or girlfriends	31	52%
9. Kidnapped their children	7	12%	9. Kidnapped their children	22	37%
10. Engaged in brainwashing campaigns	0	0%	10. Engaged in brainwashing campaigns	34	57%

professional-level skills when they married—or when they separated.

In addition, 87 percent of these mothers had never worked full time or at "careers" once they became mothers. Thus, when each separated, she had access to very little money—i.e., upon separation, her annual "income" was $5,000. This represented a combination of wages, child support payments, alimony, savings, loans—and state welfare.[20]

Of the group of mothers, 94 percent were white; 77 percent were heterosexual. Fifteen percent of the heterosexual mothers eventually remarried or had live-in boyfriends.

Half the mothers were of Protestant origin; 23 percent were of Catholic origin; 27 percent were of Jewish origin.

WERE THESE MOTHERS REALLY "GOOD ENOUGH" MOTHERS?

Fifty-eight mothers (97 percent) successfully gave birth to children after pregnancy and labor. (Two mothers adopted infants at birth.) All mothers, whether they worked outside the home or not, psychologically bonded with their children and were their primary care givers.

Most mothers personally attended to all their children's physical and emotional needs. A minority supervised others in assisting them with certain maternal responsibilities. Custodially challenged mothers fulfilled at least the following twenty-five child-related responsibilities:

1. Breast- and/or bottle-fed infants;
2. Changed six to eight diapers a day until their infants were toilet-trained;
3. Toilet-trained their infants;
4. Nursed their infants through every illness;
5. Taught each infant how to eat;
6. Taught each child how to speak;
7. Taught each child how to walk;
8. Taught each child how to read;
9. Shopped for children's food;
10. Shopped for children's clothing;
11. Cooked for children;
12. Sewed for children;
13. Ironed for children;
14. Cleaned for children;
15. Called and waited for repairmen, salesmen, etc.;
16. Helped children with their homework;

17. Helped children with their psychological problems;
18. Chose religious and private schools or special lessons for each child;
19. Chose and transported children to and from dentists and doctors;
20. Transported children to and from birthday parties, athletic and cultural events;
21. Planned and carried out all family holidays and birthday parties;
22. Planned and worked out the details of children's summer camps;
23. Met and maintained contact with teachers, parents' groups, and other parents;
24. Found, trained, and supervised baby-sitters and housekeepers;
25. Assumed responsibility for sick children, whether they worked outside the home or not.[21]

WHAT KINDS OF FATHERS CUSTODIALLY CHALLENGED "GOOD ENOUGH" MOTHERS? (TABLE TWO)

In this study, eight fathers (13 percent) were involved in the primary child care of their children. Eighty-seven percent of the fathers weren't responsible for any of the previously mentioned twenty-five chores. An exceptionally good husband sometimes "helped out" with one to three of these chores; an unusually good husband felt "responsible" for one to three of these chores.[22]

According to mothers, about 20 percent of the fathers "helped out." For example, a father might "baby-sit" for one child while a mother nursed another sick child; or a father might shop, following a list created by his wife. Some fathers "helped" their wives put children to bed, or took the children out while mothers rested or did other domestic tasks.

In general, fathers earned money—and left the children and house-work to their wives. Most mothers never expected or asked for their husbands' help with household tasks. Those mothers who did were met with disbelief, indifference, or hostility.

During marriage and/or during the custody struggle, 62 percent of the fathers physically abused their wives. More than a third (37 percent) kid-napped their children; 57 percent engaged in serious child-brainwashing "campaigns." Half the fathers remarried or had live-in girlfriends or paternal grandmothers.

As a group fathers earned *five times* as much as mothers. Half the fathers earned between $7,000 and $25,000 a year at the time of separation. A fourth earned between $26,000 and $49,000; a fourth earned between $50,000 and $300,000 a year. Although these fathers had been domestically and reproductively serviced by their wives for an average of nine years, only 10 percent paid any alimony; only a third paid any child support.

Ninety-four percent of these fathers were white; 87 percent were heterosexual and/or sexually active within marriage; 13 percent were homosexual, bisexual, or sexually celibate.

In regard to religion, 43 percent of the fathers were of Protestant origin; 38 percent were of Jewish origin; 18 percent were of Catholic origin.

The information I have about these fathers is based on my interviews with their ex-wives. In *Women and Madness*, sixty interviewees each contributed to a collective portrait of the mental health establishment. I employed this same approach with custodially challenged mothers.

I also interviewed fifty-five custodially embattled, custodial, and non-custodial fathers. Five of these fathers had been married to five of my

TABLE TWO (A).

Paternal Payment of Child Support and Alimony as a Function of Paternal Income (Based on Sixty North American Custody Battles) 1960–1981*

	Number of Fathers	Paid Alimony	Paid Child Support
TOTAL	60	10%	33%
High income ($50,000 to $250,000 plus/yr.)	16	31%	56%
Middle income ($26,000 to $49,000/yr.)	15	7%	40%
Low income ($0 to $25,000/yr.)	29	0%	17%

*Eight custody battles took place between 1960 and 1970. The remaining fifty-two battles took place between 1971 and 1981.

maternal interviewees; thirty were fathers' rights activists. These interviewees confirmed most of my findings based on the maternal interviews. [23]

HOW WAS THE *PSYCHOLOGICAL* PARENTING OF MOTHERS VIEWED?

Maternal styles of psychological parenting were closely scrutinized by fathers, relatives, neighbors, judges—and children. Highly controversial or popular (mis)interpretations of complex psychoanalytic *theories* were used to terrorize mothers—especially those involved in courtroom battles. As I've noted previously, idealized motherhood exposes all mothers. No mother can embody the maternal ideal perfectly enough to ensure her custody in a battle.

All sixty mothers had internalized certain standards of ideal mothering. These mothers were the first to blame themselves for minor or major psychological "failings." Mothers were often accused of psychologically abusing their children when they disciplined them—i.e., when they set curfews, demanded that homework be done, rooms cleaned, and domestic chores shared. Mothers were also accused of being psychologically "abusive" or psychologically "inadequate" for refusing to give up or "let go" of their children (a real Catch-22!).

Husbands, lawyers, and judges *accused* mothers of wanting their children "as meal tickets because they can't function in the real world." Mothers who worked were also viewed as psychologically abusing their children because they had to work or because they wanted careers.

HOW WAS THE *PSYCHOLOGICAL* PARENTING OF FATHERS VIEWED?

Paternal styles of psychological parenting remained invisible. Judges, lawyers, relatives, children—and mothers—minimized an individual father's long-term absence or abusive presence. As I've noted previously, the *ideal* of fatherhood is very sacred and essentially symbolic. As such, it protected these fathers, including those who really were psychologically unfit.

Fathers adopted three main fathering styles: the absent and authoritarian Patriarch (60 percent); the Peer-Buddy (17 percent); and the

Smother-Father (23 percent). Some fathers exhibited only one fathering style; others combined two fathering styles. [24]

Patriarchal fathers ruled through "symbolic" authority rather than intimacy. Some patriarchal fathers were never home; some were passive at home; some were psychologically demanding and competitive at home. All were emotionally distant or emotionally inept.

Patriarchal fathers tended to be more interested in older than younger children, "harder" on sons than on daughters, and hostile to daughters who were not sufficiently "feminine." Patriarchal fathers considered themselves "good" fathers. None was involved in child care or domestic labor.

Peer-Buddies were also patriarchs, who tended to be permissive, playful, and "boyish" with their children. Such fathers left discipline up to their wives and then opposed or mocked the need for discipline.

The Smother-Father demanded an exclusive "bond" with his children—one in which he was seen as the better "mother" or as a self-sufficient pansexual mother-father. Smother-Fathers were tenacious, seductive, and very overwhelming. They convinced everyone, including their children, that they were more generous and self-sacrificing than mothers. Their children often thought that satisfying their fathers' emotional needs, including rejecting their mothers, was a way of being paternally loved. [25]

WHERE AND FOR HOW LONG DID PARENTS BATTLE FOR CUSTODY? (TABLE THREE)

Of the battles, 58 percent took place in the American Northeast. The remaining battles (42 percent) took place in the American South, Midwest, and West and in Canada.

According to Table Three, custody struggles lasted an average of three stressful years and involved a total of 141 children, 56 percent of whom were boys. The average age of the youngest child was six when the battle commenced.*

Table Three tells us that custodially challenged mothers, and challenging fathers, did not give up easily; that mothers endured protracted litigation, poverty, and violence; and that fathers fought for children who were already toilet-trained, verbal, and of school age.

---

*Involved children's ages ranged from breast-feeding infants to teenagers.

TABLE THREE.

The North American Custody Battle (1960–1981)*

Average number of years custody battle lasted	3 years
Average number of stress points endured by mother during battle†	4 points
Total number of children involved	141
Number of girls	62 (44%)
Number of boys	79 (56%)
Average age of all children when battle begins	9 years
Average age of youngest child when battle begins	6 years
Average age of mother when battle begins	34 years
Geographic region of battle	
Northeast	58%
South	12%
Midwest	13%
West	12%
Canada	3%
Outside the U.S.	3%

*Eight custody battles took place between 1960 and 1970. The remaining fifty-two battles took place between 1971 and 1981.

†These stress points are: protracted or dramatic litigation; father withholds child support; children's visits to mother prohibited; children "seduced" and brainwashed against mother; mother not allowed to move/mother forced to move in order to see her children; mother prohibited from having a lover; father "legally" kidnaps child or receives mandatory joint or split custody of the children.

WHY DID FATHERS CUSTODIALLY CHALLENGE FIT MOTHERS? (TABLE FOUR)

Fathers battled for custody for at least eight reasons—in addition to loving their children. Two-thirds of the fathers (67 percent) had some economic motive, e.g., they didn't want to lose or share the marital homes or other financial assets with custodial ex-wives. Some fathers wanted to provide for their children—without depriving themselves or their second wives of comfortable middle-class lives. Since such a father couldn't afford to subsidize two wives, he chose to sacrifice his first wife custodially.

Those fathers (25 percent) who were fairly prosperous refused to

TABLE FOUR.

The Eight Major Reasons Sixty North American Fathers Battled for Child Custody (1960–1981)*

	Total Number	Percent
	60	100
Fathers		
1. Economically and psychologically refused to subsidize their ex-wives' motherhood by paying alimony or child support; didn't want to move out or sell marital home or liquidate and divide other marital assets; wanted companionship of and control over the children they had to support	40	67
2. Punished "uppity" female behavior (desire to return to school, work, or career or to have an independent intellectual, religious or social life)	37	62
3. Punished maternal nonmarital sexual activity (heterosexual and lesbian) during marriage and after divorce	29	48
4. Punished wives' initiation of divorce	27	45
5. Had patriarchal concept of children as paternal "property." (A) Punished and prevented ex-wives from moving away (the Apartheid factor)	19	32
6. Had patriarchal concept of children as paternal "property." (B) Initiated divorce and forcibly separated mothers from children by physically ejecting mothers.	16	27
7. Had patriarchal concept of the male as the "superior" parent, and competed with mothers for exclusive intimacy with children (the Smother-Father factor)	14	23
8. Were infertile or were remarried to infertile wives	15	25

*Eight custody battles took place between 1960 and 1970. The remaining fifty-two battles took place between 1971 and 1981. An individual father can have more than one motive for fighting. The paternal population as a whole had an average of two reasons for fighting.

subsidize their ex-wives' motherhood for both economic and psychological reasons. Such fathers were addicted to "jet set" lifestyles. They couldn't (psychologically) afford to cut back in order to subsidize their first wives' custodial motherhood.

Most fathers believed that *wifely* disobedience was a form of maternal unfitness, and that "uppity" wives deserved to be custodially punished. Nearly two-thirds (62 percent) of the fathers viewed their ex-wives as punishably "uppity."

"Uppity" behavior included non-marital sexual activity during marriage or after divorce, returning to school or work, holding independent religious or political opinions, or initiating a divorce against a husband's wishes.

Nearly a fourth (23 percent) were Smother-Fathers. These fathers believed they were the "superior" parent, and/or that their children needed only one parent. Smother-Fathers, Patriarchs, and Peer-Buddies all loved and needed their children—as obedient inferiors, as domestic servants, and as personal-genetic allies in a hostile world.

In addition, 25 percent of the fathers fought for their children because they—or their second wives—were infertile. Perhaps such fathers needed daily, visible proof of their (former) spermatic potency; or they also wanted to "award" children to their (infertile) second wives.

HOW OFTEN DID FATHERS WIN CUSTODY? (TABLE FIVE)

In court, 70 percent of the judges ordered children into paternal custody; 70 percent of the private arrangements also resulted in paternal custody. Within two years, 82 percent of all custody battles resulted in paternal custody.

Only five mothers—8 percent—retained custody without having to keep battling. These mothers either "gave up" their rights to alimony, child support, or other marital assets, or agreed to whatever paternal visitation was demanded. In addition, two of these mothers agreed in writing never to allow lovers into their homes overnight.

Table Five shows us that when fathers *fought* for custody they *won* custody, and that challenged mothers were custodially vulnerable—no matter how maternally fit they were.

TABLE FIVE.

The Results of Thirty-Seven Judicial and Twenty-Three Private Custody Battles in North America (1960–1981) Initially and Two Years Later*

Initial Outcome		Number	Percent
Judicially ordered paternal custody		26	70
Privately arranged paternal custody		16	70
Two Years Later			
Judicially ordered paternal custody		26	
Privately arranged paternal custody†		23	
Total			
Sole paternal custody	82%		
Sole maternal custody	18%		

*Eight custody battles took place between 1960 and 1970. The remaining fifty-two battles took place between 1971 and 1981.

†The additional seven privately arranged cases of paternal custody originated as judicial orders for maternal custody. Paternal legal persistence, maternal poverty, plus paternal brainwashing and kidnapping, led to maternal "agreement" in court, on the eve of a trial, or, in general, to sole paternal custody.

WHAT KINDS OF FATHERS WON CUSTODY JUDICIALLY VERSUS PRIVATELY? (TABLE SIX)

Fifty-nine percent of the judicially successful and 50 percent of the privately successful fathers physically abused their wives or initiated a violent divorce. Such fathers believed that wives can be unilaterally discarded, and that children are a form of landed personal property, and not part of a moveable maternal unit. Mothers are not "entitled" to children any more than they are entitled to the marital house or furniture. A third of these fathers (32 percent) also moved for custody when their ex-wives needed and wanted to move out of the father's immediate geographical orbit.

As for the children, 36 percent of the judicially successful and 19 percent of the privately successful fathers kidnapped their children; 45 percent of the judicially successful and 31 percent of the privately successful fathers brainwashed their children. Nearly half the judicial fathers (49 percent) and 44 percent of the privately successful fathers opposed their ex-wives with Mother Competitors.

TABLE SIX.

Fathers: Selected Variables Associated with Four Kinds of Custodial Arrangements: Judicially Ordered Paternal Custody, Privately Arranged Paternal Custody, Judicially Ordered Maternal Custody, and Privately Arranged Maternal Custody. Sixty North American Custody Battles (1960–1981)*

| | Paternal Custody | | Maternal Custody | | |
	Judicially Ordered (N = 26)	Privately Arranged (N = 16)	Judicially Ordered (N = 11)	Privately Arranged (N = 7)	(TOTAL N = 60)
Fathers:					
1. Physically abusive	59%	50%	54%	29%	
2. Brainwashed children	45%	31%	54%	0%	
3. Opposed mother with mother competitor	49%	44%	81%	0%	
4. Initiated the divorce violently	29%	50%	27%	0%	
5. Kidnapped children	36%	19%	64%	43%	
6. Saw mother as "uppity"	64%	50%	27%	0%	
7. Did not pay alimony	77%	100%	82%	100%	
8. Did not pay child support	42%	69%	64%	43%	
9. Involved in primary child care	12%	6%	27%†	14%	

*Eight custody battles took place between 1960 and 1970. The remaining fifty-two battles took place between 1971 and 1981.

†Three fathers were involved in some primary child care in 30 percent of the court cases.

After separation or divorce and prior to obtaining custody, three quarters (77 percent) of the judicially successful and all (100 percent) of the privately successful fathers refused to pay alimony. Moreover, 42 percent of the judicially successful and 69 percent of the privately successful fathers refused to pay any child support.

Mothers were not rescued from individually violent men by policemen, social workers, lawyers, or other family members. Judges did not rescue mothers from violent men either. On the contrary, the (large number of) domestically violent fathers, including those who kidnapped their children, were not imprisoned, fined, or custodially punished. Of the 12 percent of the mothers who kidnapped their children (Table Two), 80 percent were imprisoned, fined, or custodially punished.

HOW DID 82 PERCENT OF SUCH FATHERS WIN CUSTODY? (TABLE SEVEN)

Fathers had many motives for fighting; they also *won* custody for more than one reason or in more than one way. According to Table Seven, at least seven reasons were involved.

Money played an important role. Judges, relatives, children—and often mothers themselves—viewed paternal economic superiority as in the child's "best interests." Money also allowed fathers to persist in their legal battles for a long time without having to suffer economically themselves. Money allowed fathers to kidnap and seduce their children economically. The paternal withholding of money gradually devastated the maternal-child unit, both economically and psychologically.

Sixty-two percent of the fathers used violence to win custody. They physically battered, psychologically terrorized, and physically ejected mothers from their homes; they kidnapped, and, with the help of mother competitors, brainwashed children.[26]

Judges upheld the views of 59 percent of the fathers who viewed mothers as punishably "uppity" and of 57 percent who viewed mothers as punishably "sexual." Mothers who wanted (and needed) to move away were judicially prevented from doing so.[27]

TABLE SEVEN.

The Seven Major Reasons Forty-nine North American Fathers Won Initial Custody Judicially and Privately (1960–1981)*

	Estimated Median Paternal Income	Estimated Median Maternal Income
	$25,000	$5,000
	Percentage	
1. *Paternal economic superiority:* Father could purchase lawyers, baby-sitters, and time to pursue and persist in their battles; superior economic status made fathers appear the "better" parent: to judges, children, and sometimes to the impoverished mother		
2. *Paternal physical violent superiority:* Father terrorized mother by physically battering her during marriage; by kidnapping or brainwashing children; by initiating the divorce, forcibly ejecting her from the house, and physically preventing her from seeing the children	62	
3. *The mother competitor:* Father provided an active stepmother, girlfriend, or live-in paternal grandmother. This was viewed by judges and by children as a normal "two-headed" household, preferable to a single "working" or welfare-subsidized mother; mother competitors coordinated legal effort, did child care, testified in court, etc.	61	
4. *The "uppity" wife is an unfit mother:* Mother was seen as unfit or deserving of punishment by father, other family members, or by a judge	59	
5. *The sexual mother is unfit:* Mother was seen as unfit by father, other family members, or by a judge because she was sexual during marriage or after divorce	57	
6. *Paternal brainwashing campaign:* Children were brainwashed into violently rejecting their mothers or into "neutrally" preferring to live with their father	51	
7. *The apartheid factor:* Mother was seen as unfit by father, other family members, or by a judge because she wanted to move away with children; children were seen as landed paternal property, not as part of a moveable maternal unit	39	

* ... ... place between 1960 and 1970. The remaining fifty-two battles took place between 1971 and 1981.

WERE JUDICIALLY ACTIVE FATHERS DIFFERENT FROM PRIVATELY ACTIVE FATHERS? (TABLE EIGHT)

Judicially active fathers were apparently more violent than privately active fathers. "Judicial" fathers physically abused and terrorized their wives more often. Nearly three times as many "judicial" fathers engaged in brainwashing campaigns; twice as many kidnapped their children; and twice as many opposed their ex-wives with mother competitors.

WERE PRIVATE CUSTODIAL ARRANGEMENTS THEREFORE LESS VIOLENT THAN JUDICIAL ARRANGEMENTS? (TABLES SIX AND EIGHT)

"Private" custodial arrangements were violent and coercive when *paternal* custody was arranged (see Table Six).* For example, "private" fathers initiated a violent divorce more often then "judicial" fathers.

TABLE EIGHT.

Comparison of Thirty-seven American Fathers Who Battled Judicially with Twenty-three American Fathers Who Battled Privately for Paternal Custody (1960–1981)†

	Fathers Battling Judicially (N = 37)	*Fathers Battling Privately* (N = 23)
1. Fathers physically abused and psychologically terrorized mothers	68%	43%
2. Fathers opposed mothers with mother competitors	62%	30%
3. Fathers tried to brainwash children against mothers	54%	22%
4. Fathers kidnapped children	51%	26%

†Eight custody battles took place between 1960 and 1970. The remaining fifty-two battles took place between 1971 and 1981.

*Experts have (incorrectly) assumed that private custodial arrangements are essentially "voluntary"—and, as such, more desirable than court-ordered arrangements.

"Private" fathers did not (even) have to kidnap children. They merely ejected mothers from their homes with threats of killing, shooting, or psychiatrically incarcerating them if they dared to return.

The apparent "non-violence" of private arrangements is due to those fathers who privately arranged *maternal* custody. Such fathers did not initiate violent divorces, brainwash children, or oppose their ex-wives with mother competitors. They did not view their wives as "uppity." Still, 29 percent physically abused their wives (see Table Six).

Interestingly, 43 percent of the fathers who privately arranged *maternal* custody kidnapped their children. Such kidnappings were probably last-ditch emotional protests rather than serious paternal "kidnapping" custody ventures.

WERE THERE ANY APPARENT DIFFERENCES BETWEEN (THE SMALL NUMBER OF) MOTHERS WHO INITIALLY WON AND (THE LARGE NUMBER OF) MOTHERS WHO INITIALLY LOST CUSTODY? (TABLE NINE)

It is important to remember that only 30 percent of my maternal interviewees initially won custody. Within two years only 18 percent of these initially successful mothers retained custody. The following differences between maternal custodial groups are suggestive, not conclusive. However, they do "spotlight" certain stress points of maternal custodial vulnerability.

Mothers who initially won custody were married to less physically abusive husbands, gave birth for the first time at "older" ages, and initiated divorces more often than mothers who lost custody. *Judicially* successful mothers tended to have professions—more often than any other maternal custodial group.

Does this mean that "uppity" career mothers who "waited" to have their children were custodially invulnerable? It does not. What it means is that certain anti-woman biases were temporarily inoperative—30 percent of the time. For example, under certain conditions, 30 percent of the judges were willing to overlook a mother's "uppityness" if she was sexually chaste or if her husband was exceptionally violent, in terms of child kidnapping.*

---

*Only 29 percent of the judicially successful mothers committed adultery or were sexually active, compared to 47 percent of the judicially unsuccessful mothers. Of the judicially successful fathers, only (!) 36 percent kidnapped their children, compared to 64 percent of the judicially unsuccessful fathers.

TABLE NINE.

Mothers: Selected Variables Associated with Four Kinds of Custody Arrangements: Judicially Ordered Paternal Custody, Privately Arranged Paternal Custody, Judicially Ordered Maternal Custody, and Privately Arranged Maternal Custody. Sixty North American Custody Battles (1960–1981)*

	Maternal Custody			Paternal Custody		
	Judicially Ordered	Privately Arranged	(Total	Judicially Ordered	Privately Arranged	(Total
	(N=11)	(N=7)	N=18)	(N=26)	(N=16)	N=42)
Mothers:						
1. Average age at birth of first child	27	26		23	22	
2. Has profession	57%	36%		40%	38%	
3. Initiated the divorce	57%	64%		40%	31%	
4. Committed adultery	29%	54%		47%	31%	
5. Were physically abused by husbands	39%			59%		
6. Endured paternal kidnapping	56%			36%		

*Eight custody battles took place between 1960 and 1970. The remaining fifty-two battles took place between 1971 and 1981. There were no apparent differences between maternal custodial groups in the areas of paternal initiation of divorce, brainwashing, or in terms of mothers wanting to move away.

Judicially successful mothers gave birth for the first time at an average age of twenty-seven; privately successful mothers gave birth when they were twenty-six; judicially unsuccessful mothers gave birth when they were twenty-three; and privately unsuccessful mothers gave birth at the youngest age—when they were twenty-two.

How does the age at which a mother first gives birth relate to her ability to defend herself custodially? Perhaps women who married and became mothers at the youngest of ages were chosen by or "attracted" to the most violent and patriarchal husbands. Young, dependent, and isolated mothers may have been further weakened by the restrictive bonds of marriage, the burdens of motherhood, and their own predisposition to "goodness."

Woman's need to be a "good girl" results in her inability to fight with her husband in public. "Good girls" are also reluctant to lie in court or to adopt violent means to obtain custody of their children.[28]

It is important to remember that "bad girls" have an even harder time in custody struggles and that mothers are custodially vulnerable whether they married at very young or at slightly older ages.

WERE CUSTODIALLY CHALLENGING FATHERS MORE INVOLVED IN HOUSEWORK OR CHILD CARE THAN OTHER FATHERS?

Most of the "custodial" fathers (87 percent) did no housework or primary child care, although many criticized and denigrated their wives' competence in these areas. Twelve of the "custodial" fathers (20 percent) "helped out" with maternally organized child-care chores; eight (14 percent) were involved in the primary care of their children.

These eight men were all Smother-Fathers. Their child-care activities included holding their children exclusively or secretively for hours on end, keeping their children up very late, expecting their children to listen to paternal problems and assuage paternal anxiety, etc. In a sense, Smother-Fathers treated their children more as "wives" than as children.

As I have noted, "good enough" fathers in general do not physically or psychologically take care of a home or a child the way "good enough" mothers do. This seems to be true about "custodial" fathers as well.

Studies of paternal involvement in housework and child care do not exist or are too experimental in nature to permit us to compare "custodial" paternal behavior with that of other fathers.

DID CUSTODIALLY CHALLENGING HUSBANDS PHYSICALLY ABUSE THEIR WIVES LESS THAN OTHER HUSBANDS?

As we have seen, 62 percent of the "custodial" fathers physically abused their wives. Of these, 30 percent did so during marriage; 32 percent did so during their divorces or custody struggles.

Recent research suggests that anywhere from 15 to 50 percent of all American wives are physically intimidated, beaten, and/or raped by their husbands or live-in boyfriends.[29] While such research does not allow us to make a valid comparison, it is clear that "custodial" husbands are as domestically violent as the most violent of husbands studied; or are not less domestically violent.

DID CUSTODIALLY CHALLENGING FATHERS ENGAGE IN LESS CHILD ABUSE THAN OTHER FATHERS?

Of the "custodial" fathers, 67 percent impoverished their wives and children, 62 percent physically abused the mothers of their children, 57 percent engaged in anti-mother brainwashing campaigns, and 37 percent kidnapped their children. Three percent were incestuous fathers. In my opinion, these all are forms of child abuse.

As we have seen, very few studies on paternal child abuse exist. Thus, we cannot compare "custodial" fathers with the paternal population in general.[30]

DID CUSTODIALLY CHALLENGING FATHERS ECONOMICALLY ABANDON THEIR WIVES AND CHILDREN LESS THAN OTHER DIVORCED HUSBANDS AND FATHERS?

Over the years, 33 percent of the "custodial" fathers paid (some) child support; 10 percent paid (some) alimony. In 1982, in a review of all the studies on the paternal payment of child support during the 1970s, Barbara Bode, Executive Director of the Children's Foundation, confirmed:

> Fathers can pay child support; fathers can usually pay more than the courts order; fathers who do pay often do so irregularly and incompletely, creating recurrent financial hardship in the children's household; one-fourth to one-third of fathers never make the first court-ordered payment; no state or county has ever been found in which more than half the fathers are in full compliance with support orders.[31]

In 1983, the United States Census Bureau reported that in 1981, of 4 million mothers supposed to receive child support payments, only 47 percent did; that mothers who received court-ordered payments received about 55 percent of the amount due; that private arrangements resulted in mothers' receipt of 78 percent of the amount due; and that paternal child-support payments averaged $2,110 per year.

According to the Census Bureau report, the three main reasons given for the paternal non-payment of child support were "refusal to pay," the "inability to locate the father," and "financial problems." Child support payments accounted for 13 percent of the average income of fathers.

Fifteen percent of 17 million divorced or separated women were awarded alimony. Of these, 43 percent received the amount owed. The mean alimony payment in 1981 was $3,000.[32]

This information, although statistically valid and comprehensive, doesn't allow us to make an accurate comparison either. However, over the years, "custodial" fathers actually paid less child support (33 percent versus 47 percent) than did other separated and divorced fathers who were studied in 1981. Over the years, "custodial" fathers paid alimony as often as other separated and divorced fathers did in 1981.

In summary, fathers who fought for custody were probably no more domestically involved, in terms of housework and child care, than fathers are in general; were as domestically violent to their wives, perhaps even more so, than husbands are in general; were physically and psychologically abusive to their children in ways for which no comparative data yet exist; and were somewhat more economically abusive to their wives and children than separated and divorced fathers are in general.

DOES THIS STUDY PROVE THAT "MORE" NORTH AMERICAN FATHERS FOUGHT FOR OR WON CUSTODY BETWEEN 1960 AND 1981 THAN EVER BEFORE?

We do not know if mothers were custodially challenged or victimized more frequently between 1960 and 1981 than between 1860 and 1881. It is almost impossible to confirm a statistical increase in a previously uncharted area.

This study can and does confirm the custodial vulnerability of "good enough" mothers; and the ease with which a domestically violent father or one with no previous involvement in child care can win custody.

This study can and does confirm that "good enough" mothers have no enforceable right to freedom from male domestic violence; no enforceable right to alimony or child support; and no right to initiate a divorce unilaterally, pursue a "career," move away, engage in non-marital sexual activities, or hold any opinions opposed by their husbands—without risking a custodial challenge.

WHAT TREND OR HIDDEN TRUTH DOES THIS STUDY REVEAL?

As we have noted, impoverished, non-white, non-Protestant, unwed, divorced, "immoral," and criminal mothers have always been historically vulnerable to custodial victimization. They still are.

As children became more of an economic burden than an economic asset, maternal custody became more common. In the twentieth century, maternal custody has also meant maternal poverty.

This study reveals that once "respectable" mothers (white and formerly married) are divorced and impoverished, they are custodially vulnerable in the same way that members of a racially, ethnically, morally, or criminally despised group are.

Historically, fathers (and the state) claimed custody of children as their absolute religious and legal right and as their children's best economic provider. In this study fathers also claimed custody on the grounds of male economic and psychological superiority.

Historically, fathers claimed custody of children as their absolute economic right.* In this study some fathers also claimed children for paternal economic advantage; all fathers claimed children as a form of psychological "wealth."

Is the custodial scapegoating of "respectable" mothers a way of terrorizing all women into sexual, reproductive, and economic obedience? Are wealthy and powerful world leaders more willing to "re-distribute" children to their fathers than to re-distribute the world's wealth to men (and women) of all classes?

"Respectable" mothers were unprepared for the consequences of divorce. They were stunned when their unchosen poverty, their need to work, their career achievements, and their sexual independence were viewed as maternal crimes. "Respectable" mothers were also surprised when policemen, lawyers, judges, neighbors, and relatives did little to protect them from male violence—including that of a custody battle.

I would like to introduce you to these mothers in the following chapters.

---

*Children performed domestic, agricultural, and wage labor for their fathers.

PART II

The Study in Depth, I.
What "Crimes" Do "Good Enough"
Mothers Commit That Result in
Maternal Custodial Victimization?

CHAPTER FIVE

The "Sexual" Mother: Anna Karenina Today

If motherhood is the highest fulfillment of women's nature, what other protection does it need save love and freedom? (Doesn't marriage) say to woman, only when you follow me shall you bring forth life? Does marriage not place a crown of thorns upon an innocent head and carve in letters of blood the hideous epithet, Bastard? Were marriage to contain all the virtues claimed for it, its crimes against motherhood would exclude it forever from the realm of love.

Emma Goldman
"Marriage and Love"

HALF THE MOTHERS (48 PERCENT) WERE CUSTODIALLY CHALLENGED on the grounds of non-marital sexual activity. A third committed adultery—i.e., they engaged in sexual activity outside of marriage while they were still married. Two-thirds engaged in sexual activity after they were separated or divorced.

This chapter discusses only the heterosexual mothers. These mothers were married to two kinds of husbands: those who were sexually inactive within marriage—e.g., who were celibate or impotent—and those who were sexually abusive within marriage—e.g., who were adulterous, sexually inept, or neglectful.

Nearly half the "sexual" mothers (44 percent) were custodially challenged solely on sexual grounds, and 56 percent were challenged for both sexual and other reasons.

IT IS TOLSTOY'S St. Petersburg. Anna Karenina is "estranged" from her husband Karenin, and in love with Count Vronsky. When Anna discovers she is pregnant, she desperately summons Vronsky— who literally bumps into Karenin at Anna's front door.

After meeting Vronsky, Karenin drove to the Italian opera. He sat through two acts and saw everybody it was necessary for him to see. [Karenin's] feeling of anger with his wife, who would not observe the rules of propriety, gave him no rest. She had not complied with his stipulation [not to receive her lover in his house], and he must punish her and carry out his threat to divorce her and take the boy away.

Anna's morphine addiction and her suicide start here—with her right to motherhood absolutely jettisoned by her need for love. Anna is a social pariah. Karenin refuses to divorce Anna; Vronsky cannot marry her; society cannot include her. Anna gives birth to a girl. Vronsky grows more distant every day. Vronsky says:

"My daughter is by law not my daughter, but Karenin's. I cannot bear the falsity of it!"

"Someday we may have a son," he went on, "my son, and by law he would be a Karenin. He would not be heir to my name or property. There would be no legal bond between us.

"[All my children] would be Karenins. Think of the bitterness and horror of such a position. Conceive the feelings of a man who knows that his children, the children of the woman he loves, will not be his, but will belong to someone who hates them, and will have nothing to do with them! It is horrible."

Vronsky has described Anna's position exactly. However, he remains unaware that Anna's legal status is even worse than his own. Anna has lost her son, her lover, her maternal and her social identity—all for the sake of passion. Anna mistrusts herself and her world. Moments before she kills herself, Anna says:

"There go some school boys, laughing. Seriozha? I thought that I loved him, and used to be moved by my own tenderness for him. Yet here I have lived without him. I exchanged him for another love. . . . Are we not all flung into the world for no other purpose than to hate each other, and so to torture ourselves and one another?"[1]

After Anna's suicide, Karenin does claim Anna and Vronsky's love child as his legal child.

I have interviewed Anna Karenina in America today. She is here, in this chapter. For example, she greets me at her door in autumn. Her hair is as red as the falling leaves. She wears a long dress over her riding boots. Her name is Catherine.

"Come in," she says. "I'm so glad you've come by." Catherine's skin is unlined; her figure, girlish. She is the mother of four teenagers. I cross her threshold into another century.

Candelabra, love seats, footstools, crowd the room. Velvet drapes silence the chime clocks and a piano. Upstairs, there are four children's beds covered with dolls and animals. There are framed paintings and photographs of children in every room. No child appears to be more than ten years old.

She is Miss Havisham, waiting for her children to return.

"It was the fifties," she finally says. "I wanted six children to love. I married in order to have children. Dr. McQueen seemed very marriage-able, very much a family man. He had no friends or close family.

"Dr. McQueen was always very secretive. For instance, whenever he went to the dentist, he refused to let me see the inside of his mouth. I thought that was very strange. Years later, when it was clear that our marriage was floundering, he also refused to open up to discuss anything. He didn't make love to me for ten years. I tried to discuss this chastity or impotence with him. He wouldn't hear of it."

I can see her smiling at parties, ashamed to admit that her husband doesn't touch her—ever—doesn't make love to her—ever; a slight figure on her side of the bed, still awake at two o'clock in the morning, planning to bake brownies.

Catherine is weeping now. "After seventeen married years I was starved for an affectionate relationship with a man. I found someone. We were very discreet. Somehow, Dr. McQueen found out. He pinned a scarlet letter on me, one I could never rip off. He had our town buzzing. He never spoke to me again, but he spoke against me to everyone.

"Thomas convinced my two youngest children that I didn't love them because I'd slept with another man. He also made them feel that *he'd* shrivel up and die without them. My boys were thrilled by his attentiveness. They perceived me as the strong one and began turning away from me. I was devastated.

"Once I was an heiress," Catherine says. "We lived in a twenty-room mansion that my mother gave us. My money paid for the children's private schools. I let Thomas handle my inheritance. He insisted on it. He also managed my mother's money. He put all her money—and mine—into a trust for the children. When the divorce came up, he threatened to have my mother declared mentally incompetent if I didn't give up my claim to the children."

FAMILY COURT

Thomas's Lawyer: We contend that Mrs. McQueen carried on an openly adulterous affair. This seriously questions her fitness as a mother. I would like to call the family priest as my first witness. Father Greeley, did Mrs. McQueen bring the two McQueen boys for their Catholic instruction?

Father Greeley: No. Their father did. I never saw Mrs. McQueen. Of course, she's not Catholic. She didn't even attend her youngest boy's confirmation.

Catherine's Lawyer: If I tell you, sir, that Mrs. McQueen brought the two older children to their Catholic instruction before you took over the parish, and that Mrs. McQueen was in the hospital during her youngest son's confirmation, would these facts influence your opinion about her involvement in the church?

Father Greeley: No, it wouldn't.

Are they trying her for not being Catholic? Or for requiring surgery?

Catherine's Lawyer: Dr. Warren, what is your psychiatric opinion of a ten-year-old boy sleeping in the same bed with his father every night? Especially since this father has not engaged in sexual intercourse with his wife for a period of ten years. Would that give you cause to inquire about the whole arrangement?

Dr. Warren:	I don't have any immediate professional opin-ion on that. It can be perfectly all right. I would have to know more about the circumstances.
Thomas's Lawyer:	Dr. McQueen, why did you admit your son into your bed?
Dr. McQueen:	Since his mother began working a year ago, our home situation has become very unstable. Shaun was reaching out to me for security. He was traumatized by his mother's absence, by her adulterous scandal, and by this divorce. I accepted him with both arms.

What if Catherine refused to sleep with her husband for ten years and were now sleeping with her ten-year-old son?

"One night, about two months after the custody trial, there was our car piled high with suitcases in the driveway. I ran into the house. 'What are you doing?' Thomas was packing another suitcase. I was absolutely frantic.

" 'I'm taking the children away. The judge has given them to me.'

"I was horrified. My teenagers were out. My two youngest boys were already asleep. The next morning they were all gone.

"I was so lonely, so ashamed to be without my children. People avoided me. I wanted to tell my side of the story, but I was damned if I was going to explain myself to a town that thought the worst of me. I moved away. When strangers ask about my children, I either lie—or feel like a liar no matter what I say.

"I miss the children. They are my whole life."

WHAT DID BETTINA, JOSIE, AND BONNIE DO? WHAT DID THEIR HUSBANDS DO?

These mothers married as virgins before they were twenty-one. Catherine and Josie were forced into sexually celibate marriages by their husbands. Bettina and Bonnie were married to openly adulterous husbands.

In 1964, Bettina married John, her childhood sweetheart. She had three children by the time she was twenty-four. John traveled the corporate road "four out of every five weeks." He was open about his extramarital affairs. After five years, Bettina began an affair—and told

John about it. John beat her up. He became obsessed with Bettina's infidelity. Bettina said:

"John hit me each time he knew I was with my lover. I guess he was right. He was within his rights to do that. I did commit a sin. I must have hurt him terribly."

Within three months of Bettina's first affair, John had kidnapped the children. He demanded that Bettina give up her lover. She did. John then agreed to pay her rent and minimal child support—if she never had another affair. He refused to divorce Bettina, live with her, or forgive her. He threatened to take the children "any time" he heard she was "misbehaving." John moved out—and took their eldest son with him as a hostage. Bettina said:

> My eldest boy was the easiest child to live with. His father left him alone with a housekeeper for weeks at a time. He wasn't permitted to visit us. This went on for a year. Eventually my son came to visit for Easter. He refused to return to his father. He said it was too lonely. His father allowed him to stay with me. I've always blamed myself for his suffering.

Bettina's punishment for her one adulterous affair far outweighed her "crime." She was economically shorn and sexually traumatized. When I interviewed her in 1981, Bettina still had never slept with or dated anyone. Perhaps Bettina was too timid. Why didn't she bring her case before a judge?

As Josie did. Josie married at eighteen and was a mother at nineteen. After a year of enforced marital celibacy, Josie moved out. Within six months, she fell in love with a black man. "We live in the South," said Josie.

> My husband Ron's father is a former politician. They tried to have me and my boyfriend fired from our jobs. Our offices were ransacked. My boyfriend's home was fire-bombed. His friends were leaned on. Threats were made. During the custody trial, they called me a filthy whore. I lost custody of Laura when she was only three. My mother-in-law became her mother. I was only allowed to see her every other weekend for six hours.

Josie was not permitted to enter Laura's home. Whenever Laura said she wanted to live with her mother, they weren't allowed to see each other. Within a year, Josie had fallen into a deep depression. "A friend pulled me out of it. She told me that if I tried to kill myself or got admitted to a mental hospital, my ability to fight for custody or for more liberal visitation would be compromised forever."

Josie decided to go to law school. Four years later she was admitted to the bar. Josie said:

> The day I was admitted to the bar I called Ron. I threatened to ruin his business if he didn't let me have Laura for two months every summer. I told him, "If I don't get my daughter, I'll ruin your reputation and your business." I knew enough to implicate him in enormous corruption. I got my summer visitation.

Josie has never remarried, never lived with anyone, and never had another child. If only Ron's family hadn't been so powerful! If only Josie's husband had been more sexually active . . .

As Bonnie's husband was. Frederick believed in "smashing monogamy." While Bonnie stayed home taking care of their two children, Frederick had a series of one-night stands and affairs. He also "loved" Bonnie very much. Then Bonnie had an affair.

> Fred lay on the couch for three or four days, just staring at the ceiling. He repeated over and over again, "You have just taken away my manhood. My trust in the human race is gone." He really pinned the scarlet letter on my breast. He kept at me day and night, accusing me of not really loving him. He acted as if I had murdered him.

A year later, when Bonnie moved out, Frederick physically prevented her from taking the children.

WHAT DOES MY STUDY TELL US ABOUT THE CUSTODIAL VICTIMIZATION OF *DIVORCED* MOTHERS WHO ENGAGE IN SEXUAL ACTIVITY?

Ten mothers were custodially challenged for post-divorce sexual activity. Of these, 30 percent had been married to maritally celibate, inactive, or impotent men, while 70 percent had been sexually abused or neglected by their husbands. It is very dangerous for a wife to be married to a sexually inadequate husband.

LUCY, LINDA, AND LORETTA:
WHAT DID THEY DO?
WHAT DID THEIR EX-HUSBANDS DO?

In the mid-1950s, Lucy had dared initiate a divorce from an adulterous husband. Lucy was custodially challenged because she went out on a *date* after her divorce. By that time her ex-husband, Stanley, had already remarried. Lucy had no family or economic resources. She and her three-year-old son were entirely dependent on Stanley's economic largesse. Stanley became enraged when he learned of Lucy's date. "He called the man I'd dated and threatened him," said Lucy.

"He harassed this man's parents. He stopped sending rent money. I got an eviction notice. He threatened a custody battle—based on my 'sexual immorality.' I was twenty-one and terribly naïve. I believed I was some kind of outlaw."

For years Stanley's maniacal possessiveness prevented Lucy from remarrying or from forming a lasting, stable relationship with another man. Stanley's second marriage and second set of children didn't seem to diminish the ardor of his vendetta. Lucy said:

> He wanted to see me dead. I'd rejected him: I didn't put up with his sexual infidelity and his emotional absence at home. The minute I went out with another man that was justification for him to get back at me. This was proof that I was no good. He was used to controlling everything. When I became a moving piece, not a fixed piece in his universe, he vowed to get me, to slow me to a standstill. His means of doing that was by withholding child support. I once asked him, "How can you do this to us?" He said, "You're not going to let him starve. I know you're not going to deprive him of anything. What I'm doing is hurting you, and you're the person I want to hurt." He was very clear and exceedingly up front about it.

Lucy was awarded custody of Michael. However, she privately agreed to a joint custody arrangement on paper. In return, Lucy got minimal child support. Within eight years Michael had chosen to live with his father and stepbrother.

When she was twenty-one, Linda married Frank, her childhood sweetheart. Frank traveled a great deal and was openly adulterous. They battled about his constant absence from home. After twelve years Frank moved out. Two years later Linda began dating a man. "One Sunday evening, Frank walked in unexpectedly," said Linda.

He was wearing a leather jacket. He looked just like the Gestapo. He pointed his finger at Carl (my boyfriend) and said, "You, outside. You have no business seeing my wife." I was mortified. We began yelling at each other. Frank punched me in the eye. I fell. He punched me in the stomach. I doubled up. Then he left. He came back a little later to say he was sorry. By that time my eye had closed and I was vomiting blood.

Linda was hospitalized for eye surgery. Frank's rage grew when Linda refused to "forgive" him. At this point, Frank began arguing about alimony and expressing a joint custodial interest in children whom he'd never parented. Linda said: "Frank was a good provider. He was never home. He was also infertile. I wasn't. He wouldn't allow me to have artificial insemination. I agreed to adopt instead. Maybe he's afraid some other man will make me pregnant and one-up him. So he wants his 'legal' kids."

Ex-husbands were enraged by their ex-wives' non-married sexual activities. Ex-husbands were also enraged when their ex-wives remarried. For example, Loretta's husband, Peter, drove her away with his repeated (and irrational) accusations of infidelity. Loretta began a post-separation love affair. When Loretta remarried, Peter felt "replaced" in his children's affections by Loretta's new husband. He initiated an intense campaign for custody of his three sons. Loretta said:

He's made our life hell. He quizzes the boys constantly. He wants them to spy on us. He's competing with Vincent, my husband, something fierce. He believes Vincent will get the boys to love him more than they love their father. He doesn't want them to get used to a stable life with me and Vincent.

WHAT IF A MOTHER IS A SEXUAL OUTLAW?

Demure pink tongue, soft blue eyes, angel blonde hair: she is Botticelli's Venus at my door. Amber is young and very scared. She is a topless dancer with a custody problem. She removes her ballet slippers, stretches out scarlet painted toes, loosens her blouse, breathes deeply, and begins.

"I got married because I was pregnant. My family never forgave me for sinning. Victoria was born when we were both eighteen. I left Dennis when Victoria was six months old. He was too violent to live with.

"I found an apartment and got on welfare. For eight months, I was cooped up breast feeding and baby-sitting. Dennis wouldn't give us any money. He wouldn't 'baby-sit' for me. He offered to take Victoria completely. He thought it would bring me back to him.

"I took care of Victoria for two full days and nights each week. I also cleaned the house and did all the laundry for Dennis. My sister—who never helped *me*—helped Dennis during the week. She said I deserved to be horsewhipped for giving Victoria up. I enrolled in two college courses and started waitressing.

"When Dennis realized I wasn't coming back, he moved six hours away by bus. I had nightmares about Victoria. I couldn't concentrate in school. I was guilty and I missed her. That's when I decided to dance topless. As a waitress, I earned eighty or ninety dollars a week. Dancing, I earned eighty dollars a shift.

"When Victoria was two and a half, Dennis agreed to joint custody. I got to take care of her every day. Dennis was dating a lot of different women and finishing college. I was his ideal baby-sitter, child-care center, and cook—all rolled into one. He also had me right under his thumb.

"Dennis said he'd let Victoria live with me if I stopped topless dancing. I took her. He refused to give me any money. I kept dancing. How else could I support us?"

Naked women dancing are our fertility goddesses—held in contempt. Nailed him to a cross, caged her genitals in shame. Continuous red neon breasts: obscene adoration, sacred love.

"Within two months, Dennis yanked Victoria out of school and disappeared with her. When we finally found him, Dennis wouldn't let me see Victoria alone. He wouldn't even let us go into the bathroom together.

"Dennis got into a fistfight with my roommate's boyfriend. He pushed the doorman down as he ran away. He jumped into his car and nearly ran someone down in the street outside. Finally! Dennis had gone berserk in front of other people. The police arrested him. Everybody—the doorman, my roommate's boyfriend, the pedestrian—pressed charges.

"Dennis's lawyer got him out of jail in twenty-four hours. The judge released him without bail, once he understood it was a 'domestic matter.'

"Dennis practically lived on my street corner, watching my apartment. On my lawyer's advice, I snuck away like a dog to another borough. I put Victoria in private school with strict instructions not to release her to anyone but me. We never went out. We were both Dennis's prisoners.

"My lawyer was really freaked by my dancing. It really annoyed her. 'Why'd ya have to dance?' she'd ask me over and over again while she kept demanding more money. I want to mother Victoria the best way I can. Not in terror of Dennis's kidnapping her. Not ashamed of what I do to support us."

The dazzling girl dances for men only, and thinks she'll stay young forever. Do women feel betrayed by her sexual indifference to them? Or by how her dependence on men mirrors their own?

Or is it the fate of the dancing girl that frightens women, reminding them of men's contempt for female flesh, the liberties they permit themselves with it, forbid to women: ma soeur, ma mort.

These "sexual" mothers all were sexually repressed. Their sexual experiences within marriage had been limited and unsatisfactory. Their undamaged longing for sexual affection was miraculous; its consummation heroic; the resulting assault on their right to motherhood cruel and unjust.

CHAPTER SIX

The "Uppity" Mother

CREON

You, with that angry look, so set against your husband—
I am afraid of you—why should I dissemble it?—
You are a clever woman, versed in evil arts

MEDEA

Through being considered clever I have suffered much.
If you put new ideas before the eyes of fools
They'll think you foolish and worthless into the bargain;
And if you are thought superior to those who have
Some reputation for learning, you will become hated.

JASON

How hopeless it is to deal with a stubborn temper.
For, with reasonable submission to our ruler's will,
You might have kept your home.
As it is you are going to be exiled for your loose speaking.

Euripides, *Medea*

Sixty-two percent of the custodially challenged mothers were perceived as "uppity." "Uppity" behavior included: exercising freedom of thought or speech, especially if a "minority" opinion was involved; exercising civic duties, such as exposing government corruption; having a "career"; having to work; wanting to move away in order to find or accept employment; and daring to initiate a divorce.

WHAT DOES MY STUDY TELL US ABOUT FEMALE-INITIATED DIVORCE AS A FORM OF CUSTODIAL PROVOCATION?

Nearly half the mothers (47 percent), and nearly a third of the fathers (27 percent) initiated the divorce. Some fathers behaved as if they "owned" both their wives and children and "allowed" their wives to take care of their children—as long as they took care of their husbands too. Once these husbands became convinced that their wives were about to "steal" paternal property (her domestic services, "his" children), the divorce escalated into a custody battle.

After twenty years of marriage, Nora could no longer live holding her breath in fear of her husband's violence. She envisioned living under her own roof, five or ten minutes away. She dreamt of breathing properly again. Their children ranged in age from eighteen to six.

Nora talked to her husband in soothing tones. She talked to him in firm tones. She suggested divorce counseling. His rage was hot red: volcanic. She attempted suicide—perhaps to convince him or herself that she would rather die than stay married.

For nineteen years, she had been the ground beneath his feet. What would he stand on if she left? Terrified that he'd float off into space forever, he kidnapped two of their children for six months.

Nora whispers when she speaks. Her hands are never idle. Fiercely tender, they knit a child's sweater, bake whole grain bread, make tea.

"I am no longer an ordinary mother," Nora says, looking around her afternoon kitchen, lowering her voice even more. "When one of the children is late coming home, I panic. Have they been kidnapped again? For years I lived with Lester in terror. I didn't know it myself. I always had to tiptoe around him. I thought we were a very successful marriage.

"When I talked to him about a divorce, he choked me until I was unconscious. Then he tried to murder my motherhood. He told people I was unfit. Neighbors stopped looking me in the eye. Some stopped speaking to me. I thought I was imagining it—or going mad.

"When I still insisted on a divorce, Lester started a custody battle that lasted two years. I was examined by three different psychiatrists. It's hard to imagine a worse punishment. Remembering it brings tears to my eyes. One psychiatrist said my self-esteem was too low for me to be a good mother. Another one said that my career was bad for the children, that my research was a cover-up for my hatred of men.

"Those were awfully long days to sit in court." Nora closes her eyes. "It was dreadful to be there alone. Some friends and colleagues came. Some volunteers from a local women's center also came. My attorney once asked the judge, 'Is there something about Nora that bothers you?' The judge said, 'I'm bothered by that coterie of women that she continually brings here.' "

"Nora, what happened to your career?" I ask.

"My career was kidnapped together with my children. I missed appointments and deadlines. For nearly three years I was more involved with detectives and lawyers than with other scientists. My company asked me to leave. I had no savings left. All I had were the clothes in my closet and five hungry mouths to feed."

How easily respectability and security are stripped from the female body. Nora's nakedness is unremarkable. She is now undistinguishable from all other women who are not and have never been successful scientists.

"I took a job at one-third my previous salary. I borrowed money to hire a lawyer to fight for money. Five years after the kidnapping, three years after the custody trial, a judge awarded me a substantial sum of money. Lester refused to pay anything. He told the judge he'd rather go to jail. Lester has never tried to see the children. He doesn't call or write or send birthday cards."

Can a woman under torture carry on as usual? Can she keep pretending she isn't being tortured?

A clock ticks, another chimes. We sip Nora's tea in silence. "I'm in hiding," she explains. "I don't want to be looked at anymore. I just want to bring home my paycheck and take care of my children. I'm not ready to do without the pleasure of their company yet."

What if a mother not only initiates a divorce, but dares to become a successful artist? Ella Mae is a painter and sculptor. In the early 1960s, she married a lawyer. From the beginning, Donald resented and opposed Ella Mae's work—even though she worked at home; even though dinner was always ready, and the house always clean. Ella Mae was devoted to their infant daughter, Mary. She said:

During the day I would feel very happy, very whole, very satisfied with my work in my attic studio. Mary gurgled or slept right beside me. It was blissful. Donald was becoming more and more unhappy. He hated his job. He had no friends. Here I was, this happy person. When he'd come home, he'd just have to knock me down.

After I sold my first painting, he demanded that I pay for my own oils and canvases. I did. As I became more successful, he demanded household money. As long as I could actually sell one of those damn paintings—he wanted me to pay for Mary's clothes. I was like some dog he could kick. After a year and a half I decided I deserved a better life than this.

Donald wouldn't move out. He wouldn't let Ella Mae take "anything he'd paid for": the iron, the first-aid kit, her sewing machine. He wouldn't give her any child support. Ella Mae outraged him by managing to survive that first winter without heat or hot water. By spring, she had sold a painting. She made new friends. Within a year, she was under the "protection" of another man, whom she eventually married. Ella Mae said:

There was nothing Donald could do to hurt me. He was very frustrated by my successful escape. He couldn't forgive me for my strength. He thought I was a monster with no feelings. He thought I should be destroyed.

For seven years I mothered Mary. I grew as an artist. I forgot that Donald had a score to settle with me. He sent twenty dollars a week for her. He thought this was a lordly sum. He thought he was a good father. This amount didn't increase in seven years.

Ella Mae divorced her second husband. Her reputation as an artist and her feminist awareness grew. She began living with an emotionally supportive younger man. When Mary was nine years old, three things happened: Ella Mae was asked to coordinate a national show of women's paintings; Mary developed a learning disorder that required special medical and educational attention; and Ella Mae decided to request an increase in child support. "At Donald's request," said Ella Mae,

Mary was with him for one month every summer. I was working on the art show. Donald hired a detective who posed as a magazine photographer. He took pictures of my home and interviewed me about the art show. After Donald thought he had a good enough case, he refused to return Mary. He accused me of being a "bohemian" and of "having orgies."

Donald was a local lawyer with a substantial and respectable practice. Donald was remarried, and had two other children. Despite Ella Mae's unblemished record as a full-time mother, a judge ordered Mary into her father's permanent custody. He allowed maternal visitation only at "Donald's discretion." Ella Mae said:

> Seven years after I left him, Donald began to exact his revenge. First, he got custody. He didn't let me see Mary for a year. Then he let me see her, now and then, for a day at a time—if I was very grateful, and never demanded her back.
>
> After a year, Mary was no longer the child I knew. She wore tiny pearls and an expensive little suit. She wouldn't look me in the eye. She talked about her swimming pool and her ballet classes. My Mary! So quiet, so ladylike. What had Donald done to her? How could he punish a child in order to get at me? How could he do to her what he wanted to do to me?
>
> You know, I've painted women as heroines and goddesses. I'm Demeter, and Mary is my Persephone. But I couldn't force Donald to return Mary to me—not for a single summer. I lived with Mary for three thousand days. Since I lost custody nine years ago, I've spent about forty days with her.
>
> Donald is my most powerful teacher. Whenever I think my success has moved me out of the female ghetto, I remember: I am without Mary.[1]

What if a mother has no artistic "calling," no "bohemian" sexual life-style—but needs to move away in order to pursue a livelihood, a "career," or a chance at a new life?

WHAT DOES MY STUDY TELL US ABOUT FATHERS WHO WANTED TO MOVE AWAY WITH THEIR CHILDREN?

Nearly a third (31 percent) of the fathers who *won* custody moved away afterward. Half these fathers obtained court approval to do so; a third moved away without entering the court system or without "mentioning" their intended move in court. One-fifth of the fathers moved away by permanently kidnapping their children.

WHAT DOES MY STUDY TELL US ABOUT MOTHERS WHO WANTED TO MOVE AWAY?

Nearly a third (32 percent) of the mothers wanted to move away. With one exception, they all were prevented from doing so—with their children. Judges (and others) all viewed children as their fathers' "landed property," not as part of a moveable maternal unit. Judges also viewed the paternal right of visitation as more important than the maternal right to survive economically and psychologically.

For example, Beth was privately forced into a joint custody arrangement. She received no alimony and no child support. Her children lived with her for half the week. When Beth found employment in a nearby city, she petitioned the court to have the children with her for fewer days—but on weekends. She said:

> This was 1974. The judge told me to live on welfare. He said I couldn't just move these kids or change their established living pattern. I moved away. I had to in order to survive. Then I had to beg, whine, and wheedle weekend visitation on my own as a favor from my husband. I had to pay their fare down or my fare up. The court wouldn't order my ex-husband to share travel costs with me. After all, I was the one who decided to move.

The belief that working, career, or remarried mothers will neglect their children is very great. The belief that such mothers will neglect children more than their working, career, or remarried fathers will— or that divorced career mothers in large cities will abuse their children more than divorced career fathers in small towns—remains virtually unshakable.

Miki is tall and very elegant. She moves swiftly, like a samurai, across the room, her eyes masked in pain. She starts speaking abruptly.

"Ten years ago, I married a white student. Together, we organized radical demonstrations. Pretty soon, Alvin became cynical and contemptuous. He began to criticize the masses—and me.

"We were living in Alvin's two-bit hometown. I was a trapped animal, far from home; a full-time mother, with a minimum-wage factory job. I couldn't pursue politics or music. I had no child care and no encouragement. When the kids turned five and seven, I moved out. Three weeks later, Alvin moved a girlfriend in.

"When I got a lawyer, Alvin stole my car. He refused to sell our house and divide up the proceeds. He threatened a custody battle if I demanded anything. He scared me. I gave up all my economic demands.

"Over the next year I began to yearn for San Francisco. I put out feelers. My parents said I could live with them or with my brother, who had young children. I could study the piano again. The kids could spend summers and vacations with Alvin. What difference would our moving to San Francisco make? Alvin traveled four months every year. *He* wasn't stuck in the Midwest. *I* was.

"Alvin got an order restraining me from leaving the state with the kids. By this time, my daughter Suzi was hostile to the idea of San Francisco. She screamed that she would be mugged there. She cried a lot. 'It's all your fault,' she said. 'The divorce and the custody battle. You're a bad mother.' Sam, my son, kept totally quiet.

"My lawyer told me there was no way I could lose custody. I believed him. Five days before the trial, Alvin married his live-in girlfriend. He began talking about how this white stepmother would be a very stable influence.

"Alvin's lawyer mocked the idea of my having a career as a concert pianist. He accused me of wanting to go to San Francisco to have 'boy-friends.' He accused me of feeding my kids un-American (Japanese) food.

"Didn't anyone notice that my children looked Japanese? Didn't anyone care about their mother's ethnic heritage? One of Alvin's witnesses was a neighbor who had once told me to 'go back to China.' I always wondered what they called me and my kids behind our backs.

"My lawyer called me two weeks after the trial. He said: 'I've got bad news for you. The judge gave Alvin custody of both children.' Alvin pulled the kids out of bed in the middle of the night and drove away with them.

"I fell apart. I begged a close friend to persuade him to let me see the children that evening. He refused. I drove by the house alone. I sat outside in the car, crying. His new wife finally sent Suzi out. She was like a zombie, straight-faced, arms at her side. Alvin followed her out. He sat down on my fender, watching everything. I tried to hug Suzi, but she held herself very stiffly. Sam hugged me, but very carefully. I could feel how scared he was.

"Alvin finally had ultimate control over me. It's as if he had the atom bomb.

"I immediately appealed the decision. I wrote and called organizations everywhere to join me in protesting this racist and sexist decision. No Japanese or civil rights or feminist organization wanted to get involved. My only support came from a group of black women social workers. They wrote a group letter to the judge on my behalf. It only infuriated him.

"Does the state have the right to force me to remain hobbled to my ex-husband's definitions of home? Do my determined and effective steps toward independence mean I am unstable? Does wanting to live with my Japanese-American family in San Francisco define me as 'rootless'? Are white married males the only people with 'roots'?

"I feel a little like a slave whose master owns my children. I'm not supposed to be free. But if I manage to escape, I'm supposed to leave my children behind as my master's property."

What if a mother exercises her conscience and her civil responsibilities by exposing government corruption? Can an exercise in public virtue result in her private custodial punishment? Jessie is such a mother. She said:

"The Civil Air Patrol shaped my personality. I was trained to survive in the desert and to participate in rescue missions for downed planes. My mentors are American patriots, soldiers, idealists.

"Mark and I married when we were both eighteen. I became a mother at twenty, and again at twenty-three. While Mark was in Vietnam, I took care of the kids, finished college, taught Sunday school, ran our house— and still had time for political campaign work.

"Mark came back a changed man. He drank. He beat me and the kids. He refused to look for work or to go for counseling. After two years, Mark drifted off. He rarely visited or even called the kids.

"I was offered a job in the Census Bureau based on my volunteer campaign work. I was very excited until I realized that Wade, my boss, was running his own political three-ring circus. He provided girls, booze, and pot for the party regulars. My job was recruiting the 'girls'—and manipulating the census findings.

"I went to my immediate superior in tears. He calmed me down. Then Wade called me in. 'If you persist in talking against me, I'll destroy you politically. I'll spread rumors about *your* sex life.' Within hours, my office was moved. I'd come into work and find my files missing, my phones dead. I'd be ordered to travel fifty miles to a meeting. When I'd arrive, there wouldn't be any meeting. People stopped talking to me.

"Then Wade fired me. Within three weeks, I found another government job in another state. I was there when the bureau scandal hit the newspapers. Apparently, another employee had called the papers. Wade thought I was behind it. He went on a drunken rampage. He found Mark and took him into court. Wade told the judge: 'This is Mark Morehouse— you know, the guy married to the one who's causing all that trouble. She's up and left the state.' That was it. The judge gave Mark custody. Mark went into hiding with the kids.

"Four months later, my appeal of the custody decision came to trial. Mark admitted he had a bad temper and an unstable work history. He admitted hitting me and the kids. He admitted not seeing the kids for more than a year. Mark's lawyers grilled me for two hours on whether I supported the Equal Rights Amendment."

Judicial Opinion

The father can provide a more stable home environment. That doesn't mean that the mother cannot in the future provide a stable home environment, but we do have a problem with her. She's moved. She has a new job. She had other problems. She is going to have to show this court that she has become stable enough to take these two children out of their home state and provide for their needs. There has been a substantial change in conditions. Based upon that finding, and in the best interests of the children, I am remanding the children to the custody of the father.

"Mark dropped out of sight again. The judge didn't order any maternal visitation. Whenever I wasn't at work, I was interviewing lawyers and meeting with the Justice Department. After eight months, my lawyer was finally able to arrange visitation for me.

"Lea had lost a lot of weight. Devon was withdrawn. He kept picking at himself. He was covered with sores. My lawyer convinced a judge to order temporary custody on medical and psychiatric grounds. He ordered a new custody trial in my new state.

"Mark flew right up with *his* custody order. He and the local police removed the kids from school. The school called me at work. I ran over, crying. The kids were crying behind a locked door. When the police took them away, they wouldn't even let me say good-bye.

"I went into the church across the street. I threw myself on the floor before the cross and cried my heart out. I couldn't stop crying. That night I sat on the children's beds all night. I left their half-eaten breakfasts in the refrigerator for months. It was worse than if they were dead.

"A week later, my doorbell rang. It was the sheriff's department with a warrant for my arrest for having 'kidnapped' the children. I was arrested as a fugitive from justice.

"I hired two criminal lawyers: one in each state. I already had two custody lawyers: one in each state. There were three civil lawyers working in D.C. to build the criminal case against Wade.

"One of my lawyers finally convinced the U.S. attorney general's office to get beyond 'this is a family argument' and look at the custody case itself as an obstruction of justice. I was extradited one month later. I was terrified that I'd be killed in prison. Wade could easily make it look like suicide. 'Depressed mother kills herself.' I had visions of me swinging from my Sheer Energy panty hose in my cell.

"They allowed me one visit with my children—under armed guard. I had to pay a hundred dollars for the armed guard. Wade was indicted one day before my trial. Mark didn't press any kidnapping charges. He just turned the kids back to me.

"If you're going to take women's children away, none of the rest matters. If women fear they'll lose their children, we'll all just move one step backwards away from careers, and into deeper servitude. I would have done anything to get my kids back."

"Women: whatever you do, don't quit fighting for your kids."

CHAPTER SEVEN

The Lesbian Mother

I open the letter. Dear Mommy. I am fine. Daddy got me a new bike. My big teeth are coming in. We are going to see Grandma for my birthday. Daddy got me new shoes. She doesn't ask about Ellen. I imagine her father standing over her, watching the words painstakingly being printed. Coaxing her. Coaching her. The letter becomes ugly. I frantically tear it in bits and scatter them out the window.

My lawyer says there is nothing more we can do. He has custody and calls the shots. We must wait and see how long it takes for him to get tired of being mommy and daddy. I open the door to [my daughter] Patricia's room. Ellen keeps it dusted and cleaned, in case she will be allowed to visit us. The yellow and bright blue walls are a mockery. I walk to the windows, begin to systematically tear down the curtains. . . . Grunting and sweating, I am pushed by rage and the searing wound in my soul. Like a wolf, caught in a trap, gnawing at her own leg to set herself free, I begin to beat my breasts to deaden the pain inside. The word . . . lesbian. Lesbian. The word that makes [all the judges in their flapping robes and the fathers who look for revenge] panic, makes them afraid, makes them destroy children. The word that dares them. Lesbian. *I am one.* Even for Patricia, even for her, I will not cease to be! My chest gives a sigh. My heart slows to its normal speech. I feel blood pumping outward to my veins, carrying nourishment and life. I strip the room naked. I close the door.

Beth Brant, *A Long Story*

FOURTEEN MOTHERS (23 PERCENT) WERE LESBIANS. THEY ALL WERE viewed as punishably "uppity" and punishably "sexual." Lesbian mothers lost judicial custody 88 percent of the time and private custody 83 percent of the time. (Non-lesbian mothers lost judicial custody 66 percent and private custody 74 percent of the time.)

Seventy-one percent of the lesbian mothers cohabited with child-oriented mates, compared to 17 percent of the non-lesbian mothers. Lesbian mothers were very aware of their custodial vulnerability.

HOW WERE LESBIAN AND NON-LESBIAN MOTHERS ALIKE?

Lesbians and non-lesbians were all "good enough" mothers. Four mothers (28 percent) became lesbians after their husbands insisted on a ménage à trois with another woman; four mothers (28 percent) became lesbians after their husbands had become openly adulterous; six mothers (43 percent) became lesbians after separation or divorce.[1]

Dr. Ellen Lewin has suggested that "concern for [their] children" is the major reason lesbian mothers leave their marriages.[2] Several studies have suggested that the psychological "organizing principle" among both lesbian and non-lesbian mothers is "motherhood and a concern for children."[3]

Of the lesbian mothers, 57 percent left husbands who were "previously absent" fathers; 43 percent left physically abusive husbands; 36 percent left husbands who subsequently embarked on brainwashing campaigns; 29 percent left husbands who kidnapped their children; and 14 percent left husbands who physically abused their children. Some mothers left husbands who neglected them—as well as their children. For example, Elizabeth said:

> My husband was never home. He had no time for me or the kids. He put off having lunch alone with me for nearly two years. I couldn't stand the loneliness anymore. I thought I'd have a better chance either to meet someone else, or at least to concentrate on my kids in a happier frame of mind. I wasn't even gay when I started to talk about separating. It's the first thing my husband accused me of. He's treated me as a "dirty dyke" ever since.

San Francisco, 1981. Alix and I recognize each other from our TV appearances, embrace—and sit down in her company cafeteria, whispering. In press conferences, before hand-held cameras, Alix never used to whisper.

> *They won't hurt me on television, she must have thought, not in front of so many witnesses. In Dallas, they shot the president on television; in Chicago, they gagged Bobby Seale. All witch-burnings are public events. We just didn't believe it meant us, too.*

She begins. "I was a proper married lady. After ten years I moved out. My husband, Andrew, kept John, our eight-year-old. He 'allowed' me to take Luke, our four-year-old, if I was willing to accept financial responsibility for him. I moved into a household of single parents and went on welfare.

"After a year, I became emotionally involved with one of the mothers in the household. Andrew was outraged. He kidnapped John to Italy, where they lived with Andrew's parents for a year. When Andrew returned, *my* parents met him at the airport. They all demanded that I stop being a lesbian and return to my husband—who was still willing to take me back.

"Had I the remotest understanding of what court is like for any mother, let alone a lesbian, I would have done something—anything—to work things out privately. At the time I honestly believed that a judge would see that I was a good mother, and that Andrew had never been too involved with the boys.

"I was grilled about my lesbianism for one solid hour. I was blamed because the media attended the trial. The judge said he would not be 'dictated to' by a bunch of 'women's libbers.' My own parents took the stand against me.

"On a Saturday morning, two weeks after the trial, I received the judge's verdict. It was contained in a seven-page harangue against lesbianism. The judge wanted to 'save Luke from the stigma of being raised by a lesbian mother.' On Monday morning, while I was in court trying to get a stay of this order, the police came and took Luke away."

Loud silence: a house suddenly emptied, by legal violence, of a mother's child. A sneaker left behind. Crayons. A dentist appointment that won't be kept.

"I was allowed to see both boys every other weekend for one full day, but never overnight. Within a year it was clear that John had closed his heart to me. Luke was 'failing' kindergarten! After nine months of legal struggle, the same judge who'd taken Luke away from me agreed that he was doing badly, and needed some 'maternal nurturance.'

"The judge ordered Luke into my custody. Simultaneously, he granted Andrew's request to take both boys on a summer visit to their grandparents in Italy. Of course, Andrew never came back. For a year I was a shadow in slow motion: exhausted, and out of step with my life.

"When my parents finally realized they had done themselves out of their grandchildren, they helped me hire an Italian lawyer and detective who confirmed that both boys were too well guarded to 'snatch' back. After a six-month struggle, I arrived in Rome with legal custody of both boys—in America.

"Italy does not have to recognize an American order. My lawyer doubted that I could win in an Italian court. I was a radical lesbian foreigner. The case would take years. I left Rome and went to see my boys. I found them playing on the beach."

Mother-woman, stage left, watching the waves break, and the untouchable, growing sons.

"At first, Luke was afraid to come near me. Then, all at once, he came over and said, 'I'm coming back with you.' Just like that. I wanted to take him off the beach and right to the airport but I had no passport, no clothes for him. What if he changed his mind along the way? What if the police found us and arrested me?

"I decided to talk to Andrew. I asked him if he thought it was good for 'his' sons to be raised without ever seeing their mother. He said that a lesbian wasn't a mother anymore."

HOW WERE LESBIAN AND NON-LESBIAN MOTHERS DIFFERENT?

Of the custodially challenged lesbian mothers, 71 percent were "bonded" with domestically supportive mates when they battled for custody. Only 17 percent of the non-lesbian mothers were remarried or "bonded" with (supportive) mates during their custody battles.[4]

Non-lesbian mothers were totally unprepared for what happened to them; lesbian mothers knew that their lesbianism would be custodially held against them. However, lesbian mothers were devastated when their own mothers *actively* opposed them in court.

Both lesbian and non-lesbian mothers were asked to make certain inhuman choices: between their right to mother and their right to lead self-determined lives. However, judges demanded that lesbian mothers choose not only between their children and "careers", but (paradoxically) between their children and their maternal "right" to domestic, emotional, and economic support. Heterosexual fathers are not asked to choose between their children or their supportive mates. They are judicially rewarded for having domestic support.[5]

While heterosexual adultery or post-divorce sexual activity can and does result in a custody challenge, what is at issue there is a mother's *non-marital* heterosexual activity, not heterosexuality itself. Once custody is determined in a heterosexual mother's favor, she doesn't have to hide the *fact* of her heterosexuality from her children.

Lesbian mothers were warned repeatedly against exposing their children to an openly lesbian "lifestyle," lest it damage them emotionally, or lead to their social ostracism. Lesbian mothers were also warned that their children would suffer emotionally if they lived with anxiously "closeted" mothers. Judges (and others) seemed convinced that lesbian mothers would "produce" lesbian children—whether they hid or exposed their lesbianism.[6]

Both lesbian and non-lesbian mothers suffered poverty, isolation, chronic fatigue, and the absence of supportive, extended families. In addition, lesbian mothers were not, or did not feel welcome as *lesbians* among non-lesbian mothers, who were either married or husband hunting. As *mothers*, lesbians were not, or did not feel welcome among lesbian *non-mothers*, who disliked or were uninterested in children and who had not gathered together to function as an unpaid (or paid) child-care center.*

The lesbian mothers I interviewed felt most nourished by their lovers and sometimes by their lawyers; and by other lesbian mothers who had not lost their children. Lesbian mothers were welcomed by other lesbians as long as they left both their children and their maternal concerns at home.

Rae: I live in a wonderful lesbian feminist collective. No one else is a mother. No one wants to co-mother or baby-sit for me. They can't. All their energy goes into surviving and helping other women survive. They feel that children are a luxury. I guess they don't want to be reminded of what they can't afford. One of the women in the house lost her children in a custody battle. Maybe it's too painful for her to relate to kids yet.

Alix: During my court battle, the lesbian and feminist communities supported me in every conceivable way. Afterwards, when the spotlight moved on, so did the activists. These women were not interested in baby-sitting for one male child as a way of defeating patriarchy. They pitied me for being stuck with the task.

---

*For mothers, such group behavior is no worse than, no better than, and no different than male-dominated patriarchal groups.

UNDER WHAT CONDITIONS WERE LESBIAN MOTHERS ALLOWED TO RETAIN CUSTODY OF THEIR CHILDREN?

Two lesbian mothers were privately allowed to keep their children by agreeing not to live with their mates; not to allow them or any woman lover ever to spend the night; not to make any economic demands on their ex-husbands; and not to oppose or interfere with the visitation patterns of their husband's choosing. In each case, the involved children were forced to give up their ongoing ties to a second female parent, and to live with a mother deprived of all domestic and economic support and of emotional and sexual affection.

Melanie, in a jump suit, weighs a hundred pounds and looks eighteen. She is twenty-four, and the mother of two sons. A judge—and her own mother—viewed her lesbianism as more dangerous to her children than her Marine husband's alcoholism and domestic violence.

"I'm very nervous," she says. "I'd better start talking right away, okay? When I became pregnant, I refused to have an abortion. Momma wanted me to quit school, leave town, and give the baby away. I refused to do this. When I gave birth to Robert, Momma was thrilled. She took Robert over completely. I'd be warming a bottle and she'd already be feeding him.

"I met Jerry. He was willing to marry me and to adopt Robert. Momma was thrilled. Jerry started drinking as soon as I got pregnant. I thought everyone's husband did that. After Mikey was born he didn't stop. Momma threatened to take both kids away from him. It did no good. Then Jerry joined the Marines and we moved away.

"Jerry never hit the kids. He didn't see them that much. He hit me. I was bruised all the time. Sometimes he'd just slam me up against a wall or start choking me. He'd knock me down the stairs or twist my arm so badly that I'd be in pain for days. He said if I ever left him, he'd kill me."

Melanie smiles for the first time. "And then I met Molly at my factory job. We became friendly. After a few months, Jerry wanted the three of us to sleep together. I slept with Molly alone—after Jerry had shipped out. I'd never known love that was loving before. Molly started helping me with the house and with the kids.

"Somehow, my momma found out about Molly and told Jerry. One day, I was walking down the street with the kids. Before I knew it, three policemen came after me. They grabbed Robert, my six-year-old, and Mikey, my two-year-old, and drove away. An hour later, a social worker arrived with some 'papers.' It seems that Jerry had temporary custody of 'his' son, Mikey. 'My' son, Robert, would be kept in a state home until our trial.

"It took me a day to locate Robert. He was hysterical. Jerry had told him that his grandmomma was coming to get him. My lawyer convinced the authorities to release Robert to me. *Mikey must have thought I was dead.*

"After three months, a judge ordered maternal visitation with Mikey once a week, but never overnight. When I'd go to pick him up, Jerry would stand there and say, 'You can't win in court. You're a lesbian. Didn't you see *Kramer vs. Kramer*? Fathers can win now. It's about time the men showed the women that they can take care of kids, too! He's my son. I want him. I don't want him being brought up by lesbians.'

"Jerry treated Mikey like a trophy. He'd take him to a barbecue, show him off for fifteen minutes, then get rid of him. He kept Mikey in the Marine day-care center all day. At night, he left him with different sitters. Soon, Jerry was calling me to baby-sit. But he still wanted custody.

"A few weeks before the trial, I happened to call a friend back home. She said she was so glad the kids were coming back. 'Your momma has fixed up a room and is buying furniture and toys.' My momma came to court with her pink suit and her pink gloves, as Jerry's witness. She said she'd never seen him drink or beat me. 'Sad to say,' she told the judge, 'it's my daughter who's the unfit mother.' She was stabbing me with each word. 'Relax and smile,' my lawyer whispered. 'Don't break down here.' I could hardly breathe. I was dying."

THE COURT-APPOINTED PSYCHOLOGICAL REPORT

Mrs. Bates is a shy, demure and private person who is somewhat socially inhibited. Because of her passive personality she didn't stand up for herself in this marriage. She declares that she has been afraid of her husband since he forced himself upon her while intoxicated. Her eldest son, Robert, shows care and nurture. He was verbal, friendly and relaxed. He related on a most positive level.

Private Bates feels that he deserves custody because his wife is a lesbian. He is afraid that his son and stepson will be sexually confused. He is disturbed that they are so positively attached to Melanie's female lover. Bates's drinking difficulties are of some concern to this examiner.

The examiner wishes to emphasize that he considers both parents as fit caretakers: and recommends joint/physical custody of the youngest child.

"Momma expected to get Robert. She didn't. I did—at least temporarily. I don't think I'll ever talk to Momma again. She really likes kids until they're about ten years old. Then—well, I'm her child. Look what she did to me.

"The judge gave Mikey to Jerry. He said that two women couldn't raise a boy without a man. Jerry's real proud of himself as a father. Meanwhile, Mikey has grown very quiet. He won't play with other kids anymore. He calls me a 'bitch.' We just found out that he's begun to hit his head against the wall in day care.

"My lawyer asked Mikey's teacher whether she or another mother would testify for us. So far, no one is willing to testify against a Marine— or for a lesbian."

WHY IS MATERNAL LESBIANISM VIEWED AS "DISGUSTING"?

Judges sometimes allow lesbians to keep their children—if they agree not to *practice* their lesbianism. Somehow, lesbianism is viewed as an infectious disease. If a mother agrees not to engage in relations with another (still infectious) woman, then her disease is viewed as "arrested" or at least as non-infectious.[7]

By contrast, the child of a heterosexual mother is not necessarily seen as "infected" by her mother's compulsive heterosexuality. Heterosexual bonding is not viewed as an infectious disease.

Heterosexually adulterous or "uppity" mothers were also custodially challenged and victimized. They did not excite the same visceral "disgust" that lesbians did. Disgust is, in this case, a form of terror, as well as a form of revulsion against that which is forbidden—but still "enchanting."

Many heterosexual men yearn for sexually active women but cannot comfortably conceive of heterosexual women (or wives) in this role. Many heterosexual men are also terrified of their own homosexual or bi-sexual longings and remain "unaware" of the relationship between such feelings and their sexual behavior within marriage—e.g., their sexual passivity, disinterest, or selfishness.[8]

Perhaps the heterosexual male fear of being overwhelmed and consumed by *one* real woman's sexual and emotional needs requires the fantasy—or reality—of *two* sexually active and accommodating women. A man in bed with two women is neither a homosexual nor a woman hater. He loves women!*

Lesbians in general arouse disgust when they "look" or "behave" like men—i.e., like womanizers who (apparently) want to possess and control women. Heterosexual men—and women—cannot tolerate the *idea* of woman-hating and womanizing behavior in female form, nor can they tolerate the *idea* of man-hating, man-avoidance, or man-izing behavior in female form.

Both heterosexual men and women are also terrified of "gender blur." They target and scapegoat the "mannish" in lesbians and the "girlish" in male homosexuals. Lesbians and male homosexuals may themselves despise or cherish these (troublesome) bi-sexual characteristics.[9]

Lesbian *mothers* arouse disgust, terror, and envy when they act as if they, like fathers, are entitled to certain rights without reciprocal maternal obligations. For example, Cecily's husband threatened to "crucify" her as a "welfare dyke" if she didn't relinquish the children to him.

His disgust grew as Cecily began to succeed economically. Her lesbianism was supposed to lead to downward, not upward, mobility. It was also supposed to inspire disgust, not love, in her children. Cecily said: "He can't stand to see how much I've achieved. I was supposed to die in the gutter. My kids were supposed to despise me. They don't. My ex-husband feels he got robbed. He sees me as scot-free. He's tied down. He has to pay for their college tuition. I don't. He calls me the lesbian bitch who escaped."[10]

How dare Cecily have a good relationship with her children when she has not undergone the sacrifice that patriarchy demands of mothers? How dare she assume the paternal prerogatives of giving up custody and still retain her children's love?

Women are "allowed" to live with each other and apart from men as long as they are heterosexual or celibate; and as long as they obey male gods—both on earth and in heaven. When a woman lives with another woman by choice, or when a lesbian has or wants to have children without being a man's wife, she is viewed as a threat to patriarchal

---

*To "love" him! According to many prostitutes, most male clients want to "do nothing" but to have "everything" done for them by one and, if possible, by two eroticized mothers for hire.

law and order. A woman who loves and lives with another woman is not serving a man—or "absorbing" his potential for anti-social violence.[11]

In creating a non-heterosexual family, the lesbian mother sets a dangerous example for all women. What if all women refused to marry men who were not emotionally or sexually nurturing but who were at best only good economic providers? What if all women refused to mate genetically with non-"maternal" husbands or fathers?*

Lesbian motherhood also arouses disgust in heterosexual women because it criticizes the conditions under which most women have to mother—and the consequent development of maternal "machismo." A "real" woman is someone who can mother a man's child with no domestic, emotional, or economic support from that man—without becoming a "man hater" and without turning a child against his or her father or against men in general.

If a lesbian refuses to serve the needs of an adult man, how can she be trusted to serve the even more insatiable needs of his male children, as envisioned by patriarchal society? For example, Harold demanded that Laura meet their son Barry's insatiable and father-created needs for a female servant. He also demanded that Laura join him and his student Margo in bed. Within a year, Laura and Margo were in love. Within two years, Laura was facing a "lesbian custody fight."

Margo: Once Harold felt he wasn't in complete control, he began calling us dirty lesbians. He called Laura a rotten mother. He tried to convince *me* that she was schizophrenic. He started to work on Barry. He'd tell him that he couldn't trust us, that we weren't real women anymore.

Laura: Once we separated, Harold would call Barry four to five times a day. He'd interrupt him during meals and bedtime preparation. Pretty soon, Barry started saying: "I have to call my father to see if it's all right to see this movie."

Margo: We were Barry's servants. We did his laundry; we cooked for him; we cleaned his room. Harold was his real parent. Barry began to reject me. "You stole my mother away from

---

*What if some men became maternal but for this reason were unattractive to women, sexually or economically? Will men actually risk genetic or social "death" (as patriarchal fathers and husbands) for the sake of justice to women and children?

me. You stole her away from my father—you ruined our family. I hate you."

Laura: By the time Barry was seven he hated us and loved his father. He kept telling me I didn't love him. Meanwhile, his father never let him have a childhood. He had Barry wait on him hand and foot. Harold was confined to a wheelchair since his college accident.

Margo: Once, before Barry went to live with Harold, he took a picture of himself, together with me and Laura to school. His teacher refused to put it up with the other family pictures on the bulletin board. She said that we weren't a real family.

PART III

The Study in Depth, II.
What Crimes Are Committed Against
"Good Enough" Mothers That Result
in Maternal Custodial Victimization?

CHAPTER EIGHT

The Poor Mother

NURSE
And she herself helped Jason in every way.
She calls upon the gods to witness
What sort of return Jason has made to her love.

JASON
You are free to continue
Telling everyone that Jason is a worthless man, but
Consider yourself most lucky that exile is your punishment.
I have come to make some provision for you,
So that you and the children may not be penniless
Or in need of anything in exile.

MEDEA
A distinguished husband I have—for breaking promises.
When in misery I am cast out of the land and go into exile,
Quite without friends and all alone with my children,
That will be a fine shame for the new-wedded groom,
For his children to wander as beggars and she who saved him.

Medea, Euripides

IN MY STUDY, FATHERS HAD OR EARNED FIVE TIMES AS much as mothers did at the time of separation. Of these fathers, 10 percent paid alimony; 33 percent paid child support, which was paid by 56 percent of high-income fathers; 40 percent of mid-income and 17 percent of low-income fathers.

Of the mothers, 60 percent had no pink-collar or professional skills. They also had no access to the job market at the time of separation. These mothers lived on a combination of loans, savings, state welfare, and child-support and alimony payments while they battled for custody.

Thus, of the mothers, 40 percent had pink-collar and professional skills, or were artists, while 13 percent had immediate access to the job market. The professional "career" mothers all suffered declines in income as a result of having to battle for custody. These mothers lived on a combination of loans, savings, child support, alimony, and wages.

MATERNAL ECONOMICS IN GENERAL

Families headed by divorced and single mothers, especially mothers of color, constitute a ghetto of extreme poverty.[1] Stay-at-home mothers are unsalaried and horrendously underpaid by state welfare departments[2]; salaried fathers earn at least twice as much as salaried mothers[3]; and divorce is rapidly increasing in North America.[4] Upon divorce, the paternal standard of living often rises by 42 percent, while the maternal standard of living may decline by 73 percent;[5] fathers do not pay adequate child support or alimony, if they pay any at all; and judges and governments rarely order or enforce the collection of child-support payments.[6] When they do, the payments are rarely above the state levels of welfare.[7]

WHAT DOES MY STUDY TELL US ABOUT MATERNAL VERSUS PATERNAL ECONOMIC RESOURCES UPON SEPARATION OR DIVORCE?

Fathers who battled for custody earned (or had) an average income that was five times greater than their wives had at the moment of separation. *This was true both for "poor" and for "rich" fathers.* The median paternal income was $25,000. The median income for mothers was approximately $5,000.[8]

Of the custodially challenged mothers, 60 percent had no profession or marketable skill. Nearly a third of the mothers did have professional skills, e.g., nursing, teaching, social work, medicine, or science. Ten percent were artists. Moreover, 87 percent of the mothers had never worked outside the home or worked only part-time and sporadically after motherhood.[9]

Although economic disputes often escalated into custody battles, these fathers did not use custody as a *threat* to obtain economic leverage. These fathers were interested in obtaining certain economic and psychological advantages—by obtaining custody. For example, some fathers pressed for custody as a way of keeping the marital homes and all other marital assets.[10]

The same father who viewed himself—and was viewed by others—

135

as a good economic provider was often economically controlling, stingy, and vindictive toward his wife and children. Linda described a wealthy and hardworking husband who carefully supervised her every expenditure:

> If I discussed a purchase with my husband beforehand, I could pretty much have anything I needed for the children or the house. I had a credit card, but I had to clear the purchases with him first.
>
> He didn't want custody. It became an issue only because I refused to back down on my right to adequate alimony and child support.

WHAT ECONOMIC OPTIONS DID MOTHERS HAVE?

Custodially challenged mothers could return to their own families or apply for state welfare. They could attempt to live on a combination of alimony, child-support payments, and savings; or they could work for wages on the open market.

HOW MANY CUSTODIALLY CHALLENGED MOTHERS SURVIVED BY GOING HOME TO THEIR FAMILIES?

None (0 percent) of these mothers was able to "go home again"—at least not with their children. Maternal families of origin lived in another state or were poor, old, or deceased. Parents were also reluctant to take responsibility for daughters and grandchildren. Some maternal grandmothers blamed their daughters for their economic predicaments and counseled reconciliation.

Cecily: My husband's parents, who are very wealthy, said they weren't responsible because he was over twenty-one. My folks sent me a check for two hundred and fifty dollars and wished me luck. I went on welfare.

Rae: My mother thought I was crazy for getting divorced. She wouldn't give me any money to help me keep my daughter with me. She only blamed me when I was forced to give her up for economic reasons. She had no pity for me. She didn't even grant me the right to feel bitter about anything.

Abigail was the only mother who turned to her *father* for help. She said:

> My mother disapproved of my leaving my husband. She didn't think that his beating me up was a good enough reason to leave. My father hit *her*, and she managed to live with him for twenty years. My mother simply didn't understand my leaving. My father, *who lived alone*, didn't think his nervous system could withstand three grandchildren in the house.

HOW MANY CUSTODIALLY CHALLENGED MOTHERS SURVIVED BY GOING ON WELFARE?*

Approximately half the mothers became welfare recipients upon separation. This meant economic impoverishment, humiliation, and a vigorous enforcement of paternal visitation.

Janet: When I was positive that my husband was sexually molesting my two sons, I made him leave the house. He was having some kind of nervous breakdown. He went to live with his mother. I went on welfare. His union disability benefits were much higher than our welfare benefits. He wouldn't give us any money unless he saw the boys. I refused. Eventually, a judge got him to pay welfare back—but only if he got his visitation.

Emily: The welfare worker was very suspicious of me. "Why should a white educated woman need to go on welfare?" If I did, something must be seriously wrong with me. Maybe I couldn't be trusted with my daughter. Maybe I was crazy. She kept sending investigators over to look for any bank accounts or secret jobs I might have. They grilled me like I was a criminal suspect.

Welfare-wives, like the wives of individual men, are expected to account for each penny—and to be grateful for the money they receive. Welfare-wives, like the wives of individual men, must be available when

---

*Within two years only 25 percent of these mothers were still on welfare.

their "husbands" want to see them. They must make their homes, closets, and sexual lives accessible to state invasion.

The state hounds the welfare-wife into "naming" the father—not to put *him* under welfare restraint, but to force him to reimburse the state at a welfare level. (Perhaps such punishment will "teach" her to avoid sex with men; or to marry only a "wealthy" man; or to become "wealthy" herself.)

The state treats its welfare wives as lazy, parasitic, and sexually amoral. It rarely supports maternal educational or career goals. The state can easily turn a self-supporting, professional mother into a welfare dependent. For example, in 1960 Winnie, a black American mother, separated from her white husband. She says:

"I immediately went back to work as a nurse on the night shift. It paid the most money and allowed me to be with Kevin all day. At night, my upstairs neighbor checked on him before she went to bed, and again when she got up in the morning. We left our doors unlocked in case Kevin got up in the middle of the night. I wasn't thrilled by this arrangement, but it was working.

"My trouble began when I tried to get Kevin into a settlement house program. The social worker told me I could lose him or even go to jail if I didn't stay home nights. She told me to apply for welfare.

"Once your right to be a mother is questioned, it casts a shadow over your entire experience of mothering. From 1960 to 1970, I lived under a kind of house arrest. I walked around with ID and various form letters all the time. I always had to prove that I wasn't getting child support. I always had to prove that I wasn't working. I also had to prove that I let Jerry see Kevin.

"Sometimes Jerry sent support payments. Whenever he did, I had to tell welfare, and they'd deduct it from my next check. If I didn't tell, I risked being thrown off welfare. I started a food co-op with five other welfare mothers. Welfare found out and cut the food allowance for each of us. If we could manage on less by pooling our resources, we needed less money, they said.

"In family court, I saw women sit and wait all day, for days at a time. A judge finally ordered Jerry to pay a small amount of child support. Once, Kevin needed a tonsilectomy. I tried to get the court to collect some money to pay for it. The judge lectured me on 'frivolous' spending for forty minutes. You really learn to keep quiet and not show what you're feeling in these situations.

"I imagine because I was black and Jerry was white that the state thought he owed me very little anyway. Any black child whose white father actually wanted to visit him was seen as a hero. Jerry was earning sixteen thousand dollars a year, while Kevin and I lived on less than two thousand a year.

"I think Jerry wanted to put my life on permanent hold. So did the state. Kevin and I were pieces of property, little black figurines without feelings.

"I should have gone off welfare sooner. But something happened to me. I became paralyzed by the rules and the forms and all the days I spent in family court and down at the welfare office. It was my full-time career for nine years. I analyzed each letter and every welfare worker's questions as if my life depended on it.

"I guess it did."

Winnie was a nurse and the mother of a "legal" child. Imagine how the state treated Manya, an unwed teenager. Manya became pregnant in 1965. Abortion was still illegal; the pill, not widely in use. Manya was seventeen.

Manya's widowed father refused to support her. He wanted her to have an abortion—or get married. Manya refused both options. Eventually, the welfare department granted Manya $12 a week and forced her into a home for unwed mothers. She said:

I didn't consider having sex or getting pregnant wrong. They put a lot of pressure on me to give up my baby. I wouldn't. A social worker continued to call me for two years after I had my child, asking if I hadn't changed my mind and wanted to put her up for adoption.

I refused to give my child up. I got on welfare. Over the years, the caseworkers would get snotty with me: "Where did I get the money for hair dye? Why were there so many toys on the floor?" I knew this was a violation of my rights. More than once, I forcibly threw out social workers. They sent me terrible letters threatening to cut off my checks, or threatening to investigate me as an unfit mother. It was nothing but intimidation for not being humble. Also, they thought something was really wrong with me. Why would a white girl get pregnant and live on welfare?[11]

The same state bureaucracy that subsidizes mothers so inadequately is quick to blame them when anything goes "wrong" with their children. Cheryl was married to an alcoholic wife batterer. She said:

From birth, my daughter Iris had a sleeping disturbance. Iris had severe temper tantrums. Sometimes they'd last for forty-five minutes. She'd climb out of windows. She'd climb into the oven. She had no sense of fear or danger. She was very strong. At first, the doctors thought she was autistic. I could barely contain her when she was out of control. I started locking her into her room at night for her own safety. She'd scream and bruise herself on the furniture. My neighbors all thought I was hitting her. Meanwhile, I hadn't slept through the night for three years.

My husband kept denying that anything was wrong. He said I was crazy. He walked out. I applied for welfare. They suspected me of abusing Iris.

Cheryl was mercilessly interrogated. One social worker discovered that Cheryl had been an abused child. As such, she was doubly suspected of being an abusive mother.

Cheryl finally found a doctor who diagnosed Iris as an epileptic. He prescribed medication. No one investigating Cheryl's maternal "fitness" took this diagnosis seriously. No one offered Cheryl any support or encouragement for wanting to keep her extremely difficult daughter. Cheryl hired a lawyer and fought the state. She said: "I had to promise that I would work no more than forty hours per week. I had to promise to provide a separate bedroom for Iris. I had to allow the social worker to come in and check me out once a week. They said that if Iris began to have tantrums again, they'd have to investigate us again."

By the time Iris was five, Cheryl was overwhelmed by fatigue and despair.

I decided to ask Iris's father if he'd take her for a while. I heard he'd remarried. Even if he was a louse, maybe his wife could help. I was too tired to go on alone. He said he'd take her on two conditions: if I promised to stay away and not bother him, and if we made it permanent and legal.

The court proceedings took about five minutes. They didn't interrogate him as they did me. They didn't even ask if he was fit. All they cared about was that he was her father, was remarried, and said he'd support her.

IN MY STUDY, HOW MANY CUSTODIALLY CHALLENGED MOTHERS SURVIVED BY RECEIVING ALIMONY OR OTHER MARITAL ASSETS?

Ninety percent of all fathers paid no alimony; 87 percent of the fathers who battled in court paid no alimony.[12] We must remember that these mothers had been married for an average of nine years, had borne and raised an average of two children, and had performed all the traditional wifely and domestic services. For only room and board, these mothers had performed tasks far beyond the economic reach of most workingmen. In addition to being unpaid housekeepers and nursemaids, some mothers had earned money during their marriages; some had worked for their husbands as unpaid secretaries, bookkeepers, and accountants; some had brought financial dowries into the marriage.

Judges and husbands consistently overlooked such unpaid and economically invaluable labor. The same judge who removed children from "career" mothers also told non-career mothers to "get jobs" and to become "economically independent."

Few mothers fought for alimony. Some knew that their ex-husbands couldn't afford it; some mothers felt guilty because they had initiated the divorce.* Once the fathers raised custody as an issue, maternal demands for alimony usually ceased. As Lillian Kozak, Chair of New York–NOW's Committee on Domestic Relations, pointed out: "When you tell a woman 'You're going to lose your children,' or, 'You stand an even chance of losing your children,' every ounce of fight for her financial rights goes right out the window. Even when she knows it's probably a bluff, she doesn't want to take the chance."

Many husbands acted as if their ex-wives' unpaid services, real wages, and dowries automatically belonged to them. They acted as if maternal wages were more than "covered" by room, board, clothing, and whatever standard of living a husband could afford. Husbands also believed that whatever was "owed" a wife as the result of her unpaid labor or financial input was "canceled" at the moment of separation. Few judges or legislators seriously opposed this point of view.[13]

Sadie is now in her early sixties. She had worked as an accountant for ten years before she married David, gave birth to, and mothered their three children. During their marriage, Sadie worked as David's (unpaid) wife and as his (unpaid) accountant.

"When we both were in our fifties, my husband left me for a thirty-year-old woman. It turns out that David didn't just fall in love and walk out. The man planned to rob me. For two years, behind my back, he transferred everything out of 'our' name and into his name alone. Twenty-five years of hard work—wiped out. Why?

*This was not the *reason* mothers didn't receive alimony. They received no alimony because their ex-husbands refused to pay any—and because judges rarely and only sporadically ordered or enforced alimony payments.

"I hired a lawyer. David ran a business valued at three million dollars. He admitted that he gave himself an annual salary of two hundred thousand dollars. Then he offered me twelve thousand dollars a year in alimony for eight years, or until our youngest turned twenty-one. When I refused it, he changed his offer to eight thousand a year in alimony.

"I refused to agree to this. David told the kids I was delaying the settlement out of greed. Greed? He was going on expensive vacations four times a year. I couldn't afford a week's vacation. My lawyer told me not to work—that if I did, it would knock down the amount of alimony. For three years, I lived on a combination of child support, loans, savings, and secret part-time work.

"Three years later, with no settlement whatsoever, my lawyer told me to start looking for work. 'David is obviously determined to keep fighting you until you run out of money. Now he's threatening to sell the house out from under you.'

"I needed money to live on and money to keep paying my lawyer. The larger firms didn't want to hire me. They said I was too old and out of the job market for too long. I finally found a job for much less money than I'm worth. Being able to work torpedoed my argument for more alimony. I had to settle. Now David wants me to pay him the fair market value for the house I live in. He knows I can't afford to buy him out. Where does he think I can afford to live?

"Three weeks ago, David remarried. His new wife is thirty-four. He set up four trust funds to guarantee her and each of our children fifty thousand dollars a year for the rest of their lives. What if I get sick? What if I can't keep working? What will happen to me if David dies and my eight thousand dollars a year in alimony stops? My kids say they don't want to get 'involved.'

"If they saw someone stabbing me, wouldn't they get involved?"

Sadie is quite lucky. Most mothers do not have "millionaire" husbands who endow their children with trust funds. Most divorced mothers do not receive any alimony; nor do they live in spacious homes after they are divorced and their children are grown up. Most full-time mothers who are now in their sixties do not have Sadie's ability to command a salary above that of a waitress, clerical worker, or secretary.

The case of Myrna Labow of Connecticut provides us with a chilling example of what can (custodially) happen to a mother with young children who insists on alimony and child support. In 1974, Myrna filed for divorce from her wealthy lawyer husband, Ronald, who had adulterously lived apart from her and their children for years. After a *four year* fight, the court awarded Myrna $7,500 a month in child support and alimony, and continued custody of the children.

Ronald Labow refused to comply with what the court ordered. Instead, he used every maneuver to weaken his ex-wife economically and psychologically. In 1979, when he was $76,000 in arrears, he moved for custody of his son.

Labow claimed that Myrna was "mentally unfit" because of her "obsession" with money! Several psychiatrists testified for him. One psychiatrist assured the judge that, in his *psychiatric* opinion, Myrna was receiving enough money. Her demand for the court-ordered money was proof of "irrational" behavior. The New York Supreme Court "was critical of [Myrna's] behavior on the witness stand," seeing it as "an obsession with [the] enforcement of her rights." In 1980, the court awarded Ronald Labow custody of his son.

On May 11, 1982, after *two more years* of fighting, the New York appellate court reversed this decision.

In essence, what is involved here is a prosperous father living in his own apartment with a woman who he says he intends to marry, and a mother left with three young children who, in addition to raising them alone for several years, has had to resort continuously, in and out of the courts and by all means available, to obtain alimony and child support. Even though the lifestyle is higher than the average, the inability to pay bills for the co-op, tuition and other expenses imposed an irksome burden.

It is obviously easier for the father to be more relaxed with his son than the mother can be. Plaintiff's obsession has been brought about by defendant's conduct. The record is barren of evidence of the father's efforts to comply with his court-ordered support obligations. The record does not support a finding that the plaintiff is mentally unfit to properly care for Steven. It strongly suggests that if defendant were to comply with his obligation, the issue would disappear from the case.[14]

IN MY STUDY, HOW MANY CUSTODIALLY CHALLENGED MOTHERS SURVIVED BY RECEIVING CHILD-SUPPORT PAYMENTS?

In my study, 67 percent of the fathers paid no child support. However, fathers at all income levels tended to pay child support more often than alimony. Some child support was paid by 56 percent of the high-income fathers, 40 percent of the middle-income fathers, and 17 percent of the low-income fathers.[15]

Many fathers economically battered the very children they wanted to reclaim. During the 1960s, Lucy received no child support. She went back to court *thirty times* in an attempt to have her court-ordered child support enforced. The judge(s) were completely uninterested in her ex-husband's domestically violent behavior. Lucy said:

> I had not received any child support in six months. I couldn't buy my son shoes. Food was also a real problem for us. I finally decided to take advantage of the clause in the divorce papers which said if he didn't pay, he couldn't see his son. My ex-husband earned thirty thousand dollars a year in 1967. I was earning less than seventy-five dollars a week.
>
> The judge was impressed by my ex-husband's desire to maintain a relationship with my son. The judge yelled at me. "Do you want to cripple your child even more than you've already done? Don't you know he needs a father? I'm reducing this father's child-support obligation to five dollars a week for the next two years. I don't want this mother to have any legal reason for interfering with the father's visitation."

The fathers who did pay child support felt heroic about doing so. Many overlooked how insufficient their payments really were. For example, Ellie said:

> When I do my income tax every year, I figure out the portion of my household expenses actually attributed to my son. It is at least six times what his father gives me. His father earns more money than I do. He has no other dependents. He loves our son, but won't pay for what he doesn't control or enjoy on a daily basis.

Those fathers who won custody and could economically afford to subsidize maternal visitation refused to do so. *Two* fathers (4 percent) out of all the custodially triumphant fathers helped subsidize maternal visitation.

Catherine: My husband allows me three thousand dollars a year out of my own inheritance toward my visitation expenses. This includes air travel and motel costs. One round-trip ticket costs four hundred dollars. Motels are at least two hundred dollars a week. Long-distance phone calls between visits come to a thousand dollars a year. This allows me to see my children three times a year at most, for a week at a time. I earn ten thousand dollars a year. My ex-husband has my inheritance and his physician's salary.

Grace: My husband earns about sixty thousand
I'm a student and waitress. According to o[u]
I have the children summers and alternate
He pays their air transportation one way
(It's about five hundred dollars.) I'm supp[ ]
for their return flight. He gives me seventy
a week for food, during the time they're with me, which
is considered very, very generous. What if they need a
doctor? What about the cost of a baby-sitter when I'm
working? What about eating out? What about books or
clothing or toys or movies when they're with me? I can
barely manage to pay their return air fare.

IN MY STUDY, WERE CUSTODIALLY CHALLENGED MOTHERS ABLE TO SURVIVE BY WORKING FOR MONEY OUTSIDE THE HOME?

Sixty percent of the mothers had no professional or marketable skills. They worked immediately or within two years of their separation as non-unionized domestics, factory workers, laborers, clerks, sales "girls" and school aides. Some mothers worked as secretaries.

These mothers did not have jobs that promised them a better economic future. They did not enjoy the work they did. They did not learn any on-the-job skills. Their work was not rewarding enough to compete with their maternal identities. *Most important, their work didn't pay very much.*

Mothers under siege were afraid of losing custody because they were (poor) "working" mothers. They were also afraid of losing their jobs because of too many lawyer or court-related absences. Rachel said:

I missed so many teaching days that they suggested I take a leave of absence or risk losing my license. I didn't want to jeopardize my continuity in a good school. I wasn't getting any child support. I couldn't manage on my income alone. But I had to appear in court or at my lawyer's office in order to fight for child support. It was an impossible situation.

At some point, 13 percent of the mothers became convinced that the quality of their maternal care was seriously impaired by poverty—and by the stress of constant battle. They also realized that their ex-husbands would never give up fighting; and would eventually win custody because of their economic superiority. These mothers then "gave up" fighting for custody.[16]

Thirty percent of the mothers had marketable professions. Ten percent were artists. Those mothers with high-status careers lost their jobs or suffered irretrievable declines in income during stressful and time-consuming custody battles. Nora, a biochemist, was asked to resign her position because of her frequent absences and her generally "distracted" state. Ellie, an academic anthropologist, was refused tenure at her university. She said: "I know they discriminate against women, but I didn't make the best of my situation. How could I make friends or publish papers or raise grant money when my energies were all consumed by the possibility of losing my child?"

Maureen is one of the eight mothers who worked continuously during their marriages. When I interviewed her, she had been battling for custody for three years. Maureen described how a custody struggle can affect a mother who, in 1981, earned $25,000—much more than most women, but only half of what her husband earned.

"In the last three years this man—who's fighting tooth and nail for sole custody of his children—has spent more money renovating his summer home than in child support. He won't give them an allowance. He won't buy them any clothes—because that would help me. He bought baseball gloves and uniforms for the twins. He keeps this stuff at his house. He told the children, 'It's only yours when you're with me.'

"I have two jobs and no money. After taxes, my salary just covers food, transportation, and rent for the four of us. That's it. No extras: like clothes, books, or movies. No eating out, no impulse spending on a Saturday night, no vintage comic books. My part-time job pays for the baby-sitters.

"Kenneth earns much more than I do. He refuses to sell or rent our jointly owned home. What this means is that he pays two hundred dollars a month to live in a four-bedroom home with a yard. I pay six hundred and fifty dollars a month for a two-bedroom apartment.

"Kenneth doesn't view any of this as bad for the children but as good for his case. If he can show that I'm out working a lot and that we live in an unsafe neighborhood . . . well. Winning the case against me is more important than his children losing time with their mother.

"When we were first married, I worked at two jobs so that Kenneth could get his doctorate without having to work at all. I also did most of the housework and child care. Kenneth has always been very concerned about the future and therefore has a lot of retirement money accumulated.

"He has a tremendous amount of insurance, all of which was accumulated while we were married. I can remember times when we didn't have money for anything pleasant, but we continued to get more insurance for him. I have no insurance. When I had a real medical emergency last year, I wasn't covered by my own policy. I asked Kenneth for money. He asked for the children back.

"In the last three years, I've aged ten years. What will Kenneth do next? Will he kidnap the kids again? Will he burst in on me and break those few belongings of value I haven't yet sold? What if I can't keep paying my very fancy lawyer and repaying my twenty-thousand-dollar bank loan, too? Will the bank repossess the furniture I have left? Will Kenneth finally repossess the children?"

CHAPTER NINE

The Mother Married to a Violent Man

1981

Long Island, New York, March 10—
A Long Island husband whisked his
two kids off to Oregon after his wife
became paralyzed—despite the fact she
was acclaimed for her courage in sur-
mounting the disability. Her husband,
a $56,000.00 a year computer con-
sultant, yanked the 9 and 11 year old
boys out of school. [Mrs. Sylvia
Geoghegan's lawyer] said he had video
tapes to prove Mrs. Geoghegan could
do everything a mother has to do.[1]

*   *   *

Seattle, August 4—A young couple died
near a busy West Seattle intersection
yesterday afternoon in what police say
was a murder-suicide that erupted from
a dispute over custody of the estranged couple's two young children.
Witnesses said Wendelken, a real-es-
tate salesman, fired several shots as he
chased his wife into the bank building.[2]

SIXTY-TWO PERCENT OF THE "GOOD ENOUGH" CUSTODIALLY challenged mothers were the victims of physical violence during their marriages and divorces or while under custodial siege. Thirty percent were physically battered on a regular basis during marriage; 32 percent were physically attacked by their husbands for initiating separations or divorces.

Mothers were physically prevented from seeing their children, either temporarily or permanently, by husbands who physically evicted them from the marital home (18 percent), kidnapped their children (37 percent), physically prevented pre-arranged maternal visitation from taking place (22 percent), and engaged in psychologically violent anti-mother brainwashing campaigns (58 percent).

In addition, 100 percent of the mothers were psychologically abused during marriage or during the struggle for custody.

WHAT DOES MY STUDY TELL US ABOUT THE DOMESTIC VIOLENCE OF FATHERS WHO BATTLED FOR CUSTODY?

Sixty-two percent of the mothers reported being the victims of domestic physical violence. Of these mothers, 30 percent were physically battered (pushed, slapped, kicked, punched, knocked unconscious, or raped) by their husbands on a regular basis during marriage. Some mothers required hospitalization. Thirty-two percent were physically attacked by their husbands after initiating separations or divorces.

Margaret is the mother of five children. She was a battered wife who, after twenty years of marriage, finally deserted her "whipping girl" post. This so outraged her husband that he moved out, withdrew all economic support, remarried, and began a campaign for custody. Margaret weeps before she can speak, this large woman in cherry-bright lipstick.

"I was married in 1953. My first was born in 1954. My other four children were born between 1960 and 1968. My husband, Ernie, was in charge of everything. I wasn't allowed to do anything on my own. Once I enrolled in a class at our local junior college. Ernie said, 'I don't want you going to school.' I stopped right away.

"I was an abused woman. I just didn't know it. See?" Margaret says, holding her right hand. "These fingers are broken. They can never hold change. When I went to the hospital to have them set, Ernie stayed with me to make sure I would say I caught them in the washing machine.

"I was always too afraid to report him. Finally, I told him I couldn't take it anymore. Ernie told me I'd regret the day I was born if I divorced him. He smashed a chair over my head. He broke my arm. After that, I stopped lying for him.

"I hired a lawyer. He told me to take the money out of our joint account. 'Don't bother looking for the checkbook,' I told Ernie. 'I took all five thousand dollars out.' With that, everything went—the mirror, the bed. He destroyed everything in the bedroom. And he beat me up.

"I got an order of protection. I used the five thousand dollars up. Then I went on welfare. Ernie got married a year after our divorce. That's when he started to visit the kids. He also started a custody action. I wasn't even worried. What judge in his right mind would give my six-, eight-, and eleven-year-olds to this crazy man?

150

"The judge gave Ernie custody of all five kids. She said Ernie had a good income, a nice large house, a new wife—and I was living on welfare. I couldn't give my kids over to that man. Not the two youngest. I went into hiding with them at my mother's house. I wore a wig when I went out to shop. We never answered the door. Two policemen and my own lawyer said I had to give my babies to Ernie or go to jail."

How many pots of coffee can she make for herself? How many clean counters can she clean again? She turns around and around in her kitchen. She puts her fist in her mouth to stop the scream.

Why doesn't she put her twenty-year career at Motherhood, Inc., behind her and get a job as a file clerk, a waitress, a cashier? Doesn't she understand that at forty-nine she is free to start a new life?

"The kids were supposed to spend Christmas with me. At six P.M. on Christmas Eve, Ernie drove up with them. 'They won't stay unless you drop your action for alimony. This Christmas is just a taste of what you'll get. I'll take them and you'll never see them again.' I said, 'I'm not going to drop my action. I happen to need something to live on also.' He just packed them into the car and off they went. Jingle Bells.

"A few months ago, my oldest son came to see me. He told me that he'd had a drug problem, that he had been in a mental hospital and was on probation. I was beside myself. No one had contacted me. No one thought he needed his mother. He said: 'Ma, I never meant to hurt you.' We sat and cried."

Margaret laughs for the first time. "Well, I told my divorce counselor I was married to one in a million. If you turn against him, forget it. But how could Ernie get custody legally? Because I left him? Because I had no money? How could I have money? I was a mother."

Didn't that judge understand what a mother is?

WHAT KINDS OF PSYCHOLOGICAL ABUSE DID PATRIARCHAL FATHERS ENGAGE IN?

According to Jehanne Dyllan:

Bill Meadows, the father of Karen Silkwood's three children, was physically abusive to Karen throughout their marriage. Cathy, a friend of Karen's, used to babysit for them. Within six months, Bill was having an affair with her. He moved Cathy right in. Bill started telling Karen to get out and leave "his" children behind. I believe that Karen Silkwood's risk-taking and perseverance against the bosses at Kerr-McGee was due to her having lost everything. She had no home to hang her hat on. She had nothing to lose. What could Kerr-McGee do to her psychologically, that hadn't already happened?[3]

Patriarchal fathers verbally and socially humiliated their wives, withheld verbal and emotional support, were emotionally overdependent and demanding, or sexually abusive or neglectful. Some husbands were particularly sadistic.

Ella Mae: When I was at the end of my first pregnancy, Donald demanded that I iron every shirt and handkerchief he owned before I left for the hospital. He demanded a week's worth of meals all cooked and frozen. He said I shouldn't think that I could stop being a wife just because I was about to give birth.

   I was in bad shape after I gave birth. I was breast feeding. My legs were still swollen. I had difficulty walking. The first night Mary cried, I asked Donald to bring her from her crib into our bed. He started yelling at me. He said he wouldn't cater to my laziness. He said I'd have to go get her myself. I crawled on my hands and knees to her crib.

Sue Ellen: I came down with pneumonia. I had a fever of a hundred five. I called Curtis at his girlfriend's house and asked him to please drive me to the hospital. He did—with her sitting in the front seat. They took the kids back to her house.

   I was in the hospital for a month. Curtis brought the kids to see me once a week for one hour. He waited outside. When I was discharged, I took the bus home. I remember it was snowing. The apartment was very cold. All the furniture was gone except for a child's bed and some cooking utensils. The telephone was turned off. There was an eviction notice under the door. I borrowed eggs and coffee from a neighbor. Curtis came over the next day to tell me we were getting divorced. He said that since the kids were already living with him, he didn't have to support me, that I should go on welfare. He'd let me see the kids every other weekend.

A number of husbands belittled, closely "supervised," and publicly denigrated their wives' housekeeping and child care. The emotional neediness, dependence, and "passivity" of some husbands were so extreme that they exerted "cornering and paralyzing" effects analogous to that of physical violence.

WHAT DID I LEARN ABOUT MALE DOMESTIC VIOLENCE FROM INTERVIEWS WITH CUSTODIALLY EMBATTLED PATRIARCHAL FATHERS?

Many of the battling fathers whom I interviewed expressed "murderous" feelings toward their ex-wives. Defiantly, bitterly, matter-of-factly, they said, "I want to kill my ex-wife," "She doesn't deserve to live," "She should be dead," etc.[4] These fathers acted as if disobedient wives were unworthy of mercy or compassion. They were "surprised" when their ex-wives displayed human emotions upon being custodially victimized.

For example, Luke believed in the sanctity of the father-controlled family. He moved out after his wife had committed adultery. He was "too upset" to see his children for "nearly a year." When he heard that his wife was "involved" in yet another love affair, he moved for custody and divorce.

I don't know why she got so wild after the judge gave me custody. She physically attacked me outside the courtroom. Would a normal woman do that? How could I let her bring my kids up? She's really crazy. When I told her that she could only see the kids under my roof, under my supervision, she screamed and cried and hit me again.

WHAT KINDS OF PSYCHOLOGICAL VIOLENCE DID SMOTHER-FATHERS ENGAGE IN?

Fourteen (23 percent) of my custodially challenged mothers were married to Smother-Fathers. I interviewed nine additional Smother-Fathers who were also battling for custody. A Smother-Father believes that *he* is the "mother" or that he is a better "mother" than his wife is.

Beth, one of my maternal interviewees, described her husband, Simon, in this way:

> If Simon had breasts, he would have taken over nursing our son, Elliott. He had some peculiar psychological investment in not letting me mother. He would come home every day, take Elliott into the bedroom or bathroom, and lock the door behind him. He'd lie on the bed or take a bath with him for three or four hours at a time. Simon used to rock Elliott very excitedly for hours on end.
>
> Now, twelve years later, this boy can't show any love toward me in front of his father. He acts as if loving me means betraying Simon. When Elliott is at my house, he'll go into another room and shut the door, before he dials Simon's number. I get the feeling that they are two lovers having a private, intimate conversation.

Smother-Fathers experienced their intimacy with their children as primary and often "mystical." They denigrated their wives' mothering abilities and lauded their own as superior.

Shawn: From the time he was born, my son William couldn't sleep if I didn't hold him. It would take hours each night to get him to fall asleep. I'd have to have the right pitch in my voice to soothe him. I'd have to stroke his forehead just so. It took two years before he could sleep without me being in the same house. I had a harder time putting him to bed when his mother was around.

Once, when William was two and a half, I had a very loud fight with my wife. Afterward, William clung to me in a great panic. The only way I could calm him down was to take him into the bathroom, fill the bathtub with warm water, and hold him in the water. I got into the bathtub with him and turned the light out. It was dark. It was warm. It was quiet. I talked to him very softly. His mother was not part of the world for the time being. He wouldn't even let his mother into the bathroom.[5]

Linus: My daughters are the most important thing in my life. I don't think their mother appreciates or enjoys them as much as I do. From the moment they were born, just being with them gave me more pleasure than sex does. I stopped working in order to be with them. I don't want anything to get in the way of my role as a father.

Debra does not concentrate intensely every minute when the girls are with her. I do. I think they give her a headache, especially after working all day. I'm always fresh for the girls. I live each moment with them vibrantly. If I don't win sole custody of these kids, the whole purpose of my life is over.

Eric: Fran was always jealous of how easy it was for me to relate to the kids. I have more fun with them than she does. I have the nesting ability. Fran has accused me of being the mother hen. I am. That's why I work at home. I like being in touch with the flow of their lives every minute.

The idea that child care is a burden is the biggest fraud perpetrated by women on men in this country. There's nothing to it. You can do everything with kids. They don't have to disrupt your life at all.

It became clear, upon questioning, that Eric, who does work at home, does not do the cooking, the shopping, the cleaning, the laundry, the chauffeuring, or the scheduling of his children's appointments. A paid housekeeper, supervised and supplemented by his live-in girlfriend, does "all that unimportant crap."

The most extreme Smother-Fathers still exhibited an aggressively "male" strategic expertise and persistence.* For example, some Smother-Fathers physically and psychologically battered their wives, kidnapped and brainwashed their children, refused to pay child support, and, above all, refused to give up until they had obtained exclusive possession of their children, both psychologically and legally.

Eric: I will not do things the way Fran wants them to be done. I don't think kids have to go to bed *exactly* at eight P.M., lights out, no TV, and no whispering. I'm not running a concentration camp. She is. I refuse to limit the number of calls I make to the kids when they're with their mother. That's interfering with my continuity and peace of mind. I'll call back twenty times if she won't put them right on the phone. Or I'll go over and demand to see them.[6]

---

*We may remember that *all* the Smother-Fathers in my first study obtained custody.

Linus: I have joint custody now, but within a year I'll have sole custody of both girls. There's no way I can lose. I'm working on this full time. Debra has a full-time job and spends her spare time trying to meet a new husband.

I'm also smarter than she is. For example, I persuaded Debra to let me enroll our eldest daughter in a private school near me. I said I'd pay the tuition instead of child support. Tuition is deductible. Child support isn't. What this means is that my youngest daughter is hearing all about a really great school from her sister. She wants to go, too. Only I have the money to send her. And I have certain conditions for doing it.

Smother-Fathers overidentified with their sons. In some cases, this meant strict supervision of a boy's achievement. In other cases, this meant spending enormous amounts of time doing things together without a mother present. Some Smother-Fathers preferred "boyish" activities; others preferred their sons to join them in adult activities.[7]

In a father-idealizing culture, absent and emotionally distant fathers already have a mesmerizing effect on their children. Present and emotionally intimate fathers probably have twice the mesmerizing effect on their children. In my opinion, this effect was more negative than positive.

Smother-Fathers seethed with unrepressed woman and mother hatred. They envied and romanticized the female condition and disliked real women. Many were loners and "paranoid" about the entire world. Lucy's ex-husband divorced both his wives and kept all his sons. Lucy said:

For years everyone, including me, believed that my ex-husband was a devoted father. At his funeral, my son Michael unexpectedly made a speech. He said, "It's all bullshit. He was never a good father. The truth is that my father was at war with the whole world. The only people he wasn't at war with were my brothers and me. We were his little soldiers. We were his eyes; we were the only human beings he would trust to help him in his war against the world. He trusted us because he thought he controlled us completely. And he did."

1982

Bryan, Texas, April 6—Dr. Phillip Alan Linerode, a forty-seven year old physician and veterinarian, kidnapped his four year old son from his estranged wife in Bryan, Texas, on August 6, 1981. He was charged with interference with child custody and pursued by the FBI. On April 3, 1982, Linerode pulled into an abandoned gasoline station. "Shots were heard, and when the agent and the deputy approached the car, they found the child and father both wounded. The boy was dead upon arrival at a hospital, and Linerode died in surgery."[8]

*   *   *

New York, April 24—The mother of Michael Buchanan, 18, who was adopted by the New York Police Officer who saved him from [jumping off a rooftop], says that she wants very much to see her son again. The son says he has no desire to meet her. Mrs Gloria Hunsinger said that when she was divorced 15 years ago, the son's father was awarded custody of him. The father took the boy to Tennessee. She never again saw her son. She subsequently remarried. Relatives told her that Michael had been killed in a motorcycle accident. Mrs. Hunsinger was reported to be deceased.

"I'm sure he has a lot of resentment against me, but I'd like him to know that I love him," Mrs. Hunsinger said. "I'd like to try to explain to him that I didn't abandon him and I have thought about him all these years. I'd go to New York in a minute if I thought he'd see me."[9]

WHAT DOES MY STUDY TELL US ABOUT INCESTUOUSLY VIOLENT FATHERS WHO BATTLED FOR CUSTODY?[10]

Two of my custodially challenged mothers were married to incestuous fathers. Emily blames herself for having demanded her husband's participation in child care. "He wasn't properly socialized. He didn't know how to put limits on his selfishness. When my daughter was two, I was bathing her one day. The moment I touched her clitoris, she said, 'Daddy.' I touched her again, and she said, 'Daddy.' Maybe the abuse began then."

Emily had access to information about incest. In 1981 she routinely requested a file on incest from a colleague.

> The articles all suggested that incest tends to be protracted unless it is interrupted by an outside intervening factor. While I was reading, I would alternately tell myself that nothing was happening, that nothing had happened, and that nothing would ever happen again. The articles said it was the mother's responsibility to get the child away from the father. I called some friends who worked in this area. They said that I should either leave him or get counseling, but that I should never leave my daughter alone with him. Then I began reading about custody battles that incestuous fathers actually won.

When I interviewed Emily, she was plagued by fear and guilt. She was guilty for having married her husband in the first place, guilty for not leaving him sooner, guilty for finally leaving and placing her daughter at grave risk in terms of a custody battle, guilty for leaving and being unable to provide her daughter with a stable economic life.

After divorcing her husband, Janet discovered that he had begun to molest their two sons sexually during visitation.

> My ex-husband loves his children, but he had a nervous breakdown. He lives on disability. When my sons were six and eight, they began telling me that they and their father got into bed and touched each other all over. They said that penises had feeling, too. I moved heaven and earth to get visitation stopped. A woman judge in family court stopped his visitation for eight months. He kept appealing this decision. Eventually the court granted him supervised visitation, but my boys missed their father. They began working on me to see him more often—and to sleep over. For two years I resisted the pressure. Then I gave up. My sons now live with their father.

WHAT DOES MY STUDY TELL US ABOUT THE INCIDENCE AND DIFFERENTIAL TREATMENT OF PATERNAL VERSUS MATERNAL CHILD KIDNAPPERS?

Twenty-two fathers (37 percent) and seven mothers (12 percent) kidnapped their children. Of the paternal kidnappers, 18 percent were never found or returned voluntarily after an average of three years. *None* of these fathers was economically, legally, or custodially punished. Of the smaller number of maternal kidnappers, *80 percent* were both found and punished. This pattern is true in general.[11]

WERE MATERNAL AND PATERNAL KIDNAPPINGS SIMILAR?

After years of being their children's primary parent, 70 percent of my custodially embattled mothers were legally, judicially, or physically prevented from seeing their children entirely or from developing a normal visitation relationship with them.

Norma: When I'd arrive for visitation, I was told that all four kids were suddenly out with friends or relatives. By the time my lawyer got to a judge, the kids themselves said they didn't want to see me. I told the judge they'd been brainwashed. I told the judge that they obviously thought *I* hadn't wanted to see *them.* I told him that whether they wanted to see me or not, they needed me and I had a right to visitation. The judge told me that he couldn't force adolescents to see their mother.

Margaret: I had visitation every Sunday from twelve to eight. Ernie wouldn't let the kids come to me. He wouldn't let me inside his house. He lived way out in the boondocks. I couldn't afford a car. I had to take a six A.M. bus to catch a train that got me there at ten-thirty A.M. Then I'd wait in the train station for an hour.

Once I had the kids, what could we do? I couldn't afford to stay in a motel. I couldn't afford to take us all out for both lunch and dinner. We used to sit on park benches or in the train station all day. Sometimes we'd see a movie twice. After I dropped them off, I waited for an eleven P.M. train. The train and bus got me home in the middle of the night.

Rachel: I came to pick up the boys at the appointed time on Friday, late afternoon. Their father came out of the house, barring the doorway. "They're still doing their homework, you whore," he screamed, loud enough for everyone to hear. He moved sideways toward me with a snarl on his face. Then my boys came out, very quiet and ashamed. On Sunday morning, eight hours before I had to return them, this madman was pounding on my window, "I want my boys back now." He was stopping my neighbors on their way to church, to tell them I'd lost custody because I was crazy and unfit. I couldn't afford any trouble with my landlord or the police, so I dressed my boys and let them go home early.[12]

Despite such provocation, very few non-custodial mothers kidnapped their children.* Mothers were exhausted by the custody struggle and, unlike fathers, couldn't count on any economic, legal, or emotional assistance for a kidnapping venture. Unlike fathers, custodially embattled or victimized mothers had no organizations or networks to turn to for kidnapping information, advice, or support.

Most mothers were also reluctant to subject their children to a fugitive and impoverished existence, and were afraid of breaking the (male) law and being denied access to their children on a permanent basis.

In 1980, a detective in search of a kidnapped child discovered and photocopied the correspondence of one fathers' rights group, Men's Equality International, Inc. According to the detective's report:

These 35–40 groups assist fathers in legally kidnapping their children. They provide kidnapper-fathers with aliases, and a network of pro-father couples, lawyers, psychiatrists, detectives and Christian private schools who accept children for a fee with no questions asked and no records forwarded. Their anti-mother stance is equalled by their anti-child stance. Violently and repeatedly kidnapped children are being psychologically killed. . . . Most diabolic are the counselors and detectives who take a bereft mother's money and have no intention of finding her child. [The "plant" detective] is able

---

*No custodial mother kidnapped her child after the child was returned by a non-custodial paternal kidnapper.

to report back to "Men International" how much "heat" the "ex-bitch" is raising and if, in fact, it is time to run with the kids again.[13]

Of the maternal kidnappers, 100 percent had been their children's primary parent; 14 percent of the paternal kidnappers had been involved in primary child care. *All* the maternal kidnappers had been paternally prevented from seeing their children; *none* of the paternal kidnappers had been maternally prevented from seeing or maintaining a visitation relationship with their children.*

Nearly two-thirds (64 percent) of the paternal kidnappers went on kidnapping "sprees." No maternal kidnapper did this. A spree usually indicates that a parent does not intend to keep the child or that he is parentally desperate and incompetent. Children described driving around a lot, moving from motel to motel, using false names, eating junk food, and not seeing anyone they knew. After retrieving such children, mothers described them as disoriented, hostile, frightened, unwashed, and sometimes ill.[14]

Some children thought that being kidnapped by a previously unavailable father was an "adventure." However, kidnapped children were often permanently angry and disappointed that their mothers hadn't rescued them. They also blamed themselves for their father's violence or thought they were responsible for provoking it and capable of appeasing it.

Twenty-five percent of the paternal kidnappers told children that their mothers "were dead," "hadn't loved them anyway," or "must never be discussed." Many of these children rejected their mothers forever or for a long time after reunion with them. None of the maternal kidnappers told children that their fathers were "dead." They didn't have to. Maternally kidnapped children knew that their mothers had been prevented from seeing them. Children who were unhappy about this, or who were paternally abused in other ways, knew that their fathers were very much alive.[15]

One-third of the paternal kidnappers did not go on sprees. They planned their kidnappings very carefully. Such fathers were all assisted by mother competitors (girlfriends, second wives, paternal grandmothers), who took care of the children, maintained the home, and often joined in disparaging or lying about the absent mother.[16]

---

*Some mothers attempted to prevent *violent* ex-husbands and fathers from visiting. They were unsuccessful in finding legal assistance to prevent such paternal visitation.

1983

Los Angeles, March 14—Charles David Rothenberg claimed that his ex-wife was going to curtail his visitation. He decided not to return his son. Fearing an arrest for kidnapping, Rothenberg became desperate. "It was either go to jail or die. I decided to kill us both. If I couldn't have him, nobody else could." He set his 6 year old son David on fire.[17]

*   *   *

San Francisco—On Wednesday, June 19, I aired my first tape concerning children and divorce. We discussed the terror a battered woman feels when the court tells her she must keep in communication with her ex-husband for the children's sake. Two people called the next day to say we exaggerated. On Friday, July 1st, a man in Oakland shot and killed his wife and sister-in-law and critically injured his mother-in-law over custody of his two-year-old daughter. His wife was a battered woman, terrified of him. We found out afterward that she had made an appointment with legal services to discuss a divorce but did not mention she was a battered wife. Therefore, the case was not treated as a crisis.[18]

WHAT HAPPENED TO PATERNAL KIDNAPPERS?

Paternal kidnappers were rarely pursued or found. Those fathers who returned voluntarily or who were apprehended were not economically fined, jailed, or custodially victimized. This non-punishment of male domestic violence and child abuse is also true in general. Unlike mothers, paternal kidnappers are usually pitied—or heroized.[19]

On December 29, 1981, a father named Rudy Johnson entered a class action lawsuit on behalf of men as a custodially discriminated class. Johnson had kidnapped his own children from Alaska to Washington, D.C., and then to California and Spokane, Washington, where he was arrested and imprisoned. Johnson sought and received sympathetic and glamorizing attention from the media and financial and psychological support from other fathers' rights activists. Incredibly:

> One of the [fathers' rights] organizations held Johnson's children as hostages while Johnson negotiated with Spokane officials until certain of his demands were met. He was released on $1,000.00 bail and allowed back to the State of Alaska under a "good-faith" agreement. His demands being met, he received all sorts of pro-father publicity on his "imprisonment" for "loving" his children. He was arrested again in Alaska and again released. He now has many legal loopholes and technicalities to concentrate on in order to side-line the actual offense for which he was arrested.[20]

Paternal kidnappers were not apprehended or punished. Very often their maternal *victims* were the ones whom policemen, lawyers, judges, social workers, and relatives punished. In *Legal Kidnapping*, Anna Demeter describes how their small town blamed her when her husband kidnapped their two youngest children:

> Is anything justified for a man who must punish an uppity woman? [Demeter is uppity only because she wants a divorce.] Do people here really feel that a man's wife has no right to reject him and should in that event be punished; and that to steal her children and run away, especially to leave her with a perplexing tangle of debts, is an appropriate and perhaps even an admirable solution? Why do these unspoken reactions still leave me breathless with protest?[21]

Dorothy won judicial custody in her home state. Her ex-husband then kidnapped the children to another state. After a year, Dorothy found them. She appealed for custody in a second state. She said:

> The new judge held my lesbianism against me. He didn't care that my ex had kidnapped the kids, disrupted their lives, and lived on public welfare. Now he was remarried and a high earner. This judge didn't put my ex in jail or fine him or take the kids away from him because he kidnapped them. He ordered *me* to repay the welfare department. He ordered *me* to pay child support in order to see the kids. My ex-husband, together with his wife, was already earning forty thousand dollars a year. I was earning twelve thousand dollars. Where is the justice?

Leslie's ex-husband kidnapped their children. Over a four-year period Leslie spent $40,000 looking for them. When she found them, her eldest child refused to live with her. Her two youngest children had been told she was "dead." Leslie and her lawyer tried to have her ex-husband imprisoned. The judge refused to do it. What would happen to the eldest child if his father "just sat around and rotted in jail"? He ordered psychiatric evaluation and counseling before or instead of a fine or prison.

Maureen describes a mother's typically incredible contact with the police and with her children's school during and after episodes of male domestic violence:

"The first summer after I moved out, Kenneth disappeared with the children. I broke into our house to look for clues to where he might have gone. A police car pulled up, screeching. Two officers came out with guns drawn. I had proof I was co-owner of the house in my pocketbook. They still arrested me and charged me with breaking and entering my own home.

"After I found the children and brought them back, Kenneth barricaded himself in their classroom with a baseball bat. The school officials called me. They refused to call the police. They said he was the legal parent of his children and it would look bad for them to get involved in a private dispute. When I got the kids home, Kenneth broke my apartment door down. I called the cops. They came without their guns drawn. They sat Kenneth down, talked to him, actually shared a beer with him. They just made him promise to pay to fix the door.

"The second time Kenneth kidnapped the children, he 'hid' them at home with him. I first got a court order for their temporary custody and asked two policemen to come with me. I showed them the court order. I asked them to wait outside, and to help me only if Kenneth became violent. They weren't about to be dictated to by me. They went in and had a nice fifteen-minute man-to-man chat with Kenneth. They came out without the children.

"One policeman said that possession was nine-tenths of the law. The other said that Kenneth obviously loved them—he wanted them, didn't he? Kenneth wasn't going to hurt his own children. They suggested we both sleep on it, or have a friend sit down with us."

WHAT HAPPENED TO THE MATERNAL KIDNAPPERS?[22]

Two mothers were pursued by their ex-husbands and jailed by the authorities.

Rachel: After I kidnapped my sons, we moved to another state. For nearly a year I worked as a social worker. We played music together every night. I supervised their homework. Their father wasn't there to interfere or downgrade me. A year later, the FBI and my ex-husband broke the door down. My head split open. My heart cracked. They threw me in prison for three weeks. Afterward, I was not permitted to see them at all, not even under court supervision. I was not allowed to attend their school graduations or Bar Mitzvahs.[23]

Jessie: I obtained temporary legal custody of my kids the first time they were allowed to visit me in a year. My ex-husband, his lawyer, and the local police swooped down on me with a warrant for my extradition and arrest. The kids were moved from school without being allowed to say good-bye to me. Within a month, I was arrested, formally extradited, and jailed on kidnapping charges.

One mother was pursued by her ex-husband, who found her and beat her so badly she required hospitalization.

Georgia: Without anyone's help I drove clear across the state with my son. Within a week, my ex-husband and his brother found us. He beat me up so badly I thought I'd never walk again. He threatened to kill me if I ever came near Bernard again. I still send letters, but I've never gotten an answer.

Two mothers were economically penalized by their ex-husbands and physically prevented from seeing their children, who were, in turn, simultaneously subjected to intense anti-mother brainwashing campaigns.

Margaret: I hid at my mother's for a month after I was supposed to turn my two youngest sons over to my ex-husband. My lawyer told me he couldn't protect me if they came to arrest me. When I turned them over, their father said that for this reason he wouldn't pay me any of the court-ordered alimony. If I pressed for it, he'd have me arrested or legally prevented from seeing my children. Then he made visitation as hard as possible.

Maureen: I'm being sued in civil court for money, in criminal court for breaking into my own house, and in superior court for custody. Since I re-kidnapped my sons, my husband has refused to pay any child support until the other lawsuits are settled.

The maternal victims of paternal kidnappings are never the "same" again. According to John Edward Gill:

Parents withdraw in a combination of anger and apathy. They have trouble getting up each morning. Their lives stop—emotions frozen, jobs abandoned, friends and themselves neglected. Houses go uncleaned. They forget to food shop, become absentminded, paralyzed with fear and bitterness. Phones go unanswered, doorbells ignored. Some act like sleepwalkers, eyes glazed, their thinking distracted. Others spend the first day or two after their children are stolen in a burst of energy.

Housewives often feel they've lost their professions—as mothers, as wives. One day they have a job they like. The next day their job is taken away. They also feel a certain stigma. Raising children was their only job. Neighbors might think them unfit because their husbands stole the children.[24]

Mothers whose children are returned to them live in fear of a second kidnapping. Those whose kidnapped children were brainwashed against them or who suffered other psychological after-effects live with "difficult" or increasingly unmanageable children. Those mothers who never see their kidnapped children again live in acute mourning—forever. Helen's son was kidnapped when he was six years old. She has not seen him since. I interviewed her after three years of mourning.

"My husband, Willie, was my childhood sweetheart. He changed as soon as I became pregnant. Anything set him off. He'd yell, throw things at me, punch me in the face, push me up against a wall. 'The baby!' I'd scream. 'If I break your finger, will that hurt the baby?' he'd sneer.

"In 1972 our son, Justin, was born. I thought Willie would change when he saw what a beautiful child we had. He didn't. After a year of marriage, Willie moved out. He didn't see me or Justin very much. I divorced him when Justin was a year old.

"Willie began coming around when Justin was two. He'd turn up with one of his girlfriends. They'd take Justin out and 'forget' to bring him back, sometimes until the next day. Justin liked having a father. I didn't have the heart to deprive him of one just because Willie hit me and wouldn't pay any child support.

"When Justin was about four, Willie came over when my mother was visiting. He picked a fight with me. I went to call the police. Willie ripped the phone out of the wall. He slugged my mother. He grabbed Justin and ran. Willie got into an accident with another car on the corner. Justin was trying to get out of the car. Willie grabbed him by the neck and threw him into the back of the car.

"My mother took Willie to criminal court. They pooh-poohed her. They told her that grandmothers shouldn't get involved. She dropped the charges. I took Willie to court. I requested an order of protection and a psychiatric evaluation of Willie. The judge refused both my requests. He said that Willie obviously loved me and wanted me back. Why didn't I consider getting remarried—for the sake of my child?

"When Justin was five and a half, he began to refuse to see his daddy. He said, 'I love Daddy but he's fucked-up in the head.' Justin described how Willie beat up his girlfriend and sent her to the hospital. He said, 'Mommy, I was so scared.' This time Willie was indicted.

"I visited his girlfriend in the hospital and offered to be a witness for her. Willie put a thirty-eight to my head and threatened to kill me if I went through with it. Then he began threatening to kill his girlfriend if she didn't drop the charges. I decided to leave town. I went to live with a relative in another state.

"Willie went into court, claiming I was a prostitute and a dope fiend who'd kidnapped his only son. The same judge who'd refused to order a psychiatric on Willie gave him custody of Justin. Within two months, Willie found us and snatched Justin on his way to school. The police couldn't help. It seems that Willie had already shown them his custody order.

"I flew home. I went into court with my parents. This same maniac of a judge returned custody to me on paper. He didn't have the real Justin to return. I moved back in with my parents. We hired detectives. I went to meetings of other parents whose children had been snatched. I cried night and day for a year. Between the crying and the meetings, I had a hard time keeping a job.

"Then something happened to me. I don't know how to put it into words. I couldn't handle myself physically. I couldn't wash my hair. I couldn't put on any makeup. I couldn't go out of the house. I couldn't sleep. I couldn't sit still. My gynecologist checked me out and said it was mental. He put me on Valium. He gave me sleeping pills. I began to drink.

"I've been looking for Justin for three years. I fantasize a lot about how it's going to be when I find him. Will Justin run into my arms? Will he refuse to talk to me? My ex-mother-in-law told my mother that a nice girl was taking care of Justin. 'Helen isn't nice. She left my Willie, and he loved her. She made him crazy when she walked out on him. She should blame herself.'

" 'You're a mother yourself,' I cried. 'How would you feel if you could never see your son?'

" 'I can't,' she said. 'Because of you.' "

1984

Brooklyn, New York, May 26—A court-awarded visit with his two young children ended in tragedy last night when an emotionally troubled Brooklyn father apparently killed them and then hanged himself. Brooklyn detectives said Centeno, separated from his young wife and under psychiatric care, hanged his young son and daughter before hanging himself—on the first day of court-awarded visits with the children.[25]

*   *   *

Laguna Niguel, California, July 4— A contractor going through a divorce and child custody dispute appeared to be grief-stricken when sheriff's investigators showed him a photograph of his wife on a morgue slab, the authorities said today. The photograph convinced Frederick Penney, 57 years old, that his wife Susan, was dead, although the picture had been posed, they said. He was later arrested for [attempted] murder when he paid off a supposed hitman, they said.

The suspect had told investigators he was "extremely upset" over arrangements for the couple's two children and property in their divorce case, Lieutenant Olson said.[26]

1985

Hyannis, Massachusetts, March 12—A distraught father wielding a shotgun terrorized an elementary school yesterday when he demanded to see his two young daughters. Hallett had been having marital trouble . . . Jeffrey T. Hallett told his wife he wanted to see his children, Casey, 11, and Kelly, 8, one last time and then kill himself.

Hallett's daughter, Casey, told *The Herald*, "Our teacher told us to get under the desks. All the kids in the class were afraid."[27]

*　　　*　　　*

Riverhead, New York, June 4—As his estranged wife watched in court, Roland Poirel was sentenced to five years' probation after he pleaded guilty in the heat-stroke death in September of his 2-year-old son, whom he had left in a car with the windows shut.

On Sept. 1, Poirel had left his son unattended in his car, with the bright sun shining directly through the window, as he spent nearly three hours in the Cafe 111 Pub, not far from the family's Hauppauge apartment.

When Poirel came outside to the car, he found his son dead of heat stroke, the prosecutor said. Poirel then took the child out of the car and left him atop some grass near the parking lot.

"I knew my son was dead," Poirel said, explaining why he put the child on the grass and left. "I couldn't face it at the moment. I'm so sorry." Poirel returned shortly afterward with his wife, Suzanne, and he was arrested. The police had been called by a witness who saw Poirel put the child's body on the ground and leave.

The judge said Poirel had crossed "the fine line between negligence and criminally negligent homicide." But Judge Seidell also said the several witnesses who were interviewed by the Probation Department before yesterday's hearing called Poirel a loving father.[28]

CHAPTER TEN

Paternal Brainwashing

MEDEA
Jason, I beg you to be forgiving to me.
Why make myself an enemy of the authorities
And of my husband, who does the best thing for me
By marrying royalty and having children who
Will be brothers to my own?

But I shall beg that my children may remain here:
Not that I would live in a country that hates me
Children of mine to feel their enemies' insults.

Euripides, *Medea*

A year had passed since Seriozha last saw his mother. Since then her
name had never been mentioned. During that year he had been sent to
school and had learned to know and like his schoolmates. The dreams and
memories he had cherished of his mother (he had been told she was
dead) no longer filled his mind. If they did come back now and again, he
studiously drove them away, regarding them shameful and fit only for
girls, not for boys who went to school. He knew that it was his lot to
remain with his father, and did his best to get used to the idea.

Leo Tolstoy, *Anna Karenina*

THIRTY-FOUR FATHERS (57 PERCENT) ENGAGED IN ANTI-MOTHER BRAIN-washing campaigns. Paternal brainwashing campaigns included the use of physical, psychological, economic, and legal force. Custodially embattled mothers did not engage in anti-father brainwashing campaigns.

Twenty-five brainwashing fathers (74 percent) were successful; eighteen (53 percent) were very successful in getting children to reject their mothers in virulent ways. Nearly two-thirds (64 percent) of the successful fathers were assisted by mother competitors.

Seventy-seven children (forty-six boys and thirty-one girls) were targeted for brainwashing. Twenty-nine boys (63 percent) and fifteen girls (48 percent) rejected their mothers. Seventeen boys (37 percent) and sixteen girls (52 percent) resisted being brainwashed, or weren't as ardently pursued.

A third of the rejected mothers kept one child or have never seen one or more of their children; 40 percent maintained minimal contact with their children or re-established it after an average of five years. Nearly a fifth of the rejected mothers (19 percent) maintained contact with their children.

BRAINWASHING IS A form of coercion used against a foreign or domestic enemy of the state, and by many cults against its young or vulnerable members.

Prisoners and cultists are usually detained against their will, beaten, threatened, sleep-deprived, and exposed repeatedly to a specific set of beliefs.[1] Despite "informational overload," the prisoner, the cultist, and the child being paternally brainwashed are each isolated. They are without access to previous or conflicting beliefs, and without access to their families of origin. Powerful and charismatic father figures (or actual fathers) demand that they renounce all other family or ideological ties.

Cults have been viewed as psychologically destructive for separating people from their past relationships and beliefs.[2] If strangers can brainwash *adult* prisoners and cultists, imagine how easily a child can be brainwashed by a father whose authority has long been upheld by that child's mother and by society in general.

Preferring to live with one's father, while maintaining a good relationship with one's mother, is not the same as violently rejecting one's mother. The paternal brainwashing of children is a conscious and systematic attempt to force children into rejecting their mothers—i.e., into committing psychological matricide.

A successfully brainwashed child doesn't want to see his or her mother at all. A successfully brainwashed child intensely mistrusts and dislikes his mother. He may believe that she is dead, has abandoned him, doesn't love him, or is too "selfish" to be a good mother.

How can a father "brainwash" a child who has been close to his mother? In view of our cultural idealization of fathers and dislike of mothers, a father need only accelerate this pre-existing dynamic. For example, in *About Men*, I described how normal boys begin to disidentify with their mothers in order to become "men."[3] In *Every Mother's Son*, Judith Arcana imagines the "mental process" of young boys in this way:

As I was growing up, I $\left\{\begin{array}{l}\text{—was very close to} \\ \text{—preferred} \\ \text{—shared interests with} \\ \text{—really respected}\end{array}\right\}$ my mother

My father was	{	—brutal —rarely (or never) in our home —an alcoholic —harsh and insensitive to my mother and/or me
But now I realize that I	{	—have a lot in common with my father —resent my mother's guidance and the work and time she put in—*she makes me feel guilty* —admired her or loved her or enjoyed her only because she tricked me into it, one way or another —was too close to my mother —have to get away from my mother—geographically and emotionally[4]

As we have noted, mothers are expected to do more than fathers and are blamed by others, including their own children, when they fail to meet idealized standards. A father's absence, neglect, or abusive presence is, comparatively speaking, overlooked, minimized, or denied by most children.

Children are also physically, psychologically, and economically weaker than their parents. Under stress they tend to "align" themselves with the parent they're more afraid of or distant from or with the parent they newly perceive as emotionally "weak" and "needy." Children also tend to align themselves with the "winning" parent.

The Use of Physical Force in Paternal Brainwashing

Force may be defined as applying the full weight of one's power to outrival an opponent. *Physical* force may take the form of kidnapping a child—or threatening to do so. It may involve physically preventing a child from seeing his mother: totally, intermittently, or threatening to do so.

Children are easily intimidated by paternal physical violence. If a girl once observes her father hit her mother, if a boy himself once has been beaten up by his father, fathers need display little subsequent physical force to be obeyed or to be psychologically "persuasive." Physically intimidated children "know" that their fathers can use force.

Children often deal with their physical helplessness by minimizing its importance or by denying that they *were* physically intimidated. A brainwashed child may ultimately refuse to acknowledge to himself that he was *forced* to do anything. His terror, his resentment, can be measured by how intensely he rejects his mother.

Not all physically intimidated children *reject* their mothers. For example, Deena was evicted from her house and physically prevented from seeing her children. Deena "secretly" spoke to her children every day on the phone. She and her children were afraid of their father. If he could get rid of their mother, what couldn't he do to them? These children did not *reject* their mother. However, they did not resist their own physical captivity.

Many children who were physically prevented from seeing their mothers rejected their mothers for not "being there" or for not "rescuing them." Many such children became convinced that their mothers were "dead" or "bad."[5]

In *Legal Kidnapping* Anna Demeter describes how her paternally kidnapped son dealt with his endangered situation by learning to "adore" his captor and "mistrust" and "hate" the mother who rescued him.[6] Bonnie Lee Black, in *Somewhere Child,* describes regaining a four-year-old paternally kidnapped child who remained angry with and mistrustful of her for six months afterward. When Black's daughter required surgery, she began yelling at her mother in the hospital.

"My daddy is going to shoot you," she'd shout at me. "He never made me have an operation. He's going to punish you for doing this to me." Would other four-year-olds who'd lived more normal lives feel similarly angry about an operation, I wondered. I didn't know.[7]

Rose was a battered wife. Her husband decided to have her psychiatrically imprisoned for wanting to attend a meeting against his wishes.

"Mother's Day is a very sad day for me," Rose says, smiling sweetly. "When Steven was seven, a close friend found out that Larry had obtained a psychiatric commitment against me. I ran away with the clothes on my back. I borrowed money for a lawyer and sued for custody of Steven. Larry brought his psychiatric commitment order into court and waved it around. 'Your Honor, the woman's crazy. She can't be alone with my boy.' The judge let Steven stay with his father temporarily.

"Sometimes Larry turned up at my job with Steven. 'Okay, Rose. Here's your son. Look at him. Have you seen enough? Don't say I don't let you see him.' Once, I went to the house to see Steven. Larry chased me off the property with a shotgun.

"Larry's widowed mother moved in. She had a poor relationship with Larry. I guess she wanted Steven as a way of having Larry. She didn't have anyone else. I appealed to her many times in bitter tears. I was the mother of this child. Couldn't she understand? 'I don't want to talk to you. Don't bother me,' she'd say, and hang up.

"I finally had my day in court one year later, when Steven was eight. In court, Steven ignored me. He wouldn't look me straight in the eye. He kept looking down. He lied. When they asked him where he wanted to be, he said he wanted to be with his father. He said that I beat him.

"The judge gave Larry custody but did order visitation with me immediately. Steven ran away from me on the street. The police brought him into court the next day. The judge ordered him to go with me again. An hour later, Steven started talking to me as if we'd never been separated. We went to a vacation park. He kept saying, 'This is fantastic!' He was very happy. At night he had a nightmare. He screamed, 'Mommy! Stay with me, stay with me.' This was in his sleep. He really clung to me that night. During the day he acted as if everything were okay.

"Just before our next scheduled visitation, Steven called me at work. 'I don't want to be with you. I don't want to spend any time with you.' He kept repeating it over and over again, as if he were a robot. I would call Steven on the phone. I did all the talking. He might say yes or no. Afterward I'd cry. I wrote Steven cards and letters. I sent him gifts for his birthday and for Christmas. He never wrote to me.

"Whenever I ask him, 'What's wrong?' he says, 'Mom, we have no problems. You know I love you.' He refuses to discuss his father or his grandmother with me. Last year, on his eighteenth birthday, Steven called to ask me for money for college books. I was overjoyed. I offered him my gasoline credit card.

"He's visited me once or twice since then, but the only steady communication we have is when I get his credit card slips every month."

The Use of Economic Force in Paternal Brainwashing

Half the successful brainwashing fathers (52 percent) economically seduced and manipulated their children. These fathers did not (have to) use physical force or intimidation.[8] American children have been taught (by television and by their parents) that they are entitled to the "best *things* in life." Why should a child remain behind with an impoverished mother when s/he has an economic alternative?

Economic-brainwashing fathers offered their impressionable and divorce-impoverished children the following "things": a room with a television set; a pony of their own; the use of a family swimming pool; new and expensive clothes; luxurious vacations; a summer home; expensive athletic lessons. Fathers also offered their children a higher standard of living in general.[9]

These fathers went beyond material bribes. They convinced their children that their mother's poverty was her own "fault," that she *had* money but was (selfishly) using it for herself, "not for her children," that her "choice" of neighborhood was dangerous, that the "right" kind of children wouldn't "like" or "associate" with them, that their "shabby" clothes and inability to vacation "properly" were a "detriment" to their (future) social life.*

Norma: When my ex-husband remarried, he began to buy the kids really expensive toys. He planned elaborate vacation and camping trips. He promised all four of them their own room and personal TV set if they'd come and live with him.

Cindy: Kids are very materialistic. It's really very difficult to resist a bribe, especially when you're a teenager. My son's step-father built him an apartment adjoining his own new house. It had a great platform bed with a skylight, carpeting, a spiral staircase in the room, glass doors—a private pad for his friends to hang out.

The Use of Psychological Force in Paternal Brainwashing

Brainwashing fathers exerted psychological force in four major ways: by paying attention to (paternally) neglected children; by "smothering" them with paternal neediness; by devaluing their mothers; and by re-placing their mothers with mother competitors.

A mother competitor is not a "stepmother" who lives with or marries a man who already has custody of his children. A mother competitor is someone who actively participates in the battle for custody and in the brainwashing campaign.

Many fathers manipulated their children in these four ways in addition to seducing them economically, or physically separating them from their mothers.

One: The Previously Absent Father

Most children have already "had" their mothers. They assume they can "have" her again whenever they want her. However, a previously absent or minimally present father has to be grabbed, and on his terms,

---

*Children are conformists. Perhaps the children of divorce are even more so.

in order to "have" him at all. If a father (a prized "commodity") demands that his children live with him, the demand is sometimes hard to resist.

> Bonnie: My youngest wanted to live with me. His father told him: "If you live with her I won't see you or speak to you. You'll be a stranger to me. I won't let you come back to me when and if you change your mind." Of course, he must have cried a lot when he said this.

Two: The Smother-Father

Some Smother-Fathers openly demanded that their children choose between their "poor" fathers and their "selfish" mothers.

> Beth: Our kids knew that their father chose to work part time in order to spend more time with them. They knew he refused ever to hire a baby-sitter. He kept telling them I was selfish compared to him. He should have told them I was normal and he wasn't. They began to mistrust me.
>
> They acted as if I were the strong and selfish one and he were the weak and giving one. They certainly didn't think there was anything unusual or abnormal about a father's making such a total commitment of time to his children.

> Catherine: My ex-husband really had no social or emotional life other than his children. He must have burdened them terribly with his fears of isolation and loneliness if they stayed with me. He complained to them about his health a lot. Maybe they were afraid he'd have a heart attack without them.

Three: The Devaluation of the Mother

A child who is physically separated from his or her mother or psychologically and economically seduced by a previously absent father does not have to *hate* or reject his or her mother. Theoretically, such a child may still miss his or her mother—and be allowed to say so. Theoretically, such a child might insist on seeing his or her mother regularly—and be allowed to do so.

This does not occur when the mother has been systematically devalued. A child who hates and rejects his or her mother has long been encouraged to disobey her authority and to suspect her maternal altruism. Such a child has long been encouraged to gather information against the mother for the father's "custody case." Such a child has long been encouraged to criticize the mother in front of other adults; to lie (or to "forget" the truth) in court; to run away from the mother's home; and, ultimately, to refuse to see the mother at all.[10]

A mother's devaluation is in progress when children begin to speak in their father's voice. A brainwashed child also begins to imitate his father's treatment of his mother. If he is very young, he may repeat what his father says, without necessarily internalizing its meaning. For example, Melanie's two-and-a-half-year-old son:

> began to slap me and say: "Mommy's a bitch." Then he'd hit my lover and say she was a "double bitch." Then he'd hug his big brother and say: "My brother's okay." He would say: "Mommy's mean to me. Mommy whips me." It was so sad. He didn't really know what he was saying but he seemed obsessed with saying it anyway.*

Pre-adolescent children are ambivalent and "torn" about having to reject their mothers.

Bonnie: From the start, my eleven-year-old refused to visit me. My eight-year-old came regularly—at first. He'd arrive and immediately unpack his clothes. Then he'd take everything out of the dresser, put it back in his suitcase, and scream, "I'm leaving. You're no good. I don't have to stay." I would go to pieces when he did this. He was showing me myself— leaving him. He was also adopting a high hand with me. He wanted to punish me for his father's sake. Maybe for his own sake, too. Then he'd call his father and tell him to pick him up. His father encouraged him to do this.

Loretta: After I got married, my ex-husband began seeing the kids a lot. My eight-year-old began spying on me. He'd tell his father things about us. He'd tell *us* that his father hated me. He'd announce that he was going to live with his father, that his father was already working on it. Then he'd start crying and refuse to leave me. He began to have tantrums and nightmares.

I interviewed Loretta and her ex-husband, Lemuel, separately. During my three-hour interview with Loretta, Lemuel called to speak to

---

*Melanie's child was too young for us to conclude whether he had psychologically incorporated what he was saying. Melanie's case is not "counted" as a successful brainwashing.

their children twice. The older boy hovered at the kitchen doorway as I interviewed his mother. He told me that "he had to hear if his mother was saying anything bad about his father. If she did, he had to tell his father."

Teenagers were less ambivalent about "taking sides." Some did so with a vengeance. Gail's teenage son grew cold, disobedient, and physically violent toward her. She said:

> He would scream at me, "This is not your house. You don't own it. You've taken it away from my father. You've ruined my father's life. Women get everything. Men get nothing." He began to do just what his father told him to. When I said he couldn't play hockey until he did his homework, he climbed out his bedroom window, screaming that his *father* said he could play hockey. I tried to stop him. He whacked me with his hockey stick. Eventually he didn't listen to anything I said. He treated me without any respect. He treated me more and more like a servant. "Get me this, get me that."

Marta's teenage son began to treat her with contempt—just as his father did. He verbally belittled her and physically avoided her. He minimized her "complaints," called her "crazy," and occasionally cursed her. Marta said: "My son also called his ten-year-old sister a dumb cunt. He called me a lazy cunt. My daughter giggled and flirted with him in response. When I wept about losing custody, my son told me to see a shrink."

Four: The Paternal Replacement of the Mother with a Mother Competitor

Of the successful brainwashing campaigns, 64 percent involved the active leadership or cooperation of a mother competitor, 82 percent of whom were virulently competitive. In addition, 59 percent were infertile; were married to (newly) infertile husbands; or, as the paternal grandmother, aunt, or "older" housekeeper, could no longer get pregnant themselves.[11]

No mother competitor was involved in 32 percent of the successful brainwashing campaigns. "Smother-Fathers" waged 88 percent of these campaigns. Also, fewer and less virulent mother competitors were involved in the nine failed brainwashing campaigns.[12]

The mother competitor maintained a battling father's home, domestically and emotionally. She also assumed responsibility for child care. Some mother competitors merely assisted fathers in devaluing mothers; others far outdid men in this area. Some mother competitors also functioned as legal secretaries and legal strategists for the custody battle.

Lucy: My husband's new wife Mindy came right into my office, plopped her legal papers down, smirked, and left. Another time she came to my office and started talking very loudly against me. She was completely unconcerned about whether this would get me fired or not. To shut her up, I signed whatever she wanted me to.

Mindy backed my ex-husband tooth and claw. I have to conclude that their marriage was somehow based on his vendetta against me. She considered herself a good wife if she could help him get revenge against me. She was a *very* good wife.

Natalie: My husband's girlfriend balanced his checkbook. She decided that "they" should stop paying me child support and alimony. She decided that she could be a better mother for less money. She was the one who found "their" first lawyer. She documented "their" case. She served me with all the legal papers.

Mother competitors verbally attacked, publicly humiliated, and physically prevented mothers from seeing or speaking to their children.

Norma: Beverly, the new wife, told me she felt it was her Christian duty to protect her husband and *my* children from my bad temper and unpredictable behavior. "Why don't you go to court against us again, you greedy bitch? You're not fit to be the mother of George's children."

Beverly used to hang up on me whenever I'd call. When I'd arrive at their house, George would send her out to deal with me; she'd pretend he wasn't home. Beverly would lie outright about why the kids weren't around. She'd slam and then lock the doors. She'd pull all the shades down. Sometimes she'd say my kids weren't there when I could hear them. Sometimes she'd say that they didn't want to see me.

Adele: There was a reception line at my son's Bar Mitzvah. My ex-husband's live-in girlfriend was standing next to him and acting like the mother of my son. I didn't cry or run away. I tried to act very proud of my son.

PATERNAL GRANDMOTHERS AND HOUSEKEEPERS

Georgia and Ruthie both faced virulently competitive paternal grandmothers.

Georgia: She thought that my son belonged to her. She thought she was a better mother than I was. She was about forty. I was only eighteen. When her son and I separated, she wasn't about to let me steal her grandson.

Ruthie: My ex-husband was easygoing. My ex-mother-in-law talked against me to our kids. She told them I was crazy and selfish for wanting a divorce. She kept telling them that I was choosing a career over my own flesh and blood. My son got very withdrawn. My daughter began to yell at me.[13]

Adele faced three mother competitors: a live-in girlfriend, a paternal aunt, and an ex-housekeeper.

Adele: My ex-housekeeper really loved the children. She also needed her job desperately. My ex-husband offered to raise her salary if she'd testify against me. My ex-sister-in-law coached her. In court, she read aloud from a carefully constructed list that detailed all the times that I was presumably "out" or "asleep" over a seven-year period. The poor woman didn't look up or say hello. She couldn't face me.[14]

THE MOTHER COMPETITOR: IN HER OWN VOICE

When she was twenty-one, Sheela assumed responsibility for forty-year-old Leopold's home and his two genetic children. She "managed" his custody battle against his first wife. After ten years of marriage, Leopold custodially challenged Sheela for the children she'd mothered, including their genetic child. Sheela said:

"Leopold was my professor. I adored him. I thought he was a genius—and very sexy. Leopold was already involved in separating from his wife when we fell in love. At the time, Leopold's children were two and three.

"I thought their mother, Lana, was a very cold woman. She had a busy career. She traveled as much as Leopold. She must have been in her middle thirties. How could *she* mother properly? Leopold didn't want me to talk to Lana. He said she hated me and would only be looking for weak spots to use against *him* in court.

"I loved doing things like making birthday parties and 'special' dinners for them. I really hated certain chores—like taking them to and from places and keeping track of all their activities and whereabouts. But I knew how important it was that the day-care teachers saw how involved I was. I knew we'd need them as witnesses. I started keeping a diary and taking pictures of everything I did with the children.

"We won custody hands down. Lana didn't bother to see them very often after that. He told the children to call me the Sheela Momma.

"As I got older and Leopold did, too, he became more demanding and supercritical. He began to have temper tantrums. He accused me of being fat and crazy. He openly began to have affairs with his students. When I moved out, he moved my mother-in-law in. He hired the most expensive lawyer in town to get custody of all three children.

"I did get custody of my biological child. Leopold kept 'his' two children. The oldest boy keeps running away to live with me. I have to send him back. Leopold has made visitation very difficult. Do you know who gave Leopold the money for his expensive lawyer? Lana did."

Mary Zenorini Silverzweig fell in love with Stanley Silverzweig, the much older married father of three girls. Despite—or perhaps because of—this impropriety, Mary became obsessed with "proper appearances" and with the Christian and patriarchal "salvation" of his daughters. Silverzweig, in her book *The Other Mother*, writes:

> I wanted to have [everyone] say some day, "She's done wonders with those children. I don't know what they would have done without her." . . . I clothed them, groomed them, trimmed their hair, and tied it in ribbons. I'd get up early to cook breakfast—or spend hours cooking dinner, so each meal would seem like a special occasion. We baked bread and cakes and cookies together. We went shopping and read to each other, did housework and played. [15]

For two years (according to Silverzweig), Stanley called his daughters every night to discuss their "coming to live with us." During this time, Mary took them on numerous shopping expeditions for expensive and "feminine" clothing. Stanley spent $100,000 on lawyers. Mary coordinated all the legal meetings and chauffeured the children back and forth.

Mary and Stanley bought three new houses, took a Caribbean vacation, a European vacation, a trip to the Grand Canyon, and a honeymoon trip to Italy. This, plus a "white wedding," did little to eliminate Mary's irrational desire to be the "first" and "only" woman in Stanley's life:

> The overpowering urge that I felt as a second wife was to bury the first, to lose the past in the frenzy of the present, and least of all to be reminded of anything that smacked of past intimacy, sex, loving devotion, or familial bliss. I refused to acknowledge that there had been one single moment of anything resembling happiness in his first marriage.

When Mary discovered that her "enemy" had become a lesbian, her missionary zeal knew no bounds. Mary relished the victory of true womanhood over lesbianism. In her own voice she describes the following parent-school scene:

> I [sat] with the teachers, dressed in a linen suit, stockings, and high heels, the way mothers used to dress when they visited the private schools that I had attended. Roberta sat on the other side of the gym, alone, in jeans, and a peasant blouse, her bare feet in sandals. Leslie would glance over her shoulders, first in one direction then in the other.
>   When it was all over, and the two hundred youngsters broke ranks wildly for summer vacation, Leslie stood and waited, not knowing what to do with the mess that confronted her. I waved, Roberta just watched. Leslie came to me. . . . "Shall we go? We have an errand to do, and then we'll pick up the little ones for the weekend." My arm was around her shoulder; I was selfish enough to want to make the most of my triumph.

I separately interviewed "Roberta," her mate, her lawyer, and her two youngest daughters. Both girls hovered at the doorway suspiciously, asked me if their father knew who I was or what I wanted, and continued to eavesdrop on our conversation—even after they had been ordered to their rooms.[16]

HOW MANY MOTHERS OF SUCCESSFULLY BRAINWASHED CHILDREN EVER SAW THEIR CHILDREN AGAIN? HOW DID THEIR CHILDREN RELATE TO THEM?

A third of the mothers (33 percent) have never seen one or more of their brainwashed children again. Forty percent of the mothers have seen their brainwashed children "sometimes" or after the passage of five years. A fifth of the mothers (19 percent) have seen their brainwashed children regularly. Eight percent of the mothers were still struggling against a brainwashing campaign when I interviewed them.

The effects of a successful brainwashing campaign can be deep and long-lasting. I interviewed one mother whose daughter had been kidnapped and brainwashed against her when she was six years old. Ten years later this mother managed to locate her missing sixteen-year-old daughter. She told me:

> At first she refused to see me at all. She finally agreed to one meeting. The first thing she said was "I love my father very much." The second thing she said was "Why did you try to abort me? Why did you beat me up when I was a child?" The third thing she said was "My father is both a mother and a father to me. He would never, never lie to me about anything."
> She told me that she "knew" I had left her, married another man, and had other kids. (All untrue.) She said she didn't want to see me again, that it would kill her father—who has a "bad heart."*[17]

The majority of rejected mothers kept trying to see their brainwashed children. They wrote, called, and sent birthday cards and presents. Rejected mothers were angry; they also forgave their children.

Maureen: Even as I'm battling for my kids, I'm angry at them. Why should I have to compete for my kids in order to keep being their mother? Why should I hold onto children who want the best economic "deal" more than they want a mother? Why don't they offer to get part-time jobs to help me, instead of complaining about what a drag it is to be poor?

Adele: My son refused to see me for four years. Then, *he* approached me. I try not to mention the past. It might hurt him or drive him away. That's the last thing I want to do. In my heart, I've even forgiven his father in the hope it will allow *both* my children to become friendly with me.

---

*This mother was not part of the study reported in Chapter Four.

WHAT IS THE PSYCHOLOGICAL SIGNIFICANCE OF ANTI-MOTHER BRAINWASHING?

The forced separation of a child from either parent, but especially from the mother who reared him, constitutes a traumatic and lasting form of child abuse. Any child who hates and rejects his or her mother is probably doomed to guilt forever. The need to deny such guilt may lead to the suppression of *all* authentic feelings—especially those of love, anger, grief, self-confidence, and hope.

Daughters who commit psychological matricide may mistrust and dislike themselves, other women, and *their* daughters as much as paternal incest victims do. Sons who commit psychological matricide may remain emotionally armored against heterosexual intimacy. John Edward Gill, in a discussion of parental kidnapping and brainwashing, notes:

> Being kidnapped is a lot harder on a child, in fact, than a real death. In an actual death, the other parent is their support and would have experienced the loss too. But in child snatching, the child has no way of talking about it, the abducting parent doesn't want to talk about it, which alienates the child even more from that absent parent.
>
> Families come together when someone dies. Relatives fly in from other states. They support each other. Children see uncles, aunts, cousins. They know they belong. Stolen children see practically no one. There are no reunions and family dinners, no offers of help. There is just hiding.[18]

I did not formally study brainwashed children for this chapter. I did observe and interview eight such children, who ranged in age from eight to sixteen. All these children were unusually pale, guarded, and suspicious. They immediately asked me who I was, what I was doing with their mothers, and whether their fathers knew about me or had sent me. All eight children held themselves rigidly. Not one child engaged in "easy," expressive, or extensive conversation.

Dr. John G. Clark, Jr., has treated and studied five hundred current and former adolescent and adult cult members. He notes:

> Although it is possible for those who have left cults to integrate their experience into their lives in healthy ways, many are unable to [do so]. Among the common negative characteristics exhibited by the former cult members studied, are depression, guilt, fear, paranoia, slow speech, rigidity of facial

expression and body posture, indifference to physical appearance, passivity and memory impairment.[19]

Argentinian psychiatrists and researchers speak of a "new sickness"—the "forced abandonment syndrome"—to describe the children of "disappeared" parents. Such children may have witnessed their parents' seizures, been "secretively alienated" from others afterwards, and been subjected to the "prolonged stress of not knowing whether their parents were dead or alive." Preliminary research has found that such children are "hyperactive," "emotionally and intellectually passive," "unable to concentrate," and often have "dulled" or "perpetually blank looks" on their faces.

> Families often worsened [this] alienation by overprotecting the child with secrecy. The greater the silence, however, the more pathological the alienation. The child is robbed of a sense of self, uncertain of his roots, of whether the missing parent is a hero or a criminal.
> It's as if you took a photo of their life at the moment their parent was taken and they stayed suspended for years.[20]

A REJECTED MOTHER: IN HER OWN VOICE

Terry married at twenty. She had two sons by the time she was twenty-three. Her husband was a hardworking physician. She says:

"I had my boys when Clark was still in medical school. I was basically a happy mother and a completely neglected wife. I went back to college when Ricky, our youngest, started kindergarten. Clark was furious. He belittled me constantly. He said I could go to school—as long as his dinner was on the table when he came home.

"We never had much sex. Now we had none. I finally began an affair. I insisted we go for marriage counseling. It was too late. Clark moved out—six blocks away.

"He started spending more time with the boys. I was delighted. I continued my secret affair with Andy, the man I've lived with ever since. Clark was busy and very lonely. I fixed him up on some dates. Within three months he was living with a woman.

"Then 'little things' started to happen. For example, Bert, my seven-year-old, told me that he wasn't dressed properly. Ricky, my six-year-old, said he was 'dirty.' His father had told him so. Bert began questioning me about what I did with the money I got from his father. He once accused me of spending 'his' money on a plant for myself.

"Clark married his live-in girlfriend. They took the boys with them to Disneyland on their honeymoon. Their honeymoon was centered on the children. The boys were made to feel that this is the way things should be.

"When they returned, Ricky asked me why I sometimes went away overnight with Andy without taking them along. Bert said it wasn't right for Andy and me to live together without being married. Both boys started criticizing everything I did. 'Daddy says if you really loved us, you'd stop school until we're all grown up,' or 'How come you hate housework so much? Daddy's wife loves it.' Clark began a compulsive letter-writing campaign to instruct me in the duties of motherhood:

An Excerpt from One of Clark's Letters

The clothes you packed for the boys were appalling. Their sneakers are worn and dirty. Bert's outfit was a ridiculous combination of a blue and white vertical striped shirt and blue checkered pants. All the buckle holes in Ricky's belt are torn together into one large useless opening (see my diagram). Also, Ricky's red striped shirt is missing several buttons. Ricky's undershorts, pajamas and red coveralls are faded and dull. Please supervise their bathing more carefully and insist it be done daily. Your own health habits are unimportant to me but those of Bert and Ricky are of great concern.[21]

"Clark suddenly stopped all his child-support payments. His lawyer told me they were prepared to move for sole custody if I didn't agree to joint custody. In court, Clark's lawyer kept referring to me as the 'liberated lady.' He kept saying I was living in sin with Andy.

"Ricky wouldn't look at his father or at me. Bert wouldn't look at me at all. Both boys seemed very pained and torn. I didn't have the heart to put them through any more. After one day in court, I agreed to joint custody. The judge told Clark that if he interfered with our arrangement, he'd flip sole custody back to me.

"My lawyer assured me that no physician with a big practice would just pick up and disappear. Friends assured me that kids eventually resent the parent who forces them to choose. The next morning, Clark, his wife, and the boys were gone. They'd moved five hundred miles away. It was legal. They hadn't moved out of the state. I was devastated. What could I do? Start another lawsuit? Uproot myself and move next door to him? Compete with Clark in tearing the boys apart?

"Clark made visitation very, very hard for me. Although I had to travel five hundred miles, Clark literally wouldn't let me through his front door.

He wouldn't let me pick the boys up until late Friday afternoon. He demanded they be back precisely at six P.M. on Sundays.

"About a year after they moved, Clark allowed the boys to spend ten days with me at Easter time. On their ninth day with me, Ricky and Bert had a fight. By accident, Bert snapped Ricky's hand back. Overnight, it got very swollen. I asked Clark to look at it. A week later I received a letter telling me that the boys were forbidden to visit with Andy and me—because *Andy* had broken Ricky's hand!

"I tried to get through to the kids. Clark's wife refused to call them to the phone. Then Clark unlisted their number. I didn't want to put Andy through a public scandal. He was a divorced father himself. I remember telling Andy that I didn't want Clark to die before the boys came out of this on their own. I wanted them to understand what he'd done first.

"For two years and nine months Clark didn't allow me to see my sons. Then Clark wrote me, 'recommending' one two-hour visit with Ricky. 'If it goes well,' he said, we can 'discuss the possibility of another visit.' Apparently, Ricky had continued to pester him about seeing me. Now, both boys visit me regularly.

"Lately Bert has complained to me about his father. I do not encourage him. I'm afraid that Clark is capable of blaming me for Bert's normal teenage rebelliousness—and interfering with visitation again. I'm afraid of something else, too. Any man who can cut a mother out of his children's lives is capable of cutting his children out of his life.

"Clark tried to kill me. He used my flesh and blood as his weapon and his shield. He got away with torture and attempted murder."

CHAPTER ELEVEN

The "Voluntarily" Non-custodial Mother

MEDEA
Since it is the King's will to banish me from here—
I am going into exile from this land;
But do you, so that you may have the care of them,
Beg Creon that the children may not be banished.

JASON
I support what you say. In the end you have come to
The right decision, like the clever woman you are.
Medea, why are your eyes all wet with pale tears?
Are not these words of mine pleasing for you to hear?

MEDEA
It is nothing. I was thinking about these children.

JASON
You must be cheerful. I shall look after them well.
Why then should you grieve so much for these children?

MEDEA
I am their mother.

O children, O my children, you have a city,
You have a home, and you can leave me behind you,
And without your mother you may live there forever.
But I am going in exile to another land
Before I have seen you happy and taken pleasure in you,
Before I have dressed your brides and made your marriage beds.

Euripides, *Medea*

Eɪɢʜᴛ ᴄᴜsᴛᴏᴅɪᴀʟʟʏ ᴄʜᴀʟʟᴇɴɢᴇᴅ ᴍᴏᴛʜᴇʀs (13 ᴘᴇʀᴄᴇɴᴛ) ᴅᴇsᴄʀɪʙᴇᴅ themselves as partially or fully responsible for their non-custodial status, or as philosophically "positive" about it. I interviewed twelve other "voluntarily" non-custodial mothers, ten "voluntarily" non-custodial fathers, and ten "voluntarily" custodial fathers.

This chapter discusses what it means for a mother or a father to "give up" custody, and explores why a custodial father is heroized but a custodial mother is taken for granted; and why a non-custodial father is viewed sympathetically but a non-custodial mother is condemned.

ON MARCH 23, 1885, "at about five minutes to nine in the morning," Charlotte Perkins Gilman, the American feminist writer, gave birth to her daughter, Katherine. Gilman was devastated by a severe *postpartum* depression. Despite a "loving and devoted" husband, a "German servant girl of unparalleled virtue," an "exquisite baby," and a maternal grandmother installed to "run things," Charlotte "lay all day on the lounge and cried."

Psychiatrist Dr. S. W. Mitchell warned Gilman not to engage in more than "two hours of intellectual life a day." He forbade her to "pick up a pen, brush, or pencil for as long as [she] lived." He ordered a long period of "bed-rest" and a lifetime of complete "domesticity."

In 1887, after four years of marriage, Gilman and her husband agreed to divorce. "Better for that dear child to have separated parents than a lunatic mother," wrote Gilman. In 1894, exhausted by illness and by her inability to secure adequate domestic assistance, Gilman entered into a joint custody agreement with Katherine's father.

> No one suffered from [my decision to share my child] but myself. Since [my ex-husband's fiancée] was a good friend to me and to my child; since the father longed for his child and had a right to some of her society; and since the child had a right to know and love her father, this seemed the right thing to do.[1]

For years, Gilman could "never see a mother and child together without crying." She would "make friends" with any child in order to "hold it in [her] arms for a little." Thirty years later, writing about this, she had to "stop typing and cry as I tell about it." Nevertheless, Gilman was "furiously" condemned for "giving up" her child.

> To hear what was said and read what was printed, one would think I had handed over a baby in a basket. In the years that followed, [Katherine] divided her time fairly between us, but in companionship with her beloved father, she grew up to be the artist that she is, with advantages I could never have given her. I lived without her temporarily, but why did they think I liked it? She was all I had.[2]

Little has changed today. Few people distinguish between a mother who has lost judicial custody of her child, a mother who chooses joint custody, and a mother who is coerced into giving up custody of her child for economic, emotional, or "career" reasons.

All non-custodial mothers are viewed as "unfit" or as unnaturally "selfish" mothers.

WHAT DO MY INTERVIEWS TELL US ABOUT NON-CUSTODIAL MOTHERHOOD?

In a sense, forty-nine (82 percent) of my maternal interviewees were non-custodial mothers. However, only eight mothers (13 percent) viewed themselves as partially or fully responsible for their non-custodial status or as "benefiting" from it in terms of their subsequent emotional, financial, or philosophical development.

I interviewed twelve additional mothers, all of whom described themselves as "voluntary" non-custodial mothers. Strictly speaking, these twenty mothers "gave up" fighting a losing battle; they didn't give up their *children*. Most mothers caved in for economic reasons; many were also forced to choose between some form of "self-realization" and a traditional style of mothering.[3]

A number of "voluntary" non-custodial mothers wanted to leave very abusive marriages. Bonnie was hounded out of her home by an adulterous husband who couldn't forgive her single act of adultery. She was forced to leave her children behind as hostages. Bonnie remains guilty for escaping and blames herself for losing her children's "love." She told me:

If I couldn't live with him, if I thought he was a raving maniac, how could I leave my children with him? But I did. I ran from his temper, his sulking, his threats. He convinced my children that I'd abandoned them. I would still tell another mother to save herself if she was drowning like I was. You do have to swim to shore. You can't always carry everyone else with you.

A number of non-custodial mothers wanted to leave bad, rather than abusive, marriages; did not have enough money to support a child alone; and were also interested in "self-realization."

Rae: I earned thirty-nine cents on my husband's dollar. How could I support my daughter and develop myself, too? I was in an economic bind. I figured that if I moved out with Joy, it would be very difficult to make her father take her on weekends, to make him support her, to make him do anything I wanted him to do. I couldn't guarantee her a continuing father. I couldn't guarantee her a decent standard of living. His position would have been: "You wanted out. You're stuck with her."

A number of non-custodial mothers were forced by their husbands to choose between their careers and *traditional* motherhood. Lara and Alicia were in the theater long before they became mothers or decided to divorce.

Lara: I was doing all the parenting. He was leading his life as usual. I was also managing a career, for which he kept attacking me continuously. I believed there was something seriously wrong with me for wanting my work so passionately. I decided to let him have the kids. For five years after I left, my work was completely blocked. I began to drink. I suppose if he'd allowed me to hire someone to help me at home, it would have made all the difference.

Alicia: My husband couldn't stand to lose both me and our daughter. I asked him to come and live in New York. He just laughed at me. I told him I'd be willing to take her with me and move in with my mother. He fought me for custody. The first time, I won, but the judge wouldn't let me leave the state. So I gave up custody.

Things didn't work out very well for my husband that first year. I agreed to take my daughter back. I settled her in with my mother and enrolled her in a good private school. Just as things were settling down, my ex-husband wanted her back. He was newly remarried and felt he could provide a better home for our daughter. I could have fought him again. I chose not to. This is my only life. I can't live it in an unhappy marriage. I can't live it fighting a constant custody battle. I can't live it without my music.

Carla chose to give up responsibility for her pre-adolescent and teenage children. Such responsibilities, which she shouldered alone within marriage, made it impossible for her to seriously pursue a career. Carla felt "devoured" by her children's endless needs—in view of the fact that she had satisfied these needs for so long. She said:

My husband didn't understand that I wanted to concentrate totally on my work, sixteen hours a day, six days a week. After fourteen years of being a housewife and mother, I didn't want to worry about having to attend school plays or give parties and listen to everyone's troubles. My husband didn't understand why I seemed to be having so much trouble managing a career plus my grownup family.

I told him that he wasn't prepared to do for me what I'd done for him. Anyway, *I'd* developed very bad habits. I needed to be totally relieved of duty in order to concentrate. I couldn't manage two things at once any more. I wanted a studio apartment, very little furniture, and lots of quiet. Is there something wrong with a mother wanting that?

WHAT DO MY INTERVIEWS TELL US ABOUT NON-CUSTODIAL FATHERHOOD?

I interviewed ten non-custodial fathers. In two cases I was also able to interview their children and ex-wives. These fathers hadn't *wanted* sole custodial status, just as most mothers hadn't *wanted* non-custodial status. Most non-custodial fathers also believed that their children were "better off" with their mothers or that no judge "back then" would have awarded custody to a father.[4]

Fifty percent of these non-custodial fathers did not see their children at all, or very often. Sixty percent paid no child support; 80 percent paid no alimony. Lyndon is a successful businessman. His wife ended their ten-year marriage because of his open love affair with his secretary. Lyndon said:

My wife Carol was a materialistic ball-buster. She looked down at me for being so successful. She thought she was really smarter than me. Cathy was my first experience of love. I had to have her. I loved my kids. I would never have pushed Carol for a divorce. She pushed me. Her pride just couldn't stand my having an open affair. She thought she'd make out better economically if we were divorced. She thought she'd get revenge on me for having something good in my life.

I was a good father. I didn't want to choose between my kids and Cathy. I hate Carol for making me choose. I won't send her any alimony. I send the exact amount of child support my lawyer agreed to, no more and no less. I'll pay half their college if their mother comes up with the other half. If not, well, Carol should have thought of that sooner.

Morris has three college-age children. After eighteen years of marriage, Valerie, his wife, left him to "fulfill herself." She left her children behind. Morris said: "Let Valerie send her kids to college on her 'fulfillment.' I have to worry about myself now. I need my money to attract the kind of woman I want. Valerie is not the only one entitled to fulfillment. The kids are closer to her than to me. Why should I keep sacrificing to send them to college?"

I interviewed Valerie, Morris's ex-wife. She described a marriage in which

> Morris was very wrapped up in his career. He had very little time for his family. When he spent time with us, he was demanding and difficult. He rewarded his children only when they were submissive and obedient. He never rewarded them for being independent or for questioning his rules. When they were in real trouble and needed his protection, he always disappeared.
>
> I'm very bitter that he won't pay for their college. How can a man live with his own children for twenty years and just shirk off all responsibility? Did he support them only as long as I was there, giving him wifely service?

In 1981, Bruce netted between $50,000 and $60,000 a year. That same year his ex-wife earned $7,000 as a part-time school administrator. Bruce sent her "about $13,000 in child support." Thus, Bruce's ex-wife and four children lived on $20,000. Bruce lived on $42,000. He said:

> I was wrong to sacrifice my life to my family. I was in harness when I was twenty-two. My wife had everything she wanted: me, children, a big house, no pressures. My wife wanted four kids. Not me. I'm not going to mortgage my whole life so that *her* kids can go to college. *She* needed the kids. It's a neurotic thing with her. Let them learn to fend for themselves. It will probably do them some good.

Bruce's children were reluctant to "complain" about their father. The older children said they "couldn't take sides." The youngest, a twelve-year-old, said,

> I think Daddy loves us, but he's awfully busy. He can't see us very much. He sends Mom money every month, but it's not always the same amount. Mom says it's not enough to support four kids. My older brother has to work after school. I will, too. Last Christmas Daddy went to Florida. He sent each of us a box filled with the stones and shells he picked up on the beach as our Christmas present.

MARALEE AND ROGER: A COMPARISON OF A NON-CUSTODIAL FATHER WHO BECAME A CUSTODIAL PARENT AND A CUSTODIAL MOTHER WHO BECAME A NON-CUSTODIAL PARENT

Maralee is the mother of two teenage children and a ten-year-old. She was referred to me as a "feminist" non-custodial heroine. Maralee didn't work for six months after each of her children was born. She worked part time and then full time, but she was always available for children's illnesses, PTA meetings, etc. She also chose her children's clothes, baby-sitters, housekeepers, schools, camps, etc. She did or supervised the cooking and cleaning for her entire married life.

Maralee was married to an exceptionally devoted father. Upon divorce, he wanted to assume bottom-line responsibility for their children. He supported Maralee's desire to start graduate school. He assumed the children would have unlimited access to their mother. Maralee, who had married at twenty, moved four blocks away. Her mother condemned her:

> My mother had told me from the time I got married that my husband would resent me because I was a workingwoman. Then she said my children were going to resent me because I was a working mother. Then, when I told her I was leaving him and not taking the children, she said, "Well, I'm not telling anyone. I refuse to acknowledge it. Get a psychiatrist. You're really sick, and you're going to feel awfully guilty."

Maralee's former neighbors and friends condemned and ostracized her and punished her children.

> We were a close-knit group of coffee klatchers on my block. But when I left without the kids, there was suddenly this chill on the block. When I would come to pick up the kids for something, the other mothers cut me dead. I would say hello to one of my neighbors, and she would go right on walking down the street. Suddenly, the mothers didn't allow their children to sleep over. This behavior continued for years.

After interviewing Maralee in New York, I visited her in her midwestern home. As we settled down to talk, Maralee's three children burst in. Within one hour of my arrival, I observed Maralee cook "early dinner" for her children and afterward help one son with his homework and one daughter solve a "fashion" problem.

In a Mexican or African village Maralee could easily pass for a traditional mother, whose children were sleeping five minutes away in their father's house. In the eighteenth century in Europe or America, she might be an oddity among mothers: the only one who refused to send *any* of her surviving children to a wet nurse, a military academy, or a convent. Maralee might be an oddity among (working) poor mothers today—for having so much spontaneous time to spend with her children.

In the 1970s, in the heartland of America, Maralee was condemned as a selfish career woman who dared move four blocks away from her children. Maralee sees herself as a besieged feminist heroine. I see her as a traditional mother who, after years of married motherhood, moved four blocks away.

Roger is the twice-divorced father of two children. He was divorced from his first wife when his son, Jeff, was a year old and from his second wife when his daughter was two years old. For eight years, Roger didn't see Jeff at all. When Jeff was ten, Roger began seeing him sporadically. He also sent gifts and money "when he could." He said: "I knew Jeff wasn't starving. My first wife was remarried to a nice, respectable guy. My son had everything he needed. When I got divorced the second time, I began to think about really getting to know both my kids. I wanted to learn what it meant to be a father."

Roger did not view his late-blooming paternal desires as "too little, too late." The passing of youth and, with it, professional ambition made Roger's exploration of the father-child bond newly attractive. When Jeff's stepfather unexpectedly died, Roger offered to try living with Jeff "for a while."

Roger developed a buddy-like relationship with the fourteen-year-old Jeff. To the envy of single mothers everywhere, father and son divided up the tasks of shopping, cooking, and home maintenance. When Roger worked late, he said he was not "guilty" about Jeff's fixing his own dinner; Jeff's putting himself to bed; and his not having a running ticker tape in his own head of Jeff's every need. Roger said:

> Jeff has to remind me about the eye doctor, because it's something I'm not used to. So he'll say, "Hey, Dad, it's been fifteen months since I had my eyes checked, can you call the doctor?" Then he'll put a note on the refrigerator to remind me, and I'll get the doctor. This just happened last week, so it's fresh in my mind.
>
> With Jeff coming into my life, I had a very clear sense of the genetic link between us. I heard Jeff using expressions that I use all the time. Sometimes it felt like I was having a conversation with myself when I talked to him.

The things that he was interested in, the ways that he would approach things, reminded me of myself. I don't think I really felt my own identity as a father until I experienced this.

Roger was a non-custodial father for nearly fourteen years before he became a custodial father. During this time, he doesn't remember suffering any "guilt" for not building a relationship with his son, Jeff. Nor does Roger seem guilty about the "peer-buddy" relationship he adopted as his parenting style. On the contrary. Roger feels that Jeff had been "well taken care of" without him and that, to his (everlasting) credit, he was "there" for his son when he "finally needed him."

Maralee was a custodial mother for nearly fourteen years before she became a non-custodial mother. She expressed "guilt" and described frequent bouts of depression about her non-custodial status, even though she lives four blocks away from her children and is available to cook, sew, and "baby-sit" for them.

Maralee is viewed as a social pariah. By comparison, Roger is viewed as something of a social hero.[5]

Roger is respected and heroized for his apparent (but not real) break with traditional fatherhood. Maralee is not respected for her apparent (but not real) break with traditional motherhood. Roger does not blame himself for his failure as a traditional father. Maralee still blames herself for not remaining an absolutely traditional mother.

Roger can share both his negative and his positive feelings about his custodial status with *anyone*. In fact, he has become a "resource" person for fathers contemplating single fatherhood. Maralee feels she cannot share her feelings about living apart from her children, except in her non-custodial mothers' support group. She said:

> My first three years of being out on my own, the sense of not being responsible to another human being, was so overwhelming that I'd hug myself, I'd dance with joy as I was driving home at eleven o'clock at night. I didn't have to call anyone to say I'd be late. I loved it.
>
> When I tried to tell anyone how happy I was, they looked at me as if I was crazy or shameless. When I had a sudden attack of the blues and looked for sympathy, I was pretty much told I had only myself to blame and that if I was unhappy, think of how much more unhappy my poor kids must be.

I asked Roger why he wasn't exercising his visitation rights or fighting for custody of his five-year-old daughter. Matter-of-factly he said, "I can't. If I have to support Jeff, how can I support another child at the same time? I can't work any more hours than I already do. When would

I see my daughter? Where would the money come from for her baby-sitters? Who'd take her to and from school? It's a tempting thought, but I'd be crazy to take it on."

Roger is not a cold or an unfeeling man. He knows that his daughter will be taken care of by her mother. He knows that *he* doesn't have to make any suicidal sacrifices, that her mother will, if any are necessary. Roger doesn't condemn himself for not doing what can't be done. Only mothers, especially single mothers, are expected to do the impossible—and are then blamed for "failing" this responsibility in any way.

HOW DID NON-CUSTODIAL MOTHERS DESCRIBE THEMSELVES? HOW WERE THEY TREATED?

All the "voluntary" non-custodial mothers experienced their status as "deviant" or as historically "novel." No one located herself anywhere in history. These mothers had so internalized the American twentieth-century standards of ideal motherhood that at some level they judged themselves as "failures." This was true even for those mothers who were proud, defiant, or even "casual" about their non-custodial status.[6]

The self-blame and sense of deviance displayed by "voluntary" non-custodial mothers was tragic because their custodial status was essentially a forced situation; tragic because these mothers did not want to sever their psychological or physical relationships with their children; tragic because 80 percent of these mothers lived close by, continued to see their children regularly, and were available for emergencies and for continued sewing, ironing, and cooking for their children or for their ex-husbands.*

Petra: I now live eight blocks away from my son. In the beginning, I didn't see him for a year. I met a man and went West. That's when I learned how much I missed my son. I couldn't afford to bring him to visit me. His father couldn't or wouldn't pay for a visit. The blues really set in. I couldn't look at a little boy without getting depressed. I returned home. I

---

*Four "voluntary" non-custodial mothers (20 percent) were physically or psychologically denied access to their children.

began seeing my son, with his father's approval, every other weekend. I do his ironing for him. I calm him down when he's upset with his father.

Alicia: I see my daughter once a month, on all the major holidays, and on some school vacations—if her father permits it. I'm not thrilled with this arrangement, but I can live with it. I have to. Maybe I'll have a chance to live with her when she's older. If not, I did my best. I work very hard. I'm the only one I can count on to fulfill my life.

Lara: I see my kids once or twice a week, for a day at a time. For a long time they wouldn't see me at all. Their father convinced them I didn't love them. Now it's nearly straightened out. I live twenty minutes away from them by bus.

In 1982, Patricia Pascowicz published an excellent book entitled *Absentee Mothers*. All her mothers had, at one time, been their children's primary caretakers; 60 percent had become non-custodial mothers essentially against their will; and 50 percent continued to live near their children. Nevertheless, Pascowicz's mothers (like my interviewees) were denounced for "abandoning" their children—both by others and by themselves.

Some of Pascowicz's mothers lost relatives, friends, and jobs as well as children. Many mothers denied that they were being ostracized or that such ostracism "bothered" them. One mother wrote that she "attached no importance" to various "unpleasant remarks." Pascowicz notes:

Yet [she] has moved far away from all her relatives; has had no contact with them at all for many years; and changed her first and last names "because I didn't like the name I had." Although she says that her absentee motherhood "is pretty much accepted," she has kept it a secret at work. [When questioned further, she said she was] immune to encounters with strangers [and didn't want] to discuss them.

By her choice of the word "immune," one knows there have been negative encounters with strangers; stating that she cannot relate them because she is immune makes no sense. Indeed, what she is really saying, probably without realizing it, is that she cannot relate them because to dwell on them at all is too painful.[7]

Several of my maternal interviewees were ostracized or bitterly attacked by their own children.

Carla: My daughter cried all the time and said I was ruining her image at school. My son withdrew into a shell. My husband walked around feeling so sorry for himself that he "couldn't" make the proper arrangements for the house and children. I got blamed for this, too.

Glenda: Even though my ex-husband was a wonderful father, and although we presented a solid front on the custody issue, I got lots of funny looks and rude questions, even from the kids. He got lots of sympathy and praise.

Nearly a fifth (19 percent) of Pascowicz's mothers did not identify themselves with other "absentee" mothers. None of her mothers sought others "like themselves" for support, nor was sympathy or compassion extended to them by people "unlike" themselves.

HOW ARE NON-CUSTODIAL MOTHERS AND FATHERS ALIKE? HOW ARE THEY DIFFERENT?

The most apparent difference between non-custodial mothers and fathers is the overwhelming *expression* of guilt by mothers and the overwhelming *silence* of fathers on the subject of guilt. Non-custodial mothers expressed guilt for not living with their children even if they lived nearby and saw them regularly. Non-custodial fathers expressed no guilt even if they lived far away or saw their children only rarely.

In general, all non-custodial parents were economically responsible for their children during visitation. Of the non-custodial fathers, 40 percent paid (some) child support; 25 percent of the non-custodial mothers also did. Nevertheless, the higher-earning fathers expressed no guilt about paying too little or no child support; the lower-earning mothers all said they "wished" they could afford to send their children more or some money.

Why did non-custodial mothers talk so freely about their maternal guilt? Why did non-custodial fathers *not* talk about their guilt?

Fathers are men, all of whom handle guilt differently from women. As men they may also be less verbally expressive or confessional than women are during an interview.

Fathers are men who may not feel guilty about their non-custodial status and about their parental absence in general.[8] Non-custodial fathers tended to minimize the consequences of their paternal absence by claiming it was "unimportant"—e.g., "my ex-wife is a good mother"; "my kids are closer to her than to me"; "she has family money"; "the kids aren't starving"; etc.

Non-custodial fathers also minimized the consequences of their paternal absence by blaming their ex-wives for it—e.g., "if only she'd put up with my polygamy; if only she hadn't demanded a sexual life with me; if only she didn't object to my homosexual adultery; I'd probably still be living with my children."

Fathers are men and have internalized a concept of fit fatherhood as a very limited responsibility. As such, they may have felt no guilt at all about being non-custodial or absent fathers. Mothers are women and have internalized a concept of fit motherhood as an unlimited responsibility.

Non-custodial fathers are men; like absentee fathers, they were not treated as social pariahs. Non-custodial mothers were.

For these (and other) reasons it remains a mystery to me that people, including non-custodial mothers, concentrate on the similarities and minimize the differences between male parenting and female non-custodial mothering.[9]

The similarities that exist between non-custodial parents are more superficial (or situational) than psychologically substantial. A non-custodial father is treated as "ordinary"; a non-custodial mother is treated as "extraordinary." A non-custodial father may have arrived at his non-custodial status without a prolonged public or externally traumatic battle. Non-custodial mothers rarely have.

Nevertheless, many discussions of non-custodial parenting do not mention such important differences. Other subjects are emphasized, often exclusively. For example, non-custodial parents describe having to "make appointments" with or to entertain one's own children; feeling parentally "unimportant" and "awkward"; and feeling parentally "powerless" to affect a child's daily life.

Fathers, who earned more money than mothers, and who were psychologically used to "paying" for their children, nevertheless described feeling "angry" about having to "buy" or "entertain" their children. ("Why can't we just behave normally, as if we lived together?") Non-custodial mothers said similar things.

However, while fathers and mothers both disliked having to "structure time artificially" with their children, some fathers were really complaining about having to structure *child*-oriented time. As men, they weren't used to doing this. They were more comfortable integrating their children into adult activities.[10]

Mothers may dislike structuring time with their children for other reasons. Mothers who have been their children's primary caretakers are used to an organic way of relating to children. They know that intimacy and expressions of love are achieved gradually, over a long and continuous period of time. Mothers also know that children express what's on their minds only to steadily accessible parents.

Thus, many non-custodial mothers were actually suffering from an absence of intimacy with their children. Some non-custodial fathers were suffering from having to do "women's work" for the first time; others were actually enjoying intimacy with their children for the first time.

When a non-custodial father found visitation "exhilarating," this was often viewed as evidence of the "male maternal instinct," or of paternal "heroism." Paternal sadness or anger at the end of visitation, if discussed, usually evoked sympathy and respect.

When a non-custodial mother was saddened or angry by the end of visitation, she was told she "had herself to blame." When a non-custodial mother was "exhilarated" but glad that visitation was over, she was not congratulated for breaking a psychological sound barrier. She was condemned. Maralee said: "I'm really very happy as a non-custodial mother. I'm afraid to admit that I'm happy. I have to hide that. If I am too happy about my freedom or about my career, or about my wonderful new husband, I'm afraid they'll kill me. Other mothers, not my kids."

A non-custodial (or custodial) father received more domestic "help" from others than his (heterosexual) maternal counterpart did.[11] The paternal grandmother, a girlfriend, a new wife, neighbors, and the wives of colleagues were willing to keep him "company" or include him in their own family activities. Neither women nor men were as willing to help or socialize with non-custodial or single custodial mothers and their children.[12]

Dr. Deborah Luepnitz noted that divorced fathers had an easier time of it "domestically" than mothers did "economically." The fathers she studied felt that "divorced parenthood elevated their status"; her mothers believed that it "lowered" theirs. Luepnitz also noted that sole or joint custodial fathers developed a "relaxed style of authority" and fully expected their children to help them with domestic chores. She writes:

> It was a little surprising to find that even the father of a seven-year-old conceived of his relationship with his son as a "partnership." The father said:

"I'm easier than I would be with two parents in this house. It's he and I; he's my partner in our twosome—so it's important that he love me. I am more reluctant to discipline him. I'm indulgent—but at least I'm aware of it." (Professor, son is seven.)[13]

Non-custodial maternal boundaries are not particularly respected by custodial fathers or by anyone else. For example, Rae's ex-husband, Doug, has remained "oblivious" to Rae's life apart from her maternal "visitor" role.

Doug sometimes sends Joy over to her mother's house early or late. He unilaterally reserves the right to change his own plans at the last minute. Doug has sometimes left town and entrusted Joy to the first available mother surrogate willing to drop her off. This has led to many hostile encounters between Rae and these more traditional women.

One Thanksgiving, Doug and I were sharing Joy. She was with me when he suddenly got an offer he couldn't refuse. He asked a colleague's wife to pick Joy up instead of him. I had previous plans to leave town that morning. I sat and waited all day. I called Doug every half hour. Doug never answered his phone. He was already gone. The woman arrives seven hours late and has a flat in front of my house. She leaves her two kids with me while she goes off to change her tire. I'm really angry by now. She can't believe that I want to get rid of my own daughter on Thanksgiving. She understands that Doug needs a vacation, but why do I? *She* doesn't get a vacation. We just yelled and screamed at each other.

Rae has moved from rage (that she *had* to give her daughter up in the first place) to rage (for being condemned for her own victimization) to rage (at her inability to moderate any of her daughter's pro-father and anti-non-traditional-mother biases). She said:

Can any child resist the societal pull away from her mother (and women) and toward her father (and men)? Why should I lose my maternal identity and respect just because I don't want to be a man's dishrag or a child's traditional servant? Why shouldn't my choice be seen as a *better* role model for my daughter?

As a politically aware woman I don't know whether it's worth fighting for my own square foot of personal genetic territory. The "territory" is a human life. It doesn't belong to me. Anyway, it's already strip-mined.

As a biological and social mother and a lesbian feminist, Rae despairs of any mother's being able to "shape her child's soul" in pro-mother or feminist ways. At times Rae is jealous of Joy's relationship to her father or jealous of how little he has to do to maintain his daughter's good opinion:

> If I'd had the same access to a salary and support from friends and neighbors, I would have been able to keep Joy with me and still go back to school. I get sad and angry about this. I also feel guilty, even though Joy is turning out to be an exceptionally independent and resourceful kid.
>
> For the last year I've wanted to see her more than she wants to see me. Sometimes Doug gives her permission not to have to come over. I freak out. I've gone right over and gotten her. "What do you mean you're not coming? You live with me. When you're supposed to be with me, that's your home."

WHY DO *WOMEN* CONDEMN NON-CUSTODIAL MOTHERS?

Why are rather ordinary mothers condemned after they have already been custodially and violently victimized by financial, medical, or legal circumstances? Why are creative or career mothers whose husbands have forced them to choose between their maternal rights and "self-realization" condemned? Why are mothers who have done a good job of bearing or rearing their children for years condemned when they turn custodial responsibility for their children over to willing and competent fathers?

Why are non-custodial mothers condemned by women—especially by traditional custodial mothers? Perhaps such mothers believe that men, including fathers, cannot be trusted with children, that men are not capable of tender, unselfish, and non-violent behavior toward children under daily domestic stress. Perhaps such mothers (erroneously) believe that father-child violence, including abandonment, neglect, abuse and incest, occurs only when a mother is not a sufficiently obedient *wife*.[14]

Perhaps traditional custodial mothers condemn non-custodial mothers when they themselves have lost children to kidnapping or disease, when they or close friends have suffered infertility, repeated miscarriages, stillbirths, and adoption difficulties. How dare any woman "give up" what they and so many other women want so badly?

Perhaps a traditional custodial mother is also afraid of losing her husband to an "independent" non-custodial mother. Perhaps the rise in male-initiated divorce and the paternal flight from family responsibility is "blamed" on the reproductively or custodially "independent" woman.

A traditional mother is also deeply threatened by any mother's custodial victimization. She may find it easier to blame the victim (as too "rebellious") and to disassociate herself from such a "rebel" than to "hear" what the non-custodial mother is saying.*

Thus traditional mothers may *blame* rather than sympathize with another mother for her non-custodial status. Maybe she *was* too "uppity." Maybe *she* chose a superficial (male) "career" over a deep (female) "calling." How dare she champion this misguided choice as "liberating"? How dare she expect sympathy from other mothers?

Women who condemn non-custodial motherhood are also exercising a form of maternal machismo. Woman's "goodness" and her right to male protection have been based on her ability to take care of others, both emotionally and economically, under the most adverse conditions. A really macho mother-woman is not supposed to complain or to demand any emotional nurturing for herself. According to Pascowicz:

> In the case of single mothers, especially, there seems to be no limit to the supply of blood. The single mother is to comfort, clean, dress, feed, support, love, and entertain her children around the clock and the week and the year. She is to largely ignore her own needs; to avoid the company of men for the sake of preserving her children's morals and not having her own challenged by the court. And then, if she is lucky, if she is good enough at total self-sacrifice, she will be given the privilege of continuing to carry the entire and very real burden of raising her children.[15]

The image of a non-custodial mother is one that "signals" many forbidden messages: that both the price of remaining within an abusive marriage and the price of single motherhood is simply too high, that an economically overburdened, emotionally starved, and professionally undeveloped mother may be "bad" for her children, etc.

It is very painful for a traditional custodial mother to seriously contemplate any of these possibilities.

The non-custodial mother who doesn't present herself as a victim may enrage custodial mothers. *She is seen as assuming a father's prerogative.* ("How dare she when I can't?") How dare any mother behave like a

---

*This is a psychological defense against feeling overwhelmed.

(male) absentee landlord who returns at harvest-time to sample the fruits, to have them sent over regularly for her pleasure?[16]

In the early 1970s, Cecily became a non-custodial mother. When we first met, she described herself as having "freely" chosen her non-custodial status. As we spoke, the "freedom" of her choice gradually became questionable—to both of us.

"I'd been married for eight years. I had three children, a two-, a four-, and a six-year-old. After countless knock-down-and-drag-out fights, my husband, Eddie, packed his bags and moved out. I remember that he took the kids along to keep him company while he hunted for an apartment. To have five spare minutes to myself was seventh heaven.

"Eddie bought a Harley-Davidson and began careening around the countryside. I couldn't get a rational word out of him. 'What do you expect us to eat?' I said. 'That's not my problem anymore,' he said, and disappeared. Eddie comes from a wealthy family. I wrote to his parents to ask for help in feeding the children. I also wrote to my parents. Eddie's mother wrote and said, 'Sorry, he's over twenty-one, and we're no longer responsible for him.' My parents sent me two hundred and fifty dollars, told me 'there was no more where that came from,' and wished me well. I applied for welfare.

"I'd put off my own education so Eddie could start on his Ph.D. Now I was facing ten years of single motherhood on welfare. Eddie moved about five hundred miles away with a girlfriend. I called him and said I was on my way to move in with him. I asked him to meet us at the Greyhound bus terminal. Eddie panicked. He agreed to send me a hundred dollars every month and to pay the mortgage on the house.

"A year later Eddie turned up with Harriet. 'Why don't you let the kids live with us? You could go to school full time.' I went to a therapist. He said I was crazy to consider giving up my children. I told him, 'I want to do something with my life. I've been changing diapers for a thousand years. I always wanted Eddie to do his share. Now he's offering to.' Friends said I'd regret it.

"I finally decided against it. Eddie could study for days without ever 'hearing' the kids. I could never leave them alone with him. If he was working on a paper, he wouldn't smell the house burning. Back then I also believed that mothers were supposed to create a perfect environment for their children. How could I trust the creation of that perfect environment to an emotional cripple and a girlfriend who might not stay?

"Two years went by. Eddie married Harriet. I began what turned out to be a six-year relationship with a woman. Violet made it possible for *me* to go to graduate school. Violet mothered me. She helped me take care of the kids during the week. She was available to help Eddie and Harriet out on the weekends.

"It was too good to last. Violet loved the children, but after a year she didn't want to shop, cook, clean, and chauffeur them around anymore. Eddie chose this moment to announce he was moving for custody. 'You'll never be able to keep them once a judge knows you're a dyke.'

"Harriet couldn't have any children of her own. She was willing to take care of mine. I'd been living on three hundred dollars a month *with* the children. Eddie offered me four hundred dollars a month to live on for three years if I let the children live with him.

"I didn't understand exactly why Eddie wanted the children. He's a scientist and a very distant, reclusive man. Maybe he needed 'background' noise to feel like a human being. He needed something to tie him to the earth. Children are perfect for that.

"I think Eddie wanted to punish me for managing to grow educationally, and for becoming a lesbian. It offended his sense of what should happen to a mother abandoned by her husband. Then there was Harriet, who had nothing to do since she finished typing Eddie's dissertation.

"I was a very ambitious mother. I was also becoming professionally ambitious. I resented bitterly not being able to manage both. I know now that if I'd had the money to hire people to clean the house, baby-sit, and manage the children's schedules, I would have fought to keep them. Instead, I accepted Eddie's deal.

"Eddie began to feel like the one who got robbed. He saw me as scot-free. I traveled. I did what I wanted to do. He was tied down. He had to live with the children during their teenage rebellions. He began to call me 'the bitch who escaped.' He's jealous of the warm relationship that's evolved between me and the children. He feels I've gotten away with murder.

"Eddie calls me an 'unnatural' mother. He says I'm the most despicable example of humankind. If he had his way, I'd never see any of my children again. 'You sold your children to me.' I used to cry when he said this. I *was* guilty that I'd given my children to such a man.

"I was convinced that I'd be punished for it by losing them. They'd reject me or hate me. For years I never kept any of their pictures around. I guess I was ashamed not to be living with them. There's a whole area of pain and longing I never talk about. I don't think I'm as close to my children as other mothers are. Sometimes I miss my children a lot.

"But I have a career I'm proud of. I've created a whole life for myself. I can go for days without thinking about my children. And they haven't died. And they love me. And I love them.'[17]

CHAPTER TWELVE

The Price of Battle: Mothers Encounter the Psychological Law

This story (of my children's kidnapping), and the classic myth about Ceres, whose child Proserpina was stolen by Pluto, god of the underworld, remind me that (this is) a Common Woman theme. The kidnapping of our children is a threat that we all live with, a pain that cuts away at our very hearts, a loss that calls forth every reserve of strength and wit and courage.

Anna Demeter, *Legal Kidnapping*

For a long time Sally thought she actually physically felt the emptiness of the baby's going. Her arms ached for the weight and shape of that little body. She could feel the hollow between her shoulder and breast where the bright little head had rested. . . . As long as she lived . . . there would be a raw and jagged hole, a stretch of wasteland in their lives where there should have been Dodie. Not just a baby, not just a little girl, but Dodie, who was uniquely and exceptionally herself. The pitiful graves of newborn babies in old cemeteries, nameless little ones too weak to make it in a perilous time of typhoid and diptheria and other mysterious untreated fevers of infancy, did not comfort her. They were babies expected to die. They were not Dodie.

Celestine Sibley, *Children, My Children*

210

Every custodially embattled mother absorbed an enormous amount of physical, legal, economic, and psychological violence without becoming psychologically dysfunctional. Overall, 30 percent became demoralized psychologically and medically.

Of the fertile fathers, 50 percent remained "reproductively engaged," i.e., they planned to have or did have other genetic or adoptive children. Only 4 percent of the fertile mothers still of childbearing years remained "reproductively engaged."

A CUSTODY BATTLE challenges a mother's psychological identity and her intimate relationship with her child. As such, it assaults both her *perceived* status and her deepest sense of *experienced* self. In addition, it weakens her self-esteem by crippling or prematurely ending her ability to fulfill her maternal obligations.

Terry: A custody battle involves profound fears on a daily basis. The pain and anxiety it generates are intense and never-ending. Your whole identity is on the line. Your children are on the line. Your ability ever to love and trust again is at stake.

Adele: A custody fight is worse than a nightmare. Each detail in your life becomes distorted, magnified. It feels like you're the criminal on trial. Even when you win, you've lost your peace of mind forever. You can never take anything for granted again.

Of the mothers studied, 50 percent married during the 1950s and 1960s; 50 percent married during the 1970s. Each mother expected to have a primary, lifelong, and uninterrupted relationship with her child, from the moment she decided to get pregnant, knew she *was* pregnant, gave birth, decided to adopt, or met her adopted child for the first time. Such mothers had no reason to anticipate custodial challenges.

All mothers were psychologically stressed by "normal" marriage and motherhood. Many mothers were also psychologically stressed (and weakened) by physically violent husbands. Divorce itself, even from an abusive husband, was psychologically stressful, quite apart from the issue of custody.[1] The burdens of being a single mother were overwhelming, quite apart from the issue of custody.

As we have seen, custodially challenged mothers were continuously and savagely battered by physical, economic, legal, and psychological violence. For example, nearly two-thirds of the mothers (62 percent) were either legally or judicially battered. The remaining mothers were legally abandoned to their husbands' violence.

Mothers were psychologically depressed by how easily fathers could use the "law" against them and by how hard it was for them to use the "law" to protect themselves.

Lucy: I kept expecting some judge to say, "Bad man, stop doing that. Don't mistreat your ex-wife and child. You've gone too far." But no judge ever said, "Enough is enough!" No one.

Winifred: My life was put on permanent hold by the number of trial postponements. The first time it happened, I asked my lawyer if postponements were allowed. He laughed and told me to get used to it.

It is more psychologically devastating to be tormented or betrayed by an intimate than by a stranger.[2] Many mothers were paralyzed by ex-husbands who continually threatened to destroy or "murder" them psychologically. They couldn't believe that husbands could treat them as "strangers" or "enemies," and not as the mothers of their children.[3]

Edna: I lived in the shadow of his rage for so many years. To feel it out in the open against me was even worse than I'd anticipated. He needed to annihilate me totally in order to accept my wanting to leave. He lashed out as if his survival demanded my death.

Angela: Just before the first custody trial, Paul said: "Believe me, if you don't give me those kids, I am going to make it so tough for you that either you will kill yourself or you'll be ready for a mental hospital!"[4]

A number of husbands continued to punish their wives even after they had won custody. For example, whenever Norma called to speak to one of her children, her ex-husband adopted a controlled and monotonously "dead" voice. He would remind Norma to be "careful," respectful, and brief, and to assert, complain, and threaten nothing.

Then, and only then, would he agree to call one of their (brainwashed) children to the phone. Whenever Norma sounded too "uppity" or lost her emotional "cool," her ex-husband, in a voice devoid of emotion, would say,

Okay, *you* blew it. I'm starting the countdown. One, two, three. You have yourself to blame. Remember, the judge said he can't force them to visit you if they don't want to. Four, five, six. I'm hanging up now. Seven, eight. The phone will be off the hook for the next few hours. Nine. Don't call back for a month if you want my cooperation in seeing the kids. Ten.*

Mothers whose children were paternally kidnapped never stopped suffering. Gradually, with a sharp and permanent intake of breath, they began to understand how much their husbands must have hated them or not perceived them as *human*.

> Bonnie: It is a terrible thing for a mother to lose her child to Time. Death is an end; Time, a continuum. With death you grieve for days and months. With a live loss you grieve forever. The pain never ends because you can't forget your child is alive and missing.[5]

Mothers were also psychologically tormented when their ex-husbands didn't seem to be suffering economically yet forced them into grave poverty; when ex-husbands refused to assume any of the burdens of child care while they watched mothers stagger beneath that very burden; and when ex-husbands remained sadistic even after they themselves had fallen in love, re-mated, or remarried supportive women while watching mothers go without sexual and emotional intimacy or support of any kind. Mothers were psychologically stressed when other "intimates," such as their own mothers, refused to support them or actively betrayed them.

> Bonnie: My mother called me Charlie Manson. She blamed me for everything.

> Sharon: It was very hard for women to stand by me. My mother was terrified. After all, why did I want out of a marriage when she hadn't left *her* marriage—and her marriage was worse than mine? I think women weren't secure enough to support me.

Friends betrayed mothers by refusing to "get involved"; by being unable and unwilling to confirm that unjust victimization was occurring;

---

*I listened to three hours of tapes that Norma had made of such phone conversations over a four-year period.

and by being unable or unwilling to comfort or attend to mothers in a state of mourning.[6]

Ella Mae: I experienced custody as a matter of life and death. Friends said I was overreacting, that I could never lose custody. Then, when I lost, they said I was overreacting, too, that lots of mothers lost kids. My daughter wasn't even dead. The battle ate up my core identity. It forced me to question our whole social contract. How could this be allowed to happen? How could friends not understand what was happening?

Terry: My best friend told me to "stop feeling so sorry for yourself. Your kids are better off with their father. He'll pay for their education. They'll have everything you wanted them to have."

MOTHERS' PSYCHOLOGICAL RESPONSE TO PSYCHOLOGICAL STRESS

Trials by fire tend to kill, maim, or sear most people rather than to ennoble them. Amazingly, this was not true for mothers *in relation to their children*.[7] However, mothers experienced the hostility directed against them in ways that were painful and self-destructive.

Seventy percent of the mothers under siege never became apparently "dysfunctional." No one human, however, can endure such hostility and stress without becoming demoralized, psychologically or medically. Thirty percent of the mothers became dysfunctional in the following ways: four mothers developed life-threatening illnesses—adrenal failure, a brain tumor, asthma, and an immune deficiency disease. Eight mothers attempted suicide, three became alcoholic, and three had "nervous breakdowns" during or after battling for custody.

Those mothers who resorted to tranquilizers, alcohol, or tears were afraid this meant they were "going crazy" or that their husbands would use it against them. Maureen said: "I began to have anxiety attacks for the first time in my life. They were horrible. But I was more worried that my kids might tell their father, or that it might happen in front of my lawyer."[8]

Custodially challenged mothers reported anxiety, depression, insomnia, and never-ending "fatigue"; they spoke of becoming "irritable" or "withdrawn"; they described themselves as temporarily or permanently unable to experience sexual "desire" or orgasm.*

Mothers also reported becoming "silent" or "secretive" about their custodial status, as a way of coping with their pariah status. Patricia Pascowicz noted that "absentee" (non-custodial) mothers tended to "disassociate" themselves from other (bad) "absentee" mothers and "denied" or "minimized" the importance of their social ostracism. They also became "secretive."[9]

Some mothers dealt with their feelings of rage and helplessness by minimizing their loss or by "looking on the bright side."[10] However, most mothers never again felt "safe."† Mothers also suffered a serious loss of (maternal) self-esteem and self-confidence.

Ella Mae: When I heard the judge award custody to my ex-husband, I just crumpled up, sobbing. I had to be pried out of my seat. I stood up with my head down to walk out of the courtroom. The first thing I saw when I looked up was my ex-husband. I leaped on his back like a lion and clawed him. I had my bag, and I hit him with it. I never killed him. It made me wonder what I'd ever kill for. Probably not even to save my own life.

Ellie: Once I realized how easily I could lose Daniel, something in me snapped. If I kept loving Daniel as much as I did, and I ever lost him, I wouldn't survive it. I think I began to protect myself by loving him a little less. He may not know it. But I do. If Daniel ever becomes an unhappy child, I'll always think it was my holding back that did it.

WHAT IS PSYCHOLOGICALLY SPECIFIC TO MATERNAL CUSTODY VICTIMIZATION?

Most heterosexual mothers remained "mateless," i.e., sexually and emotionally celibate or sexually non-orgasmic, during and after their

---

*Overburdened mothers who are not under custodial siege often report feeling this way.

†No one is "safe" in the world. We just don't think about this until we experience a crisis or disaster personally. After being victimized, the feeling of total helplessness is very devastating. It is destructive to oneself and others to mask this feeling.

custody battles.[11] They blamed themselves for their own deprivation.

Helen: I wish I could live a normal life, even marry. But who could
         marry someone with a hollow heart? It's hard for me to have
         feelings for a new man. Would he do this to me, too? Steal
         my children?

Beth: I'm a pariah. I'm spoiled human goods. I'm not light com-
         pany anymore. I'm bitter. It makes people uncomfortable.

Cindy: I really need a deep love. But I cry a lot. I'm moody. I'm
         thirty-five. I'm not capable of putting up with too many male
         demands or tricks. Does this mean my love life is over
         forever?

Does it? Only 17 percent of the heterosexual mothers remarried (or
re-mated) before, during, or within two years of battling for custody,
while 47 percent of their ex-husbands re-mated or remarried during the
same period.[12]

What about having other children? In my study, 29 percent of the
fathers genetically reproduced other children—before, during, or after
the custody battle. An additional 21 percent were actively trying to do
so or said they would have children in the future. Thus, 50 percent of
the fathers were still engaged in the process or possibility of genetic
reproduction. Of the fathers who were not, 25 percent were infertile
or had infertile second wives.[13]

Winning custody didn't necessarily satisfy a father's reproductive
"needs." Nearly half (47 percent) of the *fertile*, custodially "triumphant"
fathers remained reproductively engaged.[14] Why wasn't custody of existing children enough to satisfy their reproductive needs? Some fathers
may have had another child in order to "reward" their new wives for
taking up the burden of primary child care or as a way of re-experiencing
the paternal role with a more obedient wife in tow.

On a bio-existential level, a father might feel more secure if the genetic
children already birthed and reared by their bio-genetic mother were
to live with him. Then he would have a more primary relationship to
them than either their non-bio-genetic caretaking stepmother or their
physically absent real mother could. Such a father might ensure his
paternal primacy further by having additional genetic children who were

not genetically related to his first wife but were related to his first set of genetic children.*

Did *losing* custody depress a father's desire or ability to reproduce himself genetically? To some extent it did. Only 19 percent of these fathers had other children. Nevertheless, 38 percent said they still wanted to have children. Thus 59 percent of the fathers who (initially) lost custody were still psychologically engaged in the practice or in the possibility of genetic reproduction.[15]

What about mothers? *Only 4 percent of the custodially embattled mothers still of childbearing age ever gave birth again.* Whether they won or lost, 96 percent of the mothers did not plan to give birth or to adopt any children in the future.[16] This is similar to Pascowicz's "absentee mothers," only 15 percent of whom ever had children again.[17]

Why did so few mothers ever have children again? The superficial answers are obvious. Custody battles drained mothers emotionally and economically. Also, most mothers viewed themselves as psychologically too "old," too "traditional," and too poor ever to have children *with* husbands or, paradoxically, without being married.

> Georgia: I never, never wanted to have another child. Losing my son thirteen years ago ruined my life. I have always used birth control or had an abortion since then. I could never face trusting another man or myself enough to risk another custody struggle.
>
> Lucy: For years, my ex-husband kept pulling our son away from me. He ruined my whole experience of mothering. When my son actually went to live with him eight years ago, I knew I would never have a child again.
>
> Cecily: Never again. No way. I already have three I wasn't allowed to keep.

The two mothers who did give birth after losing custody "denied" the biological blow to their bodies by becoming more psychologically conservative. Both remarried affluent men; both were obsessed with the importance of wifely obedience. They reacted with horror to my ques-

---

*Of course, fathers, like mothers, may have additional children because it gives them a sense of purpose, power, and pleasure. I am trying to understand some of the reasons behind such parental experiences of "pleasure."

tions about whether they would commit adultery, move for a divorce, or seek an "independent" career in the future.

There are deeper explanations of why mothers did not engage in the reproductive process again. Mothers still felt they *were* the mothers of their (irreplaceable) children. They were unwilling to admit that an irreplaceable child was lost forever, or to risk "failing" another child.

We are so used to maternal victimization that even psychological castration or sterilization remains invisible to us—because *mothers are women*.

Imagine that a *man*, whose psychological identity is based on his ability to earn a living, is accused and convicted of a crime he hasn't committed. Imagine that his wife, children, and parents testify against him, never appear at all, or desert him after his conviction. Imagine that he is forbidden ever to earn a living again, i.e., he must develop an entirely new psychological identity. Imagine that he is blamed for being victimized and not permitted to complain of his fate. Imagine that he becomes a social pariah *to women*, the only beings he has ever trusted. Imagine that he "trusts" women less. Imagine that he can therefore never have children again.

It is easy to imagine such a man as one of Stalin's or Hitler's victims; easy to summon up sorrow and pity for what has been done to him. What we cannot do is see this man's imaginary fate as analogous to that of all mothers under custodial siege.

Strictly speaking, no such analogy would be necessary if men and women were exactly alike. They are not. A custody battle would equally threaten and devastate those fathers who have been reared all their lives to be "mothers"; those fathers who became pregnant, gave birth, and were the sole primary caretakers of their children from birth; those fathers already socialized from childhood to blame themselves for any problems their children develop; those fathers who are without familial and financial support during custody battles; without the kind of public fighting spirit and support networks a legal or public battle requires; and those fathers who are then ostracized for being forced into a non-custodial parental role.

In rage, in grief, in wisdom, and in protest, mothers "closed up their wombs." Mothers didn't have any more children because the experience of having to battle for custody was psycho-biologically *castrating*. Many mothers described feelings of bodily mutilation.

Melanie: It's like taking part of your body away from you. No matter how happy you are, there's a part of you that's missing. You may have to live with a longing and an emptiness, as if your arm has been ripped off. Always you'll feel your missing arm: your phantom child.

Ellie: If you miss a year of your child's childhood, it's gone forever. Being separated from my son felt like a limb was amputated. I had terrible nightmares about bodily mutilation and family massacres.

Nora: When my children were kidnapped, it felt like a vulture had ripped out two still-lactating breasts, leaving two huge, gaping holes.

Dorothy: It's just the worst thing you could ever imagine. To me it was like my entire family was wiped out in a wreck. Everybody I ever cared about was gone all at once. But they were alive. I just couldn't see them. And I was alive, too, but somehow I was dead. I was missing some vital parts.[18]

PART IV

Maternal Custody and the Male State

CHAPTER THIRTEEN

The Mother-Lawyer Relationship

"You won't lose them," [the lawyer] said. "Don't worry."
"I daresay I won't, but I don't like the thought that I might. It's bad enough having to worry about them dying without this as well."

Margaret Drabble, *The Needle's Eye*

I warn women constantly not to hire an attorney if he's divorced or if he's in the middle of a divorce. I've heard too many stories of how female clients were screwed royally by lawyers who were acting out against their own wives.

Lillian Kozak, Chair, New York State NOW,
Domestic Relations Task Force

Forty-three (72 percent) of the custodially challenged mothers hired thirty-three male lawyers and ten female lawyers. Mothers described 90 percent of the (small number of) women lawyers and 29 percent of the (large number of) men lawyers as "good." In general, mothers described 45 percent of their lawyers as "good" and 55 percent as "bad."

The maternal criteria for "good" and "bad" lawyers are analyzed, as are the reasons for the miscommunication between most male lawyers and their maternal clients.

ACCORDING TO MOTHERS, WHAT DID A "GOOD" LAWYER DO?[1]

In general, mothers described 45 percent of their lawyers as "good." According to mothers, a "good" lawyer was:

1. Emotionally supportive, consistently patient, and never verbally humiliating;
2. Accessible during office hours and non-office hours, especially for emergencies;
3. Able to distinguish between stress-induced "nervousness" and chronic "mental illness";
4. Hard-working, knowledgeable, willing to explain what was happening, and able to "hear" maternal requests;
5. Economically reasonable, or willing to wait to be paid;
6. Dedicated to mothers on principle or to the particular mother.

Adele, Tracey, and Leslie all lost one or more children to paternal kidnapping or brainwashing. Here is how they described their "good" lawyers:

Adele: My lawyer was an angel. He was my father's friend. He knew me since I was a child. He was also part of my ex-husband's professional circle. He broke with that circle for my sake. He took a very minimal retainer. My lawyer didn't just fight for custody. He got me decent child support, alimony, and a cash settlement. He convinced the judge to let me move away. There was nothing he could do when the children decided to live with their father anyway.

Tracey: My lawyer was my friend before she became my lawyer. I felt guilty for leaving my husband. I was willing to give up everything but my children. She kept reminding me of how abusive he'd really been and how he'd turned my eldest child against me. She refused to take my case unless I'd let her fight for child support, alimony, and half the cash value of the house.

Leslie: I hired my lawyer right after the kidnapping. For years, she stayed a hundred percent behind me. I paid her very well, but she did things that money can't buy. She let me call her at home. When she saw me get psychologically shaky, when I couldn't get out of bed mornings, she just waited for me to recover my strength. She always treated me like I was a good mother.

"Good" lawyers were limited by their clients' poverty, by the domestic *law* in America, by the individual judges before whom they argued their cases, and by a husband's capacity for physical and psycho-economic violence.

ACCORDING TO MOTHERS, WHAT DID A "BAD" LAWYER DO?

A "bad" lawyer was:

1. Overbearing, impatient, self-important, and verbally humiliating;
2. Inaccessible in general and inaccessible for emergencies during or after office hours;
3. Incompetent without knowing it or being able to admit it; lazy; overcommitted elsewhere; and/or cowardly;
4. Unwilling or unable to explain the limitations of the law or to use the law creatively in order to deal with such maternal concerns as disruptive or abusive paternal visitation, non-payment of child support, brainwashing, and kidnapping;
5. Money-hungry or contemptuous of maternal "demands"—in view of maternal poverty;
6. Sexist, sadistic, and/or against alimony or sole maternal custody on principle.[2]

Mothers were initially comfortable with their self-important male lawyers. This changed as each lawyer became inaccessible—without "producing any results." Many lawyers (wrongfully) assumed that mothers always win sole custody, that fathers aren't serious about custody, but only use it as leverage to obtain economic or visitation "gains."

Catherine and Rose both had "nice" lawyers, who were custodially inexperienced, who underestimated what was needed in order to win, and who, for different reasons, were consistently underprepared.

Catherine: My lawyer was sympathetic and supportive. A friend recommended him. He turned out to be a tax lawyer, not a divorce lawyer. He handled my case very badly. He thought I was obviously such a supermother that we didn't have to line up too many witnesses. He encouraged me to get a job and move out of our bedroom. He said no judge would use this against me in a modern courtroom. He was wrong. In court they said I had completely washed my hands of the house and the children.

Rose: My lawyer didn't have the right papers prepared for our first day in court. He was also late for our first court hearing. Actually, he wasn't around very much. Years later I discovered that his wife had been dying at that time. Why didn't he tell me he couldn't handle my case? Why didn't he recommend someone else?

Once a lawyer had determined that a mother wanted her children *more* than she wanted an equitable (or equal) distribution of marital assets, he often appeared puzzled or *annoyed* by her urgent and continuing requests for child support and alimony.

Cheryl: My first lawyer kept pleading with me not to expect any child support. He said my husband didn't earn enough money. But I had no job. I was supporting my daughter. I was facing welfare. My lawyer didn't seem to understand that my husband's twenty-five thousand a year was a fantastic sum compared to my zero earnings. Did I have to be married to a millionaire in order for my lawyer to feel justified in going after what I really needed?

Sally's ex-husband kept "spontaneously" dropping in on his children and then not showing up for regularly scheduled visitation. Sally's professional and social schedule was constantly invaded, further weakening her in terms of the custody struggle per se:

My lawyer pooh-poohed what my husband was doing. He said there was nothing that could be done *legally* about it anyway. I said: "What about charging him money for lateness or depriving him of the next visit?" My lawyer got very angry. He asked if I thought my private life was more important to my kids than seeing their father was. He said he wanted no part of driving a father away from his kids.

Maureen hired a "bomber." This is the name for a very expensive lawyer with a reputation for taking rich husbands (or wives) "to the cleaners." Maureen gladly suffered his supercilious and authoritarian style. She was more troubled by his fee schedule. "He knows what he's doing, but he's a real bastard. He has me adhere to a very strict fee schedule. When I can't meet a payment deadline, he does exactly what he told me he'd do: he'll stop submitting papers and he won't take my phone calls until I'm paid up."*

Margaret went to see a "bomber" after she lost judicial custody. She described a man who

> just laughed at me. He said I couldn't afford him. I asked how much he'd cost. He finally said twenty-five hundred dollars. I told him I'd get the money. He told me not to bother, that the twenty-five hundred was only for starters. Then he'd be charging me a hundred dollars an hour, and expenses would be extra, and there's no way I could afford him. He was right. But he took such pleasure in being right.

Sixteen percent of the "judicial" mothers were challenged by ex-husbands who were *themselves* lawyers or who were politically, professionally, or personally well connected to their lawyers or to the presiding judge. In these cases, no mothers' lawyers had any incentive to risk offending a male power network. Mothers were powerless and relatively poor. Lawyers are not trained (or rewarded) for risking their careers for the sake of (abstract) "justice" on behalf of strangers.[3]

Ella Mae: My lawyer was enthusiastic until he took a good look at the lineup in the courtroom. He told me not to get my hopes up too high. He said that the judge had once been a partner in my ex-husband's current law firm. He said that any judge, but especially this one, would view my ex-husband as the more desirable parent. My husband was local. He was a lawyer. I was living in another state. I was a nobody. My lawyer really threw the fight. He had to stay in that town after I left.

---

*If a mother isn't rich herself or doesn't have a rich husband, she will never meet a "bomber."

Fathers' lawyers routinely and falsely accused mothers of "sexual promiscuity" or "mental illness." *Mothers'* lawyers believed or became "worried" about such accusations. For example, Carrie's husband had her psychiatrically imprisoned and then used her hospitalization as "proof" of her mental illness. Carrie said:

My husband's lawyer kept yelling that I was a hospitalized schizophrenic, who was dangerous to my children. He said I hated my husband and punished him by having so many children, that my fertility was part of my being out of touch with reality. I could understand it if my lawyer needed the facts to refute my husband's accusation. But my own lawyer began to believe the accusation was true. He treated me as if I were a little bit crazy.

Lucy was accused by her ex-husband's lawyer of being an "illegitimate" child. He kept threatening to confront her with (non-existent) "pictures." Lucy said: "Suddenly my lawyer yelled at me for wearing sheer stockings to court. That's just about the only kind of stockings I had. They're comfortable, and they look nice, but he told me I was presenting myself as a whore. He also kept asking me about the pictures, as if they really existed and I was lying to him."

Several mothers described lawyers who tried to talk them out of alimony "for their own good" and who urged them to consider joint custody "for their own good." Linda's lawyer kept pointing out all the advantages of joint custody:

My lawyer was a non-custodial mother herself. That may be fine for her. It's not what I wanted. She kept at me. She told me I wasn't doing my kids a favor by keeping them from their father or by staying at home full time myself. I can't help but think that another lawyer would have fought harder for what I wanted and deserved.

ARE THESE "BAD" LAWYERS REPRESENTATIVE OF MOST LAWYERS?

In her study of joint custody, Dr. Deborah Luepnitz found that half her maternal interviewees thought their lawyers had served them incompetently. Luepnitz's maternal interviewees, like my own, reported being treated with contempt and derided for asking too many questions. They had a hard time finding lawyers who would return their urgent phone calls, let alone give them moral support.

My first lawyer was just horrible. I was getting absolutely nothing [economic]. The day I was supposed to close on the house, I decided to call another lawyer. He read through the papers and asked me if I had been caught in adultery because he had never seen such a terrible settlement. I was getting $750.00 out of a property worth $14,000.00. [My husband] had forged my name on a mortgage, and the first lawyer refused to fight for me.

I went to my lawyer in January, 1976. He had done nothing about the fact that my ex has never made a single child support payment. He assured me that [my husband] does have to pay, but nothing gets done. [He] doesn't return phone calls or even answer my letters. It makes you feel like you're invisible—that there is nothing you can do to make the law work for you.[4]

DOES EVERYONE HAVE "TROUBLE" WITH DOMESTIC LITIGATION?

It is important to note that most poor people can't afford lawyers. Legal self-defense costs a lot of money in America. On June 1, 1981, the U.S. Supreme Court ruled that indigent parents (mothers) were no longer entitled to "free" legal aid in cases of wife battering, marital rape, incest, child abuse, non-payment of child support—and in custody battles.[5]

"Divorce" lawyers in general are ambivalent about practicing domestic law. Unless a millionaire husband (or wife) is involved, domestic litigation is poorly and slowly paid, never-ending, frustrating, and without status.

Some divorce lawyers therefore "take on" a spouse as if he or she were IBM or General Motors. Such a fighting spirit is often effective in terms of protecting economic and property interests (a house, stocks and bonds, etc.). However, both husbands and wives report that such an approach often escalates rather than de-escalates a divorce and custody battle and that it is ineffective in achieving custodial, economic, and visitation arrangements that either last or work.

Nevertheless, despite a unique set of biases against fathers who want custody, fathers still have less trouble with their lawyers than mothers do. Fathers have more money *than mothers* do to hire lawyers. They also have something "in common" with their lawyers—even if it is just being male and married, male and divorced, or male and fathers. Both male and (especially) female lawyers are more "sympathetic" to fathers than to mothers.[6]

In Luepnitz's study, her *paternal* interviewees all reported "positive" experiences with their lawyers. Several of her fathers cited their lawyers as important members of their support networks. One father, the owner of a company, spoke to his lawyer every morning for fifteen minutes "just for moral support" for the first three weeks of his custody battle. Many of Luepnitz's fathers found lawyers among their colleagues, peers, or relatives. "Even the father with the ninth grade education who worked as a fork lift operator had a lawyer who was a friend. They belonged to the same rifle club."[7]

Unlike fathers, most housewives and mothers have no previous experience with lawyers or are used to dealing with their *husbands'* lawyers, accountants, insurance brokers, etc. Most housewives and mothers do not have independent professional or personal "friendships" with people who happen to be lawyers, nor are they trained to choose such experts carefully, to deal with them effectively, to "stand up" to them assertively, or to leave them when it seems appropriate.

Most housewives and mothers have no old girls' network "power chips" (in addition to money), to ensure consumer-controlled legal representation. In fact, women are at risk when they behave like informed legal consumers ("too pushy"). Miscommunication is a two-way street. Most lawyers have as much "trouble" understanding their maternal clients as mothers have in making themselves understood. There are structural and psychological reasons for this.

WHAT KIND OF "TROUBLE" DO MOTHERS AND CUSTODY LAWYERS HAVE WITH EACH OTHER?

Traditional or family-oriented lawyers are often sexist—i.e., they view women as inferior, dependent, naïve—and in need of male "protection." This chivalry applies to a lawyer's mother, sister, daughter, and wife, as long as his wife isn't suing him for divorce, alimony, custody, etc.*

If a woman is not a lawyer's blood relative (or someone whom a lawyer's blood relative cares about), he is under no *familial* obligation to "protect" her from the consequences of her vulnerability. On the contrary. If she is a stranger or if she is a member of a despised class

---

*Anti-traditional or anti-family-oriented lawyers are often sexist, too.

or race, if she is sexually or economically too "uppity" for a woman, the lawyer himself may wonder about her right to custody.

In addition to—or precisely because of—such unspoken structural and ideological biases, the most serious miscommunication exists between the nicest of male lawyers and their nicest women clients. The feminist philosopher Eleanor Kuykendall describes one of the major double binds that *all* women face:

> Women, like schizophrenics, receive contradictory messages about the kinds of sentences they may speak or write in order to be taken seriously. Women are caught in a linguistic dilemma requiring them to speak and write non-assertively in order to be perceived as women, but requiring them to speak and write assertively to be taken seriously as persons. [Women] identify themselves as women when they utter such sentences as "I think that perhaps what we want is to be strong women," or else they cannot be taken seriously as women, because if they utter directly assertive sentences like "We want to be strong women," it is inappropriate for their gender.[8]

Imagine how double binds and "contradictory messages" operate between a mother under custodial siege—and her lawyer. First, it is important to understand that mothers suffer their Catch-22's without awareness and without being able to articulate them.

For example, a traditional mother is not socialized to fight *against* her husband and/or in a *public* arena. When a mother does this, she experiences herself as out of context. Her lawyer may experience her as too "nervous," too "indecisive," and too "ambivalent."[9]

Many traditional mothers say one thing when they mean the very opposite.* For example, a mother may actually smile because she is angry. She may issue "orders" as self-denigrating suggestions or complaints. ("I know I don't know anything about this, and I'm probably being silly, but don't you think you might do it this way and not that way—for my sake?")

Such double-message emotional behavior is "unprofessional." It may indeed remind a lawyer of his wife or mother. He may respond accordingly. ("Since you don't know what you're talking about—you even admit it yourself—why don't you just leave everything to me and not bother me about it anymore?") His response is also "unprofessional."

---

*They are *supposed* to behave this way in a family setting. When they do so with strangers in public, it is not equivalent to a male or female professional's *choosing* to behave this way for some public gain.

As a traditional mother grows uneasy or outraged by her lawyer's inaccessibility, neglect, or incompetence, she may complain about him privately to her women friends. She will complain to her lawyer very slowly and indirectly.

A traditional mother acts as if her lawyer is her husband. She doesn't want to go through a double divorce, one from her husband (or children) and, simultaneously, from her first lawyer. She acts as if her sexual or maternal reputation will be ruined if she behaves "polygamously" with lawyers.

Beyond the economic realities involved, mothers find it psychologically hard to move on to a second lawyer. Amber, a non-traditional woman but a traditional mother, described her fears about leaving her first lawyer:

> What if he won't give me my money back? What if he won't transfer my papers if I don't pay him in full first? What if he delays my case because he's angry I've left him? What if he convinces my new lawyer that I'm nuts? What if I leave him and no one else will take my case in the middle? What if the second lawyer doesn't trust me because I've already left one lawyer?

Mothers under custodial siege are emotionally very needy. Some male lawyers refer their women clients to psychotherapists; some routinely allot a certain quota of time for "hand holding." Some lawyers have affairs with their female clients.

Most male lawyers deal with their overly needy women clients by finding ways of keeping them "at bay." They adopt brusque, authoritarian, and supercilious styles. Some lawyers terrorize women clients into soft-spoken submissiveness before they allow them limited access to their own lawyers.

A traditional male lawyer is "unhappy"—i.e., he feels impotent—when he fails to protect a "helpless" woman client from male violence. He may therefore minimize the violence or blame it on her. Of course, a mother experiences his failure and this way of handling failure as a form of cruelty.[10]

When a father kidnapped a child, lawyers *never* blamed themselves, the "law," the judge or even the father-kidnapper. If pressed, they blamed the mother for something she did or failed to do, or they essentially told her to "relax and enjoy it." Nora's husband kidnapped their two youngest sons; Helen's ex-husband kidnapped their only child.

Nora: My lawyer told me not to worry. He said: "We know he really loves the boys. So your sons must be all right." But I (the mother) thought: Doesn't my lawyer understand that kidnapping is a violent crime, undertaken only by a very angry and distraught father? What if my husband is so distraught he just fails to take ordinary precautions against all the dangers that this world offers to little children? His state of fury and disorganization must be frightening if not actually abusive to our sons.

Helen: I had two legal aid attorneys, a woman and a man. They both were blind to my ex-husband's psychotic behavior. They were overworked, but they also had experience with what a violent man can do. They didn't really take it into account. They didn't fight hard enough to have his visitation supervised or ended. When I yelled at them, they said that even the judge's order of protection hadn't prevented it from happening. They told me to be grateful for what they had done. And that I didn't even have to pay them.

When a traditional mother lurches unsteadily into her version of "male" assertiveness or persistence, her lawyer experiences her as "unpleasant," "unrealistic," or even "crazy." ("I've submitted all the papers. I told her we have to wait for the judge to act. What does she expect me to do? Come over in the middle of the night and shoot her husband?")

Traditional lawyers, like everybody else, expect an ideal mother to be "assertive" only to help her husband or to save her children's lives. Otherwise, she is not expected to "fight like a man"—i.e., to win by any means.

What if a mother and her lawyer both think her child's life is genuinely endangered by paternal custody but she decides that fighting too hard will only hurt her child more? What if she, unlike Solomon, refuses to order the baby cut in half and her lawyer therefore decides that she doesn't really want custody or isn't a "good enough" mother and therefore stops "working" on her case—and blames her for losing custody?

What if a mother believes that her child's life is endangered by paternal custody but her lawyer disagrees with her assessment? What if he thinks she's fighting for her own "selfish" reasons and therefore isn't a "good enough" mother and he stops "working" on her case—and blames her for losing custody?

What if a custodially challenged mother decides to fight "like a man"—

i.e., to win? What if she actually tells her lawyer that she wants her husband "out of her life for good"?

One thing that may happen is that her own lawyer will view her as a potential criminal (a Medea).

Ida, whose husband paid no child support, exercised visitation only when it was "convenient" for him, and alternately threatened to kidnap or abandon his child completely, said:

> My lawyer kept checking me out to see if I was against my daughter's having a relationship with her father. I once said I thought it would be a lot easier on me and probably better for my daughter not to see her father. My lawyer bawled me out and warned me that such an attitude was legally inappropriate and made him personally uncomfortable besides. He could understand my wanting to fight for child support but he couldn't go along with my desire to "avenge" myself against my husband by interfering with visitation.

When a father talks about getting a mother "out of the picture," his lawyer may think he must be referring to an "unfit" mother. Why else would a father go so far as to fight for custody or deprive his children of their mother?

Most lawyers warned mothers not to "belittle" their children's fathers at home, no matter what they did or failed to do; not to manipulate their children into taking sides; and not to use non-payment of child support or male domestic violence as an "excuse" to prevent paternal visitation from taking place.

This is very different from what male lawyers tell fathers to do. Lawyers expect men to "fight like men"—i.e., to win by any means possible. Lawyers advise fathers to take full advantage of their superior economic status to exert psychological and judicial leverage. Lawyers do not warn fathers against spending a great deal of time with their children just before a custody hearing. Lawyers do not forbid fathers to turn children against mothers.*

Male lawyers are not *surprised* or psychologically threatened by their male clients' physical or psychological terrorization of their ex-wives. This is because they identify with or "understand" what another man (or father) may be feeling. Sharon described a three-year legal ordeal.

---

*Such lawyers do not tell mothers to take full advantage of their pre-existing psychological intimacy with their children. They unconsciously expect mothers to bypass exercising *any* (unfair) advantage.

Her male lawyer, not her husband, delivered the emotional *coup de grâce:*

> My husband swore to destroy me. He nearly did. When the jury finally announced that I had the right to be divorced, I didn't even know who was the plaintiff and who was the defendant. All along I felt that I was the one on trial, that I was the one defending myself. My ex-husband broke down in tears when this verdict was rendered.
>
> My lawyer said to me: "You bitch, if you rub his nose in it right now, I'll kill you." I didn't do anything. I couldn't even breathe at that moment. I just wanted to hold myself together and not cry in front of my lawyer and those other men.[11]

Most male lawyers don't identify with their female clients' *husbands* as shockingly as this lawyer did. However, most lawyers (male and female) are not often traditional mothers. They do not identify or empathize with traditional mothers. A lawyer may feel "protective" toward a properly "feminine" mother, *but lawyers do not see themselves in her.*

HOW DO LAWYERS EXPECT MOTHERS UNDER CUSTODIAL SIEGE TO BEHAVE?

Most lawyers expect mothers to be ideal, not merely good or "good enough." They expect an ideal mother to provide a "good" father for her children—whether one exists or not. (Hence don't tell your kids that their father won't pay child support, etc.)

If a custodially challenged mother displays genuine regret about the divorce, blames herself as well as her husband for it, feels strongly that her husband has an inviolate right to his children no matter what, refuses to "destroy" his paternal reputation, refuses to fight for economic rights harder (or as hard as) she does for custody, refrains from "annoying" her lawyer—and even manages to express her "gratefulness" to him—no matter what he has or hasn't been able to do, then, and only then, will she be seen as worthy of her male legal protector.[12]

Marta hired four successive lawyers within a six-year period. Unlike most of my maternal interviewees, she was able to borrow money to hire some really "well-recommended" and expensive lawyers. Otherwise, her story is typical.

"After ten years of marriage and three children, my husband suddenly excluded me from his life. He said he'd grown beyond me. He began to exclude me from his vacations with the children. He closed our joint bank accounts, canceled my credit cards, and ordered me to leave our home.

"I had done nothing wrong. Why was this happening?

"I borrowed money from my brother-in-law and hired the most expensive lawyer I could find. This lawyer cautioned me not to move out of the house no matter what happened. If I did, I could be accused of abandoning my children. My husband started bringing women home. He began to curse me in front of the children. He also threatened me and hit me.

"My lawyer said I had to 'sit tight' until our first hearing. Why couldn't he get me a household allowance? Why couldn't he get my husband to stop mistreating me? Why couldn't he get my husband to leave the house? Why couldn't he arrange for me to move out with my children *and* child support until our first hearing?

"Two years went by without a hearing. In the beginning, my lawyer saw me once a week. The first six months he always returned my calls. After that I could never get him on the phone. Whenever I did, he sounded angry and said he had no time for small talk with me.

"Three years later, my husband served *me* with divorce papers. I borrowed another four thousand dollars from my brother-in-law. I hired another lawyer. He took my money and also never returned my phone calls. He finally called me with an offer: I could have the house—if I gave up custody of the children. 'You could sell that house and live off the proceeds for ten years if you're careful.'

"What kind of mother sells her children for a piece of real estate? What kind of lawyer repeats such an offer so matter-of-factly?

"My lawyer knew I was economically desperate. He told me that most fathers don't end up keeping their children. 'You're always complaining about money,' he yelled. 'Well, here it is. If I were you, I'd take it.'

"I was losing weight. I wasn't sleeping. I looked ten years older than my husband. I borrowed money again, this time from one of my *husband's* relatives, to hire my third lawyer. I wanted to live with my children, and I wanted the money to support them. My husband admitted earning two hundred and fifty thousand dollars on his last income tax return. He owned four houses and had many investments.

"My third lawyer's 'strategy' consisted of letting the judge see how motherly and ladylike I was. I wanted a more aggressive strategy. I wanted my lawyer to subpoena my husband's accountant, stockbroker, fund raiser, and executive secretary. How else could the judge appraise my husband's income and assets? How else could I prove that this man couldn't be home with the children, as he claimed, if he was out at meetings every night?

"My lawyer didn't do any of this. He thought I'd appear too conniving if I concentrated on my husband's money rather than on just getting the children. In fact, he did a turnaround. He warned me to be careful of what I said about my husband. He said it might hurt his career or turn the judge against me.

"This trial is about giving him the legal right to take away my career as a mother. But I'm not supposed to defend myself by telling the truth because it might hurt my husband's career!

"The judge granted my husband sole custody of all our children as 'the more economically stable parent.' I was ordered to move out of the house. I was awarded enough money to live on for three years. 'Be grateful,' my lawyer said. 'Other women don't get anything.' After years of marriage, it turns out I wasn't the 'better half' after all. I was only the family servant who could be pensioned off.

"I tried to hire my fourth lawyer. He said I couldn't win an appeal unless my husband's economic circumstances had worsened. 'Get on with your own life,' he advised me. 'You have a golden opportunity to start over.' I'm forty-eight years old. I work in a boutique. I do needlepoint. I get up every morning. But my heart isn't in it.

"In four years my children have never once stayed overnight with me. 'Oh, Ma, they say, you don't have enough room for us.'

"I told them that the American Constitution has no room for mothers in it."

CHAPTER FOURTEEN

The Mother-Judge and the Father-Judge Relationships

The father-right ("no judge will ever deny a father access to his child") is based on the father's obligation to support his child financially, according to our social and legal customs. The mother-right is in fact *only* obligation, not to the child but to the fathers: to the one support-providing father, who is usually the biological father, and to those others who will use our children as workers. Fathers are assumed to have rights of access to their children, exactly as if they were pieces of property, without any examination of the quality of the relationship.

The mother-right, on the other hand, comes out of the obligation to take care of and *can* be challenged on the basis of an examination of the quality of care. Mothers do not have the same kind of legal property rights that fathers do.

Children themselves do not even have the legal protections that hold for actual property. If Michael (my husband) had stolen a painting of the two (kidnapped children) we could probably find him and force him to return the painting, especially if it had a known and significant monetary value.

Anna Demeter, *Legal Kidnapping*

IN MY STUDY, 70 PERCENT OF THE JUDGES ORDERED CHILDREN into paternal custody. As we have seen in Chapter Two and in the study discussed in Chapter Four, in a contest, judges are pro-father and anti-(fit)-mother, especially when the mother stays at home (on welfare); works outside the home (for too little money); has a career; needs to move; is sexually, re-productively, or politically independent; or is accused of in-terfering with the right of paternal visitation.

In this chapter, I concentrate on the judicial non-punish-ment of male domestic violence, including incest; the judicial devaluation of motherhood; and the judicial overvaluation of fatherhood in cases of contested custody. These judicial biases exist in general and in the "judicial" population I studied.

Judges in general, and in my study, do not custodially or legally penalize fathers for committing incest; for neglecting, abandoning, brainwashing, or kidnapping their children; or for not paying any child support. None of the large number of father-kidnappers in my study was legally or custodi-ally penalized; 81 percent of the small number of mother-kidnappers were.

In a custody contest, judges in general prefer divorced or remarried fathers to divorced or remarried mothers; unwed, adoptive, and sperm donor fathers to unwed, adoptive, or bio-genetic mothers.

The meaning of these judicial biases and the exceptions to them are discussed.

EACH JUDICIAL DECISION wielded a terrifying amount of power over one mother. Every mother was judged not by a jury of her peers, but by one judge.

Were my maternal interviewees judged in representative ways? To answer this question, I first surveyed judicial trends in contested custody throughout the nineteenth and twentieth centuries, in Chapters One and Two.

In this chapter, I focus on recent judicial decisions in three major areas. I do not discuss every judicial decision on record; nor do I cite all the exceptions to the major trends. I concentrate on decisions that are representative of most custody contests, or that are so morally insane that they reveal the values of patriarchal law quite clearly.

Most trial court decisions are not easily available. Cases that are *appealed* are reported in legal journals. Appeals court judges never meet the "interested" parties. Therefore, trial court judges have an enormous amount of unmonitored power and information. They are the only judges who observe, question, and draw conclusions about plaintiffs, defendants, and witnesses.[1]

Judicial decisions vary from judge to judge, state to state, and year to year. Judicial decisions also vary for the *same* judge over time. Judicial language is sometimes illiterate, sometimes literary. Judicial thinking ranges from dull to learned to brilliant. Judicial decisions can be morally "insane," radically compassionate, and sometimes practical. They are rarely just.

Non-verbal judicial behavior—the thunderously raised voice and eyebrow; the disbelieving smirk; the bored or angry face—is never conveyed in the written judicial order. Neither are the full or true stories of the embattled parents.

Most mothers under custodial siege are rarely "heard" by judges. This is the importance of my in-depth interviews. The fact that my interviewees were "good enough" mothers and still lost 70 percent of the time allows us to imagine all that is missing or overlooked in other judicial orders.

Judicial decisions are shaped by many factors—e.g., by the judicial mediocrity encouraged by political patronage; by the low prestige and financial remuneration of domestic law; by overcrowded court calendars, etc. Decisions are also shaped by the most blatant and unchecked sex, race, and class biases.

Most judges are white men who have never taken care of a child.

The token number of women and black judges are probably not practicing mothers either. If they are, they do not value motherhood any more than the law allows them to.*

In general, most American judges have one standard of justice for white or wealthy men, another one entirely for white or wealthy women; one standard for black and poor men, another one entirely for black and poor women. Most judges undervalue women, devalue mothers (doing mothers' work), and overvalue men, especially as (symbolic) fathers.

In November of 1983 the National Judicial Education Program published the results of a study which confirmed that judges are biased against female *lawyers*, as well as against female plaintiffs and defendants. Eighty-six percent of the women lawyers in the study reported that their peers made hostile remarks or degrading jokes against women; 66 percent said that judges did the same thing.[2]

Many (most?) judges do not identify with women in the courtroom. Judges also have different standards of behavior for men and women in general and for their courtroom behavior in particular.

Judges expect mothers to convey a very specific kind of white middle-class "ladylike" behavior: eyes respectfully down, bosom vulnerable and modest, knees together, and a naïve, full-bodied belief in "justice."†

Judges are not comfortable when mothers under custodial siege are "surrounded" by supporters—especially by other women. Real "ladies" are supposed to arrive in court alone, sustained by their own ideal motherhood.

During a trial a mother must be moderate in her display of emotions; she must also, on patriarchal cue, display the "right" emotions. "Hysteria" must be avoided, as must "coldness," "anger," and verbal or nonverbal expressions of hostility toward anyone. Women must not curse or lose their tempers.

For example, in 1982, Tennessee Judge Steve Daniel jailed Sheila Porter, a pregnant mother, for twenty-two hours after she had uttered the word *hell* during her custody hearing. Judge Daniel criticized Porter for her "construction site language" and awarded her ex-husband custody of their four children.[3]

As we have seen in Chapter Two, judges are custodially prejudiced against "career" and against sexually or politically active mothers. They

---

Sometimes women and blacks are "harder" on women and blacks than men and whites are—when they have the (token) opportunity and (unspoken) mandate to behave like white men.

†Judges have dress codes for fathers, too. They are not meant to convey the above.

are also custodially prejudiced against working or impoverished mothers.[4]

IN MY STUDY, HOW MANY JUDGES ORDERED CHILDREN INTO PATERNAL CUSTODY? WHAT KINDS OF FATHERS WON CUSTODY?

In my study, 70 percent of the thirty-seven judges ordered children into paternal custody.* As we have seen, 59 percent of the judicially successful fathers physically abused their wives; 45 percent embarked on brainwashing campaigns; 36 percent kidnapped their children. No child support was paid by 42 percent of the judicial fathers and 77 percent paid no alimony. Of the judicially successful fathers, only 12 percent were previously involved in primary child care.

Wife abuse, non-payment of child support, brainwashing, and kidnapping were not necessarily considered proof of paternal unfitness. Judges upheld the views of 59 percent of the fathers who viewed mothers as "uppity" and 57 percent of those who viewed mothers as punishably "sexual." Attorney Laurie Woods, director of the National Center for Women and Family Law, noted that: "The same judges who overlook or refuse to see any connection between a man hitting his wife and his fitness as a father have no trouble seeing a connection between a woman smoking marijuana or living out of wedlock or pursuing a career and her maternal fitness."

IN MY STUDY DID JUDGES TREAT THE (SMALLER NUMBER OF) DOMESTICALLY VIOLENT MOTHERS AS THEY TREATED THE (LARGER NUMBER OF) DOMESTICALLY VIOLENT FATHERS?

None (0 percent) of the mothers physically abused their husbands, or embarked on brainwashing campaigns. Twelve percent of the mothers, and 37 percent of the fathers kidnapped their children.

---

*Of the judicial decisions, 62 percent took place in the Northeast; 38 percent in the Midwest, West, South, and Canada. See Chapter Four.

None (0 percent) of these fathers was ever judicially punished. Seventy-one percent of the maternal kidnappers were judicially punished: by prison or economic fines, by the imposition of limited and supervised visitation, and by the non-enforcement of court-ordered maternal visitation.

> *Question: In My Study, How Many Mothers Described Their Judges as "Corrupt"?*
> Answer: Sixteen Percent of the Mothers.

Six mothers (16 percent) described judges who were politically or professionally connected to their ex-husbands or to their ex-husbands' lawyers. For example, Jessie exposed government and political party corruption. Her boss located her ex-husband and presented him to a politically "friendly" judge. Jessie said: "My ex-boss had warned me he'd do this if I spilled the beans. I guess I didn't believe that a judge would actually give children to an unemployed alcoholic with a history of wife battering just because he owed someone a political favor. I was naïve."[5]

Ella Mae's ex-husband is a lawyer. The judge who ordered paternal custody was once a partner in her husband's current law firm.[6] Josie's judge was her father-in-law's ex-office mate in the legislature. Josie, now a lawyer herself, said: "My lawyer was afraid to fight too hard for me. He was up against a judge who belonged to the same powerful political in group my father-in-law did. These men probably saw me as an unfit mother anyway. I wasn't grateful to be part of their rich family. They fixed that decision against me *personally*. They wanted to punish me *personally*."[7]

Rachel's judge was guilty—not of political corruption but of personal psychological "corruption." His bias against "uppity" wives was a major theme in his own divorce and custody battle. He was corrupt in using his public office to revenge himself against women (and his ex-wife) over and over again.

Rachel's judge refused to order any paternal child support. He ordered paternal visitation every week to commence "before sundown on Friday until Sunday evening," for all holidays, and for the entire summer. When Rachel demanded some modification of the above, the judge ordered paternal custody and refused to order any maternal visitation. Rachel said:

A blackness akin to death took hold of me when I read the judge's decision on custody. After not seeing my sons for nearly a year, I kidnapped them. When they found me, they put me in prison. In a desperate moment, I called the judge's *wife* from a pay phone when I got out of prison. She told me to come over. She let me sleep on her couch for three months. She tried to nurse me back to health. She was living on welfare with her five kids. She was still fighting with her husband over alimony and child support. She was afraid of him. He'd threatened to get custody if she made any trouble.[8]

I was able to confirm Rachel's story. Coincidentally this same judge's wife had consulted *me* in 1972. My notes of our meeting read as follows:

Carmen is being forced onto welfare by her husband. Her husband lives with another woman. Carmen described a physically and psychologically violent husband. She said that her husband was a powerful man and a judge, who refused to support her.

He insists that she bring the children to see him once a week, at her own expense. He forces her to wait for them outside on the street for two hours. Carmen is afraid that if she tackles him legally, he'll take the children away or take it out on them in other ways. She wanted me to recommend a lawyer—but was convinced she wouldn't win anything in court.

Question: In My Study, How Many Mothers Described Judges as "Good"?
Answer: Eleven Percent of the Mothers.

Four mothers (11 percent) described judges as "supportive," "helpful," or "just." Adele described a judge who was "a gentleman in the best sense of the word. He was gentle and protective. He really cared about the kids and about me. He made sure I got enough money to take care of myself and them. The judge let me move two hundred and fifty miles away. He said he thought I was a good mother."[9]

Maureen was still battling for custody when I interviewed her. She said: "Since 1976 I've appeared before several judges. All of them made little speeches against working moms and 'women's libbers.' None of them, to their credit, took my kids away from me. One judge insisted that child support be written into my divorce decree. I bless him for that. No one has enforced it, but it's still there."[10]

Helen divorced a wife batterer who subsequently kidnapped their son. She saw several judges. All were exceedingly sexist. There was an exception. She said:

I was trying to get some child support. My ex is a very good-looking man. He dresses like a pimp. His goal in life is to be a gigolo. He walks into court wearing Gucci shoes and a Cardin suit. The judge looks at him and asks: "Is there something wrong with you?" He said, "No." She said, "I didn't think so. You look pretty healthy. Why is this woman supporting your son? You are coming in here crying I love the child, and you tell me there is nothing wrong with you physically that stops you from working. Then why aren't you helping support this child?"

She was the only judge who upped the child-support payments and who granted my request for a psychiatric evaluation.[11]

I would now like to focus on judicial custodial decisions in general, in three major areas: the non-punishment of male domestic violence, the devaluation of real motherhood, and the overvaluation of symbolic fatherhood.

1. The Judicial Non-punishment of Male Domestic Violence. Do Judges in General Behave in the Same Way That Judges in My Study Behaved?

In my study none of the fathers who physically abused their wives or ejected them from their homes was fined, jailed, or deprived of visitation or custody. This was true for mothers who never saw judges and for those who did. In general, relatively few wife batterers and their female victims are seen by judges. Those who are tend to be discharged without penalty; ordered into (anti-mother) counseling; ineffectively ordered to "stay away"; or allowed (improperly) supervised visitation.[12]

Attorneys Joanne Schulman and Laurie Woods have observed an increase in the number of battered wives being threatened with custody battles. Louise Armstrong notes:

Where a woman is battered and threatens to leave, the batterer may counter-threaten that he will sue for custody. "Go on, leave. You'll never get the kids." At the least, he can use the threat to trade her financial demands down. Where the battered wife or mother of the sexually abused child seeks the seemingly simpler "no fault" divorce, she forgoes establishing the [claim of] battering or molestation. This makes any later claims seem no more than vindictive. With "no fault," the father will normally be awarded weekend custody, and will therefore retain constant access to her and the children.[13]

Judges do not relate wife battering to child abuse or wife battering to parental custodial (un)fitness. Judges rarely offer effective redress to a battered mother who is *also* fighting for her children's physical and psychological safety. Judges have sometimes harassed and intimidated the female *victim* of male battering. A New York woman recently pressed criminal charges against her husband:

> The judge asked her if this was the first time she had been beaten up. After observing court proceedings that morning, she knew that if she answered "yes" like all the other women had, her husband would be released with virtually no penalty. So wisely, she answered "No, this is not the first time." The judge dismissed the case, responding, "Well, it sounds like you must enjoy getting beaten up if it has happened before. There's nothing I can do."[14]

Battering husbands are learning that judges won't treat their violence seriously. Battered wives are learning not to expect any judicial help. Even when a judge hears a wife's request for an order of protection, "most [such] hearings, especially those without attorneys, last no more than minutes. Few women ever have the chance to explain to judges their unique fears about further violence or their concerns about child snatching."[15]

Child snatching is an almost all-male crime. Since the summer of 1981 the FBI has had jurisdiction to pursue and arrest parental child snatchers. The FBI "snatched" two of my maternal interviewees. Perhaps the first parent seized by the FBI was a *mother*.[16]

Nancy Lemon, staff attorney for the Mid-Peninsula Support Network for Battered Women in California, described how one mother was punished in 1983 for kidnapping her child:

> The mother was denied her court-ordered visitation totally by her ex-husband. She finally kidnapped her thirteen-year-old son and drove to another state with him. She was picked up within weeks and put in jail from October 1982 to February 1983. In April 1983 she was convicted of kidnapping as a felony. That means she can't ever vote, she can't have any friends who are felons. Her visitation is supervised by the court. I have never heard of a father-kidnapper being treated this way.

Question: Granted, Domestically Violent Husbands May Retain Visitation or Even Win Custody, but Can Sexually Abusive and Incestuous Fathers Retain Visitation or Win Custody of Their Child Victims?
Answer: Yes.

Some judges (and legislators) believe that a father has the right to discipline his child physically. This way of thinking may also be used to justify a father's sexual use of his child. Letty Cottin Pogrebin has noted:

> For some men, fatherhood means "she's mine, I can do what I want with her." For some men, getting total adoration and service from a daughter is what fatherhood is all about. I heard one father excuse his sexual demands on his child by saying, "Hey, nobody got hurt." I heard another describe his incestuous relationship with his 10 year old as "just another form of fatherly love."[17]

Most judges would not claim that incest constitutes "fit" paternal behavior. Judges do not often jail fathers for incest. Judges are reluctant to believe that a particular father is actually guilty of incest or, if he is, that he should be deprived of visitation or custody. Judges find it easier to assume the mother is "lying" or to order (anti-mother) family counseling. Judges are sometimes more concerned with the paternal right to counseling than the right of his victims to safety, redress, or counseling of their own.

In 1980 a Kentucky mother, Mimi J., discovered that her daughter was being sexually abused. At five her daughter said that "Daddy was putting something he called his 'penis' in her front and back. 'It hurt,' she said, 'and there was this sticky stuff.' " Mimi consulted a psychiatrist and a pediatrician, both of whom confirmed the girl's story and hospitalized her. Mimi then tried to prevent her ex-husband, a fifth-grade schoolteacher, from having any access to his daughter. Mimi's ex-husband admitted in court that he had engaged in "sex education" with his daughter since she was two and a half.[18]

Judge Richard Revell said that *he* didn't believe a father would sexually abuse his own child. Judge Revell ordered the girl into her father's custody. He denied Mimi any maternal visitation. In fact, he ordered her to jail for "lying" on the stand and for trying to "ruin a man's reputation."[19]

In 1982 I received two unsolicited dossiers in the mail. Both contained information about two incestuous fathers who battled for custody in Wisconsin in the late 1970s and early 1980s. Legal depositions, trial transcripts, judicial decisions, psychiatric evaluations, and accompanying "Chronologies of Events" were included in both dossiers.[20]

The first mother, Brigette O., married Anthony O. in September 1978. Anthony battered Brigette before and during her pregnancy. Their daughter, Nicole, was born in November 1979. When Nicole was five months old, Brigette left Anthony. She reported:

> He only visited when he felt like it. Sometimes he left us alone for months. Sometimes he begged me to return; or threatened and harassed me when I wouldn't. His child support was irregular at best. I applied for and received welfare. When Nicole was less than two, she began to come home very upset after each visit with her father. She cried a lot, couldn't sleep, and didn't eat right. After one visit, when she was two years old, she screamed with pain when she urinated. I saw that her vagina was red and sore. I took her to the Sexual Assault Treatment Center. They reported "suspected sexual abuse."

From this moment on in 1981 Brigette tried to suspend, restrict, or have paternal visitation properly supervised. The first welfare case-worker who investigated the situation described Brigette as a "horrifying mother with sharp teeth"—a "mad witch."

On March 29, 1982, Judge Patricia Curley removed Nicole from her stay-at-home and remarried mother. She ordered Nicole into her working, unremarried, and incestuous father's custody. Judge Curley was heavily influenced by the court-ordered psychiatric report which described Brigette as "paranoid about child abuse."* Judge Curley did not view Brigette as an unfit mother. Her "unfitness" consisted of continuously attempting to separate her daughter from her "loving" father.

The judge ordered maternal visitation "every other week." Within four months Nicole, who was by now three and a half years old, had perennially reddened genitalia. Nicole also tried to kiss and tickle adult men on the lips and on the penis. "On September 11, 1982, Nurse Cathy Mallory examined the child and found the hymen was broken and the skin around the vagina stretched to the point of being thin and raw. The vagina was open .75 cm, where it had been a pinpoint less than one year before, as noted in the medical records."[21]

A psychiatrist, a psychologist, and a child abuse counselor all confirmed Nicole's sexual abuse. A court-appointed psychologist described Nicole's behavior in this way:

> Suddenly she stopped in midstream, grabbed herself in the crotch and stated, "He touched me down here! With his peanut!" She then began to jump

---

*Another psychiatrist, whom Brigette had been seeing for a year and a half, strongly disagreed with this court-ordered assessment of Brigette's "paranoia." His opinion did not carry the judicial day.

around once again, became quite agitated and kept repeating this. The process of verbal expression was now more intense than it had been throughout the evaluative procedure. She then began to grab outward from her crotch as if holding an imaginary object and began to move her pelvic area up and down, and then made motions as if she was shaking the imaginary object and stated, "Get it all off!"

This particular psychologist still believed that Brigette "focused" on the sexual abuse to Nicole's detriment. He described Brigette as a "good" mother but one he personally didn't "like." In his report he focused more on Brigette's "paranoia" about incest than on the *fact* of paternal incest:

This mother is a decidedly unfriendly person. Although she is nervous about our interview, she exhibited bizarre laughter at inappropriate moments. This mother admits to being beaten by her own father. I believe she is paranoid and over-sensitive on this very subject and capable of ruining the relationship between a loving father and his daughter. This mother is rigid, overprotective and obsessed with incest. This obsession is unhealthy for her daughter.*

This expert persuaded the court that *both* parents should enter treatment.† He argued against separating Nicole from her father.

A complete cutting of contact with the natural father could conceivably confuse the child or send a "message" of negativity that the child has not assimilated as of yet, and most importantly, it would traumatize the child— she is strongly attached to her father.

On October 5, 1982, after an emergency hearing, Judge Curley reversed her previous ruling and returned Nicole to her mother's custody. She said:

This court is satisfied that something is happening to this child. I do not know what that is. I am going to allow, obviously, for visitation between Anthony O. and his daughter. . . . Even if [the experts] were convinced that there was some sexual abuse going on they would encourage and require

---

*As I read this report I momentarily forgot that the *father*, not the mother, was committing a crime. I began to think: Aha! so *she's* not mentally healthy either . . .
†Throughout the court proceedings, Anthony maintained his innocence. The court-appointed psychologist said he had "amnesia" about the abuse—probably caused by Anthony's own *mother's* having abused him in the past!

[Mr. O.] to remain a vital figure to this child. He's not going to go away. He's going to be this child's father.

Judge Curley allowed Anthony O. to resume his weekly visitation.* As of July 1983, *eighteen months* after Brigette first discovered that her daughter was being incestuously abused, she was still trying to find a neutral person, trained in child sexual abuse, to supervise paternal visitation.[22]

Question: What If a Mother Flees the State to Protect Her Daughter from Being Sexually Molested by Her Father?
Answer: She May Be Arrested and Extradited; Her Daughter May Be Returned to Her Incestuous Father—Unless the Governor Can Be Persuaded to Intervene.

In April 1982, Arlene W., my second Wisconsin mother, did run away. Here is a highly edited chronology of the events that led to her flight:[23]

In the summer of 1977, Arlene W. met Red E. Early in 1978 Arlene became pregnant. She moved in with Red for three months. He began drinking heavily and was physically abusive. Arlene moved out. Andrea W. was born in the fall of 1978. Red visited Arlene in the hospital but was barred by the hospital staff for his "abusive" behavior. Arlene went on welfare. When Andrea was 3 months old Red forced his way into Arlene's apartment, and beat her so badly she was hospitalized.

Early in 1979, Red's paternity was established by the Welfare Department. Visitation was allowed with 24 hour notice. Red was physically abusive to both Arlene and Andrea during several visits. Arlene decided to refuse further visitation.

In the fall of 1980, Red legally demanded overnight visitation twice monthly. Judge John E. McCormick told Arlene to "give a man a second chance." He ordered visitation for one weekend day and one half weekday. Visitation began. At this point, Andrea started "acting out" behavior: aggressive hitting, crying, clinging, not sleeping, wetting herself, vomiting. Andrea complained of being hit by her father—and marks were detectable. Arlene complained to Family Reconciliation Worker Carolyn L., who said that a father had the right to hit a child.

By early 1981, Andrea started saying that her father "hurt" her. She also cried when she urinated. She had a rash on her buttocks. Arlene noticed

---

*Note that when Brigette lost custody, she was allowed visitation every other weekend.

that Andrea's vaginal area was reddened. She took her to the hospital's Sexual Assault Treatment Center. The hospital report concluded that Andrea had been sexually abused, that her bad vaginal abrasions were caused by penile rubbing. The rash on her buttocks had been caused by ejaculation. The Sexual Assault Treatment Center ruled that there were to be no further visitations. Arlene was told that the police would be calling her for a statement.

In the spring of 1981, the Sensitive Crimes Unit of the District Attorney's Office became involved in the case. D.A. Jeffrey Kremers said he believed that Andrea had been sexually abused, but that because of her age (2½) she would not be able to testify in court. Consequently, charges could not be filed against Red. The D.A. recommended no visitation. However, this recommendation of the criminal court had no effect on the visitation order by the Civil Court.

In the spring of 1981, Red appeared in Judge John E. McCormick's courtroom. Arlene W. was charged with contempt, due to the denial of visitation. A psychological evaluation was ordered on all parties. The D.A.'s office supported Arlene in the hearing. The psychologist confirmed that Andrea had been sexually abused. Judge McCormick ordered visitation. HAVING SIX CHILDREN OF HIS OWN, HE SAID HE COULD NOT BELIEVE THAT A FATHER WOULD SEXUALLY ABUSE HIS OWN CHILD. Arlene would be held in contempt of court if she prevented visitation. Visitation was to take place under supervision in the courtroom.

In the fall of 1981, Red demanded a new court hearing on visitation. Afterwards, he was also allowed to have Andrea on visits outside the courthouse. Judge McCormick told Arlene that IF SHE INTERVENED WITH VISITATION IT WOULD BE CAUSE FOR REVERSAL OF CUSTODY. Arlene's attorney refused to represent her if she didn't comply with the visitation order. She retained a new attorney—the former D.A. of Sensitive Crimes Unit, Jeff Kremers. Supervised paternal visitation outside the courthouse was upheld.

Andrea often returned home after visitation with her vagina quite red and severely irritated. Sometimes she was not abused. When she was, her mother, feeling desperate, called all the agencies again, but no action was taken. By late fall of 1981, Arlene W. refused to allow any further visitation.

Early in 1982, Arlene appeared again before Judge McCormick. Red demanded a *male* psychologist. He claimed that the previous psychologist was a woman and biased against him. The judge ordered a new psychological evaluation done by a man. The court-ordered male psychologist presented a classic profile of an incest abuser. Supervised paternal visitation was still upheld.

Judge McCormick informed both parents that THE MATTER WAS CLOSED, THAT HE DID NOT WANT TO SEE EITHER PARENT BACK IN COURT. Again he told Arlene that INTERFERENCE WITH VISITATION WOULD LEAD TO THE HARSH PENALTY OF LOSS OF CUSTODY.

After exhausting every legal means available to separate Andrea from her sexually abusive father, Arlene fled Wisconsin to her brother's home in the state of Washington. She went on welfare and enrolled Andrea in a Montessori school and an incest treatment program. Wisconsin Judge McCormick now demanded Andrea's extradition.

In January 1983, the Tacoma welfare department sent Arlene a notice to come in for a review. It was a ruse. Police arrived with a warrant for Arlene's arrest. They separated her from her daughter, denied her bail and the use of the telephone, and jailed her for four days.

Feminists, ministers, psychiatrists, incest victims, experts, academics, jurists, the department of social services—all launched a campaign against Arlene's extradition. Washington Governor John Spellman was persuaded to hold a fair hearing on the matter. On March 31, 1983, Governor John Spellman decided not to extradite Arlene for the "crime" of protecting her daughter from incest.

Arlene W.'s unedited "Chronology of Events" documents the profound isolation and vulnerability of a battered, unwed, and welfare-dependent mother who has discovered paternal incest, and the state's absolute refusal to believe or assist her. "Sympathetic" bureaucrats continually urged Arlene to expose her daughter to more sexual abuse in order to get "better documentation." Arlene was forced to watch her daughter being destroyed—not just by her (unwed) father but also by her state "father."

Arlene and Brigette's ordeals involved facing a cabal of judicial, penal, welfare, and mental health experts, all committed to assisting incestuous fathers and failing to protect mothers and children from male physical, sexual, and psychological violence. The judges in both cases refused to punish the (male) criminal and punished their female victims instead.[24]

Judges are usually "suspicious" of what wives have to say. When custody is an issue, they are doubly suspicious of any maternal accusations against a father. (Judges are not, however, doubly suspicious of paternal accusations against a mother, under exactly the same circumstances.)

Judges have not been educated about incest. No one has. Our educators and mental health experts have often denied its existence and its importance. They have also blamed the victim's mother and assured every one that "counseling" will help. Judges rarely understand that there is a relationship between sexually molesting or abusing children and having been physically or sexually abused in one's own childhood. Thus some judges order visitation supervised by *paternal* grandparents.

In the last few years the custodially challenged mothers of incest victims have lost custody and visitation and been condemned to lifelong torment. Some custodially challenged mothers of incest victims are vowing to go to jail rather than comply with court-ordered visitation.[25] Some mothers of incest victims have begun to legally fight back.

Late in 1983, Mrs. Faye Henderson, of Los Angeles, lodged a $20 million negligence suit against the two physicians who examined her daughter, against her lawyer, and against a police officer. A journalist wrote:

> [She had] appealed to the police, doctors and lawyers to help her safeguard the child from abuse, but, in the face of the father's denials, could not prevail. "Nobody would listen to me," Mrs. Henderson said. "Everybody told me, 'You're going through a divorce, all women say that.' " So Mrs. Henderson has sued the people she says would not help. The legal battle provides insights into how issues of child abuse are handled by the legal system and raises questions about how the legal and medical professions protect children who are sexually abused by adults.[26]

2. The Judicial and Legislative Devaluation of Mothers and Motherhood

In Chapters One and Two we saw that in a contest, any mother deemed "immoral" by a state judge had no custodial right to her "tender" child. The maternal presumption (or the tender years doctrine) was always interpreted as one of several judicial options to be exercised in the child's "best interests." The maternal presumption was never interpreted as a maternal "right." In fact, the child's "best interests" were usually seen as synonymous with *paternal* rights.[27]

From 1900 to 1950, presumably the height of the maternal presumption, in a contest, *moral* mothers routinely lost custody of their "older" children. Judges seemed to think that a male child over five years of age no longer required his mother's "tenderness." Girls tended to require their moral mother's (or a moral mother surrogate's) "tenderness" somewhat longer.[28]

Until the 1920s the most moral of mothers and the most tender of children were not entitled to any child support. Actually, for

> many years, a father was entitled to the economic fruits of his child's labor even if the mother had custody. Subsequently, women with custody obtained the right to their children's economic value, but the father's support obligation ceased if he did not have custody because he had no more right to

his children's services. Because those services were worthless, only those women able to provide support through their own means, or more likely, that of their families, were even in a position to request custody of their children.[29]

Since the 1950s the maternal presumption has not only been viewed as secondary to the child's "best interests" but also viewed as "sexist." By the late 1970s two-thirds of the American states rejected it as a customary presumption.

Between 1950 and 1986 judges continued to view white married mothers as custodially worthy—until they committed an "immoral" act or became welfare-dependent. The welfare mother is married to the entire state legislature, each member of which views her as a lazy, promiscuous "cheat." The sum allotted to her for mothering is an exact measure of the state's de(valuation) of mothers, mothering, and children.

In 1983 a family of four (usually a mother and three children) received $104 *a month* in Puerto Rico; $169 in Mississippi; $229 in Georgia; and $263 in Florida. In 1983 welfare for a Midwestern family of four ranged from $327 a month in Ohio, $441 in Michigan, and $263 in Arizona, to $425 in Montana. The highest welfare allotment in 1983—$682 a month—went to a family of four in Alaska. Californians received $601 and New Yorkers, $515 monthly.[30]

Judges usually ordered child-support payments that "matched" the state's economic valuation of motherhood. Judges and legislators did not worry about child-support *enforcement*. (If necessary, a mother could always turn to welfare.) Judges increasingly refused to award any, adequate, or long-term alimony (spousal support). "Let mothers work—it's what the feminists want."

State legislators also passed "no fault" divorce and "joint distribution of property" laws. This meant that judges no longer had to "hear" about male (or female) adultery, domestic violence, or financial selfishness. "Fault" no longer existed; monetary compensation for it became unnecessary.

Joint distribution of property didn't mean that wives got 50 percent of everything. On the contrary. Where "large" amounts of money were involved, wealthy men hired expensive lawyers to delay judicial action and expensive accountants to hide their assets. Above all, they purchased time with which to terrorize and humble their wives, psycho-economically, and to persuade judges that their wives had grossly overestimated how much they were really worth.

Some lawyers argued that a wealthy father, by definition, would be the better custodial parent. Lawyers had no trouble persuading most judges that a wealthy man's wife had *already* been well subsidized up to the time of divorce, that she was lazy, parasitic, financially greedy—and financially incompetent. A wife (of any age) was viewed as perfectly capable of working—especially if she was not going to be the custodial parent, or if her children were already grown, or if her grown children were already amply provided for by their wealthy father.[31]

Judges and legislators were more willing to divide *children* "jointly" than to divide a man's business "jointly." Judges, lawyers, and legislators had no trouble with devising tortuous "comparable worth" formulas—in the service of the *male* acquisition and retention of income, assets, and property. (They had, and still have, a great deal of trouble dividing a "man's" money in half and with any "comparable worth" formulas in the service of the *female* acquisition or retention of income, assets, or property.)

Despite sentimental lip service given to the "sacredness" of the mother-child bond, most judges take female mothering for granted and view it as an "easy" job. Judges express their devaluation of *mothers'* doing mothers' work whenever they decide that past maternal performance can be "canceled" by later "uppity" behavior.[32]

Maternal labor is devalued whenever judges award children to step-mothers or paternal grandmothers, as if any female surrogate is the same as the mother; and whenever judges decide that fathers who have done no primary parenting in the past are either "more" or "equally" fit parents.

As we have noted, on October 28, 1975, New York Judge Guy Ribaudo awarded sole custody of two children to their father, Dr. Lee Salk. It was clear that Kersten Salk, and not Dr. Salk, had reared the children from birth "without the aid of a governess"; and that Dr. Salk would undoubtedly require the aid of a "third party" housekeeper-governess were he to gain sole custody. Kersten was not accused of being an "unfit" mother.

The court used "an affirmative standard" to decide which parent was "better fit" to guide the "development of the children and their future."

> It is the judgement of this court that permanent custody of both infant issue is awarded to the father Dr. Lee Salk. . . . Since the birth of the children, Dr. Salk has exhibited a vast interest in the various stages of the children's development, his interaction with the children is not due solely to the fact that the father is a child psychologist.
>
> Dr. Salk is indeed a very bright, essentially stable person whose ability

to conceptualize accurately and appropriately is quite superior—a fact which is reflected in turn in a high degree of competency to render proper and realistic judgments and skill in mastering effectively problems within himself and his environment, including those related to his children.[33]

Kersten Salk's full-time housekeeping and mothering was "discounted" in favor of Dr. Salk's psychological expertise and "intellectually exciting" lifestyle. In an unpublished paper, Kersten Salk opined: "This decision was part of the backlash against the feminist movement. I was a victim of circumstance. Judge Ribaudo filmed an interview with NBC before he released the text of his decision to counsel. . . . The basis of Judge Ribaudo's decision seems to have been Lee's professional and material attainments."[34]

A "fit" or "good enough" mother is not protected by the maternal presumption or by the tender years doctrine. According to Nancy Polikoff, "No recent appeals court decision has been found overturning a custody award to a father, or upholding one to the mother, on the basis of the tender years doctrine; several have been found which have upheld awards to fathers in spite of the supposed continued existence of the tender years doctrine."[35]

The spirit of affirmative action has consistently been custodially used against mothers by judges. For example, in 1979, a Kansas court awarded one-year-old twins to a working father rather than to a mother who could stay at home with them.

> Even though it considered the tender years presumption as one factor, the father was found to be able to provide the better home environment. The higher court, in upholding the decision, made it clear that the mother could lose even if she was fit, under the best interests of the child standard.[36]

In a similar attempt to be "sex-neutral," in 1980, a judge awarded a two-year-old son to his father. Since both parents were fit, "an award to the mother *because* she was the mother, and as such the primary caretaker, would violate the requirement of sex-neutrality. The appellate court noted the faulty logic and reversed."[37]

Nancy Polikoff has analyzed another case in which the North Dakota appellate court upheld the father's custody of three children:

> The mother argued that it was unfair for her to lose her children because she chose to stay at home with them, foregoing career opportunities. But the court, in a cruel twist of the customary logic, stated that it would not

be more fair to deprive the father of custody because he did not stay home during the day.[38]

In 1980, a New Jersey judge was hearing a routine divorce case. At issue were alimony and child support—not custody. The mother, Susan Beck, was a traditional stay-at-home mother. Richard Beck was a high earner who provided well for his family. He was also, and admittedly, an absent father.

Over the weekend of the hearing, the judge happened to attend a nearby conference on joint custody. A succession of fathers' rights activists and joint custody researchers spoke convincingly about custodial discrimination against fathers and about the "joy" of joint custody. The judge returned to his courtroom and *mandated* joint custody. He wrote:

> Even though the father did not request it, and even assuming he doesn't want it, I'm going to order this as something that I feel would be in the best interests of these children, particularly because they're adopted, and I feel that adopted children need . . . the love and security of both parents. I order that these children live for four months at a time with each parent, and while one parent has the children, the other parent will visit every other weekend. Even though there have been instances of violence on the part of the husband against the wife, and while there does seem to be some strife between them, the strife seems to be about money issues and both of them evidence caring for the children and concern for their welfare; and even though there's been no probation in court, even though there's been no psychiatric testimony, and even though I haven't interviewed the children, I feel that this case would be an appropriate case for joint custody.[39]

This precedent decision was hailed as an important victory by fathers' rights activists. Richard Beck gave paternally "heroic" interviews to the press. Mrs. Beck appealed the decision and won a reversal. Mr. Beck appealed to the state supreme court. In the summer of 1981 the Supreme Court of New Jersey upheld mandated joint custody. Mrs. Beck, in private interviews with me in 1981 and 1982, said:

> That was the worst moment of my life. Why did that judge order four months? Where did he get that magic number from? My girls were hysterical. But they had to go to their father. Luckily it didn't work out. They're back with me. Richard can see them as often as he wants. It's no more often than before. I just feel sorry for any other mother who'll suffer because of my judge's ruling.[40]

It is important to understand that the equal treatment of "unequals" is unjust. The (unwarranted) paternal demand for "equal" custodial rights; and the law that values legal paternity or male economic superiority over natural motherhood and maternal practice, ultimately degrade and violate both mothers and children.

Not all judges discriminate against stay-at-home or "good enough" mothers, nor do all judges do so in the spirit of affirmative action or "sex neutrality." In 1981, the West Virginia Supreme Court, in a land-mark decision, enunciated a "primary caretaker" presumption—i.e., whichever parent actually did the child care should be the preferred or presumed custodian in any contest. The court spelled out the chores of a primary caretaker.

1) preparing and planning of meals; 2) bathing, grooming and dressing; 3) purchasing, cleaning, and care of clothes; 4) medical care, including nursing and trips to physicians; 5) arranging for social interaction among peers after school, i.e. transporting to friends' houses or, for example, to girl or boy scout meetings; 6) arranging alternative care, i.e. babysitting, daycare, etc.; 7) putting child to bed at night, attending to child in the middle of the night, waking child in the morning; 8) disciplining, i.e. teaching general manners and toilet training; 9) educating, i.e. religious, cultural, social, etc.; and 10) teaching elementary skills, i.e. reading, writing, and arithmetic.[41]

In 1983, the Mississippi Supreme Court used a combination of the tender years doctrine and the primary caretaker presumption to uphold maternal custody. The court stated: "Factors to be considered are health, sex, continuity of care, parenting skills, employment, age of parents, stability, etc." The court also stated that "the relative financial situation of the parents is not controlling since the duty to support is independent of the right to custody."[42]

3. The Judicial Overvaluation of Genetic, Legal, Economic, and Symbolic Fatherhood

Considering the "epidemic" nature of the male abandonment of families, judges are impressed by fathers who fight for paternal recognition, visitation, and custodial rights. A father need only satisfy minimal criteria in order to be seen as a "father" and as a "good enough" father. Judges view a father as fit if he bears a genetic relationship to a child; or was once married to the child's mother; or now *promises* to support the child at least at state welfare levels.

If a mother has once been legally married to the genetic father of her child, she risks losing custody and child support, being fined and even imprisoned, if she is seen as interfering with a father's right of paternal recognition, physical access, psychological relationship, and control over "his" children.

> Question: Does a Father Who Is Alcoholic, or Mentally Ill, Who Hasn't Seen His Children for Years, or Only Infrequently, and Who Hasn't Supported His Children Still Have the Right of Visitation?
>
> Answer: Yes.
>
> Question: What Happens If a Mother Interferes with This Paternal Right?
>
> Answer: A Judge May Hold Her in Contempt of Court, Fine Her, Withhold Child Support, or Remove Custody from Her Altogether.

We have already seen how incestuous and otherwise abusive fathers can win *custody* of children. Attorney Joanne Schulman describes a case in which she represented a custodial mother who wanted her alcoholic ex-husband's *visitation* structured so that he would not drive his child anywhere. The father never responded to complaints or appeared in court. Nevertheless

> The judge literally threw a fit. He threw files at me in the courtroom. He said, "I will not slander that man. I will not give you that kind of visitation. You are putting on public record that this man has a drinking problem. That man is not even here to defend himself." The *judge* was that man's attorney. The judge cared more about the man's reputation than about the kid who might be killed driving around with an alcoholic. Even when I produced evidence that this man had been convicted of drunken driving, the judge threw a fit again. He had a tantrum. He threw files all over the bench again.*

Attorney Martha O. Eller, of the state of Washington, notes that in real life, unlike *Kramer vs. Kramer*, mothers who have physically abandoned their children can rarely regain custody. However, fathers who have abandoned children completely can, at any time, re-open their claim to custody. Eller has said: "I am defending several child custody modification actions right now where the fathers' connections with the

---

*Schulman notes that lay people usually deal with this anecdote by assuming it's an isolated example. The only people who don't see it as isolated are other lawyers.

children are astonishingly minimal since the parties' separation, and yet they are being given careful consideration for custody modification."[43]

In 1981 a New York father sued his ex-wife for allegedly refusing him visitation. This father apparently saw his daughter quite "irregularly." According to Judge Getzels, the father

> did not live up to his assurances that he would arrange his business schedule to come in from Hong Kong every three months. By visiting less frequently, he failed to exercise his right. When he came, as in November 1980, he put business before his daughter and was really available only one day out of ten he would be in New York. When he did get to visit with the child in February 1981, she was afraid to be left alone with him. After this visit [the three-year-old girl] became incontinent and her behavior regressed. She was afraid to be left alone with him. It was the opinion of a child psychologist that the regression resulted from the trauma of [the girl's] seeing her father. The child feels abandoned by her father. She has been observed walking up to strange men, tugging at their trousers and saying, "Daddy, Daddy." She tells neighbors that she has no father. Two therapists are willing to testify that unsupervised, irregular visitation is detrimental.[44]

Judge Getzels did not find the mother in "malicious" or "willful" contempt of court. Nevertheless, he ordered that visitation (with prior notice) be continued. He reminded the mother that it was her duty to

> encourage visitation and to foster the child's loving relationship with her father. No evidence was adduced that irregular visitation is harmful or that supervision is necessary. . . . So vital is the relationship between the non-custodial parent and child that *interference* with that relationship may be found to be inconsistent with the child's best interests as to raise *a question as to the fitness of the offender to retain custody* [author's italics].*

In 1983, a judge in West Virginia ruled: "Unless a divorced father's failure to support was contumacious, willful or intentional, or visitation would be detrimental to the children, visitation should not be denied on grounds of non-support."[46]

In 1983, New York Judge Ralph Diamond delayed a mother's petition for child support because she had allegedly violated the *unwed* father's *visitation* privileges. The mother claimed she "did nothing to prevent

---

*Note that the judge considers the father's visitation rights more important than the child's distress; and more important than the extra work (and pain) this distress causes her mother.[45]

the child from visiting with her father." The judge noted that the child "hated" her father and refused to see him. Judge Diamond ordered a new visitation schedule away from the mother's residence, and held her petition for support "in abeyance, pending the outcome of the new arrangement." Judge Diamond wrote: "It is clear that the law at a minimum requires a custodian to do something to encourage and to foster the relationship between the child and the non-custodial parent to aid in gaining visitation. A custodian may not simply remain mute and passive and in so doing impede the visitation order of the court."[47]

Question: What If a Mother Has to Move Away in Order to Survive Economically?
● *Answer: If the Father Argues That the Move Will Interfere with His Visitation, She May Lose Custody.*

On July 27, 1981, five years after her divorce, Frances Daghir Couglin lost custody of her children because her new husband's temporary move to France was seen as interfering with paternal visitation. Khalil Daghir had abandoned the home. Frances was a stay-at-home mother who had since "provided a good home for the three children." Khalil had, in fact, been judicially viewed as incapable of "adequately caring for the children while working full time," and as someone who "might remove the children to Lebanon on a permanent basis, if he had custody."

Frances offered to subsidize Khalil's travel expenses and to "balance out" his visitation by allowing him two continuous months each summer with the children. Nevertheless, the judge granted Khalil custody. "So zealously do the courts guard the relationship between a non-custodial parent and his child, that any interference with it by the custodial parent has been said to be an act so inconsistent with the best interests of the child as to, per se, raise a strong possibility that the offending party is unfit to act as custodial parent."[48]

Thus, the *right* of paternal *visitation*, which few judges ever monitor in terms of its frequency or quality, is considered more important to children than their ongoing relationship to their "good enough" biological and full-time married mother.[49]

Perhaps Mrs. Daghir's remarriage was judicially perceived as "selfish" or as unfair to her ex-husband's paternal territoriality. By contrast, judges *like* stepmothers and do not view their taking over a mother's children as unnaturally proprietary.

It is important to stress that such paternal rights exist without reciprocal obligations. For example, in 1981, Kimberly Anne Louden asked the California courts to compel her natural, unwed father, Owen C. Olpin, to visit her. The court decided that paternal visitation is a "right and a privilege" and that such a "right is not reciprocal, and hence, the plaintiff ha[s] no right to compel her adjudicated father to visit her."[50]

The courts claim they cannot force a father to visit his child or to behave non-violently and responsibly when he does visit. However, the courts can and do order paternal child-support payments withheld or custody removed from the mother who is perceived as interfering with the paternal "right" of visitation.

> *Question: In a Contest, We Have Seen That the Genetic-Legal Father Is Entitled to Visitation and Custody over the Objections of the Bio-genetic-Legal-Adoptive-Social Mother. In a Contest, Who Is Most Entitled to Visitation and Custody: the Mother (As Above); the Unwed Father; or the Sperm Donor?*
>
> Answer: The Genetic Father (Not the Bio-genetic Mother)—Especially If He Supports the Child.

On April 3, 1972, the U.S. Supreme Court ruled that unwed fathers cannot be denied custody of their illegitimate children. This case involved the custodial status of three children after their mother's death.[51] According to Attorney Joanne Schulman, this lawsuit also involved the father's need "to obtain welfare as a poor, single parent." She noted: "A number of cases, citing *Stanley* as a precedent, have occurred which endanger the rights of mothers and enhance the rights of sperm donors and unwed fathers."

In 1979 in New York State, unwed fathers won the constitutional right to veto adoption proceedings. New York State also has a "putative father registry" which assists the court in finding the unwed fathers of impoverished or adoptable children. The search may take a long time, delay adoption, and not be in the child's "best interest."*[52]

In 1980, Virginia Judge Joseph Peters, Jr., awarded *custody* to an unwed father *after* he had kidnapped his two-and-a-half-year-old daughter. The father claimed maternal "interference" with visitation. The judge also acquitted the father of the assault, battery, and kidnapping charges.[53] Attorney Doris Jonas Freed commented: "[This decision] is the logical extension of the rights of fathers. They [unwed fathers] now stand substantially in the shoes of wedded fathers."[54]

---

*Unwed fathers who are anti-abortion have already attempted to prevent abortions on the ground of their future right to visitation and custody. They have also tried to proscribe pregnant female behavior on similar grounds.

In 1981 in New Hampshire, an unwed father successfully won visitation rights. In this case the court overruled the state's common law provision that "the mother of an illegitimate child has a right to the custody and control of the child . . . [and] the [unwed] father has no right to custody and control of the child."[55]

In 1981 and in 1983, sperm donors in Illinois and California successfully sued voluntarily single mothers for paternal recognition and visitation rights. The mothers had been impregnated with the sperm of men who had agreed to function as donors, not as fathers. After boys were born, the sperm donors wanted to "support" and establish relationships with their sons. (In the California case the mother was partially subsidized by welfare.) Both fathers obtained parental recognition and visitation.[56]

In 1984, the California Supreme Court ruled 5–2 that a man who unknowingly fathers a child has more right to the child than adoptive parents do.*

> The three year old child, identified as "Baby Girl M," has been with her adoptive parents since she was a few days old. The father, Edward McNamara, had a three months' affair with the child's mother, during which she conceived. The mother did not tell him that she was pregnant, but after she had the baby and decided to give it up for adoption, she notified him. He agreed that the baby should be adopted.
>
> Later, McNamara changed his mind and sued for the child. The San Diego Superior Court ruled that the girl should stay with her adoptive family. But the State Supreme Court decided that a man who fathers a child in casual affairs has some right to custody because he would have a responsibility to support the child if a mother sued for support.[57]

Question: Granted, Genetic (Unwed or Sperm Donor) Fathers Have More Rights Than Bio-genetic Mothers. Can a Non-genetic "Father" Ever Cancel Out a Genetic Father's Paternal Rights?
Answer: Yes. When He Is the Bio-genetic Mother's Husband and When He Supports the Child in Question.

In 1978, an Illinois genetic father fought to establish his paternity and paternal rights. Although he *was* the genetic father, his paternal rights

---

*Christina Landaverde, the impoverished refugee mother described in Chapter Two, who was tricked out of her son, did not have such rights.

were seen as less important than those of the mother's legal husband and economic protector.[58]

Under the Uniform Parentage Act passed in 1981 in Wyoming, the husband is presumed to be the father of any child born to his wife during his marriage. In 1981, this presumption was challenged by a man who claimed paternity of a child born to another man's wife. The Wyoming Supreme Court dismissed the case despite blood tests which apparently "proved" the man's assertion of paternity.[59]

In 1981, a divorced father in New York kidnapped his daughter away from her mother. A judge subsequently transferred custody to him. Judge Kevin Fogarty ruled that even though he was not the girl's *genetic* father, he was still her *legal* father. "The court finds that illegitimating a child who would lose all her rights vis-à-vis the only father she has ever known would certainly fall within the category of objectionable consequences."[60]

On June 27, 1983, the U.S. Supreme Court ruled that a genetic and unwed father was not entitled to paternal *visitation*. This unusual decision was based on the following and crucial facts: the mother had remarried, her legal husband had assumed psycho-economic responsibility for the child, and the child's father had abandoned her for some time.

In order to justify transferring paternal rights from one *man* to another *man*, the court actually enunciated paternal obligations. This decision is positive in terms of defining the paternal obligations of a genetic father. Such standards of obligation are rarely used when genetic fathers custodially challenge bio-genetic mothers.[61]

Question: What Is Going On?
Answer: Patriarchal Law Is Going On.

In the twentieth century, under patriarchal law, (male) contractual and property rights supersede (female) natural and property rights. Mothers have obligations without reciprocal legal rights. Fathers have rights without reciprocal obligations. Economically solvent men (individuals or the state legislature) have a greater right to children than do impoverished fathers or mothers or economically solvent mothers.

Under patriarchal law, men carry more custodial weight than women do; "fathers" carry more custodial weight than do bio-genetic-legal-social mothers. This is true for "fathers" who do not support or visit their children, for "fathers" who are unwed or who are sperm donors, and for "fathers" who are the legal husbands of genetic mothers.

This progression of judicial custodial priorities is not true in every case; opposite kinds of decisions also occur. However, this progression represents what *has* happened, what *can* happen, and what *may* be happening even more in the future. This progression also underlines certain patriarchal biases.

SUMMARY/JUDGMENT

Contemporary judges are biased against mothers in custody disputes.

In a contest, judges always favor paternal custody when the challenged mother is mentally ill or accused of a crime or of maternal inadequacy or "unfitness." Judges also favor paternal custody when the challenged mother accuses her *husband* of "mental illness" or of paternal "unfitness," including incest.

In a contest judges favor paternal custody when the challenged mother has less money than her ex-husband; less money than the unwed father of her child, or, in certain cases, less money than the child's sperm donor. Judges *also* favor paternal custody when the challenged mother works, has a "career," or has to move in order to work.

In a contest, judges favor paternal custody when the challenged mother commits adultery, lives with a man out of wedlock, or has an illegitimate child. Judges favor paternal custody when the challenged mother is a lesbian, holds minority political and religious opinions, or leads an "alternate" lifestyle.

In a contest, judges favor paternal custody when the father has remarried and the mother remains single. If, however, a mother remarries or if she needs to move in order to remarry, judges favor paternal custody to protect paternal "private property" from a stepfather's encroachments and in order to guarantee paternal visitation.

Judges favor paternal custody—when the challenged mother is against joint custody; is seen as interfering with paternal visitation (without necessarily moving away); when the children are over a certain age, or are boys.

Judges *do* favor maternal custody—when the challenged mother is the Virgin Mary: white, wealthy, and backed by her father, God.

INTERPRETATION

Are judges morally insane? To what extent are judges merely being "practical" when they award children to their economically superior fathers? Is there some other explanation even for the most morally outrageous custodial decision?

There may be. Traditional judges share an unacknowledged belief that men are more violent than women and that male-dominated "families" contain or minimize male violence. According to Louise Armstrong, male domestic violence is judicially unpunished because judges perceive "household violence . . . as *domesticated* violence, with the violence potential of less powerful males perceived as a fixed quantitative phenomenon which has to go *somewhere*. It would not hurt as a hedge to leave each individual male an 'appropriate' victim or two. This is the woman and child as lightning rod theory."[62]

Most judges are apparently convinced that the law cannot prevent or punish the male abandonment of women and children. They are convinced, however, that the law can be used to stem the tide of *female*-initiated divorce. Judges view mothers who abandon their husbands as genuine threats to public law and order. When judges custodially punish mothers for adultery, they specifically write about patriarchal marriage as the "bedrock" of social order.

Each mother who displeases or leaves her husband is refusing to absorb one man's potential for public violence. Such mothers are also setting a bad "example" for other women. Most important, since the state doesn't guarantee or enforce equal or comparable wages in the marketplace for women, most (single) mothers are fated to swell the state welfare rolls.

Judges represent the interests of the state, which is always unhappy about having to support the wives and children of (other) men or of independently "promiscuous" women. The state is also unhappy about having to subsidize the imprisonment, hospitalization, and survival of a growing number of male criminals, mental patients, and the unemployed. (Perhaps these are men whose wives abandoned them. . . .)

Judicial custodial decisions demonstrate the extent to which property rights are more valued than the rights of natural or sacred relationships, the extent to which a man's right to private property or to its psychological equivalent (a child) is more important than a woman's right of relationship to her own child, and more important than a woman's right to control her reproductive life, either before or during pregnancy and after childbirth.

Patriarchal law is a system of maintaining public law and order among *men*. It has traditionally been based on the legal sacrifice of women and children in the private realm. Judges are attempting to uphold *public* law and order when they render morally insane decisions in the *private* realm.[63]

CHAPTER FIFTEEN

Fetal Politics—Who Gets Custody of the "Test-Tube" Baby?: The Reproductive Rights of Husbands, Unwed Fathers, Sperm Donors— and of Women

JASON:
It would have been better far for men
To have got their children in some other way, and women
Not to have existed. Then life would have been good.

Euripides, *Medea*

Now
technological Paradise is within male
erotic grasp. Astronauts, both communist
and capitalist, lumber on the moon like
pregnant women, while scientists on earth
try to create life in baby-blue test tubes,
the color of death, the color of boys.

In museums, in marble silence, women are
hanging, beautifully clothed and beautifully naked,
painted by great artists who
loved the female body. Strange, how few of
them are pregnant.

Phyllis Chesler, *About Men*

"I grew up on an Indian reservation. When I was eighteen, I married the man who made me pregnant. He moved out soon after Michael was born. I vowed never to marry again. In fact, we never bothered to get divorced.

"By the time Michael was twelve, I owned my own home and business. When I fell madly in love with Carl, I refused to live with him. When I became pregnant by him, I refused to marry him. I did decide to have the baby.

"I consulted a lawyer to make sure that Carl would have no right to my business, my house, or to our love child. The lawyer said he'd never heard of an unwed father's demanding to baby-sit or pay child support. Carl attended the Lamaze classes with me. He was with me at Craig's birth. Then he just disappeared.

"Okay. I now had two wonderful sons and a serious cash-flow problem. For the next two years I worked seven days a week, selling real estate. Carl? Every so often he'd come by with friends and perch Craig on his shoulder for about an hour at a time. Very sexy.

"When Craig was three, I got us passports for a vacation in Europe. Eight hours before flight time Carl stomped in and forbade me to take Craig out of the country. We had a tremendous fight. Carl wanted me to sign my house over to him as collateral for 'his' son.

"Two months later when we returned, Carl's lawyer accused me of kidnapping Craig. He demanded legal recognition of Carl's paternity and custody. I spent hours trying to reason with Carl. Why pay all this money to a lawyer? What did he really want? What emerged was Carl's incredible anger at me for not marrying him in the first place and for being able to break away from him afterward.

"Carl is a white man. If we went before a judge, how would I—an Indian mother with a half-white illegitimate child—be treated? Craig could end up in foster care. Or with his father. So I agreed to let Carl visit Craig anytime he gave me twenty-four hours' notice. I agreed never to take Craig out of the country without Carl's permission.

"I was back on the reservation. Who are we anyway? We're only the Indians. He's the U.S. Cavalry and the U.S. government rolled into a few drops of very powerful sperm."

Does Carl really think of Craig as his "land"? Does the law support Carl's right to be a (bad) absentee landlord—in the hope that acknowledgment of "ownership" per se might persuade Carl to become a (good) absentee landlord? Does the "land" itself—i.e., the mother and child—have any self-determining rights? How can we think of a woman's body, a mother's labor, or a child's life as male genetic property?

Once, long ago, the male role in pro-creation was unknown or considered secondary to woman's. The earliest human idols were pregnant-bellied, birthing, or breast-feeding women. Mother goddesses (and priestesses) must have ruled the human imagination for a very long time.[1]

This all changed. Barbarous, unbridled female fertility was "bridled" for male economic and genetic gain. The relatively peaceful family of mother, daughter, and grand-daughter was replaced by the less peaceful family of father, son, and grand-son and by the rule of husbands.

Fathers sold their daughters to husbands as "colonizable" wombs. This profitable colonial arrangement was considered more "civilized" than non-colonial or non-male-dominated reproductive arrangements.[2]

The daughter of a wealthy father was sold to a wealthy husband. As such, she had slaves, servants, and status—among women. As the mother of a wealthy man's "legitimate" son, she had more than status. If she lived long enough, she could become her son's "political" ally. On his behalf she could "rule"—his wives and their children.

It was "civilized" of men to acknowledge and protect their "legitimate" children—considering that as a caste they had exclusive control of the means of production and reproduction. For more than 5,000 years the questionably civilized arrangement of patriarchal marriage has been woman's only reproductive option.

Patriarchal monotheism both glorified and reflected the "civilized" appropriation and colonization of pagan religions, cultures, peoples, lands, and natural resources. Patriarchal myths of pro-creation deified fathers and male genetic and spermatic fertility. They also denied, minimized, and suppressed the facts of female genetic and biological fertility.

Men were portrayed as the *spiritual* and therefore the *real* pro-creators of life; women, as the passive receptacles of divine sperm spirit. Male gods were able and willing to assume mortal flesh to save the world; women were nothing more than mortal flesh and could save no one.

For example, the Jewish Father-God Yahweh single-handedly "created" the world's first humans: Adam and Eve. Throughout the Old Testament fathers are "begetting" sons who "beget" more sons; rarely are mothers acknowledged for "begetting" daughters who "beget" more daughters.

In pagan Greece and Rome, and in Catholic Europe, philosophers, physicians, and scientists insisted that a mother was only the "nurse to live (male) seed" and that sperm was the "creative principle, the Vital Spark, the Idea that altered the dead matter of the female into the living soul."[3]

Until the nineteenth century the fetus was always drawn as a fully formed little man (a homunculus). People believed that sperm both caused and genetically controlled a woman's pregnancy.[4]

The Catholic Church viewed male human nature as corrupt and impure, female human nature as more so. A human soul, of woman born, was immortal only when baptized (spiritually birthed) by a male priest. An immortal soul was "legitimate" only if its parents had been married by a priest. Marriage became a church-controlled sacrament. Divorce was forbidden.

The church gradually outlawed both birth control and abortion. The church also condemned and executed many women midwives as "witches." The church—and an all-male medical profession—reaped the advantage of this persecution. Male physicians became the preferred midwives of the human race. For the first time in human history the control of birth technology was totally in male hands.*

WHAT ARE WOMEN'S TEN (REPRODUCTIVE) COMMANDMENTS?

1. A woman must remain a sexual virgin until she marries.
2. A woman must marry.
3. A wife must not have sexual intercourse with any man other than her legal husband.

---

*In a sense, children are a poor man's only economic and psychological "crop." Perhaps the church believed that if it could guarantee obedient wives and children to disenfranchised men, male church membership would grow; male violence would diminish; and well-obeyed husbands, although poor, could be persuaded to remain sexually and economically faithful to their wives and "legitimate" children. This church teaching is one important ingredient of female "piety."

4. A wife must have sexual intercourse with her legal husband "on demand."
5. A wife must not use any artificial birth control.
6. A wife must not have an abortion.
7. A wife must get pregnant.
8. A wife must give birth to as many of her husband's legal heirs as possible.
9. A wife must rear them as well.
10. If an unmarried woman or a wife engages in pre-marital or extramarital intercourse; if either woman is discovered to be using birth control or to have had an abortion; and if either woman gives birth to an "illegitimate" child, she will be seriously punished.

I cover these commandments, and the punishments for disobeying them, many times in this book, each time in a different context and for a different reason. Not every woman who has ever lived on earth had to obey all these commandments, nor was every disobedient woman punished—or punished in exactly the same way.

For 5,000 years most of the world's women were expected to obey some or all of these reproductive commandments and were punished for the slightest disobedience. I find this extraordinary—i.e., enraging and terrifying. Do you?

Such a system of compulsory reproduction can work only if women are absolutely repressed: physically, sexually, spiritually, psychologically, intellectually, militarily, politically, and economically. And so they have been.[5]

Obeying commandments is essentially an act of faith. Obedience is no guarantee of survival or of a dignified life. A reproductively obedient woman may remain unmarried and childless—through no fault of her own. She may be raped and become "illegitimately" pregnant—through no fault of her own. She may become "legitimately" pregnant and suffer a permanent loss of health—through no fault of her own. And she may die in childbirth—through no fault of her own.

A reproductively obedient woman may—through no fault of her own—find herself married to an impotent, celibate, homosexual, or openly adulterous husband, or to a husband who consorts with prostitutes, concubines, or mistresses. He may have other "illegitimate" children. A reproductively obedient woman's husband may do any or all of these things without endangering his reputation, his income, or his paternal rights.

An obedient wife dare not "complain" or initiate a divorce over such male behavior and dare not displease or disobey her husband, without risking her reputation, her income, and all access to her husband's "legitimate" children.

How have women come to terms with having no reproductive or economic alternative outside of husband-controlled motherhood? Like other enslaved or colonized groups, women have "made the best of it." They have, with a pathetic and savage loyalty, upheld their husbands' ideas as their own. Women have also dreamed of reproductive and economic "rescue"—in terms of marriage to *wealthy* (or kind-hearted or easily manipulatable) husbands.

Women and other colonized people are not stupid. It is often better to be the wife of a (kind) wealthy man than to be a (kind) poor man's wife; or to remain childless beneath a father's roof. Most women have viewed marriage as *more protective of motherhood* than are (poorly) paid positions in a hostile workplace.

Most women have viewed motherhood as more respected and as psychologically more rewarding than careers. Most women have "chosen" to have children, even though the "choice" is compulsory.

If a child's legal father abandons him, and if his mother remains behind to support and care for him, the child she cares for still "belongs" to her husband. A father may reclaim his children at some later date. They are the "products" of his sperm; they bear his name; he "owns" them, psychologically and/or legally.

Today, most people, when confronted with an analysis of marriage as women's *only* reproductive option, have several reactions. Some people agree that this is the way things should be—because God said so. Some people, less sure of what God said, view compulsory, married motherhood as an imperfect but still "practical" social arrangement.

For example, many women have died in childbirth; most women can't support children by themselves; men do need legal heirs for reasons of inheritance, etc. However, such reasons for maintaining legal paternity are only "practical"—*once men already control the means of production and reproduction.*

A newborn "orphan" can just as easily be reared by its maternal grandmother or uncle as by its father or paternal relatives; an anti-patriarchal or non-sexist society would not economically devastate mothers, etc.

For example, it is true that mothers and children need families. Whether mothers need *husbands*, and whether children actually "get" fathers or families because their mothers are married, are other questions.

When confronted by women's reproductive enslavement or women's lack of reproductive options outside of marriage, many people today claim that this *used* to be but is no longer true: "I had sex long before I was married"; "I never married"; "I've used birth control and had abortions"; "I committed adultery and never got caught"; "I decided not to have any children and I don't"; "My husband is much less interested in sex than I am"; "My husband is as involved in raising our children as I am"; "*I know someone* who had an illegitimate child, and it was accepted in her culture"; and "I was just considering artificial insemination or adoption as a single mother."

While such statements are undoubtedly true for those who make them, they are not true for most women. More important, women's sexual, obstetrical, or reproductive "choices" are historically and scientifically quite recent, not geographically universal, very fragile, and currently, as of 1986, under intense siege—not only in Teheran, Cairo, or Jerusalem, but in the United States of America.

More important, most women in the world do not have access to "quality" gynecological or obstetrical care; many women who do have been spiritually devastated by it. Both impoverished and more privileged women have also been maimed or killed by reproductive "advances," such as birth control pills and other (female) contraceptive devices.

The reproductive science that can potentially save or even "liberate" women may also result in the corporate, state, and scientific control of women as wombs, to be bred for racially and genetically "preferred" characteristics. Reproductive science in the hands of a woman-hating, racist, and profit-oriented state could lead to the extermination of racially or genetically despised women. It could also lead to the biological extinction of all womb-men.

An individual woman's reproductive enslavement to one man often includes his needing *her* as well as her womb. It also includes a paternal desire to have "his" children reared by their mother—if she remains an obedient wife. It often (50 percent of the time?) means that a father will protect and support his family to the best of his ability.

Individual men may still conceive of women as property and of children as a "profitable" enterprise. Individual men may also be obsessed with whether a child is genetically "theirs" or not. They may also be fiercely and "unconsciously" jealous of a woman's capacity to give birth to life. Imagine how these psycho-economic concerns might be expressed: impersonally and bureaucratically.*[6]

FETAL POLITICS IN AMERICA TODAY: THE CHURCH, THE STATE AND ABORTION

Abortion is a morally and psychologically "complex" issue—for men and for male-identified non-pregnant women. It is a simpler and more immediate issue for the pregnant woman of any ideological persuasion.

I believe that every pregnant woman must have the absolute right to choose whether to have an abortion or not—*for herself*. She is the one who bears the most *personal* responsibility for her child. Priests and politicians never do. Neither do her neighbors, relatives, friends—or her child's spermatic or genetic father. It is immoral to force a woman to bear a child against her will.

The question is: Can women exercise this option freely, legally, economically, and in a medically safe way—or only as "criminals" who risk imprisonment at the hands of church and state, and rape, unwanted sterilization, or death at the hands of illegal abortionists?

Some people believe that abortion is a sin and should therefore be a crime. The fight over whose view should and must be enforced is very intense.

The Catholic Church and its politically organized followers use certain "advances" in reproductive science to bolster their traditional fight against (female-controlled) abortion.† According to the church, the fetus, from the moment of (his) conception, still belongs to a male God and to (his) genetic father. A womb-man has no right to an abortion. The fetal "property" in question is not hers.

Some anti-abortion ideologues *are* concerned with everyone's "right to life" or to a viable life—even after birth. Such anti-abortion ideologues are not necessarily activists, nor do they represent or serve Vatican, capitalist, or national interests. They speak for those who are already among the living on earth but who are starving, malnourished, enslaved,

---

*I am not saying that the private (family) realm allows women more control over their reproductive bodies. I am saying that *both* public and private realms are opposed to women's control of their own bodies.

†Many Fundamentalist Protestants and Orthodox Jews are also involved and active in the fight against abortion.

imprisoned, tortured, homeless, unemployed, illiterate, and racially despised.

Such "right to life" ideologues are interpreting Christianity as a matter of individual conscience. As such they are, and always have been, at extreme risk. They are not as well organized as those anti-abortion activists who seem to have one item on their agenda: that of the white male fetus's "right to life."[7]

Much hinges on (or is hidden by) this single-item agenda. For example, single-issue activists believe that no one (female) should go unpunished for having sex or for refusing to bear a pregnancy.

To the best of my knowledge, there has been no organized attempt legally to forbid or psycho-economically to punish male masturbation or male coitus interruptus as a form of fetus murder or any legal attempt to punish unwed fathers or married fathers who abandon their children.

Single-issue activists seem more concerned with the "right to life" of white, but not black, fetuses. For example, if a white woman becomes pregnant by a white man (via incest, rape, or married or unmarried intercourse), she must go through with the pregnancy—for the sake of her unborn fetus, and as her punishment for having sex. If the pregnant white woman is unwed or underage, she must give up her baby to a legally married white couple—for the fetus's "own good" and as her punishment for having sex.

Poor and racially despised women do not have easily "adoptable" or equally "valuable" children. Such women must therefore pay for their own (legal) abortions or must undergo abortion or sterilization against their will—as their punishment for having sex or for wanting children.

Poor and racially despised mothers must work for less money than white or middle-class men; or must live in state-sanctioned poverty on "welfare"—their punishment for having sex or for wanting children.

Single-issue activists generally oppose government interference in family matters (such as incest, wife battering, or child abuse). They oppose government enforcement of equal pay for equal work within the church. However, they welcome the government as an ally in areas such as school prayer or tax exemption for church property.

Since abortion was legalized on January 22, 1973, these single-issue activists have demanded a full-scale government *invasion*—on behalf of the reproductive rights of men.

Within three years of legalized abortion, single-issue activists had

---

*This is the infamous Hyde Amendment (1976).

successfully cut off federal (Medicaid) funding for poor women's abortions. They attempted legally to overturn the Supreme Court ruling or to undermine its intention. Between 1973 and 1986 anti-abortion activists, as individuals and in groups, also tried legally to prevent individual abortions from taking place—sometimes on the ground of a father's future right to custody of the unborn fetus.

In 1983, when the Supreme Court upheld its 1973 (*Roe* v. *Wade*) decision legalizing abortion, the anti-abortion movement increased its propaganda and demonstrations against abortion clinics. Women patients and staff were verbally harassed, intimidated, threatened, and followed. Prominent priests condemned abortion week after week in widely publicized church sermons. (At the taxpayers' expense.)

Abortion was also targeted as the key issue of local and national political campaigns. A national "Right to Life" party was formed; and President Ronald Reagan and other anti-abortion political candidates across the country were reelected.

The climate that was created in no way deterred but in fact led to more violent acts against abortion. Women's medical facilities and abortion clinics were bombed or threatened with arson. Physicians and medical staff members were beaten and kidnapped. For a long time, the federal government refused to intervene in any vigorous way.[8]

Single-issue anti-abortion activists also tried another legal tactic. In 1983, an individual (male) lawyer, representing an anti-abortion group, sought a court order in New York State to require that surgery be performed on a mentally retarded, hydrocephalic, spina bifida newborn despite her physician's (and her parents') decision against surgical intervention. The U.S. government itself joined this lawyer and argued that the hospital in question was violating federal regulations by "discriminating" against handicapped patients.

This particular "Baby Jane Doe" case raises but does not answer many important questions. For example, if the federal government refuses to reimburse each state adequately for the long-term hospitalization of the handicapped, will the church or its politically organized followers do so? Are anti-abortion activists or the government ready to force the private sector to make a really significant contribution to the fetal or handicapped newborn's "right to life"?

Does the church or politically organized church followers have the right to decide for all of us that a seriously handicapped newborn is more economically "worthy" than an impoverished toddler who will die without an organ transplant—one that is far beyond her parents' economic reach? Or that the *life* of an unborn fetus or a handicapped newborn is more important and more economically "worthy" than is the *right* of all people to survival *and* to equal opportunities?

Does the church or politically organized church followers have the right to outlaw abortion without personally assuming economic and military protective obligations for all the children they force into birth or whose lives they prolong?

For that matter, does the state or private physicians have the right to deny poor women state-funded abortions? Do they have the right to sterilize or perform abortions on underage, poor, unwed, non-white, or impoverished women—without their informed consent or against their will?[9]

I am always humbled by those few individuals, male and female, who adopt seriously ill, handicapped, and racially despised children and personally rear them in loving ways. They are saints—who do not have the time for political or religious crusades. The rest of us are less saintly. Most of us are shortsighted, contradictory, hypocritical, and all too human. Some of us do not recognize a woman's absolute right to abortion. Some of us do. Some of us express our all too human selves in the voice of power. Most of us can't.

The Baby Jane Doe case demonstrates the considerable power that the combined forces of church and state have over individuals. At apparent issue is the *fetal* or *newborn* child's absolute right to life. At issue is not the "right to life" for all human beings. (Would that it were!) If it were, then these very same single-issue anti-abortion activists who represent large political powers would try to be as creatively concerned with ending the corporate and state murder of fetuses, newborns, *and* adults in wars of class, race, religion, and gender.

They would certainly be concerned with a woman's absolute right to live without having to bear a child against her will.

FETAL POLITICS IN AMERICA TODAY: THE CHURCH, THE STATE, AND ARTIFICIAL INSEMINATION; SPERM BANKS; SURROGATE MOTHERHOOD; AND IN VITRO FERTILIZATION

Artificial Insemination and Sperm Banks

In 1884, Dr. William Pancoast, an American physician, treated a married couple for sterility by using the sperm of a medical student to fertilize the (etherized and unconscious!) wife. A successful pregnancy resulted. Dr. Pancoast told the husband, but not the wife, of the artificial insemination. The husband was pleased. The action was supported by the medical profession: four out of every five men in New York City were, at the time, afflicted with venereal disease.[10]

Today artificial insemination is a booming industry that caters to the individual male, but not to the individual female, control of reproduction. Many single women do not have the money or the health coverage that infertility tests and surgery require. Many physicians and sperm banks refuse to service unmarried women or first require a husband's permission for insemination. Out of respect for male (genetic) pride, a husband's sperm is usually mixed in with donor sperm.[11]

Surrogate Mothers for Hire

The popularity of surrogate motherhood is based on women's economic poverty, male genetic narcissism, and the greed of lawyers, physicians, and other "middlemen." Wealthy white married couples or misogynist men can now bypass adoption agency scrutiny in their pursuit of a "blond, blue-eyed, and college-educated womb" for hire.

> Surrogate babies, remember, are brought to us by the same professionals who gave us the concept of "illegitimate babies"—that is, a baby is only as real as the father's identity. The issue of surrogate mothers, as it turns around in my mind, is not the issue at all.
>
> Racism is the issue, and why thousands of babies come to be "unsuitable." Ownership is the issue, and the conceit of patriarchal genetics. "Barren women" are the issue, and why some women must come to feel an excruciating sense of failure because they cannot bear a child. "Saving a marriage" is the issue, and why some marriages might not be worth saving for the cost of a child. And guilt and money, and how women earn both, are the issues that need honest attention.[12]

The surrogate mother industry raises more questions than anyone can currently answer. For example, can a surrogate mother keep her genetic baby if she changes her mind? Can she sell a baby to a couple who operate a child brothel? To a single mother who lives in a lesbian collective? To a wealthy homosexual couple? To the highest bidder?

What happens if a surrogate mother subsequently discovers she can have no more genetic children of her own? Would she be entitled to visitation or custody of the child she "sold"? What would happen if a couple rented a woman's womb and they then divorced? Who would be the child's legal (and financial) custodian?[13]

Could the genetic father force a surrogate mother to abort? Could he refuse to honor his financial obligation to her or to the infant if *he* decided to "have the abortion"? Could he successfully be sued for child support? By whom?

There is actually a case that illustrates how many things can go wrong when a fertile man with an infertile wife turns to a surrogate mother. In 1982, Judy Stiver agreed to bear Alexander Malahoff's genetic child for $10,000. Malahoff also paid a lawyer $5,000 for "arranging" Judy Stiver's services. In January 1983, Mrs. Stiver gave birth to a microcephalic, brain-damaged boy, suffering from a severe infection.

Malahoff was present at the delivery, as was Judy's husband, Ray Stiver. (Only Mrs. Malahoff, the legal mother-to-be, wasn't there.) Malahoff signed the birth certificate. However, according to hospital physicians, Malahoff then refused to allow the administration of life-saving treatment to "his" child. "Let the baby die and have another one for me," Judy Stiver alleged he said. Unlike the physicians in the 1983 Baby Jane Doe case, these physicians performed surgery.[14]

Amazingly the newborn's blood type bore no relation to Alexander Malahoff's. The boy was the genetic child of Judy and Ray Stiver! Malahoff withheld the agreed-upon $10,000, renounced all custodial rights and obligations, and proceeded to sue the Stivers for breach of contract. In turn, the Stivers sued their inseminating physician, whose orders they followed precisely.

Suppose Malahoff had rejected his obligations to a "defective" child and Judy's husband had done the same? Whose child would he be? Suppose the newborn had died after Malahoff had forbidden any life-saving treatment? Could Malahoff be prosecuted for murder if it was discovered that the child was not "his" to kill? (Could he still be prosecuted for murder if the child *was* his to kill?) Suppose Malahoff had taken custody of a healthy child and years later discovered that the child wasn't genetically "his"? Could Malahoff have successfully sued the Stivers for fraud or for "back" child support?

I do not have the moral or legal "answers" to these questions. Nor does anybody else. Clearly, reproductive advances have been made in an absolute moral vacuum. Just as clearly, this fact has contributed to, rather than restrained, the forces of economic greed and genetic narcissism.

In Vitro Fertilization and Test-Tube Babies

In vitro fertilization is the fertilization of egg and sperm outside the womb—literally "in glass." This technique can allow a woman to give birth successfully, even if her fallopian tubes are blocked.[15] Once an egg has been fertilized outside a woman's body, it is possible to relocate and "house" the fetus in another womb or ultimately in a test tube.

A surrogate mother could be hired for gestation alone. A married or wealthy enough genetic mother, for reasons of health or personal preference, could still have a genetic child without experiencing pregnancy or childbirth. A woman could experience pregnancy and give birth to her husband's (and another woman's) genetic child.

This procedure raises but does not answer exceedingly complex moral and legal questions. For example, will the child's identity be determined legally, genetically, socially, or in terms of pregnancy and gestation? Is a child conceived "in glass" the "property" of the genetic mother, the pregnant mother, the birthing mother, the social mother—or no woman at all? What if a test-tube embryo is "orphaned" long before birth by the death of its genetic parents? Who has the power of life or death over such an embryo?[16]

What will women's fate really be in an era of test-tube babies—i.e., in an era of male *scientific* control of reproduction? What will happen to women when men can reproduce genetic children of the preferred race and sex without having to marry or share custodial rights with a wife?

In 1983, the American Society for the Advancement of Science considered the scientific techniques of animal breeding in terms of their human application. Dr. Roberta Steinbacher noted: "[Sex-selection procedures favor and reflect people's preference for boys over girls.] There may soon be as many as 140 boys born for every 100 girls in the United States. The implications for women are catastrophic."[17]

There is nothing intrinsically "wrong" with a scientist's pursuit of knowledge. There is nothing "wrong" with a physician's alleviating suffering, saving lives, or, upon a patient's informed request, performing an abortion or providing contraception. There is nothing "illegal" about profiting from scientific knowledge or selling medical services for money.*

I am not saying that individual reproductive scientists or physicians are consciously engaged in a conspiracy *not* to empower women. On the contrary. Many women are the immediate and grateful beneficiaries

---

*It is, of course, immoral to withhold such services from the involuntarily impoverished.

of such procedures as amniocentesis, genetic testing, and artificial insemination. However, reproductive technology is part of the larger (unconscious) conspiracy against the female *control* of reproduction.

Despite the sympathy of individual physicians or scientists toward individual female patients, the reproductive industry strengthens the (professional) male control of reproduction and renders an increasing number of male and female consumers dependent on an all-male and patriarchal reproductive technology.

Reproductive science is not value-free, nor is it available to all. Some women have contraception, sterilization, and abortion forced upon them—against their will, in America and *by* America, elsewhere in the world, when they are poor, unwed, imprisoned, or women of color.

Technology has not been used to solve the infertility problems of such women or to raise their standard of living so that the children they do have (or want) won't die in utero or of malnutrition, poverty, and from other forms of man-made and therefore avoidable violence.[18]

The danger of reproductive technology in the hands of the modern state, church, and multinational corporation lies in how vulnerable *individuals* are to such increasingly organized and poorly checked powers. The reproductive scientists are themselves equally vulnerable.

Only certain kinds of research and certain kinds of researchers get funded. More important, the researchers who do get funded have no control over how their findings are used. For example, those American scientists who researched atomic energy were powerless to veto the government's political and military use of their research. The scientists researching infertility or the prevention of genetic defects will have as little say over the ultimate use of their work.

WOMEN-CONTROLLED REPRODUCTIVE OPTIONS: ARTIFICIAL INSEMINATION, VOLUNTARY UNWED MOTHERHOOD, AND SINGLE-MOTHER ADOPTION

Artificial Insemination

Shulamith Firestone, Marge Piercy, Martha E. Gimenez, and others have viewed artificial reproduction—i.e., test-tube babies—as potentially in women's and children's interest.

How else can women escape compulsory biological motherhood, legal marriage, and solitary child rearing; how else can biologically "humiliated" men enter child rearing as "equals"? How else can we maximize voluntary motherhood and fatherhood as a socially productive skill?[19]

Although it is legally and economically difficult for single and non-husband-controlled women to purchase many reproductive services, a growing number of such women have begun to do so. Who, after all, can stop an unmarried woman from purchasing medically administered sperm or from impregnating herself at home privately?

Kay is a thirty-year-old unwed lesbian mother. She inseminated herself with a turkey baster, using sperm that was privately donated to her in "little jars." She said:

"When I was twenty-six, I decided that having a biological child was the most important thing to me. I solved the problem of sperm by asking Greg, a local gay rights activist, to donate his. 'I don't want to go to a sperm bank and be turned down because I'm single or gay. I don't have the money a private doctor may charge for long-term artificial insemination.'

"Greg agreed to help me. 'I don't want a child,' he said. 'But I like the idea of knowing that my genes will live on.' Greg brought over little jars of sperm twice a month for four months. Once I became pregnant, we didn't see each other anymore.

"I knitted about two dozen baby 'thingies.' I painted the house inside and out. I built a cradle and a rocking horse. I was whistling-happy for the first time in my life. Even my old collective said I could leave the baby with them for a few hours at a time to 'get my head together.'

"Starchild was born in six hours. I was home the same day. After six months I ran out of savings. I didn't want to leave Star and return to my full-time job. I got a part-time job in a nearby food co-op and applied for partial welfare.

"When Star was about a year old, we bumped into Greg on the street. 'Is that my baby?' he asked. 'I guess so,' I said. About a week later Greg dropped by. He said he wanted to develop a relationship with Star. 'That wasn't our agreement,' I said. 'I know,' he said, 'but I've changed my mind.' 'It's not what I want,' I said. 'But it's what I want,' he said. 'I spoke to a lawyer. She thinks I have some rights here. I'm not saying we have to live together. I'll just take him home once or twice a week until he's old enough to decide where he'd like to be. . . .'

"My life became a nightmare. How could I teach Star to trust and love women if he were 'fathered' by a man who didn't even relate to women?

Or to me? What if Star learned to love Greg and Greg again changed his mind about being a father?

"I was trapped in the courts for two years. I was pretty optimistic. How could a court say that a sperm donor whom I never slept with and who hadn't wanted to be a father was now a 'father'? Is the donation of sperm equivalent to fatherhood?

"The judge ruled that Greg was Star's 'father' and entitled to one full day a week of visitation. Actually, the state sold Star to his sperm donor for one hundred dollars a month. That's what Greg agreed to pay the welfare department.

"Does the child of my body belong to any man willing to pay a hundred dollars a month for it? Does my decision about how to mother count for absolutely nothing? The answers are obvious. What can I do about it? That's the really hard part."

Voluntary Unwed Motherhood and Single-Mother Adoption

Unwed motherhood has traditionally been tabooed among white and middle-class American women. "Illegitimate" children have been more readily accepted by black African, black Caribbean, and some Spanish-speaking South American (poor) families in the United States.

In a 1982 study, Dr. Sydelle Levy confirmed the extent to which many white and more non-white pregnant teenagers were choosing unwed motherhood in order to escape their mothers' domination, to have "someone to love," and to achieve instant maturity. In addition, Dr. Levy said: "These girls were very clear about not wanting to marry their boyfriends. They didn't want to have to take care of them, too, or put up with their violence, drugs, sexual philandering, and possessiveness. They wanted to be independent of men as well as of their mothers. They wanted children, not masters."[20]

During the 1970s and early 1980s, many non-white pregnant teenagers continued to have and to keep their "illegitimate" babies. An increasing (and unknown) number of white, middle-class, educated, "older," career, lesbian, and feminist women also chose unwed (biological and adoptive) motherhood.

Why would such women voluntarily choose unwed motherhood—a condition that has traditionally been tabooed, impoverished, and persecuted?

First, unmarried women's traditional access to children and family life has diminished as the result of the collapse of the extended family and a job-related increase in geographical "scattering."

Secondly, married women's traditional access to children and family life has diminished because of an increase in male and female infertility and an increase in male- and female-initiated divorce.

Thirdly, heterosexual women's access to children and family life has diminished as the result of an apparent increase in male homosexuality, male uninterest in marriage or fatherhood, and male uninterest in marriage to "older," "career" women.

Fourthly, because of reproductive and economic "advances" for women, both lesbians and heterosexual women can have children at "older" ages, when they are better able to support them independently. A number of women who are unmarried, infertile, and unable or unwilling to experience pregnancy (via artificial insemination or heterosexual intercourse) are choosing single-mother adoptions.[21]

WHAT DID I LEARN FROM MY INTERVIEWS WITH VOLUNTARILY UNWED MOTHERS?

I interviewed ten white mothers who voluntarily chose unwed motherhood. Fifty percent were biological mothers; 50 percent, adoptive mothers. Of the ten, 70 percent had middle-class professions. Of the ten, 50 percent were heterosexual, 20 percent were bisexual, and 30 percent were lesbians. They became mothers for the first time between the ages of twenty-one and thirty-eight.

Of the heterosexual mothers, 30 percent had wanted children within traditional legal marriage. When each woman reached her mid-thirties "without a man in sight," she decided to have a child alone.

Paula: I heard my biological clock ticking away by the time I was thirty-four. I convinced my boyfriend to get me pregnant. I guess I kept hoping he'd want to live with me after I gave birth. He didn't. I really think a child needs a father, but I couldn't give birth to a father. I could only give birth to a child.

Fay: I looked for a husband all through my thirties. Now, I have less time and energy to look than before. Friends tell me that Andrew doesn't need a father as much as I need a lover. I don't regret adopting a child. The burden is enormous, but it's worth it to me. I was born to mother.

Sybil and Myra are lesbian feminists. Both are "older," "career" women.

Sybil: My son's father was a graduate school classmate. We had an affair of convenience. He moved on when I became pregnant. But I'm not sure what to do now. I want another child, but I don't relate to men sexually. I could go through the hassle of shaving my legs and armpits to make myself attractive to men for a few one-night stands. I'm leaning toward artificial insemination because I don't like the inconvenience and danger involved in one-night stands. I don't want to take the risk of getting beaten or killed or contracting a venereal disease. I really don't want to risk letting a man be physically or psychologically part of my pregnancy.

Myra: I adopted a girl. I'm guilty that my daughter's birth mother was probably too poor to keep her. But adoption is the safest course. No unwed father or sperm donor can turn up.

Martha became pregnant at eighteen as the result of a love affair. She decided to keep her baby and rear her in a "perfect" alternative environment. Martha lived in a series of rural communes. She and her daughter were vegetarians, never watched television, never went to violent movies.

Despite her alternative values, Martha was a psychologically traditional mother. Like many married mothers, Martha was ultimately amazed by her teenage daughter's pendulum-swing rebelliousness. "Kendra wants us to go to church together. She wants me to be a stereotyped mother: married and willing to pamper her endlessly. She sees her friends being chauffeured everywhere. She wants to know why she can't have that, too. I refuse to be turned into a classic mother where she absorbs me like a sponge."

IS UNWED MOTHERHOOD A REAL REPRODUCTIVE OPTION FOR WOMEN?

Unwed motherhood, whether it is voluntary or involuntary, is still tabooed and under-subsidized. Voluntarily white single adoptive mothers of racially despised children are slighly more "respected" than are unwed white or non-white biological mothers, who have obviously had sex outside marriage and who have not undertaken any economic responsibility for the wretched of the earth.

Unwed mothers may not have to serve or please husbands. If a boy-friend or a sperm donor is unaware of a child's existence, or if a woman has adopted a child as a single mother, she does not risk domestic violence or an expensive custody battle at the hands of an *individual* father. She is, however, vulnerable to such violence at the hands of the *collective* male state.

For that matter, without enough inherited or securely earned money, single, married, and unwed mothers all are at the custodial mercy of the male (welfare) state or of any sperm donor who covets their wealth.

Whether a mother is voluntarily wed or unwed, she still has very little control over her child's acquisition of values. An absent father, through the dominant (male) culture, may influence a mother's child with relative ease.*

Children satisfy human longings for genetic immortality, intimacy, authority, and family life. The father-dominated family currently exists under intense reproductive siege. In view of their helplessness in the face of poverty, war, exile, chemical pollution, and planetary extinction, individual men and women need to control the "small" things—i.e., the family unit and children.[22]

This may be one of the reasons that church members who are also unpaid housewives have been anti-abortion activists.[23] This may also account for the worldwide increase in or commitment to traditional family life and for the apparent increase in paternal child kidnappings and custody battles.

Many men feel powerless. If such powerlessness gentles men; if it leads them into a less authoritarian or territorial relationship to each other and to women and children, so much the better. If it leads men into more and more violent confrontations with each other, and with women, for exclusive possession or control over the "small" things, so much the worse for us all.

The male hubris that conceived of women and children as property is the same male hubris that colonized Nature in order to turn Her "profitable," is the same male hubris that expertly supplanted women as midwives, is the same male hubris that has brought us to the brink of nuclear catastrophe, and is the same male hubris involved in appropriating the reproductive process itself.

---

*Fathers may have slightly more influence over children than mothers when it comes to *opposing* the dominant and public culture. However, like individual mothers, individual fathers are relatively powerless against the dominant culture.

CHAPTER SIXTEEN

Mothers in Prison

Most women are in prison for trying to get money. Those who actually make money and get caught doing it are in jail. That's the crime.

A man can drop his seed and walk. Who is left with the responsibility for the babies? Welfare ain't going to do it. Welfare won't give enough. So any mother that cares anything about her family and herself is going to have to make ends meet. Any way you can. Any way you can. I have done it more times than I would like to remember.

—Elaine, an ex-prisoner

The Department of Corrections is in custody of everyone who is in their custody. They are also in custody of all of their possessions. If they happen to have watches on their arms or whatever else, the department has custody of it. If they happen to have children in their bodies, then the department is inescapably in custody of them. What else could you say?

—Florida Judge Carven Angel, September 12, 1980[1]

WHAT HAPPENS WHEN a "good enough" mother commits a *legal* crime? What if she steals food, forges a check, or illegally flees the state with her incestuously abused child? What if she (illegally) rents her body to a man for money? What if she robs a store, kills her husband in self-defense, or cheats the state welfare department?

Once a mother is arrested for a legal crime, she is automatically separated from her child. Mothers who are accused of legal crimes are always and automatically punished custodially. This, in fact, sets the psychological and judicial standard for the custodial punishment of all "uppity" mothers.

In a custody battle between a mother and father, maternal adultery or a maternal career may be viewed as custodially punishable "crimes." In a custody battle between a mother and the state, maternal prostitution or check-forging is similarly viewed.*

The husband-punished mother may be stripped of her maternal identity, her self-esteem, her normal relationship to her children, her home, and her standard of living. However, she still retains her physical freedom and her right to vote, to travel, to work, or even to begin life "anew." She may also retain access to her children.

By contrast, a state-punished mother is not allowed to see her children often, regularly, or at all. She may lose them legally and forever. A prisoner-mother also loses her freedom and certain civil rights while she is imprisoned or forever afterward. She may lose the rights to vote, travel abroad, move to another state, legally carry arms, join the civil service, be employed in any but the most menial or prisoner-related of jobs, or to "associate" with other ex-prisoners.

As we shall see, most mothers in prison have not committed violent crimes. They have most often stolen Jean Valjean's "loaf of bread."† As impoverished, unwed, and racially despised "welfare wives" they have protested and disobeyed their state husband's decree of poverty, humility, and chastity. They are utterly vulnerable to state punishment.

In a sense, the *welfare* system is how mothers are punished for the

---

*Maternal lesbianism is viewed and often custodially punished in much the same way that maternal drug addiction is. Both behaviors are seen as medical diseases. If the drug addict (or the lesbian mother) repents and promises not to take drugs (or live openly with another woman), then, under conditions of perpetual surveillance, she may be allowed to live with her children.

†Jean Valjean is the hero of Victor Hugo's novel *Les Miserables*.

"crime" of being born female and becoming pregnant. The *prison* system is how poor or welfare mothers are further punished when they disobey male legal authority.

WHO ARE THE WOMEN IN PRISON?

Of all North American women in prison, 60 to 75 percent are women of color (black, brown, red, or yellow) or Spanish-speaking. They are very young and very poor. More than half are single mothers living on welfare.[2]

WHAT CRIMES HAVE THESE MOTHERS COMMITTED?

Have these young, poor black mothers shot into a crowd from a high tower perch? Have they assassinated a president or kidnapped a millionaire for ransom? Have they raped, mutilated, or killed other women or men? Have they forced children into prostitution? Have they stabbed men or women to death while drinking and brawling in a bar?

Have these young, poor non-white mothers been convicted as the armed bodyguards, assassins, or master profiteers of organized crime? Have they embezzled millions from corporate investors and fled the country? Have they been convicted for government corruption?

Have these young, poor single mothers battered, raped, or killed one husband after the other: sadistically or for money? Have they bigamously married lonely widowers to trick them out of their life savings? Have they committed incest or sexually abused their children?

The majority of women in prison have not done any of these things— not even as their boyfriends' accomplices. *Most women have committed petty economic (and victimless sexual) crimes.* According to attorney Charlene Snow, "The majority of women in prison are there for economic crimes. . . . If jobs at living wages had been available to women prisoners, many women would not have committed the crimes for which they are imprisoned."[3]

Attorney Ann Stanton studied mothers in prison and on probation in four California counties. In 1980, the majority were categorized as property offenders. She noted: "The jail mothers' property offenses included both petty and grand theft, in addition to forgery, embezzlement, credit card offenses and welfare fraud. Property offenses for the probation mothers were mostly welfare fraud and forgery."[4]

According to Sister Eileen Hogan, a New York prison chaplain, in 1981, a (white) mother was sentenced to a year in prison for stealing $12 worth of cube steaks. "It was her fourth such offense. The judge had warned her. She has five children and lives on welfare. The kids were farmed out to five different foster homes. She'll face an enormous and uncaring bureaucracy to get each of them back."[5]

In 1983, a Massachusetts mother was imprisoned in Framingham for welfare fraud. Her three-and-a-half-year-old son had special medical needs. She was arrested and convicted for trying to meet those needs by collecting welfare checks from three different states.[6] According to attorney Ellen Barry:

> Mothers in prison are often there specifically because they care about their children and are unwilling to allow their children to be deprived. Which one of us would be willing to stand idly by while our children went hungry? Which one of us could stand to see our son or daughter suffer from inadequate food, from poor housing or from insufficient clothing?[7]

Dorothy Zeitz, in *Women Who Embezzle or Defraud*, found that such women did not engage in prior criminal activities. They legally "violated a trust" in order "to bring assistance when children or husbands were in jeopardy; the men [who embezzled] sought to solve their own problems."[8]

In Stanton's 1980 study, one-quarter of the convictions were narcotics offenses.[9] Susan Reed, a corrections officer, describes the "typical" female prisoner today as someone who

> comes into the corrections system at about age twelve, having run away from home and been knocked up. Her child is taken away from her and she's told that she's a terrible person. She's locked up for a year or two, then she gets out and spends her time, sometimes successfully, trying to get her child back. Then she's knocked up again and returned to custody for some petty offense; she is doped up on Thorazine to keep her docile and told again how terrible she is; her kids are taken away. By the time she's nineteen, she probably has three kids and a heroin habit, and she's turning some tricks to support them. Then she's told that she's a lesbian because for eighteen out of every twenty-four months of her life since age twelve she has been locked up with other women, and her only contact with men has been when they've knocked her up in her time out. She'll go on in this life as long as she can take it, but her initial crime—the offense that got her into this life in the first place—was simply being female.[10]

AREN'T ANY WOMEN IN PRISON FOR COMMITTING VIOLENT CRIMES?

Only 3 percent of Stanton's interviewees were convicted of "manslaughter"; 5 percent of "assault" or "assault with a deadly weapon." In 1981, attorney Charlene Snow challenged the myth that more women are committing violent crimes than ever before. Snow asserted that the majority of women convicted of violent crimes

> are not women who have become assertive as a result of the feminist movement, but rather . . . it has been found that women usually kill men, not other women, and that women who are charged with homicide have the least extensive criminal records. A study of women in Chicago's Cook County Jail found that 40% of the women arrested for murder, voluntary manslaughter, or involuntary manslaughter were battered women. All had undergone severe beatings over a number of years. All of the women had called the police on numerous occasions because of the beatings. It should be noted that only 4 out of the 53 battered women interviewed were found not guilty.[11]

Attorney Joan Potter has noted: "Most of the women prisoners convicted of violent crimes [in North Carolina] were involved in assaults or murders of husbands and boyfriends. The majority came from rural, farming backgrounds, and, as in other states, their crimes were often based on 'violence to them over a long period of time.' "[12]

In colonial America, the punishment for a wife who killed her husband was death, as was the punishment for a slave who killed her master. The murder of a husband was apparently considered a form of treason, comparable to the murder of a king.[13]

Husband murder today is still treated as a form of regicide. Unprovoked wife murder is still treated as the prerogative or sport of kings. Wives who defend their children or themselves from violent men are imprisoned and separated from their children. They are most of the mothers in prison for "violent" crimes.

For example, in 1972, a midwestern mother fought back when her husband threatened their baby's life.

> He had beaten her repeatedly, and on the night of his death he locked her in the house, smashed the telephone into fragments, and beat her severely. When she thought he was going to attack the baby, she shot him. The jury's verdict was not unsympathetic; they had been moved by the testimony of the dead man's mother who asked that her daughter-in-law not be punished.

She was an exemplary wife and mother, the older woman said, while since his return from the army, her own son had been violent and "not himself." Nevertheless, the judge handed down the maximum sentence: ten years.[14]

In another 1970s case, a Massachusetts woman was convicted of manslaughter for shooting her fiancé when he threatened to beat her and her son.

She fled to the basement of her house to join her son and daughter, and when Feruzzo [the fiancé] kept coming, she shot him. Massachusetts law, however, requires that the defendant retreat as far as possible to avoid violence; and Roberta Shaffer had only retreated as far as the basement. Shaffer argued that she could not retreat farther with her young children, and she would not leave them behind; but in 1976 the Massachusetts Supreme Court upheld her conviction.[15]

In 1976, Luz Santana was sentenced in New York State to fifteen years to life for allegedly murdering her abusive stepfather. She steadfastly maintained her innocence. She said: "The most prominent piece of evidence presented to the jurors was a standing court Order of Protection which had been granted to my mother due to my stepfather's assaultive behavior."[16]

Luz, a mother herself, was separated from her son. Her mother not only was separated from Luz but was forced, despite poor health and advancing age, to assume sole responsibility for her grandson. Luz said: "My own child has missed out on his childhood, having to assume household responsibilities. His scholastic achievement has suffered. The question arises as to the absolute need for my ongoing incarceration, when in fact I can be fulfilling a positive and constructive role within my own family nucleus."[17]

In 1978, after a long history of marital battering, many orders of protection, and a divorce, Herman Smith "pulled a gun on [his ex-wife, Bernadette], kidnapped her, and threatened to have her pumped full of heroin—so he could get custody of their seven year old son." He drove to a motel, harangued Bernadette for another hour at gunpoint, and then fell asleep.

Bernadette Powell said that she was trying to take the gun from her ex-husband's pants so she could flee, when he started up and she pulled the trigger. He died almost instantly of a single .22 caliber bullet through the heart. Despite the murder charges filed against her, Bernadette Powell seemed confident. Neither she nor her nonchalant attorney were [sic] quite prepared for the case the prosecutor presented against her.[18]

New York State District Attorney Joseph Joch presented Bernadette as a "masochist" and a "nagging wife" who "provoked" her husband to violence by her "castrating" and "manipulative" behavior. Joch produced one male witness who, unknown to the jury, had "battered *his* wife into a hospital." He produced several male witnesses "who had been charged with a series of assaults against women, including rape."

All the while, locked in the files of the New York Supreme Court, was a private and apparently unrelated document: a transcript of proceedings only a month before when complainant Marie De Jong-Joch obtained an uncontested divorce from District Attorney Joseph Joch after almost nine years of marriage. In the uncontested proceedings, the district attorney's wife alleged that her husband had brutally and violently beaten, hit, punched, dragged, pushed, and struck her, no less than thirteen times, and tried to hit her with his car.

Beaten-wife Bernadette Powell, zealously prosecuted by the same Joe Joch, was convicted of second-degree murder and sentenced to fifteen years to life in prison.[19]

As of this writing, Bernadette Powell remains in prison in New York State.

ARE FEWER AND LESS "VIOLENT" WOMEN PERCEIVED AS MORE NUMEROUS AND MORE VIOLENT THAN VIOLENT MALE CRIMINALS?

Women in prison constitute 3 to 4 percent of the number of men in prison.[20] As we have noted, the majority of women are imprisoned for (petty) economic and victimless "sexual" crimes and for crimes of self-defense. Nevertheless, when we think of imprisoned women, images of Lucrezia Borgia, Lizzie Borden, Ma Barker, Bonnie of Bonnie and Clyde (certainly not Bonnie and Maizie) come to mind.* We also assume that the most innocent of women is doomed to become a "babe in the big

---

*We also think of Belle Starr, Polly Adler, and Mata Hari as sexual "outlaws." Sometimes we think of Ilse Koch, a sadistic Nazi prison *guard*.

house," a "female animal behind bars"—anyway, once she's imprisoned with other hardened women criminals.

It is obvious that the most violent criminals are men, whom other men and women sometimes find "glamorous" or "pitiable." ("There but for the grace of God go I.") Male criminals are often seen as similar to other men—only more so. Men "root" for Robin Hood, Jesse James, the Godfather, and James Bond, as heroes who have managed to beat the "legal" system at its own game or as individualists who heroically oppose a vastly more powerful (and hypocritical) social order.

Some men identify with the "dark satanic" impulses of a rapist, a wife batterer, or a wife killer; with the loneliness of the half-crazed killer of whole families "in cold blood"; and with literary murderers who have themselves been abused "in the belly of the beast."

Some middle-class and "liberal" lawyers arrange bail, legal committees, conjugal visits, paroles, work releases, and rehabilitation programs for the (male) criminals of their choice. These lawyers do not rob banks or hijack planes; nor do they kill anybody, including their wives. However, they may have recognized themselves or a deserving humanity in common with the men who did do such things.

Decent men forgive themselves and simultaneously satisfy their own criminal fantasies when they defend or sympathize with mass murderers, wife killers, etc. These same men, and their female professional counterparts, rarely *identify* with or defend women criminals.* Mothers who have heroically defended themselves and their children against male violence remain invisible and unheroized. If they are remembered at all, it is often with the disgust that should be—but isn't reserved for cold-blooded killers.

DOES THIS DOUBLE STANDARD OF PERCEIVED VIOLENCE RESULT IN A DOUBLE STANDARD OF PUNISHMENT?

Women are punished more swiftly and more severely than men for "male" crimes, such as spouse murder, child kidnapping, embezzle-

---

*In fact, some women even fall in love with the male killers of their choice. They attend their trials, correspond with them, subsidize their legal defenses, and sometimes propose marriage. This is essentially embarrassing: this woman's chase after Bluebeard. Such women are doing what women are taught to do with *legally* violent men who do not get imprisoned. They "embarrass" us by pointing out our own hypocrisy.

ment, bank robbery, and political terrorism. Women are also exclusively punished for "female" crimes, such as prostitution, adultery, and unwed motherhood, and for having abortions. Women are often punished more severely for "female" crimes than men are for "male" crimes.*[21]

In 1978 Dan White killed two prominent men in San Francisco: Mayor George Moscone and Supervisor Harvey Milk. White argued that he was "temporarily insane" because of all the "junk food" he ate. In 1979, White was sentenced to serve seven years for voluntary manslaughter. He became eligible for parole and was released early in 1984.†

Let us compare this with the equally notorious case of Jean Harris. In 1981, *after a year in prison,* Harris was convicted of second-degree murder for shooting Dr. Hyman Tarnower, her physician lover. The "Diet Doctor" had sadistically tormented Harris and addicted her to amphetamines for twelve years. Unlike Dan White, Jean Harris did not plead "temporary insanity" caused by her serious drug addiction. She was convicted of second-degree murder and sentenced to fifteen years to life. She has not been allowed out on bail. As of this writing, she remains behind bars.

During war, even extreme male murderousness is not punished as a legal crime. For example, in 1970 Lieutenant William Calley was court-martialed for the March 16, 1968, My Lai massacre of 206 Vietnamese villagers—mainly women and children. The army placed Calley under "house arrest" with all the privileges of "home," and assisted him in preparing his defense. Calley was sentenced to five to ten years of such "house arrest." By 1975 he was a totally free man.

During war, male "excesses" such as rape or consorting with prostitutes are not always treated as legal crimes. During peace, all officers are supposed to obey stringent army orders—women more so than men. For example, in 1982, the military court-martialed Lieutenant Joanne Newak and sentenced her to three years in Fort Leavenworth. Newak's crime? She had allegedly kissed another woman off base; and had allegedly possessed a small amount of over-the-counter diet pills and marijuana off base. Despite her good conduct record, the military au-

*There always are certain exceptions to this rule. The white wives and daughters of wealth are never as heavily punished as are the black and white daughters of poverty. However, some white/wealthy daughters are scapegoated—i.e., are treated as stand-in sacrifices for their fathers or their class.[22]
†The maximum punishment for this conviction is seven years, eight months. Here, I am picking those cases that were so well publicized that people will remember them. Countless similar and lesser known cases also exist.

thorities did not assist Newak as they had Calley, nor did they place her under privileged "house arrest" before, during, or after her trial. Newak was released after serving a full year of her sentence—probably due to the continued coverage of her plight by journalists.[23]

WHAT IS PRISON LIKE?

Prison. What if you're locked in your cell and a fire breaks out—and you die in the fire?

Prison. What if you get sick or start going crazy and call for help—and no one comes?

Prison. What if the prison guard wants sex and you resist—and he gets it anyway? What if you get pregnant?

Prison. What if you love another prisoner—and you're kept apart? What if another prisoner wants to kill you—and you're not kept apart?

What if you miss your children so badly you think you'll die—and no one cares, and you don't get to die?[24]

Historically, infants and young children were always imprisoned with their mothers. For example, the second-oldest all-female prison in America (Framingham, Massachusetts) allowed children to remain with their mothers until they were three years old.[25] In the nineteenth century

the delivery room [at Sing Sing prison] was cramped and poorly ventilated. The room in which mothers and their infants lived was only 18 feet square, and at one point, 8 women were forced to live day and night in this cramped space. This poor environment led to a shockingly high mortality rate among the infant children.[26]

Nineteenth- and early-twentieth-century prison reformers wanted to protect imprisoned women and children from male sexual assault.* They also wanted to "rehabilitate" women offenders. However, because there were far fewer female than male prisoners and because women's needs have never been considered the standard for *human* needs, the all-female prison rapidly degenerated into a separate and unequal facility—i.e., into an inferior version of the male prison.

---

*Or from male *inmate* assault. Women prisoners have never been well protected from sexual assault by male guards.

This led to the forced separation of mothers and their children: for the children's sake and as a way to punish their mothers. If male prisoners didn't keep their children with them, why should women? How could a child grow up in prison anyway? How could a child be properly socialized by a convicted criminal?

After World War II, a new type of female prisoner emerged: the drug addict, who often worked as a prostitute. For years such mothers were forced to withdraw from heroin "cold," without humane medical or psychological assistance. As these mothers trembled and vomited, wept and cursed in isolation cells, they became the emblematic madwoman of Bedlam, certainly unfit for motherhood.

Prison officials feared and scorned them. They felt little pity for them or for their motherless children. The imprisoned drug addict population—poor, young, minority, and uneducated, as well as prostitutes—frustrated liberal and reformist sentiment.

Prison today is a bleak and crowded warehouse, filled with many women-hating male and female guards, social workers, and inmates. There is little privacy or opportunity for normal lesbian or heterosexual affection. Restricted physical exercise, high starch diets, and mandatory tranquilizers make it difficult for any prisoner to persist in fighting the bureaucracy.

WHAT HAPPENS TODAY WHEN A MOTHER IS FIRST ARRESTED?

From the moment of her arrest, whether a mother is innocent or guilty, she is separated from her child. Former New York prison social worker and now Commissioner of Parole Barbara Treen outlined the general procedure in New York City:

Imagine a mother who's just arrived. The lights are still on in her apartment. The dog is out in the street. Her kids are in school and coming to a locked apartment. She's desperate to contact them. But until she "clears" a medical examination, she is held in a separate housing area. She can't get in touch with anyone. If she's a drug user, she automatically goes into a detox unit, which means methadone for a period of seven days to two weeks. Only after this medical clearance will she be released into the general population.[27]

An arrested mother can't count on a wife, girlfriend, or mother to take care of her children. As she attempts to raise bail, find a lawyer, or locate witnesses, she must live with images of her children wandering around alone or, as upsetting, alone in a state institution.

As she submits to a vaginal search and other procedures designed to humiliate her, she imagines her neighbors' calling the police to claim she's "abandoned" her children. Barbara Schwarz writes:

> Since 80% of inmate mothers are unmarried heads of households, the children may end up with inadequate care and supervision during this [initial] period unless the mother is given time to make alternative arrangements. This inescapable circumstance may be used against the mother at a later date if a neglect or abandonment proceeding is instituted against her.[28]

As a newly arrested mother experiences anger, shame, and terror, she must calmly attempt to discover what her custodial options are. She must attempt to convince some social worker that she is truly a fit mother. She must also find a friend or relative who is willing and able to assume complete child-care responsibility immediately.

If such female angels exist, if they have phones, are home at that particular moment to answer them, and agree to keep the children, they may still be unable or unwilling to travel long distances to ensure mother-child visitation. They may turn the child against his "criminal" mother. They may also abuse the child.[29] New York prison chaplain Eileen Hogan commented:

> It's *very* difficult for foster families or relatives to bring the kids to see their mothers. First, it's a long ride out—even if they have a car, which many families don't. Then there's a wait of a couple of hours for clearance and processing. After all of that, visitors have about one hour to visit with the mother before they have to start the long trip back.[30]

When an arrested mother cannot locate any friends or relatives willing to take her children, the state automatically puts them into foster care or into state institutions. Siblings are separated by sex immediately and often remain separated for this and other arbitrary reasons. In New York, foster care agencies will not release the phone numbers or addresses of foster parents to prisoners. Unless the foster mother herself initiates child visitation, the prisoner-mother may have to wait until she is freed in order to *attempt* to see her child.

An arrested mother is often badgered into signing papers she barely understands. If she stubbornly refuses to sign anything, she may be threatened with a permanent loss of her children. Mamie, one of my interviewees, describes how "they told me that it was only temporary foster care papers I had to sign. 'Temporary' turned out to be fourteen years. That's a long, long temporary. I didn't see my son from the time he was ten days old until he was eighteen months old. When I got out of prison two years later, I couldn't get him back."

If children are present when their mother is arrested or sentenced, it is a traumatic experience.

> The woman is often taken directly from the courtroom to prison and is not permitted to talk with her children or to make any plans for them. Children have watched while their mothers were handcuffed and taken away; mothers have left their children promising to return but after sentencing were unable even to call until several days later to explain to the children what has happened.[31]

The children not only lose their mothers but observe their mothers' utter powerlessness. An arrested mother's sudden disappearance and continued absence can devastate a child. Sister Eileen Hogan recalls a four-year-old child who stopped talking the day her mother was arrested. "For nine months, the length of her mother's imprisonment, this child never spoke. After her mother got out, the child began to speak, but with an impediment."[32]

IS BEING PREGNANT WHEN YOU'RE ARRESTED ANY GUARANTEE THAT YOU CAN KEEP YOUR CHILD?

Many social workers have attempted to persuade pregnant mothers in prison to give their children up for legal adoption. Lavinia, one of my interviewees, said:

> I was arrested in 1975 when I was five months pregnant. I was sentenced to two years for robbing two hundred dollars from a supermarket. The social workers started making me feel guilty. How could I do this to an innocent child? Why didn't I give the child a clean start in life and give it up for adoption? I was young, they said. I could have other children after I got myself together. They took my daughter away the day I gave birth to her.

I had nobody. I was nobody. I gave my baby up. I'm not saying I would have been a terrific mother. But I have a six-year-old daughter I've never seen. . . . I don't think I did the right thing.

The state does not view young, poor, unwed, and pregnant women of color as "sacred"—especially if they've committed crimes. Under normal circumstances, the fetus belongs to the father. In prison the fetus belongs to his surrogate father—the (male) state.[33]

Some pregnant prisoners describe being pressured into abortions or being denied the right to abortion. Karen Holt has noted:

The right to choose between carrying the child or terminating the pregnancy may be denied pregnant inmates. Prison officials have used coercion or deception to force inmates to abort. One inmate was given ten pills which she was told would start her menstrual cycle. At the time she was three months pregnant, and was warned by other inmates not to take the pills as other women had lost their babies after taking them. Under threat of solitary confinement, she took the pills. One week later she began bleeding and two weeks after that aborted a three-month old fetus. Another woman bowed to authorities' pressure to abort her child, despite her religious convictions, and subsequently suffered a nervous breakdown. But, when a prisoner *desires* an abortion, the procedure is often not made available to her. Although it is the policy of the federal prison system to arrange and pay for an inmate's abortion, this practice has not gained acceptance on the state level.[34]

When a pregnant prisoner goes into labor, her mistreatment may range from terrible to shocking. In 1984, women prisoners in the California Institution for Women were still taken to Riverside General Hospital to give birth.

[They] are routinely strapped into bed at the ankles or wrists, generally at the ankle. The express intention of officials is to prevent the women from escaping; the effect of the bonds is, among other things, to prevent women from moving freely even during labor, and even from turning over in their sleep. Twenty-four hour surveillance is the rule, even during labor.[35]

Black militant Asata Shakur was pregnant when she was imprisoned on Rikers Island in New York City.

Because she was considered by some to be a dangerous Black militant, she was virtually kept in solitary confinement during her stay. The authorities were so concerned that she might escape when she went to the hospital to deliver her child that she was shackled in the ambulance. Immediately after she gave birth, she was handcuffed and chained to her hospital bed. She was then left alone in her hospital bed and almost hemorrhaged to death. She was not allowed to keep her baby daughter with her when she was returned to jail.[36]

MATERNAL VISITATION IN PRISON

New York State Commissioner of Parole Barbara Treen noted that mothers are often accused of being "manipulative" when they cry hard enough or have the "dumb luck" of finding someone within the prison system who will help them arrange a visit from their children. Treen told me: "Trying to get a visit from a child who is in a foster home when there isn't any money is next to impossible. You could write requests until you turn blue in the face."[37]

Sister Eileen Hogan described one prisoner-mother who finally persuaded a social worker to arrange a telephone conversation with her children, whom she hadn't seen since the moment of her arrest:

The prison social worker was supposed to call the foster care agency at a specified time. The agency social worker was to have picked up the children and brought them to the agency to receive the call. The prisoner waited on the prison floor, expecting to be notified when the call had been placed. She waited for hours, but she was never called. The prison social worker had forgotten to place the call.[38]

Mamie, one of my interviewees, described the callous treatment that *she* received as a child and that her children received in turn:

My brothers and sisters, my son and my daughter were all with the same agency, and they didn't know each other. There was no attempt made to let the children know their family. None whatsoever. They told me that it doesn't help the situation. It tends to "confuse" the child. How can you confuse me by telling me where my roots are? The jails, the social workers, and the foster care programs wanted my kids in foster care more than they wanted me to have them!

Contact visits, where physical contact is allowed between mother and child, are the exception, not the rule. Typically, visitors and prisoners are restrained and separated by glass or plastic screens and watched by guards. Under such circumstances prisoner-mothers and their children have no opportunity for anything approaching normal interaction.[39]

Mamie described her first visit with her two-year-old daughter—after an eighteen-month separation:

> First I had to call the social worker and get her permission. Then she had to notify the foster family and get their permission and a convenient time. Then she'd get back to me. They brought my daughter to the agency office. I had to see her in the office. They gave me an hour with her. Not alone. The foster mother and the social worker were there. I was bitter, very bitter. I had nobody. I was a young girl. I had nobody to turn to. I had to fight for every visit I got after that.

Barbara Schwarz points out: "Under these conditions, mothers often believe that it is more detrimental for their children to visit. [They] make the difficult decision not to see them while they are in prison."[40]

WHAT KINDS OF LEGAL SERVICES ARE AVAILABLE TO PRISONER-MOTHERS IN GENERAL AND SPECIFICALLY IN TERMS OF VISITATION AND CUSTODY?

According to Charlene Snow:

> Hearings on custody matters often take place miles from the prison. Women may be unable to attend custody hearings because they do not receive timely notice, or because the prison simply refuses to take them to the court hearing.
>
> Prisons are usually in rural areas where local legal services offices already have more clients than they can adequately serve. Prisoners are easily forgotten. Blind reliance on criminal defense attorneys to represent prisoners in civil matters results in thousands of prisoners being denied representation.[41]

Attorney Ellen Barry emphasized that most state-provided lawyers are overworked, non-competent, uninterested, or anti-mother. Brenda McGowan and Karen L. Blumenthal note that a prisoner-mother may be denied probation because of her inability to locate adequate legal representation.[42] Her lengthened stay in prison may automatically constitute a stronger case against her in terms of maternal abandonment or neglect.

If a prisoner-mother doesn't allow her child to be adopted, if she somehow manages to have her child regularly brought to see her, if the child isn't turned against her by relatives, foster parents, or the absence of any pro-mother opinion, if she is not too ashamed of herself for being convicted, she still faces serious legal obstacles to custody once she is freed.

WHAT DOES A FREED PRISONER-MOTHER HAVE TO DO TO REGAIN CUSTODY OF HER CHILDREN?

Commissioner Barbara Treen has described the 1981 plight of one prisoner-mother. After her release from prison Debra (a pseudonym) was told to provide a "separate bedroom for her child." Since welfare refused to pay the required rent for a two-bedroom apartment, "this mother finally went and held up a jewelry store for the money. She was arrested. The reason for the holdup was to get a larger apartment to get her son back. She was sentenced and is now at Bedford Hills. I don't believe she's an unfit mother. Her chances of getting her son back are less than they were before."

Re-entry is very difficult.

Once the parole board gives you permission to leave, you have to have someone willing to say that you'll be living with them, while you go back to school, look for work, get a job, counseling, etc. You can't get out without some post release plans, but nothing is done to help a mother make any. Roots in the community are demanded of you. How can you have any roots if you've been in prison, usually for the most petty of economic crimes?

Once you're out, you have to prove how fit you are in order to get your children back. For example, how are you going to support your kid? There are hundreds of thousands of mothers on public assistance who have children. But if you're coming out on emergency housing and temporary welfare, you're not going to get your kids so easily. Where will they stay while you're job hunting? Will they have their own bedroom? What kinds of friends or relatives can you provide for them?

Without a sensible re-entry program, most prisoner mothers are condemned to months—or years—of heartbreaking and often futile efforts to become "fit" enough for their own children.[43]

In 1982, a New York prisoner-mother succeeded in blocking her daughter's legal adoption and retaining her parental rights. The court sympathetically noted:

[T]he sad but crushing reality [is] that, all things being equal, the poor and disenfranchised have less of a chance to keep their own children than the "haves" or the affluent. The bottom line, therefore, is not that one mother has been [judicially or legally] abused, which is bad enough, but that the potential for repetition of this terrible injustice is indigenous to the entire system.[44]

Elaine is a thirty-five-year-old black American mother who has spent twelve years in prison for prostitution, aggravated assault, drug addiction, and parole violation. When Elaine was ten, her mother died. At fourteen, she ran away from her foster home. Elaine first supported herself as a prostitute. She said:

"In 1966, this drunk white dude ran up to me on the street. He was cursing and beating on me. I stabbed him. He didn't die. The law said I was supposed to 'retreat,' not attack him back. So I got one to three. I was eighteen years old and four months pregnant at the time.

"My mother's philosophy was that if you were woman enough to make a baby, you were woman enough to have one. So I did. But I had no one in the world who'd keep my son for me while I was doing time. I didn't want him to be adopted. That would tell him that his own mother didn't love him.

"I loved him enough to give birth to him. I just couldn't take care of him.

"They put Maurice in foster care when he was ten days old. I saw him again for the first time when he was two years old. I had to pitch a bitch for that one visit. He was with a foster mother. I tried to keep in touch. But I was hustling and strung out on drugs all the time. He was better off where he was.

"In 1972, I got ripped off real bad when I went to make a buy. I was just about killed. The incident took all the get-up-and-go out of me as far as the drug scene was concerned. I was twenty-six years old. I finally got tired. I wasn't getting any younger. I was just getting beat. I stopped doing drugs.

"I didn't stop hustling. I only stopped heroin. One morning, at three

A.M., I got into an argument with another prostitute. She pulled a knife on me. I took it away from her and stabbed her with it. It was either/or. She'd have got me if I hadn't got her. I had witnesses. I got five years.

"When I got out, I chose to get pregnant. I gave birth to Clifford six years after I stopped dope. I had the agency bring us together with Maurice. I wanted my boys to know they have blood roots. Maurice didn't talk very much. His foster mother was real cool and unhappy.

"Eventually I went to some adoption proceedings. Maurice told the judge that he loved me, but he loved his foster mother, too. It was too nerve-racking. I kept getting up to go to the bathroom. I couldn't bring myself to sign him away with my own hand. I told my lawyer I wouldn't sign anything, but if they did it without me, I wouldn't fight it. Then I went to the bathroom and never came back.

"When Clifford was two, I was picked up on a parole violation. This time the state wasn't going to get my child. I didn't say I *had* a child. I left him with a girlfriend and just hoped and prayed she'd come through. I knew she snorted coke, took angel dust, smoked reefer. But she took him and kept him safe for six months.

"God protected my baby. He was waiting for me when I came out.

"A child's life is not something to play with. It's a human life. Where they go depends on us. A mother must be able to put her own needs second. I'm low man all the time now. I been kissing more ass than I did when I hustled, you hear me?

"It took me a long time to understand this, a long time to learn patience. I look at it like this. Maurice is fifteen. One day he's gonna want to spend some time with me. His curiosity is gonna get him. No foster mother can stop that. He knows where I'm at. I'll be here waiting.

"Clifford is four years old now. I have a job counseling teenagers who've begun to get in trouble with the law. I do for them what I didn't have anybody to do for me. Bedford and the old Women's House of Detention are filled with the saddest, youngest women who ain't got nobody and never did.

"The next time I go there it's gonna be through the front office with a program for getting some of them out. That's my dream."

Once a mother is accused of disobedience to male authority either as an "unfit" mother or as a "criminal," no matter what the truth is, no matter what her "station" in life may have been, she is exceedingly vulnerable to victimization at the hands of individual men and at the hands of the state.

In a sense, patriarchal law still constitutes a permanent Inquisition against women—especially against those who are vulnerable to custodial victimization and imprisonment.[45]

CHAPTER SEVENTEEN

Mothers as Prisoners of Patriarchy: A Comparison of Contemporary Custody Trials and Witchcraft Trials

Why is there no mask engraved upon men's bodies,
By which we could know the true ones from the false ones?
—Robinson Jeffers, *Medea*

Letting a sinful woman keep her illegitimate child
is a way of saving her from becoming a witch.
—Nathaniel Hawthorne

The secrets of slavery are concealed like those of the Inquisition.
—Harriet Brent Jacobs

Witchcraft was hung, in History
But History and I
Find all the Witchcraft that we need
Around us, every Day.

—Emily Dickinson

ARE MOTHERS UNDER CUSTODIAL SIEGE BEING TRIED AS "WITCHES"? In what sense are contemporary custody battles the witchcraft trials of our time?

This chapter is based on a comparison of the life circumstances and "personalities" of women accused of witchcraft and custodially challenged mothers; the specific "crimes" for which "witches" and custodially embattled mothers are tried; and the psycho-legal basis for the European and American Inquisitions and for the custody battles of today.

August 1, 1983, Denver, Colorado

The FBI arrested Karen for re-kidnapping her paternally kidnapped daughter. Within hours of her arrest Karen, who was nine months pregnant, went into labor. During labor she was shackled to her bed, hand and foot. She was unchained for delivery and re-chained immediately after the birth of her son. From the moment of her arrest Karen was not allowed to see her daughter.[1]

July 28, 1982, Toronto, Canada

As the judge announced his decision of paternal custody, he simultaneously ordered his armed court officer to "immediately remove" Carrie's nursing infant from her breast. Carrie was not allowed to see any of her children for the next eight months.[2]

June 14, 1981, Washington, D.C.

The FBI arrested Jessie for "kidnapping" her children—even though a judge had ordered them into her temporary custody. Guns drawn, policemen removed her children. Jessie was not allowed to comfort or say good-bye to them. Jessie was not allowed to see them for six months.[3]

May 10, 1979, New Orleans, Louisiana

The judge instructed his two armed court officers to "remove the child from her mother—*now*." Kate's daughter screamed "no," and clutched her mother even harder. Armed men separated mother and daughter. Kate was allowed neither to comfort her child, nor to see her for more than a year.[4]

April 15, 1977, San Francisco, California

On Saturday morning, Alix received the judge's decision in the mail. As she sat down to read it, armed policemen knocked, entered, demanded both her boys, and were gone with them within ten minutes. Alix did not see either of them for nearly a year.[5]

March 8, 1975, Baltimore, Maryland

Armed policemen and a father broke the door down. "There's the witch who kidnapped my children. She's dangerous." Half-naked, weeping, Rachel was spread-eagled, searched, handcuffed, and thrown into the back seat of a police car. She was imprisoned for three weeks. She was not allowed to see or speak to her children for a year.[6]

Every custodially challenged mother I interviewed felt as if she were the one "on trial." Some mothers also experienced being "on trial" as a *déjà vu* experience. Why?

Are all mothers afraid of being "tried" for maternal imperfection? Do mothers recognize their custodial trials as a private nightmare come true? Or do they also feel like Everywoman "on trial"?

For three centuries *all* the women of Europe and colonial America were on trial for witchcraft. What do accused witches and custodially challenged mothers have in common, if anything? Are the judges or procedures of the Inquisition in any way similar to contemporary judges or judicial procedures?

For example, if a woman "fornicates" but refuses to marry, if she commits adultery or leaves or defends herself against an abusive husband, if she has an independent career (including that of a midwife and healer), worships as a pagan, inherits property, or becomes a financial drain on her community, does this mean she is part of an organized conspiracy against the church? Or that she deserves to lose custody of her children?

A custodially challenged mother is not being accused of witchcraft; in many cases she is not being accused of unfit motherhood. Why then compare custodially challenged mothers and women accused of witchcraft? What can such a comparison yield?

Ah, nothing less than the living voices of accused and "vulnerable" women, "caught up in one of society's whirlpools of callousness, or cruelty"; nothing less than a sense of what a witchcraft trial may feel like to one accused, and a sense of how easy it is for certain women to be legally, physically, and psychologically tortured and then shunned and forgotten.[7]

Can we systematically compare a *contemporary* custody trial with a *classic* witchcraft trial? Can we transcend both time and space by intuition alone, or is more formal assistance also available? Historians and other social scientists have published factual and highly imaginative accounts of the European and colonial Inquisitions. Their work is indispensable.

But the comparison I have in mind also requires at least one eyewitness account of the witchcraft trials, preferably one sympathetic to the accused. Does one exist? The answer is yes.

In 1634, a German Jesuit priest, Father Friedrich von Spee, privately circulated just such an eyewitness account. Father von Spee was the father confessor to many accused and convicted witches. He described the Inquisition's myths and procedures in forty-six points. As I read and reread each of Von Spee's points, I became convinced that they are genuinely *analogous* to the myths and procedures of a contemporary custody battle.[8]

WHAT CRIMES DID "WITCHES" COMMIT?

On December 5, 1484, Pope Innocent VIII declared a "Holy Inquisition" against "witches"—i.e., against those who had "strayed from the Catholic Faith" and through "incantations, spells, and charms" caused "horrid offenses." The pope proclaimed:

> Witches have slain infants yet in the mother's womb, (including the offspring of cattle), have blasted the produce of the earth, the grapes of the vine, the fruits of the trees, nay, men and women, beasts of burthen . . . corn, wheat and all other cereals; these witches furthermore afflict and torment men and women (and animals) with terrible and piteous pains and some diseases; they hinder men from performing the sexual act and women from conceiving.[9]

The European witchcraft trials were based on the *Malleus Maleficarum* ("The Witches' Hammer"). The *Malleus* claimed that most witches were women because women are innately inferior and innately predisposed to "evil."

> Women are feebler in the mind and body than men, [women] are intellectually like children; have slippery tongues; are more credulous; have weak memories; it is a natural [female] vice not to be disciplined, but to follow their own impulses without any sense of what is due; [women are] inferior in understanding spiritual things; are vain, and are more subject to carnal lust, which in women, is insatiable.
>
> Three general vices appear to have special dominion over wicked women, namely, *infidelity, ambition, and lust . . . when a woman thinks alone, she thinks evil.*[10]

According to the *Malleus*, witches were responsible for male impotence, male fornication, male adultery, and marital infertility. Thus witches, not men, were responsible for the *births* of illegitimate and unholy children and for the non-conceptions and *deaths* of legitimate (father-owned) children.

Witches accomplished such deeds by performing abortions, inducing unwanted miscarriages (in other women and from afar), and killing infants at birth (as attending midwives or from afar).

Witches also prevented legal conception from taking place by themselves using birth control or by providing it to other women, by refusing to marry or remarry, and by engaging in forbidden sexual practices—i.e., by having sex outside marriage and for non-procreative purpose, including engaging in "orgies" or in sex with other women.

The anecdotes in the *Malleus* are frightening to read. Heinrich Krämer and Jakob Sprenger support their claim of "witch"-induced male impotence anecdotally. For example, they tell the story of a "certain young man of Ratisbon who had an intrigue with a girl":

> [When he] wanted to leave her [he] lost his member [i.e.,] some glamour was cast over it so that he could not see or touch [anything] but his smooth body. In his worry over this, he [decided to] use some violence to induce [the witch] to restore [him] to health. [The witch] maintained that she was innocent and knew nothing about it. He fell upon her, and winding a towel tightly around her neck, choked her, saying: "Unless you give me back my health, you shall die at my hands." The witch [then] restored his "member."[11]

According to the *Malleus*, the "devil" can rape a woman in the guise of a man familiar to her, or a witch can lie and falsely accuse a man of rape. A witch can also "entice" a man into raping her and then (falsely) accuse him of rape.

Witches are so powerful that they can cause one man to kill another man from afar. In 1651, in colonial America, Thomas Allen accidentally shot and killed Henry Stiles in the presence of many witnesses. Allen was charged with "homicide by misadventure," fined, and "bound to good behavior for a year."

> But this is not the end of the matter. Presumably, Stiles' death remains a topic of local conversation—and three years later, it yields a more drastic result. In November 1654, the court holds a special session to try a case of witchcraft—against a woman, Lydia Gilbert. The court in effect is considering a complicated question: Did Lydia Gilbert's witchcraft cause Thomas Allen's gun to go off, so as to kill Henry Stiles? Depositions are taken from

eyewitnesses and others with information bearing on the case. . . . Probate documents show that Stiles was a boarder in the home of Lydia Gilbert— and her creditor as well. Perhaps there was trouble between them, even some open displays of anger? And if so, perhaps their neighbors suspected in Goodwife Gilbert a vengeful motive toward Stiles.

In due course, the trial jury weighs the evidence and reaches its verdict— guilty as charged. The magistrates hand down the prescribed sentence of death by hanging.[12]

WHAT KINDS OF WOMEN WERE ACCUSED OF WITCHCRAFT?

Theorists, scholars, historians, poets, and visionaries have answered this question in a number of similar, overlapping, and conflicting ways. Some theorists maintain that most of the women accused of witchcraft were innocent but were condemned for being born female.[13]

The church (and those afraid of incurring church wrath) perceived women as either innately inferior or innately superior. Therefore, persecution of a witch was justified for many reasons. For example, a woman was a "witch" because she was either too "smart" or too "stupid," too "rich" or too "poor," a member of a powerful and secret organization or so isolated, so hermit-like that she must be "entertaining Satan."[14]

Some theorists concluded that women accused of witchcraft were really involved in pagan goddess worship[15]; or were midwives and healers[16]; "mentally ill"[17]; or socially "eccentric."[18]

In a scholarly and imaginative analysis of the colonial witchcraft trials, historian John Putnam Demos describes most accused witches as female and "vulnerable" rather than as "lunatics" or "pagans."

Demos's accused witches had no powerful male protector or were accused and judged by powerful men at the instigation of their wives, daughters, or servants.[19] Demos's accused witches were "middle-aged," and "socially disadvantaged," had some "knowledge of medicine," and were unusually "assertive," "aggressive," "verbally assaultive," "grasping," "greedy," "tough," "resilient," and "strong." Demos's composite portrait of a "typical" woman accused of witchcraft is as follows:

[She] was female; was of middle age (i.e. between forty and sixty years old); was of English (and "Puritan") background; was married, but was more likely (than the general population) to have few children—or none at all; was frequently involved in trouble and conflict with other family members; had been accused, on some previous occasion, of committing crimes—most especially theft, slander, or other forms of assaultive speech; was more likely (than the general population) to have professed and practiced a medical vocation, i.e. "doctoring" on a local, quite informal basis; was of relatively low social position; was abrasive in style, contentious in character—and stubbornly resilient in the face of adversity.[20]

Demos notes that the marriages of accused witches were unusually "marred by trouble and conflict" (wife battering, paternal abandonment, marital lawsuits, *etc.*). For example, Rachel Clinton was accused and convicted of witchcraft in colonial America. Rachel's adulterous husband had appropriated and squandered her inheritance, seriously battered and abandoned her, remarried illegally, had "illegitimate" children, and steadfastly refused to support her. Rachel was reduced to begging for "charity" from her neighbors. In 1671, she sued her husband for "regular maintenance" because she was "destitute." Demos asks:

> What was the effect of all this on Rachel's inner life—and outward behavior? Did she not show to the world the character of an embittered, meddlesome woman—perhaps, in short, the character of a witch? Did she not scold and "rail," threaten and fight? Was she not capable of reviling her social betters with epithets like "hellhound" and "whore-masterly rogue," or of deliberately "hunching" them as they moved past her in church?[21]

In addition to having abusive husbands and dealing with them in unusually "aggressive" ways, accused witches, according to Demos, were often "aggressive" toward men and women in general:

> Goody Cole barged in on a Selectman's meeting at Hampton "to demand help . . . for wood or other things;" when refused because "she had an estate of her own," she complained that "they could help Goodman Robie," [he] being a lusty man and [yet] she could have none. (A few days later some of Robie's livestock died very strangely.)
>
> Goody Hale of Boston had asked very inquisitively about the affairs of a young man toward whom she apparently bore a grudge. . . . Encroachment, pushiness, a stubborn and inappropriate assertion of self, thus the witch in her everyday relations with neighbors.[22]

WHY WERE *WOMEN* ACCUSED OF WITCHCRAFT? WHOSE INTERESTS WERE SERVED BY SUCH ACCUSATIONS AND CONVICTIONS?

According to Demos, Puritan child rearing was extremely harsh, repressive, and oriented to "breaking the child's will." Children were reared exclusively by women—i.e., by biological mothers or by stepmothers and by female relatives and servants. Children (and adults) were forbidden to challenge or disobey parental or church authority or to do so in "aggressive" ways.

Thus women, but not men, were (unconsciously) associated with preverbal childhood experiences of intensely repressive socialization. Women were (unconsciously) remembered as both omnipotent and as cruel. According to Demos, many adult women were also "profoundly vulnerable" and could be "pulled into badly exposed positions."[23]

John Demos's work suggests that many accused witches were also battered wives or battered wives who dared fight back.

The accusation, conviction, and execution of such "undesirable" wives as witches were the only legal means of divorce available to their husbands. We may remember that the Catholic and colonial Puritan churches considered marriage a sacrament and outlawed divorce. The *Malleus* itself claimed:

> . . . that truly the most powerful cause which contributes to the increase of witches is the woeful rivalry between married folk and unmarried women and men. . . . It is not good to marry. What else is woman but a foe to friendship, an unescapable punishment, a necessary evil, a natural temptation, a desirable calamity, a domestic danger, a delectable detriment, an evil of nature painted with fair colors! Therefore, if it BE A SIN TO DIVORCE HER WHEN SHE OUGHT TO BE KEPT, IT IS INDEED A NECESSARY TORTURE: FOR EITHER WE COMMIT ADULTERY BY DIVORCING HER, OR WE MUST ENDURE DAILY STRIFE.[24]

To what extent were both the European and the American witchcraft trials a sanctioned means of divorce—for men? To what extent were the witchcraft trials a means of keeping *all* women "humble" and at the same time a means of confiscating an "independent" woman's property?

Historian Carol F. Karlsen agrees with Demos that most accused witches were middle-aged and economically marginal married women. However, on the basis of her own research, she concluded that many accused and convicted colonial witches were also women who stood to inherit property in their own right.

These women had "daughters but no sons" and had no "living brothers" or no "living children" by the men who were their husbands at the time of their accusation or conviction. Karlsen notes:

> The women who fell into these three categories either stood to inherit, did inherit, or were denied their apparent right to inherit substantially larger portions of their fathers' or husbands' accumulated estates. . . . These women were aberrations in a society with an inheritance system designed to keep property in the hands of men. . . . Many of the younger females accused of witchcraft were the daughters and granddaughters of "inheriting" women. [Those women not in any of these categories were involved in] public battles over property transactions.[25]

There is no real contradiction between Karlsen and Demos. It *is* dangerous for a (vulnerable) woman to be either too poor or too rich. In Puritan terms, the existence of a "poor" woman excites guilt and suspicion in her wealthy neighbors. How can the Puritan wealthy justify their own "wealth"? How can the Puritan wealthy explain their ill fortune? Who other than an impoverished Puritan woman would be envious or hostile enough to "steal": money, another woman's husband, a man's legal child, a family's reputation, health, or peace of mind?[26]

Whom can the impoverished Puritan woman blame for her own unhappy condition? Karlsen notes that the main accusers of propertied women were young female orphans whose own "grim economic prospects" literally "possessed" them.

> Their dissatisfaction with their present material condition—and with their future prospects—were crucial factors in bringing on their possession. . . . [They knew that] female dissatisfaction, especially with "woman's" place in the social order, was one of the most obvious signs of witchcraft. Were they going to repress their discontent and lead virtuous lives . . . or were they going to acknowledge their discontent, thereby challenging both their faith and their social order?
>
> During their possession, they acted out both sides of this profound ambivalence—and their rage that this choice was forced upon them. [By] ex-

ternalizing the evil, [they attempted to] exorcise the witch [they] feared was within them.[27]

WHEN DID THE WITCHCRAFT TRIALS FINALLY END?

According to John Demos, they never have. As "witches disappeared from view," other "figures" were obliged to take their place. "Blacks, Indians, immigrants of various kinds; Jews, Catholics, Mormons, atheists, Masons, anarchists, Communists: around these new targets, 'witchhunting' has been repeatedly revived all through American history."[28]

Such "witch-hunts" are both like and unlike each other. They are also each like and unlike the persecution of women as witches. For example, a "witch-hunt" against "enemies" of the state ("Communists" or "capitalists") does not *necessarily* target a racially or sexually distinct group.

Genocidal wars against a racially despised group are not conducted as *formally* as a witchcraft trial. The genocidal war against a racially despised group is neither a "witch-hunt" nor a "witchcraft trial."

For example, the American and the German Nazi states waged genocidal wars against Native American Indians and against European Jews respectively. Indians were raped, killed, exiled, and their land confiscated, without each Indian's being individually or formally interrogated about his or her "crime" against the American state. Being red-skinned was "crime" enough.

For twenty-two centuries, Jews were persecuted and killed in the Roman Middle East, in Christian Europe, and in Muslim North Africa. Lynchings (pogroms), rapes, land confiscations, exilings, and other forms of economic and religious discrimination went legally unpunished or were, in fact, legal. Within ten years, Adolf Hitler legally killed six million Jews. He did not formally interrogate each Jew about his or her "crime." Being Jewish was "crime" enough.

Like Jews and Indians, women were, and still are, viewed as "inferior/superior." However, unlike the members of a despised racial minority, women are well integrated within their class-culture, domestically and genetically.

Although women are anatomically rather than racially distinct from their male counterparts, they are also as "indistinguishable" from each other as they are indispensable to their husbands and children. As such, any woman accused of witchcraft, no matter what her class, must be "properly" interrogated. The patriarchal authorities insisted that *each* accused witch be carefully interrogated—although they did not believe anything she said.*

Does the accused witch threaten the patriarchal order—i.e., is the crime "Satanic"? Are her husband's "legitimate" children guilty by association with her? John Demos could find no "lasting or disabling" stigma attached to the children of witches in colonial America.[29]

This is not surprising. Children have always been legally owned by their fathers or by the (male) state. They have never "belonged" to their mothers.

There is some evidence, both in Europe and in colonial America, that children were either forced to testify against their mothers or were executed along with them. One European judge, Jean Bodin, "openly declared that he used children as witnesses because at a very young age they could without difficulty be persuaded or compelled to inform against the accused."[30]

In 1680, Emerzianne Pichler was convicted and burned as a witch. Her two children, aged twelve and fourteen, were burned as "accomplices" or "apprentices" two days later.[31] Historians have also unearthed some examples of convicted witches' children's being accused, convicted, and executed simultaneously with their mothers or years later. The impression given is that daughters more often than sons were accused, but there is no definitive evidence of this.[32]

HOW IS A WITCHCRAFT ACCUSATION ANALOGOUS TO A CUSTODY CHALLENGE?

The comparison you are about to read summarizes the information contained in previous chapters. This same information takes on a deeper and more terrible significance when counterposed with Father von Spee's analysis of the Inquisition.[33]

Women accused of witchcraft and custodially challenged mothers were both accused of being sexually insatiable and adulterous, and of causing male impotence. Both were accused of being too economically or psychologically independent—for women.

Some accused witches and custodially victimized mothers were, in effect, accused or condemned because their *husbands* were violent and adulterous, wanted to obtain "cheap" or even "profitable" divorces—

---

*This is always less true when the accused witch is also a member of a despised racial minority or is unprotected by a powerful man.

i.e., they coveted their wives' wealth, property, and intimate relationship to their children.

On Being Brought to Trial

Incredible among us Germans, and especially (I am ashamed to say) among Catholics, are popular superstitions, envy, calumnies, backbitings, insinuations, and the like, which being neither punished or refuted, stir up suspicion of witchcraft. No longer God or nature, but witches are responsible for everything.

Hence, everybody sets up a clamor that the magistrates investigate the witches—whom only popular gossip has made so numerous.*

Women in general are still blamed for anything that "goes wrong" in the universe or within their own families. Mothers are blamed when their children are unhappy or fall ill and when their children engage in criminal or tabooed sexual activities.

For example, a male rapist's *mother* is blamed for driving her son to rape by having been too cold or too "emasculating." The rapist's *wife* is blamed for being frigid or "emasculating." The rapist's *female victim* is blamed for "provoking" the rape.

When a grown man rapes or kills a woman, it is thus seen as a (psychologically) self-defensive maneuver against his "provoking" mother, wife, or female victim.

As we have seen, mothers were custodially challenged and victimized when their husbands abandoned, neglected, or physically, sexually, or psychologically abused them—or their children.

Princes, therefore, bid their judges and counselors bring proceedings against the witches.

The judges hardly know where to start, since they have no evidence (indicia) or proof.

Meanwhile, the people call this delay suspicious: and the princes are persuaded by some informer or another to this effect.

At last, therefore, the judges yield to their wishes and contrive to begin the trials.

When a "prince" or husband custodially challenges a mother, the stage is psychologically set for a witchcraft trial. In a custody battle the

---

*Friedrich von Spee. The quotes on the following pages are all from von Spee.

myth of female (sexual) evil is palpable. Mothers are (sexually) suspected because they are *women*. A mother's pre-, extra-, or post-marital sexual activities are assumed, closely examined, and used against her.

In one case, a maternal grandmother's sexual activities were used against her custodially challenged daughter. The fact that Lucy was an "illegitimate" child made other (sexual) charges against her more believable.[34] Cheryl's "illegitimacy" made her more believably suspect as an "unfit" mother.[35]

A "prince" may custodially victimize a mother merely by "suggesting" that she is or may be sexually active. A judge and a state social worker may immediately place her under surveillance, subject her to interrogation, and watch her without ever talking to her directly.

Margaret returned home one Saturday at midnight and found all her children "gone." Her ex-husband had persuaded a judge and a state child welfare agency that she had been leaving the children alone "day and night," in order to "date" men. Without interviewing Margaret, without alerting her to the accusation, the state assisted Margaret's ex-husband to "swoop down" on her one night when she was "out."[36]

The judges need not deny that they torture on mere denunciations.

They start with the first degree, i.e. the less severe torture. Although exceedingly severe, it is light compared to those tortures which follow. Wherefore, if she confesses, they say the woman has confessed without torture!

In Germany, to offend these princes is a serious offence: even clergymen approve whatever pleases them, not caring by whom these princes (however well-intentioned) have been instigated.

Contemporary judges and other state officials no longer believe in "Satan" or in female "witchcraft." They nevertheless act as if they do.

As we have seen, custodially challenged mothers are presumed guilty and must prove that they are innocent. In courtrooms, intimations of maternal "unfitness" assume the bizarre and surreal tones that characterize a witchcraft trial.

Miki was accused of "keeping her children's clothing in wicker baskets instead of in a bureau" and of "feeding them strange [health] foods." Nora was accused of "not having a basketball hoop in her driveway." Adele was accused of her children's failure to "live up to their IQ potential" in school.[37]

Judges (and other state officials) treated mothers with barely disguised contempt and suspicion. Maternal testimony rarely carried as much weight, or received as much judicial attention, as that of the "prince."

Catherine's judge refused to listen to witnesses describe her mothering. However, he listened carefully, and at great length, to the description of Catherine's adultery by her "prince" and to all those witnesses who came to praise the "prince." More than a third of the "judicial" mothers reported this same courtroom experience.[38]

Judges, policemen, and social workers hesitated to offend any "prince." They found it easier to believe that a mother was lying than to believe that a "prince" had committed incest or any other domestic crime.[39] Many mothers were cut short when they tried to introduce evidence of a husband's reign of terror or economic greed.

> Beth: My husband forced me to sign certain agreements. In return, he promised not to kidnap the kids again. When I tried to introduce these agreements in court the judge yelled at me. He said: "I don't want to re-try your divorce. Why you signed such an agreement is between you and your husband. It's past legal history." The judge treated me like I was an idiot for signing these agreements in the first place—and a bigger idiot for insisting, over my lawyer's objections, on calling them to the court's attention. He refused to look at them as proof of my ex-husband's cruelty to our kids.[40]

As we have seen, 16 percent of the "princes" influenced judges through political and professional connections. Josie, Ella Mae, Jessie, Marta, Rachel, and Rose all described ex-husbands whose power and "glamour" led to judicial orders of paternal custody.[41]

Judges Call Expert Witnesses to Enlighten Them

Other judges who still delay, afraid to get involved in this ticklish matter, are sent a special investigator. In this field of investigation, whatever inexperience or arrogance he brings to the job is held zeal for justice. His zeal for justice is also whetted by hopes of profit, especially with a poor and greedy agent with a large family, when he receives as stipend so many dollars per head for each witch burned, besides the incidental fees and perquisites which investigating agents are allowed to extort at will from those they summon.

Yet to avoid the appearance that she is indicted solely on the basis of rumor, without other proofs, a certain presumption of guilt is obtained by posing the following dilemma: either she has led an evil and improper life, or she has led a good and proper one. If an evil one, then she should be guilty. On the other hand, if she has led a good life, this is just as damning, for witches dissemble and try to appear especially virtuous.

Moreover, if one defamed goes to the investigators and asks whether what is rumored is true, so that he may prepare his defense, this is proof that his conscience is bothering him.

Lest these should be the only proofs, the investigator has his snoopers, often depraved and infamous, ferret out all her past life. This, of course, cannot be done without turning up some saying or doing of hers which men so disposed can easily twist or distort into evidence of witchcraft.

Expert witnesses—psychiatrists, psychologists, and social workers—are our "special investigators." As we have seen, considering the anti-woman, anti-mother, anti-*non-traditional*-mother, and pro-father biases among such professionals, it is easy for any custodially challenged mother to be "diagnosed" as an unfit mother.[42]

Nora and Elizabeth Packard (in the nineteenth century) both were psychiatrically diagnosed as "paranoid" because *they* mistrusted the investigating psychiatrists. According to Nora's court-appointed psychiatrist:

[Nora] maintained a controlling posture in my contacts with her, screening my questions for "relevance," and carefully modulating her own emotionality. She evinced an increasingly wary, guarded demeanor. Nora asserted that her position was forthright and accommodating, but that the investigator's behavior was at times biased, unprofessional and offensive.[43]

Nora's court-appointed psychiatrist recommended paternal custody. He also described Nora as "paranoid" about her husband, Lester—who had tried to strangle her and who had also kidnapped their youngest children. "Nora's paranoia about the children's father would be very detrimental to the children's mental health. My opinion is that, even if her fear were founded—which I do not consider it to be—the very fear itself represents a clear, present, active repressive force on the children's emotional development."[44]

As we have seen, many psychiatrists, psychologists, and social workers refused to believe that a "prince" would sexually molest his own child. They felt that any mother who accused a father of incest was "crazy," "unfit," or herself "at fault."

A state social worker and court-appointed psychologist actually used the phrase "a mad witch" in referring to Brigette, who accused her ex-husband of incest. Brigette and Arlene (another mother of an incestuously abused daughter) were both described as "paranoid," "rigid," "overprotective," and "obsessed with incest" by court-appointed experts.[45]

Paternal rape and incest were medically established in both cases. Experts nevertheless persuaded the involved judges to continue paternal visitation. According to one expert, "A complete cutting of contact with the natural father could conceivably confuse the child or send a 'message' of negativity. Most importantly, it would traumatize the child. She is strongly attached to her father."[46]

Marie, a Canadian Indian mother and herself a state social worker, described the ways in which white female social workers continually "snoop" against Indian mothers:

> They first look for evidence of a boyfriend, a liquor bottle, drugs. If an Indian mother has serious problems, they'd rather remove her children than help her. If she's working, and has left the kids with *her* mother, she's still suspected of neglecting her children. Once a mother I know went around the corner to shop for food. She'd been under welfare surveillance. When she returned a half hour later, her kids were gone—taken by the welfare department. It took her six months to get them back.[47]

Judges Call Non-expert Witnesses to Enlighten Them

> **Any who have borne her ill now have ample opportunity to bring against her whatever accusations they please: and everyone says that the evidence is strong against her.**
>
> **If a madman's ravings, or some malicious and idle rumor (for no proof of the scandal is ever needed) points to some helpless old woman, she is the first to suffer.**

Few strong witnesses appeared on behalf of a particular mother. Those who did either had no positive effect or had a negative effect. When religious or very respectably married women testified for mothers, their testimony rarely "carried the day."[48]

Judges were incensed when too many maternal supporters crowded into their courtroom. Nora and Alix both were grilled by judges about the sheer number of *female* supporters who attended their trials. Miki's judge was outraged when he received a group letter written on her behalf by state social workers, all of whom were women of color.[49]

Many mothers were judicially viewed as "unfit" because of the *absence* of strong family support. A mother's missing relatives signaled her "profound vulnerability." Judges and lawyers suspected there was something "wrong" with any mother whose own family wasn't there to support her.[50]

Neighbors of domestically violent "princes" usually chose not to get "involved" or to "take sides." Female neighbors more often testified about the recent and highly visible male maternal heroism of a "prince" than about a woman's long-lasting and more invisible maternal heroism.

Non-expert witnesses who were anti-mother or strongly pro-father carried greater weight than any pro-mother witness. For example, mothers faced *maternal* grandmothers, ex-housekeepers, ex-neighbors, ex-in-laws, and mother competitors, who falsely testified that an absent father was really present or that an overly present mother was really absent.

One father's girlfriend (falsely) testified that she'd seen the custodially challenged mother in a "habitually drunken" state. Years later, when this girlfriend became an ex-girlfriend, she called the mother with her belated apologies.[51]

As we have seen, *no* relative, neighbor, or colleague of a "prince" testified against him or in favor of his wife. Some fathers had experts who testified for them as personal "character witnesses." Full-time mothers could not command prestigious experts as friends or as personal "character witnesses."

Some brainwashed children testified against their mothers or stated their paternal preference. Judges neither dismissed such testimony nor viewed it as proof of paternal child brainwashing.[52]

More understanding or learned priests cannot visit her in prison lest they counsel her or inform the princes what goes on. Nothing is more dreaded than that something be brought to light to prove the innocence of the accused. Persons who try to do so are labeled troublemakers.

A number of non-expert men testified *for* mothers and *against* fathers. For example, Terry's live-in boyfriend described her as a "consistently devoted mother." He described Terry's ex-husband as "physically absent" and "emotionally distant" from his children and as also involved in an anti-mother brainwashing campaign. In turn, *he* was falsely accused of "breaking Terry's son's hand"—and threatened with a criminal lawsuit, public exposure, and the possibility of losing his own paternal visitation rights.[53]

Loretta's second husband was (falsely) accused in court of beating his stepchildren.[54] Ella Mae's live-in boyfriend took the stand to describe her "supermothering." In turn, he was painted as a "moral degenerate" who "lived in sin," and participated in Ella Mae's "wild, lesbian parties"![55]

Leslie's second husband emotionally and financially supported Leslie's search for her paternally kidnapped children. Once the children were found, this husband was (falsely) described in court, and to his own relatives, as a "violent alcoholic."[56]

The Interrogation of Those Presumed Guilty

So that it may seem that the woman has an opportunity to defend herself, she is brought into court and the indications of her guilt are read and examined—if it can be called an examination.

Even though she denies these charges and satisfactorily answers every accusation, no attention is paid and her replies are not even recorded: all the indictments retain their force and validity, however perfect her answers to them. She is ordered back into prison, there to consider more carefully whether she will persist in obstinacy, for since she has already denied her guilt, she is obstinate.

Judges did not "hear" or listen to mothers (or their witnesses) with the same compassion and seriousness they accorded "princes" (or their witnesses). Descriptions of fit mothering were minimized; maternal descriptions of unfit fathering were often taken as proof of *maternal* unfitness.

As we have seen, custodially challenged mothers were judicially viewed as "unfit" (or as the "lesser" of two parents) when they worked outside the home for too little money—or for too much "career" money. Mothers were also viewed as the "lesser" of two parents for mothering on a welfare wage, or as "unfit" per se, if they protested their welfare poverty by stealing or earning money "illegally."[57]

Judges grew incensed when a custodially challenged mother insisted on her right to deprive a violent, incestuous, or kidnapping father of his visitation, and when she insisted on her own right to a sexual, professional, or political life.[58]

In these trials, nobody is allowed a lawyer or any means of fair defense, for witchcraft is reckoned an exceptional crime (of such enormity that all rules of legal procedures may be suspended), and whoever ventures to defend the prisoner falls himself under suspicion of witchcraft as well as those who dare to utter a protest in these cases, and to urge the judges to

exercise a prudence, for they are forthwith labelled supporters of witch-craft, thus everybody keeps quiet for fear.

Nearly a third of the custodially challenged mothers (28 percent) could not afford and did not have any lawyers. Few mothers hired really expensive lawyers, nor were most mothers able to purchase competent, supportive, or effective lawyers at any price.

Many lawyers suspected and often scapegoated their maternal clients. They refused to risk the displeasure of a "prince" on behalf of a powerless client, who was already under siege and "weakening fast."[59]

Imprisoned mothers either had no legal counsel or were forced to rely on state-subsidized lawyers who were anti-mother, anti-woman, overworked, underpaid, undertrained, inefficient, and ineffective.[60]

Meanwhile, ignorant and headstrong priests harass the wretched creature so that, whether truly or not, she will confess herself guilty: unless she does so, they say, she cannot be saved or partake of the sacraments.

If lawyers function like "priests," a husband's lawyer functions like the Vatican's own special emissary. *Husbands'* lawyers humiliated and brutalized mothers with a host of false accusations. During a cross-examination by her husband's (military) lawyer, Melanie was actually referred to as the "accused."[61]

Mothers who were also battered wives were disbelieved and unassisted by policemen, social workers, psychiatrists, and judges. When they finally fought back in self-defense, state lawyers prosecuted them with sadistic zeal.[62]

What is so shocking about this? Priests are treated the same way.

I interviewed seven women lawyers whose custody had been challenged during or after their legal training. These mothers were exceptionally conscious of their custodial vulnerability as women.[63] In 1983 in Louisiana, a judge actually denied a mother custody of her four-year-old daughter because she *was* a lawyer.[64]

Before torture, however, she is searched for amulets, her entire body is shaved, even those privy parts indicating the female sex are wantonly examined.

Just as witches were searched for "amulets" or other "signs" of guilt, so, too, are mothers under custodial siege. Private diaries, bedside reading, pamphlets scooped up in hallways—all were admitted as evidence of maternal "unfitness." Alix was condemned as a "man-hater" for having a Wonder Woman poster on her front door. As we have seen, the "privy parts" and sexual activities of mothers were of major concern in most custody battles.[65]

> **Therefore the old woman is put in prison. A new proof is found through a second dilemma: she is afraid or not afraid. If she is afraid (hearing of the horrible tortures used against witches), this is sure proof: for her conscience accuses her. If she does not show fear (trusting in her innocence), this too is a proof, for witches characteristically pretend innocence and wear a bold front.**
>
> **If, during the torture, the old woman contorts her features with pain, they say she is laughing: if she loses consciousness, she is sleeping or has bewitched herself into taciturnity. And if she is taciturn, she deserves to be burned alive, as later has been done to some who, though several times tortured, would not say what the investigators wanted.**

Mothers on trial were condemned as too "emotional" or as too "emotionless." For example, Marta's lawyer instructed her to behave like a "lady" at all times. While her husband (falsely) accused her of alcoholism, promiscuity, stupidity, and greed, Marta stared straight ahead. Afterward, the judge told her lawyer that Marta "must really be a very cold woman, not to have reacted at all."[66]

Rachel, on the other hand, wept when the judge denied her all child support and when he ordered her children into paternal custody. The judge ordered Rachel's lawyer to "control" his "obviously hysterical and out of control client."[67]

Herbert and Roxanne Pulitzer were fighting over custody of their two young sons. They accused each other of adultery and "promiscuity." Roxanne accused Herbert of committing incest with his daughter of a previous marriage.

> Presiding Judge Harper claimed to be moved by Herbert's doleful eyes and aging face during the trial. By contrast, the wife nonchalantly sat at the table doodling on a note pad as though unconcerned. Only [when she burst into tears once] did Roxanne prove to him that she was, after all, capable of human emotion and concern.[68]

Linda was a full-time stay-at-home mother. Her ex-husband was an absent father and an adulterous and violent husband. After ordering mandatory joint custody, the judge told Linda's lawyer that he "didn't like me. He said I looked bitter and stiff-lipped. He said that my husband looked more relaxed, and easygoing."[69]

> The result is the same whether she confesses or not. If she confesses, her guilt is clear: she is executed. All recantation is in vain. If she does not confess, the torture is repeated—twice, thrice, four times. In exceptional crimes, the torture is not limited in duration, severity, or frequency.

Custody battles lasted for an average of three years.[70] In reality, the "torture" lasted much longer. Mothers who won custody were "chained to the stake of the legal system" until their youngest child became eighteen—i.e., their custody cases could be reopened over and over. During this time children could also be brainwashed or kidnapped. The maternal battle for child support or against poverty continued forever.

Mothers who lost custody were usually denied any, or any normal, access to their children. Maternal visitation was restricted and rarely enforced; children were moved far away and became inaccessible, either psychologically (through brainwashing) or economically (mothers couldn't afford long-distance visits too often).

Mothers themselves used the word *torture* to describe having to battle and having to *keep* battling to see their children. "Princes" administered this "torture" personally. The state social workers, policemen, lawyers, experts, and judges administered this torture impersonally.[71]

> When the woman has been shaved and searched, she is tortured to make her confess the truth—this is, to declare what they want, for naturally anything else will not and cannot be the truth.
>
> And so she is hurried to the torture, unless, as often happens, she was tortured on the very day of her arrest.
>
> Next day she is brought out again, and hears a decree of torture—just as if she had never refuted the charges.

Leslie remarried and was bedridden with a difficult pregnancy when her ex-husband kidnapped their children. She lost twenty pounds, gave birth prematurely, and became seriously depressed. She felt she was "going crazy" as she searched for her missing children. "I felt as though I were screaming with no sound coming out for four years."[72]

Nora said that her "battle for motherhood" was "lifelong." She spoke in a whisper, looked over her shoulder before speaking, and wanted no "tape recordings, no evidence" of what she said. She was ashamed that "battling" had made her "overly sensitive" and unable to experience her motherhood as "normal." Nora reminded me of someone who has been physically as well as psychologically tortured.

Mothers under custodial siege were "tortured" sexually, psychologically, legally, and economically. A number of "princes" demanded that their ex-wives never remarry, never have live-in boyfriends, or male or female lovers, if they wanted to keep living with their children.

As we have seen, only two mothers of childbearing age ever had children again. "Torture"—intense and prolonged suffering from which there is no escape—may, for a variety of reasons, result in behavior that closely approximates reproductive sterilization.[73]

> While she is kept in prison and tormented, the judges invent clever devices to build up new proofs of guilt to convict her to her face, so that, when reviewing the trial, some university faculty can confirm her burning alive.
>
> On the other hand, if she does not die under torture, and if some exceptionally scrupulous judge hesitates to torture her further without fresh proofs or to burn her without confession, she is kept in prison and more harshly chained, there to rot until she yields, even if it takes a whole year.

Mothers in prison and young unwed mothers on welfare were constantly badgered to "yield" or legally to give up their children. Their refusal to do so was often treated as further proof of maternal "unfitness." Imprisoned mothers were not encouraged or assisted to exercise their legal right of visitation. Visits were infrequent and short. Imprisoned mothers were usually denied information about their children's welfare and whereabouts.[74]

> When, under stress of pain, the witch has confessed, her plight is indescribable. Not only cannot she escape herself, but she is also compelled to accuse others whom she does not know, whose names are frequently put into her mouth by the investigators or suggested by the executioners, or of whom she has heard as suspected or accused. These in turn are forced to accuse others, and these still others, and so it goes on: who can help seeing that it must go on and on?
>
> Thus those forced under torture to denounce are likely to name names.

A mother was never asked to "name" another *mother* as "unfit." She was, however, forced to "name" or "acknowledge" the legal or spermatic father especially if she was an unwed welfare recipient. Once a father was "named," a mother rarely collected any child support above the state (poverty) levels for welfare.

Once "named," a father was also legally entitled to visitation and custody—as long as he *promised* to relieve the state of its economic burden. Thus, the state forced mothers into unwanted and custodially dangerous relationships with unwed fathers or sperm donors.[75]

In a sense, each custodially challenged unwed mother was forced to become an accessory to her further victimization.

> Whatever he [the accused] does he incurs commonfame, which after a year, coupled with denunciations, suffices for torture.
>
> And even confessors and clergymen agree that she died obstinate and impenitent: that she would not be converted or desert her incubus, but kept faith with him.
>
> It is the same with those who are calumniated maliciously: if they do not seek redress, their silence is proof of guilt: if they do seek it, the calumny is spread, suspicions are aroused, and it becomes common fame.
>
> She can never clear herself. The investigating committee would feel disgrace if it acquitted a woman: once arrested and in chains, she has to be guilty, by fair means or foul.

Mothers who grew too "obsessed" with their lawsuits were often shunned by relatives and friends. Mothers were warned that they would "go mad," "kill themselves," or lose their ability to remarry if they didn't adopt a "more positive view of things."[76]

However, a non-custodial mother who tried to "get on" with her life was also perceived as "cold," "unnatural," and "unfit"—*as a person.* Non-custodial mothers became "invisible pariahs," who were condemned or ostracized by other mothers for their non-custodial status. Non-custodial mothers also lost friends, acquaintances, lovers, and jobs because of their non-custodial status. Mothers who were humiliated during visitation said they felt like "lepers," "outcasts," or "criminals."[77]

> If, however, she dies under so much torture, they say the devil broke her neck.
>
> She is therefore put to death without scruple. But she would have been executed even if she had not confessed: for when once the torture has begun, the die is already cast: she cannot escape, she had perforce to die.
>
> Wherefore the corpse is buried underneath the gallows.

Many mothers under custodial siege became anxious, depressed, and insomniac. Some attempted suicide or began drinking. Some had "nervous breakdowns." Each mother blamed herself for "breaking down." Each mother was terrified that such information would be used against her in court.

Every custodially challenged mother "died" out loud every day: for weeks, months, and years. Her normal motherhood was buried beneath stacks of legal papers, in her children's premature and unnatural withdrawal from her, and in the punitive silence that surrounded her.

The mothers of paternally kidnapped children felt as if they or their children were "dead." The mothers of paternally brainwashed children described themselves and their children as "missing," "absent," or "dead."

Sonia: My life became a shadow place. I became much quieter, more passive. Like a ghost.[78]

Norma: They put me on the rack.[79]

Helen: I've died each time I thought we'd found him but we didn't. I'm like a corpse without him.[80]

Natalie: They burned me at the stake.[81]

Father Friedrich von Spee included the following observations in his account of the Inquisition. I would like to end this chapter with them. They are still relevant.[82]

Some judges, to appear ultra scrupulous, have the woman exorcised, transferred elsewhere, and tortured all over again, to break her taciturnity: if she maintains silence, then at last they can burn her. Now, in heaven's name, I would like to know, since she who confesses and she who does not both perish alike, how can anybody, no matter how innocent, escape? O unhappy woman, why have you rashly hoped? Why did you not, on first entering prison, admit whatever they wanted? Why, foolish and crazy woman, did you wish to die so many times when you might have died but once? Follow my counsel, and before undergoing all these pains, say you are guilty and die. You will not escape, for this were a catastrophic disgrace to the zeal of Germany.

The judges must either suspend these trials (and so impute their validity) or else burn their own fold, themselves, and everybody else: for all sooner or later are falsely accused, and, if tortured, all are proved guilty.

Thus eventually those who at first clamored most loudly to feed the flames are themselves involved, for they rashly failed to see that their turn too would come. Thus heaven justly punished those who with their pestilent tongues berated so many witches and sent so many innocent to the stake.

Now many of the wiser and more learned judges are opening their eyes to this enormity, and proceed more slowly and cautiously.

From all which follows this corollary, worthy to be noted in red ink: that, if only the trials be steadily continued, nobody is safe, no matter what sex, fortune, condition, or dignity, if any enemy or detractor wishes to bring a person under suspicion of witchcraft.[83]

CHAPTER EIGHTEEN

The International Custody Situation

It was not fair, she felt, the way men cleverly used a woman's sense of responsibility to actually enslave her. They knew that a traditional wife like herself would never dream of leaving her children. Yes, I have many children, but what do I have to feed them on? On my life. I have to work myself to the bone to look after them, I have to give them my all.

[If I am] lucky enough to die in peace, I even have to give them my soul. They will worship my dead spirit to provide for them: it will be hailed as a good spirit so long as there are plenty of yams and children in the family, but if anything should go wrong, if a young wife does not conceive or there is a famine, my dead spirit will be blamed. When will I be free?

But even in her confusion she knew the answer: "Never, not even in death. I am prisoner of my own flesh and blood."

Buchi Emecheta, Nigeria[1]

I am worried that men are said to be the children's owner, yet I spend nine months carrying the baby in my stomach, and then the next twenty to thirty years looking after her or him. A woman has no property at home and she has no children. When she gets divorced, she goes away naked.

Anonymous, Zimbabwe[2]

I'm a single mother on Social Security and the state doesn't think twice about whether my son and I are starving. It's a tremendous fight to get any little bit of money out of them. How can they pretend to care about the welfare of our children? When they suggest that a woman without a man cannot be allowed to have children, who besides women do they think have been taking responsibility for our children all along?

Rachel Smith, Great Britain[3]

There was no court of appeal. Mother was sent away for labor reform. (My father disassociated himself from mother and eventually "denounced" her. When she came to visit us he would scream: "The children in this house need a Revolutionary mother, not a Rightist mother." The court awarded custody of the children to father.)

So perhaps inevitably, over the years, I came to resent my mother for making life so miserable. I began to believe that she really had done something wrong. My father and teachers said so, and my classmates hated me for her supposed crimes. At last I no longer wished to visit her despite my loneliness, and when I saw her at a distance I didn't even call out to her. I cut her out of my life just as I had been told to do, and became solitary and self-reliant.

Liang Heng, China[4]

THIS CHAPTER SURVEYS WOMEN'S CUSTODIAL AND ECONOMIC RIGHTS and obligations in sixty-five countries outside the United States and Canada: in "developing" non-Western places and in "developed" capitalist and communist places; in the Middle East, Asia, Africa, Central and South America, and Europe.

In the countries surveyed, mothers were not automatically entitled to custody of their children by law or by custom or when it was contested by an individual father or by the state. No mother could count on obtaining physical or legal custody, even of a paternally kidnapped child, in her country of origin or in her husband's country of origin.

In most countries, single and unwed mothers (and "illegitimate" children) were inadequately subsidized by fathers, families, tribes, and by the modern state.

EARLY IN 1980 the wife of a UN diplomat requested an "emergency" appointment with me. "My freedom and possibly my life are being threatened."

"Have you contacted the police or told your husband?" I asked.

"My husband is the one who is threatening me," she said.

May arrived at my office that evening. Here is what she told me:

"I was born into a fairly well-known Caribbean family. My husband and I met in Europe when we both were in school. We married upon graduation and moved to my mother-in-law's home in Africa. I rarely saw my husband after that except at large family and public events. My mother-in-law was very domineering. She did not permit me to work. I gave birth to three children in six years.

"When my husband's government appointed him to the United Nations, I was overjoyed. My husband had a good salary and an expense account. He provided for his family well. He employed many servants. He also bought many homes and, with the help of friends, had a substantial investment portfolio. He kept everything in his name only. Whenever I tried to talk to him about this, he would stare at me and ask whether I or my children were hungry or without clothing. Then he would leave the room.

"My husband traveled all the time. Over the years he began to drink and became something of a womanizer. He had two children with two different women. He could have married either of them but didn't—because he was a 'modern' man. But he did expect me to accept these children into my home without rancor and graciously.

"Whenever I suggested a separation or a divorce, he would stare at me and say, 'I can't allow you to desert my household. If you force the issue, I will have you declared mentally incompetent and put away. You will never see your children again.'

"Who would help me if I forced the issue? My husband is a tribal chief. Would his tribe or its laws find me entitled to custody and a decent settlement if I were the one who wanted the divorce? Would the laws of my own country have any power in this situation? Could I turn to the International Court in The Hague or to the United Nations itself? My own father said he couldn't help me. He said I could always return to him— but only as I left him, *without my children*.

"If I fled my marriage anyway, what would happen to my children? My husband would punish *them* for my desertion. He'd treat *them* as the offspring of an immoral mother. He'd send them back to his family in Africa. He might never allow me to see them.

"I never left. However, a year ago, when our youngest turned fifteen, I obtained my first real job since completing graduate school. My husband has been threatening to disinherit our eldest son and to have me declared mentally incompetent if I don't quit and return to running his household.

"What should I do? Can my husband really have me declared mentally incompetent when it's not true? Should I hire a lawyer or simply stop working? Does anyone specialize in persuading a husband to allow his wife to work?"

Who "specialized" in turning domestic tyrants into domestic democrats? Even the UN can't do it. Few people, including diplomats, view women within their own families or countries as oppressed or exploited. Men and women deny the "oppressor" in themselves and in their familial or national midst. When pressed, people tend to locate the "oppressor" in somebody else's family or country or to view domestic "oppression" as the result of foreign politics and ideologies.

Male diplomats do not specialize in the status or problems of women. For this reason, diplomats tend to believe that "their" women are better protected, respected, and loved than "foreign" women are. ("*We* revere our women as wives and mothers. We do not expect them to have to find their own husbands or to work among hostile men"; "*We* educate our women and allow them to choose their own husbands.")

Female diplomats do exist. They are few in number. Fewer still specialize in women. Those who do often find themselves confined to all-female ghettos and granted occasional public hearings only if they are manfully "objective"—i.e., do not experience or analyze their own lives in order to understand the female condition.

On the subject of women, female diplomats and other female tokens know less than they think and always more than they say.

The truths of women's lives are not self-evident. The truths of women's lives remain buried in denial and silenced by death, disease, poverty, and illiteracy. Such truths cannot be comprehended by "objectivity" alone but must also be studied with precise and passionate subjectivity.

This chapter is not a compendium of (non-existent) studies and statistics. It is a passionate survey of women's custodial status under non-Western tribal, religious, and nationalistic rule; under capitalist democratic rule; and under communist totalitarian rule, in sixty-five countries outside the United States and Canada.

This chapter also surveys what the capitalist democracies do when the child of a female national is custodially claimed or paternally kidnapped by his or her father within the same geographical region or when s/he is taken to a foreign region; and what both the communist and capitalist superpowers do to those mothers who live in "strategically" located countries.

This chapter is based on formal and informal interviews that I conducted between 1975 and 1985. It is also shaped by my own reading and travels, by my work at the United Nations (1979–1980), and by feminist conferences that I attended, coordinated, or read about between 1973 and 1985.[5]

My questions in this chapter are: Is there any place on earth in which mothers have as many rights as they have obligations, where mothers are automatically entitled to child custody, or tend to obtain it even when a father or the state contests it?

Is there any place on earth in which the work of motherhood is adequately subsidized or custodially rewarded, despite the fact that mothers can easily be judged "immoral" by a double standard of morality that has nothing to do with mothering per se?

Is there any place on earth in which a father is not entitled to custody or simply cannot obtain it if a mother contests it? Is there any place on earth in which fathers do not abandon their families or in which fathers are forced to support their legitimate and "illegitimate" children, even against their will?

For thousands of years pre-industrial and non-Western societies were divided into patriarchal tribes and clans; and into kings and commoners, masters and slaves, rich and poor. Such societies were also divided by caste, color, and religion.

From the Middle Ages to World War II, these societies invaded or colonized each other and were also invaded and colonized by foreigners—the Spaniards, the Portuguese, the Turks, the Dutch, the British, the French, the Belgians, the Germans, the Americans—and by private enterprise.

This chapter is not an analysis of foreign colonialism and its effects on maternal custodial rights. In a sense, it is a survey of how women's bodies are reproductively and maternally colonized by different political systems and at different economic levels.

This chapter could not have been written with as much passion and subjectivity had I never crossed any national and cultural boundaries in search of love, death, power, and family.

I understood that May, the woman whose story opened this chapter was in danger, not only because I viewed the world in feminist perspective but because I had once also been married to a powerful man in a "third world" country.

I arrived in Kabul, Afghanistan, in 1961—three years after the women were unveiled. On the streets, and huddled together in the backs of public buses(!), those city women without male servants were still sheeted from head to foot: silent moving islands in a sea of men.

Like May, I lived with many servants. All worked seven days a week, gratefully ate the family "leftovers," were often beaten, and sent all their money to village families whom they rarely had time to see.

Like May, I lived with a domineering mother-in-law. Actually, I had *three* mothers-in-law and twenty-four brothers- and sisters-in-law. I lived with women who lived in *purdah*—beneath the veil and behind high walls, as the wealthy children of a polygamous father. Everyone's marriage had been or was being arranged. I both observed and experienced family life under such conditions, between parent and child and among brothers, sisters, spouses, half-brothers, and half-sisters.

As a "foreign" woman I was allowed to attend many public events. I was (naïvely) stunned by the contrast between Asian luxury and Asian poverty and by how religiously such inequality was accepted by those who suffered and by those who profited from it.

Here, in a "foreign" country, I first learned to see what existed everywhere on earth to some degree in one form or another.

After I escaped to America, I discovered how willing some Americans were to discuss the diplomatic "high life" in Afghanistan (I wasn't) and to condemn Afghanistan as a savage and inferior country (I wasn't). I never felt that other Americans understood the specificity of my experience or the extent to which "Afghanistan" was everywhere.

No Afghan was ever willing to admit that his diplomatic "high life" was more show than substance. No Afghan was willing to criticize his monarchy, his religion, or his family life, in Western, or Christian public. Most Afghans in America or Europe, like the privileged servants of tyranny everywhere, survived in whispers and by denying to themselves that anything was "wrong."

Whenever my ex-husband Ibrahim and I met, he would describe Kabul as the Vienna or Paris of Asia. Film directors from Europe, India, and the Soviet Union sat at cafés and watched the American "hippies" float by in their rags and miniskirts. What I distinctly remembered as a feudal religious monarchy had apparently been transformed into a modern secular democracy—the day after I left.

In 1979, when Ibrahim became an exile in America, I tried to "interview" him about divorce and custody in pre-Soviet Afghanistan. His indirect denial of certain facts infuriated me (as it always had). My insistence on discussing forbidden subjects directly filled him with patient contempt (as it always had).

Phyllis: Has any Afghan mother ever lost custody of her children?

Ibrahim: Never. Not once. Not that I know of. Islam is too wise and too merciful for that.

Phyllis: According to the Shari'a, a father is entitled to his children when the boy is seven and the girl is twelve.

Ibrahim: No, no. Only "at puberty." But what father would remove children from a good wife? What would he do with them?

Phyllis: What if the mother did something unheard of—like commit adultery?

Ibrahim: Under Shari'a, women can also sue for divorce if their husbands commit adultery, or are impotent, or refuse to support them, or are cruel.

Phyllis: But when the rare divorce *does* occur, who keeps the children?

Ibrahim: Divorce never occurs. It doesn't have to. Even when the men of my father's generation took a second wife, they didn't divorce or abandon their first wives and children. That would be too Western.

Phyllis: What if a woman really disobeys her husband? Can that lead to divorce or to her loss of custody?

Ibrahim: Wives don't disobey their husbands. Why would they? Now, if a mother is genuinely incompetent, if she completely neglects her children . . .

Phyllis: Neglects her children?

Ibrahim: Perhaps a mother is overly devoted to her own family. Perhaps she insists on visiting her mother every single day. Perhaps she leaves her children in the hands of servants too much. Perhaps she is not making sure that the children are kept from evil influences. Even such a terrible mother will be given time to change her behavior. The Kauzi [the mullah] might counsel her husband to give her six months to change her ways. Our mullahs are against divorce. Everyone is.

Phyllis: There must be *one* Afghan woman who once lost custody of her children because she was married to a cruel man or because she disobeyed him in some way.

Ibrahim: Give me some time to research this minor question for you.[6]

I have re-created this conversation for a reason. If May or I had tried to tell our husbands' tribesmen that we wanted a divorce, it is doubtful they would have sympathized with us. ("May/Phyllis must be crazy to want a divorce"; "She can't expect to be immoral and have her children too"; "Maybe she *is* mentally unstable,") etc.

If May or I had applied for political asylum as wives, our respective countries and the UN would have told us they couldn't interfere in the domestic affairs of another (or sovereign) nation-state, and anyway, "we must have been crazy to marry men from such backward countries."

THE SURVEY

It is dangerous for women to talk about women to an outsider or for publication. More than a third of my interviewees asked for anonymity; they are identified by false first names only.

To avoid echo-chamber repetition or too many statistics unsupported by personal anecdote, I present some countries at greater length than others either here or in the Notes. I present countries in alphabetical order when they are located within the same geographical region.

THE NEAR AND MIDDLE EAST

Egypt

My respondent, Dr. Nawal El Saadawi, researched the question of Egyptian custody for me. She wrote:

"According to Egyptian law, it is the *father* only (and not the mother) who has the *authority* over his children, males and females, until they reach the age of twenty-one. For instance, a boy or girl cannot travel outside the country without the permission of the father. If the father is away, or dead, then the *authority* goes to another *male member* of the family (and not to the mother) such as the *uncle* or the grandfather.

"Usually Egyptian mothers try to keep their children with them whether the fathers pay support or not. Fathers try to pay the least support, or avoid paying support altogether, unless forced to by the law. After divorce, the man usually remarries. The mother usually supports the children and avoids remarriage.

"In 1979, the government modified some crucial items in the Egyptian Marriage and Divorce Law. One item is related to the right of [fit] mothers to keep custody of their children after divorce. Now, she can keep a boy until he is ten and a girl until she is twelve. The father is supposed to pay their maintenance until then.

"A judge can decide to prolong this period. He or she can allow the mother to keep her boy until he is 15 and the girl until she marries. In such cases, the father has to pay the mother only for the personal expenses of the children such as food, clothes and education, and then, only according to his income."[7]

Iran

According to Dr. Reza Baraheni, domestic life in pre-Khomeini Iran was based on "absolute male dominance":

"The children absolutely belonged to the father. He had the final say over what children can and can't do. Fathers were dictators over their children. Very traditional wives from good families could subtly influence their husbands. They could never oppose them.

"Arranged marriages were in some ways better than the odd free choice in the West. Iranian men did not see their wives as sex-symbols. In fact, many Iranian men prefer anal intercourse as a means of birth control and because they are all a little homosexual. How else can they be, if they're brought up so apart from women? Unfortunately, many Iranian men are also homophobic. Their ambivalence about sexual expression is very intense."[8]

Marva is a professor in exile from Iran since 1981. I asked her about women's custodial status in post-Khomeini Iran. She said that:

"Everyone is afraid. Everyone knows that they are only safe if they obey the Qu'ran and public opinion. Iranian children have always belonged to the fathers and to their father's family. In 1980, the husband of my close girlfriend died. They were both middle class professionals. In 1982, the paternal grandparents sued for custody of the two children. They charged my friend with being unfit because she wasn't a devout Moslem. She had many Western ideas. The grandparents won custody. Miraculously, my girlfriend still managed to escape with her life, her sanity, and her children."[9]

Iraq

Basra described what happened to her sister Maryam after her husband divorced her; Nadia responded to my questions about custody with a passionate tirade against divorce. According to Basra:

"My brother-in-law took Farida, his 8-year-old daughter, away from my sister Maryam. He allowed Karim, his 4½-year-old son, to stay. He gave Farida to his mother. The two of them brainwashed Farida against Maryam. They told her that her mother was a bad woman who never took good care of her and who could ruin her chances for a good marriage.

"In 1982 my brother-in-law was automatically entitled to his son. He took him. Karim, poor child, ran back to his mother many times. Each time Maryam had to return him. Even though my sister has a profession and strong family support, there is nothing she can do. It is the father's legal right to keep his children."

According to Nadia:

"It's not hard to prove male adultery, but it's so bad for a woman to be divorced that it's not worth it. It is very hard for a divorced mother to remarry at all, or in a desirable way. An Iraqi woman will put up with almost anything in order to remain married and with her children. If divorce is unavoidable, always, the mother wants most to keep the children. She wants that more than money."

Israel

Israel is a modern, Western, and democratic state. It is also a theocratic state and very much at the mercy of American foreign policy. Israeli women have been romanticized as swamp-draining pioneers and gun-toting soldiers. However, Israeli women do not run (nor are they well represented in) the Israeli government, rabbinate, fighting armed forces, or economy.[10]

Israeli women are not customarily or legally forced into arranged or polygamous marriages; they are not veiled, do not live in purdah, and are free to emigrate to other countries. However, most Israeli women cannot travel or emigrate with their children if their Israeli husbands contest it.

Shoshannah was born in Tel Aviv and gave birth to four children between 1964 and 1972. Both she and her ex-husband are physicians. She said:

"In 1975, my husband moved out. He claimed I was having an affair with a woman neighbor. I was. He dragged me into court ten times in one year. Every divorcing husband screams, 'My wife is an adulteress or a lesbian,' to get what he wants economically. I made a big mistake. I was terrified of the public exposure. I gave up all my economic rights. I wasn't smart enough to deny everything.

"After our divorce, I still wasn't a free woman. My ex-husband inhibited my every move. He acted as if he were an emigration official holding the kids' passports. I was offered an academic post in Europe—which I couldn't accept. My ex-husband refused to sign for the kids to leave the country with me. It's not as if he was actually seeing the kids. He never visited them, not once.

"He remarried two days after our divorce became official. His new wife gave birth to two children in two years. This new wife wouldn't let my children visit their father. She would say: 'My husband is so busy. If I let you in, my little children will think you're trying to steal their father.'

"My children blamed me for the divorce and for their father's indifference to them. They yelled at me because we never had enough money and because they were 'different' from their friends.

"I finally accepted a job in the States for a year. My eldest child wanted to stay behind with his father. At the last minute, the new wife demanded that I rent a separate apartment for my son and hire a housekeeper to attend to his needs. 'I'm not your personal servant,' she screamed. 'If you don't do what I say, my husband won't let you take your other kids out of the country.'

"This time I fought back. I told her: 'If I don't have your husband's permission to take all of my children out of this country, be assured that we will all move in with you for the whole year.' It worked."

Naomi is a battered wife and part-time prostitute. Her husband has twice kidnapped their son as a way of keeping Naomi "in line." She said:

"My parents came from Algeria in the 1950s. I was born in Israel. My father beat my mother and my older brothers beat me. When I was sixteen, I moved in with a boy from Poland. He made me sleep with him and then with other men for money. He agreed to marry me when I was eight months pregnant.

"Now, if I don't do whatever he asks, he disappears with our five-year-old son. Or he threatens to divorce me and take both children away from me. He says that the government won't let my kids stay with an uneducated prostitute whose own family won't take her in. He's right. So I do what he wants."

Lebanon*

Nasreen described what happened to her cousin Leyla:

"Leyla's husband betrayed her with one of her girlfriends. He ran off when their youngest child was two years old. In her heart, Leyla kept hoping her husband would return to her. For years, my poor cousin kept doing his laundry. She never told anyone that she was divorced. Our family worked out a private arrangement for her maintenance.

*For information on Saudi Arabia and Syria, see note 11 on page 563.

"Leyla was lucky. Her husband never demanded custody of his children. For years, he hardly saw them. Eventually, when the children were eight, ten and twelve, he began to visit them again. The children were impressed by his money and his worldliness. The eldest child, however, felt it was bad for her own reputation to visit her father at his house given that a mistress was present.

"Leyla was ordered to persuade her daughter to visit her father's house—or else. The children began regular visits. They were allowed to smoke, drink, and listen to American dance music at their father's house. As they got older, they were permitted to bring 'dates' over. Soon, two of Leyla's children were spending more and more time with their father—who permitted them all the freedom Leyla was forced to deny them. A divorced mother must be especially careful not to endanger her child's reputation any further.

"Leyla finally lost all her children when the youngest was eleven. They just moved in with their father. Leyla won't admit she lost them—just as she won't talk about being divorced. Her children are condescending to her. They each have a foreign sportscar and go abroad on vacation. Recently, my niece had the temerity to call her mother to say: 'Daddy is having financial difficulties. Would you mind cutting down your expenses?' Cutting down? Leyla lives very modestly."[11]

The West Bank

Emily is a Christian-American woman who converted to Islam when she married a Palestinian Arab. She moved to the West Bank and, by 1971, had three sons.

"I separated from my husband after eight years of a very happy marriage when he began to drink. At the time, our sons were three, eight and ten. He immediately moved for custody of the two oldest boys. I hired an Arab Jewish lawyer who knew his Shari'a inside-out.

"The Mullah made a home visit himself. He saw how my husband drank. He also knew that he'd have to rule lawfully and in a way that would save face for my husband. He ruled that the father was of course entitled to custody, but for the good of the children they should keep living with their mother, perhaps even for 99 years. A clever and practical sort of ruling.

"My eldest son has been fighting with me to live with his father. He's 13 and nearly a foot taller than me. I can't stop him. Let him see for himself what living with his father is like."

Turkey*

Naila Minai is the Turkish-born author of *Women in Islam*. She responded to my specific questions about custodial matters in this way:

"The sexual double standard in Turkey has always influenced the court's interpretation of immorality in custody litigation. Ex-wives have been dragged back into court by vindictive ex-husbands who happened to see them sitting with male friends in public restaurants.

"Under the new government, courts are more consciously pro-feminist. I could not dig up *one* case where the courts decided to take the child away from the mother just because she dined in public with a male friend. But the point is that no man has ever been dragged to court for dining out with a woman friend. He is not considered immoral or unfit as a parent even if he lives with a woman friend.

"In 1974, the Committee to Revise the Turkish Constitution was formed. One of the suggestions being seriously considered is the rights of illegitimate children to inherit from their biological father whether or not he accepts the child. The main purpose of the law is to protect the children born of "imam marriages," i.e., marriages performed by Muslim "ministers" but not registered with the state authorities. Such marriages are illegal in Turkey, but are practiced in the hinterlands.

"The state authorities have regularly passed resolutions proclaiming all children legitimate who were born before—or after—a certain date, in order to protect the children's interests as guaranteed by secular law. Some educated urban women, however, are upset by this constitutional proposal. 'It will be the end of the family,' one said."[12]

ASIA†

India

Family matters are governed by both religious and civil Indian law. Islamic law functions here as it does elsewhere. Among Hindus there is a greater probability of fathers' retaining custody if there is a contest. Fathers are also considered the "natural guardians" of children over five years of age.[13]

---

*For further information on Turkey and on Yemen, see note 12, page 563.
†For information on China and the Soviet Union see pages 368 and 370 respectively.

Madhur is a Hindu wife, mother, and university professor. She responded to my questions about custody by telling me about her marriage.

"My marriage was arranged when I was a child. We didn't marry until I was sixteen and my husband, twenty-eight. I had all my children by the time I was twenty-one. I was also able to finish college before I was twenty-three.

"I published some articles anonymously on fairly controversial subjects. My husband found them in my drawer. He pulled out a tuft of hair. He threatened to divorce me if I ever published anything again. He began to beat me to keep me from becoming too independent, too Western.

"Divorce is uncommon among women in my circle. My husband knew I would not leave him. I could not live apart from my children, or in shame in my father's house, or alone as a divorcee. I could not live apart from my past. I weathered the storm. Our eldest daughter is soon to be married. My life has remained whole."

Japan

According to my respondent Dr. Kiyomi Kawano:

"Few Japanese men *want* custody. Therefore, most divorces result in maternal custody. Men cannot raise children. They can't even take care of themselves. Japanese men tend to be 'workaholic.' They live in a culture where to be 'hung up' on children is considered 'sissy.' A Japanese man doesn't want to be 'Mr. Kramer.' He is supposed to 'die out on the economic battlefield.'

"One of my good friends got divorced about three years ago. She had a hard time winning custody of her children. She was lucky. She had the financial resources to keep fighting her husband for two years. There was no mother-in-law ready to take over.

"Most divorced mothers face severe psychological and economic problems—unless they come from very wealthy and modern families. This is the reason that so many women choose to suffer in abusive marriages rather than to leave them. Needless to say, this allows men to remain arrogant."[14]

Korea

According to my respondent Grace Liu-Volckhausen:

"All countries with a Confucian tradition have a strong tradition of paternal rights and authority. Children carry their fathers' names and belong to them. In 1960, my mother fought for women's inheritance rights in Korea. The Chief Justice met with a women's delegation. He said: 'How can a field have any rights? Only the farmer, only the seed has rights.'

"Korean women often have no [first] names. They are known as the 'Number one Daughter of Mr. So-and-So.' Many Asian women will describe themselves as 'the lady who lives next to the post office,' or 'the lady who is the mother of Mr. Ahn's Number One son.'

"Since the 1950s, Korean women have had the right to sue for divorce. Female-initiated divorce is increasing. However, divorced women do not get alimony or child support from their ex-husbands or from the government. They may also lose custody of their children. I personally have three friends, all very educated women, who lost custody of their children in the 1960s and 1970s. None have ever seen their children again. I also know some women who have gotten custody and a lump sum of money.

"As of 1984, unwed motherhood remains a great social stigma. Families will keep their daughters, but will give the illegal baby away for adoption. Korean and Japanese women have a long struggle ahead for the legal right to have and keep a child out of wedlock or after divorce. We also need an enforceable system of alimony and child support, and equal employment opportunities."[15]

Malaysia and Nepal*

In Malaysia "guardianship" is the sole right of the father. "Custody," however, denotes daily physical responsibility for a child and is often granted to the mother.[16]

According to Nepal's national code, "A mother has no right upon the issue she has given birth to. The law is based on the Hindu concept of women as *jaya* or one who bears children for her husband. The mother simply gives birth to children for her husband."[17]

---

*For information on Australia and New Zealand, see note 17, page 565.

Thailand

According to Nancy Greene, of the American Branch of International Social Services:

"In 1969, a Thai mother lost custody of her infant daughter to her Thai husband. Thailand has a paternal preference. She had no recourse. The child was given to her paternal grandmother. This mother eventually married an American who obtained American citizenship for her. They decided to try to obtain custody of her thirteen-year-old daughter.

"We investigated the matter on their behalf. We discovered that the grandmother regularly abused the girl. The father had remarried and rarely saw her. Over the years the girl had been brainwashed against her mother. Initially she refused to leave Thailand with a mother who had married an American. She promised to consider it but remained ambivalent.

"Before she turned fourteen, her father was imprisoned in an economic scandal. Shortly thereafter she ran away with a boyfriend. She had repeatedly talked of being ashamed—ashamed that her mother married an American, ashamed that her father was in jail, ashamed that her grandmother abused her. So she ran off with her boyfriend, which in Thailand is a pretty scandalous action. Now she probably has that to be ashamed of, too.

"She's lost. We can't find her. This whole tragedy could have been avoided. Here's a mother who was railroaded. She had no legal recourse fourteen years ago. For the past ten years she's not had the most stable life, but couldn't that have something to do with not having her daughter? Now, when she's finally in a position to reclaim her child, it's too late. The girl's hatred of her mother was reinforced for fourteen years. Now, two women's lives have been ruined."[18]

Vietnam

Vietnam is one of many examples of what routinely happens to the economic and custodial rights of mothers in those "developing" countries deemed "strategic" or in need of salvation, by both the communist and the capitalist superpowers.

Vietnamese mothers and children were separated from each other by death and by imprisonment. Many Vietnamese mothers were forced to give up their children for adoption to their more advantaged conquerors (or saviors). According to my respondent Lee:

"When a Vietnamese mother of an Amerasian child was left behind, she was usually isolated and very poor. Many children were placed for adoption because of their mothers' inability to support or protect them during wartime. Many of these mothers didn't understand that the adoption was permanent. Those mothers who later managed to make their way to America in search of their children soon discovered that they had no legal access to their children. Adoption agencies wouldn't even divulge their children's whereabouts.

"Because of the eventual Vietnamese anger and American guilt about 'Operation Baby-Lift,' adoption agencies now require proof of the mother's death or a signed statement that she absolutely relinquishes all future interest in her child. In a sense, the same country that killed these mothers' relatives also killed *them* off on paper to create babies for Americans to adopt."

AFRICA

Algeria

According to Nadine Claire, a divorced Algerian mother is "given" responsibility for boys until they are "nine or ten" and girls "until marriage."

> But she is only working as a maid in keeping the children—the husband can take them back whenever he feels that she is not raising the children properly. She has got to stay close to him geographically, so that he can check on her every day. Which means that she cannot build a new life, she has to be under his eye all the time.
>
> [Parents cannot adopt children.] This means . . . that at any point, the state can take the children back. So if you don't "behave properly," if you are not a "good citizen," if you have any kind of political activity this is a continual threat. And I know some trade unionists who have just emigrated, because they couldn't stand the fear. And this of course was stealing a child, because it's not their child, right? On the other hand I also know of cases in which the family was just upset after two years, or five years, and just dropped the children back into the orphanages. So this is not adoption, not at all, and women are fighting for the rights of these children.[19]

Ethiopia

According to Daniel Haile, parental rights in Ethiopia are customarily exercised by the father, by his appointed guardian, or by the other men in his family. Unless the mother is considered "unfit," she customarily retains custody of children under five.

Although the code says that this is in the best interests of the children, there is reason to believe that this practice is really based upon the proposition that it is the mother's duty to raise young children who, when they grow up, become productive members of their father's homestead or business, as the case may be.[20]

Ghana

Evelyn is a mother, a wife, and a career woman. She said:

"I was born in Accra. My father divorced my mother in 1951. He remarried and kept all four children with him. His new wife was cruel. My older brothers fought with her constantly. One boy ran away to our mother all the time. She had to send him back. We were allowed to see our mother regularly, but we couldn't live with her. This was a bitter experience. Each of my brothers vowed never to divorce their wives. They never have.

"Ghana's laws are civil [British common law]; tribal [varying from tribe to tribe]; and religious [Christian and Muslim]. Tribally and traditionally, children usually live with their mothers. A father is usually away on business, or he lives with another wife. Fathers don't always support their children. An illegitimate child belongs to his mother's family and is completely accepted. The government doesn't have to support him."[21]

Mozambique*

In many parts of Africa, including Lesotho and southern Mozambique, once a husband has paid *lobolo* (bride-price), he owns all the children his wife produces; and is entitled to keep them after divorce. In Mozambique:

Child custody is determined not by what is best for the child, but according to which lineage he is considered to belong. Muslim children always belong to the father, in matrilineal societies their guardian is the mother's brother, and in patrilineal groups, once the *lobolo* has been paid, they belong to the father's lineage. Moreover, if the children go with their mother, for whatever reason, the father feels no responsibility to help support them.[22]

---

*For information on Lesotho, Mauritania, and Morocco, see note 23, page 568.

In 1975, for the first time in Mozambique, women were allowed to initiate divorce. "People's tribunals" were established to arbitrate issues of divorce, marital property, and custody. Women's families still discouraged divorce (the *lobolo* would have to be returned). Courts tried to convince fathers that children should be allowed to remain with their mothers and that fathers should become responsible for providing food for their children.

> Fathers do not accept their responsibility to provide food for their families; they expect this to come from the plot on which their wives grow cereals and vegetables. Many men in southern Mozambique who migrate either to the South African mines or to urban or rural employment centers in Mozambique in search of paid employment use their wages to pay taxes and buy consumer goods, but never send their wives money for food. Unless their husbands comprehend their responsibility to feed their family, this attitude can lead to serious problems in urban areas where many women no longer have a plot of land to cultivate.[23]

Nigeria

According to Dr. J. O. Debo Akande, "customary" Nigerian law grants custody to the father or, upon his death, to his family. Nursing mothers are entitled to temporary custody and in some areas all children are entitled to a *woman's* care until they are seven. However:

> A woman's care is not necessarily the mother's care and if the father is able to make provision to have a woman look after the child he may take the child. . . . A father could defeat the mother's right to appoint a guardian for an infant child on his death. The guardian so appointed has a better right to custody than the mother. . . . The court [can] award the custody of an infant under seven to the mother, provided that she has not committed adultery [or is] considered absolutely unfit.[24]

South Africa*

The capitalist and the communist superpowers both have an economic, an ideological, and a military-geographical stake in South Africa. The tribal and customary laws which already prohibit maternal economic and custodial rights have been further codified by the white apartheid regime.[25]

---

*For information on the Sudan, see note 27, page 571.

Black South African mothers and children may starve together in their rural homelands, or they may attempt to join their husbands and fathers as employees in "white" urban areas. However, the laws still operate to keep mothers, children, and fathers apart.[26]

Black South African children are sometimes, and under certain conditions, allowed to remain with their mothers in "white" urban areas. However, they may not be allowed to begin primary school until they are seven. Or they can attend secondary school only if they travel long distances daily or return to their rural homelands. Or black children who are sixteen or more may remain with their mothers in "white" areas if their mothers are married and if both mother and child are listed "properly" on their fathers' residential permits. According to Hilda Bernstein:

> Some years ago, Alexandra Township, a black residential area nine miles outside Johannesburg, was gradually being cleared of its whole population for "single" men and "single" women. . . . For months on end, police raided the houses, day and night. All those who lacked the necessary permits, tax receipts or papers were arrested; then the women, [and] all their children, were "endorsed out." Sometimes women were arrested when their husbands were at work, or both husband and wife would be arrested. Then small children were left totally alone. Gradually the women were expelled to the reserves; those born in other places—Lesotho, or Swaziland—were expelled even if they had lived and worked a lifetime in South Africa.
>
> When in 1972 the press published stories of children being left alone, or ordered away from their parents, Mr. Coen Kotze, who managed the local board dealing with Alexandra, stated that the women, if they were working, were given an alternative. "They are given ample time to make up their minds. We are giving them the choice: they must send their children back to the homelands themselves. . . . This is the policy and we will enforce it." The children, he said, who were being ordered out were *illegal;* and their mothers were migrant workers recruited from the homelands on a single basis. "The law states that they are illegally in the area, so they have to go. It's as simple as that."[27]

Tanzania

According to Jane Rose K. Kikopa, children customarily belong to their fathers who paid *lobolo* for them. When a father dies, his "clan council" appoints a guardian for his children, "usually a man." In a polygamous household a mother's "eldest adult son" will act as guardian to his underage siblings. The courts have recently been instructed to consider the "welfare of the child" in its custodial determinations. However, the courts still resort to community "customs which more often recognize a father's absolute right over the children. A mother is never considered capable and competent to look after her own children and property."[28]

Uganda

Grace Akello describes the absolute right over children that Ugandan fathers of the Lugbara, Acholi, and Lango tribes have.

The Lango Kwer ceremonies employ symbols that demonstrate that, although a child is affiliated with both the mother's and the father's side, a choice must be made between the two sides, and the Lango child is more closely tied to the father's side. If a marriage breaks down and the woman is strong-willed enough to leave, her husband will be able to keep his children, unless one is breast feeding. Once that child has stopped breast feeding, the father may go to his former wife's home and demand his child back.[29]

Zambia

According to lawyer Mtaze Singele:

"Traditional [tribal] marriages have no custody disputes. The custody of the children is decided by tradition: patrilineal or matrilineal. A patrilineal society will automatically grant all children to the father on divorce if his lobolo is paid up. Many times it's not. There's always been a tacit understanding (a 'gentlemen's agreement') concerning the bride-price: the husband pays only part of it on marriage, and pays it off as each child is born. So if there are only one or two children in the marriage, his lobolo may not be paid off. He must pay the rest of it before the children are his. If not, the children may go to his brother or father—but never to the mother."[30]

Zimbabwe

In Zimbabwe, fathers pay lobolo and are entitled to custody of their children. When a father dies, "guardianship" of his children usually goes to his brother. In some tribes a woman may be appointed guardian of her children. When she is unwed, or if the lobolo has not been paid, the mother's guardian also becomes her children's guardian.

While the father is entitled to guardianship and custody of his children, the divorced mother is not denied access to them. She may visit them, stay with them for reasonable periods, and express her views on matters concerning their upbringing and general welfare. If she finds that they are being neglected or abused in any way, she may bring the matter to court, which as the upper guardian, has a duty to investigate the matter and if necessary award custody to the mother or someone else.[31]

According to Rudo Gaidzanwa:

In Zimbabwe, black women can choose to be married under the civil marriage law or under customary law; but if they decide to divorce, they are governed solely by customary law. Consequently, in divorce they lose their rights to their children and inheritance. . . . Women who have begun to contest bridewealth point out that if you have bridewealth paid for you, you are mortgaging your rights to your child and yourself.[32]

CENTRAL AND SOUTH AMERICA*

Argentina

According to Argentinian novelist Luisa Valenzuela:

"*Patria Potestad*—or fathers' rights, embodied by individual men or by the state, completely governs family life in Argentina. In the late 1960s, a mother I know was accused of being against the government—by her husband. She had to leave the country immediately. Her husband wouldn't let the children go. He didn't let the children see their mother's relatives either. For about ten years he kept moving them from school to school. Luckily, his attempts to turn them against my friend were unsuccessful. She was finally able to smuggle them out of the country. I have another close friend who couldn't get her children out of Argentina for ten years, even for a visit, because her husband wouldn't allow it. She saw her children only after they turned eighteen."[33]

Argentinian feminists have recently organized a campaign against *patria potestad*. As of 1983, 13,000 signatures were collected—"no small

---

*For information on Peru and Puerto Rico, see page 374 and note 44, page 577, respectively.

wonder" in a country that has tortured and executed people for "appearing in the wrong person's address book."[34] According to Dr. Teresa Bernardez:

"Although many Argentinian fathers are physically demonstrative and feel close to their children, they don't usually pay alimony or child support. Husbands lie about their incomes. State subsidies are very inadequate. Mothers cannot legally remarry since divorce isn't legal. There are many 'common law' marriages and re-marriages. The children of these marriages are considered illegitimate and have no rights of inheritance.

"There is no enforcement of family support in Argentina. Abortion and divorce are illegal. Middle class unwed mothers are stigmatized. Lower and upper class women are less ostracized as unwed mothers."[35]

Brazil*

According to Dr. Heleith I. B. Saffieti, Brazilian mothers are considered very "important" for children only if they are "moral" or if the father doesn't want them.

"Most men don't fight for custody. If the mother behaved badly, custody might go to the grandparents. Generally, women keep children. This is more often a burden than a right since fathers seldom pay child support. More and more, men are abandoning their families. Fathers also are away all day working, or they're drunk, or they don't want to take on family responsibilities.

"Many women tolerate violence from men because it is very hard for a mother to feed her children alone. The situation in the Northeast is dramatic. For example, an abandoned mother of five children gets up at 5 A.M., prepares a small quantity of food for her children, locks them in the house, walks 5–6 miles to work, works for 4 hours carrying stones, and walks back by evening—for $12.00 a month. With this money, a family of six cannot afford to eat more than manioc flour with water."[36]

Brazilian husbands punish their adulterous or "uppity" wives custodially and economically—and sometimes by killing them. In one Bra-

*For information on Bolivia, see note 38, page 575.

zilian city, within a three-year period, 722 men killed their wives or girlfriends in "crimes of honor."[37]

Unwed mothers and "illegitimate" children are stigmatized. For example, in the mid-1970s, a pregnant Brazilian teenager was expelled from her religious high school. She married the father of her child and got a court order to re-admit her to high school.

> The director of the school, a priest, decided to resign rather than respect the court order, so he was replaced. However, when the time came to receive her diploma, it was not given to her. Saying that the decision of the court was immoral, the Monseigneur decided to close the school. About a hundred students found themselves unable to continue their studies. But the director will not consider reopening the school unless he is sure no diploma will be given to S. He declared that the school was ruled by "Canon Right," and that it did not accept conception outside of marriage.[38]

Chile, Cuba, El Salvador, and Guatemala*

Many "developing" countries in Central and South America are war zones in which the capitalist and communist superpowers are battling for economic, military, and ideological control.

Chile

Lita is a Chilean mother and career woman. She is also a political refugee.

> "Before Allende, the Chilean authorities were worse than any husband. Many children were 'lost' forever when their parents were taken to jail or executed. My husband was murdered in prison. I was tortured and imprisoned. Afterwards, I was unable to locate our son, a teenager. I fled the country without him. I returned right after Allende came to power. I found our son alive and in despair. After Allende was himself murdered, I escaped again, this time with my boy."[39]

Cuba

Cecilia is a Cuban-born dancer.

> "I was five years old when Castro came to power. My father owned a factory. He and my mother left Cuba the night they burned his factory

---

*For information on Colombia, see note 39, page 576.

down. I was left behind with one of our relatives who was a communist sympathizer. My two older sisters lived elsewhere with other relatives. We didn't see each other too often. We didn't see my parents for six years. I instinctively kept quiet about them. It was years before I realized that our family was under constant surveillance and suspicion.

"When I was fourteen, an aunt took me on a 'trip' to the 'other side of the island.' A plane was waiting for me. My parents met me in Miami. I didn't recognize them. I was very ambivalent about staying with them. They were my parents but they were also traitors to the Revolution."[40]

El Salvador

According to Pedro, a lawyer now living in exile:

"Sixty-five percent of the population in El Salvador is rural, Catholic, and very, very poor. Divorce in the villages is very rare. For the poor, marriage is an economic necessity. When a poor couple do separate, the mother is left with many children and no means of supporting them. The state is not obliged to help her. The wealthy Salvadoran father always gets custody of the children if he wants them. Most wealthy fathers want their children, especially the boys."[41]

When war between the two superpowers intensified in El Salvador, mothers, fathers, and children were increasingly separated from each other by death and imprisonment and by maternal attempts to save their children by any means possible.

Some Salvadorans fled to the United States illegally. Mothers, like Christina Landaverde (whom I discussed in Chapter Two), were separated from their children by forced adoption or by the U.S. Immigration and Naturalization Service detention of Salvadoran (and other Central American) children as a means of "luring" their mothers out of illegal "hiding."[42]

Guatemala

Nancy L. Gonzalez, an anthropologist married to a Guatemalan man, wrote:

With considerable sadness I had made the decision to leave Guatemala, where the employment opportunities were few. As a woman, I also ran the risk, if I remained, of losing custody of my sons, since Guatemalan law gave them to the father from age seven. In any case, I would not have been permitted to take them out of the country, even on short trips, without their father's written permission. This seemed too much of a limitation for a woman whose career depended upon travel to such a large extent. Furthermore, as a noncitizen, I also worried about other limitations on my freedom of action and the security of property I might acquire. I did briefly consider becoming a Guatemalan, but upon reflection that seemed unwise.[43]

Jamaica and Nicaragua*

Jamaica

Shirley grew up on a farm in the Jamaican countryside. She said:

"In the country, a woman is considered 'bad' if she has a relationship outside of marriage—even if she and her husband are separated. However, it's not considered 'bad' for men to have other women. Also, men can be drunk. Women can't. Usually what happens when a mother commits adultery, is that her husband walks out and leaves the children behind. It is very rare for a man to want to take the kids. He doesn't want the responsibility. Sometimes, though, a man will turn children against their mother.

"My mother was married to a man who left her. She had eight children with him, and three children, including me, afterwards. My mother kept us all alive the best way she could. Whenever any of my older half-brothers asked their father for money, he would chase them away or abuse them.

"Imagine my surprise when my half-brothers joined forces with their father to throw their own mother out of the house! They would torment her and curse her. They threw her clothes out the window. They figured that if they got her out, they could move their own wives and children into our house. We girls protected our mother from these boys."

In the 1950s and 1960s, many Jamaican women traveled to England to work as domestics. In the 1970s and 1980s, they began traveling to the United States to work. According to Janice:

"It's very common for Jamaican mothers to leave their children in order to earn the money elsewhere to support them. There is no stigma attached

*For information on Puerto Rico and Uruguay, see note 44, page 577.

to doing this. I haven't seen my children for three years. I do miss them terribly. You stay depressed. Sometimes you get desperate. Here, you have come a long distance to make money for your children, but you are without them. You are absolutely by yourself, a stranger in a strange land."

Nicaragua
According to Maria:

"I'm a member of the Women's Organization of [revolutionary] Nicaragua ('AMLAE'). Our problem is not losing custody of our children. It is having to support an average of ten to fifteen children by ourselves. Half of all our households are single-mother homes. Fathers desert their children and aren't held accountable.

"Our life expectancy is about 53. Under Somoza, polio was still epidemic. In four years, polio has been eradicated. In August of 1979 our government passed a law guaranteeing everyone equality, regardless of birth, race, color, sex, language or opinion. It is also now 'illegal' to use women as sex-objects in advertising.

"In 1983, a 'Law of Nature' was passed, making fathers equally responsible for a child's needs. Birth control and abortion remain illegal. Most women are religious Catholics and wouldn't support abortion."[44]

EUROPE

Great Britain

According to Alec Samuels, the majority of English fathers do not want (or do not think they can obtain) custody of children.

The mother usually wins because the father does not contest the application or contests only half-heartedly, or is unable to provide for the care and attention of the child, especially during the day when he is at work. In other words, the mother wins on the merits and not by reason of prejudice or presumption. . . . Even where the mother does gain custody, she only gains day-to-day looking after. Unresolved disputes over major matters such as religion and education may still be taken by a father to the court for decision.[45]

When fathers *do* contest custody, they do so by accusing mothers either of sexual or "uppity" behavior[46], or by kidnapping the children. Dr. Martin Richards has noted:

"What seems to be a growing problem [in the United Kingdom] is the kidnapping of children and the taking of them overseas. Usually, but not always, the kidnapper is, of course, the father. The major problem is that very few, if any, countries will recognize the orders made in British courts so that the mother has to start afresh in the new country—assuming, of course, that she is able to trace the children. Also, British embassies have been very reluctant to provide help for parents trying to retrieve their children. . . . The major significant change in recent years [in British custody] is a growing belief that joint [not to be confused with split] custody should be the normative arrangement."[47]

The British state systematically challenges the custodial rights of poor, single, working-class, dark-skinned, "colonial," immigrant, and lesbian mothers. According to Norma Steele, a black "colonial" mother, many such mothers face state-imposed poverty and separation from their children. She has said:

Every day we have to fight the [British] State for the custody of our children. When we come to this country, because we have the least money internationally, we are forced to leave our children behind. Then after years of hard saving and long separation, we are told they are too old to come to Britain without a work permit, which is almost impossible to get. . . . Our hard-earned cash is taken away as tax, yet with the Finance Act (1976) the government is saying that parents with children abroad are not allowed to claim Child Benefits for these children. We are tired of this.

It is us mothers who have to fight the police and courts when our children are arrested. It is us mothers who have to fight at the [social services] when they are trying to take our children into care. Black women have made a big fight to get [social services] for the money and time to raise our children as we want even in the face of veiled threat of deportation.[48]

France, Holland, and West Germany*

Puissance paternelle (fathers' rights) has dominated the legal codes of northwestern Europe. Mothers could retain child custody under paternal guidance; and only if husbands and the state judged them to be "moral." According to Christopher L. Blakesley, French law has never expressly articulated a "maternal preference."[49]

---

*For information on Austria, Belgium, Luxembourg, and Switzerland, see notes 49 and 51 on pages 578 and 579.

The concept of *parental* authority *(l'authorité parentale)* was recently introduced as a legal right in France,[50] Austria,[51] Holland,[52] and West Germany.[53] According to my respondent Ellen J. Cahill:

"In both France and Holland, domestic legislation emphasizes paternal *rights* and maternal *responsibilities*. Legal formulations are ambiguous, but clearly designed to favor a patriarchal system in terms of inheritance, ownership of names, *etc.* European divorce procedures are terrible. In many cases, the children are assigned to the 'care' of the mother, but it is the father who is invested with the authority and power to decide matters pertaining to the children's education and future."[54]

Simone is a French mother who was custodially penalized for adultery.

"You must understand that France is really a class-ridden and snobbish society. The French are treacherous to women who step out of line, or who refuse to keep up appearances. Mothers must be perfect. Ordinary working girls try to look like countesses.

"In 1976, I had an affair with a man much younger than myself. My husband is a government official. He and his mother took custody of our daughter. He said I could ruin his career and my daughter's marriage possibilities by my behavior. They told my daughter that I was a woman who thought only about myself, not about her. Remember the Gabrielle Roussier affair? I see myself as another kind of Roussier. Adultery is not romantic if a mother can lose her child over it."[55]

Greece

According to Margaret Papandreou, president of the Greek Women's Union:

Until 1982, all authority and decisions involving the family resided in the husband; he could decide where the family would live, how the children would be brought up, and whether his wife would work or even take the children out of the country. Strictly speaking, a man could file for divorce on grounds that his wife was a poor housekeeper.[56]

Wives were responsible for the physical care of the house, and the physical care of the children. In the case of divorce, a boy child of ten could be taken by the father, and often, he could have the girl children too, if he desired.

Naturally, the attitudes that have to do with the man's position and role in the family do not automatically change when written into law.[57]

Republic of Ireland

Northern Ireland is a war zone. Mothers and children are being separated and lost to each other in the battle to maintain—or over-throw—English, Protestant, and upper- and middle-class power.

Like mothers in "developing" non-Western countries, Irish mothers are also losing their children unjustly, as a result of customary tribal law—i.e., Catholicism. According to my respondent Ellen J. Cahill:

"In the early 1970s, I worked as a midwife in a post-natal ward of a Dublin Hospital. Great pressure was put on a young unwed mother of nineteen to submit to the adoption of her newborn baby by unknown strangers. The medical officer, the hospital priest and the girl's parents started this pressure as part of her 'pre-natal care.' The young mother had little education, no technical skills and no job. I can still visualize her, lying on her post-natal hospital bed in great distress. She was discouraged from seeing or feeding her baby, so as to obliterate the memory of its existence.

"The identity of the father was not disclosed to the ward staff. Was he a young man, without income? Was he a married man, with several children? At the time, I was appalled at the hypocritical attitudes that would separate a child from its natural mother, to avoid social scandal for her family. The lifelong scars on mother and child do not seem to matter as much as the Catholic institution of marriage."[58]

Irish mothers have also lost custody of their children for committing adultery and for engaging in post-divorce sexual and religious activities that displease their ex-husbands or the Irish courts—i.e., for disobeying Western tribal laws.[59]

"Illegitimate" children in Ireland have fewer rights than father-owned children. According to a 1983 report, this inequality "is a deliberate one to protect the institution of marriage."[60]

Italy

According to Virginia Visani:

"Italy is a country with strong patriarchal attitudes about the family. Maternity is still considered a woman's unique destiny and her most important function. It is understood that children under seven need to be cared for by their mother or by another female relative, such as the grandmother. Children are assigned to the father only in exceptional cases—that is, in case of the mother's illness, or immoral behavior. A mother might also be deemed 'unfit' by a judge if she works or does not want to take traditional care of her children. Children over fourteen are often allowed to decide whom they want to live with. From time to time a father claims custody or visitation as his legal or natural 'right' or kidnaps his child."[61]

Alma is a sophisticated career woman. She is also a traditional Italian Catholic mother. After fifteen years of marriage Alma's husband left her for a woman half his age. Alma immediately agreed to joint custody as the "progressive" thing to do.

"I thought joint custody was the right thing. He was their father. He helped quite a lot with their upbringing. He had a right to remain close to them. I also thought I could rebuild my life if I had some time alone. I had the children during the week. He had them from Thursday to Sunday night. His girlfriend was only ten years older than our eldest child. They went to pop concerts and took skiing vacations together.

"My children didn't lose 'family-life.' Only I did. I grew more and more depressed. My ex-husband condemned me as too old-fashioned. My children all agreed with him. So did our friends. I became more isolated than ever. I had to watch what I said. If I was too angry or too depressed my children would yell at me.

"Even though I'm educated and have a profession, at heart I'm a good Catholic girl still in love with my husband. We were both forty when we separated. At forty, my mother was already a grandmother. I tried to date, but I only felt ridiculous.

"I have lost everything. I am too shy and too sad to start over again. Nature is cruel to women. I can't have any more children. I always thought that when our children left home, I'd still have my husband—and then grandchildren. A career, even a lover can't replace family life for me."

Norway

Torill is a Norwegian-American mother. She described how her Norwegian in-laws physically and psychologically "kidnapped" her American-born son:

"My family was poor and very cruel to me. I married to escape them. Unfortunately, my husband turned out to be a convicted criminal who abandoned me when our son was six months old. I was nineteen and penniless. I asked his parents, who were well-to-do, to take us in until I got on my feet.

"My in-laws were very strict, very religious. My mother-in-law opened my mail and read my personal diary. She made me do the housework. I wasn't treated like a family member, but like an untrustworthy servant. They were outraged when I started seeing a young man. After bitter quarrels, I moved out with my three-year-old son.

"I returned to America to get a divorce. My mother and her minister called me immoral. They said I must take my husband back. He came from prison and threatened me with a knife for hours. I felt trapped and doomed. My husband was arrested for armed robbery. My mother refused to help me. In desperation I took my son to his Norwegian grandparents until I could sort out my life.

"Within two years I was divorced and engaged to be married. I sailed over to get my son back. They wouldn't let me see him alone. He was withdrawn and suspicious. He'd been told I was a 'bad' woman who 'didn't love him.' I was forbidden to attend most of the family Christmas parties. 'It wouldn't do to have a divorced woman seen here,' was my mother-in-law's attitude.

"My ex-in-laws were stable and fairly prosperous. I was a divorced nobody. I was afraid to risk prison for kidnapping my son back to America. I didn't want to uproot him so that he could never return. I left Norway a defeated woman. I had a nervous breakdown. I was so guilty, so ashamed. I stopped telling anyone I was a mother. I've never had another child."[62]

Sweden*

Swedish women earn seventy cents on the male dollar. All Swedish citizens are entitled to quality and state-subsidized health care, housing, and education. Swedish homemakers are considered "productive work-

---

*For information on Denmark, see note 64, page 581.

ers" and are entitled to two-week annual vacations. Swedish men are encouraged to be involved in parenting and are given paid "paternity" leaves.[63]

Despite such enlightened social programs, Swedes, like other Europeans, still suffer from alcoholism, suicide, and "mental illness." Rape, pornography, and prostitution exist in Sweden, as do wife beating, incest, and a lack of paternal responsibility for primary child care. According to Cecilia Onfelt:

> "Custody battles are in the air in Sweden. Men almost always get normal visiting rights even if they are convicted wife-beaters or child abusers. One particularly horrible case involved a 'feminist' father who was sexually molesting his five year old daughter. Another case involved a father who had been threatening to murder the baby.
>
> "The mother fought like a tiger and refused him access to the baby. For this she was fined ($300.00). The court decided that the man could see the baby but not alone. A young social assistant took the baby to the man's flat, went into the kitchen and left the man with the two year old in the bedroom. He stabbed the baby about twenty times, swiftly and quietly, without the social assistant noticing. When she came into the room the baby was already dead. The bailiffs still went to collect the mother's fine even after the murder. I think people felt that was really a bit too much and the government stopped it all.
>
> "I discussed custody with a male colleague. Should fathers have access to children regardless of their behavior? His answer was: 'If I put a quarter into a candy machine and get out a candy bar, is the candy bar mine, or is it the machine's?' His metaphor told me he thought women are machines for male use."[64]

The Communist Bloc

China

On May 1, 1950, the Marriage Law of the People's Republic of China abolished concubinage, polygamy, arranged marriages, repudiation, wife beating, and foot binding. The communist government also outlawed prostitution, pornography, and drug addiction; and took as its mandate the eradication of starvation, disease, homelessness, unemployment, illiteracy, and all private property, including the paternal ownership of children.[65]

Margery is a mother and engineer. She escaped from communist China in the 1970s.

"I was born in 1935. My father was a bourgeois capitalist. After the Revolution, I was sent to a special school. I married another engineer in good party standing. In 1963, I became the mother of twins. I began to quarrel with my husband and with his family. They all felt I wasn't obedient enough to them.

"My husband began to spread rumors about me, implying I wasn't obedient to the Revolution. I became very afraid. I could be relocated to another province. Maybe my capitalist origins could still be used against me. I fled the country. I have not seen my children since. I have no way of knowing whether they've ever received my letters."

What could Margery have done to retain custody of or access to her children if she had been declared an enemy of the state? Could she have taken her children with her into a labor camp or into foreign exile? Margery had no claim to her children as their *mother*. Like all resources, they belonged to the Chinese state.[66]

Chinese mothers (or fathers) can lose custody and access to their children if the state views them as "unfit."* Liang Heng has described how he was separated from and brainwashed against a presumably "unfit" mother. When Liang was four, his mother was routinely asked to "criticize" her work situation. After hesitating a long time, she finally criticized her section head. "It was disastrous. [Twenty years later] when she was allowed to see her file, in 1978, she found out that she had been given a Rightists' 'cap' solely because of three [minor] criticisms [that she was pressured into expressing]. There was no court of appeal. Mother was sent away to the suburb of Yuan Jia Ling for labor reform."[67]

Liang's father disassociated himself from his wife. Eventually, as both a "party" and a "family" man, he "denounced" Liang's mother. When she came to visit their three children, he would scream, "The children in this house need a Revolutionary mother, not a Rightist mother." Eventually, after a bitter marital dispute, the court awarded custody of the children to Liang's father.

So perhaps inevitably, over the years, I came to resent my mother for making life so miserable. I began to believe that she really had done something wrong. My father and teachers said so, and my classmates hated me for her supposed crimes. At last I no longer wished to visit her despite my loneliness, and when I saw her at a distance I didn't even call out to her. I cut her out of my life just as I had been told to do, and became solitary and self-reliant.[68]

---

*This is also true in the United States and in all the countries discussed so far.

The Soviet Union

Like China, the Soviet Union has defined human rights in terms of food, shelter, medical care, education, and employment. Human rights have not included the rights to own property, to engage in free speech or religion, to emigrate, or to oppose the government politically.

Pesya is a Russian Jewish émigré. She was never a practicing Jew, finds religion "barbaric," but wanted to leave the USSR for career and economic reasons.

"In Russia, you are looked on as a traitor if you want to leave the country. No one can leave unless they have the permission of both their parents—it doesn't matter how old they are. So if a mother wants to take her children out of the country, they can't go unless the father agrees. And a father can't take children out of the country without the mother's permission. Aleksandr Solzhenitsyn [the writer] couldn't have taken his kids out of the country without his wife's permission.

"Sometimes, if a mother is allowed to travel abroad for professional reasons, she is *expected* to leave her children behind—even if their father wants them to go along. The children ensure the mother's return. I was able to get my son out with me because I was widowed and my parents had already been allowed to leave for Israel."

According to a Russian diplomat, mothers do not lose custody of their children because they have careers.

"Mothers are supposed to work. If a divorce occurs, fathers are supposed to support their children. Child-support payments are enforced by the state very vigorously. Visitation rights are enforced unless the father is really dangerous to his children.

"Only if a mother is alcoholic, a prostitute, or mentally ill will she lose her child. She may sometimes lose her child because she has committed adultery. It's very rare for a woman to get divorced and leave the children behind. Fathers don't want the responsibility for children. Mothers do."

Katja is a research psychiatrist and a mother. When I asked her about custody in general, she unexpectedly told me about her own life:

"When I was four, my father was imprisoned and executed for 'crimes' against the state. My mother was condemned for not denouncing my father. She was six months pregnant when they dragged her away. I later learned that she gave birth to a child in prison, who died of neglect. Meanwhile, I was put into a state home. It was decent enough, but there was no family warmth.

"The 1930s were a terrible time. Still, a man who was sent to a labor camp was allowed to have his wife and children accompany him. They would live in the village closest to the camp. A husband did not follow an arrested wife. Her children would usually grow up in a state house, or with a relative, if the relative was above suspicion.

"I was eventually allowed to live with one of my mother's relatives when I was eight. We never discussed my mother. Twelve years later, when she returned, I refused to live with her. For awhile, my mother was confined to a small village. I visited her there occasionally. Then my mother was officially rehabilitated. The government gave her a very decent pension and a villa.

"I was never in any way discriminated against because of my parents' conviction. But I did grow up without a mother or a father."[69]

Once a mother has been custodially challenged, she is immediately at risk—anywhere in the world. In most non-Western countries a challenged mother expects to lose custody *automatically*. The laws of her land, tribe, or church unambiguously proclaim her husband's primary right to child custody.

The non-Western mother may be terrified of such laws' being exercised against her motherhood. However, when and if they are, neither she nor her children necessarily consider her to blame.

In the West children are presumably never removed from "fit" mothers, or never *automatically* removed. First, there is a trial, in which every mother is presumed guilty until proven innocent. In the West, when a mother does lose custody, she is entitled to blame herself.

Are maternal economic and custodial rights better protected in non-Western "developing" countries, in the Western capitalist democracies, or among the communist totalitarians? According to Constantin Safilios-Rothschild, nearly half of all households in the "developing countries" are female-headed.

Regardless of the reasons for which female-headed households [in developing countries] emerge, they all share a common characteristic: they are poorer than male-headed households.

This circumstance arises because female-headed households usually include fewer income-earning adults, since they lack the important economic and labor contributions of men. In addition, women's wages are less, and women have much less access to land than do men, except as mediated through their sons.[70]

The governments of non-Western "developing" countries rarely subsidize mothers at all—whether they are married, abandoned, divorced, or unwed. These governments are poor and often at the mercy of organized religion and a corrupt ruling class. Government policy on mothers and children either doesn't exist or consists of a series of assumptions—i.e., state "policy" assumes that impoverished mothers will (or should) marry or remarry; that their families will (or should) take them in; that mothers will (or should) farm their own plot of land; that mothers will (or should) work for the minimum wage or as prostitutes for slightly more than the minimum wage. If mothers and their children can't survive in these ways, then it is their own fault or the fault of imperialists, communists, capitalists—or of fate."[71]

"Developing" country governments are impoverished. Maintaining the *status quo* often means supporting the views of organized religion against divorce and against unwed motherhood. The state also fears that if it supports unwed mothers and "illegitimate" children, this might weaken the male incentive to marry or the female incentive to *stay* married.[72]

The same "developing" state that refuses to employ women at all or equally, and that refuses to subsidize mothering and child care at all or adequately might then find itself economically responsible for the survival of a great number of paternally abandoned children.[73]

The governments of Western "developed" countries do economically subsidize married, abandoned, divorced, widowed, and unwed mothers and their children—but very inadequately. As we have seen, the American state readily sacrifices mothers and children to domestically violent men for economic reasons—e.g., in order partially to reimburse itself for "welfare" expenditures. In the richest democratic countries on earth, mothers and children are actually separated from one another for economic reasons.[74]

In the "developed" and democratic West *all* people, including impoverished mothers, have the right to own private property, to exercise free speech and religion, to join opposition political parties, and to protest anything politically—including their own unemployment or underemployment.[75] Impoverished mothers also have the right to due process—if they are (non-psychiatrically) imprisoned—and the right to emigrate if they feel their futures beckon elsewhere.

Such rights are precious. However, a mother may possess these rights and still be physically, sexually, reproductively, and economically oppressed and exploited. She and her children may live in substandard housing, receive substandard educations, work for much less than the minimum wage, and suffer from both male domestic and male public violence. If an impoverished mother is ever imprisoned, her right to due process is seriously compromised by her lack of money and power to enforce this right.[76]

Mothers and children in communist countries have certain economic rights because the state owns the means of production and reproduction. Private property is forbidden—in private hands. Thus, wives and their wombs are not their husbands' "private property," nor are children their parents' "private property." Such valuable resources are the public property of the state or of its most powerful representatives.

Communist countries do economically subsidize mothers and children adequately or at least more or less equally. Of course, the real standard of maternal (consumer) living is lower than in most capitalist countries, and the pressure to conform is greater or more efficiently enforced.

In both non-Western "developing" and communist countries most mothers do not have enough money to relocate within the same country. If they do, the state, the father, or his family can either stop them or force them to leave their children behind.

In non-Western "developing" and in communist countries, most mothers (and fathers) are too poor to travel or to emigrate or are politically forbidden to do so. Those parents who are permitted to travel are often expected to leave their families or state-owned children behind.

Does this mean that mothers are more impoverished or custodially endangered in "developing" countries, such as Saudi Arabia, South Korea, Algeria, or Cuba; in communist countries, such as the Soviet Union, China, Poland, or Hungary; or in "developed" capitalist democracies, such as the United States, Great Britain, France, or Sweden?

As we have seen, the American states custodially oppose any mother who wants to move from one city to another for any reason if her ex-husband contests the move. The American and European states (with the exception of the Scandinavian countries) also set abysmally low standards of paternal child support, do not enforce these payments, do not adequately subsidize single mothers and children, and do not always support an *impoverished* mother's right to custody.[77]

In addition, the American and European democracies do not assist their female nationals to find or retrieve a child who has been paternally kidnapped to another city or country. Few American or European mothers have enough money, support, or power to trace paternally kidnapped children. Those who do may find that their judicial orders of maternal custody are not recognized in other states or countries.[78]

According to Nancy Greene, paternal kidnappings have "increased dramatically" in the last decade, from one European country to another and from the United States and Europe to non-Western "developing" countries.

"In 1981, an American mother divorced her Peruvian husband and attempted to take her nine-year-old daughter back to the United States with her. The father refused to allow it. He sent the girl to live with his mother. The American mother returned to the States and attempted to get ISS [International Social Services] to help her. She obtained a custody order in the United States and returned to Peru to reclaim her child. The father had remarried, obtained his own Peruvian custody order, and sent his daughter away to boarding school.

"The American mother returned to Peru, found her daughter and physically took her away. The father managed to pay off some Peruvian border officials, who restrained the mother and put her in jail for several days. The mother is desperate to have her daughter. The father won't allow it. In Peru, *that is his right.* It's not as though the father even sees his child. He just wants to make sure that the mother doesn't have her. The Peruvian courts will back him all the way."[79]

Are mothers from "developing" countries treated any differently by European or American law? For example, do French judges or lawyers on "free" French soil have the power to order an Afghan child into maternal custody in a contest? Aziza is Afghan. Here is what she told me:

"I was born in Kabul but educated in Europe. My marriage was arranged, but by Afghan standards, we were a modern couple. We were living part-time in Paris when the Russians invaded. We stayed on. My husband had many financial and psychological difficulties. He took a lot out on me. I opened a boutique with another woman. Compared to him, I was a great success. My husband demanded that I stop working. I refused. He accused me of being an unfit mother. He said our children needed extra supervision because we were refugees and I was never home.

"The French court gave him custody and a divorce. For two years now he has refused to allow me to see or write to my children. I am a double refugee, not only from my birthplace but from my own children."[80]

SUMMARY

This chapter surveys the paternal right to child custody in sixty-five places outside the United States and Canada: tribally, legally, economically, psychologically, physically, and according to religious beliefs. In the countries surveyed most fathers were legally and customarily entitled to custody and to other paternal rights without having to fulfill reciprocal paternal obligations.

Just as fathers were entitled to rights without reciprocal obligations, mothers were obligated to care for and support their children without any reciprocal rights. In sixty-five places mothers were not automatically entitled to custody of their children by law or custom or when it was contested by individual fathers or by the state. No mother could count on obtaining physical or legal custody, even of a paternally kidnapped child, in her country of origin or in her husband's country of origin.

In most countries single and unwed mothers (and "illegitimate" children) were inadequately subsidized by fathers, families, tribes, and by the modern state.

In sixty-five places women had few rights as *individuals* and no rights as *mothers* to protect them from the rights that men have over women, that husbands have over wives, that fathers have over mothers, and that states have over citizens.

In general, mothers everywhere are at the mercy of legalized fathers' right—whether that right is embodied by a legal or genetic father or by the state, acting as a surrogate father.[81]

PART V

The Mothers Speak

CHAPTER NINETEEN

Mother's Wisdom: Philosophical and Political Perspectives on Having and Losing Children

"Now listen to me. I want you to get out of here. Go on down and play, I need ten minutes all alone. Anthony, I might kill you if you stay up here."

"O.K., kill me."

I had to sit immediately then, so he could believe I was his size and stop picking on me.

"O.K., Tonto. O.K. I'll tell you what, go to your room for a couple of minutes, honey, go ahead."

"No," he said, climbing onto my lap. "I want to be a baby and stay right next to you every minute . . . I'm never gonna go away. I'm gonna stay right next to you forever, Faith." . . .

I held him so and rocked him. I cradled him. I closed my eyes and leaned on his dark head.

Grace Paley, *The Little Disturbances of Man*

A short parade appeared. . . . The grownups carried three posters. The first showed a prime-living, prime-earning, well-dressed man about thirty-five years old next to a small girl. A question was asked: WOULD YOU BURN A CHILD? In the next poster he placed a burning cigarette on the child's arm. The cool answer was given: WHEN NECESSARY. The third poster carried no words, only a napalmed Vietnamese baby, seared, scarred, with twisted hands.

In a fury of tears and disgust [my son Richard] wrote—in letters fifteen feet high, so the entire Saturday walking world could see—WOULD YOU BURN A CHILD? and under it, a little taller, the red reply, WHEN NECESSARY.

And I think that is exactly when events turned me around . . . directed out of that sexy playground by my children's heartfelt brains, I thought more and more and every day about the world.

Grace Paley, *Enormous Changes at the Last Minute*

379

CUSTODIALLY EMBATTLED MOTHERS DID NOT VIEW THEM-
selves as philosophers or heroes. I ultimately did. These mothers had bonded in nurturing and non-violent ways to their
children. Under siege, they maintained their pre-existing non-
violent bond toward their children. Mothers did not use
violent or "disconnected" means to win custody. This maternal virtue was used against them.

Mothers tried to appreciate, in life-affirming ways, the practical or philosophical advantages of their custodial victimization. About half the mothers (53 percent) interpreted their
experience in religious or psychological terms; nearly a third
(28 percent) did so in political terms.

Mothers defined civilization and justice in one way; fathers
and judges, in another way. Nearly half the mothers (47 percent) verbally expressed a mothers' rights position. Ten of
these mothers' rights advocates (36 percent) became pro-mother
activists and feminists.

This chapter views maternal non-violence as a way of being
in the world and as a means of resolving conflict with one's
"own" child. This chapter explores whether such a maternal
virtue can be learned and used by all adults in public as well
as in private settings.

MOST MOTHERS DO not view themselves as philosophers or heroes. However, what mothers have to say about the experience of mothering and about children probably constitutes the sum total of human wisdom on the subject.

Such wisdom is not a means of transforming power relationships within the family or among strangers. Such wisdom is based on and describes an individual mother's bond with her "own" child.

WHAT DID CUSTODIALLY CHALLENGED MOTHERS SAY ABOUT MOTHERING IN GENERAL?

Mothers have described and theorized about their experiences of pregnancy, childbirth, and motherhood.[1] Custodially challenged mothers described being "connected" to their children in strong and intimate ways.

Ellie: The mother-child bond is the most basic relationship there is. It's the first and most primary relationship. Most relationships in the world, except those we try to have with our ideals, change or end. Mothering is the only thing that is forever.

Anita: Mothering comes from some kind of special woman place. Maybe it's an instinct. Something flows from inside you outward to your child. If a third person is present or competing for my attention, this makes the flow I have with my child harder to maintain.

To what extent is maternal "connectedness" related to biological maternity or to the *experience* of mothering?

No one scientifically "knows" whether maternal bonding exists *because* women experience pregnancy, childbirth, and lactation or because all women, including biological mothers, have been socialized as "mother"-people.

Some theorists have exaggerated, and others have minimized, the importance of *biological* maternity per se.[2] The mothers I interviewed described their pregnancy experience as powerful and as one with long-lasting consequences.

> Sally: I began my life as a mother as soon as I became pregnant. I talked to my unborn child. I dreamt about her. I planned the next thirty years for both of us. By the time I went into labor, I felt I was going to meet the person I was closest to in the world.

Pregnancy, childbirth, and lactation are psychological as well as bodily experiences. As such, they seem to reinforce and extend the socializing of women into motherhood. Caroline Whitbeck observed:

> [A] woman in labor experiences helplessness, and this experience more closely resembles the total helplessness of infants than any other experience a healthy adult is likely to have. . . . In being entirely caught up in one's bodily experience, the woman is like the infant. . . . Furthermore, in the last month of pregnancy, women not only experience some helplessness . . . but must also learn to take [care of] their own bodily functions in much the same way that it is necessary to take [care of] the newborn's.[3]

Biological mothers *know* they are the mothers of their children. They have no existential doubt about it.* Many mothers "re-member" childbirth and breast feeding as specific and transcendent experiences—i.e., as naturally religious events.

> Neither men nor women remember clearly the act of being born, but women experience birth as such in an immediate way. Both men and women know about birth, think about it, experience it as real, but experience it differently. There is, in other words, such a thing as *reproductive consciousness.* . . . By her labor, the woman confirms two very important things. One, obviously, is her knowledge of this child as in a concrete sense *her* child, the product of her labor, a *value* that her labor has created. The second is the experience of an integration with the actual continuity of her species.[4]

Mothers sometimes described their ties to a child in biological terms. Some mothers also described childbirth as an "active" part of their consciousness.

---

*This may not be as true of mothers who were heavily drugged or unconscious during labor.

Helen: A force larger than myself visited me during labor. That sense of being at one with God never left me. It sustained me during a violent marriage. It gave me the courage to leave it. Unfortunately it didn't prepare me to live without knowing whether my son is dead or alive.

Rose: Nobody realizes that the umbilical cord does stretch beyond the door. Even though I was prevented from seeing my son, my mothering umbilical cord is alive for as long as I am. My child's umbilical cord was cut, not mine.

Judith: The blood bond *is* the love bond.[5]

Long before any custodial challenge occurred, these mothers, like all mothers, felt endangered by the *public* indifference or hostility to such bio-religious feelings. This is what drove them even more deeply into *private* spaces.

Tracy: I was mistreated by the doctors and nurses each time I gave birth. My husband seemed like a haven compared to that experience. He was a father figure to me. He just didn't want me to grow up. I had to. I was a mother.

Charlene: Once I became pregnant, being married became very important to me. What if I ever became ill or died? Who else would my daughter have?

Mothers came to prefer "private" life as the best or only place to care for children. Idealized (white middle-class) mothering was accommodated only in "private," male-subsidized families.

Adele: I slept and ate when my children slept and ate. I became half-child. My adult activities weren't as real as the dream I was living with my two children.

This maternal descent into pre-industrial or seasonal rhythms was not perceived as naturally sacred. As mothers became more sensitively connected to their children, their public devaluation became more painful.

Mothers were driven into self-doubt by the absence of public recognition and support. Even the most loving or helpful of husbands couldn't prevent this from happening.

Winifred: There's nothing less pleasant than walking into a school or hospital and being treated like an idiot. What can you really know, compared to social workers, teachers, and doctors? You're "only" a mother.

Phyllis: Is it too dangerous to treat motherhood as too existentially grand an event [because] men don't become mothers? Should I [then] speak in a small voice about small things? The "cute" little baby clothes, the "darling" little baby? But to become a mother is to open the gates of your womb to admit life—and death—into the world. It is so significant an act, it is devalued. Falsely flattered. Lied about. Lived alone. A woman alone is a Mother. A Mother is a woman alone.[6]

Despite public hostility and private self-doubt, maternal experience was characterized by an altered and vivid perception of reality, by the daily remembrance of things past, and by an (uneasy) recognition that life and death are both close and far apart.

Ella Mae: My canvases were love poems to my daughter. I found myself painting scenes of death as often as scenes of re-birth and life. I felt very close to both realities.

Nora: Nothing in my life has ever surprised me so much as what happens to women when they have children. At the time I found it awful, or mostly awful, but now it seems to me as if my previous life had been a dim, flat, verbal thing. . . . My son interrupted that, and the way that interruption feels, still, is that he gave me the world.[7]

Mothers became emotionally complex and mature. They encompassed opposites and stretching, were able to sustain profound ambivalence.

Ida: I think only a mother could understand how strongly you can feel in two different directions. I mean, you can totally love your child all the time, but also feel that you never want to see the child again.

Ellie: I've come to realize that my need to be free and away from my son is large, but is nowhere near as large as my need to be with him. They're contradictory feelings but they co-exist.

Some mothers perceived motherhood as a very special learning experience.

Grace: I learned how to love only after I became a mother. The growing love I feel for my children is different from anything I've ever felt for another adult.

Winifred: I'd tell any woman who wants to know what it's like to be a mother to try walking around for a day and a night carrying an egg on her head—just to begin to get a feel for it. She'd see that she couldn't just take off. She'd learn that she'd have to be many people without losing her balance. It's actually a Zen exercise if you pay attention.

Phyllis: Little ancestor, sweet baby! How you temper me, deepen me, like an ancient smithy working slowly. You—who need everything done for you—are the most powerful teacher I've ever known.[8]

WHAT HAPPENED TO MATERNAL "CONNECTEDNESS" UNDER CUSTODIAL SIEGE?

Under siege, mothers did not behave in "disconnected" ways toward their children. Even those mothers whose children rejected them did not necessarily experience such a traumatic separation as "final."

Gail: My kids cross the street when they see me coming. It's the only way they can live with the guilt of leaving me. I'm very, very angry. I'd take them back in a minute. I'm still their mother.

Norma: My teenagers don't want to see me very often. But I'm the only person who remembers everything about them. I am their memory. I have their baby pictures. I remember what they looked like when they were born. When they want to know about themselves, they'll have to come to me. I am the guardian of their history.

Under custodial siege, mothers desperately wanted their children's emotional support and loyalty. However, they were reluctant to "lean" on their children emotionally or to abdicate their disciplinary role in order to "win" a child over.

Janet: A custody struggle, in or out of court, gives a child an exaggerated sense of his own importance and power. This is bad. Maternal authority is the first thing to go. Your child will play one parent off against the other. If you give in to him in order to have him on your side, you're condemning him and yourself.

Mothers did not brainwash their children—i.e., force them to commit psychological patricide. They lacked the requisite economic and emotional resources to underwrite a kidnapping or a brainwashing campaign. Mothers were also unwilling to hurt a child by telling him that "his father is dead" or "doesn't love him" etc.

Beth: What kind of father tries to turn children against their own mother? What kind of father thinks his kids are better off *without* a mother? My husband knew I couldn't go for his jugular if it meant hurting the kids. If I "killed" their father as he was trying to "kill" me, how could I face my children afterwards?

As we have seen, when a custodially embattled father "leaned" on a child emotionally or engaged in an anti-mother brainwashing campaign, this was often experienced by the father and his children (and perceived by expert observers) as a long-overdue form of paternal "intimacy."

However, when a custodially embattled mother tried to ward off false idealizations of a father or to defend herself against her loss of maternal authority or credibility, this was experienced and perceived as "brainwashing."

When a mother "complained" to her children about the paternal nonpayment of child support, lawyers, experts, judges, and neighbors viewed this as a savage denunciation of a child's father and as more destructive to a child's self-esteem than was his father's physical, economic, or psychological abandonment. Children refused to believe that fathers were withholding child support "on purpose." Children got angry at their *mothers* for saying so.*

For two years I remained suspicious of the maternal reluctance to "fight dirty" or to "force a child to choose between her parents." Surely this was virtue by default. Most people, including mothers, aren't saints.

Why didn't these mothers simply admit that they were unable to wage a public fight, or didn't "really" want the burden of single motherhood? Why didn't they admit that physical and psychological non-violence was their only means of "pacifying" already provoked and custodially violent husbands?

Because such reasons were not the only ones involved in how a mother chose to fight. Maternal "connectedness" meant that a mother did not consciously use violent weapons against her child even in order to "win" his custody.

Denise: How could I ethically engage in an adversarial court battle, the win/lose type of situation that was against everything I believed in? How could I maintain my integrity in a way that wouldn't hurt my son or violate my feminist principles?

Sybil: In fighting to keep our kids in a custody battle, we lose what we might call our motherhood. It's another, more painful version of trying to mother under patriarchy. This is too painful to face.

Rose, in Margaret Drabble's *The Needle's Eye*, thinks:

Even if the judge laughed at Christopher's claim for custody, it would not be an end of it: he would find some new way of assailing her, or she would of assailing him. There was no solution, through violence or law. The decisions of judges, even when in her favor, were irrelevant: they chalked up no victory. The confrontation (ah, this was it) could not end in victory, because it was a fight in which there was no winning.

Some other resolutions would have to be made, in which victory and defeat played no part, in which the boundaries did not enclose the spoils of war, and were not drawn by neutral external treaty and convention.[9]

---

*Mystification of children, if it is in the service of fathers' rights, is always preferred to honesty, if it is in the service of mothers' rights.

WHY DID MATERNALLY "CONNECTED" WOMEN LOSE CUSTODY OF THEIR CHILDREN?

Custodially challenged mothers were heroic in their barefoot and unarmed fight for their children and in their refusal to adopt violent methods in order to "win."

A mother's emotional maturity functioned as a Catch-22 against her. The maternal ability to experience emotional opposites, to love two people simultaneously, and to tolerate ambivalence creatively, was, incredibly, taken as proof of maternal unfitness. ("Do you love your children or your lover? Your career or your child?" "How can you love this child when you yourself have admitted you want to run away?")

In a battle, anyone capable of strong and opposite emotions, anyone capable of complex perceptions of emotional reality, anyone concerned with the non-violent nurturance of a child—lost custody of that child.

Few judges recognized maternal non-violence as proof that a woman was the real "mother" of her child. Few judges viewed paternal domestic violence as "violent." Many such Solomons mistook a father's violent (dis)connection to his child for "love." The violent and "disconnected" paternal bond was judicially viewed as the "civilized" bond.

HOW IS PATRIARCHAL JUSTICE DIFFERENT FROM "MATRIARCHAL" JUSTICE?

Because men are violent in general, do not give birth, and are often indifferent to their children, the male protection of "their" wives and children is *the* patriarchal definition of "civilization."

Mothers also believe that civilization means the protection of mothers and children from male violence, including a violent custodial separation. Mothers also believe that civilization means the non-violent protection of children—especially by their parents.[10]

According to Dr. Carol Gilligan, contemporary men and women seem to have different concepts of morality and justice. Male concepts of morality are based on "separation" from intimate others. Men are therefore primarily concerned with "rights" among strangers.

Female concepts of morality are based on "attachment" to intimate others and are therefore concerned with "an ethic of care." Gilligan's research "suggests that men and women may speak different [moral] languages."[11]

In (patriarchal) Greek drama, if a mother's child was killed, she sought justice by killing her child's murderer. A "matriarchal" mother could not be satisfied by the fining or jailing of her child's murderer. Thus, any murder could lead to an endless number of "vigilante" blood-feuds.[12]

"Matriarchal" justice was dramaturgically condemned as inappropriate to the needs of Western or modern man. In fact, the expanding needs of men as property owners, traders, capitalists, warriors, and patriots could not be well served by the settling of public disputes in "matriarchal" (or private) ways.

"Matriarchal justice"—passionate, intimate, concrete—was dramaturgically superseded by a patriarchal system of fines, imprisonment, and exile. Thus, serious blood-feuds could be settled in more "civilized" ways—impersonally, among strangers.

Patriarchal law is at its best in preventing and punishing the violent theft of (male) property by (male) strangers. Patriarchal law "works"— because women and children are viewed as (male) property and never as property owners.

Patriarchs have had their conceptual and administrative hands full trying to prevent and punish violence among men. Patriarchs have simplified this difficult task by legalizing certain kinds of male violence, and by refusing to recognize male violence toward women, children, and wives as a criminal offense.[13]

The natural primacy of life unbound and earth unowned is precisely what patriarchal law has sought to subjugate. It is therefore not routinely concerned with justice for the oppressed.

Patriarchal law (and its application) opposes the idea that each child's life is equal, or that the mother-child *relationship* is irreplaceable and "non-redeemable." As Rose, one of my interviewees, said: "Who are these men to tell me whether I can live with my son or not? I'm his mother. They can't do away with that fact by laws alone. They sin against nature when they use laws to do that."

HOW DID MATERNAL CUSTODIAL VICTIMIZATION AFFECT WOMEN PHILOSOPHICALLY AND POLITICALLY?

Many mothers tried to appreciate, in life-affirming ways, the practical or philosophical advantages of being forced to live apart from their children.

Adele: We don't own our children. We only have the privilege of being alive and involved with them for a limited amount of time. When children become adults, they can choose never to see us again. My lease on mothering was more short-term than most. I could be a very bitter person. I was for awhile. I made a conscious choice not to poison my life. That is my strongest response to what happened.

Beth: This custody struggle has changed me from an impulsive and unrealistic woman. The situation has kept my feet nailed to the wall. Now, before I do anything, I calculate what effect it really has on the kids and on me. This miserable battle has actually made me more responsible and realistic.

In a sense, every custodially challenged mother was "radicalized"— i.e., she became more informed about reality. This was a radical departure from her previous naïveté. No custodially challenged mother ever again confused her desire or *obligation* to mother with her *right* to mother, nor did anyone suffer her previously "normal" delusions of maternal omnipotence.

Ella Mae: Sitting in the courtroom, I began to fantasize that I was a mother lion protecting my cubs. I needed a fantasy this powerful to meditate on in a place where men had the legal right to separate a mother from her child. It took me years to regain my proper energy. I had to let this fantasy of myself as a mother lion go before I could forgive myself for losing my child.

Bettina: I always thought I could protect my kids from the whole world. I couldn't protect them from their father's kidnapping them. I can't protect them from poverty. What I *can* do is physically take care of them—if I'm allowed to. I can love them. I don't have the power to do more than this.

After a custody battle no mother had any illusions about legal justice or legal protection. On the basis of what they knew, some mothers advised *other* mothers to steer clear of the law in any way possible. A few mothers advised *other* mothers to "play dirty."

Josie: Please tell other mothers involved in custody struggles to give up being naïve. Tell them they've got to go for the balls. We're outleagued emotionally and financially. We must play to win, not to show we're "better" than men. Our children are worth fighting for.

Helen: You can't depend on the legal system; you can't expect them to find your child. You have got to be your own detective. I respected the law my whole life. I can't anymore. Forget about the law. If the child is yours, take that child and *go!* Take him. Take your child and disappear. Forget about the law. There is none.

Being traumatized by injustice is not equivalent to understanding or fighting injustice. In order to survive, mothers used their newfound real-politik in many ways.

Some mothers became *less* ambitious, more cautious, more secretive than they had been. They did not want to arouse the world's violence and indifference again. Some mothers redoubled their efforts to find and "connect" with a man for protection from (male) violence. Some mothers also reaffirmed the importance of marriage and traditional values for the same reason.

Belinda: I would never, never commit adultery again, no matter what my [new] husband does. My baby is too precious to lose. Anyway, my husband rescued me. Without him I could never have survived losing my kids.

Sally: When we fight with husbands, we're dealing with professional killers. They're trained as mental killers. You need a lot of ego strength. You must forget any feelings you have about your husband—like he's an honest man; he'd never do this or that. He will. I really needed another *man* to protect me from the first male killer. It was a big paradox.

Nearly a third (28 percent) of the mothers returned to school or embarked on careers. More than two-thirds attempted to become more self-loving and psychologically independent.

Dora: For twenty years I sacrificed myself in a bad marriage. I was dying. I decided to live before it was too late and I was actually dead. I decided to be a model against suicide—and against obedience to tyranny—for my children's sake. I'm sixty-two years old now. The price of my freedom is very high. I'm willing to pay it. I have only one person in my life whom I can count on completely. It's myself.

Terry: My strength lies in getting on with my own life. I also have a strong belief that the children whom I've loved and mothered will truly return to me.

About 40 percent of the mothers looked for "larger" explanations of reality in order to survive. Some expressed their custodial victimization in religious or psychological terms; others did so in verbally dramatic terms.

Maureen described her husband as a "terrorist who, for three years, has aimed a gun at my heart." Miki and Angela described their custody battles as analagous to the battles of enslaved or racially despised peoples.

Miki: I felt I was like a black person living under slavery or under the rules of apartheid. I had to carry identity papers with me at all times—proof that I had legal custody of my kids to show the police, in case my ex-husband ever challenged me in the street or in my apartment again. I felt I was living under military occupation. My judge was a racist. So was my ex-husband. I experienced losing my children as a form of racism.

Angela: People say I'm crazy to compare the Nazi extermination of six million Jews with my situation. Maybe six million living women have not been exterminated or sterilized. Maybe ten thousand or ten million have. Whatever the number, people refuse to recognize that a mother who loses her kids the way I have has really been held hostage, tortured, and wiped out as a mother.

Rachel and Kate viewed their custodial victimization as part of the systemic victimization of women.

Rachel: Taking a child away from his mother is a violent act of mother-hatred. My ex-husband chopped my body in half. The judge helped him.

Kate: All mothers are in an endangered political position whether they know it or not. If you were a resistance fighter during World War II, you'd make arrangements for your children in case you were caught or killed. These arrangements are almost impossible to make. But they're what you need in order to fight when everything's completely rigged against you.

Half the mothers (52 percent) did not even assert a sense of maternal entitlement verbally. They may have *felt* they deserved custody of their children, but they didn't say so.

Perhaps these mothers feared that any statement about maternal "rights" would betray their boyfriends or new husbands or their own belief in the importance of fathers or of male involvement in child care.

Such mothers displayed no anger about losing a "right" they never had. Catherine MacKinnon has described a parallel sense of non-entitlement among women in her analysis of rape victims and the law:

> Most women get the message that the law against rape [against fathers' rights]* is virtually unenforceable as applied to them. . . . Women [conclude] that we have not "really" been raped [or been good mothers]* if we have ever seen or dated or slept with or been married to the man, if we were fashionably dressed or are not provably virgin, if we are prostitutes, if we put up with or tried to get it over with. . . . If we probably couldn't prove it in court, it wasn't rape [we weren't entitled to maternal custody].*. . . Rape [fathers' rights]* from women's point of view, is not prohibited; it is regulated.
>
> Women, as a survival strategy, must ignore or devalue or mute our own

---

*Author's insertion.

desires (particularly lack of them) to convey the impression that the man will get what he wants regardless of what we want.[14]

Nearly half the mothers (47 percent) *verbally* expressed a mothers' rights position. The verbal expression of maternal rights was not correlated either with sexual preference or with political ideology.[15]

What did a verbal expression of mothers' rights sound like?

> Abigail: We get pregnant. We experience physical and psychological changes. If we give birth to a healthy baby, why isn't that more important than a few drops of sperm? We bring the kids up. Isn't that as important as economically supporting them? What about those mothers who support the kids, too? Why don't mothers automatically have the right of way in a custody battle?

> Alix: How can a child be forcibly removed from a devoted and competent mother? There's one incredible explanation. It's because mothers are *women*. If mothers had any custody rights, *women* would already have equal rights.

Some mothers who verbally opposed *anyone's* having "rights" over children made similar statements. However, in the same breath they insisted that mothers should never stand in the way of a father-child relationship and that all children need fathers. They *perceived* a difference between mothering and fathering—one that they did not translate into any verbal expression of maternal entitlement.

> Sonia: Parenting is a very delicate task. As long as men are trained to be selfish and domineering, they can't be trusted with children. They know this themselves. After men win custody, they toss the children right into another woman's lap. They won't take on the job themselves.

> Maureen: My husband did many good things for our children when they were small. Once we separated, he didn't care what he did to hurt his own children—as long as it hurt me and weakened my relationship with them. He treated them as if they were extensions of me at the very time he was claiming that they "belonged" to him.

A traumatizing experience of injustice cannot "radicalize" an isolated victim into a verbal assertion of her (non-existent) "rights." Victims need an alternative vision of justice *plus* personal support in order to become verbally self-assertive. Was there any correlation between being able to talk about mothers' rights and being supported during battle?

The twenty-one heterosexual mothers who expressed a mothers' rights position did so with very little personal or political support.[16] Only three (14 percent) of the heterosexual mothers sought any *political* support. Only one mother (Miki) received any.

Miki: A group of black women social workers came through for me. I was refused help by every male-run Asian-American and black group I managed to contact.

Jessie: No feminist organization was willing to help me. They saw what happened to me as sexist, but they didn't know how to relate to it. The women I spoke to felt that fathers should have equal custodial rights. They didn't know how to support me without seeming to be against equality or against male participation in child care.

Emily: I'm a socialist. No one I knew politically wanted to handle this issue as a political issue. Some friends tried to put on a benefit for my legal expenses. It fell through.

Nine (20 percent) of the heterosexual advocates of mothers' rights were *personally* supported by male intimates. Of these, only a third expressed a mothers' rights position. This suggests that personal (male) support does not necessarily lead a woman into verbal assertions of maternal rights or into a political analysis of her experience.[17]

Half (50 percent) of the lesbian mothers did not seek any *political* support; they were isolated or too afraid to be publicly identified as lesbians. The other 50 percent both sought and received personal and political support.

These mothers all verbally expressed a mothers' rights position. *Personal* support was as important as, or was a form of, *political* support for lesbian mothers under siege.

Dorothy: A lot of lesbians sympathized with me and came to court. The community here tried to be helpful, but they actually thought that I couldn't win, that there was no point in fighting too hard. If it weren't for my lover, I would have had no contact with the community. I only had the energy to see my lawyer and go to work. I could never have arranged a benefit or gotten publicity.

Margo: I did all the work of keeping it together. Laura [the biological mother] was barely able to get up in the morning. She was seriously depressed. I helped our daughter lead an almost normal life. I also did all the political work. Actually I fought harder for that kid than she did. Maybe I had the strength and she didn't. She'd already lost her son.

Few women are able to defend themselves effectively in public battles. Fewer still are able to face the "whirlpool of cruelty" again on behalf of another woman victim.[18] Such principled and compassionate activity requires enormous psychological strength, ideological or religious conviction, and an economic and emotional base of some kind.[19]

Ten mothers—17 percent of the entire maternally embattled population; 36 percent of the verbal advocates of mothers' rights—became pro-mother activists. All were feminists.

Seven of these activists had effectively fought their own battles—i.e., they had contacted social agencies, church groups, experts, and the media. After losing their battles, these ten advocates went on to counsel, support, or accompany other custodially embattled mothers to court.

Two mothers formed a support group for themselves and for other custodially victimized mothers. Two mothers went to law school—to have a lawyer *they* could trust and to provide such a lawyer for other women. One mother joined, and a second mother created, a small crisis and counseling network for custodially embattled mothers.

This may actually be a high rate of altruistic activity among women victims. How many victims, male or female, ever become activists? How many victims, male or female, do so with as little support as these activists had in their own battles?

WHAT EXACTLY AM I SAYING ABOUT MOTHERS?

All custodially challenged mothers "bonded" in nurturing and non-violent ways to their children. Under siege, they remained *non-violently* "connected" to their children. Mothers did not use violent or "disconnected" means to win custody of their children.

After losing custody, these mothers saw or attempted to see their children regularly even under difficult and humiliating circumstances. Remaining connected under the most adverse conditions is one measure of the optimistic resilience of the mother-child bond (or social contract).

Am I saying that every mother on earth is now and always has been a saint or psychologically perfect in white, middle-class, and married ways? I am not.[20] "Good enough" mothers do not always perfectly enact what Sara Ruddick has called "maternal thinking" or the "maternal process."

> Actual mothers have the same relation to maternal practice as actual scientists have to scientific practice, or actual believers have to religious practices. As mothers, they are governed by the interests of their respective practices. But the style, skill, commitment and integrity with which they engage in these practices differ widely from individual to individual.[21]

It is important to remember that individual mothers can and do fail Ruddick's "maternal process" in a number of ways and for many reasons. Mothers are forced to nurture children "according to the Law of the Symbolic Father and under His Watchful Eye." Many mothers "deny" this fact by controlling their children "excessively" and by socializing them into "obedience" with all the fury of long-colonized eunuchs.[22]

Adult women (including mothers) have been described as more "affiliative" and "attached" than men, as more "cooperative" than "competitive," and as preferring "intimate relationships" to "self-enhancement."[23]

However, adult women are as "competitive" with and "aggressive" toward *other women* as they are "cooperatively attached" to their "own" family men and children. Adult women rarely "affiliate" with or "nurture" other women or *their* children.[24]

Women (including mothers) are "competitive" with and "aggressive" or indifferent toward women of another race, class, "tribe," or nation-state; their female slaves, servants, employees, and employers; other family women in general; those family women who have committed "female" crimes; and any woman who has been victimized, whether she is a blood or legal relative or a stranger. Women also compete with other women for boyfriends, husbands, jobs, social reputation, and so on.[25]

> The repulsive, contorted faces of white mothers shouting at black children seeking to enter schoolrooms may haunt most women. But they are faces of

maternal practice and represent a temptation to which mothers are liable—self-righteous violence against the outsider. . . . In maternal thinking a central tension is created between the fierce desire to foster one's own children and the commitment to the well-being of all children. The more individualistic, hierarchical, and competitive the social system, the more likely that a mother will see the good of her child and her group's children as opposed to the good of children of another mother or another "kind."[26]

Most men are violently "competitive" with other men and with non-family women. Most men also bond "cooperatively" with each other, and with family women, for the sake of survival and power. In addition, as physicians, firemen, policemen, and politicians, men routinely "cooperate" to save the lives of strangers. Men are paid, often honored, and empowered for such behavior.

All mothers are expected to—and do—sacrifice themselves to nurture, protect, and "advance" their husbands and children. However, such "cooperative" behavior is unpaid, unhonored, and not publicly empowering.

A true comparison of gender-specific virtues is almost impossible. "Women's" virtues are devalued or valued only within the private realm. "Men's" virtues are valued within both the private and the public realms.

Nevertheless, Ruddick's view of mothering as a "moral process" is very useful. The fact that the human race is still here suggests that most mothers throughout evolution and recorded history have been physically nurturant and non-violent to children in ways that have been "good enough."

Despite the limitations and imperfections of individual mothers, and with all due respect to what men have also done to avert violence and save lives, Ruddick's description of mothers is fairly accurate. She says:

> *I can think of no other situation in which someone with the resentments of social powerlessness, under enormous pressures of time and anger, faces a recalcitrant but helpless combatant with so much restraint. What is remarkable is that in a daily way mothers make so much peace instead of fighting, and then when peace fails, conduct so many battles without resorting to violence. I don't want to trumpet a virtue but to point to a fact: that non-violence is a constitutive principle of maternal thinking, and that mothers honor it not in the breach, but in their daily practice, despite objective temptations to violence.*[27]

If women embody the world's most concrete and continuous practice of non-violence, is this *because* as a caste, women are powerless—or because as women they give birth to life, are socialized into motherhood (which is always under siege), and/or are personally involved in the "maternal process"?[28]

Do men and non-parents devalue maternal pacifism as a way of being in the world or as a means of conflict resolution *because* they are powerful—and because they do not give birth to life, are socialized into the habits of violence, within both the private and the public realms, and are never personally involved in the "maternal process"?[29]

Can the hand that rocks the cradle really rule the world? Can an individual mother ever "mother" more than her "own" child?

Can maternal non-violence as a way of being in the world and as a means of conflict resolution be learned and used by *all* adults?

How would the "maternal process," enacted either by men or women, function among adult strangers in the public realm? What kinds of social organization would maximize the success of "maternal thinking" in both the public and the private realms?

How can a non-violent way of being or of resolving conflict ever be enacted by powerful institutions? All the world's churches and governments have been unable to abolish human greed and violence through either non-violent or violent means. How can non-violence (or peace on earth) be enacted by powerless individuals each acting alone?

I have no definitive answers to these questions. But I am asking these questions in ways that are new to me. I am understanding these questions in a new way.

Let me share my perception of an all-male discussion about nuclear war. The discussion took place on American television in 1983, immediately after the screening of *The Day After*, a fictional film about mass nuclear death.

The male government *officials* were emotionally "flat": stiff, pompous, a bit embarrassed. The male anti-nuclear *outsiders* were emotionally "passionate."

The men all agreed that both America and the Soviet Union had more nuclear weaponry than either country needed and that nuclear weapons should be decreased and more carefully stored than they are now. The men said they didn't know how to "clean up," "get rid of," or "take out" the nuclear "garbage."

At some level the male officials seemed genuinely puzzled upon being confronted with the "messy" consequences of their (impersonal) actions. They had no personal sense of responsibility for their actions. ("They were only obeying orders; personally they loved their wives, children, dogs, etc.")

If these men had ever "mothered" a child or anyone on a daily basis, they *might* know more about what it takes to preserve one life or what it would feel like to lose that particular life to violent man-made death.

They *might* also be used to "cleaning up" after themselves and *might* make less of a life-threatening "mess" if they knew concretely that what they reaped they and their "own" children would surely sow.[30]

I was as startled by what these men said as by how I perceived them. Despite my long apprenticeship in male identification, male overevaluation, and mother hating, I found myself using a maternal virtue (and a domestic metaphor) as a moral reference point for public action.

(Maternal) virtue at the sideline hardly constitutes a world-transforming politic. On the contrary. The individual woman's subsidization of the "war game status quo," as the slaves, wives, mothers, daughters, and employees of warriors, is notorious—and legion.[31]

The modern state has been very hostile to the preservation of human, animal, plant, and planetary life. Neither as individuals nor collectively have mothers per se used non-violence, on behalf of themselves, other mothers, or children, as a tactic with which to effectively confront male violence at home, on the streets, or as embodied by both church and state.[32]

Jean Bethke Elshtain uses the tragic heroine Antigone as an example of one woman's non-violent confrontation with the violence of the (male) state.

> In her loyalty to her slain brother and to family honor, Antigone asserts that there are matters of such deep significance that they begin and end where the state's writ does not and must not run, where politics cannot presume to dictate to the human soul. . . . Maternal thinking reminds us that public policy has an impact on real human beings. As public policy becomes increasingly impersonal, [bureaucratic,] calculating, technocratic, [centralized,] maternal thinking insists that the concrete reality of a single human child be kept, ongoingly, before the mind's eye. Maternal thinking, like Antigone's protest, is a rejection of amoral statecraft and an affirmation of the dignity of the human person.[33]

Antigone is a striking symbol of female rebellion. Under Christian, patriarchal rule, too few women rebels have been presented as noble. This is a good enough reason to read *Antigone* or, for that matter, *Medea*.[34]

However, Antigone is also—and basically—a dutiful sister who confronts her king on behalf of her blood brother, not on behalf of her blood sister, blood children, or any other woman or *her* blood relatives.

Antigone confronts her king alone and as his future daughter-in-law. She does not do so as the leader of an anti-war movement or as a political rebel concerned with redefining what is "public" and what is "private."

In this Antigone is something of a "matriarchal" figure. Her limitations are those of any private person, concerned with her "own" family and willing to take risks or do public battle for their sake alone.

Sara Ruddick theorizes that Antigone or, more specifically, mothers as a group could politically confront the violence of the (male) state in non-violent ways only if "maternal thinking were transformed by feminist consciousness." (And, in my opinion, if feminists were transformed by "maternal thinking.")

> Mothers can come to realize that the good of their own children is entwined with the good of all children, that in a world divided between exploiter and exploited no children can be both good and strong, that in a world at war all children are endangered. We can as mothers learn to sustain a conflicted but creative tension between personal loyalties and impersonal moral concerns. . . . This maternal conflict can bring a sense of realism and moral humanity to political struggle; it also suggests real limits to the effectiveness of maternal thinking in political life.[35]

The maternal process is, at its worst, "selfish," arbitrary, and overly emotional. The paternal process is at its worst, and at its best, "selfish," arbitrary, and underemotional.[36]

Through a reinforced absence of feeling, patriarchal man has convinced himself (and us) that there is nothing "personal" and therefore nothing "wrong" in his legalized mistreatment of others, in both the private and the public realms. Patriarchal man has convinced himself (and us) that he is "objective" and "impartial."

As we have seen, the history, basic premise, and contemporary application of patriarchal law are sexist—i.e., more concerned with the (male) ownership of property than with the preservation of (female or male) life.[37]

As such, the patriarchal legal obsession with facts, procedures, and "objective" evidence is also a way of confusing and silencing those who view patriarchal legal methods as patently arbitrary and unjust.[38]

The maternal process is characterized by certain virtues that the paternal process lacks or devalues. For example, the maternal process is, at its best, concrete rather than abstract, subjective rather than objective, emotional rather than emotionless, flexible rather than dogmatic, "whole" rather than compartmentalized.

The maternal process is, at its best, both optimistic and pessimistic, both humble and grandiose. Once the maternal process is engaged, it is engaged continuously, and in "nurturing" ways, for life. Serious maternal disengagement or life-threatening violence is rare. Mothers do not often kill their children or go to war against them as a way of socializing them.[39]

The maternal process cannot "connect" to a large number of strangers. It cannot function in a world that is overly and impersonally organized.

This doesn't mean that the maternal process is unsuited to the world at large. On the contrary. It confirms that the larger world, as presently constituted, is unsuited to the non-violent nurturance or preservation of life.

CHAPTER TWENTY

Children's Rights

It is a degrading thought that any parent has a "right" [or] "a natural inclination" to *possess* the object of his affection. What right could one have to another person?

We have obligations to each other. We earn each other's welcome by our trustworthiness or beauty or service or nurturance. But we cannot have rights to another.

But it could be argued that children are different. They cannot take care of themselves; they must be taken care of. Perhaps it is assumed, then, that there must be, as reward, some *right* to balance the *responsibility*.

Therein lies precisely the point of the dilemma of parenting on which mothers have been impaling themselves forever. For despite the responsibility and the obligation there can be no right to the child. There can only be the myriad of small pleasures of loving and caring, the attachment that grows out of the investment of time and energy and self, and the wonder at growth, change, becoming. The mothering obligation is to finish what began in the womb.

Anna Demeter, *Legal Kidnapping*

IN A MOTHER-HATING culture it is cowardly and shortsighted to plead the case for children's rights while remaining silent about mothers' rights. Do we honestly believe that children or their fathers are entitled to "rights" but that mothers aren't? Or that a child's rights can be enforced when her mother's rights remain non-existent or non-enforceable?

WHAT DO CHILDREN NEED IN ORDER TO LIVE THEIR LIVES? WHAT MUST EXIST IN ORDER TO IMPLEMENT SUCH NEEDS AS RIGHTS?

- **Every child has the right to be considered legitimate, whether or not his parents are married. There is no such thing as a child of woman born, who is "illegitimate."**

- **Every child has the right to be wanted. The unwillingly pregnant woman, the absent father, the indifferent family, and the punitive community are the parents of sorrow. Compulsory motherhood and fatherhood are not the way to welcome a child into life on earth.[1]**

- **All wanted and legal children have the right to be wanted for the right reason—i.e., for *themselves*. A child is a unique human being. No child should be forced to satisfy the excessive or totally frustrated needs that adults have for love or power merely because children are a helpless, dependent, and captive population.**

WHAT MUST EXIST IN ORDER TO IMPLEMENT THESE RIGHTS?

The individual, the family, the church, the state, and the private sector must not discriminate against children on the basis of whether their parents were married or not.

Children have a better chance of being wanted and wanted for *themselves* if women (as well as men) have the right to sexual activity; the right to legal, high quality, inexpensive birth control and abortion; and *equal* access to love and power in work and in their adult relationships.[2]

Once a pregnant woman decides to continue her pregnancy, she should not be harassed on the job, forced to leave her job for being pregnant, or prevented from returning to work after she has given birth. Likewise, a pregnant woman must be able to count on a paid maternity leave.

- **Every unborn child and his willingly pregnant mother have the right to adequate nutrition and health care. Gynecologists and obstetricians must not "treat" an unborn child and his willingly pregnant mother as if they were sick, stupid, "crazy," or evil.**

- **Every unborn child and her willingly pregnant mother must be respectfully and fully informed about drugs, technology, and child-birth methods.**

- **Every unborn child and his or her willingly pregnant mother have the right to be born and to give birth at home or in a woman-centered hospital with any number of chosen "others" in attendance: the child's father; a mother's lover, relative, friend; and/or a midwife and obstetrician.**

No unborn child and his willingly pregnant mother should be denied these rights and options because they are poor, non-white, in prison, or because the mother is unmarried.[3]

In order for an unborn child and her willingly pregnant mother to experience as normal or as safe a pregnancy as possible, they must have access to food, shelter, clothing, and other basic necessities.[4]

WHAT MUST EXIST IN ORDER TO IMPLEMENT THESE RIGHTS?

Women must not be discriminated against within the family or by the church, state, and private sector either because they *might* get pregnant, are pregnant, or have given birth to life—or because they refuse to become pregnant.

Women must have access—equal access—to education and to employment, in order to share the economic responsibility for their wanted children with individual men or women and with the church, the state, and the private sector.

There must be training of more doctors whose standards are both higher than and different from those currently in practice. Medical education must become as pro-woman as it is currently pro-profit or pro-"specialty."

- **Every child has the right to an adequate amount of nutritious food and to adequate shelter. Every child has the right to an adequate amount of clothing that fits and to soap, shampoo, toilet paper, toothpaste, laundry services, etc.[5]**

   Every child needs and is entitled to routine medical and dental care and, when necessary, to medicine, eyeglasses, braces, etc. In addition, every child has the right to his "own" books and to some athletic and cultural equipment. In my opinion, a child is also entitled to many kinds of entertainment beyond that provided by a television set, including access to nature, museums, and educational or serious films.[6]

- **Every child and her mother require both a core and an extended family, a community, and a support network to break their existential fall into newborn motherhood and into life—*for* life.**

Every child needs and has the right to more than *one* parent and, for that matter, to more than *two* parents and one TV set. From an early age children need access to an extended family—i.e., to a number of significant adults of all ages and to other children.

I am not saying that a child should be "shuttled" back and forth between an unending number of adults, none of whom cares about or feels responsibility for that child. Nor am I suggesting that the primary and privileged relationship between a child and his or her mother and father be abrogated. I am talking about a child's right to access to a reasonable number of significant others in his or her life.

No child should be at the total mercy or have to bear the (normal) limitations of one adult for the first ten years of his life. No mother and no couple should be expected to fill all of a child's "family" needs for twenty-one years to life. They cannot.[7]

- Every child is entitled to freedom from maternal or paternal physical neglect or abuse. In the event that maternal or paternal child abuse or neglect does occur, no child should be condemned to a state institution or to an equally abusive or neglectful foster home.

WHAT MUST EXIST IN ORDER TO IMPLEMENT THESE RIGHTS?

Individual legislators have publicized the economic plight of families and of children and have forced the unwilling state, church, and private sector to provide for the victims of economic violence.[8] Much more is needed.

Dr. Paul L. Adams et al. have proposed that every child should receive an adequate and direct allowance for her basic "family" needs and "special" needs ("child support"). They have also proposed a "fatherless child insurance" policy: "[This] would do for all children what it does at the present time, through Social Security, for all who are orphaned when the father dies. The orphan is rather well compensated, and without any stigma, as a survivor of a Social Security-covered patient; the child fatherless for any reason deserves as much."[9]

Extended families should be encouraged as public policy as well as private enterprise for several reasons. First, if a child is "welcomed" at birth into a family "cluster" of five to ten adults (not all of whom must live under one roof and not all of whom must agree on everything), then no child would ever have to endure "hidden," continuous, or extreme parental abuse or neglect. Nor would any child have to face the horror of impersonal state care or be destroyed by the biases that dominate private adoption and foster care.

Also, if small family clusters were already used to integrating a living child into their genetic midst, perhaps—just perhaps—this might diminish our extreme and exclusive preference for biological and genetic reproduction. Such genetic narcissism, while understandable, is hardly civilized.

In the temporary or permanent absence of a mother or father, whoever does the work of a mother or a father, whoever the child perceives as his or her "parents," should be entitled to the rights of a "real" parent.

This means that the church, the state, and the private sector should treat a practicing parent *as* a practicing parent—whether or not that person is a child's genetic or biological parent or grandparent or is unrelated to that child by blood or marital tie.[10]

- **Every child has the right to learn about his racial, religious, and cultural history and to experience this identity with pride. Ideally, racial, tribal, ethnic, and religious wisdom should be communicated in ways that are neither fanatically separatist nor fanatically assimilationist.**

In a world seething with racism and religious persecution, in a world filled with theocratic nation-states, at a time when religious fundamentalism is, as ever, used to justify violence, it is crucial that every child be taught who she is in an expansive, not restrictive, way; that every child be taught to celebrate his or her tribal as well as unique identities; and that every child be taught to celebrate, not just tolerate, all tribal differences.

I am not saying that children should be .told nothing, or too little, about their roots, or that children should be expected to "supermarket shop" for roots on their own as adults.

I am saying that children must learn about their racial, tribal, ethnic, and religious identities in ways that maximize rather than minimize their exercise of free will and in ways that do not cut them off from, or forbid them to believe in, the humanity of those born into different tribes.[11]

- **Every child has the right to his or her sexual identity. This means that children have the right to information about their bodies and the right to take pride in them. Girls have the right not to be indoctrinated into bodily self-hatred or sexual passivity; boys have the right not to be indoctrinated into bodily overevaluation, fixation on the penis and its size, and sexual aggression.**

  Children who are sexually "active" with other children; who are bi-sexual, homosexual, or lesbian; and children who are non-sexual have the right *not* to be humiliated, ostracized, or imprisoned for these reasons.

I am not saying that children must be forced by adults into pre-adolescent sexual intercourse, promiscuity, birth control, or pregnancy. On the contrary. I am talking about children's right to informed self-respect for their own bodies and for the bodies of others, including or especially those of the opposite sex.

- Every child has the right to a *quality* education. A child's education should never be totally controlled or administered by one sex, one race, one religion, or one culture. Nor should those who fear, despise, or exploit children be in charge of educating them.

    Children have the right to learn. Obedience should not be confused with learning; competitive speed is not the same as intellectual growth; adjustment is not the unfolding of talent. Above all, every child has the right to an education that is non-sexist, non-racist, and non-culturally claustrophobic.[12]

A child's education begins at birth. Creches for infants and toddlers and pre-school or after-school day-care programs are a child's right. Education, including day care, is not second-best or meant only for "working" mothers. (We do not conceive of a governess, private tutor, or private school for the very rich as second-best.)

Day care is often the only way that children have access to each other and to non-familial adults in their pre- or after-school lives.

Day care should reflect some parental and familial values and be democratically accessible to parental input. It should also reflect some non-parental and non-familial values. This is a way of balancing a child's first view of the world.

Day care, like school, should not be a way of "warehousing" children. It should be seriously pursued as public policy as well as private enterprise.

WHAT MUST EXIST IN ORDER FOR THESE RIGHTS TO BE IMPLEMENTED?

Both public and private education (including day care) has been victimized by mammoth and heartless state and church bureaucracies. Poor children have been crowded together and segregated from wealthier children, who, in turn, have been segregated together, at a remove from the world they are expected to profit from and rule.

What is needed is both more substantial and more flexible central educational planning, to economically subsidize many, small, diverse, and mother-controlled educational ventures.

This chapter is not a blueprint or instruction manual for any existing economic system. Whatever the economic system(s) are that can and will ensure a quality education for every child, the *people* within that system must first be convinced that a quality education is every child's birthright.

- **From birth every child has a right to his or her genetic or adoptive mother, to his or her practicing mother, and to his or her presiding mother figure. All three mothers (or maternal functions) may be enacted by one or more mothers.**

A child's mother figure both represents and *is* the child's tie to the eternal mother. A mother figure is she whom the child perceives as such, and she who is profoundly changed by motherhood.

As we have previously discussed, pregnancy, childbirth, and breast feeding connect mothers to their infants in powerful and profound ways;[13] female socialization also strengthens women's potential for biological maternity and for maternal practice.[14]

Maternal practice is a way of being in the world. It is a process and a dialectic. Maternal practice consists of an unending number of visible and invisible tasks, performed in nurturing and non-violent ways.

The bond between a mother and her child is naturally sacred. It is physical, psychological, and spiritual. It is very resilient and very flexible. It can stretch very far—naturally. Any artificial or violent injury to this "stretch" constitutes a serious psychic trauma to both mother and child—for all eternity.

This means that children need their mothers and mothers need their children—whether or not a mother is married or unmarried; or obedient or disobedient to her husband or to the church, the state, or the private sector.

Female non-conformity is not the same as unfit motherhood. Too often those empowered to separate a child from her mother are not concerned with

> whether a woman is a good or bad mother but rather whether she is a "respectable" or a "deviate" woman. Is it in the interest of the state, the family, or the child to remove it from its own mother's custody if her only crime is nonconformity? Whose interests are being served? Since a mother loses her rights not by mothering poorly but by violating patriarchal rules for *women*, then "parent's rights" are but a subterfuge for *men's* rights, such as they are.[15]

Children and mothers need each other whether or not their mothers engage in non-marital heterosexual or lesbian activities and whether or not their mothers have non-marital or marital orgasms, become celibate, use birth control, have abortions, or give birth to "illegal" children.

Children need their mothers; mothers need their children—whether or not their mothers have inherited or can earn "male" salaries, or are impoverished by the church, the state, and the private sector or by divorce.

Children need their mothers; mothers need their children—whether or not their mothers' maternal practice is traditional or non-traditional; whether or not they embody or defy the state's racial, class, or cultural ideals; and whether or not they are imprisoned.

WHAT MUST EXIST IN ORDER FOR THESE RIGHTS TO BE IMPLEMENTED?

In order for children and their mothers to "have" each other, mothers must be genuinely respected and supported rather than feared, hated, enslaved, overprotected, and impoverished. (*This* is a very revolutionary proposition.)

Mothers must be guaranteed the *means* as well as the right to bear and rear a child. As of 1984, in the United States,

Women have been disproportionately hurt economically because they are disproportionately represented among the poor; because they are politically unorganized and vulnerable [particularly poor women]; because they face discrimination and have had to rely on the federal government to help them combat it; and because cutting programs that aid women [especially working women and women rearing children alone] is facilitated by the ideological glorification of the patriarchal nuclear family.[16]

In 1976, in *Women, Money and Power,* I and my coauthor suggested:

As long as women's relationship to the home exists as it now does, there is merit to the position that housewives be paid wages. As long as women are viewed as belonging in the home and as long as the family or the home is the core institution, it would be preferable to pay the person who spends some portion of his time there. Thus, if the woman is at home, the husband, instead of leaving, working, and bringing his wife an allowance, or even salary, should be viewed as *her* employee or agent, who leaves the home, the family, the "core social institution;" goes out to hunt, and brings back his catch. She is the principal.[17]

A maternal wage should not reflect the "room, board, and allowance" mentality that dominates most marriages; nor should it reflect the punitive/poverty mentality that dominates the receipt of state welfare.

"Subsidized" motherhood should not become a state means of forcing women into motherhood as a "profitable" private enterprise.

A maternal wage can be calculated and paid directly as well as indirectly. Indirect payments can entail the "free" use of a mother-controlled day-care center on each block or in each office building or the "free" use of mother-controlled housekeeping and baby-sitting services—to be subsidized by both the private and the public sectors. According to Dr. Paul Adams et al.:

> The family in the capitalistic nation is an economic unit. A thrifty instrumentality, it looks after the nurture and life maintenance of millions of young people. One of its major activities is its investment in that human capital. The family [also] decides what goods to consume, and whether to have children who will, in turn become economic producers.[18]

In May 1984 Pope John Paul II also endorsed the idea of a salary for housewives and mothers. The pope's charter stated that families have a right to "social and economic order," including "wages sufficient to maintain a family with dignity." He also stated that "mothers should not be obliged to go out to work to the detriment of family life, especially the education of children."[19]

To continue my list of children's rights:

- **From birth, every child has a right to his or her genetic or adoptive father, his or her practicing father, and his or her presiding father figure. All three paternal functions may be enacted by one father or by several fathers.**

  A child's father figure both represents and is the child's tie to the eternal father and, traditionally, to both the adult and the public worlds.

  A father figure is he whom the child perceives as such and he who is profoundly changed by fatherhood.

Children need their fathers; fathers need their children—whether or not their fathers are unmarried, heterosexual, homosexual, celibate, or engage in masturbation (one of the male "equivalents" of abortion).

Children need their fathers—whether or not their fathers have inherited or can earn a "male" salary or are impoverished by the church, the state, the private sector, or by divorce.

Children need their fathers—whether or not their fathers are engaged in traditional or non-traditional paternal practice; whether or not they defy the state's racial, class, or cultural ideals; and whether or not they are imprisoned.

In a father-idealizing culture children need fathers for all the traditional psycho-economic reasons. Children may also need fathers and/or male surrogates who are physically and psychologically present in "nurturing" ways. Sara Ruddick has noted:

It is now argued that the most revolutionary change we can make in the institution of motherhood is to include men equally in every aspect of childcare. When men and women live together with children, it seems not only fair but deeply moral that they share in every aspect of childcare. To prevent or excuse men from maternal practice is to encourage them to separate public action from private affection, the privilege of parenthood from its cares. Moreover, even when men are absent from the nursery, their dominance in every other public and private room shapes a child's earliest conception of power.[20]

A practicing mother cannot hire a male surrogate to perform surgery in her name—and call herself a surgeon. A practicing surgeon cannot hire a female surrogate to "man" the nursery for him—and call himself an equal parent or a "mother."

"Equal" physical and emotional fathering may be spiritually crucial for men and for the survival of our species. However, it is important to realize that the male (or paternal) integration into the institution of child care in no way necessarily implies the liberation of women and children or the transfusion of maternal values into public life. As Adrienne Rich has noted:

The issue of mothering-by-women has been much in the air of late, usually accompanied by the view that increased parenting by men would minimize antagonism between the sexes and equalize the sexual imbalance of power of males over females. These discussions are carried on without reference to compulsory heterosexuality as a phenomenon, let alone as an ideology. . . . I believe that large numbers of men could, in fact, undertake childcare on a large scale without radically altering the balance of male power in a male-identified society.[21]

WHAT MUST EXIST FOR THESE RIGHTS TO BE IMPLEMENTED?

In order for children and their fathers to "have" each other, fathers would have to become and be perceived as care *givers* as well as care-*takers* and economic providers. (*This* is a revolutionary proposition.)

Men (fathers) have not been socialized from birth to view child care as a male activity or to serve children in physically present and psychologically nurturant ways. Those fathers who wish to do so would have to learn the skills involved in maternal practice—e.g., the difference between "helping" and "sharing."[22]

Fathers and men in general must learn how to "nurture" children in non-violent ways, physically and psychologically, in addition to economically supporting them. Fathers, like mothers, should be entitled to paternity-related leaves without job penalties.

DO CHILDREN NEED THEIR FATHERS IN THE SAME WAY THEY NEED THEIR MOTHERS?

I have suggested that children have an inviolate right to their mothers—even to those mothers who are ill or imprisoned. Does an equally inviolate right exist in relation to a father?

In Chapter Three, I suggested that most children have traditionally survived without any *physical* fathering from birth on; that many children have (had to) survive with only minimal physical or psychological contact with their fathers or with men in general; and that many "illegitimate" children have (had to) survive without any fathers at all.

In Chapter Three, I also suggested that there is a difference between how a "good enough" father fathers and how a "good enough" mother mothers.

On the basis of what *is* known about physical child abuse, I suggested that there are more *physically* violent fathers than mothers; that under stress, fathers will resort to violence or to flight more often or more quickly than mothers; and that when fathers are violent, they are more *physically* dangerous to their children than are their maternal counterparts.[23]

In Chapters Four, Eight, Nine, and Ten I showed how a particular group of fathers *battling for custody* did not hesitate to devastate economically, kidnap, and brainwash their children—either out of revenge or because they genuinely believed that paternal custody *at any price* was in their "child's best interest."

In Chapter Eleven, I discussed the difference in how we perceive and treat custodial and non-custodial parents as a function of gender and how most custodial and non-custodial fathers are different from—and parentally inferior to—their maternal counterparts.

In Chapter Nineteen, I discussed the experiential nature of the maternal process and the (relatively) non-violent nature of the mother-child bond. I also discussed the maternal unwillingness to adopt "violent measures" to obtain custody even when mothers perceived maternal custody to be in their "child's best interest."

In what sense, then, do children need those fathers whose sperm may have contributed to their conception but who since then have not psychologically or economically acknowledged their existence; who have not seen them; or who have never engaged in any regular or responsible traditional or non-traditional paternal practice?

Do children *need* fathers whose absence and indifference constitute a form of *physical* child abuse? I am not saying that children don't need fathers. I am asking if children "need" absent, indifferent, unreliable, or irresponsible fathers.

I am not suggesting that individual mothers or the state prevent a child from knowing who his or her father is or even from seeing him. I am asking us all to consider what kind of "need" is being satisfied by an unavailable or by a minimally available father.

Do children have the "right" to a relationship which is physically abusive to them? In what sense do children need fathers who are wife beaters, wife rapists, child abusers, child molesters, or child rapists?

- **Every child and his or her mother need and are entitled to freedom from physical and sexual violence. What is known as family or domestic violence is, in reality, male physical, psychological, and sexual violence toward women and children—99 percent of the time.**[24]*

What if a child's "right" to a domestically violent father condemns the child to becoming like him or to marrying someone like him? Are

---

*I am not talking about the psychological imperfections of mothers or fathers. I am talking about physical and sexual violence.

we willing to sacrifice each generation of children on the altar of paternal violence? Why?

Do we still (mistakenly) believe that paternal physical absence, indifference, or violence toward children will somehow be diminished or eliminated by granting all fathers, including violent fathers, unlimited access to "legal" heirs?*

WHAT MUST EXIST IN ORDER FOR THESE RIGHTS TO BE IMPLEMENTED?

The recent and widespread public outcry about male domestic violence in general, quite apart from its implications for custody, was led by feminist scholars and political activists and by some elected and appointed officials.

Volunteer and state-subsidized shelters for battered women and children were created; rape, incest, and battered women counselors began counseling and testifying in the courtroom.[25]

The federal and state governments were pushed by their own elected members, by the media, and by feminist groups to hold conferences, create committees, and subsidize token efforts to protect women and children from male domestic violence.

For example, Representative George Miller (D-Calif.) started focusing congressional attention on this issue during the 1970s. In 1976, the White House held its first Conference on Domestic Violence. In 1979, a Federal Office for Domestic Violence was created; by 1981 it had been destroyed by Congress and a new administration.

In July 1981, the Federal Uniform Child Kidnapping Act was finally passed. By 1983 George Miller had formed the Select Committee on Children, Youth, and Families for the stated purpose of "holding up a mirror for Congress to see the American Family."[26]

Some cities and states have recently passed legislation to combat male domestic violence. In 1983, Susan Schecter, Wisconsin Women Against Rape, the Women of Color Task Force, and Elizabeth Thomas each published a series of specific proposals concerning the detection, prevention, and punishment of domestically violent husbands and fathers. Their proposals are praiseworthy; the adoption of their proposals, urgent. I have summarized them in one very long footnote.[27]

---

*Patriarchal law and religion have been attempting to do just this with, at best, a 50 percent success rate.

- **Every child has the right to be reared in a loving and respectful way. A child's spirit is naturally sacred and need not be broken in order for socialization to take place. Children have the right to be reared by adults who are psychologically self-aware, and who are also aware of the "stages" of psychological development in children.**

I am not saying that children must be reared in either "permissive" or "non-permissive" ways, or that children must never be physically or psychologically disciplined.

I am saying that it is cruel to deceive, manipulate, humiliate, and shame children merely because they are unsocialized and vulnerable to such treatment, and also that children must be allowed to establish *some* means of natural self-regulation from the earliest possible age.

Many twentieth-century experts have stressed that authoritarian and repressive methods of child rearing are harmful to children, that such methods "kill" spontaneous and authentic feelings, often forever, and that this constitutes a form of cruelty to children.[28]

Many parents, including mothers, "instinctively" know this; many parents, including mothers, do not.

Those mothers who do know this are what I would call empathically authoritarian with their children. This is a good way to conduct a child's daily and step-by-step socialization without excessively wounding her pride and therefore her (and a mother's) ability to function.[29]

Since family life is considered more of a private right than a public responsibility, family violence remains as unregulated by public law as public violence remains unregulated by family values.

If this is so, how can the claims of the powerless—i.e., of children—begin to hold their own against the claims of the (more) powerful?

Despite lip service, children really have few enforceable rights. Many needs that children have are recognized as such. Some of these needs can be turned into enforceable rights—with enough time, will, resources, and luck.

Some needs are ideals or goals, the true implementation of which always resides, for better and for worse, in the hands of each individual.

If the sixteen rights I have discussed were implemented, then neither a bad marriage nor a good divorce would be half as traumatic as they now are.

What happens upon separation or divorce? Are children's needs or rights always, sometimes, or never in conflict with their mothers' or fathers'?

Are maternal and paternal rights always in conflict with each other? Must parental rights always yield to the rights of children?

I would like to discuss these questions separately, in the next chapter.

CHAPTER TWENTY-ONE

Upon Divorce

I had read in the Gemara that for men and women to find their right mates is as much a miracle as the splitting of the Red Sea. A good marriage does not always happen and is different with each union. . . . Men and women craved happiness together, but instead they indulged in silly quarrels, spiteful accusations, various lies, and acts of treachery. Each wanted to be stronger than the other and often to belittle and denigrate the weaker.

Isaac Bashevis Singer, *Love and Exile*

The mistake began when God was created in a male image. . . . That makes life so perverted, and death so unnatural. We should have imagined life as created in the birth-pain of God the Mother. Then we would understand why we, Her children, have inherited pain, for we would know that our life's rhythm beats from Her great heart, torn with the agony of love and birth. And we would feel that death meant reunion with Her, a passing back into Her substance, blood of Her blood again, peace of Her peace! Now wouldn't that be more logical and satisfying than having God a male whose chest thunders with egotism and is too hard for tired heads and thoroughly comfortless?

Eugene O'Neill, *Strange Interlude*

HOW CAN SO compulsory an institution as marriage also inspire so much human longing? Is marriage our way of both reliving the dream of paradise—and of renouncing it forever? Is marriage our only social contract ("Our family against the world"), or is it also the bedrock of society ("You can count on us, we're family people")?

Legal marriages come in all sizes and shapes. "Good" and "bad" marriages may last a long time or may end abruptly. Wives experience the same marriage differently from husbands; marriage means one thing to parents and something entirely different to children.

As we have seen, few women had any economic alternatives to marriage—especially if they wanted children. For centuries, both church and state outlawed divorce—for the sake of "society" and the children. Wives trapped in the worst of marriages still feared divorce. They were the ones who were blamed and impoverished, custodially and economically, upon divorce.

A husband could always obtain a divorce more easily and more "cheaply" than any wife could. A man could also remarry more easily, with or without custody of his children, without stigma. Upon divorce women were *obliged* to care for their children alone and in poverty. Upon divorce judges rarely ordered or enforced their orders of child support, alimony, or other marital assets and property.

Today, marriage is still a mother's *only* alternative, and divorce is as hard on women and children as it ever was. At best women earn sixty-three cents on the male dollar; adequate child care remains non-existent; and at least half of all divorced fathers abandon their children physically and/or economically.[1]

An increasingly visible number of fathers also kidnap or obtain custody of their children and of other marital assets through the use of economic and legal violence.

Upon divorce wealthy fathers hire expensive lawyers to "starve" their wives into "settling" for as little as possible. The passage of no-fault divorce and of equitable distribution has made this easier for them to do.

Upon divorce the judges who refuse to equate paternal domestic violence with paternal unfitness, who tend to award 100 percent of each child to fathers in contested custody cases, are the same judges who refuse to award obedient wives and custodial mothers more than 30 percent of their ex-husbands' salaries for alimony and child support or more than 35 to 40 percent of all other marital assets and properties.[2]

The judges who themselves receive pensions and who are reluctant to "divorce" any man from his pension are the same judges who award women inadequate amounts of alimony (or "rehabilitative maintenance") and then only for a limited period of time.

"Let her get a job," they thunder, even if the woman in question has been a full-time wife and homemaker for twenty-five years, is now over fifty years of age, and literally has a millionaire for an ex-husband.[3]

Upon divorce maternal custodial poverty becomes "invisible." Legislators, lawyers, and judges deny either that such poverty exists or that it is very extreme. In fact, some say that maternal custodial victimization or custodial poverty is really a form of "progress."

Massive distortions of reality rarely spring fully grown and fully armed, as Athena did, from the "womb" of her father's head. Such distortions require a long period of gestation elsewhere—gestation that is both devalued and denied.

Children are of woman born; always this has been devalued or denied. Divorce proceeds along a strong anti-mother and pro-father "fault line"; always this has been minimized or denied.

The process of denying, minimizing, or "justifying" what happens to mothers upon divorce is now in the hands of Master mythmakers. I am referring to Hollywood film-makers, mental health experts, and the fathers' rights movement.

HOLLYWOOD FILMS. *KRAMER VS. KRAMER:* BEFORE AND AFTER

Hollywood is a dream factory. Certain films (certain *kinds* of films) allow us to satisfy our deepest and most forbidden desires by disguising or romanticizing them and by punishing others for acting them out. Such films "captivate" us. They enter our collective bloodstream. *Gone With The Wind* and *The Godfather* are two such films.

Both films are about the patriarchal ownership of families and children. Both films depict a paternal child kidnapping and the violent repossession of a child. Nobody remembers "seeing" this. How can we remember what we have seen when we are so mesmerized by longing for the father-owned family, and, as women, for heroic father-husbands?

In *Gone With The Wind,* Clark Gable's Rhett Butler kidnaps, and attempts to brainwash and obtain sole custody of his daughter, Bonnie. In *The Godfather (Part II),* Al Pacino's Michael Corleone is an absent father who violently repossesses his children after his wife has had an abortion.

Despite this, both Rhett and Michael are heroes—more so because they are criminals who are also "family men." (This is the male Hollywood equivalent of the "whore with a heart of gold.") In *Gone With The Wind* we remember Vivien Leigh's Scarlett O'Hara as a spoiled, greedy, deceptive adulteress. In *The Godfather* Diane Keaton's Kay Corleone isn't even Italian, and she does have an abortion. We do not remember either Scarlett or Kay as eternal Earth-Mothers.

We forget how hard Scarlett fights to name her daughter Eugenia Victoria. (She loses the battle. Rhett wants "Bonnie.") We forget how much harder Scarlett must work to earn so less of her daughter's love, and none of her adoration. We forget how Scarlett suffers when Rhett steals Bonnie away to Europe, and when Bonnie dies—attempting to please her father.

The unspoken passion in *Gone With The Wind* (as in so many other films) is that of father-daughter incest. Only Bonnie, pure, adoring, and unthreatening, is truly worthy of Rhett's patriarchal love. Bonnie is Rhett's child bride and Rhett's "own" little female self. Bonnie must die—in this case a sacrifice to Rhett's honor.

We do not blame Rhett for this—any more than we blame Michael Corleone for his Sicilian child bride's death. We feel sorry for both men; less so for their daughter-figure victims; and not at all for the mothers involved.

We also forget (don't discuss, never mention, barely notice) another Hollywood father's violent "re-possession" of his daughter—in the film *Ragtime*. The girl's mother is also an adulteress, just like Scarlett O'Hara. Mandy Patinkin's father, like Rhett and Michael, dotes on his daughter and will soon be rich and famous. Clearly any child is better off with a rich father than with an immoral or impoverished mother.

These films are about patriarchal fathers. The custody scenes are "throw-aways." The fathers are not presented as male mothers. Still, we are left with the impression that a good patriarchal father is someone who is *acceptably* criminal, i.e., rich. Such a father really "loves" his children and is economically better for them than any mother—especially one who "doesn't stand by her man," i.e., who commits adultery or has an abortion.[4]

Recent Hollywood films have continued to glorify patriarchal (criminal-heroic) fathers. They have also begun to glorify male motherhood and to simultaneously denigrate female motherhood. The best known of these films is *Kramer vs. Kramer*.

I would like to discuss three of the following eleven films: *Paternity; Man, Woman and Child; Six Weeks; Author, Author; Table for Five; Tender Mercies; Ordinary People; Paris, Texas; Shoot the Moon; Mr. Mom;* and *Micky and Maude.*[5]

Al Pacino, in *Author, Author,* is a successful career father whose children attend private school and are all self-cleaning little "wives." Pacino's seven-year-old son collects the laundry; his eldest son serves coffee and knots his father's tie, while listening to his troubles. The night I saw this film, the audience applauded wildly when Pacino finally calls his ex-wife a "heartless bitch."

Pacino is even more heroically maternal than Dustin Hoffman is in *Kramer vs. Kramer.* Pacino, like Father Church, is mother to many children: his own (maternally abandoned) children; various stepchildren; stray neighborhood children.

As anti-mother and pro-father as *Author, Author* is, at least the "unfit" mother is allowed to live. In *Table for Five* (shades of Shakespeare), the mother is already dead. Two *men*—the genetic father vs. the maternally heroic stepfather—battle for custody.[6]

Michael Keaton, in *Mr. Mom,* was Hollywood's next maternally heroic father of the year. After Mr. Mom loses his job, he masters more than Mr. Kramer's burned french toast. He becomes a superefficient house-husband and father.

Film critic Marcia Pally notes that Hollywood's male maternity films glorify fathers at the expense of mothers and proselytize for male control of the world's money, power—and its children too. These films view independent wives as "unfit" mothers. They may also be presenting new "role models for the Reagan-era [male] unemployed." Pally has noted:

> This is not feminism. Feminism, at the very least, must be about the equitable distribution of opportunity and power across the sexes. Paternity films, by contrast, denude women of whatever influence they have. . . . The men who made these films can't imagine sharing any sphere—including the domestic one—with women.
>
> Uncomfortable with changes in social roles, they can appropriate what they will, even behavior formerly considered feminine, as their *droit du seigneur.* And having arrived in the home, they simply silence or deport the women who linger there. Cocking the pistols in their minds' eye, they say, "This kitchen isn't big enough for the two of us."[7]

Every American divorce takes place in the cultural shadow of *Gone With The Wind* and *Kramer vs. Kramer.* As Lillian Kozak pointed out:

"*Kramer vs. Kramer* took the Oscar at the Academy Awards on Monday night and a joint custody bill passed the New York State Legislature on Tuesday morning." (Then Governor Hugh Carey vetoed it.)

Every American divorce also takes place in the shadow of the family therapist or divorce mediator. Such mental health experts have all been trained in a certain way. Also, like the rest of us, they go to the movies.

THE MENTAL HEALTH EXPERTS

It is important to remember that most psychotherapists are trained not in mother-loving, but in mother-blaming. Some therapists overcome this poor training; most do not.

It is also important to remember that most psychotherapists are trained to analyze "reality" psychologically, not politically, and to provide psychological explanations rather than economic solutions to people's problems.

Good psychotherapists are not comfortable with endless diatribes against an ex-spouse. It is not "therapeutically useful" to blame anyone but oneself. Blaming an ex-husband is often "heard" with the same suspicion or impatience that judges reserve for wives who accuse husbands of wife abuse, incest, brainwashing, kidnapping, or of not paying child support.[8]

Blaming an ex-wife isn't viewed as "therapeutically useful" either. However, wife blaming is more accepted than husband blaming; it may also put a man in touch with his long-repressed *feelings*. Upon divorce men (presumably unlike women) experience profound anger and grief. Unlike women (the experts tell us), men deal with their anguish by flight, denial, work/alcoholism, sexual promiscuity, hasty second marriages, and "instant" second families.

In any event, isn't it "therapeutically" better for a father to express his anger than to act on it? Isn't it better for a father to express his feelings in "treatment" than to refuse to see or support his children?

Thus (some) psychotherapists have begun to encourage fathers to fight for their *paternal* emotional territory, while encouraging mothers to give up *maternal* emotional territory—and to fight for financial independence instead.[9]

Such therapists are now encouraging fathers to consider co-parenting or joint custody as their *right* and encouraging mothers to consider co-parenting or joint custody as their *obligation*—"in the best interests of the child."

Claiming the "emotions" of fatherhood is therapeutically praised.

Claiming the "emotions" of motherhood is not praised—*especially when those "emotions" interfere with a father's getting what he wants:* sole custody; joint custody; liberal visitation; no visitation; the non-payment of child support; the house, the car, the boat, etc.

Every divorce also takes place in the cultural shadow of the media. Judges, film-makers, and mental health experts, like everyone else, read newspapers, watch television, and attend conferences. They have all read about the fathers' rights movement.[10]

THE FATHERS' RIGHTS MOVEMENT

The fathers' rights movement in America grew out of the male feminist movement and the anti-feminist new right. "Left-wing" (or feminist) fathers' rights activists claim that fathers have an equal right to children because men can mother also. They say that: "Mother is a verb, not a noun" and "A man can be a better mother than a woman can."

"Right-wing" (or patriarchal) fathers' rights activists claim that children need a father-dominated family. They also claim that *God* is the "father" of all children and that He appointed earthly fathers as "His" children's custodians.

Both kinds of fathers' rights activists claim that as men they are savagely "discriminated" against by lawyers, judges, and ex-wives in custody matters; that as men they are economically enslaved and controlled by greedy and parasitic ex-wives who prevent them from seeing their children. In 1968 Charles Metz asserted: "Even absent from the home, the father can supply love and guidance through a good housekeeper. When he doesn't come home, his competent presence is all the more valuable. No child needs to be in contact with a parent twenty-four hours a day."[11]

In 1973 George Gilder advocated deliberately lower salaries for women and the payment of a family allowance only to "intact" two-parent families as a way of "solving" the problems of divorce, unwed motherhood, and female competition with men for "male" jobs.[12] In 1979 Daniel Amneus declared: "Fathers should get custody of their children; all alimony should be eliminated; women who want to compete in the work world should do so unencumbered by children, and should leave those children to fathers who will remarry women who want to stay home and take proper care of them."[13]

In 1980, a detective investigating the whereabouts of a child "legally" kidnapped by her father, discovered and photocopied the correspondence of a fathers' rights network known as Men's Equality International, Inc. According to the detective's report:

> These 35–40 groups assist fathers in legally kidnapping their children. They provide kidnapper-fathers with aliases, and a network of pro-father couples, lawyers, psychiatrists, detectives and Christian private (religious) schools who accept children for a fee with no questions asked and no records forwarded. Their anti-mother stance is equalled by their anti-child stance. Violently and repeatedly kidnapped children are being psychologically killed. . . . Most diabolic are the counselors and detectives who take a bereft mother's money and have no intention of finding her child. [The "plant" detective] is able to report back to "Mens International" how much "heat" the "ex-bitch" is raising and if, in fact, it is time to run with the kids again.[14]

In June 1981, representatives from twenty-one states met in Houston, Texas, to announce the formation of the National Congress of Men (NCM). Approximately 100 men claimed that the "greatest inequality suffered by men involved the loss of child custody, loss of home, and loss of assets upon divorce." Frederick Hayward, in his keynote address, used feminist rhetoric against women. He said:

> I do not want to stop women from going out and getting high-paying jobs. I want to demand that women go out and find high-paying jobs. I am tired of being their wallet. We must give full credence to the seriousness of women's problems [but] when I look at feminists today, I don't want to call them names—I only want to call their bluff.[15]

In October 1981, John Rossler and Dr. Robert Fay, of New York Equal Rights for Fathers, proposed that mothers or "homemakers" be ordered to provide their ex-husbands with domestic services as *their* form of alimony.

> It is demeaning [to a homemaker] to imply that the only contribution valuable and essential enough to be deserving of post-marriage compensation is the financial one made by the employed spouse. We therefore resolve and suggest that "alimony" or "maintenance" be broadened to include . . . such spousal contributions as housekeeping, cooking, secretarial or bookkeeping work, . . . such services to each other [should] be assigned for a specific period of time.[16]

Fathers' rights activists began to sue for custody individually and as members of an oppressed and judicially persecuted "class." On December 29, 1981, Equal Rights for Fathers of Alaska brought a class action lawsuit against nine judges and two state experts, charging them with discriminating against fathers in custody cases.

The suit alleged that judges have a "maternal preference" or follow a "tender years doctrine." The suit also called for an affirmative action program on behalf of fathers.[17]

In 1981, Gerald A. Silver, president of Fathers' Rights of America, and the second Mrs. Silver wrote:

> Women find sympathy wherever they turn. Men are treated as if they have no feelings, almost as if they are invisible. . . . Men who fail to pay child support are ruthlessly tracked down by federal computer bloodhounds. Women who withhold visitation are not pursued at all. A woman who is beaten by her husband will receive aid and support, and then be directed to a federally funded center for victims of physical abuse. A man who is battered by his wife is laughed out of the police station.[18]

In 1983, Maurice K. Franks, a fathers' rights advocate and lawyer, offered his (nineteenth-century) solution to the (twentieth-century) problem of the paternal non-payment of child support:

> Custody of the daughter had been given to the mother many years before, and the father (my client) had neglected to pay his full child support. The mother got a judgment against my client for back child support. There wasn't much we could do about that now. But we learned that the daughter, a teenager by now, had been working for a few years as a part-time waitress. We sued the mother, and the restaurant where the girl worked, for all wages ever paid to the girl.
>
> We argued that where the duty of support remained with the father, the right to sue on behalf of the child also remained with the father. We then argued that wages received by the child were the property of the father, and it was the father who was entitled to the earnings of the daughter even though she may have been in the legal custody of the mother. We asked that the restaurant owner be ordered to pay a second time, since he never should have paid wages to a minor child without the father's permission. We won. A jury ordered the restaurant owner to pay my client, the father, wages that the restaurant had previously paid to the daughter.[19]

The National Congress of Men also met in Los Angeles in 1983. It "resolved" to "focus primarily on Fathers' Rights and divorce reform." The NCM strongly favored "joint physical and legal custody" and was concerned with ending the (unfair) economic burdens faced by divorced fathers, and with assuring the paternal rights of unwed fathers.[20]

To what extent does the publicity about fathers' rights reflect a large or truly organized movement as opposed to a media-created sensation? To what extent is this a violent movement with Ku Klux Klan or Nazi-like adherents? To what extent is this an "expressive" movement of very angry and unhappy divorced fathers?[21]

Only a study, far beyond the scope of this chapter, can accurately answer these questions. What I do have to say is based on reading and on personal interviews.

I interviewed thirty fathers' rights *activists* and *advocates*. Of the activists, 75 percent were professionals (lawyers, detectives, etc.), whose livelihoods depended on the existence of fathers as clients. Activists' incomes ranged from $35,000 to $100,000 (or more) a year.

By contrast, 75 percent of the fathers' rights advocates (the clients or consumers) earned $8,000 to $30,000 a year.[22]

THE FATHERS' RIGHTS ADVOCATE

Advocates were not obsessed with paternal custody as part of some ideological program or unspoken emotional agenda. For example, they sympathized with mothers as well as with fathers.

> Flora: What if a divorced mother needs to get "out from under"? Why can't we let her go, and respect her, and trust that the children's father can do just as good a job? Why not give fathers a chance? Why not give mothers the same chance?

Many fathers' rights advocates favored "decriminalizing" custody disputes and having them "mediated" out of court. They were very bitter about divorce economics—but didn't always blame their ex-wives:

> Lemuel: When you're dealing with average incomes of fifteen to twenty-five thousand dollars before taxes, what can you get when you chop it up? You can't divide a whole into parts and get two wholes. How can we deal with a broken family without everyone getting hurt?

Fathers' rights advocates wanted to spend "spontaneous" and relaxed time with their children. They also wanted to spend the "same" amount of time with them as before; and/or the "same" amount of time that their ex-wives did.

David: There are many fathers who won't spend time with their children. Children need both parents' love. We can't do anything about the uncommitted fathers. Why should we punish those fathers who *are* committed by depriving them of liberal access—even if they can't pay any child support? I refuse to see any less of my kids than my ex-wife can.

THE FATHERS' RIGHTS ACTIVIST

Most activists were trained as lawyers, psychologists, psychiatrists, and detectives. Many were also trained in assertiveness training or in techniques of emotional manipulation. Some activists used feminist rhetoric; others used patriarchal rhetoric.

Seth is a lawyer and fathers' rights activist. For three hours he held forth on male suffering at the hands of female stupidity and cruelty. He said he "knew I'd understand and agree with him because we were both feminists." As if on cue, Seth paused, made eye contact with me, called me familiarly by my first name, and smiled. He was very self-assured and apparently used to "winning" arguments on this subject.

Seth saw no difference between his "helping out" and his ex-wife's full-time, stay-at-home motherhood. Nor did he think of *maternal* child care as "work" or as entitling a mother to custody. He said:

If a woman changes the diapers and feeds the children, and a man doesn't, because he's working outside the home, you don't really know what special relationship the children have evolved with him. You don't know what would have happened if this man had tried or been allowed, in a sense, to *replace* his wife.

Had I known how to have children without marrying or living with a woman, I would have done it. I think I'm the better parent. Why doesn't my ex-wife become liberated?

This confusion of female liberation with whatever it is a particular man happens to want and the denigration of maternal child care were shared by many fathers' rights activists.

When I could no longer bear Seth's contempt for women as mothers and because I was curious to see how verbally agile his paternal hubris really was, I shared Ella Mae's story (contained in Chapter Six) with him.

"Seth," I said familiarly, "what are your thoughts about a father who doesn't see his daughter for nearly eight years except for one month each summer; who refuses to support her decently, despite his ability to do so; and who then, without warning, suddenly refuses to return her, obtains sole paternal custody on false grounds, and then refuses to let her see her mother for the next eight years? Is sole paternal custody good for the child or fair to the mother—*in this particular case?*"

Without hesitating, Seth said,

Phyllis, even if the father hadn't seen his child for eight years, I'd conclude that they were having a relationship without seeing each other. Maybe he felt it more at that point. Maybe he needed the child more. Maybe he was better able to take care of the child. Maybe he had his act together more. Maybe he felt that the child was now grown and he was in a sense willing to put the child under the stress of changing their relationship.

"But, Seth, why remove the child from the only mother she has ever had for nine years? Why restrict that mother to seeing her child once a year or for a day at a time for the next eight years?" I asked.

Seth's immediate and unequivocal response was: "Why *not* remove the child from the mother and let her have the only father that she's ever had?"*

Martin is a psychologist-consultant. He runs groups for divorced fathers, testifies as an expert witness for fathers in custody battles, and organizes seminars for judges, lawyers, and parents on the importance of the father-child bond.

Like Seth, Martin doesn't respect his ex-wife as a mother. His sense of outrage and victimization is very real to him—and really dangerous to the wives of his male clients. Martin can exorcise and capitalize on his "divorce demon" by winning battles against other men's wives: over and over again.†

Some fathers' rights activists sounded like football coaches, mercenary soldiers, or Marine sergeants. They handled every question as an opportunity to display their blood-and-guts "manhood":

Men! Make no mistake about it. There's a war on! We have an aggressor army attacking us! Men, you must put together a very tough team. You need a private investigator. [As a group] you must turn over all your cases to him and to one lawyer. Then you get to control what they do.

Get a local psychiatrist, throw him all your business and wow! For thousands of dollars a week is he going to say what you want? You better believe

---

*Seth had sole paternal custody of his children.
†Martin has liberal visitation but was planning his own battle for sole custody in the "near future."

it! He'll go with you to the state legislature. Why shouldn't he? With the business you throw him, he'll be building a new wing on the hospital in your name.[23]

AN ACTIVIST AND HIS EX-WIFE

John was lionized by the press as a heroic father battling for child custody. When I called, he immediately agreed to an interview. John was relaxed and very personable.

However, either he waited for me to "agree" with him after each point or he tried to "agree" with whatever I said—even if it meant contradicting himself. John also smiled a lot during our four-hour interview—especially when he distorted the facts or contradicted himself. For example, he smiled when he said:

Men are hunted down like criminals if we miss a single child-support payment, and jailed if we don't pay outrageous sums of child support. These are facts. This is not just my personal impression. Since the feminist movement, most fathers have been nurturing children just as mothers do. Fathers now have a diaper relationship with their kids.

When John discussed his divorce, he began to pace, and in a voice strangled with pain, repeatedly asked me "can a woman who has sex with every Tom, Dick, and Harry really care about her children? Marriage is forever in my book. What kind of woman leaves with young children just because she wants to? Now that she's remarried, she thinks she's a lady. But the damage's been done."

At first, John's ex-wife, Priscilla, refused to see me. She said she didn't "trust" psychologists. Unsmilingly, Priscilla described John as a very traditional father who "lost his temper a lot." She said:

Once I left the sink full of dishes to take a fast shower. John came home, pulled me out of the shower to yell about the house being a pigsty. Then he tried to strangle me. I moved out with only the clothes on my back. Even though we both worked, he felt everything we bought belonged to him. More so since I belonged to him, too, but I was leaving.

Once Priscilla remarried, John joined a fathers' rights group, sued for sole paternal custody, and attempted to brainwash the children against her. He claimed, in courtrooms and in press conferences, that Priscilla was "interfering" with his visitation. "Were you?" I asked. She answered:

No matter what kind of visitation he has, he feels inconvenienced and deprived. Once, John's visitation coincided with our daughter's hospitalization. He was very angry that he had to share his child in her hospital room with me. My husband had to leave the hospital when John arrived. Even so, John made a scene, left the hospital early, and wouldn't return.

Once our son's birthday fell on one of John's visitation days. I had planned a huge party. I asked John to join us as a member of the family. He refused. He told me to cancel the party. I suggested he take our son the day before or the day after the party. He refused. I proposed extra visitation the following weekend. He refused. Instead, he had his lawyer charge me with visitation interference.*

Why are some fathers' rights activists demanding to be recognized as "mothers"? Are they romanticizing unpaid and private labor—now that they themselves are established in positions of paid, public labor? Or is it because they aren't and thus feel as economically devalued as women—but without a maternal "cover" or "fallback" position?

Why are some fathers' rights activists so angry about "uppity" wives or divorced mothers? Are they afraid of losing their strangleholds over unpaid, obedient wives? Or do they perceive "reverse discrimination" in all domestically affirmative actions?[24] Letty Cottin Pogrebin has theorized that:

Now that men have no animals to tame and no frontiers to conquer; now that women are rebellious and machines are out-thinking and displacing men, children are the last remaining subjects of domination. Rulers need subjects. . . . Men, especially, need children to anchor the bottom of the chain of command. When gender, race, and class comforts fail, children are the last order of necessary inferiors.[25]

MANDATORY JOINT CUSTODY: POST-DIVORCE PATRIARCHY

A number of fathers' rights activists and feminist theorists have posited the "withering away" of the patriarchal state once men become involved in child care. According to Dr. Deborah Luepnitz, many feminists support the idea of joint custody as a way of "encoding" the fact that both

---

*Two months after our interview, John won joint custody of his son, and more liberal visitation with his daughter.

men and women "should remain responsible for the act of spawning mortal flesh."[26]

However, this is liberal theoretics, not scientific fact. Joint custody of children already mothered by women cannot bring about any hoped-for feminist revolution in human psychology. Awarding mother-reared children to previously absent or non-nurturant fathers cannot change a child's earliest sex-typed emotions, nor does it necessarily turn patriar-chal fathers into "nurturant" mothers.[27]

Jointly awarding mother-reared children to previously uninvolved fathers will certainly not upgrade children's opinions of the importance of *female* mothering, nor will it force fathers to get involved in child care *before* they're divorced. On the contrary. Attorney Nancy Polikoff has noted:

> Presumptions favoring joint custody upon divorce, regardless of who has provided care and nurturance during the marriage, actually discourage co-parenting during marriage by sending a clear message to fathers that they have a right to intimate involvement with their children upon divorce—if they choose to exercise it—no matter how detached they are from the ongoing care of their children during the marriage. . . . Although joint child rearing by mothers and fathers should be encouraged, joint custody pre-sumptions are not carefully tailored to this.[28]

There are many reasons a father may want joint custody. He may want to make "amends" to his children for his past unavailability or for the divorce itself. He may want to deny that his marriage is over or to protest his ejection from his castle.

A father may also want joint custody as a way of "having" his children without having to subsidize them or their mother economically and without having to contend with repeated demands for child support. According to attorney Joanne Schulman,

> Joint custody is being used as a bargaining tool by men to extract more favorable property and support terms in divorce. . . . Joint custody is being used by men to avoid or reduce outstanding support orders. In a recent New Jersey support enforcement case, the father cross-complained for sole custody. The trial court, on its own motion, awarded joint custody, reduced the original child support order, and refused to enforce payment of arrears. The trial court's ruling was, fortunately, reversed on appeal, at great expense to the mother.
>
> There has been only one study of the effects of joint custody on *children*. In that study, there were no instances of court ordered joint custody; pur-

suant to both parents' agreement and desires. The study concluded only that the effects of joint custody on children needed to be studied more before this arrangement could be presumed to apply in most or all cases. The Roman-Grief Study, which is used in support of joint custody legislation and forced joint custody awards, only studied *fathers*—the children (and the mothers) were never interviewed or studied.[29]

A father may also want joint custody as a way of retaining the marital home and other assets and as a way of monitoring, controlling, and harassing his ex-wife. According to attorney Laurie Woods:

Joint custody would allow a father to exercise maximum control over his former wife while having minimum responsibility. Joint custody is also a good threat for fathers to use to get mothers to back down from economic demands. . . . A more serious problem involves the increasing demand for joint custody on the part of wife batterers and incestuous fathers. Battered women who fear for their safety and oppose joint custody are being punished—the courts are finding them "uncooperative parents" and awarding custody to the batterer.[30]

Elizabeth Thomas has noted that many battered wives are increasingly inclined to remain married once they understand that paternal visitation will be enforced or turned into joint custody or sole paternal custody.[31]

Not all judges, lawyers, or mental health experts are in favor of mandatory joint custody. Many oppose it. For example, Judge Vincent R. Balletta, Jr., has noted:

Those who strongly advocate joint custody as the "way to go" point to . . . studies, but rarely do they fully consider the cooperation required between parents to make such a situation viable. . . . It seems almost naive to believe that parents resorting to the courts to settle their differences would suddenly interact in an imposed joint custody arrangement in a way calculated to be in the child's best interests. . . . Joint custody as a favored solution is a flawed concept.[32]

Dr. Deborah Luepnitz, who has published the best study of joint custody to date, has stated:

Much more research is needed before we could conclude with confidence what the best custodial arrangements for children of different ages would be. As long as joint custody is *voluntary*, it can work, even though neither parent initially wants it. If the fathers are not abusive or vindictive, then joint custody is clearly better for everyone involved.

Making joint custody *mandatory* is full of painful contradictions. On the one hand, we must recognize that judges, legislators, and lawyers are mostly men and that the law is always man's law. To propose statutory change which presents a chance of eroding women's relationships to children is extremely dangerous.[33]

Ideally, joint custody should begin as joint parenting—during marriage. Upon divorce it should not be judicially mandated, nor should divorce mediators or lawyers coerce mothers into it.

Joint custody works when divorced parents live within five or ten minutes of each other and have or earn the same amount of money. If fathers earn more money than mothers, some arrangement must be made to equalize both parents' standard of living.[34]

If a previously absent father is truly willing to start "sharing" (rather than only "helping"), if his motives are neither economically selfish nor psychologically punitive, then joint custody might still be just if, for example, both parents were responsible for the cost of a child's clothing and for the labor involved in convincing that child to shop or in shopping for him or her.

Joint custody parents do not have to agree on values. They must respect their ex-spouses' right to opposing values—absolutely. Joint custody is a rigorous test of parental maturity and flexibility. Few parents are capable of such maturity; fewer still are capable of such maturity after a failed marriage and a bitter divorce.

Judges and state legislators are more willing to award fathers sole or joint custody on the basis of work they *didn't* do than they are willing to award mothers sole custody, alimony, or marital assets on the basis of work they *did* do.

It is not entirely accidental that legislators all over the country were attempting to mandate joint custody at the precise historical moment they were defeating the Equal Rights Amendment.[35]

The organized *movement* for joint custody (as opposed to the theory of joint custody) is not organized on behalf of mothers and children. It is organized to obtain more rights for fathers.

There is no *movement* for mothers' rights—i.e., for custody, child support, alimony, marital property, increased levels of welfare, "free" legal counsel upon divorce, etc.

The equal treatment of "unequals" is unjust. The previously absent father's demands for "equal" custodial rights; the judge, the lawyer, the legislator, the film-maker, the psychotherapist, and the fathers' rights activist who encourage him are all valuing legal paternity or male economic superiority over biological motherhood and maternal practice. They are degrading and violating both mothers and children.

HOW SHOULD WE "SEE" THE ECONOMICS OF FAMILY LIFE UPON DIVORCE?

The mother-child unit constitutes the largest and most oppressed unit of "sex-class" society. As such, it has a basic interest in controlling the means of production and reproduction. This basic interest is not synonymous with the "interests" of men in the father-dominated family, or in the male-dominated state, church, or private sector.[36]

How can mothers seize the means of production and reproduction? Can mothers turn to the state or the church for help? Yes and no. It is foolish as well as dangerous to involve the state in such a revolutionary activity. However, the state is already deeply involved in the lives of mothers and children—often to their detriment.

The government that allots more money toward military defense and corporate profit is the same government that sacrifices the lives and the basic economic needs of its most vulnerable citizens. This must be changed: carefully, patiently—and impatiently. As Carol Brown notes:

> If we make demands on the public patriarchy for more support of female-headed families, we increase the scope of public patriarchy. Thus one might argue that we should avoid such involvement. However, if we do not make such demands, women heading families will suffer an unjustified burden of labor and cost that not only oppresses them, but also forces all women into greater dependence on individual men and the private patriarchy for lack of alternatives. Given the choice, there is no question that women must make demands on the public patriarchy.[37]

For example, the state has the power to determine accurately the amount of wages and assets available upon divorce[38], to deduct automatically a portion of this for dependent children and their mothers, and to fine or imprison those fathers who are delinquent.[39]

This may sound anti-father. It is however pro-child, pro-mother, and pro-taxpayer.

Where a father (or a mother) is underemployed, unemployed, disabled, unfit, dead, or non-existent, the state has the power to exact child support and a maternal wage from the private sector, the church, and from the individual taxpayer.

In order to expand the quantity and quality of available services, the state could make it unlawful for any bank or creditor to lend money to a private business which does not provide paid maternity and paternity leaves, adequate on-site day-care facilities, and flexible work shifts for all its employees and which does not establish and enforce an effective affirmative action program.[40]

THE MOTHER AS HER CHILD'S NATURAL GUARDIAN

A number of pro-mother lawyers, under tremendous ideological siege from other feminists and from patriarchy itself, have argued that a "maternal presumption" is far more consonant with a child's "best interest" than is the pro-father application of a sex-neutral standard.

These lawyers have argued that a "maternal presumption" would ensure the continuation of a child's "psychological" or emotional parenting and would also avoid the devastating combat of prolonged custodial litigation.

In *Beyond the Best Interests of the Child*, Drs. Joseph Goldstein, Anna Freud, and Albert J. Solnit make a strong argument on behalf of the "psychological" parent's right to custody. According to Goldstein et al., this "psychological parent" can be the child's biological or adoptive parent or any other "caring" adult. However, he or she cannot be "an absent, inactive adult, whatever his biological or legal relationship to the child may be."[41]

Judge Rena K. Uviller specifically asks feminists to re-evaluate the importance of a maternal custodial presumption:

For those of us dedicated to the elimination of rigidly dehumanizing sex-role assignments, it is disquieting to conclude that the maternal presumption should be defended and preserved. . . . The maternal preference, resting on the assumption that it has been the woman who has committed herself to care for home and children, should yield only to a showing that in fact it has been the father who has assumed that role during marriage.

If a father can prove that he and not the mother has devoted his time to domestic duties, that he and not she has compromised his work for the sake of family, then indeed he should prevail. This is not the same as determining who has been the "better" parent. . . . If during her marriage a woman has devoted herself to child care at the expense of her economic and social independence, her past commitment should be reflected in custodial priority.[42]

Uviller's argument is not a biologically supremacist one. Nor does she claim that children "belong" to their mother by constitutional or natural right, or only when they are of "tender" years. Uviller is challenging the belief that in a forced-choice situation, paternal custody—i.e., economic stability and a "father figure"—is necessarily in a child's "best interest."

Uviller suggests that a child's "best interest" consists of continued access to his or her primary caretaker or "psychological" parent.[43]

Attorney Lucy Katz, equally concerned with the reactionary erosion of the "maternal presumption" in the name of feminism, suggests an outright "maternal preference" in contested custody cases. She also proposes a reconsideration of the "maternal presumption" on its merits (in terms of the "psychological" parents' importance to the child); as a way of reducing prolonged and injurious litigation; and as a way of *encouraging* a non-custodial father's post-divorce involvement with his children:

A maternal preference is not inconsistent with a greater parenting role for divorced fathers. There is no question that children need both parents, and that they and their fathers will thrive on closeness after the divorce. This goal is ill-served by any system which places the mother under constant threat of losing custody; the closer the father comes, the greater the threat she perceives to her role as custodian. Nor is a maternal preference inconsistent with joint custody, when the parents can work with such an arrangement. A maternal preference may therefore actually strengthen the relationship between fathers and their children during and after dissolution of marriage.[44]

Attorney Nancy Polikoff of the Women's Legal Defense Fund attempts to define the "primary caretaker" parent in sex-neutral ways.

The primary caretaker's specific duties (e.g., diaper changing, cooking, shopping for food and clothes, contact with teachers and doctors). In most cases, the courts would find the mother to be the psychological parent—without incurring the charge of sex-bias through a maternal presumption.[45]

Sex neutrality should never be interpreted to mean that the traditional father role, even modified by small amounts of assistance to the mother, is as valuable to the child's development as is the traditional mother role of primary nurturance, care, and responsibility.

Such an interpretation, which is already infiltrating custody decisions and is found in the extreme pro-father rights literature, would lead to a rigidification of traditional sex roles through paternal custody rather than a destruction of those roles. Similarly, the mandate of sex equality in child-custody determinations should be interpreted to encourage male nurturance while the family is intact, in order to move society closer to genuine equality in childrearing.[46]

These lawyers were shocked by the unexamined depth of anti-mother bias among feminist lawyers and among judges, lawyers, fathers' rights activists, and legislators.[47] Helen Levine and Alma Estable have argued that in cases of contested custody we need to be

> inequitable to ensure that we are just. The scales need to be weighted in favor of mothers. We do not advocate a return to the idea that "maternal instinct" makes women inherently better parents. Rather, we suggest that in custody disputes, the courts must systematically take into account the structural inequalities faced by women. It often takes a feminist framework for even well-seasoned activists to realize that "they've given fathers the children but they haven't given mothers the money."
>
> [As Pauline Bart has noted:] "Who among us does not know women who thought they had egalitarian relationships with men with whom they were co-parenting only to see it fall apart and the male sense of entitlement re-emerge when they wanted to divorce?"[48]

At this point in human evolution, mothers as a group are *less* violent and *less* property-oriented in relation to their own children than fathers are as a group.[49] I am not saying that every mother is in every instance a "better" parent than every father. I am saying that most mothers are "better" parents than most fathers are—as of 1986.[50]

Law should not be used as a weapon over and against reality. A "good enough" mother is—and should therefore legally be recognized as—her child's natural guardian.

I believe that mothers and children have a natural and "ineffable" right to each other. This right transcends *and* is based on genetic and biological ties as well as on the chores of "psychological" parenting.[51] Denise Nadeau describes the mother-child bond as:

> indelible and ineffable. In it lies a passion and a drive for truth and life that is unique and cannot be replaced by any father-child bond. A feminism that denies the primacy of mothering denies the core of our power.
>
> The courts have taken a feminist demand, that fathers be more responsible for their child, and have turned it into a weapon against women. Our own theory must become clearer on why children should be with their mothers (when they are wanted) and why and how the qualities and value structure

of mothering, when valued by this culture, can create healthier and saner human beings.[52]

A mother should be recognized as her child's legal guardian. Nora, one of my interviewees, suggested: "At birth, every child should automatically have appointed a legal guardian, who should in every case, unless otherwise specified, be the mother. No matter what else parents argue about later in life, custody should not be arguable. Every child should have a legal guardian—his mother."

If a mother is automatically her child's legal guardian, she should have no reason to deprive a (non-violent) father of "organic" access to his children. This should be true whether a father is unwed, married, or divorced; whether he can afford to pay adequate child support or not; and whatever his sexual persuasion is.

If a father's child-"sharing" activity is stridently paternal, if his child-"sharing" activity is bent on building as strong a case as possible for sole paternal custody, then the most desperately overburdened mother will understandably be terrified and become "proprietary" about her child-care responsibilities. Sara Ruddick notes that:

> Those of us who live with the fathers of our children will eagerly welcome shared parenthood—for overwhelming practical as well as ideological reasons. But in our eagerness, we must not forget . . . that male presence can be harmful as well as beneficial. It does a woman no good to have the power of the Symbolic Father brought right into the nursery.[53]

We must begin to question if violence—physical, economic, psychological, or legal—should ever be used to separate a child from his or her mother and if fathers who use violence to obtain custody of their children do so out of love for them.

We must begin to ask what "love" means to such a father. We must at least begin to shift our sympathies toward mothers by *one inch* and view mothers as entitled to some of the *rights* that fathers already take for granted.

I am not saying that fathers should be barred from the family hearth or allowed nightly access only if they can afford the admission price. I in no way relish such a division of labor and what it entails (the divorce of feeling from reason, public from private life, the oppression of women and children, etc.).

I am not saying that "good enough" fathers should be punished for the failings of "unfit" fathers. I am saying that a father's right to parent should never be obtained by separating a child from her mother. I join several pro-mother attorneys in suggesting: "Any father who puts a child and his mother through the pain of a custody battle or who attempts to separate them from each other is, by definition, an unfit father."[54]

If a father's approach to "sharing" responsibility for a child is "selfless" rather than calculating and competitive, gentle rather than violent, then a mother who remains assured of custody will hardly resist his involvement. This is doubly true if the mother and father in question are divorced.

WHAT IS THE DIFFERENCE BETWEEN RESOLVING THE QUESTION OF LEGAL CUSTODY AND RESOLVING CUSTODIAL ARRANGEMENTS?

As a society we tend to focus more on individual custody *disputes* than on our collective custodial *arrangements*. "Custody" is viewed as a contest between a "winner" and a "loser," not as a series of questions about the conditions under which we mother, father, and grow up and about who determines these conditions.

For example, should a judge (or the state legislature) order a father to "baby-sit" and do half the housework instead of pursuing his career? Should a judge (or the state legislature) order a father to attend "parenting" classes and put 60 percent of his wages toward the support of his family—or risk going to jail and losing his paternal right of visitation?

Should a judge (or the state legislature) force a mother to pursue a dead-end job away from home, live in celibate poverty, and work for less than the minimum wage (welfare)—or risk going to jail and losing custody of her child to her ex-husband or to the state?*

These are questions about custodial *arrangements*. Our focus must shift from resolving custody disputes by force, and on an individual basis, to a more civilized resolution of all our custodial (or child-care) arrangements.

I believe that *legal* custody must be determined as quickly as possible on behalf of the child's natural guardian: his or her mother. Once determined, custody should not be raised as an issue over and over again.

---

*Obviously, judges and the state legislature already force mothers to do this. They are unwilling to exert equally unjust pressures against fathers or to treat mothers and fathers equally.

However, I favor spending a great deal of time working out custodial arrangements.[55] Goldstein et al. state:

> Once it is determined who will be the custodial parent, it is that parent, not the court, who must decide under what conditions he or she wishes to raise the child. Thus, the noncustodial parent should have no legally enforceable right to visit the child, and the custodial parent should have the right to decide whether it is desirable for the child to have such visits. What we have said is designed to protect the security of an ongoing relationship— that between the child and the custodial parent.
>
> At the same time, the state neither makes nor breaks the psychological relationship between the child and the noncustodial parent, which the adults involved may have jeopardized. It leaves to them what only they can ultimately resolve.[56]

This seems very harsh to the non-custodial parent. Do we really want to condemn non-custodial parents and children to the tyranny of *one* custodial parent?

However, this is no different from what now happens when *one* father kidnaps or brainwashes a child, when *one* judge orders a child into paternal custody, and when *one* judge refuses to "believe" or act on a mother's report of paternal incest, harassment, or non-payment of child support.

Goldstein et al.'s idea of "leaving to [the parents] what only they can ultimately resolve" is neither harsh nor tender. It is based on an accurate understanding of the law. Patriarchal law, lawyers, and judges are at their best in solving disputes over property and capital *in terms of property and capital*. They are at their worst in solving disputes about intimate, private relationships *in relational or private terms*.

We cannot expect a patriarchal judge to order a custodial arrangement that "works" when we refuse to do so, either as individuals or as a society. We should not use the law to punish individual mothers and children because we refuse to "work out" custodial arrangements beforehand as a matter of policy. Attorney Nancy Polikoff notes that most judges

> have little understanding of what is involved in taking daily primary responsibility for a child. They are therefore very impressed with [any father's] changing of a fraction of the number of diapers, preparing a fraction of the number of meals, presiding over a fraction of the number of baths, providing solace for a fraction of the scraped knees and hurt feelings.
>
> Similarly, mothers know that [the judicial] equating [of maternal] em-

ployment with an abdication of nurturing is an oversimplification of parenting functions and not a true reflection of contemporary family life.[57]

Many lawyers and judges recommend that judges be assisted by social scientists to "arbitrate" or "mediate" custodial arrangements, preferably away from a courtroom setting[58]; and that children have their own legal and psychological advocates upon divorce.

> What is lacking, if the interests of the child are to be protected properly, is legislation *requiring* that the child be independently represented by a lawyer, guardian ad litem or committee . . . in the determination of his or her own custody and support.[59]

I agree in theory. However, in practice, such advocates (as well as divorce counselors, mediators, and arbitrators) have also been trained to overvalue fathers (and white parents) and undervalue mothers (and black parents) and to do so for the "good of the child." Seattle attorney Martha O. Eller notes a disturbing trend:

> We are very disheartened by social workers' and psychologists' willingness to ignore issues of domestic violence, over-emphasize the value of a working father and under-value the contributions of a full-time homemaker, and [their] general tendency to despise a woman for having boyfriends without carefully inquiring of the father along the same lines.
> The [child] guardians *ad litem*, including psychologists, tend to evaluate the mothers harshly, even more so than the judges, finding them to be unstable for not having had jobs for years, or finding them weak and dependent for having a "series of boyfriends" meaning two or three in two years. Our office is finding that we have to struggle time after time against negative guardian recommendations.[60]

Ironically, when a child advocate recommends an arrangement that opposes what a father wants or that offends a judge's pro-father bias, s/he is frequently overruled. Paul L. Adams et al. give an example of how both a mother and a child advocate were unable to prevent a joint custody father from sexually molesting his daughter:

> Under the guise of sharing custody and outmothering the mother, the father began performing vaginal examinations on his little girl; he cloaked his sexual abuse under the guise of "cleaning her vagina" when the little girl reported his actions to her mother. He ranted against the mother's "neglect of the

girl's vaginal cleanliness" and discounted the mother's objections as emanating from her "puritanism about everything sexual."

The therapist reported the case to protective services and made every effort to help the child but the protection agency found that what the father did—although admitted to be a bit bizarre—was not harmful to the girl. The court said there was no reason to change the child's life from its former status of shared custody by her parents. The therapist realized that child therapy and child advocacy may be hampered in the 1980's and had to yield, contenting herself with being available to the mother if needed.[61]

Judges do interview or interrogate children of all ages, both formally and informally. Such interviews rarely result in any judicial "discovery" of paternal brainwashing or non-payment of child support. Judges are rarely guided by children's statements when those statements oppose what a father wants or oppose the judge's own pro-father bias.

Nevertheless, when children are interviewed and judicially "heard," how can we be sure that they haven't been intimidated or brainwashed into stating or into refusing to state a parental preference? Why should we expect children to be more evenhanded than their expert advocates?[62]

In a father- and money-idealizing culture, how can we be sure that children will not automatically undervalue their ever-present and impoverished mothers and overvalue their previously absent and financially attractive fathers—to their own detriment? Should we use children to legalize such values?

Upon divorce mothers are even more poorly represented than children are. No one is suggesting maternal advocates. I am. As we have seen, judges and experts, including a mother's own lawyer, may be biased against her—or incompetent on her behalf.[63]

According to Laurie Woods, the mediation process can only hurt women and children, upon divorce.

Mediation is a (1) private, (2) non-appealable, (3) non-enforceable approach to resolving differences (4) which is not required to be and (5) does not attempt to be consistent with any set of laws and (6) is not required to have consistent outcomes. . . .

Mediation trivializes family law issues by relegating them to a lesser forum. It diminishes the public perception of the relative importance of laws addressing women's and children's rights in the family, by placing them outside society's key institutional system—while continuing to allow corporate and other "important" matters to have unfettered access to that system. Loss of one's children and protection of one's physical safety should be considered too important to entrust to any other legal system.[64]

Joanne Schulman notes that:

Mediation is conducted behind closed doors. There are no court reporters; there are no rules of evidence; there are no rules for mediation or for mediators. The politics of "behind closed doors" is woman's herstory and women's oppression. We have seen this in rape, we have seen this in battering. We are now seeing it in mediation.

What we know is that mediation is based on a therapeutic theory. That is, divorce is an emotional problem first and foremost, rather than legal, political and financial. What we know is that women's issues have traditionally been deemed emotional and therefore trivial, and that on this basis women have been denied equal access to the legal system. What we know is that women do not need more therapy or more therapists. What we need is access to a legal system that is responsive to our issues—that is, equal justice.

Finally, we know that mediation is big money, and once again this money is being made off the backs and the lives of women.[65]

WHO IS A CUSTODY "EXPERT"? WHAT PROCESS SHOULD S/HE USE TO RESOLVE CUSTODIAL ARRANGEMENTS?

Legislators, judges, lawyers, and mediation experts are rarely held personally accountable for the decisions they make or enforce. They do not have to live with the consequences of their actions. Their decisions are often wrong, imperfect, unworkable, and unjust for this very reason.

Judges and other experts are "effective" in silencing a mother's own heartbeat because they have the *power* to do so and because mothers, who are women, have been trained to obey male "law," to idealize others as experts, and to sacrifice their own self-interest when it conflicts with male self-interest.

Such experts are therefore "effective" in resolving the question of who "wins" custody. They are not effective in resolving custodial arrangements in a way that is just and workable or in a way that is pro-mother and pro-child as well as pro-father.

The majority of lawyers, judges, and legislators are born male, socialized as "men," and trained to use a paternal (or public) process to settle disputes. This process is authoritative because it is presumably "objective" *and because it is violent.*

As such, it is a process completely at odds with the psychological needs of family or "private" relationships.[66]

Once legal justice is enforced, the ensuing disputes or human dilemmas are better resolved by a process that is empathic, patient, and non-violent. As Sara Ruddick has noted, although individual mothers are far from perfect, "maternal thought" as a *process* is a way of "thinking, feeling, and acting" that is essentially "peaceful":

> By "peacefulness" I mean a commitment to avoid battle whenever possible, to fight necessary battles non-violently and to take, as the aim of battle, a reconciliation between opponents and restoration of connection and community. I will call this the "pacifist commitment." Its most prominent controversial feature is the renunciation of violence even in cases whose justice is undisputed.
>
> By "violence" I mean strategies or weapons which are intended to damage an opponent. By damage I mean at least physical or psychological harm for which there is no compensatory benefit to the person damaged and which is, or is likely to be, indefinitely lasting. Military strategy is opposed to pacifist commitment in that it accepts violence . . . and values victory over reconciliation.[67]

Ruddick's way of "thinking" or of resolving conflict may characterize methods of conflict resolution within a small community. However, we are no longer part of a small community. We are a large and fragmented society, which resolves its conflicts in bureaucratic and violent ways.[68]

Large, bureaucratic, and paternal process methods of conflict resolution never lead to *everyone's* psychological satisfaction. Nor do they lead to justice, the genuine "preservation of the social fabric," or to the protection of children.[69]

If the mother is "good enough" and the father is non-violent, then parents require *as much time as it takes to resolve custodial arrangements.* (This is however different from resolving the question of legal custody.)

In a dispute about custodial arrangements, everyone is essentially "on trial"—mothers more so than others. As non-criminals on trial, mothers and fathers should at least have the same rights as accused criminals, i.e., the right to equal protection under the law and the right to be heard by a jury of their peers.

Judges, lawyers, and other experts (both male and female) already function as paternal advocates. Many are men and fathers themselves. Many have already proved how sympathetic they are to any father on trial.

Who is a mother's peer or advocate? Is it any other mother? Is it any other woman? Considering most women's competitive dislike of other women and their identification of self-interest with male-interest, would an all-female or all-mother "jury" be any more pro-mother or pro-child than female judges or female experts have been?

Who are our real experts in custodial arrangements? Perhaps an expert is any mother, older child, and father who have *personally* survived their own custody battles and/or who have *personally* prospered under more than one custodial arrangement. They are members of a custodially embattled "community."

Under the right conditions (obviously to be determined), with training to counterbalance our existing pro-father and pro-patriarch as expert biases, such grass-roots experts of both sexes, and of many ages and colors, may constitute an untapped, golden resource.

The ideas in this chapter deserve our immediate and passionate attention, as does every issue raised by this book. Can this be done in a way that views custody in its proper perspective and that involves the greatest number of people?

I propose that we hold a series of town meetings or speakouts in every state of our nation. Perhaps a congressional committee could hold legislative hearings based on the information, proposals, and energy generated by the hearings.

Such hearings would inform the public that *all* mothers are custodially vulnerable because they are women; that *all* fathers, including incestuous, violent, absent, passive, and "helper" fathers, can win custody, not because mothers are "unfit" or because fathers are truly "equal" parents, but because fathers are men; and that all custodial mothers and children are impoverished against their will, both by individual fathers and by state legislators.

Perhaps custodially embattled and economically endangered mothers could form self-help and self-interest groups, much as corporate, religious, consumer, fathers' rights, and other groups have done.

Such hearings would also allow a large number of disenfranchised parents, non-parents, and parents-to-be to understand what is at stake in a custody dispute and therefore to understand and question our child-rearing (custodial) arrangements.[70]

I envision a spirited gathering and a gathering of spirits. Many mothers' and children's voices will be there, voices written on the wind, living and dead, come to tell their stories, come to speak in the many voices of the heart, long silenced.

CHAPTER TWENTY-TWO

Mothers' Voices, Written on the Wind

Broud seldom stood face to face with Ayla. She was much taller than the tallest man in the clan, and Broud was not among the tallest. He barely reached her shoulders. She knew he didn't like looking up at her.

"As you know, I am your new leader," Broud started, "I will take Ayla as second woman to my hearth. I will not have [her son] living at my hearth." Ayla's head jerked up. "What does he mean? If I have to move to his hearth, my son comes with me." Children belonged with their mothers until they were grown. Why would Broud take Ayla, but refuse her son?

"Broud, you can't take Durc away from me. He's my son. Wherever a woman goes her children go with her." "Are you, woman, telling this leader what he can or cannot do? Every woman in the clan is mother to him. What difference does it make where he lives? He obviously doesn't care, he eats at everyone's hearth," Broud said. . . .

"You're going away," [Durc] accused [Ayla]. "You're all dressed and going away." "Yes, Durc, I'm going away. I have to go away." "Take me with you, Mama. Take me with you! Don't leave me!" "I can't take you with me, Durc. I love you, Durc. Never forget that, I love you."

The last thing Ayla heard as she disappeared behind the broken ridge was Durc's plaintive wail—

"Maama, Maaama, Maamaaa!"

Jean M. Auel, *The Clan of The Cave Bear*

448

WHAT IS A CUSTODY BATTLE REALLY ABOUT?

"A custody battle is *the* quintessential power struggle between men and women. It's about who controls a woman's mind and body. It's also about who gets to control the future. Children are the future."

"My husband loved me very much. He couldn't bear to lose me *and* our children, too. He fought to keep what he could."

"A custody battle is a reminder to women that our children are only on loan to us. We can lose children to death, and to insecure and angry fathers."

"Men think of children as the necessary chains to keep wives from flying away. If we fly away anyway, they transfer their needs to their children."

"Having to fight for custody is like being raped; only it's worse. It never stops. And there is no crisis intervention center for it."

"My husband was already jealous of how close I was to our kids. If I lived alone with them, he was afraid I'd get even closer. He did what he could to prevent that from happening."

"In a custody battle your children are blinded, turned into sleep-walkers. They do not see their mothers. They do not see her grieving. They do not understand her anger. They act as if she's crazy or as if 'nothing's wrong.' For me, losing custody was the way my husband had me legally sentenced to death. It was also his way of denying his part in my murder. After all, it was the judge's decision, not his."

"My ex-husband had a drinking problem. He needed our kids to help him lead a respectable life."

"In many ways a custody battle is a psychological war. The greatest danger lies in colluding with the enemy in self-doubt. I had to become

449

a spiritual warrior to convince myself that I was a good mother. This personal conviction helped me endure."

WHAT TO DO WHEN A CUSTODY BATTLE INVADES YOUR LIFE

"First, take a deep breath and calm down. Save your strength for the long haul. Find out what all your options are. Find a therapist for some immediate support. You'll need him or her as a witness if you go into court."

"Any mother involved in a custody struggle is the one who's on trial. You'll need people to hold your hand, to hold you, to take care of your kids, to cook a meal, to say 'I care.' You'll need people to keep telling you that you're sane and that you have rights. Find those people *now*."

"Never leave home without taking your kids with you—not if you're fighting over custody. Don't leave your kids behind to take a weekend vacation. If you've just been beaten up and you're on your way to the hospital, you'd better take your kids along."

"You'll need to be on permanent good behavior in order to fight this fight. Your husband or someone will always be breathing down your neck trying to make your life miserable."

"I allowed things to get very bad before I started to fight back. I would never have waited so long if I knew what I know now: that for me *not* fighting was worse than fighting."

"If you open up a power struggle with your husband, be prepared to learn how to win. Don't go on believing that your husband won't lie and manipulate to cheat you. He will. If he doesn't, his lawyer will. In order to win on their turf you've got to be as rotten as they are. Being fair means you're going to lose."

"Keep a record of how often your ex-husband visits and whether he's on time or late. Tape-record your phone conversations with him so you'll remember everything. Record any threats he makes to you. Record what he does with the kids. Do they come back unfed, unwashed, late?

Are they suddenly critical or distant from you? That could be the sign of brainwashing."

"Organize your family photos into a 'Mom and Kids' showpiece album. Reconstruct a diary of what you did with and for your kids from your old calendars or appointment books. You'll have to prove that you're a good mother."

"No matter what happens, no matter what they say, never let any social worker or lawyer or judge or policeman make you doubt yourself or your self-worth."

"*Believe* that you're stronger than you think you are. Become very assertive about getting what you need from others, but depend only on yourself. You have the most to lose and the most to gain."

ON HIRING A LAWYER

"Get a copy of your Legal Bill of Rights. Refer to it when you're talking to your lawyer. Interview more than one lawyer. Be prepared to leave a lawyer who doesn't treat you well and to sue him or her for legal malpractice."

"Once you're involved in the court system, you must ask your lawyer's advice about everything. You can't start a new job or love affair without first weighing the legal consequences involved. You must assume that everything you do will be used against you."

"Your lawyer isn't God. He or she is your employee. Don't let your lawyer pressure you into anything 'temporarily' that you wouldn't want permanently."

"Talk to other women who've been through custody battles. Find a lawyer who's experienced in *custody* battles, not just in matters of divorce."

"It's important to find a good woman lawyer. Treat her with more respect than women usually treat each other. Don't expect her to be your therapist or your friend. Expect her to treat you with respect and to use the law vigorously and creatively on your behalf."

ON LAWSUITS

"A man can sue for damages if someone alienates his wife's affections or if he loses her services. He can also sue for damages if he loses his penis or his mind in an industrial accident or as a result of a robber's chasing him down the block. How much money would a jury award him as compensation for such losses? Why should a mother who loses her children get any less compensation? She should really get a lot more."

"Why can't kids sue their father if he refuses to visit them at all? The money could pay for a house-husband, a male baby-sitter, or a shrink."

"Any mother who is alienated from the affections of her own child should sue whoever did this for a lot of money. No mother should be deprived of this most fundamental right of nature. Money is the only language men understand."

"A father should be sued for damages if he says he's going to visit but doesn't show up at the last minute. He should pay for a baby-sitter to replace him. If his irresponsibility causes a mother to lose her job or her mental health, he should be responsible for her lost wages. His kids should sue him for losing the services of their mother and for a diminished standard of living."

WHAT TO TELL YOUR CHILDREN

"In a custody battle children challenge maternal authority right away. Don't let them do this. Remind them that you're still their mother, even if you're fighting with their father."

"If one parent is blatantly destructive to the children, it's the job of the other parent to say so, loud and clear. I don't believe that cover-ups are good for children."

"If the state takes you away from your kids, tell them that you love them and always will. Tell them that you'll always be their mother. Tell them you'll be out looking for them as soon as you can. Tell them whatever happens, it's not their fault."

"I kept quiet for too long. I didn't believe it was right to involve kids in private adult matters. But my kids needed to hear my point of view, *too*. They needed to know that I loved them, *too*, and would fight for them. They also needed to know that I would keep loving them no matter what happened."

"My children really wanted to leave me. I fought this for a long time. I should have let them go. They already had my love. They couldn't have their father's love if they lived with me."

ON CHILD KIDNAPPING

"If your child is kidnapped by his father, don't be surprised if you lose your job and have a nervous breakdown. I did. Don't be surprised by how much money it takes to keep looking for your child. Don't be surprised if you never see your child again. I never have."

"After your child has been kidnapped, be prepared to become your own detective. Don't put your faith in some detached person who's doing it only for the money and who doesn't know your child or your husband. Plan your own strategy. Think of your lawyer and your detective as *your* assistants."

"One day I met a woman who had kidnapped her kids. She asked me if I was ready to spend the rest of my life under a false name. *I wasn't.* She asked me if I was sure my kids would come with me. *I wasn't.* For six months I contemplated kidnapping them. I didn't want my kids to lead an abnormal life. They'd already suffered through a divorce and a custody battle. How could I subject them and myself to an underground life? *I couldn't.*"

"As a mother, you owe it to yourself and your child to kidnap her away from a violent father. Kidnapping a child is very risky. You have to cut all your ties so that no one can trace you. You have to keep a low profile. You have to be willing to lead a secret and isolated life. You have to learn whom to trust with what information. But how can a mother live with herself knowing that her child is being seriously abused? You are the most important person in your child's life. No one else will save her but you."

"If your husband threatens to kidnap your child, go to court immediately and get temporary custody. Get an order of protection and demand that his visitation be supervised by the court. Demand that he get some counseling. Get a judge to spell out to your husband that he can't move out of state with your child even if you're not divorced. Make sure you have your husband's credit card numbers and the names and addresses of his employer, relatives, and friends. Make sure you have recent photos of your child and his or her fingerprints."

A CHILD, NOW A GROWN MAN OF FORTY, TALKS ABOUT LOSING HIS MOTHER IN A CUSTODY BATTLE, LONG AGO

"I was two and a half years old when my father got custody of me. I have no memory of living with my mother. I do recall sitting under the table, which I wasn't allowed to do, and asking about my mother, saying that I wanted to see her.

"I remember the house we lived in as dark and badly lit. I remember my friends' houses as much brighter. Early on, I acquired the skill of being 'adopted' for a few hours at a time by other people's mothers. I think this shows resourcefulness on my part.

"I didn't want to believe that my mother had left me. I remember pretending that I had a young mother like everyone else did, instead of a grandmother. I fantasized a mother who came to see me once or twice a week instead of once a year.

"My mother was permitted to come to the house once a year at Christmas. In the morning I always received many lavish gifts from my grandmother and my father. In the afternoon my mother came, bearing less lavish but carefully chosen gifts. I was always glad to see her. I don't remember feeling angry toward her.

"My grandmother never left my mother alone with me. My mother would have to talk to *her* while she was trying to talk to me. My father would also be in the room, watching and listening. It was an odd and embarrassing situation.

"My father was happy enough to have me around. He was great to play games with. But he was also a spoiled and only child who expected hot meals prepared for him at odd hours. When he was impatient or angry, it was tough to be around him. He was arrogant and very selfish.

"I don't remember how he was to my mother. When I knew him, he had a terrible temper. Maybe my mother couldn't bear living with him anymore, not even to keep her child—to keep me.

"As I got older, my grandmother wasn't strong enough to control or amuse me. I know this hurt her a lot. Having a child at home is what kept my grandmother alive. She literally died the day I left home. I refuse to take any responsibility for her death, but it was a powerful event.

"In college, friends always complained about how their mothers wouldn't let go of them. The most obvious cases were some Jewish friends from New York. They were my favorite people. My very oldest and dearest friend, Robert, is a Jew from New York whose mother called him every Sunday night, saying the most inane things. And then Robert's voice would be reduced to this little puppy laughter, and the rest of the people in our house would say, 'Ah, it's Robert's mother. . . .'

"Soon after I started college, my mother invited me to her home for the first time. It seems that my father's family were the wealthy ones. My mother was a poor farm girl. My father eloped with her against his mother's wishes. It seems she was pregnant. It was easy for them to get rid of her once I was born.

"My mother remarried when I was about five. She went on to have three other sons. Had we been neighbors, I would have been a part of it. I met these other children. I'm fond of them, but we're not close. Maybe it's just plain jealousy. They got all my mother's love. I see them regularly, once or twice a year.

"My father remarried and got divorced again. Then he retired early. He lives on his inheritance in the same house we both grew up in. He sits home alone in the shadows. I see him regularly, about once a year.

"My mother is this short woman who seems very healthy. She has good skin color. She wears earth-colored clothes and smiles easily. It recently occurred to me that it would be nice having her nearby. If she were close—I mean geographically—then we could talk to each other whenever one of us felt like it.

"Not having my mother is the trauma of my life. It's a loss that never ends. I have never lived with a woman—even with one that I loved. That's the most painful part of my legacy: my fear of getting too close to anyone.

"My mother always invites me over on the holidays. Thankfully she doesn't insist that I come. She knows how painful holidays are for me. She knows I don't like being there, at her house."

i knew you before you had a mother,
when you were newt-like, swimming,
a horrible brain in water.
i knew you when your connections
belonged only to yourself,
when you had no history
to hook on to,
barnacle,
when you had no sustenance of metal
when you had no beat to travel
when you stayed in the same
place, treading the question;
i knew you when you were all
eyes and a cocktail,
blank as the sky of a mind,
a root,
neither ground nor placental;
not yet
red with the cut nor astonished
by pain, one terrible eye
open in the center of your head
to night, turning and the stars
blinked like a cat. we swam
in the last trickle of champagne
before we knew breastmilk—we
shared the night of the closet,
the parasitic
closing on our thumbprint,
we were smudged in a yellow book.

son, we were oak without
mouth, uncut, we were
brave without memory

                        Toi Derricotte

Notes

PREFACE

1. "In His Own Words: Dr. Lee Salk Speaking for Babies," *People*, March 11, 1974; quoted by Sheila Moran in "Courts and Custody: A Break for Fathers?", *New York Post*, November 22, 1975. This case is known as: *Salk* v. *Salk*, NY 393, 2nd 841, 1975.

2. The Kansas case is known as: *Neis* v. *Neis*, Kansas App. 599, p. 2d 305, 1979. The North Dakota case is known as: *Porter* v. *Porter*, N.D. 274 N.W. 2nd 235, 1979. Both cases are cited and discussed by attorney Nancy Polikoff in "Gender and Child Custody Determinations. Exploding the Myths," in *Families, Politics and Public Policy. A Feminist Dialogue on Women and the State*, Irene Diamond (ed.), (New York: Longman, 1983).

3. The Oregon case is known as: *Van Dyke* v. *Van Dyke*, Oregon App. 965, 618, p. 2nd, 465, 1980.

4. This phrase is taken from a poem by Rosalie Sorrels and quoted by Anna Demeter in her book *Legal Kidnapping* (Boston: Beacon Press, 1977).

CHAPTER ONE: AN HISTORICAL OVERVIEW

1. In 1861, the slave Harriet published her autobiography under the name Harriet Brent Jacobs: *Incidents in the Life of a Slave Girl. An Authentic Narrative Describing the Horrors of Slavery as Experienced by Black Women*, L. Maria Child, ed. (1861; reprint ed., New York: Harcourt, Brace, Jovanovich, 1973). New introduction and notes by Walter Teller.

   This is a precious document, the only one ever written by a woman fugitive about her life as a Southern slave. It is a moral and literary gem; a passionately Victorian work; and a work that Jacobs published on her own. In the autobiography, Harriet is "Linda Brent"; Dr. Norcom is "Mr. Flint"; Mr. Sawyer is "Mr. Sands"; and her children Joseph and Louisa are "Benjamin" and "Ellen."

Dorothy Sterling in *We Are Your Sisters: Black Women in the Nineteenth Century* (New York: Norton, 1984), unearthed the real names and places of Jacobs's life. According to Sterling, Harriet Brent Jacobs escaped to the North around 1842 and found employment as nurse and housekeeper "in the family of Nathaniel P. Willis, a popular journalist. After Mrs. Willis' death, Jacobs had full responsibility for the Willis' baby daughter. She remained in his employ until 1861, except for an interval in 1849–50 when she helped her brother John establish an anti-slavery reading room in Rochester, New York. John S. Jacobs had escaped from slavery in 1841 and had become an anti-slavery speaker, sharing platforms with Frederick Douglass and other notables. Like other creative black women . . . Harriet Jacobs labored in the nursery and kitchen by day and wrote at night."

Jacobs traveled to England as governess to the dead Mrs. Willis's child. She moved in bohemian, abolitionist, and upper-class circles. Jacobs also observed the lives of England's peasants and factory workers, and concluded that she would "ten thousand times" prefer her children to be the "half-starved paupers of Ireland than the most pampered among slaves in America." "The most ignorant and the most destitute of these peasants was a thousand fold better off than the most pampered American slave. In England, the relations of husband and wife, parent and child, were too sacred for the richest noble in the land to violate with impunity."

The first and the second Mrs. Willis, and Amy Post, were abolitionists and feminists. They encouraged Harriet Brent Jacobs to write her autobiography. Lydia Maria Child, a prominent writer and anti-slavery activist, agreed to write the preface. Thayer and Eldridge of Boston agreed to publish the book. One month before publication, they went out of business. Undaunted, Harriet bought the plates and published the book herself.

2. Dorothy Sterling, *We Are Your Sisters: Black Women in the Nineteenth Century* (New York: W. W. Norton, 1984), and Jacqueline Jones, *Labor of Love, Labor of Sorrow: Black Women, Work, and the Family from Slavery to the Present* (New York: Basic Books, 1985). Both discuss and cite many examples of white men's sexual harassment and rape of black slave women and of the jealousy, powerlessness, and cruelty of many white wives toward black slave women.

Sterling quotes Lewis Hayden, a leader of Boston's black community, on his mother's sexual persecution: "[My mother's owner] made proposals of a base nature to [her]. My mother would not consent to live with this man. He sent her to prison and had her flogged, and punished her in various ways, so that at last, she began to have crazy turns. She tried to kill herself several times, once with a knife and once by hanging. . . . When she had her raving turns, she always talked about her children. They let her out one time, and she came to the place where we were. She caught my arms, and seemed going to break them, and then said, 'I'll fix you so they'll never get you!' I screamed, for I thought she was going to kill me. They tied her, and carried her off."

According to Jones, "Husbands who flaunted their activities in the slave quarters essentially dared their wives to attack a specific woman or her offspring. Some promiscuous husbands made no attempts at gentlemanly discretion (or 'transcendent silence') within their own households, but rather actively sought to antagonize their wives. . . . Divorce petitions provide one of the few sources that reveal white wives' outrage in response to their husbands' provocative behavior. For example, a witness in a Virginia divorce case in 1848 offered the following testimony: A master one morning told his favorite slave to sit down at the breakfast table 'to which Mrs. N [his wife] objected, saying . . . that she [Mrs. N] would have her severely punished.' The husband then replied 'that in the event he would visit her [Mrs. N] with a like punishment. Mrs. N then burst into tears and asked if it was not too much for her to stand.' Like at least some other masters, Mr. N freely admitted that his initial attraction to his future wife stemmed from her 'large Estate of land and negroes.' (Thus a favorable marriage became one more consideration for the ambitious slaveholder.) However, this particular husband went out of his way to demonstrate his 'strong dislike and aversion to the company of his bride by sleeping with the slave woman on a pallet in his wife's room and by frequently embracing her in the presence of his wife.' Mrs. N's first response was to lay 'her hands in an angry manner on the said servant.' Her husband, besides threatening his wife with bodily harm, told her if she did not like his course, to leave his house and take herself to some place she liked better. Although the outcome of this case is not known, the patriarchalism of the southern legal system dictated that the odds would be against the humiliated Mrs. N. In any case, the considerable dowry she brought to the marriage would remain in the hands of her spouse."

For accounts of slave life also see: Mary Boykin Chestnut, *A Diary from Dixie*, Ben Ames Williams, ed. (Cambridge, Mass.: Harvard University Press, 1980); Eugene D. Genovese, *Roll Jordan Roll: The World the Slaves Made* (New York: Random House, 1974); Paula Giddings, *When and Where I Enter: The Impact of Black Women on Race and Sex in America* (New York: William Morrow, 1984); Herbert C. Gutman, *The Black Family in Slavery and Freedom, 1750–1925* (New York: Pantheon, 1976); Mattie Griffiths, *Autobiography of a Female Slave* (Redfield, N.Y., 1857; reprint ed., Miami: Mnemosyne Press, 1969); Gloria T. Hull, Patricia Bell Scott, and Barbara Smith, eds., *All the Women Are White, All the Blacks Are*

Men, but Some of Us Are Brave: Black Women's Studies (Old Westbury, N.Y.: Feminist Press, 1982); Frances A. Kemble, *Journal of a Residence on a Georgian Plantation in 1838–1839* (London: Longman, Green, 1863); Suzanne Lebsock, *The Free Women of Petersburg: Status and Culture in a Southern Town, 1784–1860* (New York: W. W. Norton, 1984); Leslie Howard Owens, *This Species of Property: Slave Life and Culture in the Old South* (New York: Oxford University Press, 1980); Dorothy Sterling, ed., *The Trouble They Seen: Black People Tell the Story of Reconstruction* (New York: Doubleday, 1976).

3. Jacobs, op. cit. Jacobs describes the facts and accompanying emotions of her seven years' separation from both her children. She revealed herself *once*, to her seven-year-old daughter (after a five-year separation), on the eve of Louisa's ("Ellen's") departure north.

" 'Ellen, my dear child, I am your mother.' She drew back a little, and looked at me; I folded her to [my] heart. 'You really *are* my mother?' . . . She wept, and I did not check her tears. Perhaps she would never again have a chance to pour her tears into a mother's bosom. All night she nestled in my arms. Once, when I thought she was asleep, I kissed her forehead softly, and she said, 'I am not asleep, dear mother. . . . Mother, I will never tell.' And she never did."

Harriet also had one very emotional "interview" with her son Joseph when he was twelve, after a seven-year separation, on the eve of her own escape to the North. Joseph never revealed his mothers' whereabouts either.

Sterling, in *We Are Your Sisters*, recounts a number of extremely painful first-person accounts of the separation of slave mothers, slave children, and slave families. Here are two descriptions, the first by an anonymous ex-slave, the second by ex-slave Emma Brown, of Petersburg, Virginia, in 1858.

Anonymous: "O, dat was a terrible time! All de slaves be in de field, plowin', hoein', and singin' in de boilin' sun. Old Marse, he comes through de field with a man call de speculator. Dey walked round just lookin'. All de darkies know what dis mean. Dey didn't dare look up, just work right on. Den de speculator he see who he want. He talk to old Marse, den dey slaps de handcuffs on him and take him away to de cotton country. . . . When darkies went to dinner de ole nigger mammy she ask where am such and such. None of de others want to tell her. But when she see dem look down to de ground she just say: 'De speculator, de speculator.' Den de tears roll down her cheeks, cause maybe it her son or husband and she knows she never see 'em again."

Emma Brown: "It was durin' cottin chopping time dat year, a day I'll never forgit, when the speckulataws bought me. Ma come home from de fiel' 'bout haf after 'leven dat day an cooked a good dinner, I hopin her.

O, I never has forgot dat last dinner wid my folks: bout de middle of the even' up rid my young master an' two strange white mens. Dey hitch dere hosses an' cum in de house. Den one o' de strangers said, 'Get yo clothes, Mary: We has bought you from Mr. Shorter.' I c'menced crying' an' beggin' Mr. Shorter to not let 'em take me away. But he say, 'Yes Mary, I has sole yer, an' yer must go wid em.'

"Den dese strange mens drive off wid me, me hollerin' at de top' my voice an' callin my ma! Den dem speckulataws begin to sing loud—jes to drown out my hollerin. We passed de very filed whar paw an' all my fokes wuz wuckin, an' I calt out as loud an' as long as I could see 'em, 'Good'bye Ma! Good-bye Ma!' But she never heard me. I ain't never seed nor heared tell o' ma an' pa, an' bruthers, an' susters from dat day to dis."

Sterling recounts the story of Harriet Tubman's mother, Harriet Ross, who saved one of her sons from being sold.

"Late at night [master] came to the door and asked the mother to let him come in, but she was suspicious and she says, 'What do you want?' Says he, 'Mr. Scott wants to come in to light a segar.' She ripped out an oath and said: 'You are after my son: But the first man that comes into my house, I will split his head open.' That frightened them, and they would not come in. So she kept the boy hid until the Georgia man went away."

4. Mattie Griffiths, *Autobiography of a Female Slave* (1857; reprint ed., Miami: Mnemosyne Press, 1969). Mattie Griffiths's *Autobiography* was written after Emancipation; she doesn't recount a fugitive life, only her life as a slave. It is priceless, and similar in style to Harriet Brent Jacobs's *Incidents*.

5. This article is cited by Dorothy Sterling, *We Are Your Sisters*. Jacobs wrote it in response to an article by Julia Taylor, the wife of ex-President Taylor, who claimed that "slaves were not sold away from their families, except under 'peculiar circumstances.' "

6. Griffiths, op. cit.

7. Jacobs, op. cit.

8. When Jacobs arrived in Philadelphia in 1842, her ship was met by a "colored man, the Rev. Jeremiah Durham, minister of Bethel Church." The Anti-Slavery Society offered to find lodgings and employment for her, and to pay her expenses to New York. Harriet was deeply moved by the sight of his wife and home—all part of a legal, Christian household. For her it is a rare sight.

Throughout *Incidents*, Jacobs, like Mattie Griffiths and other women writers of the era, is very romantic about womanly virtue, God, marriage, motherhood, children, and loving *lawful* family relationships. Jacobs remains deeply "ashamed" of her illegal love affair with Sawyer.

9. This story and all direct quotes for it are contained in Elizabeth Parsons Ware Packard, *Modern Persecution*, vol. I, *Insane Asylums Unveiled. Report of the Investigating Committee of the Legislature of Illinois*, and vol. II, *Married Woman's Liabilities, as Demonstrated by the Action of the Illinois Legislature*, published by the authoress, 1875. The printers were Case, Lockwood and Brainard.

I have previously written about this extraordinary American heroine in *Women and Madness* (New York: Doubleday, 1972). Beyond surviving an abusive marriage, psychiatric imprisonment, separation from her beloved children, and poverty, she became a self-supporting published author. From 1864 on, Mrs. Elizabeth Packard supported herself by writing, publishing, and selling 28,000 copies of the account of her persecution. Packard also went on to lobby state legislatures on behalf of mental patients. In 1867, the Illinois legislature passed her Personal Liberty Bill, granting certain legal rights to all imprisoned mental patients, and to those accused of "insanity." She also lobbied for the rights of married women. Where is the Hollywood film about her? I have longed to see one.

10. *People, ex rel. Uriel M. Rhoades, Sophia Rhoades* v. *George Humphreys,* county judge of Cayuga County, Cayuga General Term, June 1, 1857. New York State Supreme Court, Johnson, T. T. Strong and Smith, Justices. This decision overturns a previous one that granted Sophia custody of the "tender" child.

It is important to remember that throughout the eighteenth and nineteenth centuries in America, judicial decisions were based on English Common Law. Some American judges were as—or more—conservative than the most conservative of English jurists; others attempted to Americanize (democratize) the English Common Law. Some judges attempted to use the law on behalf of children; others bowed, with enormous regret, to the need to enforce laws that were clearly cruel to mothers and not in their children's "best interest." According to Jamil S. Zinaildin in "The Emergence of a Modern American Family Law: Child Custody, Adoption, and the Courts, 1796–1851," *Northwestern University Law Review*, vol. 73, no. 6, (1979):

"The nineteenth-century English judge adopted a patriarchal paradigm of family relations and applied it to the law with such force and vigor that it had the effect of creating new paternal rights, the existence of which had only been vaguely hinted at by previous judges. . . . During the first part of the nineteenth century, many American courts declared an increasing independence from precedent, especially British precedent. . . . Not all American jurists, however, were willing to make an abrupt break with the past. Moreover, European laws and decisions were often powerful forces in shaping American legal thought. Highly influential figures such as Supreme Court Justice Story and New York's Chancellor Kent supported their views of modern law by citing the rulings in contemporary English cases."

Rather than cite a string of illustrative lawsuits by name only, I would like to describe two cases from the 1830s and 1840s. In 1834, in Massachusetts, Mrs. Samuel Thacher left her "cruel and intemperate" husband. She and her three-year-old daughter returned to her parents. The Judge ordered the child into paternal custody, saying that:

"The Court 'ought not to sanction an unjustified and unauthorized [marital] separation, by now ordering the child into the mother's possession. In general, the father is by law clearly entitled to the custody of the child.' " (*Commonwealth* v. *Briggs*, Chief Justice Shaw, Massachusetts, Supreme Judicial Court 73 Mass [16 Pick] 203 [1834]).

Between 1840 and 1842 a more notorious case occurred. In 1835, Eliza Anna Mercein married John Barry, a widower with four daughters. Mrs. Barry described her husband as a man of irascible temper, domineering and vindictive spirit, unfeeling, harsh, tyrannical, and cruel. In 1838 (after his business failed), Barry returned to his native Nova Scotia. He asked Eliza to move to Nova Scotia and to have her father establish him in business there. Mrs. Barry refused. Barry said he would force her to go by taking their three-year-old son. The boy was surrendered. Barry now demanded possession of their nineteen-month-old daughter. At first, Mrs. Barry was allowed to keep her "tender" daughter. Then Justice Bronson of New York overturned the decision that granted her (and her wealthy father) temporary custody. He wrote that:

"Mrs. Barry cannot expect to deprive a father of his children. The husband may be at fault in relation to his conjugal duties [and may still have] paramount right to custody, which no court is at liberty to disregard. By the law of the land, the claims of the father are superior to those of the mother. Ordered accordingly."

Bronson ends his decision in sarcasm. "It is possible that our laws relating to the rights and duties of husband and wife have not kept pace with (the) progress of civilization. It may be best that the wife should be at liberty to desert her husband at pleasure and take the children of the marriage with her. . . . I will however venture the remark, even at the hazard of being thought out of fashion, that human laws cannot be very far out of the way when they are in accordance with the law of God." (*Mercein ex rel. Barry*, 25 Wendell [NY] 64 [1840]: 3 Hill NY 399 [1842]).

11. There is an eerie parallel between Mrs. Packard's house arrest and confinement to her bedroom and that of Mrs. Charles (Catherine) Dickens in England during the 1850s and 1860s. According to Phyllis Rose:

"Mrs. Charles Dickens had given birth to ten children in sixteen years of marriage, and [also had] miscarriages. Almost always pregnant or caring for an infant, she was exhausted. If Catherine would commit adultery, [Dickens] could be free of her. But that was preposterous. Immobile conventional Catherine would never do anything so daring. . . . The first gesture [Dickens] devised to express outwardly the separation from Catherine that existed in his [already adulterous life] was to [ask] the servant at Tavistock House to arrange for separate bedrooms for himself and his wife. Mrs. Dickens was to have the bedroom which they had formerly shared. His dressing room was to be turned into a bedroom for himself. The connection between the two rooms was to be walled up and covered over with bookshelves. He was to have a new iron bedstand. Who was being walled up?" (Phyllis Rose, *Parallel Lives: Five Victorian Marriages* [New York: Knopf, 1983]).

12. Rose, ibid. Rose notes that: "Catherine felt she had been wronged and hoped that posterity would vindicate her. Near the end of her life, she gave the letters which Charles Dickens had written to her in the course of their life together to her daughter Kate. . . . It took George Bernard Shaw, whom she consulted on the matter, to convince Kate to save [her mother's letters] and donate them to the British Museum. It took Shaw to get her to see that a case could be made for her mother. For Kate was an old-fashioned romantic, and she liked the story of a great man mismated and dragged down by an inferior woman. Shaw did not. He argued that the sentimental sympathy of the nineteenth century with the man of genius tied to a commonplace wife had been rudely upset by a writer named Ibsen. He predicted that posterity would sympathize more with the woman sacrificed to her husband's uxoriousness to the extent of being made to bear ten children in sixteen years than with the man whose grievance only amounted to the fact 'that she was not a female Charles Dickens.' "

Countess Sophie Tolstoy was also married to a much-beloved novelist. She was as conservative as Catherine Dickens, although far more energetic and efficient. Nevertheless, she was also "rejected" by her children, especially by her eldest daughter, who, like Dickens's children, preferred their charismatic father. Sophie writes in her *Diaries*:

"Everyone, [Tolstoy] as well as the children who follow him like a flock of sheep—have come to think of me as a *scourge*. [Masha and Tanya] have embraced Tolstoy's philosophy and become distant to me. After throwing on me the whole responsibility of the children and their education, household duties, money matters, and all the other material things, they come along, and with a cold, officious, and pious expression, tell me to give a horse to a peasant, or some money. God! I am so tired of all this life and the struggle and suffering! How deep is the unconscious hatred of even one's nearest people, and how great their selfishness."

This information is contained in Anne Edwards, *Sonya: Life of Countess Tolstoy* (New York: Simon and Schuster, 1981), and in Sophie's diaries of 1886, reprinted in Mary Jane Moffat and Charlotte Painter, eds., *Revelations: Diaries of Women*, (New York: Vintage Books, 1975).

13. Packard, op. cit., vol. II. A bill concerning the economic and property rights of married women was passed in Illinois in 1872. It did not deal with custody issues. Women obtained the legal right to property and an equal (male) court-decided right to their children in Kansas in 1859; in Massachusetts in 1869; in Oregon in 1880; and in Pennsylvania in 1895. According to Peggy A. Rabkin, in *Fathers to Daughters: The Legal Foundation of Female Emancipation* (Westport, Conn.: Greenwood Press, 1980):

"As Elizabeth Cady Stanton observed, the fathers in the Dutch aristocracy 'desired to see their life-long accumulations descend to their daughters and grandchildren rather than pass into the hands of dissipated, thriftless sons-in-law.' In the nineteenth century, sound commercial reasons existed for a desire to protect married women's property. The economy had been developing rapidly, bringing with it concomitant speculation, business failures, and general fluctuations in the business cycle. Insolvencies became frequent. Protection of a married woman's property more often than not meant protection from the creditors rather than from the husband. . . .

"The Married Women's Property Acts were part of a long series of legislation that aimed to defeudalize real property and convert it to an item of commerce. . . . In some cases, particularly with regard to the earliest bills, feminist agitation slowed the passage of the acts because of the fear of changes in intergender relationships, while it was their appeal to commercial necessity that ensured their passage."

14. Packard, op. cit., vol. II. It is important to note that three of Elizabeth's older sons risked being disinherited in order to correspond with and visit their mother (once) in the insane asylum. Also, she was later assisted by her son Samuel, a lawyer, in preparing her case for custody in Massachusetts.

Elizabeth never got divorced. When she returned to her house on Prairie Avenue in Chicago with the children, Theophilus followed her. He visited the children liberally in Elizabeth's home. He never "repented" his actions. Against her wishes, Theophilus apprenticed their youngest son Arthur to a farmer—frustrating Elizabeth's desire to provide him with a "superior education."

15. This speech is fictionalized. It is based on the account of the Phelps story contained in Kathryn Anthony's biography of Susan B. Anthony, *Her Personal History* (New York: Doubleday, 1954); on the account given by Lois W. Banner, *Elizabeth Cady Stanton: A Radical for Women's Rights* (Boston: Little, Brown and Co., 1980); and on the account given by Alice Felt in *Freedom's Ferment* (New York: Harper/Torch, 1944); and on Rita Childe Dorr's work on Susan B. Anthony, published in 1928, and now out of print.

16. According to Kathryn Anthony, op. cit., Susan B. Anthony first placed Mrs. Phelps with Abby Hopper Gibbons, daughter of the Quaker phil-

anthropist Isaac Hopper, and then with Mrs. Elizabeth Ellet, author of *Women of the Revolution.*

17. Anthony's "reverence" for the abolitionists Phillips and Garrison is quoted by Kathryn Anthony, op. cit., where their letter to her also appears. Alma Lutz, in *Susan B. Anthony* (Boston: Beacon Press, 1959), reports the following anecdote:

"It was incomprehensible to Susan that neither Garrison nor Phillips recognized woman's subservient status in marriage under prevailing laws and traditions. The Rev. A. D. Mayo, Unitarian Clergyman of Albany, heretofore Susan's loyal champion, now made a point of reproving her. 'You are not married,' he declared with withering scorn. 'You have no business to be discussing marriage.' To this she retorted, 'Well, Mr. Mayo, you are not a slave. Suppose you quit lecturing on slavery.' "

18. This quote is taken from Felt, op. cit., pp. 459–460. The source for Tyler's anecdote is a book on Susan B. Anthony by Rita Childe Dorr, *What Eight Million Women Want* (Boston, 1910 and 1928). It was first called to my attention in 1981 by historian Miriam Schneir, and again by playwright Mary Vasiliades. Kathryn Anthony quotes in her biography from a letter written by Susan B. Anthony to Phillips and Garrison: "Trust me, that I ignore all law to help the slave, so will I ignore it all to protect an enslaved woman."

There is a long (and forgotten) history of feminist agitation on behalf of maternal custody. For example, in 1852, "As women's rights campaigner Clarina I. Howard Nichols traveled from Vermont to Massachusetts, an elderly man and a sheriff boarded her train and tried to seize the youngest children of a female passenger. Nichols immediately stood up and told the startled passengers:

" 'It means, my friends, that a woman has no legal right to her own babies; that the law-givers of this Christian country (!) have given the custody of the babies to the father, drunken or sober, and he may send the sheriff . . . to arrest and rob her of her little ones!' Learning that the husband had transferred his custody rights to his own father, Nichols quickly explained that a recent Massachusetts court decision held that only a father could take children away from their mother. The passengers then threw the pair out."

This anecdote appears in several places, including Michael Grossberg's article, "Who Gets the Child? Custody, Guardianship, and the Role of a Judicial Patriarchy in Nineteenth Century America," *Feminist Studies* 9, no. 2, Summer 1983.

19. Elizabeth Cady Stanton, "Speech to the McFarland-Richardson Protest Meeting," May 1869. Reprinted in Ellen C. Dubois, ed., *Elizabeth Cady Stanton/Susan B. Anthony: Correspondence, Writings, Speeches* (New York: Schocken, 1981).

Susan B. Anthony and Elizabeth Cady Stanton both argued for custodial rights on behalf of married women; and both saw analogies between slavery for black people and legal marriage for women. See Dubois, op. cit.

20. While some American judges sometimes allowed a non-adulterous mother *temporary* custody of her children—especially if her father was wealthy and her husband was flagrantly abusive—custody was "temporary," and decisions like this were rare. For example, in 1809, in South Carolina, Mr. Prather deserted his wife for his mistress. In what was regarded as a highly "radical" decision, the judge allowed Mrs. Prather to keep her young infant "temporarily," with the clear understanding that she would return the child to his father. (*Prather* v. *Prather* [S.C. 1809], 4 Deseau., 33, 34, 44.) See Grossberg, op. cit., p. 471.

More characteristic of most judicial decisions was the following one. In 1813, in Pennsylvania, a judge allowed Barbara Lee to keep her two young daughters "temporarily." Barbara had been beaten and deserted by her adulterous husband. For years she was her family's sole economic provider. However, Barbara had begun living with a Mr. Addicks *before* she obtained her divorce. (She subsequently married him.) By law, Barbara Lee could not marry a man she had lived with in adultery, as a "paramour," during the lifetime of her (former) husband. In 1816, the court ordered the girls back into their father's custody. The judge "could not allow two potential wives to be reared by a mother who thought a marital vow could be so easily broken. At present, [the girls] may not reflect upon it, but soon they will, and when they inquire why it was that they were separated from their mother, they will be taught, as far as our opinion can teach them that in good fortune or bad, sickness or in health, in happiness or in misery, the marriage contract, unless dissolved by the law of the country, is sacred and inviolable." (*Commonwealth* v. *Addicks*, S. Binn S20 [PA 1813]: 2 Serge and Rawle, 174 [Pa 1816].)

In 1854, Mrs. Lindsay sought custody of her daughter. She claimed that her husband's cruelty and lack of financial support drove her to seek asylum with another man. Her petition was denied by the Georgia Supreme Court, which claimed that:

" 'There may be no difference in the sins of the man and the woman who violate the laws of chastity, but in the opinion of society it is otherwise.' When a man commits adultery he isn't excluded from associating with 'decent people.' . . . The frail female is reduced to 'utter and irredeemable ruin, where her associations are with the Vulgar, the Vile and the Depraved. If her children be with her, their characters must be, more or less, influenced and formed by the circumstances which surround them.' " (*Lindsay* v. *Lindsay*, 14 Ga 657 [1854]; see also *Matter of Viele*, 44 How. Pr. 14 [1872].)

As late as 1884, in New York, an (unmarried or separated) "adulteress" and petty thief "lost her children, was forbidden from visiting them, and evidently not even told where they were." *In re Diss. Debar*, 3 N.Y.S. [1889]. Cited by Douglas R. Rendleman, "Parents Patriae: From Chancery to the Juvenile Court," *South Carolina Law Review*, vol. 23, [1971].

21. "Sergeant Talfourd's Argument for the British Infants' Custody Act," *Hansard's Parliamentary Debates*, vol. 39 (1837). This act became law in 1839. Talfourd reviews a number of cases in which virtuous mothers were abused and abandoned by adulterous and profligate husbands—who also removed their children. The cases read like Gothic novels or tales of horror. For example:

In 1804, in England, Monsieur de Manneville, a Frenchman, left his English wife for his mistress. He returned during a storm, "ripped his eight-month-old daughter from her mother's breast," and disappeared into the night. Despite his threats to remove his child to France, the English court upheld his absolute right to custody. (*The King against De Manneville,* 1804 [In the Forty-Fourth Year of George III], Hil. 38. Geo 3.)

In 1824, in England, the court refused to "interfere" with paternal custody—even though the father had abused his wife, abandoned her for his mistress, kidnapped the child, and was, at the time, in jail! His mistress brought the six-year-old boy to visit him in jail. The mother was denied custody. Visitation did not exist as a maternal right. (*Ex parte Skinner,* In the Fifth Year of Geo. IV. 9 Moor. 278–283. King's Bench, Monday, May 31, 1824.)

In 1831, in England, a mother was denied the right to *nurse* her ailing child. The Court's decision is as follows:

"Mary M'Clellan, the mother of the child, came to have possession of [Eliza] in consequence of [her] being afflicted with a scrofulous complaint while at school, at which the father had placed her: that in consequence of that complaint and the fact of two others of her children having died of it, she had taken [Eliza] from the school: that the child is in a very delicate state of health, and requires very great care and attention: that it has been for some time under the mother's care . . . and that during the whole of that period, the treatment by the mother of her child was most kind and attentive.

"The application [of habeas corpus is] made at the instance of the father. There is no instance of the King's bench having taken the custody of the child from the father. I feel myself, therefore bound to say, that the child must be delivered up to the father. Rule absolute." (*Ex Parte McClellan* 1831.)

In 1836, in England, Mr. Greenhill lived in "open adultery." Mrs. Greenhill returned to her parents with her three daughters, all under five. She asked the court's permission "to continue bestowing upon her children the same personal care and attention which they had hitherto received from her, and which was necessary to their welfare; she further stated that she would consent even to relinquish the custody and control of her children, if she might be assured of permission to give them her personal care and attention during their tender years." The court refused her request. First, Mrs. Greenhill was not a good enough "Christian" wife; she remained unwilling to "forgive" her husband. Second, the children belonged to their father by law—and were so remanded into his custody. (*The King Against Henrietta Lavinia Greenhill*, Lord Chief Justice Derman presiding. 4 Adolphus and Ellis, King's Bench Reports 624 [1836].)

In 1837, in England, Mrs. Ball was driven out of her home by her husband's physical violence and adulteries. Mrs. Ball offered to support her adolescent daughter with the funds she herself had. Nonetheless, she was denied both custody and visitation with her daughter. Talfourd asked: "Should a child be deprived, by the brutal conduct of the father, of the company, advice and protection of the mother, against whom no imputation can be raised? . . . I know of no act more harsh and cruel than depriving a mother of proper intercourse with her child."

22. My account of Frances (Fanny) Wright is primarily based on Cecilia Morris Eckhardt, *Fanny Wright: Rebel in America* (Cambridge, Mass.: Harvard University Press, 1984).

23. My account of George Sand is based on Curtis Cate's biography, *George Sand: A Biography* (Boston: Houghton Mifflin, 1975); George Sand, *My Life,* trans. Don Hofstadter (reprint ed., New York: Harper/Colophon, 1979); George Sand, *The Intimate Journal,* trans. Marie Jenny Howe (reprint ed., Chicago: Academy Press, Cassandra Editions, 1977); and George Sand, *Winter in Majorca,* trans. Marie Jenny Howe (reprint ed., Chicago: Academy Press, Cassandra Editions, 1978).

24. Eckhardt, op. cit. It is important to remember that under common law, in England and America (and under equivalent laws in all countries), husbands were legally entitled to their wives' dowries, inheritance, and earnings. Common law made it illegal for married women to contract, sue, or collect debts without their husbands' consent. Women married to untrustworthy husbands could not engage in business without encountering enormous obstacles. (They were denied credit.)

25. Eckhardt, ibid.

26. Many accomplished and wealthy women were custodially punished for adultery, or for displeasing their husbands. For example, the British-born feminist Caroline Sheridan Norton was trapped in a disastrous marriage. In 1836, her husband accused her of committing adultery with the British prime minister.

"Although she was judged innocent, Caroline's reputation was permanently tarnished. Separated from her husband, she was denied access to their three children; meanwhile, he took legal action to obtain the proceeds from her writings. These tribulations left Caroline bitterly conscious of the inferior legal status of married women and led her to condemn publicly the laws regarding divorce and child custody. In 1857, prodded by her protest and the activities of other feminists, Parliament passed the Matrimonial Causes Act, which established special civil courts to grant judicial separations and divorces."

This account is contained, together with Norton's writings, in Erna Olafson Hellerstein, Leslie Parker Hume, and Karen M. Offen, eds., Estelle B. Freedman, Barbara Charlesworth Gelpi, and Marilyn Yalom, assoc. eds., *Victorian Women: A Documentary of Women's Lives in Nineteenth-Century England, France and the United States* (Stanford University Press, 1981).

27. At this time in America, Victoria C. Woodhull and Elizabeth Cady Stanton were publishing their views on voluntary motherhood, women's suffrage, and "free love." In 1873, the infamous Comstock Laws were passed in America, prohibiting the advocacy of birth control. Margaret Sanger would later be forced to leave America for England because of these laws.

28. *In re Besant*, Chancery Division, vol. XI, 508–522.

29. Ibid.

30. Ibid. There are other cases of prominent English (male) atheists losing custody of their children. In 1817, the poet Percy Bysshe Shelley, who had previously abandoned his wife and children, was denied their custody after their mother's death. According to the English court, Shelley "avowed himself an atheist; he had written and published a work in which he blasphemously derided the truth of the Christian revelation and denied the existence of a God as creator of the universe." Shelley was considered morally unfit to parent. The maternal *grandfather*, Mr. Westbrooke, who presumably believed in God, assumed custody of his grandchildren. (*Shelley* v. *Westbrooke*, Jacob Chancery Reports 226, 1817.)

31. William Shakespeare, *A Midsummer Night's Dream*, in *The Complete Works of William Shakespeare* (London: Abby Library, 1977). Based on the 1623 Folio. The Indian child is only the dramatic "excuse" for a domestic quarrel among immortals.

32. The Christian king's right to his genetic children symbolized and maintained patriarchal order. It ensured *every* man his legal and obedient heir and every heir his rightful inheritance. The medieval Arthurian legends are essentially about the importance of father-owned and father-controlled children. The natural—or naturally "political"—relationship between a queen and her child must be sacrificed for the sake of Christian patriarchal order. Arthur's father, Uther Pendragon, "mates" with the Lady Igraine to beget his "once and future King." He demands that Igraine

give the newborn Arthur away at birth—which she obediently does.

"When the lady [Igraine] was delivered, the king commanded two knights and two ladies to take the child, bound in a cloth of gold. . . . So the child was delivered unto Merlin, and so he bore it forth to Ector, and made an holy man to christen him, and named him Arthur; and so Sir Ector's wife nourished him with her own pap." Sir Thomas Malory, *La Morte d'Arthur* (New York: Everyman, 1967). See Marion Zimmer Bradley's excellent popular retelling of the Arthurian myths in *The Mists of Avalon.*

While it is true that mothers of all classes routinely gave their children "away" to wet nurses, governesses, tutors, etc., it was not always done at birth, or in a way that denied the mother all access to her child—if she wanted it. The mother-surrogates were usually social inferiors and employees, rather than another woman of the mother's own station, as Sir Ector's wife was. I view Igraine in the legends as a role model of Christian wifely obedience, which includes worshipping one male God and no Goddesses.

Female-initiated sexual activity or unwed motherhood is politically dangerous. In the legends, the adolescent Arthur is "bewitched" into impregnating Morgana LeFay—a half-sister who is also a fairy queen. Their "illegitimate" son, Mordred, is later blamed for plunging England into civil war.

33. Despite a double standard of sexual morality (between queens and kings, and between queens and their non-royal female "inferiors"), some queens and some royal ladies did take lovers and did give birth to illegitimate children. Obviously, our information is somewhat limited on so "sensitive" a subject as the legitimacy of future kings, lords, and ladies.

34. Joseph Dahmus, *Seven Medieval Queens* (New York: Doubleday, 1972).

35. Elizabeth Jenkins, in her biography of *Elizabeth the Great* (New York: Berkley Medallion, 1958), notes that: "Apart from (two indirect) instances there is no record of Elizabeth having uttered her mother's name. But with this determined silence, there went a marked kindness toward her mother's connections. In her kindness to these, she paid a mute tribute where she could not speak."

In the sixteenth century, King Henry VIII married, divorced, imprisoned, or beheaded queen after queen in his obsessive search for a male heir. His first wife, the pious Catherine of Aragon, refused to agree to a divorce. Henry separated her from Mary, their only child, for five years. Despite this enforced separation, and despite the humiliation of house arrest, Queen Catherine continued to refuse to consent to a divorce. How could she? At stake were Mary's legitimacy—as well as Catherine's own religious beliefs. See Nora Loft, *The King's Pleasure* (London: Coronet Books, 1969).

36. Lady Ann Roos eventually gave birth to another son, retained custody of "Ignoto," moved to Ireland, and was duly divorced "in the ecclesiastical court" for adultery. Her children, John and Charles Manners, were subsequently declared "illegitimate," by an act of Parliament. See Antonia Fraser, *The Weaker Vessel* (New York: Knopf, 1984).

37. In 1796, when Catherine the Great died, a sealed envelope of her memoirs was discovered, addressed "To his Imperial Highness the Czarevich and Grand Duke Paul, my dearly loved son." Her memoirs were suppressed— because she admits that her son and royal heir had "no Romanov blood," i.e., was an illegitimate child. My information about Catherine the Great of Russia is contained in *The Memoirs of Catherine the Great*, trans. Moura Budberg, Dominique Maroger, ed. (London: Hamish Hamilton, 1955). The volume is as extraordinary as it is little known.

38. Maroger, op. cit. Peter (who is Elizabeth's nephew and heir) is obviously insane. Catherine recounts this scene in her memoirs:
    "One day when I walked into His Imperial Highness's [apartment], I was struck by the sight of an immense rat which he had hanged, with all the paraphernalia of torture, in the middle of the small room which he had partitioned off. I asked what was the meaning of this; he then told me that the rat had been convicted of a crime and deserved the severest punishment according to military law. . . . I could not help laughing at the madness of the whole thing, but this greatly displeased him, because of the importance he attributed to procedure. I retired and apologized, pleading womanly ignorance of military law, but he continued to sulk with me for having laughed at him."

39. Count Sergei Saltikov is considered the father of Catherine's son Paul I for several reasons. Maroger notes: "Everything: the Empress's suspicion, Saltikov's cautiousness, the speed with which Saltikov is removed as soon as the child is born (but not beforehand so as not to endanger Catherine's health), the Grand Duke's attitude, that of the Empress who snatches the new-born child from Catherine, everything seems to indicate that Catherine's entourage had no doubt whatsoever that Saltikov was the father of the child. The secret had to be closely guarded as in these circumstances the heir to the throne was no longer of the blood of the Romanovs. It is surprising that Catherine should have half-revealed it in memoirs which were essentially destined for her son and her grandson, Alexander."

40. Maroger, op. cit.

41. Catherine's memoirs give us a glimpse into the kind of power a queen (like the Empress Elizabeth) can exercise—if she had no king, and if her heir (in this case her nephew) is insane and incompetent.

42. Sophie-Catherine is never clear about what her role is in her husband's

assassination, or about whether she knew beforehand of the plans to assassinate Peter. There was one other contender for the throne: a four-year-old boy named Ivan. In the 1740s, the Empress Elizabeth "dethroned" him, separated him from his mother, and had him imprisoned for the rest of his life. Sophie-Catherine met him once; described him as "stammering" and as "insulting" to her. She probably had him murdered after she assumed the throne.

43. Maroger, op. cit. In her private writings and letters (some of which are reprinted together with her memoirs), the Empress Catherine, a devotee of the French Enlightenment, envisions the emancipation of the serfs, and mourns the existence of "slavery" and the "high infant mortality" among the peasants. She reminds herself to avoid "flatterers," to be "kind, gentle, accessible, and liberal-minded," and to "behave so that the kind love you, the evil fear you, and all respect you."

44. Rendleman, op. cit.

45. Ann Jones, *Women Who Kill* (New York: Holt, Rinehart, 1980). Jones notes that the colonial lawmakers fell back upon English common law, which defined the murder of a husband or master as petit treason. Since the husband was "lord" of the wife, the common law said her killing him was treachery comparable to murdering the king—though on a lesser scale. A Virginia judge defined the gravity of the crime: "Other offenses are injurious to Private Persons only, but this is a Public Mischief, and often strikes at the Root of all Civil Government."

46. Lorena Walsh, *Child Custody in the Early Colonial Chesapeake: A Case Study (1658–1720)*, Regional Economic History Research Center, May 1981. Unpublished, on file at Radcliffe's Schlesinger Library. Walsh notes that the law in seventeenth-century Maryland condemned mulatto offspring to be sold for thirty-one years of servitude. In some ways, unwed mothers had more rights over their children than did married mothers. Walsh cites some examples of unwed maternal rights to wages of an apprenticed child, even when the natural father sought the non-legitimated child for his own economic purpose.

   Ann Jones, op. cit., notes: "When Eve Sewell, a free white woman, bore a child in 1790 by a black slave, under Maryland law her white husband received an automatic divorce and both she and her child were sold into slavery."

47. Ann Jones, op. cit.

48. Walsh, op. cit.
   Rape was also a serious colonial offense. Unwed pregnant girls who were neither servants nor paupers who claimed that their pregnancies were the result of rape were sometimes *formally interrogated* in the throes of child-

birth. If they stuck to their story of rape, could name the father, and were believed, the father was then ordered to support his child. According to Ellen Fitzpatrick, in 1686, Elizabeth Emerson of New England accused Thomas Swan of raping and impregnating her. She was "examined" during childbirth, and her charges were confirmed.

"The child was a year old before a Salem court settled the case in the Emersons' favor. Swan was ordered to pay ten shillings six pence per week in child support. But the Emersons were back in court shortly after the child's second birthday. They had yet to receive any money from Swan. Instead, the reluctant father had offered molasses, lumber, a cow, and other goods which the Emersons complained were 'useless and frivolous things which will afford said Child no maintenance.' " (Ellen Fitzpatrick, "Childbirth and an Unwed Mother in 17th Century New England," *Signs*, vol. 8, no. 4 [Summer 1983]).

49. In colonial America, both men and women were punished for fornication and adultery by economic fines, public whipping, imprisonment, or death by hanging. Needless to say, women were far more vulnerable than men to the consequences of such crimes.

In Nathaniel Hawthorne's 1850 version of Puritan New England, Hester Prynne was imprisoned and forced to wear the scarlet letter "A" (for adulteress) over her heart forever. Hester refuses to name Roger Dimmesdale as her daughter's father. He is also Hester's pastor and a prominent member of the community. Hester is allowed to keep her daughter, Pearl, "as a way of saving her from becoming a witch." Hester's ostracism is total and lifelong. Crowds reject her or follow her. Children jeer at her. If Hester "entered a church, trusting to share the Sabbath smile of the Universal Father, it was often her mishap to find herself the text of the discourse. . . . Another peculiar torture was felt in the gaze of a new eye. When strangers looked curiously at the scarlet letter—and none ever failed to do so—they branded it afresh into Hester's soul. The spot never grew callous; it seemed on the contrary to grow more sensitive with daily torture." When Pearl is three years old, the town magistrates decide to remove her from her mother's "un-Christian custody." Hester now threatens Dimmesdale with exposure. He persuades the magistrates to allow Hester the solace and rights of natural motherhood (Nathaniel Hawthorne, *The Scarlet Letter* [1850; New York: Bantam, 1965]).

50. Jones, op. cit., notes that just about the same time that Hanna Piggin and Abiel Converse were hanged in Northampton, Massachusetts (for concealing the birth of a bastard or for infanticide), six male leaders of Shays's Rebellion, convicted in the same jurisdiction of treason and sentenced to hang, were pardoned. Still others, guilty of far more brutal crimes, got off with light sentences. When Robert Thompson was convicted of assault in the same Northampton jurisdiction, he was whipped twenty stripes, set

on the gallows for one hour, whipped nineteen more stripes, jailed for one year, and ordered to pay costs. He had beaten up his wife, Agnes Thompson, and "dug out both her eyes with his thumbs and a stick so she is entirely blind."

In the 1860s, Elizabeth Cady Stanton referred to one "Hester Vaughan," then "under sentence of death for the alleged crime of Infanticide, which could not be proved against her [and who] has dragged the weary days of a whole year away in the solitude and gloom of a Pennsylvania prison, while he who betrayed her walks this green earth in freedom" (Dubois, op. cit.).

Also see Nicole Hahn Rafter, *Partial Justice: Women in State Prisons, 1800–1935*, (Boston: Northeastern University Press, 1985).

51. Walsh, op. cit. The Watts children were lucky; they had a maternal grandfather who petitioned for their custody. It took three years of persistent effort before he obtained it.

52. M. Jerigan, *The Laboring and Dependent Classes in Colonial America,* 157, 1960, cited by Rendleman, op. cit.

53. Walsh, op. cit., also notes that *un-remarried* colonial widows attempted to have their children released from bondage to a cruel master.

54. Ibid. In her study of colonial custody in Maryland, Walsh concludes that the "preferred custodial solution" was to grant custody to the "closest surviving and nurturing kin," a decision that "strongly reinforced the rights of the natural mother and also encouraged strong kin networks."

Perhaps such widows, if they remained unmarried, were in the unusual position of being single women of property. As such they may have been vulnerable to accusations of witchcraft for just this reason, just as their married, abused, and property-less female counterparts were vulnerable to similar accusations for another set of reasons. See Chapter 17 for a discussion of this.

55. Jones, op cit.

56. Nancy F. Cott, "Eighteenth-Century Family and Social Life Revealed in Massachusetts Divorce Records," in Nancy F. Cott and Elizabeth H. Pleck, eds., *A Heritage of Her Own: Toward a New Social History of American Women* (New York: Touchstone Books/Simon & Schuster, 1980), notes that between 1692 and 1786 women clung to married status longer than men did, even when aware of their spouses' wrongs. Aggrieved wives waited a longer time before suing for divorce than aggrieved husbands did. On the average, wives waited almost five years, while husbands petitioned after only two-and-a-half years.

"Of course, other considerations besides pure tolerance or resignation must have figured in an individual's decision to wait or to sue for divorce. Awareness of divorce procedure, estimation of how likely a divorce was to be obtained, or appraisal of what benefit or shame a divorce would produce, could counterbalance the desire to be rid of an unworthy partner, and more effectively did so, it seems, for wives than for husbands. Some cases are truly remarkable. Abigail Daniels of Grafton finally petitioned in 1781 to divorce her husband of thirty years, when for as long as eight years he had been cohabitating at home with her sister, as well as frequenting taverns and failing to support Abigail and her children. Several wives who sued on the grounds of cruelty said they had endured five or ten years of physical abuse, and women often waited as long, or longer to petition after being deserted."

It is important to remember that female and maternal poverty continued throughout the nineteenth century. For example, in 1845, the *New York Tribune* published an article on the economic plight of white mothers: "It was but a week or two ago that a respectable woman, reduced from competence to poverty by a sudden calamity, traversed the streets of our city for two or three days in search of some employment by which she could earn bread for herself and her children. In this case, the woman found paid home work as a seamstress, worked for a week, and received only 'credit.' With this she was to return to her desolate, destitute home. Such scenes are occurring daily in our city and in all cities. . . . Many who dance in jewels one year are shivering in garrets the next, willing to labor for the humblest fare, yet unable to labor to produce it" (Julie Matthaei, *An Economic History of Women in America* [New York: Schocken Books, 1982]).

According to Elizabeth Pleck, during the nineteenth century, free black mothers and their children worked as field hands and in domestic service. Poorly paid laundry work was an economic mainstay of many black mothers (Elizabeth H. Pleck, "A Mother's Wages: Income Earning Among Married and Black Women (1896–1911)," in Cott and Pleck, op. cit.).

According to Sterling, in *We Are Your Sisters*, "Freedwomen were always paid less than the men. On one Georgia plantation male hands received $140 a year, women from $60 to $85. In Adams County, Mississippi, Sarah Nelson was promised $10 a month; John, a man working alongside her, received $15. . . . In June 1866 [black washerwomen] published a politely worded ultimatum [asking for] $1.50 per day for washing; $15.00 per month for family washing; $10.00 per month for single individuals."

57. There are always many exceptions to any rule, including that of fathers' rights. A close reading of some of these judicial exceptions reveals that an "intemperate" and wealthy father's custodial petition failed only when *his* own father, the paternal grandfather, refused to back him, but instead backed his wife, or his dead wife's equally wealthy family. The best example of this is the case known as *Wellesley* v. *Wellesley* or *The Wellesley Children*

v. *Duke of Beaufort*, 2 Russell Chancery Reports, I., 1827. Cited by Grace Abbott, *The Child and the State* (Westport, Conn.: Greenwood Press, 1938).

58. *Nickols* v. *Giles*, 2 Root 461 (Conn. 1796), cited by Zinaildin, op. cit.
    There are other cases in which a wealthy maternal grandfather was granted custody of a grandchild. For example, in 1816, John Waldron petitioned for custody of his daughter, Margaret Eliza. He claimed that his father-in-law, Andrew McGowan, had "improperly restrained" her. Waldron also claimed that McGowan had on numerous occasions "repulsed" his attempts to visit his wife and child. McGowan described Waldron as "insolvent" and unable to pay "trifling debts" and as a man who (had) to "live with his mother." Waldron was Margaret's father. His mother was offering to help him economically. Nevertheless, the court denied Waldron's petition. Andrew McGowan was a ". . . very affluent [man], and abundantly able to maintain his grand-daughter [who] would most probably receive the greater part of the property of her grandparents, on their death" (*In re Waldron 13 Johns*, 418–419, New York 1816, cited by Zinaildin, op. cit.).

59. *Ex parte Crouse*, 4 Whart. 9 Penn. 1839. Earlier, in 1810, where the *child* was not charged with "immorality," but her parents were, the state acted as the child's superior guardian. However, it did not establish any precedent in so doing. In 1810, Levi Nutt of Pennsylvania petitioned the court for custody of his daughter. Nutt had no property or income. He also "cursed in front of his wife and daughter."
    "Mrs. Nutt was also of a 'disgusting character.' She frequently 'kept house for Amos Howell,' a tavernkeeper who had separated from his wife. 'There is every reason to believe they lived in constant habits of adultery.' The virtue and innocence of the child, a girl named Acha, 'could not be trusted with safety' in 'either party's custody. . . . The father has a right to custody of his children' but Acha will be placed with a relative 'where her mind and morals [were] in the least danger of being corrupted' " (*Commonwealth* v. *Nutt*, 1 Bro 143 [Philadelphia County] 1810, cited by Zinaildin, op. cit.).
    Rendleman, op. cit., explains the state's misuse and misinterpretation of *parens patriae* as a way of controlling, punishing, and profiting from the poor—without a guilty conscience, and without having to find better or more costly programs to rehabilitate the impoverished. According to Rendleman:
    "The Latin phrase 'parens patriae' had acquired meaning over a long period of time and was sensibly applied between private parties, usually where property or guardianship was an issue. The Crouse [court used this phrase] to justify the state statutory schemes to part poor or incompetent parents from their children."

Rendleman also observes (here he is quoting from *The Honest Politicians Guide to Crime Control*): "The juvenile court emerged from what was a legal misinterpretation of the *parens patriae* concept. This concept was developed for quite different purposes—property and wardship—and had nothing to do with what juvenile courts do now. Though we keep on practicing *parens patriae*, we might as well burn incense. Historical idiosyncrasies gave us a doubtful assumption of power over children. With the quasi-legal concept of *parens patriae* to brace it, this assumption of power blended well with the earlier humanitarian traditions in churches and other charitable organizations regarding child care and child-saving. The juvenile court is thus the product of paternal error and maternal generosity, which is not [the] usual genesis of illegitimacy."

60. *Ackley* v. *Tinker*, 26 Kansas 485 (1881), cited by Zinaildin, op. cit.

61. *Harrison* v. *Gilbert*, 71 Conn. 724, 43A 190 (1899), cited by Zinaildin, op. cit. The last sentence is Zinaildin's comment on the case.
    Strictly speaking, the state was not legally involved in human slavery. Rendleman, op. cit., notes that "the practice of breaking up families by sale [slavery] was a private enterprise." The state was neither a buyer nor a seller and not an integral party to the transaction. The state, however, was intimately involved in the economic benefits or savings of child apprenticeships.

62. Sterling, *We Are Your Sisters*.

63. This is a fictionalized account of one Indian mother's response to being separated from her children. It was written by Beth Brant and entitled "A Long Story." It appeared in *Sinister Wisdom: A Gathering of Spirit. North American Indian Women's Issue* 22/23 (Iowa City, Iowa: Iowa City Women's Press, 1983). Brant's Indian name is Degonwadonti, of the Bay of Quinte Mohawks. She belongs to the Turtle Clan and her "place of spirit" is Tyendinaga Reserve in Ontario. Brant counterposes a late-nineteenth-century Indian mother's loss of her children with a late-twentieth-century lesbian custody battle.
    In the same issue, Elizabeth Cook-Lynn, in another short story, "A Family Matter," writes about an Indian mother's poverty and consequent "abandonment" of her children to their white paternal grandmother; and about how her ex-mother-in-law brainwashes them against her and against their Indian heritage.

64. Most contemporary historians have been forced to focus on the parental mistreatment of *poor* nineteenth-century children. Fewer records were kept charting the parental mistreatment of middle- or upper-class children. Private and state organizations began to keep records of child abuse only after the Civil War. Even then, such records are more suggestive than comprehensive.

In 1821, Sir William Blackstone in his *Commentaries on the Laws of England* (8th ed., 1821), noted that "The rich indeed are left at their own option, whether they will breed up their children to be ornaments or disgraces to their family."

65. According to Charles Loring Brace, founder of the Children's Aid Society of New York, "As Christian men, we cannot look upon this great multitude of unhappy, deserted and degraded boys and girls without feeling our responsibility to God for them. The class increases; immigration is pouring in its multitudes . . . of helpless foreigners who crowd into the tenements in the Russian, Polish, Bohemian, Hungarian, and Italian quarters of our city. . . . They must be taught our language. They must be trained to be clean, obedient to authority, industrious and truthful, and must be instructed in the elements of an English education.

"These boys and girls, it should be remembered, will soon form the great lower class of our city. They will influence elections; they may shape the policy of the city; they will assuredly, if unreclaimed, poison society all around them. They will help to form the great multitude of robbers, thieves, and vagrants, who are now such a burden upon the law-respecting community."

These words are taken from a series of circulars written in the 1820s by Brace. See Charles Loring Brace, "The Children's Aid Society of New York: Its History, Plans and Results," in Anthony Platt, ed., *History of Child-Saving in the United States* (1893; reprint ed., Montclair, N.Y.: Patterson Smith, 1971). Bruce also described the overwhelming and serious problems faced by impoverished children.

In 1797, Isabella Graham founded the New York Society for the Relief of Poor Widows with Small Children. In 1806, she privately opened the first orphan asylum in the United States. This effort attempted to keep families together, as well as to shelter and educate both mothers and children. This information is contained in William Pryor Letchworth, "The History of Child-Saving Work in Connecticut," in Platt, op. cit.

66. Robert S. Pickert, *House of Refuge: Origins of Juvenile Reform in New York State, 1815–1857* (Syracuse: Syracuse University Press, 1969).

67. The boy was beaten to death as Russian prisoners are under the knout. It was shown that the father had continued his brutal conduct for months. The man was sentenced to be hanged, but applied for a new trial on a technicality. A new trial was granted, conditioned on his pleading guilty, as the jury had coupled a recommendation of mercy with their verdict. He was then sentenced to imprisonment for life (Oscar L. Dubley, "Saving the Children: Sixteen Years Work among the Dependent Youth of Chicago," in Platt, op. cit.).

For other accounts of abused, impoverished children, see Letchworth, op. cit.; Pickert, op. cit.; Brace, op. cit.; Douglas R. Rendleman, op. cit.;

Zinaildin, op. cit.; and Anne B. Richardson, "The Massachusetts System for Caring for State Minor Wards," in Platt, op. cit.

68. For example, in 1833, in South Carolina, the judge was creative in "saving" a young man from his abusive father. The court ruled: "The father had severely beaten his son, Frederick. He later placed the child with Mrs. Mary Thompson, who gratuitously clothed, fed and housed the boy. Kottman demanded the return of his son. Mrs. Thompson refused to cooperate. Frederick was now fifteen years of age and insisted on remaining with Mrs. Thompson. While the father does possess the legal right to custody of his son, the court can permit Kottman to 'take' his son 'where he can find him.' He must not commit a trespass on retrieving him. 'It must be at his own risk' " (*In re Kottman 20 S.C.L.* [2 Hill] 363 [1833], cited by Zinaildin, op. cit.).

69. *Commonwealth* v. *Coyle*, 160 PA. 36, 576, 28 A. 634 (1894), cited by Rendleman, op. cit.

70. For example, in 1833, in South Carolina (*In re Kottman*), a judge awarded an adolescent male to the kind mother-surrogate who took him in and reared him after his father beat him savagely. The judges made no legal ruling in this case *against* a father's right to custody.

In 1846, in Tennessee (*Ward* v. *Roper*), a judge awarded a child to her maternal grandparents who had raised her, and refused custody to her paternally appointed guardian. The "ties" to her maternal grandmother "should not be broken."

In 1851, in Pennsylvania (*Gilkeson* v. *Gilkeson*), a judge awarded custody to a girl's paternal aunt and uncle who had been acting as her adoptive parents for six years. The father's claim was dismissed.

In 1881, in Kansas (*Chapsky* v. *Wood*), a father's custodial claim was dismissed in favor of the child's pre-existing live-in relationship with her maternal aunt, who was "like a mother to her."

Such exceptional cases must be contrasted with the cases I've referred to in which moral or economically solvent mothers, such as Fanny Wright, Elizabeth Packard, Abby McFarland, etc., were denied custody of their own children when custody was contested by an immoral and economically solvent father.

71. An 1810 case illustrates the point I am making. A widowed biological mother was forced to apprentice her daughter "in upper Canada." Later, the child returned to Massachusetts with her master, William Hamilton. The child's now remarried mother petitioned the court for her daughter's return. However, since the mother was remarried, she "ceased to have any power of controlling her own actions"; and her new husband was under no legal obligation to provide for the girl. Without any precedent, the court

cautioned the mother not to "molest, interrupt or disturb" her daughter "in respect to her residence in the family of said Hamilton" (*Commonwealth v. Hamilton*, 6 Mass 273 [1810], cited by Zinaildin, op. cit.).

In certain cases throughout the nineteenth century, some widowed biological mothers who could afford a lawsuit were judicially found to be entitled to the services or wages of their children. For example, see *Osborn v. Allen* (26, New Jersey Law Reports, 388, 1857). This was not true if a father was alive, or if the mother was seen as "immoral."

72. Michael Grossberg, op. cit. See also Elizabeth Badinter, *Mother Love: Myth and Reality* (New York: Macmillan, 1981), and Carol Brown, "Mothers, Fathers and Children: From Private to Public Patriarch," in Lydia Sargent, ed., *Women and Revolution* (Boston: South End Press, 1981).

73. In addition, women and men were both imprisoned and/or custodially penalized for "male" crimes, including poverty, vagrancy, alcoholism, atheism, robbery, and homicide. Women were often more severely punished for "female" sexual crimes than men were for "male" crimes. Barbara Hobson studied prostitutes in Victorian Boston. She cites proof of discrepancies in treatment of males and females brought into court on charges of immoral behavior. Greater numbers of females were found guilty, and, upon sentencing, a larger proportion were imprisoned; men were often fined. Women were overwhelmingly accused of moral turpitude, and were tried for offenses against the public order more often than they were charged with crimes against persons or property. Impoverished deviant women suffered more than their more well-to-do sisters in the criminal world. (Barbara Hobson, "Sex in the Marketplace: Prostitution in an American Victorian City, Boston, 1820–1880," Ph.D. dissertation, Boston University, 1981; cited by Barbara M. Brenzel, *Daughters of the State: A Social Portrait of the First Reform School for Girls in North America, 1856–1905* [Cambridge, Mass.: MIT Press, 1983].)

Ann Jones, in *Women Who Kill*, documents this same point for both colonial, Victorian, and contemporary women in America.

74. Brenzel, op. cit.

Rendleman, op. cit., also notes the anti-Catholic, anti-Irish, and anti-immigrant biases of nineteenth-century "child saving." He notes the *O'Connell* case (1870), which on appeal returned a Catholic child to a Catholic home. "Justice Redfield commented after O'Connell that a Catholic 'child cannot be torn from home and immured in a Protestant prison, for ten or more years, and trained in what he regards as a heretical and deadly faith, to the destruction of his own soul.' The O'Connell decision did not stop this practice."

75. Brenzel, op. cit. Perhaps impoverished families—like all other families— had less patience with or placed less value on daughters than on sons;

perhaps they feared "immorality" in girls and judged it more harshly than "immorality" in boys. Perhaps such families genuinely wanted to save their daughters from a life of prostitution; perhaps the victims of incest had to be sacrificed and exiled for the sake of "the family."

76. Brenzel, ibid.

77. Brenzel, ibid., quoting the "14th Annual Report regarding Lancaster, to the Board of State Charities," Public Document 20, 1869.

   Later in the century, when factories required cheap female labor, Lancaster inmates were trained accordingly—despite the continued probability of sexual harassment and rape on the job. Perhaps Lancaster (and its many counterparts) really tried to "save" as many individual girls as possible—given that their poverty rendered them and their mothers so vulnerable to male sexual aggression and exploitation.

78. "According to Dr. Walter E. Fernald of Massachusetts, one strong indicator of feeble-mindedness in young girls was sexual activity: 'Imbeciles of both sexes show active sexual propensities and perversions at an early age' " (an unpublished record of Dr. Walter E. Fernald, The Walter E. Fernald State School, 1910; cited by Brenzel, op. cit.).

79. Brenzel, op. cit.

80. Grossberg, op. cit.

CHAPTER TWO:
A CONTEMPORARY
OVERVIEW

1. *In re Abdullah*, 80 Ill. App. 3d. 1144, 400 N.E. 2d. 1063 (1980). *In re Abdullah*, 85 Ill. 2d. 300, 423 N.E. 2d. 915 (1981). The Abdullah decision is contained and discussed in *The Family Advocate* (1981) in an article by attorney Michael Minton, "Should a Divorced Mother Lose Custody Because She Has a Lover?" Mr. Minton is Mrs. Jarrett's attorney. The *Abdullah* decision was reversed three years later, as the result of mounting pressure. When the Abdullah child was six years old, he was legally "adoptable."

2. Minton, op. cit. The dissenting judge in the *Abdullah* decision concluded: "We acquiesced in depriving a woman of the custody of her children. . . . We held that the fact of open and notorious cohabitation alone made it in the best interests of the children that they live with their father. In this case, however (Abdullah), the majority holds that the unrebutted murder of the child's mother . . . is insufficient to justify dispensing with

the murderer's consent before the child may be placed for adoption. In other words, cohabitation [with no tangible evidence that her conduct harmed the children in any way] may justify losing custody of children, but the murder of one's wife, the mother of the child, will not."

3. It is important to realize that each judicial decision is interpreted differently both by lawyers and by judges, in each state, over time, and in different cases. It is also important to realize that custody remains an open matter until a child reaches his or her majority. Thus, decisions are sometimes appealed endlessly; private custodial arrangements are appealed for the first time in courts years later; judicial custodial decisions are also modified by the parents and children involved on a daily basis.

The fact that such decisions as I cite here can happen *even once* in contemporary America is important. The effect they have on each mother involved and on any other mother who hears about it is important. What it tells us about judicial practice is important. Please see Chapter 14 for a discussion of judicial trends in general.

4. "Natural Parent Entitled to Custody Absent 'Extraordinary Circumstances,' " 9 *FLR* (August 16, 1983).

5. Ibid.

6. *Landaverde* v. *Howie*. Reported in *Family Law Reporter* 8/16/83, 9 *FLR* 2601. In a sense, Christina was initially impoverished and endangered by the American state. Fleeing for her life, she was then deprived of her natural son—by that same American state. There have been other women in Christina's position, whose cases have been resolved differently.

In 1978, for example, a white, unwed, and native-born mother was in Christina's position. She too was tricked by an adoption agency. She, however, managed to get her child back. According to the *Chicago Tribune* of May 12, 1978: "A circuit judge ruled Friday that Catholic Charities used 'fraud' and duress to persuade an unmarried north suburban woman to put her two month old son up for adoption in 1977. Therefore, Judge Irwin Cohen ruled, Linda Polales, thirty, of 1300 S. Chester Ave., Park Ridge, should get custody of eighteen month old Sean Patrick Polales, the son she has not seen for sixteen months. Miss Polales, a former administrative secretary for a pharmaceutical firm, was not married to the baby's father, a thirty-six-year-old married man who she said lives in California. She said that a month after the birth of Sean, the father began harassing her, so she placed Sean in the care of Catholic Charities while she got legal help to terminate the man's parental rights. Catholic Charities changed its case records to make it look as though she had agreed to the baby's adoption. The organization had warned her that the baby's father could 'bother you for life'—though he had signed a form denying being the father and surrendering any parental rights."

In 1984, Elizabeth Wuertz, a mother who lost custody of her baby daughter because of an error by her former attorney, was awarded custody by the Louisiana Supreme Court following a two-year legal battle. Wuertz was nineteen and unwed in December 1980, when she gave birth to her daughter, Christina. The two lived with Wuertz's mother, court records showed, until her mother was imprisoned for burglary.

Wuertz was taken to see a lawyer who arranged for the child's adoption, court records show. Wuertz was quoted as saying that she was told if she did not surrender the child, she might be charged with child abuse. She reportedly said she unwillingly signed an adoption consent form, and she was told she had thirty days to change her mind. She did change her mind, but a trial court ruled that her request to get the child back was invalid because her former attorney did not send it back by certified mail.

7. *In re Marriage of Gould*, 112 Wisc. 2d 674, 333 N.W. 2d 733 (March 1983). This decision was reversed on appeal, 342 N.W. 2d 426 (Wisc. Supreme Court, 1984). I am indebted to Nancy Polikoff's discussion of this case in her review of case law, op. cit.

Please see Chapter 14 for a discussion of the judicial and legislative devaluation of mothers in terms of the levels of child support set by the state ("welfare") and the levels of child support therefore set by individual judges.

8. *Porter* v. *Porter*, 274 N.W. 2d 235 (N.D. 1979). The comments are Nancy Polikoff's, op. cit.

9. *Dempsey* v. *Dempsey*, 95 Mich. App. 285, 292 N.W., 2d 549 (1980); 409 Mich. 495, 296 N.W. 2d 813 (1980), quoted by Nancy Polikoff, "*Why* Are Mothers Losing? A Brief Analysis of Criteria Used in Child Custody Determinations." *Women's Rights Law Reporter*, 7, 3 (Spring 1982).

10. *Gulyas* v. *Gulyas*, 75 Mich. App. 138, 254 N.W. 2d 818 (1977). According to Nancy Polikoff's review of the *Gulyas* case (op. cit.): "There was no evidence that the father spent any more time with his child than her mother did. The record offered no factual support for an implicit finding that the mother's career, and not the father's, interfered with the giving of love, affection, and guidance to the child.

"It should be noted that the child in *Gulyas* has resided with her mother for over one and a half years during the marital separation, but the father had snatched her in New York four months before the hearing. As a result, the judge gave the father an edge on the factor of continuity."

11. *Simmons* v. *Simmons*, 223 Kansas 639, 576 P. 2d 598 (1978).

12. *In re the Marriage of Milovich*, 105 Ill. App. 3d 596, 434 N.E. 2d. 811 (1982).

13. Judge Duran's decision was discussed in the *National Law Journal* on September 26, 1983. His opinion is partly paraphrased. Margaret Gaines

(Mrs. Raoul Bezou) appealed this decision. Judge Duran's decision was upheld on June 28, 1983.

A. *Raoul Bezou* v. *Margaret Gaines, wife of A. Raoul Bezou,* Court of Appeal of Louisiana, June 28, 1983.

14. Tina Fishman was originally awarded legal custody of Riva in Indiana. She then lived with Riva in Illinois for seven years, where her order was recognized as valid. Ted Fishman moved to California after the original Indiana custody order. Riva visited and was detained by him in California. Tina was a member of the Revolutionary Communist Party. Its members— American citizens—demonstrated in Washington to protest the state visit of the Communist Chinese Premier. Tina was arrested, indicted, and acquitted for exercising her civil rights.

15. *In re the Marriage of Fishman,* Superior Court of the State of California, #255665. Commissioner Browning had spearheaded the government investigations of the Revolutionary Union (forerunner of the Revolutionary Communist Party) in the early 1970s. As the U.S. attorney in San Francisco he had also presided over Patricia Hearst's trial.

16. Leslie Guevarra, *San Francisco Examiner,* quoting Judge Ragan, June 24, 1983.

17. Communication from Tina Fishman's Defense Committee.

18. *Anon.* v. *Anon.,* reported in the *New York Law Journal,* July 20, 1981. This mother is convicted by her own hand. The diary allows or forces her to convict herself. In reading this decision, I was reminded of a study by Shirley Angrist that I described in *Women and Madness* (1972). The ex-mental patients returned to the mental asylum by their husbands were the same as those not returned except for one thing. The returnees refused to do any housework, cooking, shopping, or cleaning.

In a number of decisions mothers lost custody of their children for a combination of "life-style" reasons. This includes economic and working status, social and sexual status, and political or religious status. For example, in New York in 1982, another mother was found less fit by the judge to have custody of two girls (eleven and eight) because her own best interests and social life appeared to be of "paramount concern to the exclusion of best interests of her children." She (presumably) left the eight- and eleven-year-olds alone until late at night. She permitted a male friend to stay in the apartment and share her bed. She failed to take the children to Sabbath services (Frederwitzer v. Frederwitzer, 55 NY 2d 89, Ct. of App. 2/16/82).

19. Roxanne Pulitzer lost her appeal of the custody decision in April 1984. Herbert sharply curtailed her visitation (during a subsequent period of "intimacy"), when she asked for an increase in alimony, in December 1984. The judge denied Roxanne's request for $38,000 in legal fees, and cut it

back to $26,000 in March 1985. "The judge was apparently unimpressed by Roxanne's claims that her $160 earnings as an aerobics instructor can't cover her monthly expenses of $2740." I obtained this information from coverage in the *New York Times, New York Post,* and *Miami Herald.*

The *Pulitzer* appeal is: *Pulitzer* v. *Pulitzer,* 449 Southern Reporter, 2nd Series 370, May 24, 1984.

This middle-class standard of maternal "fitness" had been used against the upper-class mother in the notorious Vanderbilt custody trial. See Barbara Goldsmith, *Little Gloria: Happy at Last* (New York: Dell, 1981).

Mothers who inherited wealth in their own names or whose wealth derived from their marriages have been custodially challenged and punished for their sexual, social, and political activities. For example, the English aristocrat Julia Strachey lost custody of her mother when she was five years old, in the early part of the twentieth century.

"On the surface, Julia's was a heritage of enviable privilege. Her father, one of Lytton Strachey's brothers and a product of Eton and Balliol, was a failed concert pianist who was given a sinecure with the East India Railway Company by his father, Sir Richard, the Company's chairman. Born in India, Julia always remembered her first few years as 'a perfect paradise' of family life. Then the idyll was shattered.

" 'I was five years old when the guillotine fell,' she recalled later. Her parents were divorcing, although Julia was not told the truth about that or anything else. Her adored mother, pregnant by another man, took Julia to Rome with her and then sent her on to England in the care of a temporary nursemaid. Her mother's assurances that she would soon follow proved heartbreakingly false; Julia did not see her mother again for decades, and it was years before she learned that her father, who remained in India at the time, had forbidden his departing wife to have any contact with Julia. Deposited with an elderly English aunt and an 'unbelievably repressive and grim' Scottish nanny, Julia was inconsolable, rarely speaking except when overcome by her frequent 'despairing fits of crying.' "—Leslie Bennets, *New York Times Book Review* (October 16, 1983), review of *Julia: A Portrait of Julia Strachey by Herself and Frances Partridge* (Boston: Little, Brown & Co., 1983).

In the 1930s the Lindbergh child was kidnapped. Mrs. Gloria Vanderbilt became a widow. Her governess, her ex-husband's sister, Mrs. Gertrude Whitney, and her own mother, Mrs. Morgan, challenged her right to custody on several grounds and in various ways. Gloria was a "social butterfly, also (presumably) promiscuous, an adulteress, and a lesbian. Her own child was now deathly afraid of her. Barbara Goldsmith, op. cit.

In the 1940s, Woolworth heiress Barbara ("Babs") Hutton was custodially (and economically) challenged by her Danish husband, Count Reventlow (A. E. Hotchner, *Choice People* [New York: Morrow, 1984]).

In the 1950s the wealthy film actress Joan Fontaine was custodially challenged by her ex-husband, William Dozier, for their daughter, Debbie. Her right to a sexual life, to a "career," to travel, and to take Debbie along with her—all were at issue (Charles Higham, *Sisters* [New York: Coward-McCann, 1984]).

In the 1960s Sarah, the battered wife of the wealthy singer Bob Dylan, was custodially as well as economically challenged, as was the wife of Dr. James Murphy, who later became Mrs. Nelson Rockefeller. Happy Rockefeller lost legal custody of her four children by her first husband and of her fifth child, presumably a blood child of Nelson Rockefeller's, because she had committed adultery with Rockefeller and because she wanted a divorce from her first husband.

In the early 1970s Yoko Ono lost her daughter to "kidnapping" custody because she committed adultery and moved in with her future husband, John Lennon. Quite by accident, years later, I found myself interviewing a psychiatrist who had been part of that kidnapping conspiracy. He justified his actions, these many years later, by saying "Yoko Ono was too ambitious. She was going to leave her first husband with nothing. She was moving into the big time and was going to get everything. Why should she also have his child?" To the best of my knowledge, Yoko Ono has never been able to find this child again.

20. The *Pulitzer* v. *Pulitzer* decision was reported in the *New York Post* in 1983; her appeal was reported on April 19, 1984.

21. *Simmons* v. *Simmons*, 223 Kan. 639, 576, P. 2d 589 (1978); *Blonsky* v. *Blonsky*, 84 Ill. App. 3d 810, 405 N.E. 2d 112 (1980).

There are many, many cases in which the mother's sexuality is the key issue. In 1983 a mother in Louisiana lost custody solely because she openly lived with a man for eight months before marrying him (*Stewart* v. *Stewart*, 430 S. 2d, 189, La. App. 2 Cir. 1983). Some other recent cases are: *Krabel* v. *Krabel*, 12/18/81, summarized in 8 *FLR* 2249, v. 8, #18; *Ryan* v. *Ryan*, Mo. Ct. App. E. Dist., 5/17/83, summarized in 9 *FLR* 2489; *Cleeton* v. *Cleeton*, 6 *FLR* 2577; *Stephenson* v. *Stephenson*, La. Sup. Ct. 9/28/81, 7 *FLR* 2774.

As recently as 1978 in Kansas and in 1980 in Illinois, fathers with live-in girlfriends (who slept with them in studio apartments when children also slept over) won custody away from "working" mothers because *they* had live-in boyfriends. Attorney Nancy Polikoff commented on the Kansas case: "The [Kansas] court felt that the mother's work, but not the father's, interfered with childcare. Both parents had sexual relationships. The mother was engaged, and although her fiancé sometimes spent the night with her, the children were unaware of any sexual activity. The fiancé also stopped spending the night when it was suggested that this behavior would jeopardize the mother's custody.

"The father lived with his woman friend, and on two of his three visits to the children prior to filing the change of custody suit his woman friend accompanied him and they stayed overnight with the children in one hotel room. The father remarried five days after he filed for custody. The judge's derogatory references to the mother's 'social interests' and 'private life' presumably referred to her relationship while no attention was paid to the father's conduct" (Polikoff, "Gender and Child-Custody Determinations: Exploding the Myths").

22. *Bunim* v. *Bunim*, 273 App Div 861, 76 N.Y.S. 2d 456 (Feb. 10, 1948).

23. Ibid.

24. *Grimditch* v. *Grimditch,* 71 Ariz. 198, 225 P.2d. 489 (1950).

25. Ibid. In Maryland in 1967 a remarried Mr. Miller sued his ex-wife for sole custody of their three children on the ground that she had verbally "confessed" to a two-month adulterous affair. The ex-Mrs. Miller was allowed to retain custody because, in the presiding judge's opinion, "There had been a true repentance of the illicit relationship. When the mother realized that her relationship with the children was jeopardized by this one affair, she broke off relations and has not seen the man. . . . [Since the divorce the mother] has not had improper relations with a subsequent admirer. . . . [The children] seemed to have good training in school, church and home, for much of which the mother was responsible." *Miller* v. *Miller,* 228 *Atlantic Reporter,* 2nd Series, April 8, 1967, pp. 311–312.

26. *Blain* v. *Blain*, Ark. 346, 168, S.W. 2nd, 807 (1943).

27. *Blackburn* v. *Blackburn*, 249 Ga. 689, 292 S.E. 2d., 821 (1982). *Blackburn* v. *Blackburn*, 168 Ga. App. 66, 308 S.E. 2d., 19 (1983).

28. Judge Hawkins's and Kathleen Blackburn's comments were quoted by Katie Wood in the *Florida Times Union,* September 7, 1983. There is another case similar to the Blackburn case (*Palmore* v. *Sidoti,* Fl. Ct. App. 2nd District 1982). According to *Off Our Backs* (June 1984): "Melanie Sidoti, who is now six, went to live with her mother when the Sidotis divorced in 1980. Two years later a Florida court of law decided to protect Melanie from the 'social stigmatization that was sure to follow' from continuing to live with her mother and her mother's husband, Clarence Palmore. The judge awarded custody of Melanie to her father, a white man who had remarried a white woman. This April 26, the Supreme Court unanimously struck down that ruling.

"What was not decided, however, was the outcome of the custody battle. One day after the Supreme Court decision, Anthony Sidoti, who now lives in Texas, was able to obtain a temporary restraining order from Judge Tom McDonald, Jr., forbidding Palmore to remove Melanie from her father's custody. *In These Times* reported in mid-May that the action would give

Sidoti 'a few more weeks to come up with a tactic to try to win Melanie permanently.'

"Linda Sidoti Palmore put in an emergency request to Chief Justice Burger asking him to block the Texas court's attempt to interfere in the case. Burger ignored the request, though he did return the case to Florida rather than wait until May 20, when the Supreme Court ruling would normally take effect.

"In the meantime, *In These Times* reports that Sidoti seems to have the support of his local community in Bryant, the small town in which he and his new wife, and Melanie now live; he was able to raise $6,000 in court expenses by raffling off a rifle."

In a related case, *New York Womannews,* quoting *Off Our Backs* (May 1984), reported that "Michigan Judge Daner convicted Frederick Luna of having murdered his wife with an ax, but downgraded the charge from murder to manslaughter when he learned Luna killed his wife after learning she was having an affair with a black man. What was at stake, the judge said, was 'not only an infidelity—and I do not wish to be called a racist, but we are in a court of law and a spade must be called a spade—but infidelity with a Black man.' "

29. *Schuster* v. *Schuster,* No. D–36863 (Washington Sup. Ct. King Cty., Dec. 22, 1972); and *Isaacson* v. *Isaacson,* D–36867 (Washington Sup. Ct. King Cty., Dec. 22, 1972).

In *Schuster* and *Isaacson* and, for example, in *People* v. *Brown* (1973), a judge allowed a lesbian mother to keep her child under certain conditions; or decided that lesbianism per se was not relevant to a determination of parental fitness. Cited by D. R. A. Basile, "Lesbian Mothers I," *Women's Rights Law Reporter,* vol. 2, no. 2 (December 1974).

The first recorded lesbian mother case was *Nadler* v. *Superior Court Cal.* (1967). The mother lost on the grounds of her lesbianism at the trial level, and upon appeal.

30. *In re Matthews* (California, 1975), reported by Donna J. Hitchens and Barbara E. Price, "Trial Strategy in Lesbian Mother Custody Cases," *Golden Gate Law Review,* 9:451–479 (1979).

31. *In re Tammy F.,* 1 Civ. No. 32648 (Cal. 1st App. Dist., Div. 2, August 21, 1973); and *In re Deanna P.,* No. 10447–J (Sup. Ct. Sonoma Cty., July 12, 1973).

Ms. Driber and Ms. Koop, two lesbian mothers, were living together with their children. Ms. Driber was awarded custody of her three children. Ms. Koop, tried on the same day by a different judge, lost custody of two of her three children, although all three stated that they wanted to live with their mother. The other two were sent to live with their father, but when they ran away several times Ms. Koop filed for custody, claiming that their behavior constituted a change in circumstance. The judge denied the request and ordered the children to be placed in a juvenile home when they said that they would not return to their father. They were later given into the custody of their married half-sister. The judge ultimately decided that the children should remain in the "neutral" home of the half-sister because it would not be in the children's "best interests" to live with their mother.

Driber v. *Driber*, No. 220748, Wash. Super. Ct., Pierce County, Sept. 7, 1973, and *In re Koop*, nos. 28218 and 28219 (Wash. Superior Court, Pierce County, Juvenile Dept. Feb. 6, 1976), cited in "Lesbian Mother Custody Cases," an unpublished paper by Robin G. Burdulis.

32. This California case is a "closed case." It was reported to me by San Francisco attorney Donna Hitchens, the director of the Lesbian Legal Rights Project (1983).

33. Ruth Snyder's account of what happened is contained in a 1928 interview in the *New York Mirror* while she was on death row, waiting to be electrocuted. Ann Jones quotes it and describes the case, op. cit.

34. Ibid. According to Jones, Willard Mack, the district attorney, arguing "that both Gray and Snyder should be executed, gave away the vindictiveness behind the equal rights argument. [She] has wanted 'ONE BED' with her lover, Mack said. Let her have 'ONE CHAIR.' . . . [Ruth] claimed for herself sexual prerogatives that belonged only to men: through her execution the full implications of 'equality' could be brought home to feminists and flappers alike."

35. Ann Jones makes this point and presents many cases of battered women's mistreatment by the law. Also see Susan Schecter, *Women and Male Violence: The Visions and Struggles of the Battered Women's Movement* (Boston: South End Press, 1982).

36. Jones, op. cit.

37. Jones is quoting the first detective assigned to the case, "Jerry Piering, a Catholic father of six," one of the jurors, and many, many reporters.

For a good book on the Alice Crimmins case, see Kenneth Gross, *The Alice Crimmins Case* (New York: Knopf, 1975). *People* v. *Crimmins*, 33 A.D. 2d. 793 307 N.Y.S. 2d. 81 (1969). *People* v. *Crimmins*, 26 N.Y. 2d. 319, 310 N.Y.S. 2d. 300 (1970). *People* v. *Crimmins*, 41 A.D. 2d. 933, 343 N.Y.S. 2d. 203 (1973). *People* v. *Crimmins*, 48 A.D. 2d. 663, 367 N.Y.S. 2d. 532 (1975). *People* v. *Crimmins*, 381 N.Y.S. 2d. 1, 343 N.E. 2d. 719 (1975).

38. Ibid.

39. Ibid.

40. Men psychologically project a great deal of their own insatiable sense of imperfection onto both women and nature. They then attempt to "perfect"

both, instead of themselves, for peace of mind and for profit. Paradoxically, while men fear untamed nature in women, they also despise and rebel against women who oppose a little male "fun"—i.e., drunkenness, debauchery, corruption, etc.

41. I will be quoting from two *Medeas:* Euripides' (contained in *The Complete Greek Tragedies,* translated by Rex Warner, introduced by Richard Lattimore [Chicago: University of Chicago Press, and London: 1955]) and Robinson Jeffers's, as "freely adapted" (New York: Samuel French, Inc., 1948).

42. Here Medea embodies the patriarchal "good girl" who must leave her parents and her homeland, never to return, to live in her husband's house and to bear her husband's children.

43. Marrying Creon's daughter Glauce confers Corinthian citizenship upon Jason. By renouncing Medea, but asking her to stay on he is "demoting" her to the position of hetaera—a legal prostitute/male companion. As such Medea would have no rights whatsoever to dwell within the city without being "kept"—and complying with every whim of her "keeper."

A legal prostitute cannot be employed anywhere, by anyone, for any reason; she cannot trade in the marketplace or take advantage of the considerable state benefits afforded to citizens. Jason's offer to make "some provisions" for a legal prostitute, or to keep her sons, is a reasonable offer by Greek ("civilized") standards. The offer outrages Medea.

44. Euripides, op. cit.

45. In Jeffers's play, op. cit., Medea refuses to let Jason bury her sons. She says:

> . . . You would betray even the little bodies:
> coin them for silver.
> Sell them for power.

46. Ibid. Euripides's *Medea,* op. cit., says:

> Let no one think me a weak one, feeble-spirited,
> A stay-at-home, but rather just the opposite,
> One who can hurt my enemies and help my friends;
> For the lives of such persons are most remembered.

47. Jeffers, op. cit.

48. Ibid.

49. Euripides, op. cit. If she does not kill her "enemies," then she is not the "barbarian" Medea, but some other woman, a humbled Greek woman perhaps.

50. Jeffers, op. cit.

51. Euripides, op. cit.

52. Why does Medea *have* to kill her children? Why can't she just take them with her in her dragon-drawn chariot? Can't a half-goddess and priestess find some way to avoid poverty and ostracism?

But Medea is as mortal as she is divine. "Magical" solutions are available to her only in the service of inevitable tragedy. "Magical" solutions (such as saving Jason's children) would not destroy Jason. Nor would they punish Medea for having renounced her "barbarian" ways.

53. Medea's murder of her brother (king-consort?) constitutes the murder of a sacred blood tie. It is not a ceremonial murder. It is done for "love" of Jason, not as part of a pre-ordained religious ritual. As such it is a profound betrayal of Medea's own self; of her religion, family, and homeland. This betrayal dooms Medea.

Medea's offstage murders haunt us precisely because they are so invisible, so impersonal. Are her murders part of a "foreign" ceremony? Are they reminders of the son-consort-king's ritual death, presided over by priestesses, memories of pagan "crucifixion," now forbidden?

According to Barbara G. Walker, quoting Briffault and Herodotus, "Mycenaean Demeter made a god of the sacrificial victim Pelops by resurrecting him from her magic cauldron. The same regenerative magic was performed by Demeter's Colchian counterpart Medea, who came into Hellenic myth as a mortal queen, but who was an eponymous Crone Mother of the Medes. Her name meant "Wisdom." She was known as an all-healer; our word medicine descended from her." Barbara G. Walker, *The Crone, Woman of Age, Wisdom and Power* (New York: Harper & Row, 1985).

54. Euripides first presented and won a prize for his *Medea* in 431 B.C. in Athens. His audience was long familiar with the figure and with the clash of cultures the play represents.

In classical Greece and Rome, fathers, not mothers, had the legal right to commit infanticide. (Oedipus' father did so, although it did lead to his downfall.) Fathers also had the right to own, abuse, or kill their slaves, their prostitutes, and their wives.

Classical Greek and Roman literature is *about* the male right to wage war for the sake of male "honor" as well as for greed or adventure. Few women are depicted engaged in such "heroic" tasks. (A legendary band of Amazons do come to fight at Troy, to preserve it. Homer describes them with beauty and power.) See Homer's *Odyssey* and *Iliad*, and Vergil's *Aeneid*, for many examples of this.

CHAPTER THREE: WHAT IS A FIT MOTHER AND FATHER? AN UNFIT MOTHER AND FATHER? WHO DECIDES?

1. Judith Arcana, *Every Mother's Son* (New York: Doubleday-Anchor, 1983).

2. Ibid.

3. The biblical Abraham didn't ask his wife Sarah for permission to sacrifice their son Isaac. See my book *About Men* for a discussion of this in contemporary terms (New York: Simon & Schuster, 1978; Bantam, 1980).

4. This is how slaves or prisoners are treated—when revolt is feared when one prisoner has tried to escape or fight back. Most mothers do not view themselves as "alike" or as "imprisoned."

5. We forget that Oedipus' father, Laius, ordered his newborn son placed on a mountaintop to die. We do not remember Oedipus' mother, Jocasta, as the "good" mother who saved her son. We remember her as the "bad" mother who, many years later, married him.

    In the twentieth century, Laius has actually been popularized, psychoanalytically, as his *son's* victim. Few experts theorize about the "Laiusian" complex among fathers.

6. Philippe Arriès, *Centuries of Childhood: A Social History of Family Life* (New York: Knopf, 1962); Badinter, op. cit.; David Bakan, *Slaughter of the Innocents: A Study of the Battered Child Phenomenon* (Boston: Beacon Press, 1971); Cott and Pleck, eds., op. cit. (Touchstone, 1980); Ruth H. Bloch, "American Feminine Ideals in Transition: The Rise of the Moral Mother, 1785–1815," *Feminist Studies*, 4 (June 1978), and "Untangling the Roots of Modern Sex Roles," *Signs*, 4 (Winter 1978); Ann Dally, *Inventing Motherhood: The Consequences of an Ideal Childhood* (New York: Schocken Books, 1981); Carl Degler, *At Odds: Women and the Family in America, from the Revolution to the Present* (New York: Oxford University Press, 1980); Lloyd de Mause, ed., *The History of Childhood* (New York: Harper & Row, 1974); John Demos, *Entertaining Satan* (New York: Oxford University Press, 1982); Alice Miller, *For Your Own Good: Hidden Cruelty in Child-Rearing and the Roots of Violence* (New York: Farrar, Straus & Giroux, 1983); Morton Schatzman, *Soul Murder: Persecution in the Family* (New York: Random House, 1983); Abigail Stewart, David G. Winter, and David A. Jones, "Coding Categories for the Study of Child-Rearing from Historical Sources," *Journal of Interdisciplinary History* 5 (Spring 1975).

7. Miller, op. cit.

8. Demos, op. cit.

9. Degler, op. cit.

10. Bloch, "American Feminine Ideals in Transition: The Rise of the Moral Mother, 1785–1815"; Bloch, "Untangling the Roots of Modern Sex Roles: A Survey of Four Centuries of Change," loc. cit.; Degler, op. cit.; Badinter, op. cit. Badinter suggests that too many children died in infancy, that colonialist European countries wanted their native populations to survive, and that mothers were viewed as crucial to this effort.

11. Jean Jacques Rousseau as quoted by Badinter, op. cit. Badinter also notes the economic and ideological advantages involved in persuading large numbers of women to concentrate on (unpaid) child care rather than on employment and single motherhood.

12. Dr. Daniel G. M. Schreber has been used as an example of an exceedingly popular and influential nineteenth-century scientific father whose harsh "regimes" probably led to his own son's insanity and, in psychoanalyst Wilhelm Reich's and Alice Miller's opinions, also led to the twentieth-century "obedience" of the German masses to charismatic fascism. See Badinter, op. cit.; Dally, op. cit.; and Schatzman, op. cit.

13. Ann Dally reviews Schreber's twentieth-century English counterpart, Dr. Truby King. King recommended "a scheme of rigidly regular four-hour feedings. No baby was to be fed until the clock struck, no matter how much he cried. Most particularly, they were not to be fed at night. They had to learn to sleep at the proper times and not be allowed to manipulate and dominate their mothers by their demands. Regularity of bowel movements was important and he advised pot-training from the age of two months, aided by enemas if the baby did not perform."

14. Ibid. I have drawn on Dally's review of D. W. Winnicott, R. Spitz, and J. Bowlby.

15. Ibid. Dally notes that such beliefs made it unnecessary for the British government to provide tax-supported child care. Nor was private industry pressured to provide on-site child care or other benefits for its parent-employees.

16. In the late nineteenth century, the most "moral" of full-time middle-class wives and mothers were probably plagued by maternal guilt. In 1887, Charlena Anderson wrote to her husband that her "daily round of household chores [is] overwhelming and difficult to organize. She recognized that a mother could not adequately care for the children and maintain a house at the same time. If only she had 'relief from the time-consuming details of housekeeping,' she wrote her husband in 1887, so that she might spend more time with the children. 'Every night when I go to bed my heart sinks at the thought of opportunities lost for drawing out some faculty or doing just a little toward it, for directing them into better habits, or for having

some pleasant impressions upon minds.' " Charlena Anderson, 1887, quoted by Degler, op. cit.

17. See Barbara Ehrenreich and Deidre English, *For Her Own Good* (New York: Doubleday-Anchor, 1978). The authors analyze the ultimately destructive influence exerted over mothers by nineteenth- and twentieth-century experts in obstetrics and gynecology. Tempting promises were made to mothers in this area also.

18. Donald Winnicott, quoted by Dally, op. cit.

19. I am thinking about Sigmund Freud's Oedipal theory and its widespread acceptance by other experts and by ordinary people (*Sigmund Freud, The Basic Writings of Sigmund Freud*, trans. and ed. A. A. Brill [New York: Modern Library, 1938], and *Moses and Monotheism* [New York: Random House Vintage Books, 1939]). See my book *About Men*, and Judith Arcana's *Our Mother's Daughters* (Calif.: Shameless Hussy Press, 1980) for some interpretations of why Freud and so many other child development experts remained silent about (or denied) the existence of tyrannical, incestuous, or cruelly absent fathers.

20. Louise Armstrong, *The Home Front: Notes from the Family War Zone* (New York: McGraw-Hill, 1983); Judith Lewis Herman, *Father-Daughter Incest* (Cambridge, Mass.: Harvard University Press, 1981); Ann Jackowitz, "Anna O./Bertha Peppenheim and Me," *Between Women* (eds.) Carol Ascher, Louise De Salvo, and Sara Ruddick (Boston: Beacon Press, 1984); Jeffrey Moussaieff Masson, *The Assault on Truth: Freud's Suppression of the Seduction Theory* (New York: Farrar, Straus & Giroux, 1984); Florence Rush, *The Best Kept Secret: The Sexual Abuse of Children* (Englewood Cliffs, N.J.: Prentice-Hall, 1980).

21. Compared to what? To past non-reports on child abuse? Child-abuse data are based on official reports, not on studies of incidence. Reports are not filed in each state equally, nor do they always indicate the severity and kind of abuse involved. Reports do not always indicate the abuser's sex, nor do they define "abuse" in psychologically complex ways.

22. Naomi Feigelson Chase, *A Child Is Being Beaten: Violence Against Children, an American Tragedy* (New York: Holt, Rinehart, & Winston, 1975).

23. Leontine Young, *Wednesday's Children* (New York: McGraw-Hill, 1964), cited by Chase, op. cit.

24. Chase, op. cit.

25. David Gil, ed., *Violence Against Children: Physical Child Abuse in the United States* (New York: AMS Press, 1978).

26. Gil's composite of "serious" child abusers, based on 6,110 cases, was under twenty-five; had appeared before in family courts; had been in foster care; had an annual income of under $3,500, and/or were single mothers.

27. Chase, op. cit.

28. This study was done by Drs. Byron Egelund, Ellen Farber, et al. I did not read the study itself—only the newspaper coverage of the study. My point here was not to analyze the study's methodology but to rely on newspaper accounts, the way most people do, to draw certain emotional conclusions. If I or the newspapers have in any way misrepresented or drawn the wrong conclusions about this study, I apologize (*New York Times*, December 20, 1983).

29. If our state fathers pay attention to such a study, it is doubtful they will triple the welfare levels and expand support services to single mothers in order that they can "nurture" well. The state is more likely to use such a study to justify forced abortion and sterilization among such a maternal population.

I interviewed ten unfit mothers for this chapter. Eight mothers called me in response to an ad for "mothers who were involved in custody battles." Some mothers responded to the ad because they wanted sympathy and advice on how to deal with state bureaucrats and with relatives. Two mothers were referred to me by colleagues. Three mothers were black; one was Chicana; six were white.

Of the ten, 80 percent were teenage mothers; 60 percent were unwed; 80 percent were very poor. No mother was economically supported by her child's father or by her own parents. Most mothers were, in fact, *persecuted* by their own families and by the state when they were children and when they gave birth to children.

Ninety percent of these mothers did not starve, beat, torture, abandon, or try to kill their child or children. They were, however, unable to provide emotional care and an adequate level of economic care. Two mothers (20 percent) were, in my clinical opinion, suffering from mental illness.

Most of these mothers could, in my opinion, have been helped to assume more responsibility for their children. Certainly they could have maintained regular contact with them. This would have required massive infusions of emotional, economic, and educational support. This particular group of unfit mothers had no truly vicious or callously sadistic member. Another group might have such mothers.

These unfit mothers did not present themselves as unjustly accused—only as unjustly punished. I would not want to be the child victim of any one of these mothers. However, they are unfit—not inhuman. They are not fire-breathing dragons.

30. In 1979 Lenore E. Walker (*The Battered Woman* [New York: Harper & Row, 1979]) estimated that 50 percent of all married women in America were or would be battered in marriage. In 1980 Drs. Murray Straus, Richard Gelles, and Suzanne Steinmetz (*Behind Closed Doors: Violence in the American Family* [New York: Doubleday-Anchor, 1980]) estimated a domestic violence rate of 50 to 60 percent based on a 28 percent *reported*

rate. In 1980 Irene Frieze ("Causes and Consequences of Marital Rape," a paper presented at the American Psychological Association meeting, Montreal, Canada, September 1980) reported that 34 percent of geographically selected women reported "some marital violence."

In 1982 Dr. Diana E. H. Russell (*Rape in Marriage* [New York: Macmillan, 1982]) reported that "21 percent of her [randomly selected] 644 women who had ever been married reported being subjected to physical violence by a husband at some time in their lives." Dr. Russell explained the discrepancy between her own estimate and Dr. Frieze's estimate as a function of Frieze's "much broader definition of marital violence." She also noted that Walker's estimate was extrapolated from a battered female population.

In 1983 the National Center of Child Abuse and Neglect reported that "the number of women beaten yearly by their husbands ranges from two to six million." Of 18,000 incidents of domestic violence *reported* in 1983, women were the victims 86 percent of the time (*New York Times*, December 11, 1983). This study was based on reported cases in New Jersey from January to September 1983 (reported in the *New York Times*, October 5, 1983).

In 1984 Dr. Louie Andrews ("Family Violence in the Florida Panhandle," *Ms.* magazine [March 1984]) found that "one in six wives [surveyed] say their husbands force them to have intercourse against their wills. One in eight say their husbands physically abuse them or threaten them with weapons. One out of 23 wives surveyed were threatened with guns by their husbands. One in 66 had the guns actually fired at them." These findings are extrapolated from a survey of 400 married women who *did not* fit the classic description of the isolated, abused wife. The incidence of wife battering and abuse may actually be higher among more isolated wives. The original survey was conducted by Drs. Louie Andrews and Diane Patrick.

31. Mildred D. Pagelow conducted a study of 306 battered mothers between 1976 and 1980. Of the mothers in her study, 76 percent reported that their children were present at the beatings. One-third of all the children were victims of parental violence as well, half of them beaten in conjunction with their mothers, half of them separately: Mildred D. Pagelow, "Children in Violent Families," in *Young Children and Their Families*, eds. Shirley Hill and B. J. Barnes (Boston: Lexington Books, 1982). See also Mildred D. Pagelow, "Violence in Families: Is There an Intergenerational Transmission?," paper prepared for a meeting of the Society for the Study of Social Problems, 1982.

A 1980 study of hyperactive and socially deviant boys reemphasizes the correlation between a child's disruptive behavior and wife or child abuse. The researchers found a high rate of psychiatric disorders among the fathers of boys who exhibited antisocial conduct. Boys who were unusually aggressive tended to have fathers who were alcoholic, antisocial, and physically abusive to their wives (Mark A. Steward, C. Susan DeBlois, and Claudette Cummings, "Psychiatric Disorder in the Parents of Hyperactive Boys and Those with Conduct Disorders," *Journal of Child Psychology and Psychiatry,* 21 [1980]).

According to Elaine Hilberman's 1977 study of battered wives, "half of the women we studied reported violence between their parents (usually the father assaulting the mother)." (Elaine Hilberman, "Overview: The Wife-Beater's Wife Reconsidered," *American Journal of Psychiatry,* 137 [November 1980]: 11).

32. See Chapters 9 and 14. Armstrong, op. cit.; Kathleen Brady, *Kiss Daddy Goodnight: A Speak Out on Incest* (New York: Hawthorn, 1978); Herman, op. cit.; Mary Haneman Lystad, "Sexual Abuse in the Home: A Review of the Literature," *International Journal of Family Psychiatry, 1982: The Urban and Social Change Review,* 15, 2 (1982). U.S. Department of Health and Human Services, *Sexual Abuse of Children* (Washington, D.C.: Government Printing Office, 1980); Masson, op. cit.; Rush, op. cit.; William Stacey and Anson Shupe, *The Family Secret: Domestic Violence in America* (Boston: Beacon Press, 1983); Walker, op. cit.

33. Russell, op. cit., and "Incest: An Unpublished Study of Incidence," 1983. Russell's random sample survey of women for her study of marital rape also asked about childhood sexual abuse. Her findings will be published in 1986. (Personal communication, 1983). Incest includes stepfathers within the home.

34. Dr. Mary Rimsza, quoted in the *New York Times,* April 4, 1984. It is unclear whether Rimsza is talking about incest plus a variety of other sexual crimes against children, committed by older brothers, uncles, schoolteachers, etc.

35. Dr. David Finkelhor, quoted in *Newsweek* (May 14, 1984).

36. Mothers sometimes "confess" to child abuse in order to keep the family intact or in the false belief that they will receive lighter sentences than men. The ideal mother is not supposed to accuse her children's economic provider and "symbolic" father of child abuse.

When she does, the church counsels patience and prayer; psychological experts wonder whether the abuse has really occurred; the state is reluctant to invade a father's castle—especially if he pays the rent on it. As we have seen, the state will invade a "poor" man's castle more quickly than a wealthy man's castle. Women have no castles. If they do and they live in them alone, they are physically and custodially vulnerable to any man who enters or pays any of the bills there.

When it is clear that a father has abused his child, church, state, and experts still wonder if the mother isn't "really" to blame—for marrying such a man in the first place, for allowing him to abuse his children, for not seeking help, and for not leaving him sooner.

When a mother flees a domestically violent father, she is immediately punished by the state's imposition of (welfare or wage) poverty and then blamed for impoverishing her children.

37. Sara Ruddick, "Preservative Love and Military Destruction: Some Reflections on Mothering and Peace," *Mothering: Essays in Feminist Theory,* ed. Joyce Treblicot (Totowa, N.J.: Rowman and Allanheld, 1984).

I do not know how "common" an occurrence maternal physical or psychological violence is. Has there ever been a study measuring the incidence of physical and psychological violence toward children, practiced by mothers and compared to fathers who spend the same amount of time with children as mothers do?

38. Paul L. Adams, Judith R. Milner, and Nancy A. Schrepf, *Fatherless Children* (New York: John Wiley & Sons, 1984); N. D. Coletta, "The Impact of Divorce: Father Absence or Poverty?" *Journal of Divorce,* 3, 1 (1979): 27–36; M. E. Lamb, ed., *The Role of the Father in Child Development* (New York: John Wiley & Sons, 1976); David B. Lynn, *The Father: His Role in Child Development* (Belmont, Calif.: Wadsworth, 1974); J. O. Wisdom, "The Role of the Father in the Minds of Parents, in Psychoanalytic Theory and in the Life of the Infant," *International Review of Psycho-Analysis,* 3 (1976): 231–39; E. Herzog and C. E. Sudia, "Fatherless Homes: A Review of Research," *Children,* 15, 5 (September–October 1968), pp. 177–82.

39. Adams et al., op. cit.

40. Often these researchers have observed or studied what fathers experimentally (not actually) *do* with their children, what fathers *think* they do, and what fathers say they would *like* to do.

41. For reviews of this research, see Adams et al., op. cit.; Grace Baruch and Rosalind Barnett, *Life Patterns* (New York: McGraw-Hill, 1983); S. W. Leonard, "How First Time Fathers Feel Toward Their Newborn," *American Journal of Maternal Child Nursing* (November–December 1976); Robert MacTurk, P. Nettelbladt, N. Uddenberg, and I. Englesson, "Father-Child Relationship: Background Factors in the Father," *Acta Psychiatrica Scandinavia,* 61 (1980); Frank Pederson, ed., Joseph Pleck, *Men's New Roles in the Family: Housework and Child Care,* Institute for Social Research, 1976; V. Reiber, "Is the Nurturing Role Natural to Fathers?," *American Journal of Maternal Child Nursing* (December 1976); Martha Zaslow, Lamb, op. cit.

There are many, many studies I haven't mentioned here.

42. In 1974 one study estimated that fathers spent from 37.7 seconds to 10

minutes and 26 seconds daily with infants (F. Rebelsky and C. Hanks, "Fathers' Verbal Interaction with Infants in the First Three Months of Life," *Child Development* [1971]).

Another 1974 study estimated that fathers spent between 15 and 20 minutes a day with one-year-olds and 16 minutes daily with children between the ages of six and sixteen (P. L. Ban and M. Lewis, "Mothers and Fathers, Girls and Boys: Attachment Behavior in the One-Year Old," *Merrill-Palmer Quarterly* [July 1974]).

A 1976 study found that fathers spent 15 minutes a day feeding their babies, compared to mothers who spent $1^1/_2$ hours a day doing so. Nearly half these fathers had never changed the baby's diapers (I. Rendina and J. D. Dickerschand, "Father Involvement with First-Born Infants," *Family Coordinator* [October 1976], cited by Letty Cottin Pogrebin, *Family Politics* [New York: McGraw-Hill, 1983]).

43. There are always exceptions to this rule. Such exceptional men are probably capable of doing many more domestic and infant-related chores than most men currently perform. However, even exceptional men who perform 50 percent of all domestic and infant-rearing chores are not the same as mothers. They remain (socialized) men, who therefore experience the same things differently from (socialized) women.

44. Adams et al, op. cit. According to Wisdom, op. cit., "The father avoids the nursery where breasts and nurture really matter, fearing his feminine yearnings stirred by the milieu, fearing that his femininity can't compete with his wife's: In his dealings in the nursery, the man's deepest envy is aroused . . . he loses the battle—if there is one—over the nursery, takes second place, and is a sort of second-rate mother, because he wants to avoid any indication of femininity . . . feeling uncertain of masculinity and having a deep-seated identification with motherhood provide him with a problem.

"So though the experts agree that a baby can attach to the father, given the opportunity, it rarely does because both men and women view infant care as women's work."

45. K. E. Walker, "Time Spent in Household Work by Homemakers," *Family Economic Review* (1969), and "Time Spent by Husbands in Household Work," *Family Economics Review* (1970); M. Meissner, et al., "No Exit for Wives: Sexual Division of Labor and the Cumulation of Household Demands," *Canadian Review of Sociology and Anthropology*, 12 (1975); K. Walker and M. Woods, *Time Use: A Measure of Household Production of Family Goods and Services*, Center for the Family, American Home Economics Association, 1976; J. Robinson, *How Americans Use Time: A Social Psychological Analysis* (New York: Praeger, 1977); S. F. Berk, ed., *Women and Household Labor* (Beverly Hills, Calif.: Sage, 1980), cited by Pogrebin, op. cit.

Perhaps there really is little new under the sun. For example, in a study of American missionary mothers in Hawaii, Patricia Grimshaw notes that:

"Some of these [American] missionary women believed that fathers should take a more than nominal part in childrearing. Lucia Smith, as yet unmarried, had watched with dismay how seasick missionary mothers were dispatched to the hold on voyaging with their miserably vomiting children, while selfish fathers sat in peace on the deck. 'I found myself revolving the question in my own mind many times, why all this thrown on the mother? Is it right? I fear I had been in the place of some of them I should have [said] no. Enough of this!!'

"When an *Address to Mothers* was read at the Honolulu Maternal Association stressing the incessant duties of mothers from morning to night till they reached the grave, while they might expect no return for their labors except consciousness of duty done, 'some objections were made to the recent practice of fathers throwing *all* the care and responsibility of training on the Mother.' Over and over women hoped that their husbands would soon be able to play a more active part in the training of the children, but at present they seemed particularly busy. The time seldom seemed to arrive."

Patricia Grimshaw, " 'Christian Woman, Pious Wife, Faithful Mother, Devoted Missionary': Conflicts in Roles of American Missionary Women in Nineteenth-Century Hawaii," *Feminist Studies* 9, 3 (Fall 1983).

46. Drs. Philip Blumstein and Pepper Schwartz, *American Couples* (New York: Morrow, 1983).

47. Pogrebin, op. cit.

One of my interviewees said, "My ex-husband was once unemployed for about a year. I taught full time and rushed home at three, collected the kids, shopped, and cooked dinner. I was very tired by the time I put the kids to bed and finished the dishes. I begged him to cook dinner. He refused. After much battling he agreed to cook every Friday night. He finally cooked dinner about twice a month. We all had to praise him and eat everything. I had to clear the table and do the dishes. Everyone said I had to be very understanding because he wasn't employed."

48. As I have noted, contemporary sons tend to remain silent about their fathers in public—*especially* if their fathers have been abusive. Many daughters who achieve public voices remember their fathers as far more encouraging and "maternal" than their mothers. It is hard for them—and for us—to remember that paternally nurtured daughters who become women of "male" achievement are the exception and not the rule.

Most mothers and fathers do not and cannot nurture their daughters or their sons into public intellectual achievement. This is usually a privilege of class—not of gender. It is also true that most mothers do not "like" daughters to achieve like men, and do little to psychologically nurture them. Dr. Ann Oakley describes a fairly common twentieth-century "memory" of a patient "maternal" father and an angry "masculine" mother in

Taking It Like a Woman: A Personal History (New York: Random House, 1984).

Kate Simon, in *Bronx Primitive* (New York: Harper Colophon, 1982), does describe another kind of father—one less often described by a twentieth-century woman intellectual or artist. She writes: "There were no sacks of candy and cookies, no dolls, no perennial summer that meant America. America was a stern man whose duty it was to cure us of being the cosseted spoiled little beasts our mother and her idiot sisters had allowed to flourish. At the far remove of decades, I can understand how infuriating it was for this indulged semibachelor, [my father] to be saddled with a wife and two noisy children whom he hadn't the courage to abandon nor the wish to live with. Nothing to do but mold us with speed and force into absolute obedience, to make his world more tolerable and, I often suspected, to avenge himself on us for existing."

49. Please see what I've written about the destructive quality of the mother-daughter "bond" and about the lack of circumscribed nature of maternal nurturance for daughters in *Women and Madness*, in *Women, Money and Power* (New York: William Morrow, 1976), and in *With Child,* (New York: Lippincott-Crowell, 1979). Please see what I've written about the mother-son bond in *About Men* (New York: Simon & Schuster, 1978).

There is a growing psychoanalytically oriented feminist literature on the mother-daughter relationship. Most often and deservedly quoted are: E. M. Broner, Nancy Chodorow, Dorothy Dinnerstein, and Adrienne Rich.

50. Drs. Joseph Goldstein, Anna Freud, and Albert J. Solnit, *Beyond the Best Interests of the Child,* new edition with epilogue (New York: Macmillan, The Free Press, 1979). They note that "Children may also be deeply attached to parents with impoverished or unstable personalities . . . where the tie is to adults who are 'unfit' as parents, unbroken closeness to them, especially identification with them, may cease to be a benefit and become a threat. In extreme cases this necessitates state interference. . . . [However,] whatever beneficial qualities a psychological parent may be lacking, he offers the child the chance to beome a wanted and needed member within a family structure; ordinarily this cannot happen even in the institutions where care, safety and stimulation may be provided, but where the individual child has no psychological parents."

51. Miller, op. cit.

52. See Chapters 4, 8, 20, and 21 for a discussion and for reference to the paternal non-payment of child support.

53. See Chapter 4 for this list. More than one and a half years after I chose these chores, the Supreme Court in West Virginia chose the performance of such "chores" as the way to 'identify" the primary and psychological parent

in a custody contest. See Chapter 14 for a discussion of the 1981 West Virginia case known as *Garska* v. *McCoy*.

CHAPTER FOUR: DO "GOOD ENOUGH" MOTHERS STILL LOSE CUSTODY OF THEIR CHILDREN IN NORTH AMERICA TODAY?: THE RESULTS OF AN ORIGINAL STUDY

1. It is hard to chart an "increase" in a previously unstudied area. The following studies all attempt to do so, in different ways, for different reasons, using different kinds of basic materials, and with different degrees of methodological success. From one point of view Lenore J. Weitzman and Ruth B. Dixon have published the most comprehensive and methodologically generalizable study to date (Weitzman and Dixon, op. cit.).

   From another point of view, Nancy D. Polikoff has published the most comprehensive analysis of case law. Polikoff's article is an excellent description of anti-mother judicial trends in contested custody, based on case law (Polikoff, "Gender and Child Custody Determinations: Exploding Myths").

   Attorney Joanne Schulman, of the National Center for Women and Family Law has published alone, and together with Adele Hendrickson, articles on the increase in joint custody awards to fathers from the mid-1970s to the mid-1980s (Schulman and Hendrickson, op. cit.).

   Studies of "child snatching" or parental kidnapping confirm that most parental child kidnappers are fathers, and that this phenomenon has been increasing (Gill, op. cit., and Gelles, op. cit.).

   From yet another point of view are three separate studies by psychologists from which we can *infer* some kind of increase in paternal custody. The studies were done by Dr. Deborah Anna Luepnitz, *Child Custody: A Study of Families After Divorce* (Lexington, Mass.: Lexington Books-D. C. Heath, 1982); Patricia Pascowicz, *Absentee Mothers* (Totowa, N.J.: Allanheld Universe, 1982); and James R. Turner, "Divorced Fathers Who Win Contested Custody of Their Children: An Exploratory Study," *American Journal of Orthopsychiatry*, 54, 3 (July 1984). I read this last study long after I completed my own. In Turner's words, his study is "preliminary" and not "statistically significant." As we shall see, I think his two major motivational patterns among fathers are true, although my interpretation of what a "close" relationship with a child means to such fathers may not be as "positive" as Turner's is.

   A number of other studies also exist regarding an increase in paternal custody when custody is contested. They are each limited methodologically or to a specific geographical region. Based on a study of one New York judge's custodial decisions over a five-year period during the 1970s, in sixty to seventy cases, Michael Wheeler found an "increase" in paternal custody (M. L. Wheeler, *Divided Children: A Legal Guide for Divorcing Parents* [New York: Norton, 1980]).

Betty Blair reports an "increase" in judicial paternal custody decisions in Michigan between 1972 and 1974. This "increase" is based on the recommendations made by court referees to judges in three Michigan counties (Betty Blair, *Detroit News*, March 16, 1976).

Dennis K. Orthner and Ken Lewis suggest an increase in judicial paternal custody in Minnesota based on a survey (Dennis K. Orthner and Ken Lewis, "Evidence of Single Father Competence in Child Rearing," *Family Law Quarterly*, 8 [1970]).

M. Ricke, quoted by Blair, op. cit., reports an increase in paternal custody judicially in the state of Washington, based on a study of three counties, between 1972 and 1974.

The Legal Aid Society of Alameda County, California, reported that of thirteen contested custodial trials in 1979, five (38 percent) resulted in paternal custody (Adele Hendrickson, attorney, Family Law Unit, Oakland, California).

Since the mid-1970s lawyers have *observed* (rather than studied) an increase in the number of divorcing fathers who threaten, fight, and win custody battles in court. For example, attorneys Laurie Woods and Joanne Schulman of the National Center for Women and Family Law; Nancy Polikoff of the Women's Legal Defense Fund, in Washington, D.C.; and Donna Hitchens of the Lesbian Rights Project in San Francisco, California; have observed such an increase in general, and among domestically violent fathers in particular. Fathers' rights lawyers, such as Edward Winter, Jr., Maurice K. Franks, and Ken Lewis, have also observed such an "increase."

2. Weitzman and Dixon, op. cit. This study found that 33 percent of the fathers who fought for custody in 1968, and 37 percent of the fathers who fought for custody in 1972, won custody. This is the most comprehensive and methodologically generalizable study done to date.

3. Ibid.; Lenore J. Weitzman and Ruth B. Dixon, "The Economics of Divorce," *UCLA Law Review*, 28 (1981): 1181, 1245; Ruth Sanders, "Child Support and Alimony," U.S. Bureau of Census, 1983; Nan D. Hunter, "Women and Child Support," in *Families, Politics and Public Policy*, loc. cit.

4. Polikoff, op. cit.

5. Group for the Advancement of Psychiatry, *Divorce, Child Custody and the Family* (New York: Mental Health Materials Center, 1980); K. Lewis, *fare*, 57 (1978): 643–51. They estimate that as of 1976 a half million fathers had custody of their children.

Weitzman and Dixon, op. cit., estimate that 30,000 fathers won sole custody and 10,000 fathers won joint custody each year in the United States.

Patricia Hoff, of the American Bar Association Family Law Section, quoted in the *New York Times,* January 20, 1981.

6. Privately coerced "agreements" to paternal custody remain statistically unstudied. Several researchers, in passing, do note that "more" mothers seem to be "agreeing" to paternal custody.

7. Gill, op. cit. In 1984 Senator Arlen Specter (R-Pa.) also estimated that 100,000 cases yearly are parental kidnappings. Specter is the Chairman of the Senate Sub-Committee on Juvenile Justice.

8. Gelles, op. cit., did not analyze these data as a function of parental gender. In a personal communication he notes that the majority of parental child kidnappings were "probably" carried out by fathers.

9. I am using Weitzman and Dixon's extrapolated estimate of 40,000 cases of paternal custody *each year* beginning in 1977 as a stable and continuous (rather than an increasing) number. I am also arbitrarily using a paternal kidnapping rate of 200,000 each year—less than Gelles's estimate of 459,000 to 751,000; more than Gill's estimate of 100,000 to 125,000 annually.

10. Imprisoned mothers always lose their children when they are arrested. This is a form of state "kidnapping." Between 1974 and 1984 approximately 150,000 mothers were arrested and imprisoned for petty economic crimes. The majority of these mothers were young, poor, black welfare-recipients. Suddenly they were prevented from seeing their children—often for life. This number of 150,000 *mothers* is approximate and probably an underestimate. It is based on many sources. See Chapter 16.

11. Mavis Hetherington, M. Cos, and R. Cox, "Divorcing Fathers," *Family Coordinator* (October 1976) and Mavis Hetherington, et al., "Play and Social Interaction in Children Following Divorce," *Journal of Social Issues,* 35, 4 (1979): 26–49; Deborah Luepnitz, "Children of Divorce: A Review of the Psychological Literature," *Law and Human Behavior,* 2 (1978): 167–79; Judith Wallerstein and Joan Kelly, *Surviving the Break Up* (New York: Basic Books, 1980).

12. Kelen Gersick, "Father by Choice: Divorced Men Who Received Custody of Their Children," in *Divorce and Separation,* eds. G. Levinger and O. Moles (New York: Basic Books, 1979); K. Rosenthal and H. Keshet, *Fathers Without Partners* (Totowa, N.J.: Rowman and Littlefield, 1981); Judith Greif, "Fathers, Children and Joint Custody," *American Journal of Orthopsychiatry* (1979): 311–19. M. Roman and W. Haddad, *The Disposable Parent* (New York: Holt, Rinehart & Winston, 1978).

13. Luepnitz, *Child Custody,* op. cit.

14. Pascowicz, op. cit., 61 percent of her mothers were "intimidated" or coerced by their husbands, physically, psychologically, and/or economically. (They lost outright in court, were rejected by their children, or were economically impoverished. Four percent were forced to relinquish custody by their second husbands.)

15. Turner, op. cit.

16. I am purposely concentrating on parents rather than on children in this particular study. However, please see Chapters 8, 9, 10, and 14 for a discussion of the effect on children exerted by paternal physical and economic abandonment, paternal incest, kidnapping, and brainwashing. See Chapters 20 and 21 for a discussion of children's rights.

17. Twenty mothers had such materials.

18. Each mother had from one to five children; each marriage lasted from two to twenty years. At the time of our interviews these mothers ranged in age from twenty-one to sixty.

19. Maternal education ranged from non-completed high school to completed graduate and medical school.

20. This median maternal "income" remained depressingly stable for nearly two decades in America.

21. This list is similar to what the Supreme Court of West Virginia specified as the tasks of a primary care-giver, in 1981. See Chapter 14. This list does not include what a wife does for a husband. For example, mothers also wrote checks, balanced the checkbook, and budgeted money; listened to their husbands' problems; shopped, cooked, and cleaned for husbands and their guests, etc. A number of mothers also worked as bookkeepers, secretaries, nurses, and receptionists in their husbands' offices.

22. Please see Chapters 9, 10, 11, and 21 for a discussion of these independent interviews with fathers. I studied 25 and surveyed 30 fathers.

23. Accurate information about fathering was hard to elicit. Traditional mothers are not used to evaluating men in terms of child care. They are not used to saying "bad" things even about ex-husbands. Mothers found it difficult to describe what their ex-husbands did, exactly, in terms of child care, without fearing they were being "unfair" or "biased."

24. Jules Henry, *Culture Against Men* (New York: Random House, 1965), describes the American phenomenon of the father as an "imp of fun," who, instead of allowing the children to share his activities, shares the children's. Some Peer-Buddies also involved children in adult activities.

25. I independently interviewed nine additional Smother-Fathers. See Chap-

ter 9 for a discussion of this. All Smother-Fathers in this study won custody—despite the fact that a strong judicial bias presumably exists against fathers competing with mothers for the "maternal" role.

26. Only 15 percent of the heterosexual mothers compared to 52 percent of the heterosexual fathers remarried or had a grandmother or a live-in lover willing to provide child care. Unfortunately a mother's heterosexual remarriage didn't always work to her custodial advantage. A lesbian remarriage never worked to maternal custodial advantage.

27. Once they won custody, an almost equal number of fathers moved away without being prevented from doing so. See Chapters 6 and 14.

28. This is discussed in Chapter 19.

29. See Chapter 3 for a discussion of this, and for a review of the relevant studies.

30. See Chapters 3, 14, and 20 for a discussion of what constitutes parental unfitness and for a review of the studies on paternal incest, and other forms of paternal child abuse. Two of the custodial fathers (3 percent) were involved in the sexual molestation of their children. This may be less of a paternal incest incidence rate than in the population at large. However, see Chapter 14 for a discussion of incestuous fathers battling for custody.

31. Barbara Bode, "Background Facts on Child Support Enforcement" (Washington, D.C.: Children's Foundation, 1982). Also see Nan P. Hunter, "Women and Child Support," in *Families, Politics and Public Policy, A Feminist Dialogue on Women and the State*, Irene Diamond, ed. (New York: Longman, 1983).

In 1984, the U.S. Internal Revenue Service published the results of its "experiment" to attach unpaid child support payments from *tax refunds* due the fathers. It discontinued this approach after it was clear that such targeted fathers then refused to comply with filing their income tax returns (David Burnham, "Diverting Refund to Child Support Raises Tax Cheating, Study Finds," *New York Times*, June 7, 1984).

In 1985, a study subsidized by the Social Security Administration and the Federal Office of Child Support Enforcement was published. According to *New York Times* reporter André Brooks,

" 'One of our most shocking findings,' said Dr. Ron Haskins, Associate Director of the Bush Institute, 'was that middle-class fathers feel at greater liberty not to pay a substantial amount either because the courts never insisted or the collection agencies never took their family situations seriously. . . . Census figures show that the average male wage earner made $24,120 in 1984.' . . .

"The study found that a national formula was only a partial answer. Dr. Haskins, commenting on the much-discussed problem of delinquency in payments, said that in his own view if these fathers were going to pay their fair share the amount should be withheld from the father's paycheck from the start, instead of waiting for him to fall behind in payments.

"The study suggested that middle-income fathers should provide more support for the custodial mother in nontraditional ways, such as setting aside a night or two a week to babysit (if they live nearby) or helping her get special job training.

"Low-income noncustodial fathers, the study found, seem to be far more involved in the daily lives of their children and the mother than most middle-income absentee fathers." (Andree Brooks, *New York Times*, February 22, 1985.)

32. Ruth Sanders, op. cit.

The economic vulnerability and degradation of American mothers and children is truly shocking. Everyone "knows" that stay-at-home mothers are unsalaried, received no social security or pensions for housework or mothering, and are horrendously underpaid by state welfare departments, and that salaried fathers earn at least twice as much as salaried mothers. (The median income for women in 1983 was $6,320, while for men it was $14,360.)

According to the 1983 welfare levels (for a family of four), not even the highest paying states of Alaska ($682/month), California ($601/month), and New York ($515/month) match the poverty level of $10,178/year. The lowest paying states are in the Southern region and in Puerto Rico: (Mississippi, $120/month; Alabama, $148/month; Arkansas, $164/month; South Carolina, $169/month; Texas, $141/month; and Puerto Rico, $104/month).

The majority of welfare recipients in these areas are black and Hispanic-American mothers. In 1983, only 28 percent of the white women heading households were living on incomes below the poverty level, whereas 54.9 percent of women of color who headed households were living below the poverty level. The white mother's average income was $13,496; almost twice the $7,458 average income of a woman of color.

"Welfare" mothers are not subsidized as well as foster care mothers are to care for the very same children; welfare and foster care mothers are certainly not subsidized as well as governesses or housekeepers are in the homes of the wealthy.

See the U.S. Bureau of Labor, Commerce and Census Statistics 1970–1984; Frances Fox Piven and Richard A. Cloward, *Regulating the Poor: The Functions of Public Welfare* (New York: Vintage Books, 1972); *Women's Equity Action League Bulletin*, 13, 3 (June–July 1984); Robert Pear, "Rate of Poverty Found to Persist in Face of Gains," *New York Times*, August 3, 1984. (The poverty level was defined as a family of four with a cash income of less than $10,178 per year); and Joyce Purnick, "The Changing Face of Poverty," Community Service Society of Greater New York Report,

New York Times, Dec. 16, 1984. The report notes that the "number of poor households headed by women with young children increased 72 percent between 1970 and 1980.

CHAPTER FIVE: THE "SEXUAL" MOTHER: ANNA KARENINA TODAY

1. Leo Tolstoy, *Anna Karenina*, trans. Rosemary Edmund (New York: Penguin, 1979).

2. When husbands are impotent or sexually inept, when husbands insist on marital celibacy, or when they are "forced" into the beds of girlfriends or prostitutes, it is wives whom they blame. When a father who wants custody is sexually celibate, he is seen as "pure" rather than as "disturbed." Celibacy presumably entails more suffering for a man than a woman. Therefore, he is seen as "saintly," compared to his "evil" and "selfish" ex-wife, as we have just seen in Catherine's case.

    Women accused of "witchcraft" were often charged with causing male "impotence" and "adulterous fornication." Please see Chapter 17.

CHAPTER SIX: THE "UPPITY" MOTHER

1. In 1983 Leslie Silko, the poet and writer and one of the few women awarded a grant from the MacArthur Foundation, said: "I paid and paid and paid in my personal life for not being more conventional. The very qualities that got me the award made me lose custody of my younger son. Society makes it real hard for a woman to excel in the ways rewarded by the MacArthur Foundation" (Quoted in the *Village Voice*, December 7, 1983).

CHAPTER SEVEN: THE LESBIAN MOTHER

1. The overall rate of lesbian and non-lesbian maternal loss, judicially and privately, was 70 percent. The number of lesbian mothers in my study is too small to allow me statistically to compare the lesbian to non-lesbian "loss rate." Lesbian mothers did not give up fighting any sooner than non-lesbian mothers did. All mothers who agreed to paternal custody privately ended their struggle sooner than judicial mothers did.

2. Ellen Lewin, "Lesbianism and Motherhood: Implications for Child Custody," *Human Organization*, 40, 1 (1980).

3. Martha Kirkpatrick, "Lesbian Mother Families," *Psychiatric Annals*, 12, 9 (September 1982); Mildred I. Pagelow, "Heterosexual and Lesbian Single Mothers: A Comparison of Problems, Coping and Solutions," *Journal of Homosexuality*, 5, 3 (Spring 1980). Lesbian and non-lesbian mothers differ in this way: The non-lesbian mothers have a greater desire to remarry. Otherwise, lesbian and non-lesbian mothers seem to have similar child-hoods and parenting histories and similar attitudes toward marriage, di-vorce, sex roles, and sex education. See my book *Women and Madness* for a discussion of the psychological similarities between heterosexual and lesbian women in general.

4. Perhaps single men do not want the responsibility for another man's chil-dren and do not want to live through a prolonged custody battle. Perhaps lesbian mothers and lesbian non-mothers are more interested in creating or supporting family life than heterosexual men are.

5. Homosexual fathers are also custodially persecuted. However, they are rarely the primary parents that lesbian mothers are. If they *are,* judges see that as doubly "abnormal." If they're *not,* their claim to children is often seen as non-existent. Homosexual fathers face overwhelming judicial fears about homosexual paternal incest from the same judges who deny the existence of far more widespread paternal incest on the part of het-erosexual fathers.

6. This belief holds fast despite the overwhelming reality that most lesbians and homosexuals come from heterosexual families, and despite expert observations that the children of lesbian and homosexual parents tend to become heterosexual. See Richard Green, "Children of Homosex-uals Seem Headed Straight," *Psychology Today* (November 1978); Rich-ard Green, "Sexual Identity of 37 Children Raised by Homosexual or Transsexual Parents," *American Journal Psychology*, 692 (1978); Martha Kirkpatrick, M.D., Ronald Roy, M.D., and Katherine Smith, "A New Look at Lesbian Mothers," *Human Behavior*, vol. 5, no. 8 (August 1976).

7. In *Townsend* v. *Townsend*, 1 Fam. L. Rep. p. 2830, Ohio Court Common Pleas, 10/21/75, cited in *Mom's Apple Pie*, the Lesbian Mothers National Defense Fund Newsletter, June 1975, the tone of judicial disgust is very clear.

   Larraine Townsend lost custody of her three children in March 1975. "Judge Albert Carais, a retired judge who heard the case by special as-signment, said that if Larraine had indicated that she would abandon Les-bianism while the children were young, 'the court might have been tempted to experiment' with giving her custody. He said that there was no doubt that Larraine and Vicky 'intend to continue the relationship they began. They intend to live together. They intend to engage in Lesbianism. . . . I would think for the sake of the children, a Lesbian would abandon the practice. . . . Orgasm means more to them than children or anything else.'

"Larraine was denied custody because her Lesbianism was 'clearly to the neglect of supervision of the children' (no apparent nexus), the father was denied custody because 'he ignored the children for ten months and, at one point, attempted suicide in the mother's presence.' The children were instead awarded to the 65 year old paternal grandmother, who neither asked for the children nor testified in court." Cited by Burdulis, op. cit.

In *Spence* v. *Durham,* a lesbian mother was allowed to keep her child on the grounds that she was no longer involved in lesbian activity; in *Mitchell* v. *Mitchell,* a California court allowed a lesbian mother to keep her child on the condition that she not associate with her lover (both cited by E. Carrigton Boggan, Marilyn G. Haft, Charles Lister, and John P. Rupp, in *The Rights of Gay People* [Toronto: Clarke, Irwin & Co., 1975]).

In 1981, a custodially embattled lesbian mother was judicially castigated for *acting* on her lesbian impulses. If she would control herself, and give up her lover, the court said, it "would" or "might" allow her to keep her children. This mother didn't lose her children because she was a lesbian— but because she *behaved* like a lesbian. *Jacobson* v. *Jacobson,* 314 N.W. 2d 78, 8 *FLR* 2154, N.D. (1981).

8. Nearly a third of the lesbian mothers were married to men who tried to bully them into bed with another woman. Lesbian sexual activity is a popular pornographic theme. The reasons for this are complex, and may also involve heterosexual women's "prurient" interest in other women. Please see my book *About Men* for a discussion of pornography.

9. They may project this self-hatred outward—and condemn it in other lesbians and homosexuals.

10. See Chapter 11 for Cecily's story.

11. See Chapters 2, 14, 15, and 20 for further discussion of this. For a review of lesbian mother custody cases and legal strategies, see Donna Hitchen's *Lesbian Mother Litigation Manual* (San Francisco: Lesbian Rights Project, 1982), and Nan Hunter and Nancy Polikoff, "Custody Rights of Lesbian Mothers: Legal Theory and Litigation Strategy," 25 *Buffalo Law Review*, 691 (1976).

CHAPTER EIGHT: THE POOR MOTHER

1. See the U.S. Bureau of Labor, Commerce, and Census, *Statistics*, 1970–1984 (Washington, D.C.: Government Printing Office); Marilyn Powers, "Falling Through the 'Safety Net': Women, Economic Crisis, and Reaganomics," *Feminist Studies*, 10, 1 (Spring 1984): 32–53. See *Signs: Journal*

of Women in Culture and Society (Winter 1984—issue on "Women and Poverty").

2. See Chapters 14 and 20 for some recent welfare statistics.

3. U.S. Bureau of Labor statistics, op. cit.; Power, op. cit.

4. U.S. Bureau of Census statistics, op. cit.

5. Weitzman, op. cit. See the National Center for Women and Family Law's comments on this and similar studies, 1981–1984 (available from National Center for Women and Family Law, New York).

6. U.S. Bureau of the Census, op. cit.; Sanders, op. cit.

7. Hunter, op. cit.

8. According to Table Two(A), page 75, half these fathers earned between 0 and $25,000; a quarter earned between $26,000 and $49,000; a third earned between $50,000 and $200,000. A father who earned only $10,000 still earned two to three times more than his wife did on welfare. These are estimated medians. Maternal income includes welfare, savings, wages, child support, and alimony.

9. As noted in *Women, Money and Power:* "Unlike businessmen, wives and mothers cannot convert skills and time into experience that 'counts' in some (other) job—nor can they convert their labor into liquid capital. Mothers are not automatically promoted to other positions after they have completed the job of child raising. ('Dropping out' of the job market to have children usually means a permanent crippling of direct money-making capabilities)" (Phyllis Chesler and Emily Jane Goodman, *Women, Money and Power* [New York: Morrow, 1976; Bantam, 1978]).

10. Deborah Luepnitz found that 81 percent of the fathers who won sole custody retained the marital home (*Child Custody*, op. cit.).

11. I interviewed Manya after I formally closed my first study.

12. Of the fathers, 44 percent of those with high incomes, 7 percent of those with mid-incomes, and none of those with low incomes paid alimony. See Table Two, page 72.

13. There are some exceptions to this rule. For example, in 1982 the New Jersey Supreme Court ruled that spouses are entitled to "reimbursement alimony" for putting their partners through professional schools. The cases involved three women who supported their husbands by paying tuition and living expenses while the men earned professional degrees. The judge who wrote the decision said, in part: "Marriage should not be a free ticket to professional education and training, without subsequent obligations." (Tim Weiner, *Philadelphia Inquirer*, December 16, 1982)

14. *New York Law Journal*, 5/17/82. The New York *Labow* decision is a clear-sighted and sensitive opinion. It is a rare one. The National Center for Women and Family Law advised me, that as of 1985, Mrs. Labow was still being forced to fight for her economic rights.

15. See Table Two(A), page 75.

16. See Chapter 11 for a discussion of these eight and other mothers. Maternal motives for conceding custody battles include psychological motives as well. For example, some mothers thought that children needed their fathers; some mothers saw no point in "hanging on" to brainwashed children over whom they exerted no authority.

CHAPTER NINE: THE MOTHER MARRIED TO A VIOLENT MAN

1. *New York Post*, March 10, 1981.

2. *Seattle Times*, August 4, 1981.

3. Jehanne Dyllan. Personal interviews 1981 and 1982. Dyllan wrote and starred in a play about Karen Silkwood, primarily for union audiences around the country. Dyllan also told me that when Bill Meadows later left Cathy (his babysitter-mistress) for another woman, he or Cathy then "offered" Karen's children to their maternal grandparents.

4. Mothers also harbor equally intense and murderous feelings toward their ex-husbands. However, they hide or minimize such feelings—even to themselves. I don't think mothers are allowed to express such emotions. Fathers are.

5. Nora Ephron, in her novel *Heartburn* (New York: Knopf, 1982), describes a potentially smothering father in a bitterly humorous way: "[He's the kind of man] who goes through the whole business [of pregnancy and childbirth] under the delusion that it's as much his experience as it is yours. All this starts in Lamaze classes, where your husband ends up thinking he's pregnant, and let me tell you he's not. It's not his body, it's not his labor, it's not his pain—it's yours, and does any man give you credit or respect for it? No. They're too busy getting in on the act, holding their stop watches and telling you when to breathe and when to push. . . . Beware of men who cry. It's true that men who cry are sensitive to and in touch with their feelings, but the only feelings they tend to be sensitive to and in touch with are their own."

6. I asked Beth to listen to my taped interview with Eric. Here are some of her comments: "Eric reminds me of Simon. They are both desperate to

have their kids constantly engaged with them. By not setting any rules, limits, structures for his kids, Eric forces them to stay engaged with him at all times. Daddy says, 'I'll let you stay up late' (which really means, I don't want to let go of you and experience the emptiness), 'if you promise not to be tired in the morning.'

"Eric doesn't let his kids learn to control themselves or to tolerate frustration because if they were self-controlling, self-generating people, then he could not be all-controlling and all-central. It really does make Eric crazy (irrational, impulsive, out of control, emotionally violent) if he's separated from them. All this has less to do with the welfare of his children, and more to do with his needing them to supply the missing center of his own life. In order to 'have' his kids, he'll even hurt them by separating them from their mother totally, by keeping them up late, by letting them eat junk food, by kidnapping them.

"Eric puts his ex-wife down because she wants an adult 'private' life. He says she's cold and uncaring because she sets limits and provides structure. Eric is worse than the 'clutchiest' of mothers. His poor kids! He thinks that playing with them is a form of child-care. His kids already know that they have to stay attached to Daddy to keep Daddy from falling apart. If Daddy falls apart, so will they."

7. In my study, daughters were either unimportant; less important; or important only as "cute little mothers." Smother-Fathers (with one exception)—did not seem to encourage their daughters to achieve anything beyond domestic subservience. For example, according to Catherine, her husband ". . . Thomas prefers the boys to the girl. I feel he sees me in my daughter and mistrusts her. She tries very hard to please him. She baked him a cake for Christmas. He never thanked her for it. He didn't give her a Christmas present. But Thomas refuses to cover her tuition if she switches colleges to live closer to me."

According to Miki, "My daughter treats her father just like I used to. She agrees with him, flatters him, keeps her eyes down a lot. He treats her like he treated me: as stubborn, but stupid. Maybe she's also learned to behave in self-demeaning ways by watching me do it. She certainly doesn't identify with me as a woman, or an abused wife. Maybe she thinks she can escape her father's violence if she completely gives me up and tries very hard to please him."

Maureen is still battling against her children's brainwashing. She says: "My sons have never seen any physical warmth between their father and mother. Now that we're battling, all they see is physical violence: kidnapping, beating, banging on doors. They see him beating me down economically too. How will my sons relate to women? Like their father related to me?"

8. *New York Daily News*, April 6, 1982.

9. *New York Times*, April 24, 1982.

10. See Chapter 14 for a more extensive discussion of how judges handle incestuous fathers. During the course of this book, I interviewed three additional mothers after I had closed my study, each of whom lost custody of her daughter to an incestuous father. All three were recommended by psychiatrists who had interviewed them and their daughters. One of these mothers said: "My daughter is six. I think she's going crazy. I'm allowed to see her every other weekend. I don't know which of us is in worse shape. I've exhausted all my economic resources. By the time I begin another legal action, my daughter will be permanently destroyed. How can one trust a legal system that would do this in the first place?"

11. See Chapters 14 and 20. In my core population (Chapter 4) both custodial and non-custodial fathers and mothers "legally" and "illegally" kidnapped or re-kidnapped children. I have counted all such incidents. With one exception the custodial fathers who "legally" kidnapped their children did so before the divorce was final. Like non-custodial or "illegal" paternal kidnappers, they took children on "sprees," cutting all contact with their ex-wives. Twelve percent of the non-custodial mothers and 23 percent of the non-custodial fathers kidnapped their children. In general, half the paternal kidnappings were "legal"; half were not. See Chapter 14 for an additional discussion of parental kidnapping.

12. Judges take fathers' accusations of maternal interference with parental visitation far more seriously than they take similar accusations by mothers. Also, fathers are less frightened by maternal threats than mothers are of paternal threats to sue or kidnap.

Judges did economically penalize mothers for presumably interfering with paternal *visitation*. For example, Sally was perpetually victimized by her ex-husband's lateness. After two years of having all her plans disrupted by his late arrivals or returns, she "put her foot down." When he arrived two hours late, Sally told him to wait an hour until the family finished dinner. She says: "He had a screaming episode. He hurled rocks at my window. He went to court and actually got a judge to fine me $500 for holding the children for three hours when they judicially belonged to him. I was devastated." Please see Chapter 14 for similar examples.

13. Confidential Detectives' Report based on a one-year investigation. Filed in 1982. Shown to me by attorneys at the National Center for Women and Family Law, 1982.

14. In the Australian film *Smash Palace* we see a kidnapper-father unable to emotionally handle his daughter's sudden fever without panicking and becoming enraged. Jack Olson, *Have You Seen My Son* (New York: Atheneum, 1982); Joy Fielding, *Kiss Mommy Goodbye* (New York: Doubleday, 1981); and Bonnie Lee Black, *Somewhere Child* (New York: Viking Press,

1981); and Norma Foxmaier, *Taking Terri Mueller* (New York: Morrow, 1983) all describe the "spree" phenomenon; the paternal refusal to talk about the mother left behind; the paternal lying about a mother's "being dead" or not "loving" the kidnapped child anyway; and the paternal phenomenon of exaggerated domestic and emotional dependence on a kidnapped child, coupled with paranoia about the rest of the world.

15. See John Gill, op. cit.

16. Ibid. cites the case of a kidnapped, brainwashed, and apprehended child who was unwilling to be taken back. This girl was taken by her father when she was three. When she was recovered, she was about five. She'd grown to know her father's girlfriend as her mother and when the natural mother confronted her, she didn't know what to think. She'd been calling the girlfriend "Mommy."

"It took her a few days to realize and remember who her mother was. She was told her natural mother had died in an automobile accident and that she would now have the girlfriend as her mother. The child accepted this." How did she adjust? " 'It took her grandmother,' Cerone said. 'Her father had never said anything about her grandmother, so she knew she could trust her grandmother. It was sad. When she was first recovered, she called for "Mommy" but it was for her surrogate mother. . . .' 'A man in Tennessee told his girls their mother didn't love them and didn't want them. We've had a lot of them say the other parent is dead. That's *much* more damaging than an actual recovery.' "

17. *New York Post*, March 14, 1983.

18. Rana Lee, Station KPFA, San Francisco, California.

19. See Chapter 14 for a discussion of this.

20. This information is based on a private detectives' report. The investigation turned up correspondence between Johnson and various fathers' rights activists around the country. One activist offered Johnson the babysitting services of his second wife if Johnson would help him kidnap his children, etc. I read the photocopied correspondence at the National Center for Women and Family Law in 1981 and 1982.

21. Demeter, op. cit.

22. One maternal kidnapper re-kidnapped her child back from Europe. Her husband was psychiatrically imprisoned by his own family and died shortly thereafter. He never pursued her. One maternal kidnapper who lost custody and was prevented from all access to her children, both physically and psychologically, kidnapped them in 1970, when they were ten and twelve years old. She was never pursued or found.

23. Rachel's husband did find her with the assistance of the FBI—in the mid-

1970s, before the FBI was legally empowered to do this. Rachel's story is discussed in Chapter 14.

24. Gill, op. cit.

25. *New York Post*, May 26, 1984.

26. Associated Press, July 4, 1984.

27. *The Boston Herald*, March 12, 1985.

28. Thomas J. Maier, "No Jail in Death of Son Left in Car," *Newsday*, June 4, 1985.

CHAPTER TEN: PATERNAL BRAINWASHING

1. This is true even after they have voluntarily participated in their own psychological "hi-jacking."

2. Dr. John C. Clark, Dr. Stanley H. Cath, Dr. Robert Jay Lifton, and Dr. Margaret T. Singer all have studied brainwashing in prisoner-of-war camps and/or among cults.

3. Chesler, *About Men*.

4. Arcana, *Every Mother's Son*.

5. Gill, op. cit., has many examples of kidnapped children rejecting their mothers. Thirty-seven percent of all battling fathers in my study kidnapped their children. Sixty-two percent were physically abusive to the mothers of their children.

6. Demeter, op. cit.

7. Black, op. cit.

8. It is important to note that *none* of these economically forceful fathers engaged in long-term or "spree"-like kidnappings. Only two of these fathers engaged in short term kidnapping skirmishes. Four fathers physically prevented maternal visitation by legally moving far away after obtaining court-room custody.

9. One previously absent and economically superior father allowed himself to be used by his daughter against her mother—although he didn't really want her. Ida said: "Bernie left us when Kim was five. He never visited. Sometimes, he called or sent a gift. When Kim turned eight, *she* began to use Bernie's existence as a weapon against me. She threatened to move out whenever I wanted her to clean her room. Bernie would tell her "that he'd buy her clothes and let her do whatever she wanted.

   "When Kim was ten, she insisted on spending the summer with Bernie and his wife. I had to secretly beg him to take her. When Kim returned she was real unhappy about how we lived compared to how her father lived. She kept asking about why we split up. I tried to explain about his violence. 'If he's so violent, why does his other wife stay with him?' Kim is fourteen now. I think she'll go back and forth between us in her mind, comparing us, putting me into competition with Bernie, for a long time.

"I can't say he's brainwashed her. It's a cultural set-up. All Bernie had to do was have a penis and keep his distance."

10. Gill, op. cit., quotes a mother whose children were "indoctrinated" against her: " 'You could call it brainwashing, I guess,' the mother, Elena Hoffman, thirty-one, said. 'It wasn't anything you could notice directly. But every now or then my son would say something like, "Mommy likes her work more than me," or "Why do you have to use the typewriter when I'm here?" I think he'd been taught to say that by his father, who worked on a ranch and lived with a woman who stayed home,' [Hoffman] said. 'In fact, my son even complained once that I wasn't doing enough housework. He'd found dirty dishes in the sink.' "

11. Paternal grandmothers made up 39 percent of all mother-competitors.

12. One of these Smother-Fathers was also assisted by a virulent paternal grandmother for a limited period of time.

13. A number of autobiographies and biographies describe the competitive role of paternal grandmothers. For example, Black, op. cit., describes the paternal grandmother who assisted her husband in kidnapping and initially brainwashing their daughter:

" 'Let me teach you how to cook,' Jim's mother said soon after I moved in.

" 'Thank you,' I said, as tactfully as I could, 'but I already know how. I've been cooking for my family since my mother went back to work when I was eleven.' I didn't add that I'd been studying cookbooks religiously for years. She seemed insulted. 'Well, Jimmy likes things done a certain way. *My way.*' She showed me how she prepared asparagus, 'one of Jimmy's favorites,' by boiling it in a large potful of water for twenty minutes, then pouring all the water down the drain, burning some butter in a frying pan until it was black, stirring in some breadcrumbs, and pouring this all over the platter of soggy spears.

" 'I think I would do it a little differently,' I said after she finished her demonstration.

"She left the kitchen then without a word, but when Jim came home from work she complained to him that I was 'pigheaded,' 'ungrateful,' 'insolent,' and 'stubborn.' "

14. Goldsmith, op. cit., describes a *maternal* grandmother, *paternal* aunt, and maternally hired *governess* who fought a widowed mother for custody.

Mother Gloria's own (fortune-seeking) mother (the maternal grandmother) testified that her daughter pursued a "gay life" and treated her granddaughter "like an orphan." Gertrude Whitney, the paternal aunt, said she was appalled at little Gloria's "terror" of her own mother. Gertrude Whitney won custody. Goldsmith writes: "[A lawyer] told several associates that Gertrude Whitney was everything she accused Gloria of being: she loved to travel and had left her children for months at a time while she pursued her own life; she was extravagant, she liked to drink alcohol, she'd had many lovers and there were rumors of lesbian relationships. But there were essential differences which protected Gertrude Whitney: Gloria led her life in print while Gertrude's was shrouded in a secrecy purchased by her vast wealth. And at twenty-nine, Gloria could not disguise her sexuality while Gertrude at fifty-nine seemed the quintessential conservative, austere widow."

Henry James, in *What Maisie Knew*, describes a divorce and joint-custodial arrangement. Both parents battle for their daughter Maisie, by trying to "make the little girl a burden to the other." The father is a Smother-Father of sorts. The mother forbids Maisie's governess to follow her into her adulterous father's house. She said that it was a house that "no decent woman could consent to be seen in." The governess, named Ms. Overmore, "explained to Maisie that she had had a hope of being allowed to accompany her to her father's, and that his hope had been dashed by the way her mother took it. 'She says that if I ever do such a thing as enter his service I must never expect to show my face in this house again. So I've promised not to attempt to go with you. If I wait patiently till you come back here we shall certainly be together once more.' 'Then who'll take care of me at papa's?' "

The governess can't bear to be separated from Maisie and tells her frankly what had happened. "That she had really been unable to hold out. She had broken her vow to Mrs. Farange, she had come straight to Maisie's papa and told him the simple truth. She adored his daughter; she couldn't give her up; she'd make for her any sacrifice. On this basis it had been arranged that she should stay: her courage had been rewarded; she left Maisie in no doubt as to the amount of courage she had required."

15. Mary Zenorini Silverzweig, *The Other Mother* (New York: Harper & Row, 1982). Mary uses everyone's real name in her account of this brainwashing and custody battle—except for the biological mother.

16. I also tried to interview Mary and Stanley Silverzweig, but the interview never "worked out." I felt I knew more than I wanted to know once Mary's book was published. After our interview, Roberta "agreed" to joint custody of her two youngest daughters on the eve of her third or fourth separate court date. Her eldest daughter still refused to see her.

17. Barbara Goldsmith, op. cit., depicts a child who is terrified of her mother;

a child who physically runs away from her mother—screaming "I hate you . . . don't kill me"; who cannot identify her mother's photograph in court and claims she never loved her anyway.

Goldsmith theorizes that little Gloria's Nurse Keislish (along with others) somehow convinced her charge that her mother would kidnap her—just like the Lindbergh child. According to Goldsmith, two physicians examined little Gloria. They concluded that she had "been poisoned against her mother." Their testimony didn't persuade the judge to remove little Gloria from those who had "poisoned" her.

In 1985 Gloria Vanderbilt published *Once Upon A Time: A True Story* (New York: Alfred A. Knopf, 1985). She describes how she was coerced into the "game" of betraying her mother. Despite this, and the fact that Gloria's mother led a socialite's life, Gloria still needed, longed for and romanticized her socially and legally absent but psychologically present mother. She describes maternal visitation after the custody trial in this way:

"Then Aunt Gertrude said something in her graceful way, and—to my horror—my mother reached out to take my hand. I was torn apart not knowing what it meant or what exactly was going on or what I was supposed to do. No one had ever said this might happen—no one ever said that my mother might reach over and take my hand into the beauty of hers. I left my hand there, dumped on the cushion, as if it were a dead thing. I kept staring at Aunt Gertrude's hat, holding my eyes onto it, as if something about it would tell me something and give me a clue as to what I should do and what to expect next. But no answer came.

"So there we all sat . . . my mother, on the other side, her veiled beauty now turned from me. I sat in the middle, half wanting to throw myself into her arms, half wanting to yank my hand away from hers so fast and hard that it would tear her soft fingers off into mine—for then she would belong to me forever!"

18. Gill, op. cit.

19. Glenn Collins, "The Psychology of the Cult Experience," *New York Times*, March 15, 1982. Dr. Clark and Dr. Stanley Cath are based in Boston. They have treated former members of the Unification Church, the International Society for Krishna Consciousness, Scientology, the Way International, The Divine Light Mission, the Children of God, the Church of Bible-Understanding, etc.

20. Edward Schumacher, "Children of the Disappeared: Argentine Doctors Find a Syndrome of Pain," *New York Times*, February 21, 1984.

21. These letters were long, single-spaced, and handwritten in a very neat script. I read five such letters. Similar letters arrived weekly for at least a year.

CHAPTER ELEVEN: THE "VOLUNTARILY" NON-CUSTODIAL MOTHER

1. Charlotte Perkins Gilman, *The Living Charlotte Perkins Gilman: An Autobiography* (New York: Arno, 1972). In 1892, Gilman wrote a story entitled "The Unnatural Mother." The fictional mother is condemned for her willingness to sacrifice her child's life in order to save an entire community. The child and the villagers survive. The mother and her husband die. After her death the mother is still condemned as "unnatural."

2. Ibid. Gilman's story has a happy ending. In her old age, when she was ill and dying, her daughter and her co-mother, Grace Channing, together came to nurse her and love her in California.

3. "Self-realization" included leaving an abusive marriage; accepting a meaningful job, (often) in another city, state, or country; continuing to work at an artistic career; or "giving up" the losing battle of single motherhood with still existing career ambitions. Pascowicz, op. cit., first used the term *self-realization* to describe one of the motives involved in maternal non-custodial status.

4. I interviewed ten non-custodial fathers who had never battled for custody. I found them through newspaper ads, and through professional and personal referrals.

5. Luepnitz, *Child Custody*, loc. cit., found that sole (and joint) custodial fathers were "very welcome at school functions" and were treated as "heros" for being able to work and simultaneously raise a child.

6. Alice Walker's heroine Meridian, in the novel of the same name, does locate herself historically. Her historical perspective only leads to more guilt and a greater sense of deviance. "Meridian knew that enslaved women had been made miserable by the sale of their children, that they had laid down their lives, gladly, for their children, that the daughters of these enslaved women had thought their greatest blessing from 'Freedom' was that it meant they could keep their children. And what had Meridian Hill done with *her* precious child? She had given him away. She thought of her mother as being worthy of this maternal history, and of herself as belonging to an unworthy minority, for which there was no precedent and of which she was, as far as she knew, the only member." (Alice Walker, *Meridian* [New York: Harcourt Brace Jovanovich, 1976].)

7. Pascowicz, op. cit.

8. See Chapter 19 for a discussion of how men, especially in official positions, rarely take *personal* responsibility for their public action.

9. Many non-custodial mothers in television and newspaper interviews insist

that they have "everything" in common with non-custodial fathers. Some things—yes; everything—no. Perhaps such mothers have been too hurt by the harsh judgments of other mothers and find that fathers are more "reasonable" or merciful about non-custodial parenthood. Perhaps as divorced heterosexual mothers in search of mates, they may need to demonstrate an acceptable level of compassion for men to attract them; to feel "attractive" to them; or to make common cause with them as non-custodial parents.

I am not suggesting that a non-custodial mother disassociate herself from men, hate men, or refuse to work with men. I am pointing out the importance of her being absolutely clear about her own status. What she *does* about her situation is entirely up to her as an individual.

10. Some fathers like to integrate themselves into their teenage sons' activities as a way of "rebelling" against mothers. See Chapters 4 and 8 for a discussion of the "Imp of Fun," "Peer-Buddy," and "Smother-Father" styles of parenting.

11. For those fathers who did not wish to remarry or who did not wish to "share" their children with a *woman,* such "help" was perceived as a potential problem. My point is that fathers had this option; mothers did not.

12. There are exceptions to this rule. Some mothers were "helped" by boyfriends or second husbands. Some fathers were unable to get anyone to "take over" for them. I interviewed only *one* blue collar widower who single-handedly reared his six-year-old twins after their mother's death. He didn't remarry. He rarely dated. He started bringing his children to work with him when necessary. Ultimately, he insisted on working part-time.

13. Luepnitz, loc. cit.

14. This is not necessarily my view of all fathers, nor are all fathers deserving of this view. It is, however, one of the major unspoken reasons that non-custodial mothers are instinctively condemned. See what I have written on the subject of father-child violence in *About Men*, loc. cit. and in other chapters of this book.

15. Pascowicz, op. cit.

16. Pascowicz, op. cit., notes that "married life is best enjoyed by the child-free; studies indicate that the most content people are married couples with no children. This supports [her] assertion that a portion of the anger displayed toward absentee mothers results from repressed resentment among custodial parents that they must bear the burdens of childrearing while absentee mothers go free."

17. In 1984, three years after our initial interviews, Cecily called to tell me that her college-age children were living with her weekends, vacations,

and summers. She said: "Harriet left Eddie. He didn't want to run a large house on his own, especially since the kids were all in college. He 'dumped' them on me. I'm really thrilled to have them. He knows I can afford only a one-bedroom apartment. It is a bit crowded. . . ."

CHAPTER TWELVE: THE PRICE OF BATTLE: MOTHERS ENCOUNTER THE PSYCHOLOGICAL LAW

1. Research has described a higher incidence of suicide attempts, depression, and unhappiness among divorced women as well as men. See Dr. Gerald F. Jacobson, "The Multiple Crisis of Marital Separation and Divorce" (New York: Grune & Stratton, 1984); Dr. Gerald F. Jacobson and Dr. James J. Lynch, *The Broken Heart: The Medical Consequences of Loneliness* (New York: Basic Books, 1979); Mavis Hetherington, M. Cox, and R. Cox, "Divorced Fathers," *The Family Coordinator*, October 1976.

2. Armstrong, op. cit., notes: "It is more, not less, serious to do severe harm to those toward whom you stand in a relationship of trust—than to do similar harm to a stranger."

3. For a long time such mothers behave like incestuously abused children who can't name what is happening to them. When they do, they aren't believed. They sometimes don't believe themselves. All female victims of paternal domestic violence become self-destructive (and blame their mothers) more readily than they blame their fathers or become "other"-destructive.

4. Sonia Johnson, *From Housewife to Heretic* (New York: Doubleday-Anchor, 1982), describes a confrontation with her husband, Rick: "Back at his office, [Rick] asked me calmly, in a detached sort of way, which two of our four children I wanted to keep. . . . There in his office, his face an expressionless mask, he pointed out coolly that the agreement I had signed (!) divvied up the kids equally between us, and that he wouldn't mind getting me in court (*and here his voice got ugly, and I saw such astonishing hatred in his face I felt faint*), because if he ever did, he would show me a thing or two. He would make me wish I had kept quietly to our 'agreement.' "

5. Black, op. cit.

6. Gill, op. cit., has many examples of how woman friends betray or are not supportive to the mother of a paternally kidnapped child.

    Susan Jacoby writes: "Simple acknowledgment—regardless of whether the words are poetic—is a powerful form of consolation. Lack of acknowledgment is especially common when people are suffering from grief that is not covered by conventional social expectations. We all expect people to be in mourning if a close relative has died, but we tend to ignore grief that is somewhat removed from the predictable social order. . . . The rising incidence of divorce means that we are likely to see more varieties of unconventional grief. Ex-husbands and ex-wives will grieve for one another; stepchildren will grieve for stepparents. Who will console these people in a society that finds it difficult to confront conventional grief for conventionally admissible losses?

"There are so many ways in which friends can help the bereaved—ways that have nothing to do with the futile search for the 'right thing to say.' To begin, we can listen. . . . When grieving people attempt to speak of their loss, many of us try to change the subject. We feel there is something unhealthy about dwelling on the past—and this sensibility is one factor in the prevalence of ill-timed suggestions about remarriage or having another baby or getting a new dog." (*New York Times*, April 21, 1983)

7. See Chapter 19 for a discussion of maternal heroism and non-violence under siege.

8. We may remember that Anna Karenina was profoundly "indifferent" to her newborn daughter. Being without her son, she knew how easily she could lose her daughter. Karenina's way of "denying" or "expressing" this blow to her body consisted of drug addiction and, ultimately, suicide.

Marilyn French, in *The Women's Room*, describes how Mira, a mother, experiences divorce and single motherhood.

"Mira was thrust into freedom just as she had been chuted into slavery, or at least that is how she thought of it. She could have refused Norm a divorce or she could have acceded easily, demanding nothing, but she agreed to the divorce and submitted a bitter bill, totting up the cost of her services for fifteen years. Norm was horrified that she could view their marriage in that way, but at the same time he argued that she had not deducted her food, lodging, and clothes.

"Their separation and divorce did not feel like good freedom to her, it felt more like being thrown out of the igloo in the middle of a snowstorm. There is lots of space to wander in, but it's all cold. . . . Some days she raged like an out-of-control train, charging through the house, cleaning it with compulsive ferocity, purging basement and attic and every closet of fifteen years of shit. Still pieces of Norm remained: there were the boys, to begin with, and at times she turned that fury on them. Other times she wept, inconsolably, ceaselessly and would have to wear sunglasses to the market next day.

"She began to drink during the days. Several times she was staggering when the boys came in from school. Norm found her drunk once when he came in to get something he had left behind, and he warned her severely that if she did not 'shape up,' as he put it, he would take the boys away from her."

Just after Mira is "rescued" from a suicide attempt, she says: "I kept thinking I ought to care about the boys, but I didn't."

"No. I know. Nothing else matters when you feel that much pain."

"No. Not even getting even with Norm. Because, you know, he might feel guilty for a little while, but mostly he'd be annoyed at the crimp I put in his plans, saddling him with the boys. But he could even handle that: he had enough money. There's just nothing I can do to him except kill him. If I could beat him up, I'd feel better, but I can't, I'd have to shoot him or something. And that's not very satisfying. What I want is to make him cry, to see him living in pain the way I am."

9. Pascowicz, op. cit., finds that this was most pronounced among mothers who lost custody in court; next, among those who were physically or financially "intimidated" into relinquishing custody.

   Pascowicz notes that 40 of her 100 respondents (40 percent) led "happy well adjusted lives" after becoming non-custodial mothers. "Not that they have not experienced sadness . . . but they coped [with it] with or without support.

10. It is psychologically dangerous to "gloss over" a genuine loss. Jane Brody, in the *New York Times*, January 17, 1984, summarized the research on victims done by Dr. Linda S. Perloff; Dr. Ronnie Janoff-Bulman and Dr. Irene Hanson Frieze; Dr. Shelley E. Taylor; and Dr. Camille B. Wortman. Brody notes that: "Sometimes, victims may adopt a falsely optimistic attitude solely for social reasons, since a person who continually bemoans his fate is not likely to be popular with other people. But while keeping one's emotional distress within manageable limits may be seen as a sign of a good adjustment, letting out one's feelings of deep distress appears more therapeutic. Thus, taking the disaster 'very well' may be thwarting recovery."

11. Of the (smaller number of) lesbian mothers, 71 percent co-habited with mates during or immediately after their custody loss—compared to 17 percent of the heterosexual mothers.

12. Pascowicz, op. cit., also found that more husbands than wives remarried after a custody struggle—and that they did so more rapidly. Pascowicz found that 9 percent of her maternal respondents and 20 percent of their ex-husbands remarried within a year, and 50 percent of her mothers eventually remarried.

   It is important to note that my maternal population all reported battling against their will. Pascowicz claims that 40 percent of her population either "wanted" or "accepted" custody losses because of emotional incapacity or creative ambitions.

13. It is important to remember that nearly half—twenty-nine fathers—did

not reproduce or did not say they would. One of these fathers died, and one father's subsequent reproductive activity is unknown—inasmuch as he disappeared with his child.

14. Of the fertile, custodially "triumphant" fathers, 33 percent genetically reproduced themselves again and 14 percent said they still wanted to have children. Of the "winning" fathers, 12 percent were infertile or had infertile wives; 12 percent were Smother-Fathers.

15. Remember, we are talking about a small number of fathers: eighteen to be exact, 13 percent of whom had infertility problems; 13 percent were Smother-Fathers.

16. Forty-three (72 percent) of the mothers were still of childbearing age when they ended their initial fights for custody. They were between the ages of twenty-one and thirty-nine. I interviewed these mothers anywhere from two to seventeen years after they had fought for custody. Eighteen (40 percent) lost custody two to five years prior to the interview; 18 (40 percent) lost custody six to ten years prior to the interview. Seven (16 percent) lost custody eleven to fourteen years prior to the interview; two (4 percent) lost custody fifteen to seventeen years prior to the interview. Seventeen mothers (28 percent) were forty or more at the end of their initial fight. Their ages ranged from forty to forty-eight. They did not view themselves as capable of biological reproduction.

17. Pascowicz, op. cit., notes that 50 percent of these mothers said they had made a conscious "decision" not to have any more children. Eighty-five percent had none. Again, it is important to note that her population is somewhat different from mine. Forty percent of her interviewees did not lose custody legally or through violent intimidation.

18. Alice Walker's heroine Meridian in the novel *Meridian* gives her child up for adoption "with a light heart" because she wants him (and herself) to live and to have good lives.

"But she had not anticipated the nightmares that began to trouble her sleep. Nightmares of the child, Rundi, calling to her, crying, suffering unbearable deprivations because she was not there, yet she knew it was just the opposite: Because she was not there he needn't worry, ever, about being deprived. Of his life, for instance. She felt deeply that what she'd done was the only thing, and was right, but that did not seem to matter. On some deeper level than she had anticipated or had even been aware of, she felt condemned, consigned to penitence, for life.

"After she had figuratively kissed the ground of the campus and walked about its lawns intent on bettering herself, she knew for certain she had broken something, for she began hearing a voice . . . A voice that cursed her existence—an existence that could not live up to the standard of motherhood that had gone before. It said, over and over, until she would literally reel in the streets, her head between her hands: Why don't you die? Why not kill yourself? Jump into the traffic! Lie down under the wheels of that big truck! Jump off the roof, as long as you're up there! Always, the voice. Mocking, making fun. It frightened her because the voice urging her on— the voice that said terrible things about her lack of value—was her own voice. It was talking to her, and it was full of hate."

CHAPTER THIRTEEN: THE MOTHER-LAWYER RELATIONSHIP

1. Of the forty-three mothers who retained lawyers, thirty-eight were able or willing to describe or "rate" their lawyers afterward. Altogether ten women lawyers and twenty-eight male lawyers were described or rated. Some mothers hired more than one lawyer. I counted a mother's description of only one lawyer: either the one she had the strongest feelings about, whether they were positive or negative, or her last lawyer.

2. In terms of lawyers' sexism, in 1979 Weitzman and Dixon, op. cit., studied the conditions under which the "maternal preference" broke down. They asked lawyers to predict the factors that influence judges in custody battles. Lawyers ranked maternal "sexual promiscuity" as the third most important factor, after maternal physical and psychological neglect of children. They didn't mention fathers' "sexual promiscuity" at all. This may be a measure of lawyers' accurate perception of judicial sexism. It may also be a measure of lawyers' pre-ordained complicity with such sexism.

3. See Chapter 14 for a discussion of this.

4. Luepnitz, *Child Custody*, loc. cit.

5. Poor people are still entitled to "free" counsel if they are accused of murder, rape, robbery, etc.

6. There are exceptions to this rule. However, in a woman- and mother-hating culture and a man and father-idealizing culture, few people are absolutely "equal" in their pro-mother and pro-father sentiments or are genuinely capable of treating their clients equally, regardless of sex. For a variety of reasons, this is true of feminist, non-feminist, and anti-feminist lawyers.

7. Luepnitz, op. cit.

8. Eleanor Kuykendall, "Breaking the Double Binds," *Language and Style*, 13 (1980).

9. Non-traditional female clients have another kind of "problem" with male or female lawyers.

10. A male expert's need to be effective and to "know" more than his clients is very frustrated by the practice of domestic law.

11. Sharon is not officially part of the study reported in Chapter 4.

12. How different are these expectations from those held by nineteenth-century judges in England and America, who custodially condemned wives who were unwilling to forgive their husband's past cruelties or unwilling to drop their divorce action as "Unchristian," as no longer the Victorian Angel at Home?

CHAPTER FOURTEEN: THE MOTHER-JUDGE AND THE FATHER-JUDGE RELATIONSHIPS

1. See Nancy Polikoff, "Gender and Child-Custody Determinations: Exploding the Myths," loc. cit., for a description of what is available and/or accessible to the public.

2. Seventy-eight percent of the women lawyers reported that they were "treated disadvantageously" by judges in the courtroom because of their sex. Housewives involved in personal injury suits received smaller awards because these awards are "unfairly skewed" to earning potential, and homemakers are unpaid for their labor. Divorced women are forced into "deepening cycles of poverty" because of awards of insufficient child and spousal support—which is not even enforced. Police, judges, and probation officers all failed to enforce New Jersey's 1982 Prevention of Domestic Violence Act, aimed at wife-beating.

   This study was commissioned by New Jersey Chief Justice Robert N. Wilentz and coordinated by Attorney Lynn Hecht Schafran, Chair of the National Judicial Education Program to Promote Equality for Women and Men in the Courts. (This program is a project of the National Organization for Women's Legal Defense and Education Fund.)

3. *Off Our Backs*, May, 1982.

4. See Chapters 1 and 2. Also see Mary Dunlap, "Toward a Recognition of a Right to Be Sexual," *Women's Rights Law Reporter*, 7, 3 (Spring 1982). She gives several examples of rulings against female sexuality including the case of a sixty-seven-year-old woman being ejected from her nursing home in 1979 because of her sexual activity (*Wagner* v. *Sheltz*, Connecticut, 1979). Mary Dunlap, "Where the Person Ends, Does the Government Begin? An Exploration of Present Controversies Concerning the 'Right to Privacy,' " *Lincoln Law Review*, 12, 47 (1981): 54–63.

5. Jessie's story is described in Chapter 6.

6. Ella Mae's story is described in Chapter 6.

7. Josie's story is described in Chapter 5.

8. Rachel's story is contained in Chapter 9. In the course of researching this book I was sometimes able to "match" a particular judge's custodial order with some knowledge of his own divorce, child-support, and custody battle. For example, Judge W. had refused to pay child-support for more than ten years. In 1982, when his wife finally got an order of child-support, he sued for custody and claimed she'd moved far away and alienated his children's affections.

   This particular judge then rendered a decision in 1983 in another divorce and custody battle. In effect, he awarded the children to their father; and also awarded the father the house purchased by his ex-wife's money and use of his ex-wife's summer house. The reason? The mother was "hysterical" and "psychiatrically unstable." How? She was "hysterical" about her husband's threats to get custody, to alienate her from her children, and to get her house and her money, too. The judge saw the father as the more "stable" parent.

9. Adele's story is described in Chapter 10.

10. Maureen's story is in Chapters 8 and 9.

11. Helen's story is contained in Chapter 9 and in this chapter.

12. See Schecter, op. cit.

13. Armstrong, op. cit.

14. Schecter, op. cit.

15. Ibid.

16. Harriet Berne fled Rochester, New York, with her two sons. Family Judge Bruce Wettman ordered Scott Berne, eleven, and his seven-year-old brother, returned from Texas to their father, who had been awarded custody of the boys after the divorce. The boys wanted to live with their mother. Ms. Berne was so distraught by losing her sons that she attempted suicide shortly after her sons were removed. (*Family Law Reporter*, [Summer 1981].)

    In December 1980, the Federal Parental Kidnapping Prevention Act was signed into law.

17. Letty Cottin Pogrebin, op. cit. Pogrebin is here specifically referring to the legislative actions of the Reverend Greg Dixon. Dixon personally maneuvered a weakening of Indiana's child abuse restrictions, stating that "welts and bruises are a sign that a parent is doing a good job of discipline."

18. It is my initial impression, gained through the National Center for Women and Family Law, that Mimi "J." prefers that her case not be publicized by name. I am honoring her request. There was, however, media coverage of her case in the Washington based feminist newspaper *Off Our Backs*. The name of the judge is known.

19. Mimi "J." has never served this one day sentence. My information about this case was first obtained through media coverage and then through the National Center for Women and Family Law. Recently, Dr. Paul L. Adams told me that he was the expert witness for both mother and child in this case. He has written a book about his experience—one that, to date, no publisher has been interested in publishing. Dr. Adams told me that Mimi "J." has not been allowed to see her daughter at all.

20. The National Center for Women and Family Law suggested that the mothers and their lawyers forward this information to me.

21. This information is contained in Brigette's unpublished "Chronology of Events."

22. The mental health profession has to date or until very recently been resistant to take reports of incest seriously, or to *blame* the fathers for it. They tend to blame the mothers for paternal incest. In 1984 Dr. Deborah Luepnitz, a researcher and child analyst who had worked with me on sections of this book, suddenly shared the following information with me:

    "Before 1983 and our work together, I never 'noticed' how the mothers of paternal incest victims were scapegoated in family therapy and in incest therapy. I remember a recent case I was involved in, in which a mother lost custody of her daughter when the mother's boyfriend was jailed for raping a woman. The 16 year old daughter was then placed in the custody of her natural father, a 'respectable' Naval officer. In the course of therapy, it was discovered that the natural father had sexually molested the girl several years beforehand.

    "The father said he felt 'badly' about what had happened, but 'relieved' that they were finally discussing it and that 'it's all taken care of now.' He proceeded to request that the girl come and live with him—although the daughter stated that he was still fondling her as recently as last year.

    "Meanwhile, the mother is targeted from every side. The attitude of professionals and counselors is, 'Imagine what kind of *mother* that woman must be! First she marries a child molester, and then her boyfriend is a rapist!' "

23. The report was prepared by Arlene White with the assistance of many involved professionals and groups. On file with the National Center for Women and Family Law.

24. I knew that when adult women reported incestuous assaults they were disbelieved, or viewed as neurotic or psychotic. Mental health experts have

accused female victims of "imagining" paternal sexual molestation, of "seducing" their fathers, and of secretly "wanting" (what never happened) to happen anyway.

I knew that female victims were usually blamed for their victimization. I didn't know that incestuous fathers, with the help of psychiatrists, psychologists, and judges, were actually getting custody of their daughters.

Feminist researchers and writers such as Louise Armstrong, Kathleen Brady, Judith Herman, Florence Rush, and Diana Russell (to name only a few) have been writing about this since the early 1970s. Recently, a scandal erupted when Jeffrey Moussaieff Masson in *The Assault on Truth*, op. cit., added his voice to this growing body of literature.

25. Tom Vesey, "Claims Children Are Molested. Mother Defies Custody Terms," *Washington Post*, March 24, 1984.

26. Robert Lindsey, "A Mute Girl's Story: Child Abuse and the System," *New York Times*, May 12, 1984.

27. According to Judge Rena K. Uviller, "Unfortunately, the 'best interest of the child' formulation, while high-toned and well intended, is devoid of substance. A 'child's best interest' comprises any and all of the deciding judge's child rearing prejudices. These may range from the need for religious training to the respective virtues and pitfalls of permissiveness and authority. A 'child's best interests' may involve a judicial preference for living in the country as opposed to the city, as in *Shaw* v. *Shaw*, where the court noted disapprovingly that the mother lives 'in an apartment complex' whereas the father lives 'in a rural community with an environment of the minor child concerned' " (Rena K. Uviller, "Father's Rights and Feminism: The Maternal Presumption Revisited," *Harvard Women's Law Journal*, 1, 1 [1978]: 107–30).

28. In the *People* v. *Sinclair* (95 N.Y. Supp 861 [1905]), a five-year-old boy was awarded to his mother when he was three. Two years later, the judge considered him "old enough" to do without his mother, and "ready for paternal custody."

In *Jenkins* v. *Jenkins*, (173 Wis. 592, 181 NW 826 [1921]), a mother was awarded custody of her three-year-old. He was still judicially considered "tender." However, on appeal, the judge decided that the mother could not retain custody of her "older" sons, aged five and eight.

In *Butler* v. *Butler* (222 Alabama 684 [1931]), the judge determined that "older children, even if they were forcibly prevented from remaining with [their] mother, are now happily adjusted in the household of two paternal aunts. They can remain there. A four-year-old girl, however, still needs her mother."

In *Tuter* v. *Tuter* (Springfield Court of Appeals, Missouri 120 S.W. [2 Oct. 1938]), a judge decided that "older children can remain with [their] father in [an] environment hostile to mother, but that the younger child must be returned to mother."

29. Brown, op. cit.; Polikoff, op. cit.; Hunter, op. cit.

30. National welfare (AFDC) statistics obtained from the National Conference of State Legislatures (Denver, Col.). There is a long history of judicial, legal, and popular opposition to low welfare levels and procedures and as long a history of judicial, legal and popular support for an even more stringently controlled welfare policy. I would like to quote Justice Thurgood Marshall in *Wyman* v. *James*, arguing against the majority position that a citizen's welfare allotment could be cut off because the recipient refused to allow a government agent to enter her home:

"Would the majority sanction, in the absence of probable cause, compulsory visits to all American homes for the purpose of discovering child abuse? Or is this Court prepared to hold as a matter of constitutional law that a mother, merely because she is poor, is substantially more likely to injure or exploit her children? Such a categorical approach to an entire class of citizens would be dangerously at odds with the tenets of our democracy." (*Wyman* v. *James*, 91 S. Ct. 381, 399 [dissenting opinion] [1971], cited by Douglas R. Rendleman, op. cit.)

31. Interviews with Lillian Kozak, Chair, New York State NOW Committee on Domestic Relations 1981–1984.

32. Women are rarely rewarded for "following orders." Their reward consists of avoiding the punishment meted out to women who "disobey orders." I noted this in 1976, in *Woman, Money and Power*.

33. *Kersten Salk* v. *Lee Salk*, 393 NY 2nd 841 (28 Oct. 1975). Even though Dr. Salk had a very busy career, the court "consider[ed] it more important to ascertain the quality, rather than the quantity of time a parent devotes to his or her children, in determining the best interest of the child."

34. Kersten Salk, unpublished paper, 1976.

35. Nancy Polikoff, "Gender and Child-Custody Determinations," op. cit.

36. Ibid. Polikoff is commenting on *Neis* v. *Neis*, 599 P. 2d 305 (Kan., App. 1979).

37. *Van Dyke* v. *Van Dyke*, 48 Or. App. 965, 618, P. 2d, 465 (1980). Commented on by Nancy Polikoff, "Why Are Mothers Losing: A Brief Analysis of Criteria Used in Child Custody Determinations," *Women's Rights Law Reporter*, 7, #3 (Spring 1982).

38. Polikoff, in "Gender and Child-Custody Determinations," commenting on *Porter* v. *Porter*, 274 N.W. 2d 235 (N.D. 1979).

39. *Beck* v. *Beck,* New Jersey, Supreme Court, Docket #A-76; 86 N.J. 480, 432 A 2d 63 (1981); 173 N.J. Super. 33 App. Div. (1980).

40. Strictly speaking, the Supreme Court reversed the Appellate decision, by *upholding* the right of the trial court judge to mandate joint custody. The Supreme Court concluded that it did not retain jurisdiction in this matter, and that since two years had elapsed since the original joint custody decree, a new trial court hearing should take place.

    The Appellate court had noted that Mrs. Beck was a "more than adequate mother"; that Mr. Beck had not been an "involved parent" and that he used his "custodial time" to play golf and "utilized the services of the maternal grandmother" in his stead. The trial court judge relied on expert testimony that insisted that, although Mr. Beck enjoyed liberal *visitation,* that joint custody would be "better" for an uninvolved father than is visitation. "Visitation for all its liberality is not the same thing . . . it's just entertainment time."

    The Supreme Court did note that other experts counseled against joint custody *in this particular case;* and that both children did not want joint custody. "Although required to do so by the N.J.S.A., the trial judge did not, as previously indicated, interview the children to determine their preference as to custody before arriving at his June 12, 1979, disposition of the matter. And, even after he did interview the two girls during the proceedings which followed the entry of the June 12 judgment, he failed to give to their clear preference the "due weight" required by that statute. It appears that he summarily brushed aside their wishes with the comment that "they may not fully understand" the alternating custody plan which he had imposed. "But children are not pawns to be maneuvered and molded into agreement with an arbitrarily produced way of life which they strongly oppose and which neither parent had sought."

41. *Garska* v. *McCoy,* 278 S.E. 2nd 357, 361 W. Va. (1981). The case itself concerns Gwendolyn McCoy, a young unwed mother who, at the age of fifteen, was impregnated by her mother's boarder, Michael Garska. Garska did not see or support McCoy after the birth of Jonathan. In order for Jonathan to become eligible for medical coverage, his grandparents agreed to adopt him. At this point, Garska began sending $15 a week and moved for custody.

    The trial level court which awarded Garska sole custody found that he "is more intelligent than the natural mother"; is "better able to provide financial support and maintenance than the natural mother"; "has a somewhat better command of the English language than the natural mother"; "has a better appearance and demeanor than the natural mother."

    The Supreme Court reversed this decision. Nancy Polikoff (in "Gender and Child-Custody Determinations") notes that this case "developed a standard which preserves sex neutrality, encourages paternal involvement in child rearing, and guarantees that the child's bond with the parent providing daily care and nurturance will be maintained." Unfortunately, this "primary caretaker" presumption may apply only to young children. Once a child is "older," custody determination may not have to take past primary care into account."

42. *Albright* v. *Albright,* Miss. Sup. Ct. (9/21/83).

43. Communication to the National Center for Women and Family Law.

44. *In re Herbert A.D.* v. *Charlene D.,* reported in *New York Law Journal* (September 3, 1981).

45. Ibid. In 1983, in California, a custodial mother's "interference" with paternal visitation was "proper grounds for change of custody" (*In re Wood,* 9 *FLR* 2414; Cal. Ct. App. 5th Dist., 4/5/83).

46. *Ledsome* v. *Ledsome,* 51 LW 2591, 9 *FLR* 2331 (West Virginia Ct. of App. 8/11/83).

47. *Joye* v. *Schechter,* 460 NYS 2d 992, 9 *FLR* 2384 (New York Family Ct., 4/15/83). Note that this judge holds the *mother* responsible for both implementing a court order and for persuading her child to "love" her father.

48. *Daghir* v. *Daghir,* 441 N.Y.S. 2d 494 (N.Y. App. Div., 2d Dept. 1981); N.Y. 439 N.E. 2nd 324. Frances Daghir Coughlin's appeal of this decision was also unsuccessful.

49. Some judges have allowed mothers to move away. For example: *Auge* v. *Auge,* 61 L.W. 2768 Minn. Sup. Ct., 6/30/83; *Klein* v. *Klein* 93 A.D. 2d 807, 460 N.Y.S. 2d 607, *FLR* 2049, 4/4/83. These are exceptions to the rule.

50. *Louden* v. *Olpin,* App. 173 Cal. Rptr. 447 May 14, 1981, June 24, 1981.

51. *Stanley* v. *Illinois,* 405 U.S. 645, 92, S. Ct. 1208, 31, L. Ed 2nd 551 1972. It is important to remember that decisions about the paternal rights of unwed fathers vary widely and often contradict each other. For example, in 1979, a Wisconsin judge denied an unwed father's *custodial* claims. Willie Hill was imprisoned for kidnapping his three-year-old son. Hill claimed that he was discriminated against by laws that favored [unwed] maternal over [unwed] paternal custody. Judge John Desher ruled: "the classification [denying unwed fathers equal custodial rights] is based upon a fact of nature. The mother is present at birth. The maternal parentage is unquestioned and the mother continues to provide care and nurture for the child after birth."

52. N.Y. Soc. Serv. Law, sec. 372-c *McKinney.* Unwed fathers have many reasons for fighting for paternal recognition and for paternity rights. For example, an unwed father may want to force a pregnant woman into mar-

riage against her will; he may want to prevent an abortion by claiming custody of the pregnancy, based on his future paternal custodial rights. He may want a child of his own without having to marry, pay a surrogate mother, or share the child with her mother.

An unwed father may also want to "legitimize" and/or support a genetic child; or to make the child his legal heir. An unwed father may want to adopt his child, or to prevent his child's adoption by genetic strangers. For example, in 1980, Jeff Claypool, a twenty-year-old adopted child, sued the Associated Catholic Charities of Washington for custody of his genetic son. The child's mother was sixteen. "He's the only flesh and blood I know," said Claypool. Reported by the *San Francisco Examiner and Chronicle*, August 5, 1980.

See Nanette Dembitz, "Child's Rights and Exaggerated Concern for the Out-Of-Wedlock Father," *New York State Bar Journal*, May 1984 (reprinted in *The Single Mothers By Choice Newsletter*, Sept./Oct. 1984).

53. Thomas Grubiscich, "Unwed Father Wins Custody of Daughter," *Washington Post*, August 13, 1980.

54. Doris Jonas Freed, quoted ibid.

55. *Brauch* v. *Shaw*, N.H. Supr. Ct. 6/26/81; reported in 7 *FLR* 2648, 8-25-81.

56. Attorney Donna Hitchens reported the California case to me. I discuss it in Chapters Two and Fifteen. The Illinois case is *Myer* v. *Alvarado*, Ill. App. Ct. 4th Dist., 9/9/81; 7 *FLR*.

57. Reported in *Off Our Backs*, December 1984.

58. *Happel* v. *Mecklenburger*, Ill. App. Ct. 1st Dist. decided 10/8/81; reported in 9 *FLR* (11/3/81). Happel was Mrs. Mecklenburger's lover. Mrs. Mecklenburger was artificially inseminated with sperm from an anonymous donor which was mixed with her legal husband's sperm. Artificial insemination did not result in conception; Happel "proved" he was the genetic father.

59. *New York Times*, November 6, 1981.

60. *Virginia E.* v. *Alberto P.*, cited in *New York Post*, April 22, 1981.

61. *Lehr* v. *Robertson*, 103. S. C. 2985, 1983. Also see *Caban* v. *Mohammed*, 441 U.S. 380, 1979; and Dembitz, op. cit.

62. Armstrong, op. cit.

63. Please see Chapter 19 for a discussion of "patriarchal" (public) and "matriarchal" (private) visions of justice. Patriarchal law has been used to bring about some justice for women as *workers* in the public realm; rarely as *mothers* in the private realm.

CHAPTER FIFTEEN: FETAL POLITICS—WHO GETS CUSTODY OF THE "TEST-TUBE" BABY?: THE REPRODUCTIVE RIGHTS OF HUSBANDS, UNWED FATHERS, SPERM DONORS—AND OF WOMEN

1. Johann Jakob Bachofen, *Das Mutterrecht Gesammelte Werke* (Basel: 1948), and *Myth, Religion and Mother Right: Selected Writings*, Bollingen Series, LXXXIV (Princeton: Princeton University Press, 1967); Robert Briffault, *The Mothers* (London, New York: 1927); Elizabeth Gould Davis, *The First Sex* (New York: Putnam, 1971); Helen Diner, *Mothers and Amazons: The First Feminine History* (New York: The Julian Press, 1965); Friedrich Engels, *The Origin of the Family, Private Property and the State* (New York: International Publishers, 1972); Elizabeth Fischer, *Women's Creation, Sexual Evolution and the Shaping of Society* (New York: Doubleday-Anchor, 1979); Sir James G. Frazer, *The Golden Bough: A Study in Magic and Religion* (New York: Macmillan, 1968); Erick Neumann, *The Great Mother: An Analysis of the Archetype*, Bollingen Series, XLVII (New York: Pantheon, 1955); Evelyn Reed, *Woman's Evolution: From Matriarchal Clan to Patriarchal Family* (New York: Pathfinder Press, 1975); Merlin Stone, *When God Was a Woman* (New York: Dial Press, 1976); Barbara G. Walker, *The Woman's Encyclopedia of Myths and Secrets* (New York: Harper & Row, 1983).

2. There are many theories about how this changed. Each theory accounts for or explains *some* things. Each theory is provocative, plausible, and limited, and raises as many questions as it answers. As yet, these theories are conjectural, correlational, and descriptive, rather than casual. They are also discussed only by feminists; and rendered invisible or hotly disputed by anti-feminists. Some of these theories are as follows:

   A. Men were essentially indifferent or abusive to children. It was in women's interest that male genetic narcissism be engaged to protect children from male infanticide, cannibalism, abuse and neglect. Reed, op. cit., theorized that men were the original cannibals of the human race. If this is so, then the conception of women and children as male property would be a "step up" the ladder of survival. However, if men were truly dangerous to children, how could Goddess-worship or fertility worship have existed? How could the human race have survived at all if half its members were dangerous to the other half—and to children?

   B. Conceiving of women and children as male property allowed men to barter women as a way of settling male disputes. Male enemies could become allies through the sharing of blood-children. Male debts could be settled by a peaceful exchange of reproductive wealth, i.e., women in patriarchal marriage.

C. Conceiving of women and children as male property allowed men to "progress" from primitive "communism" to capitalism and from the (male) ownership of women and children to the (male) ownership of "real" property. Engels, op. cit. and Janet Farrell Smith, "Parenting and Property," op. cit.

D. Conceiving of women and children as male property is the only way that womb-less men can feel reproductively equal to women. Mothers are absolutely certain that their children are "theirs." Men never are. Men are in the humiliating position of having to buy and then guard a womb-man in order to be sure of their genetic paternity. Because men are psycho-biologically "alienated" from pregnancy, child-birth, and breast-feeding, they have related to children in controlling and authoritarian ways. They have also forced women into child care and then devalued it.

Please see my book *About Men*, loc. cit., for a somewhat poetic discussion of male uterus-envy. A number of twentieth-century social scientists have posited male uterus-envy; they include Bruno Bettelheim, Karen Horney, Wolfgang Lederer, Margaret Mead, Theodore Reik, Una Stannard, and Clara Thompson.

3. Una Stannard, *Mrs. Man* (Calif.: Germain Books, 1977).

4. The mammalian ovum was scientifically confirmed in 1827.

5. An individual woman may love an individual man or child, but her reproductive behavior follows a compulsory pattern. See Adrienne Rich, "Compulsory Heterosexuality and Lesbian Existence," in *Powers of Desire: The Politics of Sexuality*, Ann Snitow, Christine Stonsell, and Sharon Thompson, eds. (New York: Monthly Review Press, 1983).

6. Sometimes an individual woman may win more reproductive control within the family unit; sometimes, outside of it. The state control of single mothers, in terms of the level of welfare granted to them, is an example of state cruelty toward mothers and children. An individual man's abandonment of such a mother and her children to the (male) state is an example of individual male cruelty toward mothers and children.

7. Multi-issue "pro-life" activists who independently speak their conscience are not always considered "newsworthy." Individual thinkers are never granted the same attention as are well organized power blocs, which, in this case, represent the interests of the powerful (the organized male church) against those of the powerless (unorganized and impoverished) women.

8. The church and its politically organized followers have succeeded in barring Roman Catholic social workers from referring homeless women to a Los Angeles shelter run by a nun who signed a news advertisement saying Catholics disagreed on abortion. (Reported in the *New York Times*, Jan.

25, 1985.) The church and its politically organized followers succeeded in legally barring two Planned Parenthood clinics from providing abortions in upstate New York. (Reported in the *New York Times,* Feb. 1, 1985.) In March 1985, anti-abortionists successfully blocked an unmarried pregnant prisoner from having an abortion—until another judge reversed this order after the woman was nearly twenty-four weeks pregnant. (Reported in the *New York Post,* March 18, 1985.)

On April 16, 1985, the Reagan administration ordered doctors and nurses to provide medically "necessary treatment for severely handicapped 'Baby Doe' infants—except in cases where death appears inevitable. The rules were tacked onto a child abuse law. States must implement them by October 9 to qualify for child abuse prevention grants" (*New York Post,* April 16, 1985).

Please see Barbara Ehrenreich's article ("Hers") in the *New York Times,* February 7, 1985, about the abortion "controversy."

9. See Jeff Lyon, *Playing God in the Nursery* (New York: W. W. Norton, 1985), for a discussion of the legal and moral implications of genetic engineering, and the unspoken economic priorities of the "Right to Life" movement.

   Sterilization is the most popular form of (female) birth control. When a medically sterilized woman becomes pregnant, she cannot recover damages or the cost of rearing her unwanted child from her physician or his hospital. On March 27, 1985, Judge Mathew Jasen wrote for the New York Court of Appeals: "In view of our society's acknowledgement of the sanctity of life, it cannot be said, as a matter of public policy, that the birth of a healthy child constitutes a harm cognizable at law. The moral, social and emotional advantages arising from the birth are to be preferred to the protection of purely economic interests." (*New York Times,* March 27, 1985)

10. Robert Francoeur, *Utopian Motherhood: New Trends in Human Reproduction* (New York: Doubleday, 1970).

11. In England, a "scandal" erupted in the early 1980s when it was learned that (unwed) lesbians were attempting to become pregnant through artificial insemination. Surrogate mothers have mainly been hired by men—not by single women.

    I interviewed one mother whose husband's infertility led to legal adoption rather than artificial insemination. His pride wouldn't allow her to get pregnant if he couldn't be the genetic father. Her pride in being legally owned and accounted for was so great that she didn't consider or insist on any other reproductive option.

12. Mary Kay Blakely, "Surrogate Mothers: For Whom Are They Working?" *Ms.,* (March 1983).

13. Reluctance to part with a new-born child is not surprising. In September of 1981, a surrogate mother, Elizabeth Kane, said of the child she bore for a Kentucky couple, "If I had the opportunity to hold him again, I would have to turn it down because I couldn't trust myself." ("And She's a Mom In Mourning," *New York Post*, September 8, 1981.)

   The same year, surrogate mother Denise Thrane was forced into a custody battle in California for the child she was still bearing. During her pregnancy Thrane had decided to retain the child she had originally conceived for another couple. ("Whose Baby Is It, Anyway?" *Newsweek* [April 6, 1981]).

14. Ivor Peterson, *New York Times*, February 6, 1983. Malahoff has since denied that he refused to allow life-saving procedures to be administered.

15. This is the way Drs. Patrick Steptoe and Robert Edwards engineered "test-tube" baby Louise Brown's birth on July 25, 1978.

16. This happened in Australia when a South-American, California-based couple died without heirs, leaving two fertilized embryos behind in a Melbourne, Australia hospital. Physicians have asked "an ethics committee for advice on whether a surrogate mother should give birth to them so that they can grow up and claim their multi-million dollar fortune" (*New York Post*, June 18, 1984).

17. "Study of Sex Selection Gains," *New York Times*, May 28, 1983. She is referring to the universal preference for male over female children. This preference explains the rise in female infanticide in post-revolutionary China in the 1970s and 1980s. If government family planning restricts each couple to one child each, the desire for a boy remains overwhelming—and unchecked by the Chinese government.

   Evelyn Le Garrec of France published a story entitled "City of Fathers" in *Connexions: International Women's Quarterly*, 15 (Oakland, California: Winter 1985). Le Garrec envisions a logically savage patriarchal "take over" of the reproductive process:

   "The prehistoric time ended in 1980, nearly 100 years ago, with a discovery by the genius, St. Levin. He wasn't considered a saint in his own time. He practiced in a now non-existent town named Louisville in the U.S.A. Like many other inventors, he couldn't foresee the possible ramifications of his research. In former times, it had been his modest aim to help couples in which the woman was sterile. He wanted to enable them to buy a child like a car. In those primitive societies the father didn't live by himself; the father lived with a human-female, who was called 'wife.' Pre-scientific categories classified these creatures as human beings. In the old religion, even the priests acknowledged, after lengthy discussions, that these creatures had a 'soul.' These 'wives' gave birth to children, like the workers do today in the Factories of the Sons. But despite the fact that the father gave his name to the children, the 'wives' also possessed the children and had the task of raising them. As a result, they wanted to keep the children for themselves. Those times were filled with trouble and fear for the men. Until then, the fathers had not shown much interest in their children—no more than for their other possessions, like furniture. But when they felt that they were about to lose this particular possession, and when they noticed that their name, their insurance against mortality, was threatened with extinction, they suddenly discovered the pleasant side and the honor of fatherhood. Fathers went on hunger strikes in order to force their pregnant 'wives' to reimburse them with the product of their sperm. Organizations for the defense of fatherhood were established. There was a renaissance of film and literature whose themes celebrated the special bond, the holy connection between father and son.

"But success was really due to a discovery by Dr. Levin. He had the idea of fertilizing an anonymous woman with the sperm of a man whose wife was sterile. The woman signed a contract that she would remain anonymous and that she would give away the fruit of her pregnancy.

"This revolutionary practice led to the differentiation between pregnancy and motherhood. Pregnancy became a profession. The public got used to the idea that fathers could have children without 'wives.' This all led to the present population of single fathers. They had to keep the human-female as long as the even cleaner, more sterile test tube was not yet perfected. The human-females were locked into factories, and robots began performing all the tasks which in former times had been performed by humans. The number of humans on the earth was reduced to one million. These humans, all very healthy, distributed themselves into the remaining cities."

Please see Andrea Dworkin, *Right Wing Women* (New York: G. P. Putnam, 1982), for a discussion of these issues.

18. This is one of Germaine Greer's points in her well documented polemic against Western culture and technology, *Sex and Destiny* (New York: Harper & Row, 1984). Unfortunately, she romanticizes compulsory, non-Western motherhood and erroneously believes that in countries where marital rape, the genital mutilation of women, and female sexual slavery are taken for granted, that *women* can choose a natural method of birth control that men will obey.

See Rita Arditti, Renate Duell Klein, and Shelly Minden, *Test Tube Women: What Future for Motherhood?* (Boston: Pandora Press, 1985), for a discussion of these issues.

19. Shulamith Firestone, *The Dialectics of Sex* (New York: Morrow, 1971); Marge Piercy, *Woman on the Edge of Time* (New York: Knopf, 1976); Martha Gimenez, "Feminism, Pronatalism and Motherhood," in *Moth-

ering: Essays in Feminist Theory, Joyce Trebilcott, ed., (Totowa, N.J.: Rowman & Allenheld, 1984).

20. Personal interview, 1982, New York City. Dr. Levy is an anthropologist. The study is as yet unpublished.

21. In view of the number of sperm donors and unwed fathers now fighting to establish their paternal rights, a small number of legally informed women believe that single mother adoption is the safest *custodial* course for any woman to take.

22. Perhaps individual or family control over anything is only an illusion. If public labor is alienated, so is private labor. It may be *experienced* differently. To the extent to which it *is* different, it may function as an opiate— as long as it in no way threatens church, corporate, or state control over anything.

23. Kirsten Luker, *The Politics of Motherhood* (Berkeley: University of California Press, 1984).

CHAPTER SIXTEEN: MOTHERS IN PRISON

1. Judge Angel Carven, Florida State Clearinghouse Commission, 1980.

2. The FBI has estimated that 15,000 women are in jail on any given day (see the Justice Department, *FBI Uniform Crime Reports*, 1970–1984).

   Ann Stanton, *When Mothers Go to Jail* (Lexington, Mass.: Lexington Books–D. C. Heath, 1980), did a study of prisoner mothers. She found that 78 percent of her interviewees were living on welfare prior to their arrest and that 50 percent came from families in which a family member had also spent time in jail.

   The Florida Clearinghouse on Criminal Justice, in a 1978 publication, noted that the "typical" female offender is black (64 percent); is twenty-seven years old or younger (50 percent); has a tenth grade education or less; is serving a sentence of five years or less; "is usually the mother of one or more children under the age of three" (70 percent); and is usually a single parent and the sole support of the household.

   Julie Jackson, "The Loss of Parental Rights as a Consequence of Conviction and Imprisonment: Unintended Punishment" (*New England Journal of Prison Law*, 6: 1 [1979]), notes that recent estimates allow that 56 to 80 percent of imprisoned women leave behind dependent children. Convicted female felons leave 2.43 children behind.

   Brenda G.McGowan and Karen L. Blumenthal, *Why Punish the Children?: A Study of Children of Women Prisoners*, (Hackensack, N.J.: National Council on Crime and Delinquency, 1980), confirm the extent to which women prisoners are poor single mothers; as do attorney Ellen Barry, Director of Legal Services to Women Prisoners in California; Evelyn Machtinger, Family Support and Advocacy Coordinator, Aid to Incarcerated Mothers (AIM), (1982–1983); and Charlene Snow, "Women in Prison" (*Clearinghouse Review* [February 1981]).

3. Snow, op. cit.

4. Ann Stanton, op. cit.

5. Personal interview, Rikers Island, 1981.

6. Enid Gamer and Charles P. Gamer, "There Is No Solitary Confinement: A Look at the Impact of Incarceration Upon the Family" (April 12, 1983).

7. Ellen Barry, "Legal Service Available to Incarcerated Parents and Their Children: An Assessment of Needs and Services," presented at the National Institute of Mental Health Conference, October 1979, plus personal interviews in 1981, 1982, and 1985.

8. Dorothy Zeitz, *Women Who Embezzle or Defraud: A Study of Convicted Felons* (New York: Praeger, 1981), quoted by Sarvara Raffel Prince in *Signs* (Summer 1983).

9. Ann Stanton, op. cit.

10. Susan Reed, quoted by Jones, *Women Who Kill*, op. cit.

11. Snow, op. cit.

12. Joan Potter, *Corrections* Magazine (December 1978).

13. Jones, op. cit., notes that "The colonial lawmakers fell back upon English Common Law, which defined the murder of a husband or master as petit treason. Since the husband was 'lord' of the wife, the Common Law said, her killing him was treachery comparable to murdering the king—though on a lesser scale. A Virginia judge defined the gravity of the crime: '. . . Other offenses are injurious to Private Persons only, but this is a Public Mischief, and often strikes at the Root of all Civil Government.' "

14. Ibid.

15. Ibid. Jones gives many examples of wife-battering and murder going unpunished—or more lightly punished than husband-murder in self-defense. Noting the 1978 *maximum* sentence given to Ruth Childers in Indiana, she writes: "The last two people charged with murder in Benton County (Indiana), both men, seemed in comparison to have gotten off rather easily: one who shot his wife was convicted of voluntary manslaughter and given the minimum sentence of one to ten years, while the other, the man who beat his wife to death and raped her while giving her 'a good thumping'

was never tried for murder (despite what the sheriff called 'a lot of evidence') but allowed to plead guilty to manslaughter and given a six-year sentence."

16. Luz Santana, information circulated privately, 1981.

17. Ibid. As of 1985, Santana was still imprisoned.

18. Jones, op. cit.

19. Ibid.

20. Snow, op. cit.

21. See Chapters 1, 2, and 14. Jones, op. cit., has given us many historical examples of this double standard of crime and punishment. She notes: "Many other people, guilty of crimes far more damaging to society, escaped the hangman. Just about the same time that Hanna Piggin and Abiel Converse were hanged in Northampton, Massachusetts [for concealing the birth of a bastard and/or for infanticide], six leaders of Shay's Rebellion convicted in the same jurisdiction of treason and sentenced to hang, were pardoned. Still others, guilty of far more brutal crimes, got off with light sentences. When Robert Thompson was convicted of assault in the same Northampton jurisdiction, he was whipped twenty stripes, set on the gallows for one hour, and ordered to pay costs. He had beaten up his wife, Agnes Thompson, and 'dug out both her eyes with his thumb and a stick so she is entirely blind.' "

22. For example, the white and wealthy Patricia Hearst was convicted for bank-robbery. No weight was given to the fact that she'd been kidnapped, raped, terrorized, isolated, and brainwashed. Her upper class origin and the fact that she was *female* were apparently used against her in her first trial. The white and middle class Jane Alpert was also more severely punished than were Abbie Hoffman or Mark Rudd, both of whom were white, male and committed a variety of political crimes during the 1960s and 1970s. Neither Hoffman nor Rudd was kidnapped, raped or brainwashed. Both men spent no or very little time in jail. Hoffman was allowed to enter a work-release program and continue his new life as an environmentalist and husband.

23. See Nat Hentoff's excellent coverage of her case in the *Village Voice*, 1983. According to Paula Martinac in the October 1983 issue of *Womanews* (4, 9), Newak was finally released on parole on August 17, 1983, after serving one year of her three year sentence.

24. Donna Hansen in *Prisons* eloquently describes prison experience. "Barbed wire" and "cement floors" imprison "gray levi bodies" into "loneliness, isolation, helplessness and kicking cold turkey"; shrinking cells, echoing halls and metal doors surround women forced into "mindless labor" and watched suspiciously, twenty-four hours a day by police and by flashlight. Hansen misses her "family, her children adopted away" and wants to know "when can I go home?"

25. Personal interview with Framingham prisoner rights activist Susan Saxe, 1982.

26. Barry, op. cit.

27. Barbara Treen, personal interview, 1981. Also, see Barbara Swartz, *Inmate Mothers*, op. cit. McGowan and Blumenthal, op. cit., note that the New York City Police Department had no guidelines for handling an offender mother until 1972. Now, under Patrol Guide Procedure #106-12, "When an officer arrests a woman, he is required to ask whether she has a dependent for whom she is responsible."

28. Swartz, op. cit.

29. Swartz, op. cit., gives a tragic account of a friend's mistreatment of a prisoner's children:

"Selma Jones (a pseudonym) is serving up to a three-year sentence at Bedford Hills Correctional Facility in New York for possession of a small quantity of narcotics. She is young, black and a first offender. She also has two small children. When she went to prison, she asked a friend to care for her son and daughter. Through the Department of Social Services in her home county, the friend was made the children's foster mother. Shortly after Ms. Jones arrived at Bedford Hills, her four year old son was found beaten to death. There were human teeth marks covering his body. Her prison caseworker says the foster mother is suspected of the murder. The daughter, who is suffering from a rare blood disease, has been taken from the foster home and placed in an institution. When Ms. Jones is released from prison she will have to go to court to try to regain custody of her child. She may not win."

30. Personal interview, 1981, conducted by Ellen Whitford.

31. McGowan and Blumenthal, op. cit.

32. Personal interview, 1981.

33. See Florida Judge Angel's comments about this. Florida State Clearinghouse Commission, 1980.

34. Karen Holt, "Nine Months to Life: The Law and the Pregnant Inmate," *Journal of Family Law*, 20 (1981–1982).

35. "No More Cages," *Off Our Backs* (July 1984).

36. *New York Daily News*, August 1, 1983.

37. Personal interview, 1981.

38. Sister Eileen Hogan, Personal interview, op. cit.

39. In 1982 Kathy Boudin was imprisoned and at first denied all visits with her infant son. Even Dr. Benjamin Spock couldn't persuade prison officials of the importance of "contact" visits.

Recently, Judith Clark, also associated with the Black Liberation Army and the Brinks truck robbery, was sentenced to seventy-five years as an accessory to murder in the killing of a Brinks guard. Clark was, of course, not allowed to take her toddler daughter into prison with her. Nor were her pre-arranged plans for her child's upbringing honored by her parents or by the state. In 1984, her daughter, Harriet, was custodially awarded to her maternal grandparents. It is up to them if and how often Harriet will visit her mother; and if and how often Harriet can see those with whom her mother wanted her to live. See the interview with Judith Clark in *Off Our Backs* (December 1984).

40. Swartz, op. cit.

41. Snow, op. cit.

42. McGowan and Blumenthal, op. cit.

43. Treen, op. cit.

44. *In re Tricia Lashawanda M*, New York Family Court, Queens County, 4/23/82, reported in 8 *FLR* 2387 (5/11/82).

45. As we have noted, the majority of mothers in prison are not necessarily unfit or unloving mothers. Some are. The majority of imprisoned mothers have committed petty economic crimes; victim-less sexual crimes; crimes of drug addiction; and crimes of self-defense. They can and should be "rehabilitated" and assisted to remain in contact with their children.

In my opinion, it serves no one to imprison such mothers. Their imprisonment is a major disservice to their children and ultimately to other taxpayers. The money spent on punitively warehousing prisoner-mothers and their children (over and over again), would be better spent on their education, housing, employment, and psychological counseling. Employed mothers with decent-sized paychecks could "pay back" the small amounts of money they originally stole.

In my opinion, it serves no one to imprison women for the "victimless" crime of prostitution. Actually, there is a victim involved—the prostitute and her children, if she is a mother. Men who patronize prostitutes are rarely fined, imprisoned, or custodially endangered.

Prostitution is essentially a petty economic crime which should be decriminalized—not legalized. Wherever prostitution is legalized, the government becomes a profit-hungry pimp. The almost all-female and/or male-oriented sex-worker has no job security, job advancement, or other benefits, as she rapidly grows "too old" to practice her profession.

The state might seriously consider fining those who purchase the services of prostitutes, and those who profit from such services, such as pimps, landlords, politicians, club and hotel owners, etc. The state definitely must imprison those men and women who seduce, kidnap, terrorize, rape, drug, and imprison young girls into pornography and prostitution.

Drug addiction is, unfortunately, an American and twentieth-century way of life. Many addictive drugs are legal and easily available to adults, white people, and to the middle and upper classes. Although drug addiction is a serious problem, drug addiction is not always permanent; and it is amenable to a wide variety of treatments.

Drug addicted mothers are not necessarily without "mother-love"; or necessarily unfit mothers. It is clear that a heroin addict who is poor and denied legal access to drugs will lead a "criminal" life; and that a "criminal" life is far less than ideal for any participant. It is also clear that many children of drug addict mothers would rather live with or retain a relationship to their mothers—than live mother-less.

To the extent to which addiction is a genetic predisposition and/or a chemical and metabolic problem, it may be medically treated. To the extent to which addiction is a psychological problem, it may be psychologically treated. To the extent to which addictions reflect the normal self-destructive response to poverty, racism and sexism, more extensive measures may be needed to combat it. Even then, drug addiction may not totally disappear from American or modern life. What *may* disappear is its widespread use among the young, the poor, the non-white and the female.

The majority of mothers imprisoned for crimes of violence are battered wives who finally defended themselves and their children. While I don't insist that such mothers be given ticker-tape parades at taxpayer expense, I do think it important that such mothers be subsidized to tell their stories: in schools, churches, synagogues, and on television. It is important that battered wives who rose to their own self-defense be given an opportunity to function as deterrents to male domestic violence—and as role models.

I have no immediate suggestions about how to punish those women in prison, including mothers, who have no respect for human life. They probably should be treated exactly as their male counterparts are. (This may improve their treatment immediately.)

According to attorneys Ellen Barry and Charlene Snow, and various prison-activists and social workers, some programs do exist to facilitate an infant's or child's access to her imprisoned mother. They are extremely recent, limited, under-budgeted, and bureaucratically monstrous. For example, California has long had legislation allowing children to remain with incarcerated mothers. This legislation has not been enforced until recently. Women eligible for the California program must have less than two years to serve; must be first time offenders; must be the primary parent of the children; must have children who are two years old or less; and must be judged by the state as fit mothers. Attorney Charlene Snow comments on this California legislation which, on paper, allows prisoner-mothers to live with their children:

"Although the legislation appears to be progressive, there are a number of exclusions which make it almost impossible for women to qualify for the program. *A recent survey of approximately 800 women prisoners in California found only 7 women who were qualified to participate in the program.*"

In New York, the Women's Prison Association has developed several programs to aid prisoner-mothers. For example, Hopper House is a halfway house for eighteen female prisoners and ex-prisoners which provides a supportive re-entry shelter for prisoner-mothers while they attend school and hunt for jobs. *This halfway house unfortunately cannot accommodate any children.*

Attorney Ellen Barry proposes that in place of prison nurseries (which house infants and mothers separately), a separate prison facility be built to house mothers with their children. Alternatively, Barry suggests that prisoner-mothers and their children be housed in a sheltered environment away from prison grounds. "Mother-Release" programs, analogous to the "work-release" programs available to male prisoners, should be established. This would maintain the continuity and quality of the mother-child relationship. It would also facilitate a prisoner-mother's re-entry into society.

In 1980, Aid to Incarcerated Mothers (AIM), a program geared to the women prisoners in Framingham Prison in Massachusetts, began. According to director Evelyn Machtinger and ex-prisoner activist Susan Saxe, AIM functions as a crucial intermediary between mother-prisoners and the bureaucracies which control their lives: social services, foster care agencies, social workers, and the Department of Corrections. AIM assigns volunteers to help mothers on a one-to-one basis, with a variety of needs. AIM also encourages, arranges, pays for and expedites children's visits to their imprisoned mothers.

For a comprehensive review of existing prison programs for mothers and children, see Barry, op. cit.; Harvey S. Perlman, "Incarcerated Parents and Their Children: The Uniform Commissioners' Model Sentencing and Corrections Act," National Institute of Mental Health Conference, Oct. 16–17, 1979; Stanton, op. cit.; and Gamer and Gamer, op. cit.

CHAPTER SEVENTEEN: MOTHERS AS PRISONERS OF PATRIARCHY: A COMPARISON OF CONTEMPORARY CUSTODY TRIALS AND WITCHCRAFT TRIALS

1. In 1983 Karen Daskam went into labor just after her arrest for re-kidnapping her paternally-kidnapped child. Deputy Fred Nigh "suggested it was sick to think the treatment of [the woman in labor] was not proper. Where is the difference between her and anyone else? We've had people here with broken necks that cut the chains and left. Any prisoner in the hospital [is] chained twice—leg and arm. It's been that way for twenty-one years." (*New York Post*, August 1, 1983; August 2, 1983.)

2. Carrie's story is contained in Chapter 13. The exact date and geographical location have been changed to protect the innocent from being further victimized by the guilty.

3. Jessie's story is contained in Chapter 6. The exact date and location have been changed to protect the innocent from being further victimized by the guilty.

4. Kate's story is discussed in Chapter 19. The exact date and location have been changed to protect the innocent from being further victimized by the guilty.

5. Alix's story is discussed in Chapter 7. The exact date and location have been changed to protect the innocent from being further victimized by the guilty.

6. Rachel's story is discussed in Chapters 9 and 14. The exact date and location have been changed to protect the innocent from being further victimized by the guilty.

7. The eloquent phrase "vulnerable women caught up in one of society's whirlpools of callousness or cruelty" belongs to John Putnam Demos, *Entertaining Satan: Witchcraft and the Culture of Early New England* (New York: Oxford University Press, 1982).

8. Freidrich von Spee, *Cautio Criminalis (Precautions for Prosecutors)*, reprinted in Douglas Russell Hope Robbins's *The Encyclopedia of Witchcraft and Demonology*, (New York: Crown, 1959). Von Spee described the European witchcraft trials in forty-one points. Some of these points are repetitive. He made five additional points which I quote at the end of this chapter.

9. The Bull of Innocent VIII, reprinted in Heinrich Krämer and Jacobus Sprenger, *Malleus Maleficarum*, trans. Montague Summers (London: Arrow Books, 1928).

10. Krämer and Sprenger, op. cit.

11. Ibid.

12. Demos, op. cit.

13. Matilda Joslyn Gage, *Women, Church and State* (1893), quoted by Mary Daly, *Gyn/Ecology: The Metaethics of Radical Feminism* (Boston: Beacon Press, 1978); Robbins, op. cit.; Von Spee, op. cit.

14. The title of Demos's book is *Entertaining Satan*.

15. Z. Budapest, *The Holy Book of Women's Mysteries—Parts One and Two* (Los Angeles: Susan B. Anthony Coven No. 1, 1979, 1980); Phyllis Chesler, *Women and Madness* (New York: Doubleday, 1972); Chesler, "The Amazon Legacy: An Interpretive Essay" in *Wonder Woman* (New York: Holt Rinehart & Winston/Warner Books, 1973), also excerpted in Charlene Spretnak, (see below), 1982; Chesler, *About Men;* Daly, op. cit.; *Pure Lust* (Boston: Beacon Press, 1984); Frazier, op. cit.; G. B. Gardner, *The Meaning of Witchcraft* (New York: Samuel Weiser, 1959); Judy Grahn, *Another Mother Tongue* (Boston: Beacon Press, 1984); Robert Graves, *The White Goddess: A Historical Grammar of Poetic Myth* (New York: Farrar, Straus, & Giroux, 1948); C. Kerenyi, *Eleusis Archetypal Image of Mothers and Daughters.* Bollinger Series 4 (New York: Pantheon, 1967); T. C. Lethbridge, *Witches* (New York: Citadel Press, 1962); Jules Michelet, *Satanism and Witchcraft: A Study in Medieval Superstition* (New York: Citadel Press, 1939); Margaret Murray, *The Witch Cult in Western Europe* (London: Oxford University Press, 1921); Margaret Murray, *The God of the Witches* (London: Oxford University Press, 1931); Neumann, op. cit.; Demosthenes Savramis, *The Satanizing of Women, Religion Versus Sexuality* (New York: Doubleday, 1974); Stone, op. cit.; Charlene Spretnak, *The Politics of Women's Spirituality: Essays on the Rise of Spiritual Power Within the Feminist Movement* (New York: Doubleday-Anchor, 1982).

16. Ehrenreich and English, op. cit.; Barbara Ehrenreich and Deidre English, *Witches, Midwives and Nurses* (New York: Feminist Press, 1978); Jean Donnison, *Midwives and Medical Men: A History of Interprofessional Rivalries and Women's Rights* (New York: Schocken Books, 1977); Michelet, op. cit.

17. Thomas Szasz, *The Manufacture of Madness: A Comparative Study of the Inquisition and the Mental Health Movement* (New York: Harper & Row, 1970).

18. Demos, op. cit., and Robbins, op. cit.

19. According to Demos, op. cit., women most often accused women of witch-craft. They then persuaded their husbands, fathers, or male employers to have the accused witch arrested. Men alone sat in formal judgment at a witchcraft trial.

20. Ibid.

21. Ibid. Demos states that "sometimes the witch and her [his] spouse squared as antagonists. Jane Collins was brought to court not only for witchcraft, but also for 'railing' at her husband and calling him 'gurly-gutted Devil.' Bridget Oliver and her husband, Thomas, were tried, convicted and pun-ished for 'fighting with each other.' The estrangement between Sarah Dib-ble and *her* husband was so bitter that he actively encouraged suspicions of her witchcraft. Moreover, his general 'carriage' toward her was most inhumane, e.g., beating of her so that he caused the blood to settle in several places on her body."

22. Ibid.

23. Ibid. Demos consciously draws on feminist and psychoanalytic sources such as Dorothy Dinnerstein and Nancy Chodorow, to arrive at this explanation. His use of the concept of "vulnerability" was extremely helpful.

24. Krämer and Sprenger, op. cit. It is important to note that many individual husbands opposed their wives' arrests and sought to help them. They were rarely successful. Many were themselves accused of being "witch lovers" or accomplices and also executed. See both Demos and Robbins for such examples.

A number of theorists, occultists, and poets have suggested that men's involvement with "witchcraft" or with "witches" signified male involvement in pagan religious practices.

However, there are important distinctions to bear in mind about the nature of the male involvement in paganism or Goddess-worship. For example, the mythic male images involved in Goddess-worship range from son-consorts with whom goddesses have children; son-consorts who rape, kill, and dismember their mothers; surrogate (earthly) sons who as kings, warriors, or youths are ritually sacrificed to ensure harvests, ward off dis-ease, transcend the need for warfare, etc.; and surrogate sons who castrate themselves, are castrated, or remain celibate in order to become more like the priestesses of a goddess.

Then there are patriarchal surrogate sons who castrate and exile the priestesses, put on their long skirts, worship the male ritual sacrifice (cru-cifixion and a male godhead, instead of the female godhead); patriarchal surrogate sons who participate in European coven activities as women's spiritual superiors, equals, or subordinates; patriarchal surrogate sons who engage in group heterosexual or homosexual sex for the sake of male-dominated sex; and surrogate sons who are accused of witchcraft simply because they love individual women or individual men, sexually, and out-side of marriage and who also believe in Goddesses.

25. Carol F. Karlsen, "The Devil in the Shape of a Woman: The Witch in Seventeenth Century New England." Unpublished paper. Presented at the American Historical Association annual meeting, December 28, 1983. This paper is a summary of her unpublished book.

26. This is Demos's interpretation, paraphrased.

27. Karlsen, op. cit.

28. Demos, op. cit.

29. Ibid. Demos notes that the "four sons of the Windsor witch, Lydia Gilbert, became substantial citizens of Wethersfield and Hartford. (Two were fre-quent office-holders.) David Lake, the younger son of Alice (convicted and executed in the town at Dorchester in 1651), was a leading man in the town of Little Compton, Rhode Island. Erasmus James, Jr., son of Jane (perennial suspect in Marblehead), rose up from humble beginnings as a carpenter to the status of 'merchant and shipwright'; eventually he was a local Selectman, his name prefixed by the honorific 'Mr.' The sons of Mary (Bliss) Parsons of Northhampton attained various forms of civic promi-nence, while her daughters married prominence (e.g., merchants and min-isters)."

30. The source for this is given as Ronald Seth and is quoted by Daly, op. cit.

31. Robbins, op. cit.

32. Ibid.

33. For aesthetic reasons, I have taken the liberty of re-ordering Father Von Spee's presentation.

    The colonial and European Inquisitions were different in many important ways. My comparison of custodially challenged mothers and accused witches is based on an account of the European Inquisition and on an account of contemporary custodially challenged mothers in North America. Demos's and Karlsen's historical research on colonial witches could have been in-cluded, as could my own interviews with custodially challenged mothers in contemporary Europe, and under Catholic and Islamic rule in South America, the Middle East, and Africa. These mothers are here in spirit. Strictly speaking, they are not part of this analogical comparison.

    All the custodially challenged "good enough" mothers in my formal study are represented in this comparison. Twenty-six women are mentioned by name. All these women were involved in judicial battles. They represent 70 percent of the judicially challenged mothers.

34. Lucy is discussed in Chapters 5 and 8.

35. Cheryl is discussed in Chapter 8.

36. Margaret is discussed in Chapter 9.

37. Miki and Nora are discussed in Chapter 6; Adele is discussed in Chapter 10.

38. For example, Catherine, Lucy, and Josie are discussed in Chapter 5; Ella Mae, Jessie, Miki, and Nora in Chapter 6; Rachel in Chapters 9 and 14; Carrie in Chapter 9; and Marta in Chapters 13 and 14. Nora is also discussed in Chapters 2 and 9.

39. See Chapters 9 and 14.

40. Beth is discussed in Chapter 9.

41. See Chapter 14.

42. Please see my book, *Women and Madness*, for a discussion of this. Also, note my discussion of the first study which demonstrated that clinical experts routinely perceive normal women as "unhealthy" adults (Inge Broverman et al., "Sex Role Stereotypes and Clinical Judgments of Mental Health," *Journal of Consulting and Clinical Psychology*, 34, [1970]).

43. Elizabeth Packard is discussed in Chapter 1; and in *Women and Madness*. Nora is discussed in Chapters 2, 6, and 9.

44. Ibid.

45. See Chapter 14 for a discussion of Brigette and Arlene. Neither mother is part of my formal group.

46. Ibid. Also, see Armstrong, op. cit., and Sarah Begus and Pamela Armstrong, "Daddy's Right," in *Families, Politics and Public Policy*, op. cit., for a fuller discussion of the role of experts in blaming the mother for paternal incest.

47. Marie is not part of my formal study. See Chapter 20, "Children's Rights," for Marie's further comments.

48. For example, Catherine is discussed in Chapter 5, Ella Mae in Chapter 6, and Adele in Chapter 10.

49. Nora and Miki are discussed in Chapter 6; Alix is discussed in Chapter 7.

50. See Chapter 12.

51. Marta is discussed in Chapters 9, 13, and 14.

52. Catherine is discussed in Chapter 5; Miki and Nora are discussed in Chapter 6; Melanie and Alix are discussed in Chapter 7; Rachel is discussed in Chapters 9 and 14; Marta is discussed in Chapters 9, 13, and 14; Grace and Adele are discussed in Chapter 10. Adele is also discussed in Chapter 2.

53. Terry is discussed in Chapter 10.

54. Loretta is discussed in Chapter 5.

55. Ella Mae is discussed in Chapter 6.

56. Leslie is discussed in Chapter 9.

57. See Chapters 8 and 14.

58. See Chapters 5, 6, 7, 9, and 14.

59. See Chapter 13.

60. See Chapter 16.

61. See Chapter 7 for Melanie's story.

62. See Chapters 14 and 16.

63. See Chapter 5, for Josie's story, and Chapters 7, 10, 13, and 19.

64. This is discussed in Chapter 2. Judge Duran said of mother and lawyer Margaret Bezou: "She is indeed interested first and foremost in herself and in furthering her own career. . . . [she had shown no sign of being] 'willing to sacrifice advancement of her career.' . . . [the handicapped child] 'had been cursed with two ambitious parents, especially a mother who wants to be a lawyer more than she wants to be a mother' " (*National Law Journal*, September 26, 1983).

65. See Chapters 2, 7, and 14.

66. Marta is discussed in Chapters 9, 13, and 14.

67. Rachel is discussed in Chapters 9 and 14.

68. See Chapter 2.

69. Linda is discussed in Chapter 5.

70. See Chapter 4.

71. See Chapters 8, 9, 10, 12, and 14.

72. Leslie is discussed in Chapters 9 and 14.

73. See Chapter 12 for a discussion of what I mean by maternal "sterilization" or castration.

74. See Chapter 16.

75. See Chapters 8, 14, and 15.

76. See Chapters 11 and 12.

77. Ibid.

78. Sonia is discussed in Chapters 12 and 19.

79. Norma is discussed in Chapter 10.

80. Helen is discussed in Chapters 9 and 14.

81. Natalie is discussed in Chapter 10.

82. The only one of Father Von Spee's points not reprinted in my comparison is: "Now what prince can doubt her guilt when he is told she has confessed voluntarily, without torture?" This is perhaps analogous to the responses of husbands whose wives "admitted" they committed adultery or became lesbians, who "admitted" that they *did* want careers, or who admitted that battling for custody was becoming unbearable and wearing them down.

83. Most of the judicial orders that I cite in Chapters 1, 2, and 14 read, in part, like documents gathered during a witchcraft proceeding. I would like to present an excerpt of only one case, that of Mildred Milovich, whom I didn't interview, but whose case I describe in Chapter 2. The excerpt summarizes the trial court's decision of paternal custody and upholds it at the Appellate level. (*Milovich* v. *Milovich*, March 31, 1982, Ill. App. 434 N.E. 2d 811).

    "On May 14, 1979, after approximately 12 years of marriage, petitioner filed a dissolution action, alleging that his wife was guilty of adultery and requesting various forms of relief. Respondent answered and counter-petitioned, denying the adultery allegations and alleging that petitioner was guilty of mental cruelty.

    "On May 16, 1980, the child custody hearing began. The court heard the testimony of 15 witnesses in 6 sessions over a five-month period. Petitioner's first witness was Dr. Dean Dauw, a clinical psychologist and published author with 15 years of experience in marriage counseling. He testified that he consulted with the parties 10 times between March 13 and May 8, 1976. Mrs. Milovich had told him of her wish to "better relate" to her daughter, Nicole, and her desire to have a "more effective career" than being a mother or a housewife. The doctor conducted psychological tests on the parties and concluded that respondent had certain needs which led her to be impatient with her daughter.

    "George Lebseck, petitioner's supervisor at the Chicago Housing Authority, next testified. He had known Peter Milovich for 20 years, at work as well as socially. He testified that on two occasions he had seen Peter display a concerned, responsive attitude toward the two Milovich children.

    "Dmitor Rakich, president of the congregation of petitioner's church, testified that he had known Peter for 30–35 years, through church activities. He testified that petitioner attended church regularly and brought the children to Sunday School. He thought that Peter exhibited more "warmth" toward them than had Mrs. Milovich. He stated his opinon that Mr. Milovich was the more responsible parent, although he admitted that he had only observed the mother 3–5 years ago for a few minutes during infrequent church social functions.

"Another neighbor and a friend of the parties, Mariangela Castogiovanni, testified that she had seen both parents interact with their children. She related that Mrs. Milovich had told her she would not have children if she had her life to live over again. Since the dissolution proceedings began, Mrs. Milovich had not socialized with any of the neighbors.

"Peter Milovich's niece babysat for the children every other week from 1972–1977. On occasion she saw both parties discipline the children. The father spanked them and the mother sometimes dug her fingernails into their arms. She saw the mother kiss the children on the tops of their heads only. The children were more "physical" with their father, who played with them. In the niece's opinion, he was affectionate toward them but Mrs. Milovich was not.

"Petitioner's sister, Sorka Lester, testified that she had enjoyed a good relationship with her brother's wife for several years but that they had not been on friendly terms for the last few years. She had talked to respondent approximately 6 months before the parties' marriage. At that time respondent expressed her feelings that she did not want to have children. Ms. Lester further testified that her brother would always check on the children when the families visited but that her sister-in-law rarely did so.

"Petitioner then testified on his own behalf. He further testified that his wife had been very upset after the birth of Nicole and, in the delivery room, screamed that she did not want the baby and hoped it was dead. He stated that he helped his wife feed the baby and change her diapers. He also described several incidents when Nicole or Jason were ill and he had taken care of them, even missing a day of work in one instance.

"After the dissolution proceedings began the parties' relationship deteriorated rapidly. They both continued to live in the marital home with Nicole and Jason. Petitioner testified that one night in June of 1979 he was prevented from eating with his family because his wife refused to set him a place and then threw his food out and called him a name. The next day when he again tried to eat with them she said she would poison him.

"Petitioner further testified that his wife's employment required her to be out of town approximately 73 days total, from January to September 1980. Finally, petitioner testified that his wife did not demonstrate affection toward the children and told them not to "mess up" her hair or dress. He, on the other hand, would hold them, carry them, and kiss and hug them.

"After petitioner rested, respondent called as her first witness, her sister, Sally Ann Radick, a Pennsylvania attorney. She related that she had observed Mrs. Milovich on several occasions playing with the children and also observed affection between them and their mother.

"A college student who works at the neighborhood pool next testified that he saw Mrs. Milovich bring the children there 2–3 times a week during 1980. He never saw Mr. Milovich bring them.

"Wayne Basch, associate pastor of a church, testified that he knew Mrs. Milovich from her work as a Brownie Scout leader. The pastor observed that the mother and son appeared to be close and responsive to each other. He had never met Mr. Milovich.

"Respondent's mother, Mildred Radick, testified that she had taken care of the children at her daughter's request, approximately 6 times between January and May of 1980 when Mrs. Milovich was out of town on business. She stayed in the Milovich home with the children and Mr. Milovich for periods ranging from one to five days at a time. During her stays she would do the cooking and cleaning also. Mrs. Radick also testified that on occasions that she visited her daughter and son-in-law, her daughter was always the one who cooked and cleaned for the family. She had never seen Mr. Milovich help.

"Mrs. Milovich testified on her own behalf. She is a technical representative and local salesperson for Perma Alloys. Presently, her job only requires her to travel during the day although prior to September, 1980, she had to make overnight trips. In 1980 she was gone for a total of 56 days.

"When she was in the recovery room following Nicole's birth she was groggy and tired. She testified that she did not ever reject having the baby in the room with her. She took care of the baby and all the household chores. When Jason was born, she fed him most of the time, but Mr. Milovich sometimes gave him the midnight feeding. He would not change diapers but occasionally bathed Nicole.

"Mrs. Milovich had been home until May of 1979, when she found employment as a salesperson. Her hours were flexible and she usually left after the children were taken care of in the morning and returned by 4 P.M. Mr. Milovich's schedule was to leave for work at 7:30 A.M. and return home at about 6 P.M. She further testified that . . . respondent had taken care of all domestic chores when she was home and that she still did all the housework in addition to her job. Mr. Milovich further told Ms. Sillman that he could learn to take care of the house or hire a housekeeper if he had custody of the children.

"The court then ruled that after considering all of the relevant factors it would be in the best interests of the children to be placed in their father's custody. [The judge] noted that Mrs. Milovich is entitled to pursue her own career, but that the children were entitled to a stable environment.

"Nicole told the court that she wanted to be with her mother as much as possible. At first she did not care who she was to stay with but had since decided that she could not stand being with her father because he had been hitting her. They had arguments during which she refused to do what he told her to do.

"Finally, while Nicole did tell the judge during the March 5, 1981, interview that the father was 'hitting' her, at that time the parents were still living together in what undoubtedly was a tension-filled environment with the children caught in the middle of the parent's battle. Nicole's statements in this second interview also indicated that part of the problem was her failure to obey her father. We conclude that the record contains no persuasive evidence that Mr. Milovich was violent or abusive toward the children.

"On March 27, 1981, Joel Ostrow offered a petition that alleged that Mr. Milovich had physically and emotionally harassed his ex-wife and Nicole. The relief requested was a rule to show cause and a re-opening of the custody determination.

"Regarding the mother's evidence, we recognize that much of it indicates that she also is a good parent. She took the children to their lessons and activities and had primary responsibility for household chores, even after taking a full-time job. The job has flexible hours and no longer requires her to travel out of town overnight. Other evidence, however, indicates that she attempted to keep the children away from their father while the parties lived together during the proceedings and that she refused to allow him to eat with the family. While there is no question that both parties love their children, that is not the crucial issue here. A custody determination does not require a showing that one parent is a 'better' or 'worse' person than the other; it is the children's best interest that is paramount. As we have noted, neither parent emerges as a monster or a saint. After our careful scrutiny of the record we conclude that there is nothing to indicate that this judgment is 'manifestly unjust' or against the manifest weight of the evidence."

"Respondent theorizes [that] the judge in the pending cause allowed his personal and political interest to become adverse to the wife's interests because his custody ruling was publicized in newspapers, television, and radio. According to respondent, his decision was highly criticized by the media and, as a result, he was subjected to adverse publicity just before the judicial retention election in which he was up for consideration. Respondent takes the position that after he won retention the judge 'punished' the wife by his subsequent rulings.

"Respondent next contends that the court erred in refusing to allow her to add or substitute attorneys. The first time a motion was presented to add counsel was October 15, 1980, when Alan Rugendorf sought leave to appear as additional counsel.

"The court denied the motion and the custody hearing was concluded. Thereafter, several other motions to add or substitute attorneys were presented and denied.

"On November 10, 1980, a hearing on respondent's motion was held. She testified that she had lost faith in Karton, believed him to be incompetent, and refused to pay him any further fees. She did not explain why she needed four attorneys. The attorneys for petitioner and the children strongly objected to the motion, citing the disruptive impact that four new attorneys would have on the remaining proceedings. The four attorneys denied that there would be any delay in the trial on the remaining issues. The court denied the motion.

"On November 21, 1980, the court denied Karton's motion to reconsider its refusal to allow him to withdraw.

"On December 4, 1980, the court heard Mrs. Milovich's *pro se* petition asking the judge to recuse himself for being biased against her. Karton unequivocally disassociated himself from the contents and allegations of the petition. Mrs. Milovich first told the judge to swear himself in as a witness to answer her 96 questions.

"On January 21, 1981, while Judge Grupp was in the hospital, Karton presented his motion to withdraw before another judge.

"On March 4, 1981, Judge Grupp denied respondent's motion to add (rather than substitute) the four attorneys and the remaining issues were heard.

"Respondent now argues that the trial court's actions constitute 'the world's most compelling case of a judge's abuse of discretion,' and maintains that she had an unconditional right to discharge Attorney Karton. We disagree.

"Perhaps the most striking fact involved in this issue is respondent's unexplained need, mid-trial, for four attorneys from separate law firms.

"We conclude that the trial court did not abuse its discretion in refusing to allow respondent to substitute or add counsel."

"On March 13, 1981, just before closing arguments, petitioner's counsel presented an emergency petition to bar Mrs. Milovich from entering the marital home because she had allegedly removed items from the home and ordered a moving van to take away furniture. Respondent threw printer's ink on the living room furniture. The court also enjoined her from removing household effects.

"The final issue before us involves the distribution of the parties' marital property and the allocations of attorney's fees.

"Respondent argues that the trial court awarded a disproportionate share of marital property to the husband.

"Mrs. Milovich was awarded one-half of the stocks, bonds, and investment fund; one-half of the equity in the marital home; the Pinto and one room of furniture. Petitioner was awarded the other 50 percent interests as well as his pension funds and the Lincoln Continental. Both parties kept their personal property and were barred from maintenance. Mr. Milovich, as custodian of the children, was awarded possession of the marital home and all the furnishings except the specific items awarded to respondent. The judgment provides for the marital home to be sold when the younger child attains majority, petitioner remarries, or the home is sooner sold. Respondent must pay weekly child support of $15 per child.

"We therefore affirm the trial court's apportionment of the marital property."

CHAPTER EIGHTEEN: THE INTERNATIONAL CUSTODY SITUATION

1. Buchi Emecheta, *The Joys of Motherhood* (New York: George Braziller, 1979).

2. Two anonymous informants from the Fingo and Mtoko tribes. Quoted by Kate McCalman, "We Carry a Heavy Load: Report of a Survey Carried Out By the Zimbabwe Women's Bureau," December 1981, distributed by the UN.

3. Rachel Smith, in an address to the House of Commons, published in *Gay News* (London, January 26, 1978).

4. Liang Heng and Judith Shapiro, *Son of the Revolution* (New York: Alfred A. Knopf, 1983).

5. In 1973, global feminists from at least four geographical regions began meeting in the United States, in South America, and in Europe. Between 1973 and 1985, feminist demonstrations on behalf of imprisoned, raped, tortured, or executed women in other countries, took place in the United States and in Europe.

   In 1975, global feminists met in Mexico City, at the first UN Conference on Women. In 1976, feminists from forty countries attended the first international and non-governmental Tribunal on Crimes Against Women, held in Brussels, Belgium. See Diana Russell and Nicole Van de Ven, eds., *Crimes Against Women: Proceedings of the International Tribunal* (Millbrae, California: Les Femmes, 1976); new edition with introduction by Charlotte Bunch (Millbrae, California: Frog in the Well, 1984).

   Between 1975 and 1980, global feminist conferences took place in Europe, South America, Asia, and in the United States. In 1980, I coordinated a conference under UN auspices that took place in Oslo, Norway. See *Creative Women in Changing Societies: A Quest for Alternatives,* edited by Torrill Stokland, Mallica Vajrathon, and Davidson Nicol (New York: Transnational Publishers, 1982). Missing from this volume are my foreword, and papers by Marilyn Waring (New Zealand) and Motlalepula Chabaku (South Africa).

   Contained in this volume of the Oslo proceedings are papers delivered and/or submitted by participants Ama Ata Aidoo (Ghana); Astrid Asting (Norway); Teresa Bernadez (Argentina and the United States); Sylvia Ardyn

Boone (United States); E. M. Broner (United States); Chang Li-Chu (China); Claire de Hedevary (UN, Belgium); Nawal El Saadawi (Egypt); Therese Gastaut (France); Dorothea Gaudart (Austria); Manjula Giri (Nepal); Svetlana Goncharova (Soviet Union); Hema Goonatilake (Sri Lanka); Keiko Higuchi (Japan); Antonia Khripkova (Soviet Union); Gwendoline Konie (Zambia); Carmen Lugo (Mexico); Lucile Mair (UN, Jamaica); Robin Morgan (United States); Gladys Mutukwa (Zambia); Olayinka Burney Nicol (Sierra Leone); Ann Oakley (United Kingdom); Ulla Olin (Sweden); B. Marie Perinbam (United States); Sheila M. Pfafflin (United States); Hilkka Pietila (Finland); Maria Lourdes Pintasilgo (Portugal); Nana Pratt (Sierra Leone); Isel Rivero (Cuba); Sissel Ronbeck (Norway); Maria A. Tagle (Chile); Prathoomporn Vajrasthira (Thailand); and Mallica Vajrathon (Thailand).

In 1980, immediately following the Oslo conference, global feminists met in Copenhagen, Denmark, at the Second International UN Conference on Women. Between 1980 and 1985, global feminist conferences were held in the United States, Europe, the Middle East, Africa, the Far East, and in South America. In April 1983, feminists from twenty-four countries attended a conference on the Sexual Slavery of Women, held in Rotterdam, Holland. See *International Feminism: Networking Against Female Sexual Slavery. Report of the Global Feminist Workshop to Organize Against Traffic in Women*, Rotterdam, the Netherlands, April 6–15, 1983, distributed by the International Women's Tribune Center, Inc., 777 U.N. Plaza, New York, NY, 1984, Kathleen Barry, Charlotte Bunch, and Shirley Castley, eds. In July of 1985, the UN sponsored another conference on women in Nairobi, Kenya.

Since 1973, newspapers, magazines, news services, and books have reported on women and on feminism from a global perspective. Most are available in English and/or in the United States, and are widely read. To the best of my knowledge, they are, in chronological order as follows:

1972	Off Our Backs (*newspaper*), *Washington, D.C.*
1973	*Naomi Katz and Nancy Milton*, Fragment from a Lost Diary and Other Stories: Women in Asia, Africa and Latin America *(New York: Pantheon, 1973)*.
1974	*Bonnie Charles Bluh*, Woman to Woman: European Feminists *(New York: Starogubski Press, 1974)*.
1975	*Mary Jane Moffat and Charlotte Painter, eds.*, Revelations: Diaries of Women *(New York: Vintage, 1975)*.
1976–1985	Crimes Against Women, *op. cit.*
1976–1985	Spare Rib (*newspaper*), *England* Women's International Information and Communication Service *(ISIS), Geneva, Switzerland, and Rome, Italy.*

1977–1985 Women's International Network News *(WIN), Fran Hoskin, ed., Lexington, Mass.*
Women in Europe *(periodical).*

1978–1983 Quest *(a Feminist quarterly), Washington, D.C.*

1979 *Kathleen Barry,* Female Sexual Slavery *(Englewood Cliffs, N.J.: Prentice-Hall, 1979).*

1982–1985 Connexions: An International Women's Quarterly, *Oakland, Calif.*
D' Elizabeth Paquot, ed., Terre des femmes: Panorama de la situation des femmes dans le monde *(La Decouverte/Maspero Boreal Press, Paris, Montreal, 1982).*

1983 *Annette Fuentes and Barbara Ehrenreich,* Women in the Global Factory *(Institute for New Communications/South End Press, Boston, Mass., 1983).*

1984 *Barry, Bunch, and Castley,* op. cit.
Robin Morgan, ed., Sisterhood Is Global: The International Women's Movement Anthology *(New York: Doubleday-Anchor, 1984).*

6. My first published short story about Afghanistan was "Memoirs of Afghanistan" in *Mademoiselle* (June 1969). I also wrote about Afghanistan in *About Men* (Simon & Schuster, 1978; Bantam, 1979).

   According to Naila Minai in personal interviews and in her book, *Women in Islam: Tradition and Transition in the Middle East* (New York: Seaview Books, 1981), the Islamic Sha'ria guarantees men the absolute right to custody of their children "at puberty" (seven for boys, twelve for girls); sooner if a mother is divorced or deemed "unfit." She writes that:

   "Some [Muslim] women live in ulcerous insecurity with husbands who [threaten to] use the repudiation or male-initiated unilateral right to divorce on the slightest provocation. The terror lies in the fact that if the husband is spiteful, the divorcee is left virtually without support. . . . The wife's father or brother is expected to take her back, but this causes inordinate hardship in poor families.

   "Although the Qu'ran calls for 'maintenance on a reasonable scale' for divorced women, it is customary among those who claim to adhere to the letter of the Sha'ria to pay her the balance of the dowry agreed upon and support her only during the three months of chastity that she must observe after the divorce in order to see if she is pregnant by her husband. If she is, the child must be turned over to her ex-husband when it is born, along with her older children."

   On this subject, also see: Leila Ahmed, "Western Ethnocentrism and Perceptions of the Harem," *Feminist Studies* 8 (Fall 1982); William Bayer,

Visions of Isabelle (New York: Delacorte, 1976); Lois Beck and Nikki Keddie, eds. *Women in the Muslim World* (Cambridge, Mass.: Harvard University Press, 1978); Lesley Blanch, *The Wilder Shores of Love* (New York: Touchstone-Simon & Schuster, 1954); Sir Richard Burton, *The Arabian Nights,* Halycon House (New York: Garden City, 1948); Sir Richard Burton, *Personal Narrative of a Pilgramage to Al-Midinnah and Meccah,* vols. I & II, 1893 (New York: Dover Press, 1964); Lewis A. Coser, *Greedy Institutions: Patterns of Undivided Commitment* (New York: Free Press, 1974); Elizabeth Warnock Fernea, *Guests of the Shiek: An Ethnography of an Iraqui Village* (New York: Doubleday-Anchor, 1965); Elizabeth Warnock Fernea and Basima Quattaw Bezirgan, eds., *Middle Eastern Muslim Women Speak* (Austin, Texas: University of Texas Press, 1977); Edward Hunter, *The Past Present* (London: Hodder and Staughten, 1959); Robin Jenkins, *Dust on the Paw* (New York: Putnam, 1961); Alison Legh-Jones, *English Woman, Arab Man* (London: Elek Books Ltd., 1975); Cecily Mackworth, *The Destiny of Isabelle Eberhardt: A Biography* (New York: Ecco Press, 1975); Fatima Mernissi, *Beyond the Veil: Male-Female Dynamics in a Modern Muslim Society* (New York: Schenkman-John Wiley, 1975); Edward W. Said, *Orientalism* (New York: Pantheon, 1978); Freya Stark, *East Is West* (London: John Murray, 1947); Germain Tillion, *The Republic of Cousins: Women's Oppression in Mediterranean Society* (London: Al Saqui Books-Zed Press, 1983).

7. Egypt is, strictly speaking, part of Africa. I am including it in the Middle East because that is how Egypt chooses to view itself, and is seen. Dr. Nawal El Saadawi is an Egyptian-Moslem physician and the author of many books. *The Hidden Face of Eve* was published in English in 1981. I first interviewed El Saadawi in New York in 1980, and again in Oslo in 1980. El Saadawi subsequently responded to my request for information on child custody. Dr. El Saadawi and my other respondents, responded to a form letter and to a series of questions.

8. During the 1970s, Dr. Reza Bareheni was the head of CAIFI (Students Against the Shah). He is the author of many books, including *The Crowed Cannibals: Writing on Repression in Iran,* introduction by E. L. Doctorow (New York: Random House-Vintage Books, 1977).

9. For a powerful view of Iranian domestic life see Nachid Rachlin's novels, *Foreigner* (New York: Norton, 1978) and *Married to a Stranger* (New York: E. P. Dutton, 1983), and Marva Nabili's film *Ramparts of Clay*—a haunting evocation of pre-Khomeni Iranian domestic life.

10. In fact, Israeli women are legally forbidden to engage in combat. They are not trained to do so. An anthology of writings by early Zionist Pioneers, *The Ploughwoman,* dispels the myth of gender-equality among East Eu-

ropean pioneers. A more recent book by Lesley Hazelton, *Israeli Women: Myth and Reality* (New York: Simon & Schuster, 1979), dispels the myths about Israel's women from 1948 to today. Also see Natalie Rein, *Daughters of Rachel: Women in Israel* (New York: Penguin Books, 1979).

11. I interviewed a number of women from Saudi Arabia, Syria, and the Gulf States. Like other Middle Eastern women, they all had tales to tell—but always about "someone else." Many women confirmed what has already been said. Some concentrated on the economic problems of divorce; others, on the injustice incurred by so many different double standards. Sahura, a Syrian mother, had this to say: "Many divorced men remarry. Most divorced women do not. Most men dump their kids on their first wives. They know that they'll have other kids. If they don't have other kids, or if they're angry at their first wives, they may refuse to pay maintenance or child support. They may also legally take the children at puberty. . . . If a married father dies, the wife only gets one-eighth of everything. The children inherit everything else. It is possible, if a woman has strong support, to be very creative with the inheritance law, so as to benefit the mother somewhat more."

Rozia, a Saudi Arabian mother who had also lived and worked in Kuwait and Bahrain said: "Divorce is terrible for women. We can lose our social standing, our means of survival, and our children. It is preferable to suffer marital abuse. While wealthy men allow themselves to travel, drink, keep foreign mistresses or visit prostitutes, wealthy wives are much more circumscribed. If one falls in love or commits adultery, she can even be killed. In the late 1970s they publicly beheaded a young Saudi princess for trying to leave the country to marry a man of her choice. Can you imagine what might happen to her as some man's wife and the mother of his children? Whatever women do must be kept very, very quiet."

12. The Turkish film *Yol* portrays the fate of an adulterous mother whose husband has been in prison. Her own father chains her up in a dark room after her sexual misbehavior, to await her husband's "justice." On a pass from prison her husband decides she must die. He kills her by forcing her to accompany him and their ten-year-old son on a forced march in winter—dressed for summer.

Against an endless and pitiless expanse of frozen white wasteland, she stumbles, calls out, falls. Her husband resolutely marches on, deaf to her cries for "mercy" and "help." Their ten-year-old is uneasy. Finally, he becomes wildly agitated. At his son's pleading the husband walks back—to pick up his wife's corpse. In the Turkish provinces a child belongs to his convict father, not to his adulterous mother.

In *Women in Islam*, Minai also notes: "Yemeni courts which punish men's crimes of honor lightly are also prone to interpret the law in the husband's favor. The women independence fighters of the People's Democratic Republic of Yemen scored a feat of poetic justice on this point in 1974 when the Ministry of Justice ordered divorce cases to be heard by the Social Committee of the Women's Union before being judged by the courts.

"This resulted in extraordinary *de facto* trials of husbands by all-women courts packed with women spectators. The reversal of the usual courtroom scene garnered so much publicity for the divorcées cause that the predominantly male courts which were legally empowered to pass the final verdict could not ignore the judgment reached by the women's courts."

13. *Women in India: A Handbook* (Bombay: Research Unit on Women's Studies, Shreemati Nathibai Damodar Thackersey Women's University; Bombay, 1975). The report also notes: "Christian wives in India have to establish more grounds for dissolution of marriage than men. Women cannot get a divorce on the ground of adultery alone, but have to prove adultery with cruelty or adultery with desertion."

14. I first met Dr. Kiyomi Kawano in Copenhagen in 1980. She is a Japanese-born and Tokyo based feminist psychotherapist and the translator of my book *Women and Madness* into Japanese.

In 1968 in Japan, Keiko, a twenty-five-year-old kindergarten teacher, was raped by the father of one of her pupils. He threatened to expose their sexual "relationship" if she didn't become his "mistress." Keiko became pregnant. The man tried to force her to abort. A week after giving birth, Keiko asked this man to acknowledge paternity legally. His response was to have the infant kidnapped. Eventually Keiko found her kidnapped son. He had already been adopted with Keiko's forged consent.

Keiko sued for legal custody. She lost her suit in 1971. The court noted that "Keiko was unmarried," that she "kept company with the father of a pupil"; and that she had had the child "without any solid plan"; and therefore, probably had not "true love for the child." In 1975 Keiko rekidnapped her (by then) five-year-old son. She obtained legal custody also—only after paying "consolation money" to her rapist's legal wife.

Keiko's "case" was reported in Russell and Van de Ven, op. cit.

According to Nancy Greene, of the American branch of International Social Services, "Twenty years ago an American serviceman fell in love with a Japanese woman. They had a child. He wanted to marry her. The Army would not permit it. The father, having lived in Japan, was aware of the difficulties the child would experience as an Amerasian 'illegitimate' child. When he returned to the U.S., he wrote the mother and asked her to bring the child to America. By then it was too late. The economic difficulties of single motherhood had forced her to put the baby into foster care. The child had quickly been adopted by an American couple, with the mother's [forged] 'consent.' Both the mother and the father were unable to locate the child."

15. Grace Liu-Volkhausen is a Korean-born intellectual, businesswoman, and healer.

16. According to the Malaysian Federation of Planning, the Guardianship of Infants Act serves as a uniform child custody code for the Buddhist, Christian, and Muslim population—except where it conflicts with Muslim Law. "Guardianship" is the sole right of the father—and entails legal and economic responsibilities. They note that: "Under the Guardianship of Infants Act, the father has the right to the guardianship of the child/children, but the court may deprive him of his right. In doing so, the most important consideration is the welfare of the child/children. Because the welfare of the child/children is of paramount importance in the granting of custody, a woman who has been found guilty of adultery need not lose custody of her child/children" (Women Today in Peninsular Malaysia, Federation of Family Planning Associations publication, 1976).

17. Lynn Bennett, "Tradition and Change in the Legal Status of Nepalese Women," in The Status of Women in Nepal, I, Part 2 (New York: United Nations, 1978). According to Bennett, Nepalese mothers are entitled to custody of children under the age of five. Mothers may retain custody of children until they are sixteen if they do not remarry—and if the father doesn't want custody. Divorced Nepalese women automatically lose custody of children when they remarry. However, divorced women have some new custodial rights to children over five: the right to custody if the father permits it and the right to "meet the child occasionally."

The "right of visitation" shall be enjoyed even by a mother who has remarried. "When the child is under the custody of the mother, the father is under obligations to pay for the expense of the child's maintenance (i.e., the expenses of food, clothing, education, and medical care)."

New Zealand

Although New Zealand is located in South East Asia it is essentially an outlying province of the British Commonwealth. Catherine Mallon traces the history of custody in New Zealand. She writes: "The courts have made it clear that the presumption [of the child's best interests being served by the mother] is not in any sense a rule of law and is liable to be displaced by other considerations in the child's best interests. The law has never recognized the mother principle as having the status of a rule of law. It is a factor of importance which varies from case to case. The courts over the years have consistently taken the view that where all other considerations are equal, it is in the best interests of growing boys that they should be in the care of their father" (Catherine Mallon, "Joshua Williams Memorial Essay 1973: A Critical Examination of Judicial Interpretation of a Child's Best Interest in Inter-Parental Custody Disputes in New Zealand," Otago Law Review, 3 [August 1974]: 191–204). Mallon also notes that the courts do not consider it ". . . in the child's best interest for custody to be given to the mother where her relationship with the child is destructive, where she is significantly mentally ill, or where someone else has replaced her in the child's life as the established mother-figure."

Australia

According to Maureen, an Australian businesswoman now living in Europe: "In the mid-1970's, my children were brainwashed against me because I had a career. My working was held up to them as proof that I didn't love them. My refusal to be tied down in a traditional way to motherhood or marriage caused me endless suffering. My own family turned against me, once it was clear that I was not willing to fight for custody if it meant losing my job, or if it meant winning and having to be a traditional mother. No one allowed me to mother in my way. No one encouraged or supported me in my fight for liberal visitation. No one believed that I really loved my kids."

18. Historically Thailand was known as Siam. In 1873 Anna H. Leonowens published an account of her experience in Bangkok as governess to the King's children. Anna described the City of Veiled Women, which had a population of 9,000 royal princesses, wives, concubines, servants, and slaves, all "completely dependent on every whim and passion of King Mongkut."

One day Anna sees a wild-haired woman "naked to the waist, and chained— chained like a wild beast." The woman is sitting beneath the "fierce tropical sun," calmly nursing a child. This woman was born Muslim—and a slave. She was once "chief attendant" to the king's daughter Princess P'hra Ong Bittry. When she was repulsed in her attempts to buy her freedom, she escaped by jumping into a river. She lived and eventually married a wealthy Muslim merchant.

Four months after her very "happy" marriage she was "seized, gagged, and bound hand and foot"; and returned to the city. She has not seen her husband since. Her mistress the Queen, had her "chained to this post" until she gave birth. Four years ago, when her infant was one month old, " 'I was chained here again, and my child was brought to me to nurse; this was done until he could come to me alone. But they are not unkind; when it is very wet the slave-woman takes him to sleep under the shelter of her little shed. I could free myself from these chains if I promise never to quit the palace. That I will never do.'

"In the afternoon of the same day I [Anna] went to the house of [her husband] Ibrahim, and told him that I had seen his wife and child. He was much affected when he heard they were still alive, and was moved to tears when I told him of their sad condition. That night a deputation of Mohammedans, headed by the Moolah Hadjee Baba, waited upon me; we drew up a petition to the king, after which I retired, thankful that I was not a Siamese subject" (Anna H. Leonowens, *Siamese Harem Life,* with an introduction by Freya Stark, originally published in 1873 [New York: E. P. Dutton, 1953]).

I found this out-of-print book in the mid 1970s. I was aghast when I realized that the popular musical, *The King and I* actually romanticized King Mongkut—a sadistic despot—as a Zorba of the nineteenth-century Orient. Mongkut's torture and enslavement of women alone demand a serious drama, not a glamorizing, light-hearted musical. *The King and I* is like a musical about Genghis Khan or Attila the Hun.

19. Nadine Claire is an Algerian feminist interviewed by the English feminist magazine *Trouble and Strife.* The interview was reprinted in *Off Our Backs* (March 1985).

20. Daniel Haile, "Law and the Status of Women in Ethiopia" (Addis Ababa, Ethiopia: African Training and Research Centre for Women, 1980). Haile also notes that in Ethiopia: "In any marriage, parental rights are exercised by the father. Next, the person appointed guardian by the father, next the eldest brother, then the grandfather, the paternal uncle and then the paternal nephew. Similarly, pursuant to the Sha'ria rules, the father is the guardian, [and in] order of priority: the father's executor, the father's father or the paternal grandfather's executor. However, it must be emphasized that even though both the Fetha Negast (the Ethiopian civil codes) and the Sha'ria do not recognize the mother as legal guardian, they do not prohibit her being a guardian by appointment.

"Normally, unless there are serious grounds for deciding otherwise, the children are entrusted to their mother up to the age of five years and to the father over the age of five. The father is obliged to assist the mother by providing maintenance to the children under her custody. However, the amount is usually insignificant since the raising of children is more or less a full-time job. The end result of divorce is the transformation of the woman from a relatively unequal partner in the marriage to having full responsibility for caring for the children and no assistance from the children's father."

Haile notes that divorce and custody are often handled by family arbitrators, who are "close relatives or persons who know the spouses [and] are more inclined to listen and follow the advice given by their friends, neighbors or relatives, rather than a judge who may be unknown to them. This procedure for resolving marital dispute by family arbitrators is certainly a better device for enhancing the security of women than the more impersonal court procedures.

"Moreover, a good wife is always [supposed] to know her place. A wife should always show proper deference to her husband, especially when they have guests, and when the couple are in public. A common sight today is a woman walking a few paces behind her husband. At mealtime, a wife is expected to serve her husband first, then she takes her meal later with her daughters and young sons, and sometimes they eat apart from the men. If young children or servants are not available, she is expected to wash nightly the feet of the husband, father and head of the *abarus* [household], then the wife is expected to do this for her husband's guests who stay overnight. When her husband retires the wife must sleep beside his bed."

21. Evelyn also pointed out: "A traditional man will divorce his wife for adultery or for indulging in sorcery against him. Otherwise, he will simply move out and take another wife. This is what leads to female wealth in Ghana. Yes! Some of the richest people in Ghana are woman traders. Yes! This is the best way for most women, especially those without an education, to make and keep money. If your husband lives with another wife, you don't have to be his housekeeper anymore. You can invest the money he usually gives you in trade. Polygamy is the only path of independence for women in Ghana if you're the first wife."

   For a view of Ghanaian life, also read Ama Ata Aidoo, *Dilemma of a Ghost* (New York: Collier Books, 1965) and "The Message," Katz and Milton, op. cit.

22. *Mozambique: Women, the Law and Agrarian Reform* (New York: United Nations, 1980). This report notes: "Women's productive and reproductive potential, at least in patrilineal societies, was [controlled and] regulated by the practice of brideprice. Once brideprice was paid by the husband's to the wife's lineage, all children born of the union belonged to the husband's lineage, whether or not he was the biological father. When brideprice was not given or was only partially paid, the children belonged to the lineage of the mother's father. Since the husband's family had bought both the woman's services and her fertility, she was from that date onward expected to obey and serve her husband's lineage."

23. Ibid.

Lesotho

According to Gwen Mphokho Malahleha, in an article written for *Change* and reprinted in *Off Our Backs* (March 1985), Lesotho practices Bohali (lobolo or sepekele, the tradition of the brideprice). Unwed mothers and their "illegitimate" children are stigmatized; but still under male dominance.

Mauritania

According to Barbara Abeille, most Mauritanian women are economically devastated by divorce and reduced to "handouts" from their family or to prostitution. Divorce is especially rare among those tribes where custody is retained by fathers. "One of the reasons why there are fewer divorces among the Toucouleur is [their] polygamous tradition [in which] the husbands retain the children."

"Among the Bidans, the women keep the children when they are divorced. However, among the Toucouleur and Wolofs the man normally assumes the responsibility for his children, either by keeping them with him and his new or second wife in a polygamous marriage or by sending them to his mother" (Barbara Abeille, "A Study of Female Life in Mauritania" [Washington, D.C.: Office of Women in Development, Agency for International Development, 1979]).

Morocco

Dr. Fatima Mernissi, in *Beyond the Veil: Male and Female Dynamics in a Modern Muslim Society* (Cambridge, Mass.: John Wiley-Schenken, 1975) notes that in Morocco, "heterosexual love" is severely inhibited by practices such as the importance of female virginity, arranged marriage, repudiation (unilateral male divorce), polygamy, the segregation of the sexes, the veiling of women, the paternal custody of children, the lack of domestic privacy, etc. Such practices are at war, ideologically, with modernization.

Mernissi observes that *all* state power (colonialist and religious-nationalist) also suppresses the "heterosexual" unit. She says: "The average polygamous man in [Morocco] is fifty years old and takes as his second and third wives, women who are a generation or two younger. Seldom does he survive long enough to support his younger children to adulthood, and he may not leave enough wealth to allow his wives to educate them adequately after his death. The older wives' children suffer especially, for a fifth of all divorces in urban areas are initiated by women who prefer not to live with co-wives and either leave the offspring with their father or take them out into a life of poverty."

Dr. Mernissi is a Moroccan sociologist whom I interviewed in New York and in Copenhagen in 1980. According to Mernissi, the "revolutionary" new social structure of Islam was "historically" based on male dominance. "Polygamy, repudiation, the prohibition of *zina* and the guarantees of physical paternity were all designed to foster the transition from a family based on female self-determination to a family based on male control. The Prophet saw the establishment of the male-dominated Muslim family as crucial to the establishment of Islam. He bitterly fought existing sexual practices where marital unions for both men and women were numerous and lax."

24. Dr. J. O. Debo Akande, "Law and the Status of Women in Nigeria," Nigeria: Economic Commission for Africa, African Training Center for Women, 1979.

In *The Joys of Motherhood,* Nigerian novelist Buchi Emecheta dramatizes the effects of modernization on her rural heroine, Nnu Ego. Her husband has taken another wife; he has also refused to give her any money to feed their children. (Buchi Emecheta, *The Joys of Motherhood* [New York: George Braziller, 1979]).

25. In general, superpowers run great political risks when they attempt to overthrow tribal customs and laws—especially those regarding women. The superpowers tend to align themselves with the most reactionary and religious forces in a country in order to maintain or obtain a greater leverage in that country.

For example, the United States supported the Shah in Iran. Despite his incredible corruption and tyranny, the Shah *was* "Westernizing" and "democraticizing" Iran, especially in terms of women. The Ayatollah Khomeini has driven women back by ten centuries in less than a decade.

The United States has learned from its Iranian failure. It is currently backing the most reactionary and religious Afghan refugees and "freedom fighters" against their Soviet invaders. The USSR had been attempting to communize and de-feudalize Afghanistan politically before its military invasion. Perhaps the Soviet attempts to defeudalize women's status is what touched off the most popular and long-lasting resistance to their political and ideological take-over.

In Africa, the United States claims South Africa is a military-geographical base against Communist totalitarianism. The United States justifies its support of an apartheid regime for many reasons. For example, it argues for the importance of slow evolution under capitalism as opposed to quick revolution under communism—in terms of South Africa's need for human rights (as defined by the West). The U.S. administration also argues that in surrounding African countries where Communist regimes are in place or influential, tribal warfare has decimated the lives, social fabrics, and standards of living of many tribal and ethnic enemies and minorities.

26. See Hilda Bernstein, *For Their Triumph and for Their Tears: Women in Apartheid South Africa* (Cambridge, Mass.: International Defense and Aid Fund, 1978); Jim Morrell, *International Institutions and Economic Sanctions on South Africa* (Geneva: International University Exchange Fund, 1980).

The United Nations Centre Against Apartheid regularly publishes information on women under apartheid. Some information is factual; some is slanted; all is used as a Communist weapon against the West. None of the UN material focuses on women's *maternal* rights or the rights of mothers although unmarried. See the following publications: Elizabeth Landis, *Apartheid and the Disabilities of African Women in South Africa* (New York: UN Centre Against Apartheid, 1973); *Notes and Documents: Women Against Apartheid* (New York: 1975, reprinted in July 1981); Carolyn Roth,

Apartheid: A Threat to Public Health in South Africa (New York: UN Centre Against Apartheid, 1979); *The Plight of Black Women in Apartheid South Africa,* based on the United Nations report prepared for the 1980 World Conference (New York); *Women Under Apartheid: In Photographs and Text* (New York: International Defense and Aid Fund for Southern Africa, in cooperation with the UN Centre Against Apartheid, 1981).

27. Bernstein, op. cit.

According to Dorothy, a black South African mother whom I interviewed in Oslo and Copenhagen in 1980, "Whatever you've read about apartheid can't convey its destructive effects on daily life. No. I was educated and helped by church women to leave Johannesburg in 1976. I left one daughter buried behind me, dead of misfortune. I have one daughter left. She is really my sister's child, whom I informally adopted after both her parents died. How can I get her out? I'm an illegal alien. Even at home my daughter wasn't listed as mine on my identity cards. She lived with me illegally."

The Sudan

In the Sudan fathers are also entitled to custody if they want it. In general, drought, famine, and female (agricultural) poverty are a greater problem for mothers than is their automatic loss of custody. Farmers in the Sudan are traditionally women—who also sell their crops in the marketplace. According to Fran Hosken, "Many men have abandoned their villages long ago. They can be seen in cities and towns, hanging around, unemployed, often drunk. Left behind in the drought-stricken rural areas are their help-less victims, the women, responsible for feeding their many children. A typical male returns to his village once a year or so, fathers another child and eats the food his wife produces. Many men have another wife in the city. Moreover, women traditionally have no ownership rights to land . . . land ownership is conveyed on the male head of the family even when he is not present.

"Subsaharan Africa's food production is steadily decreasing while its pop-ulation is steadily increasing. [Western] Development assistance, where agriculture production is concerned, is being provided for men only. . . . By now, the results of the discrimination against Africa's women farmers are visible to all. . . . Still, the decision makers at the World Bank, theUN Development Program and the U.S. Agency for International Development won't listen" (Fran P. Hosken, *New York Times,* March 21, 1984).

28. Jane Rose K. Kikopa, "Law and the Status of Women in Tanzania" (African Training and Research Centre for Women, 1981; distributed through UN). Kikopa notes that where a mother "chooses to remain a widow, then she is assisted in the upbringing and care of her children and their property. In case a guardian acts beyond his powers, perhaps by attempting to sell

the land he is supposed to administer for the children, a mother can institute proceedings for recovery—if requested to do so by her children."

29. Grace Akello, "Self Twice-Removed: Ugandan Women," *Change: International Reports on Women and Society* (1982).

Akello notes that "a woman's worth is determined most of all by her children, particularly male children. They afford her security, and a woman will therefore hang onto a marriage for as long as there are children in it, especially since they belong to her husband and she cannot take them to her own lineage. Apart from the emotional attachment to her children, most women know they cannot divorce their husbands. Incompatibility means that a woman has failed to adjust to her husband. It in no way implies that a husband has failed to adjust to his wife. The Teso, Langi or Acholi wife must adjust to the extent that, if her husband deserted her, she would have no grounds for divorce, so long as there was some male relative remaining in the family home.

"Mugisu women have been freer than most others. Muhima women are not permitted any sexual activity before marriage. They are their father's means of acquiring cattle. On marriage, she becomes part of her husband's family. She must obey her mother-in-law and husband. If not, she will be beaten, shamed or divorced."

Okot P'Bitek writes of life among the polygamous Acholi in her "Song of Lawino." She protests her abandonment by a rapidly Weternized husband, who also holds her in contempt because she is neither educated nor baptized. She pleads for the chance to "praise" him and to "dance" her "love" for him, to "show" (him) the wealth in (his) house. Her husband's second wife has turned him against the "noise" and "mess" of children. P'Bitek cannot imagine wanting to live without "muddy fat kids." (Katz and Milton, op. cit.)

30. Sinjele notes: "Zambia is governed by both tribal and European statutory law. The court's main criteria for deciding on custody are: the financial status of the parents, and the best environment for the children. The courts do believe that children are better taken care of by their mothers. However, this is only the initial custody determination. The domestic laws of Zambia are a very complex integration of traditional practices and European statutory law.

"The court may grant mothers custody—without enforcing their order. A court will often look the other way if a father refuses to pay his maintenance and child support. Although the statutory court may have ordered maternal custody and paternal child support payment, these are alien practices. The concept of maintenance [alimony] is a Western idea. Women have always worked outside the home and contributed to the family earnings as much as the men. Only very wealthy women stay home and rear the children by themselves.

"Generally, if a father wants his children, especially in a patrilineal culture, he'll get them. This often means that the couple goes into court over and over again until one or the other decides to give up."

31. *Women's Guide to Law Through Life: A Woman's Guide to the Laws and Regulations Relating to Marriage, Birth, Children, Death and Widowhood, and the Position of Women in Zimbabwe-Rhodesia* (Women in Development Research Unit, University of Rhodesia, April 1979).

   One woman in Zimbabwe was quoted as follows: "I am worried that men are said to be the children's owner, yet I spend nine months carrying the baby in my stomach, and then the next twenty to thirty years looking after her or him. My husband is in charge of everything I do or can make with my hands, which is so rough and cruel. He says that the lobolo that he paid to my parents means that he bought me. So I have to follow his orders and work for him and his family" (Kate McCalman, ed., "We Carry a Heavy Load: Rural Women in Zimbabwe Speak Out" [Zimbabwe's Women's Bureau, circulated though UN December 1981]).

32. Gaidzanwa's comments were made at an international conference on female sexual slavery and are contained in Barry, Bunch, and Castley, op. cit.

   McCalman, op. cit., notes that those women who refuse to have lobolo (bridewealth) paid for them "are considered 'bad' women and accused of being prostitutes. It is unheard of for a woman to receive and dispose of her own bridewealth. Only prostitutes [do] that and it is not accepted socially. For women, it is a no-choice situation. Choice, if it is there at all, is to be under the husband's exploitation or to be exploited generally, but in a personal way [as in prostitution]."

33. Luisa Valenzuela is the author of *Strange Things Happen Here* (New York: Harcourt Brace Jovanovich, 1979). She also notes: "Children who were born in jail to tortured mothers were given to unknown people. Some children left behind when their parents were arrested, were put in parks. Sometimes they'd be wearing a sign: 'I'm a Lost Child. Take me with you.' Children were given away at airports. Some were simply taken by military officials who needed to adopt. These young children 'disappeared'—just like thousands more adult 'children' 'disappeared.' Mothers of the Plaza de Mayo gathered daily to protest the disappearance of their [adult] children, and to find out where they were."

34. Dr. Ximena Bunster and Nancy Saporta Sternbach both describe the numerous, horrifying cases of "disappearing" mothers and children as well as the sexual torture and execution of women. According to Bunster, "Amnesty International has documented numerous cases of the disappearance of mothers and children, where the child was either born in prison or abducted with the mother. In Argentina, all pregnant women who survived interrogation were taken to a Naval Training College and attended by a doctor. After the birth, the mothers were usually 'transferred' and the

infants sent to official or clandestine orphanages, or adopted by childless couples in the armed forces. 'Transfer,' according to surviving witnesses, is the name given to massive assassination in Argentina. Evidence, documentation concerning the sale of some of these children, both in Latin America and abroad, is just surfacing" (Barry, Bunch, and Castley, op. cit).

Nancy Saporta Sternbach described her meeting with Argentinian feminists in 1983: "One of their first projects was a campaign against *patria potestad*, a law based on the Napoleonic Code which grants the father full and exclusive rights over his children regardless of whether he participated in their support and raising. In order for a woman to take her children out of the country, she must have her husband's permission. Thus, many exiled Latin American women are afraid to visit their families for fear that their ex-husbands will kidnap their children with the support of the law.

"Together with Organización Feminista Argentina (OFA) begun and headed by feminist organizer and activist Maria Elena Oddone, they are currently gathering signatures to be presented to the congress of the new government. In July 1983, some 13,000 people had signed. Considering that so many of the desaparecido were murdered for appearing in the wrong person's address book, it is no small wonder that so many women (and men, although fewer) were willing to wait in line to get their names on the list, a petition for what is called *joint patria potestad*." (Nancy Saporta Sternbach, "Argentine Feminism: Gaining Speed," *Off Our Backs* [March 1984]).

35. Dr. Teresa Bernardez is a psychiatrist and now lives in the United States. I interviewed her in New York and Oslo in 1980. Since then, she has responded to my specific questions about custody.

Argentinian lawyer Patricia Zayas also responded to my queries. She wrote: "Argentinian law is based on Roman law and the Napoleonic Code. Mothers usually get custody, unless they commit adultery, are lesbians, or are otherwise improper. Fathers are supposed to pay child support. Divorced fathers visit their children often (about 48 hours a week). Unwed mothers are not entitled to any state subsidies. Illegitimate children have different [lesser] rights than legitimate children."

36. Dr. Saffieti, a Brazilian sociologist, responded to my specific queries about custody.

37. For example, in 1980, Mario Stanciolli of Belo Horizonto, Brazil, murdered his thirty-two-year-old wife, Eloise, who had wanted to leave him to marry another man. The all-male seven-member jury exonerated Stanciolli because his wife was an adulterous "career" woman with a thriving clothing business. Stanciolli received a suspended two-year sentence for the premeditated murder—the same sentence he would have received for "accidentally running over someone with his car." According to the Chief of homicide: "These men who killed their wives had almost always pleaded legitimate defense of honor and generally received 'light' sentences, if any"

(Warren Hoge, "Machismo Murder Case," *New York Times*, May 23, 1983).

38. Reported in Russell and Van de Ven, op. cit. European Catholicism is the major religion of most Central and South American states. Africa, Native Indian, Muslim, Hindu, and, of course, Protestant forms of worship also exist—but to a lesser extent. While Catholicism has comforted the "wretched of the earth"; and sometimes functioned as a symbolic form of resistance to the state (as it does in contemporary Poland), it has also meant that divorce, abortion, birth control, and unwed motherhood are illegal and/or socially tabooed.

In certain parts of Central and South America "illegitimate" children are completely accepted. Carolina Maria de Jesus is a mother-writer who lives in the Brazilian slums (*favelas*). She has written about the "advantages" of unwed motherhood: "My kids are not kept alive by the church's bread. I take on all kinds of work to keep them. And other women have to beg or even steal. At night when they are begging, I peacefully sit in my shack listening to Viennese waltzes. While their husbands break the boards of the shack, I and my children sleep peacefully. I don't envy the married women of the favelas (slums) who lead lives like Indian slaves" (Carolina Maria de Jesus, in Moffat and Painter, op. cit.).

Bolivia

As in most other Central and South American countries, abandoned, divorced, widowed, and unmarried Bolivian mothers are *obligated* to support their children. A Bolivian male child over the age of five must remain with his father—if his father wants him. A mother may retain custody of her male and female children if the father allows it. Fathers retain "guardianship," i.e., the right to make decisions ("Leyes de Divorcio en los Paises Americanos," *Comisión Interamericano de Mujeres*, Serie Estudios 1 [Washington, D.C., 1974]).

In both Bolivia and Mexico, if the mother commits adultery or abandons her wifely or maternal responsibilities, "the children are entrusted to their father. . . . Grounds for divorce in Bolivia are: adultery, or the attempt to commit adultery; attempting to kill or endanger the spouse; various misdemeanors; the attempt to prostitute either the spouse or one of the children; malicious or voluntary abandonment of a spouse; cruelty; drunkenness; insanity, terminal and contagious illness; and mutual consent" (ibid.).

According to Blanca, a peasant mother in Bolivia, "A man falls once and he gets up again. A woman falls but once and she is marked. A man can choose what he wants, but women have to get married, and then come the children. Men don't know what it is to be a mother and cry for a child." Blanca is quoted by Audrey Bronstein, *The Triple Struggle: Latin American Peasant Women* (Boston: South End Press, 1982). Cited by Jan Adams, "Lesbian Connection," Spring, 1984.

39. The divorce and custody laws in Colombia are similar to those in Chile. In Colombia boys are "entrusted" to their father after they are five; once a boy is fourteen, he is "entrusted" to his father even in a "grave" situation. Girls may stay with their mothers if neither they nor their mothers are "immoral." Fathers exercise "guardianship" over their children, "whether they live with them or not" ("Leyes de Divorcio").

40. According to Margaret Randall, in 1953, Cuban women occupied only "9.8 percent of the total labour force, and this included 70,000 domestic servants who earned starvation wages. . . . In addition to widespread prostitution, humiliation, sickness, hunger, unemployment, illiteracy and premature death, organized asassination and large-scale torture were Batista's answer to the growing revolutionary struggle" (Margaret Randall, *Cuban Women Now* [Toronto: Women's Press, 1979]).

   In Communist Cuba women, but not men still work as domestics and illegally as prostitutes. Women have many employment alternatives to prostitution or marriage. If they are obedient workers, they are entitled to social dignity and to food, medical care, education, housing, etc. Cuban children have many rights—but not the right to associate with anti-revolutionary or non-Communist parents.

41. Isabel is a peasant mother in El Salvador. She said: "I had 17 children but only 10 of them are living. . . . The priest who married us said we should be ready to receive all the children that God wanted to send us. My husband said to me that if I didn't want a big family, he would go and find another woman. . . . Having children isn't [all] bad . . . it is good because children are useful. I have six girls, for example. My husband comes home and wants to eat, and they serve him" (Bronstein, op. cit.).

42. In Chapter 2 I discuss the case of Christina Landaverde who fled El Salvador illegally when she was pregnant and was forced to give up her baby "temporarily" when she gave birth. She was then forced to fight for her son Mauricio's return after he had been legally adopted by an American couple and lost her heroic three-and-a-half-year legal battle—"in the best interests of the child."

   On September 4, 1984, a class action lawsuit was filed accusing the Immigration and Naturalization Service of trying to lure undocumented workers out of hiding by holding their children. At the center of the controversy is Orlando Ramirez, then a four-year-old boy who left El Salvador for the United States on August 5, 1984. The child's father was killed the year before, and his mother was already in Los Angeles, working as a domestic. The boy and other Salvadorans were intercepted, and Orlando had been in custody for more than two weeks.

   "The lawsuit, filed in Federal District Court here, contends that the service, as a matter of policy, seeks to use Orlando and 200 other youngsters as 'hostages.' The suit was filed by the National Center for Immigrants' Rights and El Rescate, a legal service center. Last week the Board of Immigration Appeals upheld the rule requiring a parent to pick up a child. 'We have no objection to that,' said Peter Schey of the Center For Immigrants' Rights. 'What we do object to is that the I.N.S. insists she be subjected to interrogation and give up her constitutional right to remain silent' " (*New York Times*, September 4, 1984).

Also see coverage in the *Village Voice* and *New York Times* during 1984 and 1985 regarding the "sanctuary movement" in the United States; and the movement among Salvadoran women known as "The Mothers of the Disappeared."

43. Nancy L. Gonzalez, "The Anthropologist as Female Head of Household," *Feminist Studies*, 10, 1 (Spring 1984).

According to Carmen, "Guatemala is the only Latin American country with a legally sanctioned 'joint custody' option for parents. However, 'guardianship,' i.e. the legal accountability and decision-making power for children, still belongs to the father. A divorced mother who is innocent of wrongdoing may retain physical custody of her young children (usually until the age of seven). Her ex-husband can supervise what she does if he wants to. He can take the child away if she had committed adultery."

44. Many Puerto Rican women have been sterilized without their knowledge or consent. They have "lost" their right to children as the result of international racism and sexism. Puerto Rican women, like other "expendable" third world women (in India for example), have been the uninformed or all too grateful "guinea pigs" in testing birth control pills. In 1976 a group of Puerto Rican women declared: "Puerto Rico has the highest rate of sterilization in the world. In 1968, 35% of Puerto Rican women of child-bearing age had been sterilized. This compares with 5% in India and 3% in Pakistan—both countries that also have public sterilization programs. . . . We do not condemn sterilization *per se*. We condemn it when it is manipulated or forced. While traditionally our ability to have children has been used to create myths about our inferiority in other endeavors, when that ability is economically counter-productive, it loses all mystique and becomes a 'function' that must be disposed of. It should also be noted that the Catholic Church, which is strong in Puerto Rico, does not oppose sterilization" (Russell and Van de Ven, op. cit.).

In Uruguay there is no specific law stipulating either parent as the de facto custodian after divorce. "A judge determines custody according to the party who can financially afford it. This would probably be the father, who has the capacity to do so; or a third party of an official institution" ("Leyes de Divorcio").

45. Alec Samuels, *"Kramer vs. Kramer* in England," *Solicitor's Journal,* 125 (July 10, 1981):470.

46. For example, Samuels, op. cit., describes *Owen* v. *Owen* (1974), 4 *Family Law* 13; *B.* v. *B.* (1975), 119 *Sol. Journal* 610; *Hutchinson* v. *Hutchinson* (1978), 8 *Family Law* 140; *T.* v. *T.* (1974).

47. Dr. Martin Richards, "Post-Divorce Arrangements for Children: A Psychological Perspective" (unpublished paper, 1981). Richards, in a personal communication (1983), confirmed that there is enormous prejudice against lesbian and homosexual parents, and that more mothers are "agreeing" to paternal custody than in the past. Like most researchers in America, Richards fails to take into account that most mothers who "agree" to paternal custody have essentially been forced into it. He does note that the vast majority of custody battles are fought by relatively wealthy parents who can afford both the initial trial and a series of appeals.

48. Norma Steele, quoted in *Gay News* (London), January 26, 1978. Steele is a member of "Black Women for Wages for Housework," a London-based group. An extraordinary film made in the 1960s, *Tears for Cathy,* depicts how the English welfare state drives a white father away from his family, denies housing and employment to the abandoned mother and children; and then takes the children away from their impoverished and state-debilitated mother.

49. Christopher L. Blakesley, "Child Custody and Parental Authority in France and Louisiana," *Boston College International and Comparative Law Review,* 4, 2 (Fall 1981), states: "Notwithstanding the de facto maternal preference that developed, the concept of 'paternal power' continued to have an impact under the [Napoleonic] Code, as the father maintained his power of control over the children, even when the court did not award custody to him."

   As Blakesley shows, mothers in northern and western Europe may retain custody of their children—unless they are judged "morally" or "maternally" unfit, i.e., adulterous; sexually active after divorce; a lesbian; relatively impoverished; a "career" woman; an atheist; "unstable;" alcoholic; or mentally ill.

Belgium and Switzerland

According to Blakesley, fathers in Belgium still retain all decision-making power over children—regardless of who takes care of them. Mothers must petition the Belgian court to contest the fathers' decision in each specific matter. In Switzerland, fathers' rights are upheld during and after marriage. The Swiss mother cannot legally contest paternal decision-making. Mothers could retain (uncontested) custody in Belgium and Switzerland and still be responsible for carrying out paternal decisions by "remote control."

Luxembourg

Luxembourg's archaic divorce laws were reformed at the end of 1978. Mothers became entitled to child support and alimony regardless of whose "fault" the divorce was. However, in the attempt to modernize its divorce law, Luxembourg also made women equally liable for paying child support—despite the fact that women earn less than men and have already done most of the primary child care and housework.

"[In 1983], for the first time in Luxembourg legal history, a woman was given a three-month (suspended) sentence for refusing to pay maintenance (child support) to her ex-husband and the children living with him" (*Women of Europe*, 30 [March–April 1983]).

50. Blakesley, op. cit.

51. Ibid.

   Dr. Ingrid Djalinous of the Austrian Federal Ministry of Justice wrote: "Austrian mothers of young children are not discriminated against in custody decisions unless she has ever left them or wants to move away" (personal communication). However, Greta, who is also Austrian, describes a very painful battle she recently fought first for child support and then against paternal brainwashing.

52. Blakesley, op. cit..

53. Ibid.

   West German mothers usually get (non-contested) custody; fathers are obligated to pay child support; and custodial mothers have some legal control of paternal visitation (Ruth Lester, quoting Hanna Lambrette of Verband Alleninstehender Mutter und Vater, Personal communication).

54. I met Ellen Cahill at a feminist conference in Salzburg, Austria in 1982. We corresponded, and she answered my questions about custody for many European countries, especially, France, Holland, and Ireland. Cahill runs a consulting agency, "Les Resources," in Bordeaux, France.

55. In the late 1960s Gabrielle Roussier, a young French teacher, fell in love with one of her seventeen-year-old (male) students. Roussier lost her job, was imprisoned, and, in shame and despair, killed herself.

56. In an interview given to the Canadian journalist Jacqueline Schwartz.

57. Haris Livas, "Breaking the Mold: An Interview with Margaret Papandreou," *Ana: Athens News Agency*, 62 (March 28, 1983).

   According to the revised Greek civil code, mutual agreement between husband and wife has legally supplanted a man's traditional right to rule his family legally. However, alimony and child support are not automatic or fixed. The Synergazomena Gynekia Somatia (Common Front of Women's Associations) has been organizing to protect both the lives and the rights of divorcing women. The Synergazomena proposed that in some situations, divorced women should receive a percentage of their ex-husband's pension, or another form of compensation. My respondent, Ellen J. Cahill gave me this information.

58. Cahill, September 1983. As of 1983 contraceptives were illegal and hard to obtain in the Republic of Ireland.

59. J. O'Reilly, "Custody Disputes in the Irish Republic: The Uncertain Search for the Child's Welfare," *The Irish Jurist*, 12 (June 1977):37. O'Reilly discusses the contradictory but basically pro-father and conservative opinions of the Irish Supreme Court. For example, in 1974 the Irish Supreme Court upheld paternal custody because: "The life which is being led by the [divorced and sexually active] mother in this case is a manifest repudiation of the social and religious values with which the children should be inculcated. . . . [How can she teach such values] while clearly repudiating them herself in the sight of her own children?" (Unreported, Supreme Court, 31 July, 1974, quoted by O'Reilly, op. cit.) The court refused to hear arguments on behalf of one child's continued need for her mother's nursing for a medical ailment. The "adultery" was paramount.

60. "However, in a recent report, the Law Reform Commission proposed that the concept of 'illegitimacy' should be abolished. This document says that it is unjust to deny rights to innocent people in order to protect the institution of marriage. The Law Reform Commission also proposed that father's rights should be guaranteed outside marriage, but this suggestion raised a storm of protests from women's organizations" (*Women of Europe*, 30 [March/April 1983]). This publication was forwarded to me by Ellen Cahill. Mrs. Nuala Fennell, Minister of State for Women's Affairs, has organized a recent public conference on this issue.

61. Virginia Visani, who lives in Milan, Italy, provided me with several examples of recent or "notorious" custody battles in Italy. For example, a ten-year-old girl had been living with her mother for five years, from the time her parents separated. The separation agreement contained a clause allowing the mother and daughter to keep living in the marital home in Salerno. The mother could no longer afford the rent and moved to a cheaper apartment in a nearby village. In 1981 the father demanded that the girl be turned over to him. The girl threatened to kill herself if she had to leave her mother. After many exhausting meetings the girl was finally allowed to remain with her mother.

In 1979 a remarried father kidnapped his ten-year-old son twice. The father claimed he had remarried a "housewife" who could stay at home with the boy. He deemed her a better mother than his ex-wife because the latter had worked outside the home for three years, since their divorce.

62. Norwegian director Vibekke Lokkborg's film *Kamilla* dramatizes how the Norwegian state "kidnaps" the children of a battered wife away from her. The children try to flee, then beg the social workers to allow them to remain with their mother. The mother herself chases after the car, weeping, and pitiful. The scene is set in Norway right after World War II.

63. Birgitta Wittcorp, "Joint Custody of the Children of Divorced Unmarried Parents," *Current Sweden* (February 1977). In terms of joint custody, Wittcorp points out, "No child maintenance allowance is payable to the other partner when divorced or unmarried parents share the custody of their children. Joint legal custody means that the parents have no legal recourse to advance payments of maintenance-allowance from the state."

64. Cecilia Onfelt writes, edits a feminist magazine, and works in a shelter for battered women; I interviewed her in New York in 1981. She also responded to my questions about custody.

Denmark

The incidence of child abduction by unwed fathers in Denmark is so severe that a special legislative commission has been established to cope with the problem. Danish laws tend to favor mothers over unwed fathers. One out of every four children is born out of wedlock (Ann Mariager, "Custody for Unwed Father," *San Francisco Chronicle*, May 25, 1980).

65. According to the *Li Chi, Quang*, "If a [Chinese] husband and wife should separate [a rare event], the sons would stay with the father's family. The grandson of Confucius said: 'She who was my wife was also my son's mother. When she ceased [by repudiation] to be my wife, she ceased to be the mother of my son' " (quoted by Molly Spitzer Frost, "Chinese Matriarchy: Clues from Legends and Characters," Ph.D. diss. Georgetown University, 1982).

In *The Woman Warrior*, Maxine Hong Kingston remembers an aunt who is "never discussed." Pregnant and unwed in pre-revolutionary China, this aunt endangers her family and her village. Children *must* have a father. If not, it is feared they will prey on their neighbors. Kingston imagines her terrified aunt giving birth, alone, in the family pigpen. This unlucky "ghost" of an aunt decided to "protect this child as she has protected its father. It would look after her soul, leaving supplies on her grave. But how would this tiny child without family find her anywhere, when there would be no marker for her anywhere, neither in the earth nor in the family hall? No one would give her a family name. She had taken the child with her into the wastes. At its birth the two of them had felt the same raw pain of separation, a void that only the family pressing tight could close. A child with no descent line would not soften her life but only trail after her, ghost-like, begging her to give it purpose. At dawn the villagers on their way to the fields would stand around the fence and look. Carrying the baby to the well shows loving. . . . Otherwise, abandon it. Turn its face into the mud. Mothers who love their children take them along. It was probably a girl; there is some hope of forgiveness for boys" (Maxine Hong Kingston, *The Woman Warrior: Memoirs of a Girlhood Among Ghosts* [New York: Knopf, 1976]).

See Agnes Smedley, *Portraits of Chinese Women in Revolution*, 1938 (Old Westbury, N.Y.: Feminist Press, 1976).

66. Under Communist totalitarianism women as *mothers* have no special place. Women as *workers* are at best, part of middle management. The government has been run by men, not by men and women. According to Roxanne Witke, the biographer of Chiang-Ch'ing, Mao's imprisoned widow, and member of the infamous "Gang of Four," Chiang-Ch'ing's real crime was having too much power—for a woman. Her misuse of power is another matter. She also supported the entrance of too many other women into visible positions in "middle management") Roxanne Witke, personal interview, 1981).

67. Liang's mother "said that her Section Head sometimes used crude language and liked to criticize people, that he should give his housekeeper a bed to sleep on instead of making her sleep on the floor, and that sometimes when it came time to give raises, the leaders didn't listen to the masses' opinions" (Liang Heng and Judith Shapiro, *Son of the Revolution*, [New York: Knopf, 1983]).

68. Ibid.

According to Amanda Bennett in the *Wall Street Journal*, on July 6, 1983, and Bernard Nossiter, in the *New York Times*, July 23, 1983, the Chinese state attempted to limit population growth by punishing pre- or extra-marital sex; by legalizing abortion and contraception; and by encouraging "late" marriage. By the mid-1970s, the state had to restrict every legally married couple to only one child. The results were an increase in female infanticide.

"Many people have turned to killing their baby girls in order to try for a son that China's newspapers have been publicizing the problem. China's papers have printed horrifying stories: a father stuffing a roll of cotton into his baby's mouth, a man dropping his infant daughter into a well. . . . The Chinese Government has said female infanticide stems from a 'feudal mentality' and that those who practiced it would be punished. The punishment was fairly light, however, in a country where simply having an affair has brought life imprisonment."

The Chinese government did not deny the problem; and was in fact, attempting to grapple with it. On July 23, 1983, despite some protest, the United Nations Fund for Population Activities awarded China and India joint prizes for their family planning programs.

69. Katja also pointed out that "between the 1930's and the 1950's, it was very common for a village woman to have a child—and then come to the city to find work. She usually left her child in the village, or sent the child back. It wasn't stigmatizing, but it was very emotionally difficult for the mothers. A whole generation of women had to do this. This still goes on, but not as much."

Newspapers in the United States cover the defection of parents from the USSR and from the Soviet bloc, and their entreaties to have their children sent out to join them in the West. A Polish couple had to wait for seven years before their (then) infant daughter was allowed to join them in the United States (Robert Weddle, "Polish Couple Await Reunion with Daughter," *New York Post*, July 28, 1984).

Stalin's daughter, Svetlana Alliluyeva, born in the Soviet Union, married an American man, William Peters, the son of Frank Lloyd Wright's wife. After having a daughter, Alliluyeva and Peters divorced. Peters sent no child support nor did he visit his daughter, Olga, for ten years. Alliluyeva and her daughter moved to England; became disillusioned with life in the West, and moved to the USSR. William Peters (and the U.S. State Department) began to worry about Olga's "willingness" to move to Russia (Stuart Taylor, Jr., "Stalin's Kin: Legal Issues," *New York Times*, November 24, 1984).

Another Russian mother, Ludmila Morrow, was not allowed to move back to Russia with Anatasha, her four-year-old daughter. The girl's father, American-born David Morrow fought for custody; and to prevent Anatasha from being removed forever to Russia. A judge granted Ludmila custody on the condition that she remain here (Hal Davis, "Tot in Cold War Tug of Love," *New York Post*, February 14, 1985).

The most notorious recent U.S. versus USSR international custody battle was that of twelve-year-old Walter Polovchak who in 1980 chose to remain in the United States and not return to the USSR with his parents. A juvenile court declared Walter a ward of the state.

"But Walter was still too young to make such a major decision on his own, they argued. The parents bitterly objected to intervention by the state in what they viewed as a family affair. . . . 'Who is the government to take away my child?' Mr. Polovchak said at the time. 'It is against the law and against the constitution.' Soviet officials said Walter had been 'brainwashed.' The United States accused the Russians of mounting a 'propaganda campaign' on the parents' behalf. . . . The legal issues are still winding their way through the Federal court system and the publicity has subsided. Life has taken on a steadier pace for Walter and Natalie, who live with their cousin in a quiet neighborhood on the Northwest side [of Chicago]" ("U.S. Life Agrees with Soviet Boy Who Fled," *New York Times*, April 15, 1984). In July 1985, Walter lost his case to remain in the United States (Alan Dershowitz, "Rights of Children in Conflict," *L.A. Times*, July 27, 1985).

70. Constantin Safilios-Rothschild, "The Role of the Family: A Neglected Aspect of Poverty." In "Implementing Programs of Human Development," World Bank Staff Working Paper, No. 403 (Washington, D.C.: World Bank, July, 1980).

71. Many developing countries rely on the family or tribal systems to subsidize their mothers and children. Those families (and states) that do not reject their daughters' "illegitimate" children may demand that such daughters work as prostitutes or in geographically remote areas of wage labor. For example, see *Connections: An International Women's Quarterly*, 836LL (Spring 1984) for reports of the seduction and sale of women into forced prostitution, by their own (impoverished) families or states in Thailand, Pakistan, and Korea and "sacred" institutions in India and Iran. Also see Barry, op. cit., and Barry, Bunch, and Castley, op. cit.

72. It may also lead to an increase in female-initiated sexual and procreative activities—a more "dreadful" prospect.

73. Mothers are single for many reasons beyond unwed sex and wanting "illegitimate"children. They may have been raped and abandoned; their husbands may have died or emigrated to urban areas; they may have been divorced or abandoned against their will; their husbands may not be able to afford any child support or may also be responsible for another family, etc.

74. See Chapters 8, 13, 14, 15, 16, 20, and 21.
    According to my respondent Ellen J. Cahill, the Commission of European Communities has confirmed that the "collection of maintenance has always been a problem . . . 56% of all maintenance is not paid or is paid irregularly. Twenty-five percent is not paid at all." Yvette Roudy, French minister for women's rights, confirms the inadequate level of "maintenance" (child support) and its non-enforcement.

75. See Tina Fishman's story in Chapter 2; and "Jessie's" story in Chapter 6 for examples of how politically "uppity" women are custodially punished.

76. See Chapters 20 and 21 for a discussion of the needs and rights of mothers, children, and families.

77. See Chapters 4, 6, 8, and 14.

78. Regional, national, and international attempts have been made to establish some legal reciprocity between governments in the areas of child custody and the rights of "illegitimate" children. These attempts have met with limited success; they have also encountered governmental opposition, indifference, and "bureaucratic" non-compliance.

For example, in 1981, the United States adopted a Uniform Child Custody Act, which made parental kidnapping illegal. To date women have been more quickly and harshly prosecuted for this essentially all-male crime than males have (see Chapter 14). In 1981 the Council of Europe attempted to establish a "central authority" for custodial matters. Of primary concern was the increase in "parental" child-kidnapping across state borders. It did not succeed in doing so. See R. L. Jones, "Council of Europe Convention on Recognition and Enforcement of Decisions Relating to the Custody of Children," *International and Comparative Law Quarterly*, 30 (April 1981):467.

In 1970 the United Nations' Commission on the Status of Women drafted a resolution to eliminate economic and legal discrimination against unwed mothers and "illegitimate" children. The resolution recommended "recognizing" maternal filiation as a fact of birth; "granting" unwed mothers the same parental rights as married mothers; "transmitting" an unwed mother's nationality to her child; "assisting" the unwed mother in establishing paternity and collecting paternal maintenance; "eliminating" discrimination against "illegitimate" children; and "awarding" equal state welfare benefits to both unwed and married mothers ("Legal and Social Status of the Unmarried Mother," UN Commission of the Status of Women, May 21, 1971).

Only thirteen UN members—Australia, Czechoslovakia, Denmark, Finland, Jamaica, Maldives, Netherlands, New Zealand, Romania, Tunisia, Ukrainian SSR, USSR, and United States—accepted this resolution. Three countries—Afghanistan, Kuwait, and Pakistan, rejected it entirely. Pakistan stated: ". . . the 'normalization' of legal and social attitudes towards extra-marital relations which seem implicit in the resolution, would have adverse effects on social progress and better standards of life. The institution of marriage is a social institution, and if a man and woman is to live in a society, he or she shall have to conform to the norms which . . . have got legal sanction behind it. Otherwise there would be no necessity for having the institution of marriage and the laws for the purpose."

Fifteen countries expressed serious reservations about specific clauses— especially the following clause: "The unmarried mother should be vested in law with full parental authority over her child, in all cases, as an automatic consequence of the fact of birth."

Austria could not reconcile this proposition with existing Austrian law because, "Austrian family legislation does not yet [as of 1971] include the concept of 'parental authority' even though a tendency exists to introduce it. The children born in wedlock are only subject to the 'paternal authority' exerted by their father."

Senegal agreed in principle, but had the following reservation: "A child whose filiation at birth is established *vis-à-vis* the mother only, shall be subject to her authority, it being provided that the *juge de paix* may transfer such authority to the father if he subsequently acknowledges the child, but only if the interests of the latter so require."

79. Greene, op. cit. According to Nancy Greene, "In the late 1970's an American woman lived with a Nigerian man in the United States. The father died before they could marry. She gave birth to a son. The mother took her infant son on a visit to his grandparents in Nigeria. The paternal grandmother offered to take care of the boy for a year while the mother returned to finish school in the United States. The Nigerian family then refused to give up the child. Since the boy is the only son of their only [deceased] son, they feel—and in Nigeria . . . they *have* the legitimate claim to custody. The only thing this mother can do is to go to Nigeria and physically take her child. If she makes it back to the U.S., she's home free. But how many single women have the money to do that?"

80. According to Jamila, an Algerian mother, "My husband Achmed is a cruel and violent man. When I got a temporary job offer as a governess in France, I accepted it with Achmed's permission, and then stayed on illegally. For a year I worked eighteen hours a day, seven days a week, as a cashier, waitress, and domestic. I sent money home and also saved enough money to send two of my children tickets to visit me for the summer. Then I refused to send them back. Achmed actually came and found us. He beat me in the street. The police came. They understood that I was illegal. They only locked Achmed up overnight.

"The lawyer said that in Algeria Achmed—not I, was entitled to custody. How could I expect French custody when I wasn't even a French citizen and was in fact, already breaking the French laws? Legally I had abandoned my husband and kidnapped his children. The lawyer advised me to go back to Algeria and live with Achmed if he would still have me."

81. Whether the patriarchal state is formed by analogy to the family or is based on institutions such as the army or the church, the modern state is engaged in a struggle against all other organized powers and against all individuals for control of the means of production and reproduction, i.e., for control of fertility, population, children, etc. and for control of children as tax-paying citizens, soldiers, obedient workers, etc.

It is important to note that some mothers do have *privileges* (not rights) as a function of their national, family, and class origin, and their race, skin color, caste, and good fortune.

CHAPTER NINETEEN: MOTHER'S WISDOM: PHILOSOPHICAL AND POLITICAL PERSPECTIVES ON HAVING AND LOSING CHILDREN

1. Alta, *Momma: A Start on all the Untold Stories* (New York: Times Change Press, 1984); Judith Arcana, *Every Mother's Son;* Virginia Barber and Merrill Maguire Skaggs, *The Mother Person* (Indianapolis: Bobbs-Merrill, 1975); J. Bernard, *Self-Portrait of a Family* (Boston: Beacon Press, 1978), *The Future of Motherhood* (New York: Dial, 1974), and *Women, Wives and Mothers* (Chicago: Aldine, 1975); E. M. Broner, *Her Mothers* (New York: Holt, Rinehart & Winston, 1975), and *A Weave of Women* (New York: Holt, Rinehart & Winston, 1978); Phyllis Chesler, *With Child* (New York: Thomas Y. Crowell, 1979); Nancy Chodorow, *The Reproduction of Mothering* (Berkeley: University of California Press, 1978); Toi Derricott, "In Knowledge of Young Boys" in *The Empress of the Death House* (Detroit: Lotus, 1978); Dorothy Dinnerstein, *The Mermaid and the Minotaur* (New York: Harper & Row, 1976); Jean Bethke Elshtain, "Feminist Discourse and its Discontents: Language Power and Meaning," and "Antigone's Daughters: Reflections on Female Identity and the State," in Diamond, ed., *Families, Politics and Public Policy: A Feminist Dialogue on Women and the State*, op. cit.; Oriana Fallaci, *Letter to a Child Never Born* (New York: Simon & Schuster, 1976); Joan Goulianos, ed., *By a Woman Writ: Literature from Six Centuries By and About Women* (Indianapolis: Bobbs-Merrill, 1973); Joanne Haggerty, *Daughters of the Moon* (New York: Bobbs-Merrill, 1971); G. E. Hanscombe and J. Forster, *Rocking the Cradle: Lesbian Mothers—A Challenge in Family Living* (Boston: Alyson Publications, 1982); Gladys Hindmarch, *A Birth Account* (Vancouver: New Star Books, 1976); Brigitte Jordan, *Birth in Four Cultures: A Cross-Cultural Investigation of Childbirth in Yucatan, Holland, Sweden and the United States* (St. Albans, Vt.: Eden Press Women's Publications, 1978); Eleanor H. Kuykendall, "Toward an Ethic of Nurturance: Luce Irigaray on Mothering and Power," in *Mothering: Essays in Feminist Theory*, Joyce Treblicot, ed. (Totowa, N.J.: Rowman & Allanheld, 1984); Jane Lazarre, *The Mother Knot* (New York: Dell, 1976); Angela Barron McBride, *The Growth and Development of Mothers* (New York: Harper & Row-Perennial Library, 1973); Mary O'Brien, "Feminist Theory and Dialectical Logic," in *Feminist Theory: A Criticism of Ideology*, Nannerl O'Keohane, Michelle Rosaldo, and Barbara C. Gelpi, eds. (Chicago: University of Chicago Press, 1981, 1982); Tillie Olsen, *Silences* (New York: Delacorte Press-Seymour Lawrence, 1978); Alicia Ostriker, "The Mother/Child Papers," *Feminist Studies* (1978); Shirley L. Radl, *Mothers Day is Over* (New York: Warner Books,

1973), and Radl, *How To Be A Mother and a Person Too* (New York: Rawson-Wade, 1979); Adrienne Rich, *Of Woman Born: Motherhood as Experience and Institution* (New York: W. W. Norton, 1976); Sara Ruddick, "Maternal Thinking," and "Preservative Love and Military Destruction: Some Reflections on Mothering and Peace," in Joyce Treblicot, ed., *Mothering: Essays on Feminist Theory* (Totowa, N.J.: Rowman & Allanheld, 1984); Jain Nyborg Sherrand, *Mother Warrior Pilgrim: A Personal Chronicle* (Kansas City: Andrews and McMeel, 1980); Alice Thornton, "The Autobiography of Mrs. Alice Thornton," in Joan Goulianos, ed., 1973, op. cit.; Viva, *The Baby* (New York: Alfred A. Knopf, 1975); Alice Walker, *In Love and Trouble* (New York: Harcourt, Brace, 1968); Caroline Whitbeck, "The Maternal Instinct," in Treblicot, op. cit.; Elizabeth Whelan, *A Baby? . . . Maybe: A Guide to Making The Most Fateful Decision of Your Life* (New York: Bobbs-Merrill, 1975).

2. Feminist theorists are, understandably, very concerned with patriarchy's use of biological differences as a way of keeping women, including mothers, economically dependent or impoverished. Some feminist theorists are also concerned with minimizing women's unique biological role in relation to children in order to persuade men to assume domestic and "maternal" responsibilities at home.

     It is important to remember that women *can* and do perform "male" activities. Women have been denied proper training—and wages—for doing so, because of presumed biological differences.

3. Caroline Whitbeck, "The Maternal Instinct" (1972), and "Afterward" (1982) in *Mothering: Essays in Feminist Theory*, Joyce Treblicot, ed., ibid.

4. Mary O'Brien, op. cit. I don't know whether biological mothers are significantly different from adoptive mothers in either their experience or practice of motherhood. They may/must have differences in feeling and perception. However, both biological and adoptive mothers have been socialized as women; both have experienced daughterhood; both have experienced being mothers under similar patriarchal conditions.

5. Judith Arcana, *Our Mothers' Daughters*, op. cit.

6. Phyllis Chesler, *With Child*, op. cit.

7. Nora Bartlett, "An Excerpt from my Unpublished Writing," in Michelle Wandor, ed., *On Gender and Writing* (Boston: Pandora Press, 1983).

8. Phyllis Chesler, *With Child*.

9. Margaret Drabble, *The Needle's Eye* (New York: Alfred A. Knopf, 1972). Rose's ultimate solution to her dilemma is reunion and remarriage to her children's father.

10. Sigmund Freud once observed that women seemed to lack (a male) "su-

perego" or sense of "ethics." Freud and others failed to consider that women and mothers, as well as the enslaved, the colonized, and the powerless, may possess a non-patriarchal code of ethics.

11. Carol Gilligan, *In a Different Voice: Psychological Theory and Women's Development* (Cambridge, Mass.: Harvard University Press, 1982).

12. Aeschylus, in the *Oresteia*, dramatizes the defeat of such matriarchal justice. Queen Clytemnestra's daughter, Iphighenia, is murdered by her father, King Agamemnon (infanticide); Clytemnestra kills her husband, Agamemnon, a blood stranger, to avenge her child's death (husband murder). In turn, Clytemnestra is betrayed by her daughter, Electra, and killed by her son, Orestes (matricide). Orestes, however, is legally and morally exonerated by the presiding tribunal of Greek gods.

Euripides, in the *Bacchae*, is the only classical dramatist to explore pro-mother justice sympathetically. He depicts Dionysus avenging the unjust murder of his mother, Semele. Dionysus, of course, is not a daughter, a mother, or a "female force."

13. The administration of law and order among violent male strangers is more "manageable" if women and children are conceived of as male property and if certain male crimes against women and children therefore aren't considered "crimes."

For example, until recently any man who abused, abandoned, or killed his slaves, his wife, or his children was not breaking the law. "Justice" did not have to intervene in such private matters. "Justice" is still reluctant to intervene on behalf of women and children who are domestically abused by husbands and fathers.

Unconsciously (or psychologically) men are guilty about their (mis)treatment of women. The man-child always fears retribution from his "mother." Aristophanes portrayed the male fear of an organized "matriarchal" presence in politics and in matters of honor. Since evolving patriarchal law didn't—and still doesn't—protect the rights of mothers and children, the male fear of female "vigilante justice" must remain a powerful fear.

It is also true that a white person's crime against someone who is racially despised often goes unpunished, lightly punished, or isn't seen as a crime. Whatever the racially despised do, including the defense of their own lives or the exercise of their civil rights, is often viewed and punished as a crime. Patriarchal law and its application does not protect the poor and the racially despised from each other as well as it protects wealthy, white men from all others who stand in their way, refuse them their way, or attempt to use the law as if they, too, were wealthy, white men.

14. Catherine MacKinnon, "Feminism, Marxism and the State," *Signs*, (Summer 1983).

15. Nearly half of the heterosexual mothers (46 percent) and 50 percent of the

lesbian mothers verbally expressed a mothers' rights view, while 30 percent of the heterosexual mothers and 43 percent of the lesbian mothers identified themselves as feminists at the time of the interview.

16. All custodially embattled mothers experienced maternal "connectedness." Both maternally assertive and non-assertive heterosexual mothers had achieved the same average education and had mothered for the same average number of years. None of the maternally assertive mothers ever won in court; nearly a third (27 percent) of the *non-assertive* mothers did, at first. Perhaps an initial courtroom victory confused mothers about the existence of their rights or about the willingness of the law to protect them from subsequent paternal harassment. Perhaps those mothers who were able to settle privately, as 20 percent of the *assertive* mothers had, were already "clear" about their natural maternal rights and the non-existence of their maternal legal rights; perhaps, as we have seen, they were also married to less violent husbands.

17. It is important to realize that the numbers involved here are relatively small and that no statistical significance is involved.

18. This excellent phrase belongs to John Demos, author of *Entertaining Satan.*

19. Profound and lasting intimacy was experienced by "political" women who never lived together but who joined each other in battle. I have been privileged, not often enough, to know such incandescent intimacy.

20. But I have enjoyed being able to write about mothers, seriously and positively, for eighteen pages, without feeling obliged to demonstrate my understanding of maternal limitations and imperfections sooner or all along the way. This is a very useful exercise in a mother-hating culture.

21. Ruddick, "Preservative Love and Military Destruction"; and "Maternal Thinking."

22. The phrases in quotes are Sara Ruddick's, ibid.

23. Some recent feminist theorists have described women and men as "similar"; other theorists have described women and men as profoundly "different." The majority of these studies of women (and men) have been psychological rather than political or historical; theoretical or experimental, rather than based on field studies of the real lives of adult women. They are also written from the point of view of white, Western, middle-class, educated, married, or heterosexual women. This is not meant as a criticism. It is a description of the unspoken or unacknowledged angle of vision. See, for example, Phyllis Chesler, *Women and Madness,* Doubleday, 1972, and *About Men,* Simon & Schuster, 1978; Nancy Chodorow, *The Reproduction of Mothering,* University of California Press, 1978; Dorothy Dinnerstein, *The Mermaid and the Minotaur,* Harper & Row, 1976; Jean Bethke Elshtain,

"Antigone's Daughters: Reflections on Female Identity and the State," Irene Diamond, ed., Longman, 1983; Carol Gilligan, *In a New Voice*, Harvard University Press, 1982; Jean Baker Miller, *Toward a New Psychology of Women*, (Boston: Beacon Press, 1976).

24. Sitting in the same playground and engaging in parallel co-mothering are not ways of maternally nurturing another woman or her child, although the company is always appreciated. Taking over the care of a blood-daughter or blood-sister's child is more common among the impoverished or the racially despised. However, this is a psychologically complex "take-over." It is a *familial* form of affiliation. It is sometimes, but not always, a form of female-female competition within the same blood family.

25. See my forthcoming book, *Woman's Inhumanity to Woman*.

26. Sara Ruddick, op. cit.

27. Sara Ruddick, op. cit.

28. It is important to remember that parents, both men and women, absorb and accept violence for the sake of children and inflict violence on others for the sake of their own families.

29. Jean Baker Miller in *Toward a New Psychology of Women*, Ibid., noted that: "It is certainly clear that we have not reached a very high level of cooperative living. To the extent that it exists, women have assumed the greater responsibility for providing it. Although they may not label it in large letters, women in families are constantly trying to work out some sort of cooperative system that attends to each person's needs. Their task is greatly impeded by the unequal premise on which our families are based, but it has been women who have *practiced* trying."

30. This is never the case as long as powerful people personally do not have to suffer the consequences of their impersonal actions. I am essentially describing a public show of officials.

    However, in 1983, I listened to an all-female panel of European anti-nuclear pacifists describe an important male-female difference at the Greenham Common Peace Camp in England. Apparently it had been impossible for the (powerless) male pacifists to remain non-violent when they saw policemen brutally assaulting women, and when they themselves were assaulted. The women finally asked the men not to participate in actions of civil disobedience for this reason.

    Surely, "gentle" men do exist—i.e., men who are emotionally nurturing, and non-violent toward children and women, men who have "maternal" desires or feelings. Surely men committed to principles of non-violence also exist. (In most cases economic as well as psychological necessity does not permit such men to engage in maternal practice.)

    Most men committed to non-violence are spiritual or political *leaders*.

As such they are involved in commanding or organizing large numbers of strangers. They are rarely involved in the daily non-violent nurturing of dependent intimates.

It is as hard for men to overcome and oppose their socialization into a dependent dominance and into violence as it is for women to overcome ours.

31. Jean Baker Miller, op. cit., has noted: "Some of the things I have written may sound like things our grandmothers would have told us: 'Men will be boys. We let them play their little games with each other. We know it isn't about the important things, but they think so. So we let them. We take care of them so that they can go on playing. Without us they couldn't.' But the games are not fun anymore, if they ever were. Many end in war games. What grandma did not tell us is that men are capable of something altogether different. (If they are not, then perhaps women had better take over completely!) But even though men are untapped wells of potential, they will not move forward if women continue to subsidize the status quo." Jeffner Allen, in "Looking At Our Blood: A Lesbian Response to Men's Terrorization of Women" (*Trivia: A Journal of Ideas* [Spring 1984]), has written about women's adherence to non-violence as a self-defeating trap. Allen identifies such adherence as "heterosexual" and as part of the "society of mothers." She identifies women's desire for survival and freedom from terror as "lesbian." Allen writes: "Adherents to the ideology of heterosexual virtue hold in common the claim that violence is brutalizing. Women are held to be better than men, either wholly or in part precisely because women are nonviolent. Women's superiority is frequently attributed to feminine qualities of nurturance, understanding, and concern for others. The history of nurturance, in which women give freely, expect nothing in return, and remain powerless while partaking in unsatisfying relationships, is dismissed. Obliterated, as well, are women who have rejected feminine qualities as restrictive, false virtues that are useless for women's daily lives.

"The heterosexual virtue which binds women to male-defined nonviolence is preeminently self-destructive, leading to the sole form of action permitted to women: martyrdom and suicide. . . . Men's terrorization of women need not, however, be endured at all. . . . I no longer regard myself as a woman, she who exists to be empenised, or as a mother, she who produces for the sake of men.

"We must decide which actions are necessary for women's survival and freedom. If we are to live free from terror, the most effective actions are those which make impossible men's acts of sexual terrorism. Men's terrorization of women is most effectively stopped before it can happen. In a world of female friendship and freedom, rape becomes a form of sexual violation against which all women act to secure that it never exist again.

"The claim that 'an all-female army in patriarchal society *is* necessary for the liberation of women,' as articulated by Susan Cavin, should be adopted wholeheartedly and immediately by women everywhere."

32. Industrialization, for example, from which we all profit today, meant centuries of horror for men, women, and children who worked and died in factories. While advances in science and technology potentially preserve more lives and at a higher economic and spiritual standard of living, this has not yet been accomplished.

Women as *workers* or as consumers of medical and other services *have* legally confronted the male state with some success. Women as wives and mothers have been less successful in confronting the male state on their own behalf.

33. Jean Bethke Elshtain, "Antigone's Daughters: Reflections on Female Identity and the State," in *Families, Politics and Public Policy: A Feminist Dialogue on Women and the State*, op. cit.

34. The Living Theatre has presented Antigone as a passionate anti-war and anti-state rebel.

35. Sara Ruddick, op. cit.

36. The maternal process can also be called matriarchal or private; the paternal process can also be called patriarchal or public.

37. Chapters 1, 2, 4, 9, 10, 13, 14, 17, and 18. Also see Chapters 20 and 21.

38. MacKinnon, op. cit., notes: "If objectivity [is important] then the [legal] state will appear most relentless in imposing the male point of view when it comes closest to achieving its highest formal criterion of distanced aperspectivity. When it is most ruthlessly neutral, it will be most male; when it is most sex blind, it will be most blind to the sex of the standard being applied. When it most closely conforms to precedent, to 'facts,' to legislative intent, it will most closely enforce socially male norms. . . . Justice will require change, not reflection—a new jurisprudence, a new relation between life and law."

39. I am not saying that practicing mothers don't have breaking points or are not entitled to sabbaticals as well as assistance and support. They are. I am saying that few practicing mothers voluntarily leave their children for long or, if they do, in "disconnected" ways. Mothers remain "connected" to their children for life.

CHAPTER TWENTY: CHILDREN'S RIGHTS

1. According to Dr. Paul L. Adams, "We believe that the future augurs well for the child whose mother chose positively to bring the child into the

world. Children who are wanted have a prospect to live worthwhile lives. The unwanted child is fated, by contrast, to be abused and neglected. . . . For that reason, *we insist that wanted children should become a societal premium, and the wanting of children should be a national goal*" Paul L. Adams; Judith R. Milner; and Nancy A. Screpf: *Fatherless Children* (a volume in the Wiley series in Child Mental Health); New York: John Wiley & Sons, 1984.

Martha Gimenez suggests that "the highest incidence of child abuse and battered wives, the high divorce and remarriage rates, the high increases in illegitimacy and teenage pregnancy, and the growth of female-headed households are phenomena which [suggest] the negative consequences of prescriptive parenthood [which] pressures women and men, sometimes at very early ages, to enter into relationships for which they might not be entirely suited" (Martha E. Gimenez, "Feminism, Pronatalism, and Motherhood," in *Mothering: Essays in Feminist Theory*, Joyce Treblicot, ed., op. cit). See also Jeffner Allen, "Motherhood: The Annihilation of Women," in *Mothering: Essays in Feminist Theory*, Joyce Treblicot, ed., op. cit.

2. If children have the right to be wanted, then those willing to parent must have the right to have children. This means that no one (male or female) should be unwillingly or unknowingly sterilized, forced into an abortion against her will, or forced to give up her infant at birth either because she is too young, unmarried, impoverished, unemployed, or underpaid or because she is denied access to basic family support services.

This is especially true for racially despised and impoverished people, who are routinely channeled into military, industrial, or sexual occupations that either kill or sterilize them; and into prison, where their right to mother (or father) is non-existent or highly circumscribed by the state.

In cases of female or male infertility or in cases where women or men want to adopt, rather than genetically to reproduce children, discrimination must cease against the unmarried, the non-affluent, and the non-white.

3. See Brigitte Jordan, *Birth in Four Cultures: A Cross-Cultural Investigation of Childbirth in Yucatan, Holland, Sweden and the United States*, St. Albans, Vt, Eden Press Women's Publications 1978, for some superb descriptions of communal childbirth in culture. See Suzanne Arms, *Immaculate Deception: A New Look at Women in America* (Boston: Houghton-Mifflin, 1975) for a description of the savage limitations of childbirth in America.

4. I am reluctant to talk about the pregnant "couple." While fathers-to-be can play (and are playing) increasingly supportive roles during their wives' pregnancies and childbirths, they themselves do not experience pregnancy or childbirth. I will discuss the role of fathers in the lives of children separately.

I am also reluctant to outline what the precise educational, political, legal, and especially economic systems are that must be retained, eliminated, or modified in order that what I'm talking about can truly be implemented. The reason is simple enough. For us, as a civilization, to shift to a concern for people before profits would require many complex, simultaneous evolutionary and revolutionary changes. This is the subject of many other books.

5. In 1962 and 1963 I worked as a welfare "investigator" for the City of New York on Manhattan's Lower East Side. I kept a diary but have never published it. The mothers on welfare were not then, and still are not today, adequately subsidized in terms of their own or their children's food or hygiene needs. Shelter was subsidized in the highest crime-rate areas without adequate space, sunlight, or heat. The state (and philosophers) claim that everything is "relative." And so it is. In India whole families live on the street for their whole lives; in Africa whole families are starving to death; in Asia whole families have been killed by war.

  They all are our "relatives."

6. I am not making an argument for immediate economic communization of the United States. However, what a child "costs" is not what women alone can earn here, nor is it what the state (or church) gives toward a child's existence. See recent welfare levels cited in Chapters 4, 8, and 14.

7. Conversely, mothers and fathers do not "own" their children and should not act as if they did. Children should be free to love other people and to manifest "preferences" for people other than their mothers and fathers. The development of such "preferences" does not mean that a mother and father have failed or that a child doesn't love them.

8. We do have a state "welfare" and Social Security system that is still operative. More recently, in 1984, the United States House of Representatives and Senate passed part of an Economic Equity Act which called for better child support enforcement, prohibited pension penalties for women on maternity leaves, apportioned pension benefits in divorce proceedings, and protected spousal pension rights in the event of death before the age of retirement. The pension bill was introduced by Representative Geraldine Ferraro, the Democratic candidate for vice president in 1984 ("Pension Measure Aiding Women Goes to Reagan," *New York Times,* August 10, 1984).

  The Family Law Project seeks legislation to define marriage in economic terms and to provide recognition and support to the *economic* value of the homemaker. In California, Assemblyman Art Agnos sponsored a bill that set mandatory standards on child-support payments. A formula was proposed to take into consideration the combined net incomes of both parents, number of children, and other factors. The state welfare levels would be used as a minimum for the amount of child support ordered. The formula would be used in excess of welfare levels (A letter from Art Agnos, Assemblyman, California legislature, Sixteenth District, February 1984).

In December 1984 Governor Mario Cuomo of New York formed a state commission to study the problem of the nonpayment of child support.

9. Adams, et al., op. cit.

10. I am not saying that grandparents, maternal aunts, and first cousins all should be economically subsidized by the already overtaxed taxpayer. I am saying that a family consists of a core of at least two parents and should extend outward to include from three to eight more adult and child-oriented family members.

It is dangerous to make children too profitable an enterprise. In the past children were easily exploited for the incomes they represented. Their wealth was easily and cruelly squandered by adults. A middle ground must be created so that every family (as described above) can function well above the poverty level.

11. America's "melting pot" history is also one of forced assimilation to the racial and cultural status quo. This always involves a psychologically dangerous denial of one's own roots, one's family, and oneself. Successive waves of white immigrants and light-skinned black ex-slaves lost as much as they gained in their efforts to "pass" for white, Protestant, or middle class.

Native American Indians constitute an extreme and extremely tragic example of how the American state forced children apart from their mothers, fathers, and tribal identities, thereby forcing Indian children into a self-hating and self-destructive obedience to a white and racist Christianity. (This also occurred with dark-skinned blacks, but not in the exact same way.)

There exists a literature describing the *negative* effects of being forcibly separated from one's social, tribal, ethnic, and religious identity. For example, Doris Lessing and Richard Rodriguez both have written about the pain involved in choosing "superior" cultures over one's own culture of origin.

Most Native American Indian writers describe being forcibly separated from their *real* mothers and fathers and from their cultural history and identity. See, for example, Brant, op. cit.

Native Canadian Indian social worker Marie Baker, in a personal interview in 1983, spoke to me about this. I would like to quote her at length:

"Indian children in Canada and the United States used to be sent to boarding school to 'civilize' them. They were taught white culture and English. Foster care is the modern form of cultural genocide. It separates mothers and children from each other and from their roots. Unwed Indian mothers are regularly pressured by the state authorities to give up their babies for legal adoption.

"In 1983 one young mother was delayed for eight days in the hospital after giving birth, in order to convince her to give up the child. The white social workers acted as if the maternal grandmother wasn't actively on the scene. When an Indian mother runs away from a very abusive husband, the state begins to move in on her children. If an Indian mother already under welfare snooping has to leave her kids unattended for an hour, the state might just snatch them. She'll find them gone when she comes back.

"Once a child has been snatched by social services, it usually takes seven months for the Indian mother to even see her kids again. In that time a mother may start drinking. Then she's easy to call unfit.

"When Indian kids run away from abusive foster homes, they can't always find their mothers. Teenage girls are becoming street prostitutes. The state doesn't hurry to return them from *this* unfit environment back to their mothers. You can get eleven thousand to twenty thousand dollars for an infant. Some kids are shipped down to the American South to work as unpaid farm laborers. Several Indian women, myself included, have just started Native Family Services (Nokomus Consultants) to help Indian mothers retain or regain custody of their kids from the state, and to reach out to Indian kids who've run away from foster care and want to return to their natural mothers."

12. According to Alma Estable and Helen Levine, "The Power Politics of Motherhood" (Ottawa, Canada, Carleton University, 1983), and "Occasional Papers," (Ontario), "Children have the right to grow into full 'parenthood' without girls being reduced to subservience and limited definitions of womanhood; and boys being exempted from nurturant behavior in the name of masculinity."

13. See Chapter Nineteen. Also see the following works: Julia Kristeva, "Women's Time," in *Feminist Theory: A Critique of Ideology*, ed., Nannerl O. Keohane, Michelle Z. Rosaldo, and Barbara C. Gelpi (Chicago: University of Chicago Press, 1982); Lynda Lange, "Woman Is Not A Rational Animal: On Aristotle's Biology of Reproduction," in *Discovering Reality: Feminist Perspectives on Epistemology, Metaphysics, Methodology, and Philosophy of Science*, ed. Sandra Harding and Merrill B. Hintikka (Boston: D. Reidel Publishing Co., Holland: Dordacht, 1983); Barbara Love and Elizabeth Shanklin, "The Answer is Matriarchy," *Mothering: Essays in Feminist Theory*, Joyce Treblicot, ed.; Mary O'Brien, "Feminist Theory and Dialectical Logic," in *Feminist Theory*, Sara Ruddick, "Preservative Love and Military Destruction: Some Reflections on Mothering and Peace," and "Maternal Thinking," *Mothering: Essays in Feminist Theory*, Joyce Treblicot, ed.; Caroline Whitbeck, "The Maternal Instinct (1972)" and "Afterword (1982)," *Mothering: Essays in Feminist Theory*, Joyce Treblicot, ed.; Barbara Walker, *The Women's Dictionary of Myths and Secrets* (New York: Harper and Row, 1984).

14. There are many, many descriptions of how women are so socialized to become mothers and what this means, in terms of male-female parenting differences. For example, Nancy Chodorow, *The Reproduction of Mothering* (Berkeley: University of California Press, 1978); Dorothy Dinnerstein, *The Mermaid and The Minotaur*, (New York: Harper & Row, 1976); Linda Gordon, *Woman's Body, Woman's Right: A Social History of Birth Control in America*, (New York: Penguin, 1976); Jean Baker Miller, *Toward a New Psychology of Women*, (Boston: Beacon Press, 1976); Eleanor Kuykendall, "Toward an Ethic of Nurturance: Luce Irigary on Mothering and Power," *Mothering: Essays in Feminist Theory*, Joyce Treblicot, ed., Sara Ruddick, in *Mothering: Essays in Feminist Theory*, notes: "Not all women are mothers, nor is maternal thinking the whole of women's thought. Equally important, maternal thinking is not the whole of a *mother's* thought any more than maternity is the whole of a mother's life. . . . Although maternal thinking arises out of the care of actual children. . . . maternal thought does, I believe, exist for all women in radically different ways than for men. It is because we are *daughters*, nurtured and trained by women. . . . We are alert to the values and costs of maternal practice whether we are determined to engage in them or to avoid them." See Chapters 3, 4, and 19 for a description of maternal practice. Also see Sara Ruddick, op. cit.

15. Letty Cottin Pogrebin, op. cit.

See Chapter 3 for a discussion of our standards for maternal and paternal fitness and unfitness and for a description of what most mothers actually do for children. For example, a large research literature documents a wide variety of positive effects exerted on children by working or career mothers. This literature has been recently and comprehensively reviewed by Paul L. Adams, Judith R. Milner and Nancy A. Schrepf in *Fatherless Children*, a volume in the Wiley Series in Child Mental Health, Joseph D. Noshpitz, ed., (New York: John Wiley and Sons, 1984); by Mary Joan Gerson, Judith L. Alpert, and Mary Sue Richardson, "Mothering: The View from Psychological Research," *Signs*, 9, 3 (1984).

A decent-size research literature documents either the positive or negligible effects of children having lesbian and/or sexually active mothers. For example, Mildred D. Pagelow, "Heterosexual and Lesbian Single Mothers: A Comparison of Problems, Coping and Solutions," *Journal of Homosexuality*, 5, 8 (Spring 1980); and Martha Kirkpatrick, "Lesbian Mother Families," *Psychiatric Annals*, 12, 9 (Sept., 1982). See Chapter 7.

16. Powers, "Falling Through the Safety Net: Women, Economic Crisis and Reaganomics," *Signs* (Summer 1984). Powers cites an article in *Newsweek*, indicating that 60 percent of the cuts in federal entitlement programs in fiscal 1982 came from programs for the poor. Aid to Families with Dependent Children (AFDC) was cut by approximately $1 billion, Med-

icaid by $800 million, and Food Stamps by $700 million. These programs were dealt another blow in the 1983 budget. *Newsweek,* April 5, 1982. *New York Times,* September 21, 1981 and June 24, 1982; *Washington Post,* June 25 and August 14, 1982.

Powers also notes that President Reagan's policies are "consistent—with political support for capital and the 'free' market, consistent with an ideological strategy of weakening the power of labor and redistributing income towards profits. *These policies provide a perfect illustration of how the sexism embedded in a society's structures and institutions can be reproduced without requiring a conscious effort to do so."*

17. See Phyllis Chesler and Emily Jane Goodman, *Women, Money & Power* (New York: Morrow, 1976; Bantam, 1978), for a discussion of the role that private industry and the state could and should play in effecting a direct maternal wage. See also Sheila B. Kamerman's proposals for a policy agenda for the United States in "Women, Children and Poverty: Public Policies and Female Headed Families in Industrialized Countries," *Signs* (Winter 1984).

18. Paul L. Adams, et al., op. cit.

If mothers and children were valued, humane quality child care would already be provided for everyone—not just for mothers in prison. Also, if we had direct maternal wages, benefits, and a family allowance, instead of welfare levels of poverty, few mothers would have to work illegally as prostitutes, shoplift food, write "bad" checks, or engage in welfare "fraud" in order to adequately support themselves and their children.

Until our society engages in a massive redistribution of economic security and opportunity, young, unmarried, non-educated, and impoverished mothers, especially those reduced to welfare levels of poverty, will continue to be convicted of petty economic and victimless "crimes."

19. "Pope: Pay Moms to Stay Home," *New York Post,* May 1984.

20. See Sara Ruddick, op. cit.

21. Adrienne Rich, "Compulsory Heterosexuality."

22. Richard Cohen, "Men Sharing," *Ms.* magazine (August 1984).

23. See Chapters 1 through 4 and Chapters 9, 10, and 14.

24. L. Armstrong, op. cit.; Herman, op. cit.; Kenneth Hermann, *I Hope My Daddy Dies, Mister* (Philadelphia: Dorrence, 1975); Faith McNulty, *The Burning Bed;* Diana Russell, *Rape in Marriage* (New York: Macmillan, 1982); Schecter, *Women and Male Violence: The Visions and Struggles of the Battered Women's Movement* (Boston: South End Press, 1982); Elizabeth Thomas, "Custody Litigation Strategies for Battered Women," in *Domestic Violence: Are Lawyers Prepared to Meet a Growing Crisis?* CLE

Seminar, Seattle, WA, Northwestern Womens' Law Center, January 27, 1983; Women Against Rape (Wisconsin) *Newsletter*, July 1983; Helen Yglesias, *Sweetsir* (New York: Simon & Schuster, 1981).

It is important to realize that certain acts of male domestic violence devastate children directly as well as indirectly. In terms of child kidnapping, according to J.E. Gill in "Stolen Children," op. cit.: "[Kidnapping] is a lot harder on a child, in fact, than a real death. In an actual death, the other parent is their support and would have experienced the loss, too. But in child snatching, the child has no way of talking about it. The abducting parent doesn't want to talk about it, which alienates the child even more from that absent parent.

"Families come together when someone dies. Relatives fly in from other states. They support each other. Children see uncles, aunts, cousins. They know they belong. Stolen children see practically no one. There are no reunions and family dinners, no offers of help. There is just hiding. When they come home, they may have to hide again. Everyone fears a second kidnapping."

25. Quoted by Steven V. Roberts, "Now a Select Committee for Families," *New York Times*, February 23, 1983.

26. For example, in 1983 and 1984, in the states of Minnesota and New Jersey, police officers were trained and ordered to arrest domestically violent men as they would any violent criminal. In Minnesota, the lowest rates of repeated domestic violence occurred in those cases where male offenders were jailed—even for a day.

27. Wisconsin's Women Against Rape (WAR) recommend that:
"A parallel to the right to a speedy trial [as used in Criminal Court] must be established in Family Court for cases of battery within marriage and child abuse, assault and/or neglect. [When the alleged abuse includes incest] visitation must be suspended from the time such complaints are made until the Court completes a hearing which determines whether or not abuse, assault or neglect has occurred and who is the abusing party. There must be *no* visitation between a complaint and the final Court determination because:
"—it jeopardizes the child's testimony and places the child in physical and emotional danger;
"—visitation provides the abuser with an opportunity to suppress the child's allegations and distort the child's version of the incident by allowing the abuser to be in a pseudo-friendly relationship with the victim.
"When all testimony and evidence has been entered, the Courts must make a determination as to whether the allegations are 'indicated' or 'unfounded.' If the Court finds that abuse occurred, court proceedings must come to an end, and visitation must be terminated or supervised.
"Determination of abuse must be recorded—if the abusing parent de-

sires to re-open the matter, he or she must bear the cost of all resulting fees and must prove to the Court that he or she has met the criteria to allow supervised visitation to occur.

"If the Court does not find that enough material evidence is present in order to make a determination of abuse (the norm with children under 9 or 11) yet there is concrete evidence of other abusive behavior in the alleged offender's past, then supervised visitation with a neutral professional, third-party, trained in the dynamics of abuse must be ordered."

Wisconsin's Women Against Rape also recommend:

"A Special Unit on Family Protection within the Family Court must be created. Personnel staffing this special unit must be hired on the basis of the skill and training they possess.

—They must pass an examination based on bibliography of current material in the field which is agreed upon by survivor advocacy/community groups and experts in these issues;

—the performance of these workers must be monitored and evaluated on a continuous basis (bi-annually). . . .

"This unit should coordinate and maintain records on individuals who have been determined to be abusers in complaints heard in Family, Criminal and Children's Court."

Resumption of visitation rights for the abusing father must be conditional. Wisconsin's Women Against Rape propose: "The court must insure that the vulnerable child's wishes and preferences regarding visitation are presented and given strong consideration, as well as the child's safety.

"1. The child should be able to refuse visitation in light of the abusing parent's behavior.

"2. However, the non-abusing parent should also have the paramount right not to have abuse in their own or their child's life.

"3. In cases where the child has been conditioned by the abusing parent and socialized to be a lover, the non-abusing parent has the right and the responsibility to request that the Court suspend visitation to prevent further danger to the child and the Court should respond positively.

"4. When visitation has been terminated because the Court finds that a parent has endangered the child's physical, mental or emotional health, visitation may not be resumed unless:

"—the Court has completed proceedings to determine whether or not the allegations are indicated or unfounded;

"—the abusing parent meets the criteria for resuming visitation in a supervised setting;

"—the child wishes to visit with the abuser and is old enough to understand how to terminate unwanted contact and seek help;

"—the non-abusing parent consents to allow visitation;

"—visitation is supervised by a trained professional supervisor;

"—the abusive parent demonstrates to the Court that [he or she has] met the following criteria: the abuser acknowledges that [he or she] committed the offense and does not project blame or responsibility on some external factor (victim provocation, intoxication, etc.). The abuser verbalizes [his or her] acceptance of responsibility for the incidents to the child, in the presence of the child's therapist. The abuser must explain how [he or she] manipulated and coerced the child into submission and was physically, sexually, emotionally abusive/or was neglectful of caretaking responsibilities.

"5. The abuser demonstrates that [he or she has] become sensitized to the chain or patterns of behavior that led to [his or her] sexual involvement with children or adolescents, or other abusive or neglectful behaviors, so that the offender can detect early warning signs or symptoms."

28. None of the popular psychoanalytic accounts of child development or child abuse is written from a feminist or antisexist point of view. Their views are all compatible with a yet-to-be enunciated feminist view of ideal and normal human development. See Alice Miller's description of the normal child abuse rampant in most families (Alice Miller, *Prisoners of Childhood,* op. cit., and *For Your Own Good: Hidden Cruelty in Child Rearing and the Roots of Violence,* op. cit.). Many others address this issue. For example: Adams, et al., op. cit.; David Cooper, *The Death of the Family* (New York: Pantheon, 1970); Sigmund Freud, *The Basic Writings of Sigmund Freud,* trans. and ed. by Dr. A.H. Brill (New York: Modern Library, 1938); Wilhelm Reich, *The Mass Psychology of Fascism* (New York: Noonday Books, 1970); Morton Schatzman, *Soul Murder* (New York: Random House, 1973).

29. A reminder: "good enough" mothers may *psychologically* fail maternal practice in the service of "protecting" their children from a violent world. Mothers may also *psychologically* fail maternal practice by projecting their own sense of worthlessness onto their children or by trying vicariously to "perfect" themselves through their children.

It is therefore miraculous and heroic that so many mothers are physically non-violent and "empathetically" authoritarian with their children.

To the extent to which this is true for a mother, we must ask: "why?" Perhaps those mothers who are "empathetically" authoritarian remember that their children were once part of their own bodies. Perhaps some mothers identified with or grew "tender" toward helpless, dependent, or breast-feeding infants. Perhaps maternal (physical) non-violence also evolved for non-biological reasons.

Perhaps mothers, all of whom are women and most of whom are (or once were) wives or heterosexual, have learned non-violence as a means of domestic survival with men, as unequal dependents.

CHAPTER TWENTY-ONE: UPON DIVORCE

1. See Chapters 4, 8, 9, and 20. Also, a December 1984 National Institute of Mental Health (NIMH) study found that 52 percent of the children of divorce hadn't heard from their fathers in the last year, and 36 percent of such children had had no contact with them for five years. The paternal non-payment of child support has been discussed elsewhere.

   The NIMH study also suggests that divorce doesn't do long-term harm to children and that it hurts them less than living with two parents in conflict. This finding is based on a survey of 1,423 children. It is apparently at "odds" with several earlier studies, including the most-quoted one by Dr. Judith Wallerstein, which was based on 131 children.

   This kind of finding is important for several reasons. For example, not all parents need stay together for the sake of their children. Doing so may actually cause the children more harm than good. Also, the loss of one parent (usually the father) as the result of divorce need not necessarily harm children in the long run.

2. See Chapters 8, 14, and 20.

   In many personal interviews in 1981 and 1982 Lillian Kozak, of New York NOW, convinced me that no-fault divorce and equitable distribution of property laws which eliminated alimony were actually being used *against* women. Materials on file with the National Center for Women and Family Law.

   Attorneys Harriet Cohen and Nancy C. Deming analyzed twenty-six of the first equitable-distribution cases decided by the courts in New York State. Seventeen of these decisions, including every one of those that involved large sums of money, favored the husband. Seven cases couldn't be categorized because the assets were negligible, the husband had defaulted, or the decision was too close to call. Only two decisions were considered "pro-wife."

   A NOW-sponsored New Jersey Supreme Court study, based on U.S. Census reports and other data, found that divorce impoverished mothers and children but not men and that judges contributed to this state of affairs. According to this study, judges justified what they did by claiming that women "remarried" and could now "earn equal pay for equal work." Judges also had no idea of what "feeding or clothing a family" and "child care" actually cost.

   Therefore, according to this study, "judges rarely give a wife more than 30 percent of her husband's salary in combined maintenance (which he can deduct for tax purposes) and child support, thus leaving him with 70 percent for himself. As for jointly held marital assets, women rarely receive more than 35 to 40 percent, slightly more than the nationwide estimate of one-third. The study found that many judges see rehabilitative maintenance as a short-term award even in the case of long marriages in which the wife has little chance of ever earning what her husband does. Finally, the report said, the courts are reluctant to award adequate fees for appraisal and accounting services, thus making it difficult for women even to make a case for truly equitable distribution."

This study is also referred to in Chapter 14, and is covered by Katherine Bouton, "Women and Divorce: How the New Law Works Against Them," *New York* magazine (October 8, 1984).

On March 28, 1985, New York Appellate Division Judge John Carro made headlines when he ruled that alimony ends when a wife, in this case of fifteen years, "lives with a lover." Her past labor and services are, in effect, canceled when she takes on a private relationship or a new job. In a sense, this is equivalent to a man or worker losing his or her pension after fifteen years of work because they enter into a private relationship or begin a new career (*New York Post,* March 29, 1985). *Bliss* v. *Bliss*, decided March 28, 1985, reported in 11 *FLR* 1292–1293.

3. Lillian Kozak showed me a number of well-known and scandalous cases in which very wealthy and millionaire fathers are assisted by the courts to impoverish their ex-wives and children. (See Chapter 8 for a discussion of the Labow case.)

Katherine Bouton, op. cit., cites the case of one "Elizabeth Connell": "Elizabeth Connell," who was married for 30 years and divorced on the grounds of her husband "Daniel's" abandonment. Elizabeth stopped working in order to work as a wife and mother. Trouble arose when Elizabeth sought an equitable or equal share of her ex-husband's considerable business assets. Bouton notes that: "Elizabeth's accountant had testified that the business was worth more than $3 million. Daniel's experts valued it at $241,577. The judge determined that the value lay 'somewhere between the two claims'—and set the amount at $480,000, awarding Elizabeth half of that. She believes her own lawyer, a man, was partially responsible for the judge's low valuation. The lawyer didn't energetically support her accountant's testimony because, he later admitted to her, he thought that since her accountant was a woman she must be merely a friend and therefore not fully competent to make an accurate assessment."

4. Passion is forbidden in patriarchal Puritan culture. Male power is eroticized in its place. In *Gone With The Wind,* passion (or true love) is largely unrequited. Rhett loves Scarlett; Scarlett loves Ashley; neither gets what he or she wants. Rhett, however, remains a hero; Scarlett becomes and remains a fallen woman—abandoned and lost.

5. We also forget (don't discuss, never mention, barely notice) another

recent Hollywood father's violent "repossession" of his daughter—in the film *Ragtime*. The girl's mother is also an adulteress—just like Scarlett O'Hara. Mandy Patinkin's father, like Rhett and Michael, dotes on his daughter; he will soon be rich and famous. Clearly, any child is better off with a rich father than with an immoral or impoverished mother.

Single mothers, especially if they are divorced, are rarely glorified in Hollywood films. *Alice Doesn't Live Here Anymore*, *Heart Like a Wheel*, and *Without a Trace* are three major exceptions. These films, however, do not glorify (single) female motherhood per se. They focus on other matters. They are remarkable because they present single divorced mothers as sympathetic *workers* or career women.

Widows (*Places in the Heart*) and married wives (*The River*) show us women who are neither glorified nor denigrated as mothers; but who *are* glorified as loyal and feisty wives or fighters against adversity. The divorced mother in *The Exorcist* isn't glorified for her motherhood—but at least she isn't *blamed* for her daughter's "possession." The divorced lesbian mother in *Lianna* is not glorified—but she is presented sympathetically. (Strictly speaking, John Sayles, *Lianna*'s director-writer, is not a Hollywood studio writer.)

One recent film, *Silkwood*, has presented a custodial father as violent and sadistic, and a mother sympathetically—not as a glorified mother, but as a union activist. Otherwise, the daily Hollywood fare is profoundly anti-mother (*Ordinary People*).

The film *Hanna K.* also touches on the question of custody. Jill Clayburgh is the mother and lawyer who decides to go through with the pregnancy on her own, as she defends the civil rights of a Palestinian on the West Bank. Clayburgh is married; her lover, and the genetic father of her son, is the Israeli DA. The DA begins talking about "my son" when Clayburgh's politics frighten and offend him. Clayburgh says: "Such fuss over a few drops of sperm." In one scene, in disgust, she says: "Take your son." The genetic father walks off, leaving the two-month-old infant with the mother who chose to remain pregnant, who gave birth to him, lived with him, and took full responsibility for him.

6. Desdemona in *Othello* has no mother. Neither does Ophelia in *Hamlet;* Regan, Goneril, and Cordelia in *King Lear;* Miranda in *The Tempest;* Portia in *The Merchant of Venice*, etc., etc. Please see Myra Glazer Schotz's "The Great Unwritten Story: Mothers and Daughters in Shakespeare," in *The Lost Tradition. Mothers and Daughters in Literature*, Cathy Davidson and E. M. Broner, eds. (New York: Ungar, 1980).

7. Marcia Pally, "The Suit for Paternity," *Village Voice* (October 5, 1983).

8. Like judges, many therapists are traditionally used to "treating" more

women than men; and used to seeing many more mothers than fathers accompany their children into family therapy. As this began to change, both judges and therapists "maternally" overresponded to those (relatively few) fathers who did turn up. (So few fathers fight for custody in courtrooms —so few think they have to—that those who do are seen as heroic pioneers.) See Paula Caplan and Ian Hall-McCorquodale, "Mother Blaming in Major Clinical Journals," *American Journal of Orthopsychiatry*, July 1985.

9. No one is encouraging fathers to choose between their male incomes and their children; only mothers are expected to choose one or the other.

10. The number of mass magazine articles and books that are pro-single father, pro-divorced father, and pro-paternal custody are far greater than the number of articles and books that are pro-single mother, pro-divorced mother, and pro-maternal custody. The fathers are usually photographed *alone* with their children, as if no mother exists. Custodial fathers rarely express sorrow or guilt over the absence of a mother-figure.

   I have yet to read an article about a paternal kidnapper who weeps with joy when he reunites a mother and her child, or about a "reformed" father who now joyfully babysits and pays alimony and child support to his financially drowned ex-wife and children.

11. Charles Metz, *Divorce and Custody for Men* (New York: Doubleday, 1968).

12. George Gilder, *Sexual Suicide* (New York: Quadrangle, 1973).

13. Daniel Amneus, *Back to Patriarchy* (New York: Arlington House, 1979). Amneus and Metz both are cited by Nancy Polikoff, op. cit.

14. Detectives' report based on a one-year investigation, filed in 1982.

15. William K. Stevens, "A Congress of Men Asks Equality for Both Sexes," *New York Times*, June 15, 1981. The NCM also "resolved" to "extend sexual equality to men and women."

16. John Rossler, president, and Dr. Robert Fay, consultant, Equal Rights for Fatherhood, New York State. *Contributions of the Homemaker,* October 21, 1981, organization pamphlet. I have chosen one of several propositions fashioned by Dr. Fay and endorsed by Rossler for the organization.

17. This suit was ultimately denied. Similar class action lawsuits on behalf of fathers have been attempted before and since in at least ten American states. *Equal Rights for Fathers of Alaska* v. *Superior Court Judges, U.S. District Court,* No. A82-008 CIV, reported in 8 FLR 2702, February 9, 1982.

18. Gerald A. Silver and Myrna Silver, *Weekend Fathers* (Los Angeles: Stratford Press, Harper & Row, distributors, 1981).

19. Maurice K. Franks, *Winning Custody: A No-Holds-Barred Guide for Fa-*

thers (Englewood Cliffs, N.J.: Prentice-Hall, 1983). Maurice Franks's book is accompanied by a lawyer-geared brochure outlining 75 "special custody-winning strategies to enable you to handle the ever-increasing demand for child custody by fathers"! Some of the 75 techniques high-lighted include:

"*How to keep temporary orders from permanently damaging the father's case . . .*" To give the father the custodial edge, Franks describes a simple strategy for getting the mother to agree voluntarily to sole or joint temporary custody by the father. And he shows you how to use this initial leverage to turn a de facto custodial situation into a de jure one! In addition, should you *fail* to gain temporary custody, Franks gives you special tactics to keep interim support payment to the mother low. And he shows you how to take advantage of this unfortunate stopgap custody situation to prove that the father is a more capable parent than the mother.

"*Using tape recorders and private investigators to 'get the goods' on your client's wife.* Your client is well aware that his wife neglects the children. But how can *you* help him prove it in court? First you get a comprehensive briefing on the law regarding the use of taped telephone conversations. And—if such evidence is legal in your state—you get the most up-to-date advice on what taping equipment your client should buy, how he should install it, and what pitfalls to avoid when you replay the tapes in court."(!)

"In addition, you get clear-cut procedures for establishing round-the-clock surveillance of your client's spouse. And you see how to use this information to present 'A Week in the Life of Mrs. A——— and Her Children' in court."

20. As reprinted in *Marriage and Divorce Today*, 9:6, (September 12, 1983). The NCM "resolved" that children must be assured of "frequent and continuing contact" with both parents; that the Federal Parental Kidnapping Act should be enforced regardless of the custodial status of the parent's sex. It also "resolved" to "support all efforts to replace the adversarial system of custody litigation by a system of mediation; to 'support' the education of fathers in birth and parenting and [the] increased participation by fathers in their children's lives."

21. Fathers' rights spokesmen have claimed up to "one million members" in "two hundred different groups." In 1984 a National Organization for Men was founded; it claims 2,700 members.

22. Sixteen interviewees were activists; seven were advocates; seven were expert observers; twenty-four were men; six were women; four were homosexual fathers.

23. This quote is taken from what two activists said on a program aired on National Public Radio early in 1983. They also said that "a man doesn't know the meaning of viciousness in comparison with a woman. If a man's

got his opponent on the ground, he'll back off. A woman won't. A female-dominated society [is to blame] for many of today's social problems. [Think of] Indira Gandhi, Golda Meir, and even the infamous Bitch of Buchenwald, who committed atrocities as head of a Nazi concentration camp. Every time a woman's been in that kind of position of power, it ain't been good!"

I called several well-known fathers' rights activists for an interview. One man refused to see me unless I paid for his time. He said, "I don't do freebies. I can't talk to you for more than fifteen minutes—unless you're paying. I'm very busy. I'm always on a plane flying somewhere for important custody cases."

Within those fifteen minutes Dick took four urgent phone calls, yelled at his secretary twice and at me once. Dick recommended that I call Lloyd. In a telephone interview Lloyd talked about ". . . children's needs for a strong father figure. Not these namby-pamby types who give up their kids without a fight and walk around with their tiny tails between their legs. No, ma'am. I'm talking about Christian, God-fearing fathers who know how important a father is to their children's normal Christian development. I'd go through fire for God's sake. I respect and would help any man who'd do the same."

24. The "right-wing" demand for fathers' rights is somewhat analogous to the demand for white rights in a racist society. Indeed, those whites who are not privileged by class *feel* discriminated against when efforts to redress racial or sexual discrimination succeed, even in token ways. ("Women and minorities are the only ones being hired today because of affirmative action quotas. What about men?")

25. Letty Cottin Pogrebin, *Family Politics*, op. cit.

26. Deborah Luepnitz, author of a study on joint custody (*Child Custody*, private interview, 1984.)

27. Luepnitz's custodial and joint custodial fathers *do* describe becoming less "authoritarian" and more "relaxed" in their single fathering style. None of her fathers passed along child-care responsibilities to girlfriends, mothers, or wives.

28. Nancy Polikoff, "Gender and Child-Custody Determinations: Exploding the Myths," in *Families, Politics and Public Policy: A Feminist Dialogue on Women and the State*, Irene Diamond (ed.) (New York: Longman, Inc., 1983).

29. Joanne Schulman, "The Truth About Joint Custody: Some Current Myths Exposed," *The Woman's Advocate*, Newsletter of the National Center on Women and Family Law, III No. 2 (June 1982), and personal communication. Dr. Deborah Luepnitz's study on joint custody is frequently cited

as proof that joint custody "works" and is "better" than sole maternal custody. According to Luepnitz, her study was "a) based on only 11 families with joint custody b) in all but one case, both parents had agreed to joint custody c) the sample was self-selected, meaning that the parents had agreed for their own reasons to be interviewed. I did locate a number of families who declined to participate because their arrangements were not working well. d) Finally, the study includes no follow-up of the 11 families. Each of these points is contained in my book, but I fear they are easily overlooked by readers who are eager to plead one or another cause."

A number of studies are also cited as proof that joint custody decreases re-litigation and/or leads to adequate and continuous child support payments. These studies have all been concerned with *voluntary*, as opposed to mandatory (court-imposed or mediation-coerced) joint custody.

Drs. Susan Steinman, Steven F. Zemmelman and Thomas M. Knoblauch have recently completed the first study that compared 48 voluntary and mandated joint custody families. Of these 48 families, 32% "failed;" 42% were severely "stressed;" and 27% were "successful." Steinman et al. note that:

"The characteristics that seem to be associated with a negative outcome for the joint custody arrangement included: 1) intense, continuing hostility and conflict that cannot be diverted from the child; 2) overwhelming anger and the continuing need to punish the spouse; 3) history of physical abuse; 4) history of substance abuse; 5) fixed belief that the other is a bad parent; 6) inability to separate their own feelings and needs from those of the child."

Thirteen of Steinman's families were "successful." All (100%) of these families were voluntary. 15% engaged in re-litigation. Physical (male domestic) violence occurred in 23% of these families.

Twenty families were "stressed" by their joint custody arrangement. 90% of these families were voluntary. Nevertheless, 65% engaged in re-litigation. Physical (male domestic) violence occurred in 50% of these families.

Fifteen families "failed" at their joint custody arrangement. 47% of these families had joint custody mandated. *Eighty seven percent* of these families engaged in re-litigation. Physical (male domestic) violence occurred in 57% of these families.

Susan B. Steinman, Steven Zemmelman and Thomas M. Knoblauch, "A Study of Parents Who Sought Joint Custody Following Divorce: Who Reaches Agreement and Sustains Joint Custody and Who Returns to Court." *Journal of The American Academy of Child Psychiatry*. In Press. Sept./Oct. 1985.

30. Laurie Woods, personal interviews, 1981–1984.

31. Elizabeth Thomas notes that an abused wife may now "stay [in an abusive marriage] because of the batterer's threat to take the children, which she has reason to believe [he will do] in light of his history of violence, the unresponsiveness of the legal system, her own lack of funds to hire an attorney to defend a custody suit, and her lack of funds to find a stolen child. . . . Expert testimony may demonstrate that the problems stem from the abuse and are likely to abate with separation from the abuser. . . . After separation, a client may appear unstable because she moved frequently, but the moves may be necessary for her to escape the batterer. Likewise, apparent 'uncooperativeness' about visitation may result from the father's use of visitation as an occasion for renewed physical or mental abuse." (Elizabeth Thomas, "Custody Litigation Strategies for Battered Women." In press. *Women's Rights Law Reporter;* paper presented at Continuing Legal Education Seminar, Seattle, Washington, January 27, 1983.)

32. Justice Vincent R. Balletta, Jr., "A View from the Bench: Joint Custody Revisited—Who Will be Given Custody of the Children?", *Family Law Review,* 15 (March 1983):1.

    Pittsburgh lawyer Harry Gruener, in his 1983 address to the Association of American Trial Lawyers, warned against the wave "of joint custody presumptions. You should candidly ask whether or not your client regards it as getting a foot in the door in order to fight for sole custody later. Next, what has been the parenting pattern of each parent? [Has] the child's relationship to both parents been one that indicates that joint custody is appropriate—or has the child been brainwashed by one of the parents so as to hate the other?" (Harry Gruener, *United States Law Week,* 52 (August 2, 1983):2065.

    Carol S. Bruch, a Family Law professor at the University of California at Davis and a 1983 consultant to California's law revision commission, sees "a knee jerk reaction on joint custody. In one recent case, a judge took a nursing infant and said, 'Two weeks with the mother, two weeks with the father.' Now that's insanity." Professor Bruch was quoted by Georgia Dullea, "Wide Changes in Family Life Are Altering Family Law," *New York Times,* February 7, 1983.

33. Deborah Luepnitz, private communication, 1984.

34. When mothers (or women) are not allowed to earn a "male" salary, and when fathers don't earn enough money to support two families adequately, they shouldn't have two families to support. Male polygamy should not be exercised at the expense of mothers and children.

    Unfortunately (serial) polygamy is outlawed in theory but not in practice in America. When fathers don't earn enough money to support two families in middle-class style, enormous friction develops between the "new" and the "old" wife, each pressing her claim to the American Dream.

35. In a private interview in 1981 Lillian Kozak noted: "The New York legislature recently passed a joint custody bill. The governor vetoed it. [The legislature] wanted the fathers to have joint *decision making*, not joint physical custody. They didn't vote for joint custody because they wanted mothers to have the time to pursue careers. They didn't imagine that joint custody would stop a father from having a career. But as joint custodians, fathers would be able to control decisions about schooling, vacations, medical care, religious education, without having the daily physical responsibility for that child."

36. In my *Women and Madness* (Doubleday 1972) and in the chapter on "Marriage and Motherhood: The Psychology of Total Commitment" in my and Goodman's *Women, Money and Power* (Morrow, 1976), I discuss what it means for women not to control the means of production and reproduction. I discuss how women's biological and domestic labor is never counted as part of any government's gross national product.

    The phrase *sex-class society* has been used by Andrea Dworkin in *Right-Wing Woman* (New York: Putnam, 1982). Jeanette Silveira, "Why Men Oppress Women," *Lesbian Ethics* 1, 1 (1984), uses this concept to clarify certain theoretical questions. Love and Shanklin, "The Answer Is Matriarchy" in *Mothering: Essays in Feminist Theory*, Joyce Treblicot, ed. (Rowman & Allenheld, 1984), also address some of these issues.

    Fortunately I have no simple "position" on the question of feminist revolution, biological motherhood, patriarchal oppression, or test-tube technology. On the contrary. I am unwilling theoretically to barter away any woman's option of biological motherhood and child rearing *because* this is colonized territory and because despite such colonization, certain (devalued) maternal traits *in relation to children* that are very desirable traits have evolved: practicality; nurturant non-violence; the ability to sustain emotional opposites and ambivalence, etc.

    I am also reluctant to entertain the concept that a feminist struggle for liberation is possible only after patriarchal men control test-tube technology and when women no longer have to become biological mothers.

    Perhaps after so many years as an intellectual I am frightened by too much abstract or intellectual purity. Such formulations may be "beautiful," but they are not always "right" in human terms. I have seen how human beings—men, women, Marxists, royalists, feminists, capitalists, nationalists, religionists, etc.—use intellectual formulations over and over again to justify violence and tyranny.

37. Carol Brown, *Women and Revolution*, Lydia Sargent, ed. (Mass.: South End Press, 1981.)

38. At the time of marriage both husband and wife could file with the state

copies of their tax returns for the preceding five years and proof of any other income-producing assets they might have. New contracts, property, stocks, sales, or employment agreements could automatically be filed as they come into existence.

If this were done—really done—then lawyers and judges, as well as wives, would be able to take into account whether a father has deferred his income for the sake of the divorce battle or diverted his income somewhere else to his own tax advantage. Judges could ascertain how much child support a father can genuinely afford without starving himself or so that his children won't have to starve.

Such information, if reliable, would be relevant in every instance in which fathers earn or have more money than what the state allots as welfare to mothers and children and in every instance in which fathers, because they are men, earn and have more money than mothers, because they are women, do.

Requiring such information legally is never a guarantee that everyone will comply and "tell the whole truth." A law is never a guarantee that someone won't break it. However, such legally acquired information would begin to place the burden of economic sacrifice on individual fathers, rather than on taxpayers or on already impoverished mothers and children.

There are many other state-subsidized solutions to the problem of child support. For example, any man whose name is listed on a child's birth certificate could automatically be required to forfeit X percent of his income to that child until the child grows up.

39. Representatives Barbara Kennelly (D-Conn.) and Marge Roukema (R-N.J.) both have proposed bills in this area. Roukema's bill proposes that child-support payments be automatically withheld from fathers' paychecks as soon as the court order is issued. She has said: "Why should the custodial parent wait for two months or more before any support is received? The bills do not stop coming in. The children still need to eat and be clothed. There is no national enforceable system of justice for these children. No mother and no child should have to bear the burden of endless and debasing legal battles before they can receive the rightful support which due process had decreed" (quoted by Beverly Stephen, "Child Support Legislation Is Overdue," *New York Daily News*, August 25, 1983).

One state-subsidized solution to the problem of fathers in default is noted in Florida, where Judge Charles McClure of Tallahassee and four fellow justices have confiscated $3.7 million in cash, plus numerous cars, boats, etc., in 4,000 child-support cases. Judge McClure et al. have also jailed 400 non-paying parents (397 fathers and 3 mothers) during the same nineteen-month period (reported in "Controversy," *People* magazine, 1984).

The IRS did do a (1981–1983) pilot project involving the withholding of *tax return refunds* to those fathers who were in arrears of their child-support payments. The IRS decided not to pursue this approach when those fathers underreported their taxes the following year. Nevertheless, individual states (such as Illinois, as of 1984) were giving the names of such fathers to the IRS. The state of Illinois collected more than $3 million from the program in 1983 and does not want individual taxpayers to foot the bill for irresponsible fathers (*Chicago Sun-Times*, December 7, 1984).

Many fathers claim that they want to support their children but that they cannot "tolerate" supporting their ex-wives. Several of my interviewees proposed arrangements whereby paternal child support could go directly to the child. Winifred said: "The money should bypass me altogether. What this will do is calm my ex-husband down. He'd be sure that his money is going directly to the store, the ex-wife never touches it. I've been exploring ideas like this. You could have an automatic inflation adjustment as the tuition bills go up or the charges at the store go up. A mother shouldn't have to go back and ask for more money each time."

The state could also encourage (subsidize) private insurance companies to underwrite child-support insurance. One Dallas, Texas, insurance company, the Republic Insurance Group, charges a premium in advance of 6 percent of the court ordered payments, in exchange for a renewable three-year agreement in which the company makes up any default or payment in arrears for at least two months. However, the father or the state should pay the premiums for the divorced mother. A mother who has just finished an emotionally and economically debilitating divorce or custody trial cannot afford such insurance. Such insurance should be made available to mothers directly. Elaine Fromm, secretary of the Organization for the Enforcement of Child Support, doesn't think that parents will be interested in the idea. She has said: "The man usually has full intentions of making those payments in the beginning, so he won't think it's necessary. And the woman isn't likely to insist because she still believes the law will force him to pay. It's only later she finds out how difficult it is to get that enforcement. And anyway, most women believe it will never happen to them" (Andree Brooks, "When Divorce Payments Lag," *New York Times*, April 12, 1983).

40. I am referring to corporations which have more than fifty employees or assets above a certain dollar amount.

For a series of related proposals, please see Paul L. Adams, op. cit.; Phyllis Chesler and Emily Goodman, Deborah Anna Luepnitz, *Child Custody*.

41. *Joseph Goldstein, Anna Freud, Albert J. Solnit, Beyond the Best Interests of the Child*, (London: The Free Press, Division of Macmillan Publishers, 1979).

42. Rena K. Uviller, "Father's Rights and Feminism: The Maternal Presumption Revisited," *Harvard Women's Law Journal* 1 (1): 107–130, (1978).

43. Uviller is not saying that children need their "psychological" parent only

during infancy or until they can reach less "tender" ages. Under the American and European "tender years" tradition, children automatically reverted back to their fathers' custody at any one of several arbitrary ages between five and thirteen.

Those who conceived of and fought for the "tender years" presumption sincerely believed that access to maternal (or female) tenderness was in the child's "best interest." The presumption itself was used to maximize the amount of time that children could be assured of access to their mothers—*without eroding the principle of father rule and father right.*

As we have seen in Chapter 1, the "tender years" presumption was also immediately used to justify state paternal power over children who were abused, abandoned, or delinquent or whose parents were impoverished or culturally and racially despised.

Today, under Jewish and Islamic law, children automatically "belong" to their fathers anywhere between the ages of five and fourteen—sometimes sooner if a divorce occurs or if wifely disobedience is at issue. (See Chapter 17.)

44. Lucy Katz, "The Maternal Preference and the Psychological Parent: Suggestions for Allocating the Burden of Proof in Custody Litigation," *Connecticut Bar Journal*, 53, (1979):343–48.

45. Attorney Nancy Polikoff, personal interview, 1982.

46. Nancy Polikoff, "Gender and Child-Custody Determinations: Exploding the Myths," in *Families, Politics and Public Policy: A Feminist Dialogue on Women and the State*, Irene Diamond, ed., (New York: Longman, Inc., 1983).

Also see Nancy Polikoff and the Women's Legal Defense Fund, *Representing Primary Caretaker Parents in Custody Disputes: A Manual for Attorneys*, Women's Legal Defense Fund, 2000 P Street NW, Suite 400, Washington, D.C. 20036, 1984.

47. Many feminist lawyers are more concerned with "equal" rights even for unequals, and for fathers' rights, as opposed to mothers' rights. Three pro-mother lawyers (a minority among feminist lawyers to date) have interpreted this in different ways.

Lucille: Feminist lawyers for fathers' rights seem compelled to offer men an incentive or reward for remaining involved with mothers and children. I don't understand why else feminists would be emotionally invested in fathers' custodial rights at all when there's so much undone for mothers. Is this their way of personally working out their feminism, their careers, or their heterosexuality?

Barbara: Some feminists for fathers' rights are so male-identified they don't like to behave like mothers in their office or in the courtroom. They either have no children, or if they do, they don't parent themselves. They see biological reproduction as messy or as a woman's own responsibility. Just like the department of welfare does.

Peggy: Feminists for fathers' rights are mainly interested in getting publicity and money. Fathers' rights is more dramatic, sexier, better-paying than trying to get child support enforced for a mother who has no money.

Reading the proposals of the pro-mother lawyers was a great pleasure. It is always a pleasure for me, as a psychologist, to contemplate the ways in which human reason remains nobly and creatively at the disposal of human emotions: necessarily subjective, not objective.

48. Helen Levine and Alma Estable, "The Power Politics of Motherhood," and occasional papers. Unpublished Canadian manuscript, 1983 Carlton School of Social Work.

The last sentence is a quote from Pauline Bart's review of Nancy Chodorow, *The Reproduction of Mothering* in *Off Our Backs* (January 1981).

49. Janet Farrell Smith in her essay, "Parenting and Property," writes: "[While] the property model as it applies to parenting captures many of the traditional powers and duties of fathers, it conflicts with many of the traditional responsibilities and feelings of mothers. Whereas male roles in parenting [historically] emphasized the rights of parenthood, the female role emphasized its responsibilities in the day-to-day care-taking of children. This division of labor may be analogous to that between the owner of property who has rights over it and the manager of the property who deals with the mundane daily transactions concerning property.

"An ethic of care and concern associated with the traditional responsibilities of mothering has several key philosophical advantages over the values associated with the property model. It emphasizes care rather than proprietary control, interdependence rather than exclusion, and recognition of individuality rather than possessive individualism. Its central theme is developmental rather than extractive power. Treating children on the literal premise that they are property, or on the analogy that children are to be controlled as property is controlled, conflicts with the most humane ideals for care of children."

The essay is contained in *Mothering: Essays in Feminist Theory*, Joyce Treblicot, ed., (Totowa, N.J.: Rowman & Allenheld, 1984).

50. Those fathers who do not abandon their families are usually better *economic* providers than mothers are. However, many mothers have provided for their children both parentally and economically. Fewer fathers have taken over both roles in equivalent situations of impoverished isolation.

51. The "psychological" parent presumption is potentially as fragile as the "tender years" presumption. The "psychological" parent presumption does not claim that the mother-child relationship is as "ineffable" or as non-replaceable as patriarchal law has claimed of the father-child relationship.

   More important, the "psychological" or primary caretaker parent presumption does not address certain contemporary realities—e.g., that of working or career mothers who delegate many caretaking tasks to others. The "psychological" parent presumption cannot by itself correct the legal or judicial (mis)conception that paternal "helping" is equivalent to paternal "sharing," and that paternal "sharing" is equivalent to a woman's responsibility for maternal practice.

52. Denise Nadeau, mother and theorist, unpublished communication.

53. Sara Ruddick, "Maternal Thinking," op. cit. Ruddick also believes that male involvement in child care will lead to "serious social reform. . . . Responsible, equal childcaring would require men to relinquish power and their own favorable position in the division between intellectual/ professional and service labor as that division expresses itself domestically. Loss of preferred status at home might make socially privileged men more suspicious of unnecessary divisions of labor and damaging hierarchies in the public world. Moreover, if men were emotionally and practically committed to childcare, they would reform the work world . . . in response to human needs as well as to the demands of productivity with an eye to growth rather than measurable profit."

54. Private interviews, 1981–1984.

55. Joseph Goldstein, Anna Freud, Albert J. Solnit, *Beyond the Best Interests of the Child* (London: The Free Press, Division of Macmillan Publishers, 1979). Goldstein, et al, notes: "The lack of finality, which stems from the court's retention of jurisdiction over its custody decision, invites challenges by a disappointed party claiming changed circumstances. This absence of finality coupled with the concomitant increase in opportunities for appeal are in conflict with the child's need for continuity. As in adoption, a custody decree should be final, that is, not subject to modification."

56. Goldstein, Ibid.

57. Nancy Polikoff, "Gender and Child-Custody Determinations: Exploding the Myths That Mothers Always Win," in *Families, Politics and Public Policy: A Feminist Dialogue on Women and the State*, Irene Diamond, ed., (New York: Longman, Inc., 1983).

   Lawyers, judicially battered parents, and some judges have recommended that judges be specifically or better trained in the domestic area and that more such judges be appointed or elected so that each judge has enough time to review a custody arrangement properly.

Lawyers also need special training and retraining in the area of domestic law. Domestic law itself needs to be better-valued and better-paid. Within a legal and economic system that values profits and property over human life, this is a revolutionary reform.

58. For example, New York Judge Sol Wachtel proposed that custody be determined "by a panel dominated by trained behavior specialists. Panels should be made up of psychiatrists, psychologists and members of the bar who have specialized in family law" (quoted by Bernard S. Meyer and Stephen W. Schlissel, "Child Custody Following Divorce: How Grasp the Nettle?," *N.Y. State Bar Journal* [December 1982]).

Judge Donald King believes that custody decisions should be removed from the legal system entirely. King says: "I seriously dispute the wisdom of having child custody and visitation disputes decided by the adversary system. Frequently, the judge hearing such disputes is a short-timer as a family law judge, with little or no training in psychology or child development . . . child custody is not a legal problem. It is a human problem, a psychological problem, and a child developmental problem" (Donald B. King, *Family Advocate* [Summer 1978]).

King recommends a three-month period of mandatory family counseling and arbitration. Psychiatrists Elissa and Richard Benedek also recommend the participation of "behavioral science" experts but who function in a setting that is "less inhibiting than the courtroom. The idea is to make a basically unpleasant experience more tolerable for the participants, and more revealing as well" (Elissa P. Benedek, M.D., and Richard S. Benedek, J.D., "New Child Custody Laws: Making Them Do What They Say," *American Journal of Orthopsychiatry*, vol. 42, no. 5 [October 1971]).

59. Bernard Meyer and Stephen W. Schlissel, "Child Custody Following Divorce: How Grasp the Nettle?" *N.Y. State Bar Journal*, December, 1982.

It is important to remember that until very recently, family law (and lawyers and judges) protected fathers exclusively and children not at all. "Fatherless" children had no legal rights. According to Paul L. Adams, Judith R. Milner and Nancy A. Schrepf, *Fatherless Children*, op. cit., "The Supreme Court first acknowledged children's rights in 1967. . . . Children's rights are still extremely abstract: 'Nowhere in the standard juvenile court law of the new Model Juvenile Court Act [the act concerning neglected, dependent and delinquent children] are there any specifications of the rights of a child or the procedures that he may invoke for his protection or to obtain redress for wrongs done to him' . . . in the late 1960's the Supreme Court [decided] that the Equal Protection Clause of the 14th Amendment must be extended to illegitimate children."

According to a 1984 New York Bar Association study, 50 percent of the time legal representation for abused and delinquent children was "seriously inadequate or marginally adequate." Legal representation was found to be "effective or acceptable" less than one-third of the time. The report also noted that children's lawyers were so ill-prepared that they were often ordered to leave the courtroom. (This study was cited in the *New York Times,* June 25, 1984.)

60. Martha O. Eller, letter to the National Center for Women and Family Law, 1982.

My passion for evenhandedness and my own maternal vulnerability are outraged by experts who overlook and deny paternal unfitness or who argue eloquently on behalf of fathers who have abandoned, beaten, or raped their wives or children. I am terrified when these same experts see maternal failings where none exist and who are simply more pro-father than pro-mother.

61. Paul L. Adams, Judith R. Milner and Nancy A. Schrepf, *Fatherless Children,* (New York: John Wiley and Sons, 1984). Also, see Chapters 8, 9, and 14.

Dr. Judith Herman, author of *Father-Daughter Incest,* a psychiatrist and psychotherapist, has also testified as an expert witness on behalf of sexually abused children whose incestuous fathers were fighting for their custody. Her testimony rarely "carries the day." See Chapter 14.

62. I am not saying that methods of using children as witnesses, especially in matters of their own victimization, do not exist or can't be developed and refined. I am saying that this is a new area and still quite vulnerable to traditional anti-mother or pro-father biases.

Adams et al., op. cit., cite the case of a thirteen-year-old-boy who perjured himself in court on behalf of the same father who had sexually abused both him and his sister: "Reginald had good reason to hate his father, but he also loved him and tried to protect him. Under pressure from the paternal grandmother and other relatives, he had perjured himself during the latest trial of his father. What Reginald lied about was [to be truthful]: His father had forced Reginald to have sexual intercourse with a younger sister while the father performed sodomy on Reginald. Reginald had lied in the courtroom but his sister stuck to the truth; Reginald was rewarded with a motorcycle for his courtroom report and the sister consoled herself with the rewards of a clear conscience."

Reginald's true story was not revealed by lawyers or a judge. It was uncovered over a long period of time by a therapist afterward.

63. See Chapters 13, 14, 16, and 17.

64. Laurie Woods, "Mediation: A Backlash to Women's Progress on Family Law Issues in the Courts and Legislatures," National Center on Women and Family Law, Inc., 1985. Woods notes further that:

"In divorce or family law mediation there is no process by which the dependent spouse can verify the extent of the assets or attempt to discover hidden assets of the propertied spouse. A full, honest and forth right accounting of marital assets by a self-interested spouse is unlikely. The legal system offers various means of obtaining this disclosure, including depositions, subpoenaing of records and coercive sanctions for non-compliance or false representations. Similarly dissipation of assets may go unnoticed and unaccounted for in the mediation process, while the legal system offers various safeguards. The parties are not informed of their legal rights and have no rules or precedents to guide them as to what is equitable or reasonable under the circumstances. The parties deal directly with each other without an independent advocate who can deal with the issues without the emotional baggage burdening the parties. Thus the parties are susceptible to giving away rights out of guilt, domination, intimidation, lack of resources or coercion. Settlements may be agreed upon, but not equitable. Settlements may be agreed upon, but not enforceable. Only those items which both parties wish to put on the table are settled. And not all issues are foreseen by the parties. There is no guarantee of confidentiality of communications made either to the mediator or in the mediation sessions. Accordingly, the parties may use the statements made in mediation as admissions in a later court proceeding. In many jurisdictions mediators made recommendations to the court but can not be cross-examined with respect to their recommendations.

Mediation is problematic whether the mediator is a lawyer or a non-lawyer. Lawyer mediators can not represent either side and cannot exercise professional judgment and at best can only offer "impartial legal advise." The dangers of lawyer mediation are that each party may assume that the lawyer-mediator is looking out for his/her interest and that every statement is based on legal expertise. The American Bar Association Standards of Practice for Divorce Mediators would require the mediator, whether or not he is a lawyer, to recommend that each party seek independent legal representation during the process. This recognition of the need for independent counsel is implicit recognition of the fact that mediation is not and cannot be an *alternative* to legal representation.

A non-lawyer mediator may be able to define the points of agreement which are at the moment consuming the parties' attention, but it is unlikely that a non-lawyer could knowledgeably deal with all forseeable contingencies such as the moving of the custodial spouse or the future unemployment of the paying spouse. A non-lawyer would not understand the legal, tax or public assistance effects and consequences of alternative compromises such as the form of custody agreed upon, how to valuate different forms of property, such as pension benefits, closed corporations, and loss of inheritance; what constitutes marital and separate property; how to valuate appreciation of separate property through active or passive contributions of the non-titled spouse; and how to valuate non-monetary contributions of the homemaker spouse. Lay mediation is, in the words of one commentator, "(a) self-determined process between two uninformed spouses guided by a neutral person unfamiliar with the legal rights of the parties, operating without standards or rules which may produce an unenforceable agreement."

It is not a concidence that, just when the state legislators are passing strong laws with respect to battery, marital property and child support enforcement, and when the U.S. Congress and U.S. Supreme Court are acting for the first time in history on family law issues, we have a movement to exclude these issues from the courts. It is no coincidence, that as battered women are gaining increased access to the courts, through *pro se* civil procedures or increased arrests, we have a movement that would exclude these cases from the jurisdiction of the civil and criminal courts. Nor is it a coincidence that as standards and enforcement are beginning to be developed by the legal system in the areas of child and spousal support, mediation, which would offer no enforcement, is being pushed.

"Only the legal system has the power to remove the batterer from the home, to arrest when necessary, to enforce the terms of any decree if a new assault occurs, to discover hidden assets, to prevent dissipation of assets, and to enforce support orders. Only the legislatures and courts can create, develop, expand, and enforce women's rights. Mediation offers no protection, no deterrence, no enforcement, and no opportunity to expand women's rights."

65. Joanne Schulman, paper presented at *Mediation and Battered Women Panel*, Washington, D.C., April 9, 1983, *14th National Conference on Women and Law*, available from the National Center on Women and Family Law, Inc.

66. As I have noted, women and racially despised men in public positions must use the same process. In fact, they must use it very well because they are tokens or exceptions to what is conceived of as "normal" (white male) among the population of experts in authority.

67. Sara Ruddick, "Preservative Love and Military Destruction," op. cit.

68. Many scholars have described matrifocal, matrilineal, or "matrist" societies as apparently more cooperative, egalitarian, peaceful, and sexually permissive than patriarchal, patrifocal, patrilineal, or "patrist" societies. Although I've read and quoted from Briffault, Bachofen, Engels, Harrison, and Taylor on this subject in previous works, I am indebted to Barbara G. Walker's excellent *The Women's Encyclopedia of Myths and Secrets*, Harper & Row, New York, 1984, for summarizing such information in her essay on motherhood.

69. The state's recent attempts to treat male domestic violence as criminal acts are too little, too late, long overdue and, in limited ways, highly successful.

These attempts fall far short of economically compensating the female and child victims of male domestic violence.

70. I am using the word *parent* here because that is what I mean. In general, I have refrained from using the word *parent* when I mean "mother" or "father." Sara Ruddick, ibid., gives a good explanation of why my refraining is appropriate.

I try throughout to make a comparative evaluation between "parenting" and the terms it appears to be meant to replace, i.e., "mothering" and "fathering." Using ordinary common sense, my own experience of progress made by the Women's Movement, and statistical information, I conclude that "parenting" ought not be used for four reasons. First, using "parenting" is ahistorical, since there is currently no set of social activities that can be called "parenting"; the term lacks a historical or material base. Second, encouraging this change in language does not further feminist goals, because language is relatively powerless to effect changes in material conditions of women's oppression, and because using the term can falsely create the impression that women's condition has improved more than it actually has. Third, using "parenting" in any given case may be morally wrong, insofar as it deprives those doing "primary child care," i.e., the laborious, day-to-day nurturing of children, of the proper credit they deserve, whether they are men or women. Last, using "parenting" can have dire political consequences because it can disguise illegitimate and anti-feminist motives and social actions. Really, "parenting" is an elite, obfuscatory euphemism that does much more harm to women's condition than good. I prefer "mothering" to refer to day-to-day child care whether done by women or men, but I also accept the compromise term "nurturing."

Resources

Organizations that provide services to the custodially and economically embattled mother are understaffed, overworked, and sometimes legally prohibited from dispensing advice or providing any direct service. The following organizations may or may not be pro-mother, experts in custody or family law, or providers of direct service. They will, however, refer custodially and economically embattled mothers to educational, legal, legislative, psychological, feminist, and self-help groups within each state and region.

Battered Women

Center for Women Policy Studies
2000 P Street, N.W.
Suite 508
Washington, D.C. 20036-5997

Publishes *Response,* a newsletter on battered women's issues.

National Coalition Against Domestic Violence
1500 Massachusetts Ave., N.W.
Suite 35
Washington, D.C. 20006
(202) 347-7017
Executive Director: Sharon Parker

Referral to state battered women's coalitions (who will then make referrals to local battered women's programs). Policy analysis; legislative advocacy.

U.S. Attorney General's Task Force on Family Violence
Department of Justice
Washington, D.C.
Attn: Lois Harrington

Legislative hearings; recommendations; investigation; educational reports.

Women's Law Project
112 South 16th St.
Suite 1012
Philadelphia, PA 19102
Attn: Katherine Kolbert

Impact litigation.

623

Child Abuse

National Coalition Against Sexual
Assault
430 Metro Square
St. Paul, MN 55101

Referral to state rape crisis
conditions.

National Legal Resource Center for
Child Advocacy and Protection
1800 M Street, N.W.
Washington, D.C. 20036
(202) 331-2250

Resource materials.

National Organization of Victim
Assistance (NOVA)
U.S. Department of Justice
1757 Park Road, N.W.
Washington, D.C. 20010
(202) 232-8560
Director: Marlene A. Young

Legislative advocacy; newsletter.

Incest Survivors Resource Network
c/o Adelphi University
School of Social Work
Garden City, NY 11530
Coordinator: Anne Eriksson
(516) 935-3031

Referrals; information; self-help
groups.

Child Support

American Bar Association
Child Support Project
1800 M Street, N.W.
Washington, D.C. 20036
(202) 331-2250
Co-Director: Diane Dodson

Resource and educational materials.

Center for Enforcement of Family
Support
9570 Wilshire Blvd., Suite 368
Beverly Hills, CA 90212
(213) 557-3001
Attn: Dennis Cohen, Esq.

Private law firm concentrating on
child and spousal support
enforcement

Center for Law and Social Policy
1751 N Street, N.W.
Washington, D.C. 20036
(202) 872-0670
Attn: Paula Roberts

Legislative and policy analysis.

Child Support Project
National Conference of State
Legislators (NCSL)
1125 17th St., Suite 1500
Denver, CO 80202
(303) 623-6600
Project Manager: Deborah Dale

Information on state legislation.

Children's Defense Fund
1520 New Hampshire Ave., N.W.
Washington, D.C. 20036
(202) 483-1470
Director: Marian Wright Edelman,
Nancy Ebb

Policy analysis; child support.

The Children's Foundation
815 15th Street, N.W.
Suite 928
Washington, D.C. 20005
(202) 347-3300
Director: Barbara Bode

National organizational network.
Information; local legislation; low
and moderate income mothers.

National Child Support Enforcement
Reference Center
6110 Executive Blvd.
Beltway View Building, Room 820
Rockville, MD 20852
(301) 443-5106

Resource materials on child support
laws and issues.

National Women's Law Center
1751 N Street, N.W.
Washington, D.C. 20036
(202) 872-0670
Director: Nancy D. Campbell

Child support; litigation policy
analysis.

Custody

Dr. Phyllis Chesler
c/o Elaine Markson
Literary Agent
44 Greenwich Ave.
New York, NY 10011

Expert witness; lecture and
consultation services.

National Center on Women &
Family Law
799 Broadway, Room 402
New York, NY 10003
(212) 674-8200
Director: Laurie Woods
Staff Attorney: Joanne Schulman

Battered women and custody
project; child custody project; legal
advocacy for poor women; national
child custody task force; national
child support advocacy network.

Women's Legal Defense Fund   Legal advocacy and referral;
Child Custody Project   education; policy analysis.
2000 P Street, N.W.
Suite 400
Washington, D.C. 20036
Project Director: Nancy Polikoff

Custody Handbooks

The Custody Handbook: A Woman's Guide to Child Custody Disputes
(Women's Legal Defense Fund, 1984), 74 pp., $4.00. Available from the
Women's Legal Defense Fund, 2000 P Street, NW, Suite 400, Washington,
D.C. 20036

> Written specifically for women facing contested custody cases; covers
> every step in a custody determination, from understanding the law and
> choosing an attorney to preparing for trial and appealing an unfavorable
> decision.

Representing Primary Caretaker Parents in Custody Disputes (Women's
Legal Defense Fund, 1984) 70 pp., $7.50. Available from the Women's
Legal Defense Fund, 2000 P Street, NW, Suite 400, Washington, D.C.
20036

> A manual for lawyers representing the primary caretaker parent in custody
> disputes. Includes a list of cases and questions for disposition on trial
> designed to establish which parent has been the primary caretaker.

Child Custody Resource Packet, from the National Center on Women and
Family Law, Inc., 799 Broadway, Room 402, New York, NY 10003. Price:
$2.00

> List of selected articles, books, and organizations covering custody, joint
> custody, battered women and custody, parental kidnapping.

*Interstate Child Custody Disputes and Parental Kidnapping: Policy, Practice
and Law* (ABA/LSC, 1982): available from the National Center on Women
and Family Law, Inc., 799 Broadway, Room 402, New York, NY. 550 pp.,
$35.00 plus postage.

> 550-page manual on the use of civil and criminal laws in parental
> kidnapping cases for lawyers and clients.

Lesbian Mother Litigation Manual, by Donna Hitchens (1982); available
from the Lesbian Rights Project, 1370 Mission St., 4th Floor, San Francisco,
CA 94103. $35.00

> Guide to lawyers representing lesbian mothers in child custody litigation,
> giving practical advice and guidance on potential strategies and legal

approaches; includes model briefs/pleadings, and annotated bibliography of legal and psychological materials.

Imprisoned Mothers

AIM (Aid to Incarcerated Mothers)   Advocacy and research.
Family Support and Advocacy
100 Arlington St.
Boston, MA 02116
(617) 482-6695
Family Services Coordinator: Evelyn
Machtinger

Bucks County Rehabilitation   Advocacy.
Center's Prison Playroom Project
18 Brantwood Lane
Stamford, CT 06903
(203) 322-3257
Co-Directors: Ann Adalist-Estrin,
Susanne Blough Abbott

Legal Assistance for Mothers in   Advocacy.
Prison
104 E. Main St.
Durham, NC 27701
(919) 683-1280
Exec. Director: Christine J.
Herlinger

Legal Services to Women Prisoners   Advocacy and research.
433 Turk St., 2nd Floor
San Francisco, CA 94102
(415) 777-2379
Attorney & Director: Ellen Barry

National Prison Project   Referral.
ACLU Foundation
1346 Connecticut Ave., N.W.
Suite 402
Washington, D.C. 20036
(202) 331-0500
Attn: Urvashi Vaid and Mary
McClymont

No More Cages   Journal for and about women
Women Free Women in Prison   prisoners.
P.O. Box 90
Brooklyn, NY 11215

Prisoners' Legal Services of New York 105 Chambers St., 5th Floor New York, NY 10007	Advocacy and referral
State of New York Executive Department Division of Parole 314 W. 40th St. New York, NY 10018 (212) 964-6307 Commissioner: Barbara Treen	Parole; mothers and children.

Parental Kidnapping

American Bar Association Child Custody Project 1800 M Street, N.W. Washington, D.C. 20036 Director: Patricia Hoff	Resource and educational materials on parental kidnapping.
Child Find, Inc. P.O. Box 277 New Paltz, NY 12561 Director: Gloria Yerkovich	Location of missing children; attorney and support group referrals.
International Social Services, American Branch 20 West 40th St. New York, NY 10018 Director: Lemina Cashel	Information on children kidnapped abroad.
National Center for Missing and Exploited Children 1835 K Street, N.W., Suite 700 Washington, D.C. 20006 (202) 634-9821 (800) 834-5678 (hotline)	Information and referrals.
State Department Office of Citizen Consular Services Room 4811 Washington, D.C. 20520 (202) 632-3444	Information.

Lesbian Rights, Custody and General

Custody Action for Lesbian Mothers   Legal advocacy and referral.
Avenue of the Art Building
1346 Chestnut, Room 1109
Philadelphia, PA 19107
c/o Rose Eisenberg

Lambda Legal Defense and   Legal advocacy and referral.
Education Fund
132 W. 43rd St.
New York, N.Y. 10036
(212) 944-9488
Director: Timothy Sweeney

Lesbian Mothers' National Defense   Referral and information.
Fund
P.O. Box 21567
Seattle, WA 98111
(206) 325-2643

Lesbian Rights Project   Legal advocacy, referral and
1370 Mission St., 4th Floor   resource materials/handbooks
San Francisco, CA 94103
(415) 621-0674
Director: Roberta Achtenberg

Women's Rights, General

Chicana Rights Project   Information and referrals.
201 N. St. Mary's Street
Suite 517, San Antonio, TX 78205
Coordinator: Barbara Aguirre
(512) 224-5476

Equal Rights Advocates   Referral assistance.
1370 Mission St., 4th Floor
San Francisco, CA 94103
(415) 621-0505
Director: Nancy Davis

Legal Defense and Education Fund   Referral assistance.
National Organization for Women
99 Hudson St., 12th Floor
New York, NY 10013
Legal Director: Marsha Levick

National Organization for Women   Referral assistance.
425 13th St., N.W.
Suite 1048
Washington, D.C. 20004
(202) 347-2279

Northwest Women's Law Center   Referral assistance.
701 N.E. Northlake Way
Seattle, WA 98105

Puerto Rico Legal Defense and   Referral assistance.
Education Fund
950 Madison Ave., Suite 1304
New York, NY 10016
(212) 532-8470

Women's Rights Project, ACLU
132 West 43rd St.
New York, NY 10036
(212) 944-9800
Director: Isabelle Pinzler

Index